HANDBOOK OF QUALITATIVE RESEARCH METHODS IN MARKETING

Handbook of Qualitative Research Methods in Marketing

Edited by

Russell W. Belk

Kraft Foods Canada Chair of Marketing, Schulich School of Business, York University, Toronto, Canada

Edward Elgar
Cheltenham, UK • Northampton, MA, USA

Published by
Edward Elgar Publishing Limited
Glensanda House
Montpellier Parade
Cheltenham
Glos GL50 1UA
UK

Edward Elgar Publishing, Inc.
William Pratt House
9 Dewey Court
Northampton
Massachusetts 01060
USA

A catalogue record for this book
is available from the British Library

Library of Congress Cataloguing in Publication Data

Handbook of qualitative research methods in marketing/[edited by]
    Russell W. Belk.
        p.   cm.
    Includes bibliographical references and index.
    1. Marketing research—Methodology. 2. Consumers—
Research—Methodology. 3. Qualitative research—Methodology.
I. Belk, Russell W.
HF5415.2.H288   2006
658.8'3—dc22

                                        2006004283

ISBN-13: 978 1 84542 100 7 (cased)
ISBN-10: 1 84542 100 0 (cased)

Printed and bound in Great Britain by MPG Books Ltd, Bodmin, Cornwall

Contents

PART V   DATA ANALYSIS METHODS

PART VI   PRESENTING QUALITATIVE RESEARCH

PART VII   APPLICATIONS

PART VIII   SPECIAL ISSUES

Contributors

Eric Arnould, Professor of Retailing and Consumer Sciences, University of Arizona, USA

Shalini Bahl, Assistant Professor, David Eccles School of Business, University of Utah, USA

Stacey Menzel Baker, Associate Professor of Marketing and Governor Geringer Scholar, Department of Management and Marketing, College of Business Administration, University of Wyoming, USA

Russell W. Belk, Kraft Foods Canada Chair of Marketing, Schulich School of Business, York University, Canada

Anders Bengtsson, Department of Marketing, Sawyer Business School, Suffolk University, USA

Stephen Brown, School of Marketing, Entrepreneurship and Strategy, University of Ulster, UK

Miriam Catterall, The Queen's University of Belfast, UK

Julien Cayla, Australian Graduate School of Management, Sydney, Australia

Jason Chambers, University of Illinois, USA

Manli Chen, PhD Candidate, Marketing, Rensselaer Polytechnic Institute, USA

Suraj Commuri, Assistant Professor, Department of Marketing, University of Missouri–Columbia, USA

Daniel Thomas Cook, Department of Advertising, University of Illinois, USA

June Cotte, Assistant Professor of Marketing, The Ivey School of Business, University of Western Ontario, Canada

Robin A. Coulter, Marketing Department, University of Connecticut, USA

Fabian Faurholt Csaba, Copenhagen Business School, Denmark

Andrea Davies, Senior Lecturer in Marketing, University of Leicester, UK

Rita M. Denny, Practica Group, LLC, USA

Jonathan Deschenes, Concordia University, Canada

Jeffrey F. Durgee, Associate Dean for Academic Affairs, Associate Professor, Marketing, Rensselaer Polytechnic Institute, USA

Karin M. Ekström, Associate Professor and Director, Center for Consumer Science, School of Business, Economics and Law, Göteborg University, Sweden

Richard Elliott, Professor of Marketing, School of Management, University of Bath, UK

Eileen Fischer, Schulich School of Business, York University, Canada

James W. Gentry, Maurice J. and Alice Hollman Professor in Marketing, Department of Marketing, University of Nebraska-Lincoln, USA

Güliz Ger, Department of Marketing, Bilkent University, Turkey

Stephen J. Gould, Professor of Marketing, Baruch College, The City University of New York, USA

Elizabeth C. Hirschman, Department of Marketing, School of Business, Rutgers University, USA

Margaret K. Hogg, Department of Marketing, Lancaster University Management School, UK

Morris B. Holbrook, W.T. Dillard Professor of Marketing, Graduate School of Business, Columbia University, USA

Gillian C. Hopkinson, Department of Marketing, Lancaster University Management School, UK

D.G. Brian Jones, Professor of Marketing, Quinnipiac University, USA

Annamma Joy, Professor, John Molson School of Business, Concordia University, Canada

Steven M. Kates, Simon Fraser University, Canada

Geoffrey Kistruck, Doctoral Student in Strategic Management, The Ivey School of Business, University of Western Ontario, Canada

Dannie Kjeldgaard, University of Southern Denmark

Robert V. Kozinets, Associate Professor of Marketing, Schulich School of Business, York University, Canada

Sidney J. Levy, Department of Marketing, Eller College of Management, University of Arizona, USA

Tina M. Lowrey, Professor of Marketing, College of Business, University of Texas at San Antonio, USA

James H. McAlexander, Department of Marketing, Oregon State University, Corvallis, Oregon, USA

Pauline Maclaran, De Montfort University, UK

Diane M. Martin, Assistant Professor of Marketing at University of Portland, USA and a senior research associate at Ethos Market Research, LLC

David Glen Mick, McIntire School of Commerce, University of Virginia, USA

George R. Milne, Associate Professor of Marketing, University of Massachusetts, Amherst, USA

Risto Moisio, University of Nebraska, USA

Jeff B. Murray, Professor of Marketing, Walton College of Business, University of Arkansas, USA

Jacob Ostberg, Stockholm University, Sweden

Laura R. Oswald, Department of Marketing, ESSEC Business School, France

Cele C. Otnes, Professor of Marketing, University of Illinois – Urbana-Champaign, USA

Julie L. Ozanne, Professor of Marketing, R.B. Pamplin College of Business, Virginia Tech, USA

Donald Panther-Yates, DNA Consulting, USA

Lisa Peñaloza, Emma Eccles Jones Professor of Marketing, David Eccles School of Business, University of Utah, USA

Linda Price, Department of Marketing, Eller College of Management, University of Arizona, USA

Dennis W. Rook, Professor of Marketing, Clinical, Marshall School of Business, University of Southern California, Los Angeles, USA

Julie A. Ruth, Associate Professor of Marketing, Rutgers University/Camden, USA

Özlem Sandikci, Assistant Professor of Marketing, Bilkent University, Turkey

Shay Sayre, Professor of Communications, California State University, Fullerton, USA

John W. Schouten, Associate Professor of Marketing at University of Portland, USA and a principal of Ethos Market Research, LLC

Linda M. Scott, Professor of Marketing, Said Business School, Oxford University, UK

Jonathan E. Schroeder, Professor of Marketing, University of Exeter, UK

John F. Sherry, Department of Marketing, Mendoza College of Business, University of Notre Dame, USA

Katherine Sredl, University of Illinois, USA

Patricia L. Sunderland, Practica Group, LLC, USA

Gabriele Troilo, Bocconi University, Italy

Terrence H. Witkowski, Professor of Marketing, California State University, Long Beach, USA

PART I

HISTORY AND SCOPE

1 History of qualitative research methods in marketing
Sidney J. Levy

This chapter traces the history of qualitative research methods in marketing. These methods include a variety of techniques such as personal interviewing (sometimes designated as 'open-ended', 'non-directive', 'depth', 'casual' etc.); group or focus group interviewing, projective techniques, participant observation, ethnography, case studies, photography and story telling. Also the analysis of data, however gathered and even if they include measurement, may be characterized as a method that is 'interpretive', 'subjective', 'hermeneutic', 'introspective' or 'post-modern', indicating that it is a qualitative version, as is exemplified by the variety of topics in this *Handbook*. In this history I have emphasized the early days of qualitative research lest they be lost to the memories of modern students who tend to focus attention on the recent decade of their field.

Historic roots of qualitative inquiry
The field of marketing became an academic discipline early in the twentieth century, but its practice and the gathering of intelligence about the market extend far back in time. There have always been explorers, scouts, runners, agents, representatives, salesmen, spies, tax gatherers, census takers, other government functionaries and so on, to provide word of the market. Even Joseph's interpretation of the Pharaoh's dream in the Hebrew Bible led to a form of marketing planning for the storage and distribution of grain. Aristotle, Plato, Cicero and other ancients criticized merchants; and throughout history there have been ambivalent attitudes toward the consumption of goods and services. Qualitative analysis of consumption takes various forms because it interests scholars in different disciplines. Historians, economists, anthropologists, sociologists, psychologists and marcologists (scholars who study marketing [Levy, 1976]) have all paid attention to consumption as an outgrowth of concern with human life.

A History of Private Life: Passions of the Renaissance, conceived by Phillipe Ariès and edited by Roger Chartier (1989), chronicles changes in consumption in France coming out of the Middle Ages. 'People learned to read, discovered the seductions of the self, and retreated into domestic intimacy' (p. 610). Wealth made possible the creation of houses with separate rooms and attention to furnishings and décor; issues of comfort and aesthetics spread from elites to the general public. The elites resisted with sumptuary laws forbidding common folk to emulate them, and they regarded the spread of printed materials as a profanation of knowledge. It is ironic that the growing wealth and freedom of the Enlightenment produced the child-centered family that the wealth and freedom of modern times are often accused of destroying.

The necessity and pleasures of food and eating, their variety and complexity, make them intrinsically appealing. In 1825, Jean Brillat-Savarin (a lawyer and politician) published *The Physiology of Taste*. He is noted for having said, 'Tell me what you eat and I will tell you what you are!' Peter Farb and George Armelagos later wrote a volume, *Consuming Passions: The Anthropology of Eating* (1980), an overview aimed at 'understanding society and culture through eating'. The great anthropologist, Bronislaw Malinowski (1939) addressed the biological and psychological foundations of need satisfaction. Given his analysis of the Trobriand Island exchange system called the *Kula* (1961), Malinowski may be regarded as one of the founders of the behavioral science approach to marketing. The classic study by his student, Audrey Richards, *Hunger and Work in a Savage Tribe* (1948), illustrates his functional method, as applied to nutrition among the Bantu of Africa.

To accomplish such a comprehensive undertaking in modern societies is hard to conceive, but partial attempts are made. 'Hunger and work in a civilized tribe' (Levy, 1978) is regularly addressed by the major food companies. Researchers examine attitudes toward food, the preoccupation with weight control, the relation of diet to health and the use of food to communicate complexities of social status and interaction. For example, *Better Homes and Gardens* has sponsored research on changes in these outlooks; such investigations have been carried out by General Foods, Kraft and so on, usually privately published.

The historian Daniel Horowitz (1985) provides a detailed examination of consumer society in America from 1875 to 1940. He notes the changes in budgets among different social groups, and tells how family behavior was judged by social critics, social workers, home economists and other social scientists. In these materials there is a tension between traditional values of hard work, thrift, the self-controlled family focused on production, and the emerging family with discretionary income seeking new levels of consumption. Many writers disparaged consumers' responses to more money, appliances, indoor plumbing and advertising as profligate and dissolute, and they exhorted the public 'to heed the call of prudence and refinement' (Horowitz 1985, p. 82). The critics hoped that the rigors of World War II might restore traditional morality and sensible frugality.

The post-war period instead brought the Consumer Revolution. Accumulation of capital and personal prosperity joined with pent-up demand for consumer goods and desires for liberated forms of self-expression. The impact of increasing education, contraception, sexual freedom, feminism and the assertion of civil rights became more pronounced. In long qualitative essays, critics offered negative depictions of contemporary life. David Reisman regretted the rise of other-directedness in *The Lonely Crowd* (1950), preferring conformity to inner-directedness and tradition. John Galbraith, in *The Affluent Society* (1958), lamented the squirrel-cage character of consumers motivated by advertising rather than by the public good. And Vance Packard (profitably) exposed and viewed with alarm *The Hidden Persuaders* (1957) who were allegedly corrupting consumers with their insidious analyses and advertising subtleties.

Some social science scholars studied consumers in less visibly moralistic fashion. In 1954 and 1955, New York University Press published two volumes titled *Consumer Behavior*, edited by Lincoln H. Clark. Volume I had the subtitle 'The Dynamics of Consumer Reaction' and Volume II, 'The Life Cycle and Consumer Behavior'. These volumes were sponsored by the Committee for Research on Consumer Attitudes and Behavior, and contain thoughtful articles by economists, sociologists and psychologists. Only the editor, Clark, was a professor of marketing. Nelson N. Foote (1954) wrote on

'The Autonomy of the Consumer', pointing to economic changes in America: growth of middle-income families, a substantial rise in real income every year, and mounting discretionary income (ibid., p.15). He interprets growing opportunities for consumers to make choices and show self-determination. At the same time, William H. Whyte (1954) writes on 'The Consumer in the New Suburbia', but emphasizes the conformity he sees among the residents of a development in Park Forest, Illinois.

Scholars in the Clark volumes mainly study choice and decision making. Introducing the discipline of psychological economics, George Katona says that 'actors on the economic scene have significant latitude or discretion in their behavior . . . (or) . . . there would be hardly any need to introduce psychological variables as explanatory principles of economic behavior' (1954, p.30). Similarly, James Tobin, a professor of economics, says, 'Perhaps an even more fundamental and difficult research program would center on the values, aspirations, and goals of families . . . and their effects on consumption behavior' (1954, p. 108.) Thus, to the agendas of home economists, social workers, Bureau of Labor statisticians and moralists are added the research slates of sociologists, psychologists and the emerging marcologists.

Robert Hess and Gerald Handel (1959) studied family life in a volume titled *Family Worlds: A Psychosocial Approach to Family Life*. Their case studies were derived from intensive interviews with family members, held individually and together, written essays, and projective methods such as Incomplete Sentences and the Thematic Apperception Technique. These qualitative methods illuminated especially the fine dynamic detail and complexity of individual patterns and variations among the families.

The role of marketing research
Following the first US Census in 1790, and spurred by the English work of Charles Booth in 1886, many large-scale projects were carried out (Young, 1939; Parten, 1950). Similarly, psychological testing grew, stimulated by the use of IQ measurement in World War I, adding to the desire to gather data about the public. Awareness of public opinion grew with the writing of Walter Lippmann in the 1920s, with studies of newspapers and their readers. In the 1930s, psychologists (notably Gordon W. Allport and Hadley Cantril) examined the role and impact of radio. The 1940s and 1950s were a golden age of communications study as psychologists, sociologists, political scientists, historians and journalists (led especially by Samuel A. Stouffer, Robert K. Merton and Bernard Berelson) delved into the various media (Klapper, 1960).

The history of qualitative research methods occurs within two main contexts. First, qualitative methods are applied to the marketplace as *marketing research*. Second, academic personnel are drawn to develop theories about the nature of marketing with *research into marketing*. Donald M. Hobart tells how modern marketing research began.

> There was a time when marketing research did not exist. About the year 1910 an idea was born . . . The father of this idea was Mr. Stanley Latshaw, at that time the advertising representative in Boston for The Curtis Publishing Company . . . He was not satisfied with the way in which he and his salesmen sold advertising space. Neither they nor their customers knew much about markets and the wants and habits of consumers and dealers . . . The plan was to hire a competent man, turn him loose with a roving commission, and then see what happened. The man whom Mr. Latshaw hired for this untried work was the late Charles Coolidge Parlin, a schoolmaster from a small city in Wisconsin. (Hobart, 1950, pp. 3–4)

We can see here numerous issues arising: the dissatisfaction of a manager with a marketing problem, the nature of salesmanship, the business-to-business relationship, the role of the media and communications, the desire to understand the end users' motives and actions, involvement of an academic intelligence and the early, open-minded, exploratory attitude.

In 1926, General Foods established a panel of homemakers for testing new products; in 1932, the Psychological Corporation set up a continuous poll of buying behavior. This survey work was aimed at measuring audience characteristics, with emphasis on learning what people did, and on statistical differences among them in terms of age, sex, education, income, occupation and marital status. The goal of understanding behavior was central, of course, but finding out what the actions were, per se, was an important first step. By comparing the characteristics of groups that did different things, insight was gained, and findings could be speculated about and taken to affirm or question previously held hypotheses.

The rise of qualitative research

Despite the centuries of marketing activity, the *Journal of Marketing* was first published only in 1922; and, despite all the work after World War II on consumers and communication, the *Journal of Marketing Research* arrived only in 1964, and the *Journal of Consumer Research* ten years later. In the 1930s, dissatisfaction with polling and surveying appeared in the marketing literature. The information gained seemed descriptive, mechanical and not explanatory enough. Psychology was moving from a measurement phase to a clinical phase, with personality analyses and projective techniques adding an interpretive dimension to the traditional laboratory focus. Instead of IQ measurement, qualitative personality assessment was emphasized by the Office of Strategic Services (OSS), precursor to the CIA.

The European migration

Harold H. Kassarjian (1994) describes the move to the US in the 1930s of influential researchers such as George Katona, Hans Zeisel and Herta Herzog. Alfred Politz became a successful commercial surveyor who believed that valid marketing research required national probability samples of at least 1200 people; and he opposed qualitative methods. Kassarjian names Paul F. Lazarsfeld for bringing 'the techniques of introspection as well as introducing qualitative research and small samples to marketing and advertising research' (p. 269). Kassarjian's own work as a researcher, teacher, reviewer and editor made major contributions in reports on projective techniques, personality theory and numerous other topics, as is visible in his vita (2005).

Consumer goods companies pioneered, often using research consultants, including academicians who applied behavioral science ideas to business problems. In 1939, Ernest Dichter, Lazarsfeld's student, carried out qualitative analyses of Ivory Soap and Plymouth cars. He was a leader in qualitative work that came to be called 'motivation research' (Dichter, 1947). He was notorious for his free-wheeling approach and psychoanalytic ideas, as well as his popularity among executives; and Lazarsfeld joined in the criticism of Dichter, despite the merits and practical value of Dichter's ideas.

Having a traditional receptivity to psychology (Scott, 1917), advertising agencies were aware of new work in the communications field (Strong, 1913; Poffenberger, 1925). They

played a major role in the competition among brands and were sensitive to market segmentation. Demographic data were not always sufficient or satisfying. Sometimes there
were no significant differences between two user groups in their age, sex and income distributions, so those characteristics did not appear to account for their different marketing
behaviors. Often, too, user groups gave the same reasons for different brand preferences,
showing that there are discrepancies between what people say they do or think or like and
what they actually do, think or like. The reasons people give may not be all the reason,
and they may not be able to explain their own behavior. Because the usual structured questionnaire was often found to be insufficiently informative, research workers found it useful
to develop more conversational interviews. Sometimes these interviews were carried
out by psychiatric or psychological personnel and were compared to the free association
sessions connected with psychoanalytic therapy. Because of this, such interviews were
called 'depth interviews'. Also the work of Carl R. Rogers (1956) gained fame for the
'non-directive interview'. Despite theoretical differences between Freud and Rogers, both
relied on the subject freely introspecting and talking so that thoughts and feelings are
explored and brought forth fully.

The post-World War II surge
Social science technology grew fast after World War II. Social Research, Inc. (SRI) was
established in 1946 to apply the interests of faculty members of the Committee on Human
Development at the University of Chicago: W. Lloyd Warner (social stratification and
symbol systems, 1949), Burleigh B. Gardner (human organization, 1945) and William E.
Henry (analysis of fantasy, 1956). News of company-sponsored research appeared in
trade publications such as *Advertising Age, Sponsor, Printers' Ink* and *Advertising &
Selling*. A magazine of advertising, marketing and public relations, *Tide* (1947), reported
SRI's work that used projective methods and ethnographies adapted from social anthropology and psychology to analyze symbolic meanings of greeting cards and of soap
operas.

Qualitative research methods were not readily accepted in academic marketing departments, despite their common use in history, anthropology, sociology and literary criticism. The receptivity by business offended people who look down on business and its
minions. Morris Holbrook (1995) said that such consultants were obsequious dogs
(p. 303). In *The Theory of the Leisure Class*, that pioneering study of consumption,
Thorstein Veblen (1899) commented that 'knowledge of latter-day men and things is . . .
"lower", "base", "ignoble" – one even hears the epithet "sub-human", applied to this
matter-of-fact knowledge of mankind and of everyday life' (p. 391). Some contemporary
sociologists have an awakened interest in studying consumers, but they commonly ignore
work in the marketing literature, at times as a result busying themselves re-inventing the
wheel. A professor of finance recently raved in my presence that he hated the behavioral
people he asserted were ruining his field.

In 'Alternative Approaches in the Study of Complex Situations', Robert Weiss (1966)
calmly and objectively contrasts research methods. But contention and lack of scientific
objectivity about methods persist. Dominant paradigm people often resist, show hostility and, at many schools, refuse to hire or promote faculty who are qualitatively oriented.
They are defensive, unrealistically acting as though their livelihoods are jeopardized by
the projective techniques and ethnographies that they imagine will replace their surveys,

regressions and multivariate methods. At the 1998 conference of the Association for Consumer Research, such persons complained that qualitative researchers were taking over the conference.

Nevertheless, results of the early work on social-psychological aspects of consumer behavior worked their way into the academic literature. Warner and Henry (1948) published 'The Radio Day Time Serial: A Symbolic Analysis', in *Genetic Psychology Monographs*. The *Harvard Business Review* published Dichter's 'Psychology in Marketing Research' (1947), illustrating the distinction between 'rationalized' explanations for actions and customers' deeper, unconscious reasons. Such thinking attempted to get past the 'lists of motives' that used to make up much of the psychological approach to explaining customer behavior (Kornhauser, 1923; Copeland, 1924; Duncan, 1940).

The kind of indirectly derived insight that a projective method might yield was famously dramatized for the marketing profession by a single simple experiment reported by Mason Haire in 1950. He showed samples of women a brief shopping list and asked for a description of the woman who had prepared the list. The list was varied by including or omitting a brand of instant coffee. Subjects who saw instant coffee on the list projected their ideas about instant coffee by describing the buyer as less oriented to home and family, compared to the descriptions given by those who saw the list without instant coffee (Haire, 1950).

Motivation research

S.I. Hayakawa's *Language in Action* (1941) introduced me to General Semantics, announcing that words and things were different. Hayakawa led me to a weighty and esoteric tome, *Science and Sanity*, by Count Alfred Korzybski (1933), and his model of the Structural Differential. This interest foreshadowed the attention to semiotics that flared up years later (Umiker-Sebiok, 1987). With this background, I was drawn into interdisciplinary study with the Committee on Human Development at Chicago, and in 1948 at SRI began my career of investigating the significance to people of companies, products, brands, media, advertisements, persons and life styles. I was increasingly struck by the way motivation interacts with perception: that is, how people's motives lead them to perceive meaning in the objects they encounter and how the meanings of those objects affect their motives. I studied the Thematic Apperception Technique with William Henry (1956), learning to interpret people's story telling. I saw how they symbolize their lives in the products and brands they consume, and how they tell each other stories in pursuit of their aims.

The excitement about behavioral science methods and theories spread in the mid-1950s, linking marketplace behavior with personality traits, exploring consumer motivations and analyzing perceptions of products and brands. *The Chicago Tribune*'s Pierre D. Martineau commissioned from SRI basic studies of beer, cigarettes, soaps and detergents, and automobiles, which he publicized via numerous industry presentations, where they were usually the first of their kind. We called these studies 'motivation research'.

Cigarettes: Their Role and Function analyzed the physical, psychological, sociological, and cultural significance of cigarettes and smoking. *Motivations Relating to Soaps and Chemical Detergents* analyzed how these products helped housewives cope with and control negative aspects of their social role. *Automobiles: What They Mean to Americans* explored the ramified significance of the automobile in people's lives as an extension of the self, in terms of its practical use, economic value, social status symbolism, psychological motives, and perceptions of the cars' images. (Newman, 1957)

In the 1960s and 1970s, the excitement moderated. Attention shifted to the systematic measurement that was aided by the rise of the computer. New promise came from the experiments of cognitive psychology, not from depth psychologies. Motivation research (like Freudianism and God) was said to have died. Still, motivation research never died. It settled down to be carried out by Dichter and other workers, including my associates at Social Research, Inc. and myself, under the heading of motivational studies, qualitative analyses, sociopsychological studies and the like.

The 1970s saw the rise of the focus group. This method had a history in the study of group dynamics (Lewin, 1947), small groups (Bales, 1950) and convenient survey methods (Parten, 1950). It showed up in marketing literature with a piece by Alfred Goldman (1962) on the group depth interview in the *Journal of Marketing* and in reports in the *Marketing News* and other trade press. The business community loved the focus group. In many organizations it was (and is) considered synonymous with qualitative research and was the only method used to get qualitative information. Marketing managers need information to nourish their decisions, and focus groups are the fast food of marketing research.

At times, hostility to the new methods and practitioners was intense. Motivation researchers were accused of offering false panaceas or, conversely, dangerously effective insights. The vice of subjectivity, with its supposed lack of validity and reliability, was especially emphasized. The conflict can be seen in titles of news articles of the period: 'Politz Tags Motivation Research "Fake", "Hah!" Hahs Dichter Group', *Advertising Age* (1955b); 'Battle of Embittered Ph.D.s', *Advertising Age* (1955a); 'Research Rivals Trade Blows', *Business Week* (1955); 'Is motivation research really an instrument of the Devil?' (William D. Wells, 1956).

By 1958, the pros and cons had been pretty thoroughly reviewed. A compendium of these views was compiled by Robert Ferber and Hugh G. Wales (1958) in *Motivation and Market Behavior*. Joseph Newman (1957) also provided a comprehensive view. Using a case approach, he shows the breadth of understanding that was sought in qualitative studies. The results of personality studies were critically reviewed (Kassarjian and Sheffet, 1975). Books by Martineau (1957), George Horsley Smith (1954), Harry Henry (1958) and Vance Packard (1957) presented concepts, methods, applications, criticism and defense.

Pioneers in qualitative research

Two sets of pioneers were especially important in fostering the initial wave of motivation/qualitative work. Such figures as Ernest Dichter; my colleagues Burleigh B. Gardner, Steuart Henderson Britt and Harriett Bruce Moore; Dietrich Leonhard, Hal Kassarjian, Louis Cheskin, Herta Herzog, Virginia Miles, William D. Wells and several others, were knowledgeable and spread the word. The second group who played a special role were the daring business people who had the curiosity and imagination to support innovative research projects, who were willing to learn about unconventional methods. These included George Reeves and Sandy Gunn of J. Walter Thompson, Henry O. Whiteside of Gardner Advertising and later J. Walter Thompson, Hugh McMillan and Jack Bowen of

Campbell-Ewald, Leo Burnett of Leo Burnett Advertising, Pierre D. Martineau of *The Chicago Tribune*, Gerhardt Kleining of Reemstma in Germany, Dudley Ruch of Pillsbury, John Catlin of Kimberly-Clark, Robert Gwynn and Dan Bash of Sunbeam Corporation, George Stewart of Swift and Company, Beland Honderich of the *Toronto Star*, Margaret Rogers at N.W. Ayers, and many more.

The influence of Social Research, Inc.
The work at Social Research, Inc., where I became a principal, spread qualitative research methods in both practical and theoretical directions. We embedded projective devices (Levy, 1985) within the more or less nondirective approach of the so-called 'depth interview'. These were variants on the clinical techniques of the time, such as the TAT, the Rorschach, Sentence Completion, Word Association, Draw-A-Person and the curious Szondi test (Rainwater, 1956). We created devices such as matching people, animals, cars, pictorial symbols and soliciting dreams. We took pictures of houses and living rooms, we sent interviewers to spend days observing and making detailed notes on what respondents did and said. Essentially, we engaged in accumulating case studies, personal histories and ethnographies; and we conducted group interviews before they came to be called 'focus groups'. A later variation on these methods is reported in 'Autodriving: A Photoelicitation Technique' (Heisley and Levy, 1991). Gerald Zaltman (2003) has recently combined pictures in collages, metaphors and story telling in his Zaltman Metaphor Elicitation Technique.

Using Warner's Index of Status Characteristics (Warner et al., 1949), we classified our respondents to examine the effects of social class on consumer behavior. *Workingman's Wife*, by Lee Rainwater, Richard P. Coleman and Gerald Handel (1959), was based on studies of readers of romance publications for Macfadden-Bartell Corporation. We taught clients about social stratification in American society. Along the way, to apply my multidisciplinary training, I wrote one article to show the use of sociological concepts ('Social Class and Consumer Behavior', Levy, 1966), another arguing for the psychological perspective ('Mammon and Psyche', Levy, 1968) and another to show the relevance of anthropology ('Hunger and Work in a Civilized Tribe', Levy, 1978). Assisting in the spread of ideas from SRI, Lee Rainwater (1974) became a professor of anthropology and sociology at Harvard; Gerald Handel taught sociology at CCNY; and Richard Coleman and I taught in marketing departments, he at Kansas State and I at Northwestern and now the University of Arizona.

The brand image
One concept that emerged from our work was that of the brand image. I remembered William James (1892) writing that 'a man has as many social selves as there are individuals who recognize him and carry an image of him in their mind . . . But as the individuals who carry the images fall differently into classes we may practically say that there are as many different social selves as there are distinct groups of persons about whose opinion he cares (p. 180)'. At SRI we saw that this idea was true for organizations, their products and their brands, and the notion of imagery as a marketing apperception was used to interpret them. Consequently (with Burleigh B. Gardner), I wrote 'The Product and the Brand', for the *Harvard Business Review* (1955), explaining that each product or brand exists in people's minds as a symbolic entity, an integrated resultant of all their

experiences with it in the marketplace. The notion was seized upon by the advertising community and, if I may immodestly (or guiltily) say so, the brand image idea subsequently swept the world, becoming part of the lingua franca of modern times.

Symbolic analysis
The brand image was also a vehicle for spreading the notion of symbolic analysis. Reinforced by Warner's work on symbol systems (1959), the symbolic interactionists at the University of Chicago, and experience with projective methods, our consumer studies were exercises in the interpretation of symbols and symbolic behavior. Ira O. Glick and I wrote *Living with Television* (1962, re-issued in 2005), based on studies of television shows' audiences conducted for Chevrolet and Campbell-Ewald, its advertising agency. Warner described it as a 'contribution to our body of knowledge about the meanings and function of the symbol systems commonly shared by most Americans' (p. 6). We did the first qualitative study for the Coca-Cola Company on why people drink soft drinks, the first study for AT&T on the meaning of the telephone. For the Wrigley Company we studied what baseball meant to Cubs fans. A study for FTD, the flower delivery system, analyzed the poignancy of flowers in representing the life cycle, symbolizing its beauty, its fragility and the inevitability of death. With this work in mind, I wrote the article 'Symbols for Sale' (1959) and other related reports: 'Symbolism and Life Style' (1963) and 'Interpreting Consumer Mythology: A Structural Approach to Consumer Behavior' (1981).

Broadening the concept of marketing
From the variety of SRI's innovative qualitative research for corporations, hospitals, schools, banks, associations, politicians and government agencies, it became evident to me that marketing was a function of all individuals and organizations. Philip Kotler and I wrote 'Broadening the Concept of Marketing', that appeared in the *Journal of Marketing* (1969). The broadening idea created a stir. Our article led to the 'broadening' title being given to the 1970 American Marketing Association Summer Educators' Conference, and diffused the marketing concept into the management of education, health, government and the arts. It was criticized by some people as obvious, wrongheaded and evil. One piece (Laczniak and Michie, 1979) accused us of creating social disorder by distorting the definition of marketing. In reply (Levy and Kotler, 1979), we defended the 'uses of disorder' (Sennett, 1970).

Recent history
Historically, marketing departments had one major qualitative method. Emulating Harvard by using case studies was accepted as a respectable tradition. However, in the late 1950s and 1960s, scientific research hit marketing departments, affecting the personnel and the nature of their work. Northwestern University hired a stream of social scientists with qualitative interests, such as Steuart Henderson Britt, then me, Philip Kotler, Gerald Zaltman, Bobby Calder and John Sherry. Doctoral program graduates who did qualitative work include John Myers (1968), Thomas Robertson (1967), Richard Bagozzi (1974), Fuat Firat (1978), Dennis Rook (1985, 1987), Aaron Ahuvia (1998), Güliz Ger (1992), Douglas Holt (1995) and Deborah Heisley (1990). Marketing scholars at other schools similarly recognized the contribution of the behavioral sciences, and some among them turned to qualitative work.

From the establishment of the Association for Consumer Research in 1970 and the *Journal of Consumer Research* in 1974, there has been a steady flow of reports from the qualitative workers of the last 35 years. Major integrations were provided by Engel, Kollat and Blackwell in 1968, with *Consumer Behavior*, by Howard and Sheth in 1969, with *The Theory of Buyer Behavior*, Joel B. Cohen's editing of *Behavioral Science Foundations of Consumer Behavior* (1972) and lately by Shay Sayre (2001). Michael Solomon (2005), in his textbook, gives an overview of the progress that has been made in studying consumption, including the work of qualitative researchers. In the critical vein, consumers are still blamed for their supposedly unhappy materialism, but postmodernists tend to find greater villainy in corporate power and policies, and the negative hegemonies of the age (Firat and Dholakia, 1998; Askegaard and Firat, 1997).

Feeding these currents was a second major wave of European influence. The French stand out for the contributions of Roland Barthes (1957), Michel Foucault (1969), Jean Baudrillard (1981) and Pierre Bourdieu (1987); and the whole semiotic movement, for which see David Mick (1986) and Hanne Larsen et al. (1991). Dominique Bouchet (2005) has fostered the qualitative approach at the University of Southern Denmark, along with his students and colleagues Per Østergaard (1991) and Søren Askegaard (1991). From Ireland came the provocative voices of Stephen Brown and Darach Turley (1977).

Not all contributors to qualitative research can be listed, regrettably, but some are notable for promoting the modern entrenchment of qualitative endeavors. To describe the remarkable productivity of Russell E. Belk could fill a chapter, as Belk is an industry in himself. Readers are referred to his vita (2005) to see his publications, both in text and in film. His leadership led to *Highways and Buyways: Naturalistic Research from the Consumer Behavior Odyssey* (1991) a milestone in qualitative research history. Morris B. Holbrook (1981, 1995) stands out for his prolific contributions as he veered between systematic technical work and his qualitative interest in symbolic materials, expressed especially in his love of animal metaphors. Individually and jointly, he and Elizabeth C. Hirschman (1992) illuminated a great variety of topics. Barbara Stern (1988), Edward McQuarrie (1991), John Schouten (1991) brought their special literary sensibilities to bear on marketing communications.

Along the qualitative trail are the distinctive contributions of anthropologists: John Sherry (1995, 1998), Eric Arnould, Linda L. Price and Cele Otnes (1999), Eric Arnould (2001), Grant McCracken (1988) and Annamma Joy (1982), with creative and provocative work. Robert V. Kozinets (2002) brings his acuity to cultural phenomena such as *Star Trek* and *Burning Man*. Emphasizing postmodern thinking and its application are Fuat Firat and Alladi Venkatesh, editors of the journal *Consumption, Markets and Culture*. A prominent figure in the qualitative field is Melanie Wallendorf, with an important stream of work, individually (1980) and jointly with Arnould (1991), Belk (1987), Sherry (Belk, Wallendorf and Sherry 1989), Zaltman (1983), and others. Among contemporary colleagues are Craig Thompson (Thompson, Loccander and Pollio, 1989) and Douglas Holt (Holt and Thompson, 2002) whose work together and individually illuminates diverse cultural issues such as baseball, Starbucks and masculinity. Cele Otnes and Richard F. Beltramini (1996) and Mary Ann McGrath (1989) have highlighted gifting; and Jeffrey Durgee makes lively and thoughtful connections between qualitative theory and application (2005). These scholars and several others speak further for themselves in the subsequent chapters of this *Handbook*.

References

Advertising Age (1955a), 'Battle of Embittered Ph.D.s', 19 September, 3.
—— (1955b), 'Politz Tags: Motivation Research "Fake", "Hah!" Hahs Dichter Group', 19 September, 3.
Ahuvia, A.C. (1998), 'Social criticism of advertising: on the role of literary theory and the use of data', *Journal of Advertising*, **27**, 143–62.
Ariès, Phillipe and Georges Duby (eds) (1989), *A History of Private Life: Passions of the Renaissance*, Vol. III, Cambridge, MA: Harvard University Press.
Arnould, Eric J. (2001), 'Ethnographic contributions to marketing and consumer behavior: an introduction', *Journal of Contemporary Ethnography*, special issue (August).
Arnould, Eric J., Linda L. Price and Cele Otnes (1999), 'Making (consumption) magic: a study of white water river rafting', *Journal of Contemporary Ethnography*, **28** (1), February, 33–68.
Askegaard, Søren (1991), 'Toward a semiotic structure of cultural identity', in Hanne Hartvig Larsen et al. (eds), *Marketing and Semiotics*, Copenhagen: Handelshøjskolens Forlag, pp. 11–30.
Askegaard Søren and A. Fuat Firat (1997), 'Towards a critique of material culture, consumption, and markets', in S. Pearce (ed.), *Experiencing Material Culture in the Western World*, London: Leicester University Press, pp. 114–39.
Bagozzi, Richard P. (1974), 'Marketing as an organized behavioral system of exchange', *Journal of Marketing*, **38**, 77–81.
Bales, R.F. (1951), *Interaction Process Analysis: A Method for the Study of Small Groups*, Cambridge, MA: Addison-Wesley Press.
Barthes, Roland (1957), *Mythologies*, Paris: Editions du Seuil.
Baudrillard, Jean (1981), *For a Critique of the Political Economy of the Sign* (tr. C. Levin), St. Louis: Telos.
Belk, Russell W. (ed.) (1991), *Highways and Buyways: Naturalistic Research from the Consumer Behavior Odyssey*, Provo, UT: Association for Consumer Research.
Belk, Russell W. (2005) (http://www.home.business.utah.edu/~mktrwb/russ2.htm).
Belk, Russell W., Melanie Wallendorf and John F. Sherry (1989), 'The sacred and the profane in consumer behavior: theodicy in the Odyssey', *Journal of Consumer Research*, **16** (June), 1–38.
Bouchet, Dominique (2005) (http://www.bouchet.dk/nukedit/content/bibliographies.asp).
Bourdieu, Pierre (1987), *Distinction: A Social Critique of the Judgement of Taste* (tr. Richard Nice), Cambridge, MA: Harvard University Press.
Brillat-Savarin, Jean ([1825] 1994), *The Physiology of Taste*, New York: Viking, Penguin.
Brown, Stephen and Darach Turley (1977), 'Travelling in trope: postcards from the edge of consumer research', in Stephen Brown and Darach Turley (eds), *Consumer Research: Postcards from the Edge*, New York: Routledge, pp. 1–21.
Business Week (1955), 'Research Rivals Trade Blows', 29 October.
Chartier, Roger (1989), in Phillipe Ariès and Georges Duby (eds), *A History of Private Life: Passions of the Renaissance*, Vol. III, Cambridge, MA: Harvard University Press.
Clark, Lincoln H. (ed.) (1954), *Consumer Behavior*, Vol. I, New York: New York University Press.
—— (1955), *Consumer Behavior*, Vol. II, New York: New York University Press.
Cohen, J.B. (ed.) (1972), *Behavioral Science Foundations of Consumer Behavior*, New York: The Free Press.
Copeland, Melvin T. (1924), *Principles of Merchandising*, Chicago: A.W. Shaw Co.
Dichter, Ernest (1947), 'Psychology in marketing research', *Harvard Business Review*, **25** (Summer), 432–43.
Duncan, Delbert J. (1940), 'What motivates business buyers', *Harvard Business Review*, **18**.
Durgee, Jeffrey F. (2005), *Creative Insight: The Researcher's Art*, Chicago: The Copy Workshop.
Farb, Peter and George Armelagos (1980), *Consuming Passions: The Anthropology of Eating*, Boston: Houghton-Mifflin.
Ferber, Robert and Hugh G. Wales (1958), *Motivation and Market Behavior*, Homewood, IL: Irwin.
Firat, A. Fuat (1978), 'The social construction of consumption patterns', doctoral dissertation, Northwestern University.
Firat, A. Fuat and Nikhilesh Dholakia (1998), *Consuming People: From Political Economy to Theaters of Consumption*, New York: Routledge.
Foote, Nelson N. (1954), 'The autonomy of the consumer', in Lincoln H. Clark (ed.), *Consumer Behavior*, Vol. I, New York: New York University Press, pp. 15–24.
Foucault, Michel (1969), *L'Archéologie du Savoir*, Paris: Gallimard.
Galbraith, John Kenneth (1958), *The Affluent Society*, New York: Houghton Mifflin Co.
Gardner, Burleigh B. (1945), *Human Relations in Industry*, Homewood, IL: Richard D. Irwin.
Gardner, Burleigh. B. and Sidney J. Levy (1955), 'The product and the brand', *Harvard Business Review* (March–April), 33–9.
Ger, Güliz (1992), 'The positive and negative effects of marketing on socioeconomic development: the Turkish case', *Journal of Consumer Policy*, **15** (3), 229–54.

Glick, Ira O. and Sidney J. Levy (1962), *Living with Television*, Chicago: Aldine Publishing Company.
Goldman, Alfred E. (1962), 'The group depth interview', *Journal of Marketing*, **26** (July), 61–8.
Haire, Mason (1950), 'Projective techniques in marketing research', *Journal of Marketing*, **14** (April), 649–56.
Handel, Gerald, (1967), 'Psychological study of whole families', in Gerald Handel (ed.), *The Psychosocial Interior of the Family*, Chicago: Aldine, pp. 517–46.
Hayakawa, S.I. (1941), *Language in Action*, New York: Harcourt Brace.
Heisley, Deborah D. (1990) 'Gender symbolism in food', doctoral dissertation, Northwestern University.
Heisley, Deborah D. and Sidney J. Levy (1991), 'Autodriving, a photoelicitation technique', *Journal of Consumer Research*, **18** (3) (December), 257–72.
Henry, Harry (1958), *Motivation Research*, London: Crosby Lockwood & Son, Ltd.
Henry, William E. (1956), *The Analysis of Fantasy*, New York: Wiley & Sons, Inc.
Robert D. Hess and Gerald Handel (1959), *Family Worlds: A Psychosocial Approach to Family Life*, Chicago: The University of Chicago Press.
Hill, Reuben, (1961), 'Patterns of decision-making and the accumulation of family assets', in Nelson N. Foote (ed.), *Household Decision-Making*, New York: New York University Press, pp. 57–102.
Hirschman, Elizabeth C. and Morris B. Holbrook (1981), *Symbolic Consumer Behavior*, New York: Association for Consumer Research.
—— (1992), *Postmodern Consumer Research: The Study of Consumption as Text*, Thousand Oaks, CA: Sage Publications.
Hobart, Donald M. (ed.) (1950), *Marketing Research Practice*, New York: The Ronald Press.
Holbrook, Morris B. (1981), 'The esthetic imperative in consumer research', in Elizabeth C. Hirschman and Morris B. Holbrook (eds), *Symbolic Consumer Behavior*, New York: Association for Consumer Research.
—— (1995), *Consumer Research: Introspective Essays on the Study of Consumption*, Thousand Oaks, CA: Sage Publications.
Holman, R. (1981), 'Apparel as communication', in E. Hirschman and M. Holbrook (eds), *Symbolic Consumer Behavior*, New York: Association for Consumer Research, pp. 7–15.
Holt, Douglas B. (1995), 'How consumers consume: a typology of consumption practices', *Journal of Consumer Research*, **22**, 1–16.
Holt, Douglas and Craig J. Thompson (2002), 'Man-of-action heroes: how the American ideology of manhood structures men's consumption', HBS Marketing Research Paper No. 03–04 (November) (http://ssrn.com/abstract=386600).
Horowitz, Daniel (1985), *The Morality of Spending*, Chicago: Ivan R. Dee.
Howard, John B. and Jagdish N. Sheth (1969), *The Theory of Buyer Behavior*, New York: John Wiley & Sons.
James, William (1892), *Psychology*, New York: Henry Holt.
Joy, Annamma (1982), 'Accommodation and cultural persistence: the case of the Sikhs and the Portuguese in the Okanagan Valley of British Columbia', PhD dissertation, University of British Columbia (Canada).
Kassarjian, Harold H. (1994), 'Scholarly traditions and European roots of American consumer research', in Gilles Laurent, Gary L. Lilien and Bernard Pras (eds), Boston: Kluwer Academic Publishers, pp. 265–82.
—— (2005) (http://www.anderson.ucla.edu/documents/areas/fac/marketing/kassarjian_vita.pdf).
Kassarjian, Harold and M.J. Sheffet (1975), 'Personality and consumer behavior: one more time', in E. Mazze (ed.), *Combined Proceedings*, Chicago: AMA, pp. 197–201.
Katona, George (1954), 'A study of purchase decisions', in Lincoln H. Clark (ed.), *Consumer Behavior*, Vol. I, New York: New York University Press, pp. 30–87.
Katona, George and Eva Mueller (1954), 'Study of purchase decisions', in Lincoln H. Clark (ed.), *Consumer Behavior*, New York: New York University Press, pp. 30–87.
Klapper, J.T. (1960), The *Effects of Mass Communication*, New York: Free Press.
Kornhauser, Arthur W. (1923), 'The motives-in-industry problem', *Annals of the American Academy of Political and Social Science* (September), 105–16.
Korzybski, Alfred (1933), *Science and Sanity*, New York: International Non-Aristotelian Publishing Co.
Kotler, Philip and Sidney J. Levy (1969), 'Broadening the concept of marketing', *Journal of Marketing*, **33** (July), 10–15, also in S.J. Levy (1999).
Kozinets, Robert V. (2002), 'Can consumers escape the market? Emancipatory illuminations from burning man', *Journal of Consumer Research*, **29** (June), 20–38.
Laczniak, Gene R. and D.A. Michie (1979), 'The social disorder of the broadened concept of marketing', *Journal of American Academy of Marketing Science*, **7** (3) (Summer), 214–32.
Larsen, Hanne Hartvig, David Glen Mick and Christian Alsted (eds) (1991), *Marketing and Semiotics*, Copenhagen: Handelshøjskolens Forlag.
Levy, Sidney J. (1959), 'Symbols for Sale', *Harvard Business Review* (July–Aug.), 117–24, also in Sidney J. Levy (1999).
—— (1963), 'Symbolism and Life Style', 'Proceedings', American Marketing Association Conference, (December), 140–150, and in Sidney J. Levy (1999).

Levy, Sidney J. (1966), 'Social class and consumer behavior', in J. Newman (ed.), *On Knowing the Consumer*, New York: John Wiley and Sons, pp. 146–60.
—— (1968), 'Mammon and psyche', in M.S. Sommers and J.B. Kernan (eds), *Explorations in Consumer Behavior*, Austin, TX: University of Texas, pp. 119–34.
—— (1976), 'Marcology 101, or the domain of marketing', in K.L. Bernhardt (ed.), *Marketing: 1776–1976 and Beyond*, Chicago: American Marketing Association, pp. 577–81, also in S.J. Levy (1999).
—— (1978), 'Hunger and work in a civilized tribe: or the anthropology of market transactions', *American Behavioral Scientist* (March–April), **21** (4), 557–70.
—— (1981), 'Interpreting consumer mythology: a structural approach to consumer behavior', *Journal of Marketing*, **45**, 49–61.
—— (1985), 'Dreams, fairy tales, animals, and cars', *Psychology and Marketing* (Summer), also in Sidney J. Levy (1999).
—— (1999), *Brands, Consumers, Symbols, and Research: Sidney J. Levy on Marketing*, Thousand Oaks, CA: Sage Publications.
Levy, Sidney J. and Philip Kotler (1979), 'A rejoinder: toward a broader concept of marketing's role in social order', *Journal of the Academy of Marketing Science*, **7** (3), 233–7.
Lewin, Kurt (1947), 'Frontiers in group dynamics', *Human Relations*, **1** (1).
McCracken, Grant (1988), *Culture and Consumption*, Bloomington, IN: Indiana University Press.
McGrath, Mary Ann (1989), 'An ethnography of a gift store: wrappings, trappings, and rapture', *Journal of Retailing*, **65** (4), 421–41.
McQuarrie, Edward F. (1991), 'The customer visit: qualitative research for business-to-business marketers', *Marketing Research*, **3** (1), 15–28.
Malinowski, B. (1939), 'The group and the individual in functional analysis', *American Journal of Sociology*, 44.
—— ([1922] 1961), *Argonauts of the Western Pacific*, New York: Dutton.
Martineau, Pierre D. (1957), *Motivation in Advertising*, New York: McGraw-Hill.
Mick, David Glen (1986), 'Consumer research and semiotics: exploring the morphology of signs, symbols, and significance', *Journal of Consumer Research*, **13** (September), 196–213.
Myers, John G. (1968), *Consumer Image and Attitude*, Berkeley, CA: IBER Special Publications.
Newman, Joseph W. (1957), *Motivation Research and Marketing Management*, Cambridge, MA: Harvard University.
Østergaard, Per (1991), 'Marketing and the interpretive turn: ontological reflections on the concept of man', in Hanne Hartvig Larsen et al. (eds), *Marketing and Semiotics*, Copenhagen: Handelshøjskolens Forlag, pp. 211–26.
Otnes, Cele and Richard F. Beltramini (1996), *Gift Giving*, Bowling Green, OH: Bowling Green State University Popular Press.
Packard, Vance (1957), *The Hidden Persuaders*, New York: Pocket Books.
Parten, Mildred (1950), *Surveys, Polls, and Samples: Practical Procedures*, New York: Harper.
Poffenberger, Albert T. (1925), *Psychology in Advertising*, Chicago: A.W. Shaw Co.
Rainwater, Lee (1956), 'A study of personality differences between middle and lower class adolescents: the Szondi Test in culture–personality research', Genetic Psychology Monographs, **54**, 3–86.
—— (1974), What *Money Buys: Inequality and the Social Meanings of Income*, New York: Basic Books.
Rainwater, Lee, Richard P. Coleman and Gerald Handel (1959), *Workingman's Wife*, New York: Oceana.
Reisman, David (1950), *The Lonely Crowd*, New Haven: Yale University Press.
Richards, Audrey ([1932] 1948), *Hunger and Work in a Savage Tribe*, Glencoe, IL: The Free Press.
Robertson, Thomas S. (1967), 'The process of innovation and the diffusion of innovation', *Journal of Marketing*, **31** (January), 14–19.
Rogers, Carl R. (1956), 'Client-centered theory', *Journal of Counseling Psychology*, **3** (2), 115–20.
Rogers, Carl R. (1967), *On Becoming a Person. A Therapist's View of Psychotherapy*, Boston: Houghton Mifflin.
Rook, Dennis W. (1985), 'The ritual dimension of consumer behavior', *Journal of Consumer Research*, **12** (December), 251–64.
—— (1987), 'The buying impulse', *Journal of Consumer Research*, **14** (September), 189–99.
Sayre, Shay (2001), *Qualitative Methods for Marketplace Research*, Thousand Oaks, CA: Sage Publications.
Schouten, John W. (1991), 'Life among the Winnebago', in Russell W. Belk (ed.), *Highways and Buyways: Naturalistic Research From the Consumer Behavior Odyssey*, Provo, UT: Association for Consumer Research, p. 13.
Scott, Walter Dill (1917), *Psychology of Advertising*, Boston: Small, Maynard & Co.
Sennett, Richard (1970), *The Uses of Disorder*, New York: Knopf.
Sherry, John F. (1995), *Contemporary Marketing and Consumer Behavior*, Thousand Oaks, CA: Sage Publications.
—— (1998), *ServiceScapes*, Lincolnwood, IL: NTC Business Books.
Smith, George R. (1954), *Motivation in Advertising and Marketing*, New York: McGraw-Hill.

Solomon, Michael (2005), *Consumer Behavior*, Upper Saddle River, NJ: Prentice-Hall.
Stern, Barbara (1988), 'Medieval allegory: roots of advertising strategy for the mass market', *Journal of Marketing*, **52** (July), 84–94.
Strong, E.K. (1913), 'Psychological methods as applied to advertising', *Journal of Educational Psychology*, **4**, 393.
Thompson, Craig J., William B. Loccander and Howard R. Pollio (1989), 'Putting consumer experience back into consumer research: the philosophy and method of existential phenomenology', *Journal of Consumer Research*, **16** (2), 133–46.
Tide (1947), 17 October, 5 December.
Tobin, James (1954), 'Subcommittee report on research program', in Lincoln H. Clark (ed.), *Consumer Behavior*, New York: New York University Press, pp. 105–8.
Umiker-Sebiok, Jean (ed.) (1987), *Marketing and Semiotics*, Berlin: Walter de Gruyter Co.
Veblen, Thorstein (1899), *The Theory of the Leisure Class*, New York: Macmillan Company.
Wallendorf, Melanie (1980), 'The formation of aesthetic criteria through social structures and social institutions', in J.C. Olson (ed.), *Advances in Consumer Research*, Vol. 7, Ann Arbor, MI: Association for Consumer Research, pp. 3–6.
Wallendorf, Melanie and Eric J. Arnould (1991), 'We gather together: consumption rituals of Thanksgiving Day', *Journal of Consumer Research*, **18** (June), 13–31.
Wallendorf, Melanie and Russell W. Belk (1987), *Deep Meaning in Possessions* (Videotape), Cambridge, MA: Marketing Science Institute.
Warner, W. Lloyd (1949), *Social Class in America*, New York: Harper.
Warner, W. Lloyd (1959), *The Living and the Dead*, New Haven: Yale University Press.
Warner, W. Lloyd and William E. Henry (1948), 'The radio day time serial: a symbolic analysis', *Genetic Psychology Monographs*, **37**, 3–71.
Warner, W. Lloyd., Marcia Meeker and Kenneth Eells (1949), *Social Class in America*, Chicago: Science Research Associates.
Weiss, Robert S. (1966), 'Alternative approaches in the study of complex situations', *Human Organization*, **25** (3) (Fall), 198–206.
Wells, William D. (1956), 'Is motivation research really an instrument of the Devil?', *Journal of Marketing*, **21** (October), 196–8.
Whyte, William H. (1954), 'The consumer in the new suburbia', in Lincoln H. Clark (ed.), *Consumer Behavior*, New York: New York University Press, pp. 1–14.
Young, Pauline V. (1939), *Scientific Social Surveys and Research*, Englewood Cliffs, NJ: Prentice-Hall.
Zaltman, Gerald (2003), *How Customers Think: Essential Insights into the Mind of the Market*, Boston: Harvard Business School Press.
Zaltman, Gerald and Melanie Wallendorf (1983), *Consumer Behavior: Basic Findings and Management Implications*, New York: John Wiley.

PART II

PARADIGMATIC PERSPECTIVES

2 Breaking new ground: developing grounded theories in marketing and consumer behavior
Eileen Fischer and Cele C. Otnes

Across the social science disciplines, there is probably no book more widely cited by those who analyze qualitative data than Glaser and Strauss's (1967) *The Discovery of Grounded Theory*. Within the fields of marketing and consumer behavior, it is featured frequently in the reference sections of articles published in the top journals. However, references to grounded theory in marketing studies often seem casual and rarely explicated. There is limited appreciation of what the actual traditions of grounded theory development are, as they compare and contrast with other traditions of qualitative research.

It is the purpose of this chapter to focus on grounded theory development as a distinctive research tradition and to draw attention to important aspects of the origins and evolution of the approach. Grounded theory development can be distinguished from most other approaches to qualitative data analysis in that the constructs and frameworks developed using grounded theory resemble those deployed by scholars who use quantitative data and work within neopositivist traditions. In this chapter, we will briefly highlight the origins of the grounded theory approach. Next, we will consider the kinds of research questions that it can address, and the types of theory it lends itself to developing. We then highlight three key techniques central to this approach that can assist students of marketing and consumer behavior in developing contributions using a grounded theory approach.

Origins and assumptions of the grounded theory tradition
As Denzin and Lincoln note (2000, p. 14), grounded theory emerged in a modernist epoch and was a major feature of the 'golden age of rigorous qualitative analysis'. Barney Glaser and Anselm Strauss, the original proponents of the approach, situated grounded theory within the 'received view of scientific theory . . . [which conceives theory as] a linguistic mechanism or language term composed by researchers that organizes and describes an empirical world' (Bacharach, 1989; cited in Locke, 2001, pp. 35–6). Their approach was rooted within the traditions of American pragmatism, insisting that the outcomes of research should be useful to their audiences. The following were fundamental tenets of the original grounded theory approach. First, the topics and concepts appropriate for the researcher to explore should be relevant to the context under study. Second, researchers should maintain an attitude of healthy skepticism toward prior work in an area, and enter the context relatively free of a priori assumptions. Third, outcomes of the researcher's data collection and analysis – that is, the conceptual categories and linkages developed to explain the processes and relationships connecting concepts – should result from the researcher's immersion in the field, and reflect the dynamics of the context under study (Locke, 2001).

A primary goal for Glaser and Strauss was to challenge the superior status then invariably accorded quantitative research and the assumption that qualitative research could produce only description and not theory. However, Glaser and Strauss did *not* seek to challenge the basic ontological or epistemological assumptions that were shared by many self-professed social scientists of the time. While the authors were sensitized to the social constructionist view of reality (Locke, 2001), their approach treated social construction, in pragmatic fashion, as a provisional reality about which positive types of theories could be developed. Thus something of a realist ontology and a positivist epistemology undergird the original articulation of grounded theory methods (Charmaz, 2000).

Although its original proponents parted company and advanced differing views on how to develop grounded theory (see, for example, Glaser, 1978, 1992; Strauss and Corbin, 1990, 1998), they remained largely faithful to their original philosophical assumptions and goals. Glaser and Strauss intended grounded theory to act as a 'polemic against hypothetico-deductive, speculative theory building' (Locke, 2001, p. 34), but they did not seek to undermine the scientific enterprise of theory building and refining. Both proponents were largely unmoved by the philosophical challenges to positivism or the postmodern critiques of social research that gained ascendancy soon after their original book was published (Charmaz, 2000). As a result, a neopositivist ethos pervades much of the contemporary work that draws explicitly on the grounded theory approach (along with the closely allied tradition of case-based qualitative research; see Eisenhardt, 1989; Yin, 2002).

Responses to the positivist heritage of grounded theory
One response to the fact that the grounded theory approach was conceived in modernism, and remains considerably rooted in its objectivist origins, is to treat grounded theory as though it were historically interesting but of limited contemporary relevance. Given that it is rooted in the second moment of the development of qualitative research (Denzin and Lincoln, 1994), it is often regarded as a research artifact associated with qualitative researchers who shared 'with quantitative investigators a concern for the nature of the relationship between their discovered facts and the observable world that they purport to explain' (Locke, 2001, p. 8).

A second response to the association of grounded theory with modernism, advocated in particular by Charmaz (e.g. 2000, 2002), has been a constructivist approach to grounded theory development – that is, one that seeks solely to understand how subjects in a study socially construct their own realities. Charmaz argues that the techniques of coding and categorizing that are central to grounded theory methodology can be adapted so as to produce theory sensitive to the fact that researchers are part of, rather than separate from, what is researched. She believes grounded theorizing can result in an interpretive type of theory in which informants' 'meanings and actions take priority over researchers' analytic interests and methodological technology' (2000, p. 524).

Our response differs from both of these summarized above in that it recognizes that the grounded theory approach, as it has evolved, provides contemporary qualitative researchers with a pragmatic means of building theories that import constructs and logics from existing work developed in quantitative traditions, and that are readily exportable for use by those who wish to build quantitatively on qualitative insights. Indeed, marketing and consumer behavior have many such scholars whose works are sometimes subsumed within the constructivist, critical or postmodernist traditions, but who in fact seek to develop constructs and hypotheses that are more closely linked to work in quantitative traditions.

We believe that qualitative researchers (neophyte and experienced) face no greater challenge than that of developing theory (ask anyone who has ever submitted qualitative work to a major journal, and received the nearly universal request to make the work more theoretical). We believe that scholars who want to develop work that builds upon that of their quantitative peers need guidance that acknowledges the possibility of pragmatic theory building based on qualitative data. Thus our response to the heritage of grounded theory is to highlight the benefits of this approach as it has evolved in contemporary usage. We enact this perspective by first distinguishing the kinds of questions suited to a grounded theory approach.

The questions grounded theory answers
In their original articulation of the grounded theory approach, Glaser and Strauss (1967) imply that researchers will find, not only their answers, but also their questions, in the research contexts they choose to investigate. They recommend that researchers immerse themselves in the setting of interest to them, essentially ignoring prior research that might impede the development of an understanding of that particular setting. This is intended to ensure that an appropriately grounded theory of the setting might arise, or that, at a minimum, healthy skepticism is maintained toward pre-existing theories that on their face might seem salient to a particular research context.

For those who seek to publish research today, adhering strictly to this approach is simply impracticable: prior research cannot be ignored. It *must* shape research questions, though its influence on the research questions asked is likely to unfold over the course of an investigation. At whatever point in the process of an inquiry the research question(s) of interest become distilled, they are invariably situated within the prior literature, and refined through the researcher's experience in the context under study. The contemporary practice of posing research questions that link to a wider literature is consistent with more recent articulations of grounded theory methodology (e.g. Strauss and Corbin, 1998) and of the closely related case study methodology (e.g. Eisenhardt, 1989).

In what sense, then, are the questions addressed by those who used this approach grounded? We believe contemporary marketing and consumer behavior research offers four distinct answers to this query. First, a study may be grounded in that its investigation of a specific context gives rise to *questions about the nature of a new construct.* Consider the question posed in a recent paper by Flint, Woodruff and Gardial (2002). They state, 'Our guiding research question was, "What does desired value change mean to customers?" ' The question they pose and the construct they identify and explore in response (i.e., customer-desired value change) emerge in part from their reading of the literature, and in part from the context of their investigation. They studied customers at different levels in US automobile manufacturing supply chains, which they characterize as being typical of mature, manufacturing-oriented industries in that country.

This context thus grounds the study in a meaningful way because customer-desired value change may not have garnered attention in early studies, in part because this construct is not salient to all customers in all industries. Instead, it may be a context-embedded construct (c.f., Teagarden and von Glinow, 1995) that is relevant specifically to the industry, the national setting and the time period, or to an even more delimited context. Thus the question asked and answered in their study enables the authors to make contributions at the level of substantive theory, which explicates relationships between constructs within a particular context where such constructs and relationships are particularly salient (Strauss and Corbin, 1994).

A second way prior marketing studies ground the questions they ask and the answers they provide is by raising *queries about the adequacy of prior conceptualizations of a relatively well established construct*. In the process of exploring a context that differs meaningfully from those previously employed, questions about the nature of well-recognized constructs often arise. An example can be found in Coupland's (2005) work: she asks, 'What are "invisible brands"?' (p. 107). She notes that the construct of invisible brands arose (i.e. emerged in an unanticipated manner) from her multi-month investigation into the pantries and kitchens of her informants. Prior studies of brands often investigate how brands are consumed in more public contexts. Yet Coupland's revelation that sometimes consumers disassociate products from their brand identifiers in the more private spaces in informants' homes led her to supplement conceptualizations of brands that stress how these phenomena are implicated in identity construction. Thus, in asking and answering questions about the nature of invisible brands, Coupland essentially adds a previously undisclosed dimension (i.e. degree of visibility) to our understanding of one of the most well established constructs in our field: the brand.

A third way qualitative studies of this kind can ground the questions and answers is by asking about *previously unrecognized facilitators or implications of a construct*. Often, when a construct has been discussed infrequently in the earlier literature, a study grounded in a particular context will offer a preliminary set of insights on some of the major factors that give rise to or follow from that construct. Drumwright (1994) studied socially responsible buying using a grounded theory approach. She did not seek to identify the nature of the construct called 'socially responsible buying'. Rather she focused on the questions pertaining to the way socially responsible buying comes about in an organization. The context she chose for investigation was firms recognized by external agencies as having engaged in buying practices that were socially responsible with regard to the environment.

Grounding her study in data from the buying center members of ten such firms, Drumwright generated a range of ideas about the individual and organizational factors likely to lead organizations to be more (versus less) socially responsible in their purchasing behaviors. She argued there was a void in prior research with respect to the reasons non-economic criteria might influence organizational purchasing behavior. As a result, she implemented a research design that essentially started from scratch in order to theorize causes of the focal phenomenon. Arguably, had she studied firms that varied in their degree or type of frequency of socially responsible purchasing behavior, different factors might have surfaced. Similarly, were the study undertaken now (ten years and many debates later), additional factors might be noted, and some of the original ones may have diminished in importance.

The final way qualitative researchers in marketing can ground questions and answers is by addressing *questions about the adequacy of prior conceptualizations of facilitators or implications of a construct*. Often, when a construct has been discussed frequently in the earlier literature, certain factors that influence or are influenced by that construct have been thinly or inconsistently conceptualized. In such cases, a grounded-theory perspective may challenge what has been taken for granted about processes or relationships involving that construct. Thus, and in line with Glaser and Strauss's original motivation for creating the grounded theory approach, questions may confront and challenge a priori theorizing with theory that emerges from data.

A case in point is Workman, Homburg and Gruner's (1998) study. In this research, the central question pertains to illuminating the set of environmental factors that influence how a marketing function will be organized, and what role this set of factors will have in shaping performance. In justifying their inquiry, the authors acknowledge that considerable prior work had addressed one factor or another in isolation. However, they observe, there has been an inadequate appreciation of the range of environmental factors that might influence both the makeup of the marketing function and the location of marketing activities within a firm. By purposefully grounding their data collection in manufacturing firms that varied in terms of size categories, technology intensity, consumer versus business focus and national location (Germany versus the US), the authors hoped to address limitations of prior work that had lacked such contextual elements and that had thus been unable adequately to capture, conceptualize and emphasize their potential theoretical significance. Moreover, because they conducted their study across a wide variety of contexts, they were more aptly suited to contribute on the level of general theory – or that which is salient to more than one context.

Figure 2.1 summarizes the distinctions drawn between the types of questions asked in grounded theory inquiries, identifying two dimensions that help delineate the four types of questions discussed above. One dimension is the purpose of the research, which may be either to identify new constructs or relationships, or to refine understandings of already acknowledged constructs or relationships. The other dimension is the focus of the question being asked. That is, questions may pertain either to the nature of a focal construct or to the nature of the relationships between constructs or processes. The intersections of these two dimensions produce the four types of research questions discussed above. Of course, any given study may seek to answer more than a single research question. For example, studies that identify a new construct will also explore the facilitators and implications of that construct (e.g. Flint, Woodruff and Gardial, 2002). Likewise, studies that question the adequacy of conceptualizations of an existing construct may also attempt to amplify previously underdeveloped understandings of particular factors that influence or are influenced by the newly refined construct. The kinds of theory that any given exemplar of research in this tradition produces will be linked inextricably to the particular nature of the research question raised. We now turn to a discussion of the nature of the theoretical contributions produced by research that adopts a grounded theory approach to analysis.

Prototypical grounded theory contributions
The specific contributions made by any given paper will be largely unique, yet, across the various papers that go beyond mere mention of the words 'grounded theory', and that actually make use of some of the techniques outlined in recent discussions of the approach, some prototypical theoretical contributions can be identified. Specifically these papers offer four distinct 'theoretical products' (Locke, 2001, p. 39): (a) they identify properties and/or dimensions of constructs; (b) they formulate and articulate typologies; (c) they present conceptual frameworks and/or models; and (d) they generate propositional statements. The first two are typical of the theorizing developed when the scope of the grounded theory investigation includes focusing on a construct. The last two are common

Purpose of the Research

	Develop new constructs or relationships	Refine constructs or relationships
Focus of Inquiry		
Focus on construct	What is the nature of this newly emergent construct? Example: Coupland (2005) identified and analyzed the new construct 'invisible brands'	How adequate are prior conceptualizations of an established construct? Example: Fournier (1998) reconceptualized the construct of 'brand relationships'
Focus on facilitators and/or implications	What previously unacknowledged factors influence and are influenced by a construct of interest? Example: Flint, Woodruff and Gardial (2002) identified factors influencing and influenced by a new construct, customers' desired value change	How adequate are prior conceptualizations of facilitators or implications of a construct? Example: Workman, Homburg and Gruner (1998) reconceptualized factors influencing and influenced by marketing function organization

Figure 2.1   A typology of the questions asked in grounded theory studies

when the scope of the investigation focuses on relationships linking a construct with facilitators and implications. We discuss each below, providing illustrations drawn from exemplars of grounded theory research in marketing.

Construct dimensions and properties
When grounded theorists are concerned with questions about the nature of a construct (whether that construct is new to the field or previously identified), one theoretical contribution they may make is to identify the properties or dimensions of this construct. This practice is directly traceable to the analytic strategies laid out by proponents of grounded theorizing. For example, Strauss and Corbin (1998) suggest that an important step in analyzing data is to identify two characteristics of constructs: (a) properties, which they describe as 'general or specific characteristics or attributes' of a category, and (b) dimensions, which they define as 'the location of a property along a continuum or range' (p. 116). The goal is to develop concepts that have analytic generalizability; that is, that 'can plausibly account for a large number and range of empirical observations' (Locke, 2001, p. 39).

The value and relevance of identifying dimensions of a construct depend, of course, on the existing understanding of the construct in question. When a construct is newly coined, such mapping is helpful in fully articulating its definition. Even when a construct is seemingly well developed, however, the value of an insightful assessment of properties and dimensions can be considerable. For example, in Fournier's (1998) study of consumer–brand relationships, she deepened current understanding of the construct of 'relationships' by her careful analysis of relationship properties and dimensions. Moving beyond the simple dichotomization of relationships as strong or weak, or close or distant (as was common in other in marketing studies based in business-to-business contexts), Fournier furnished the discipline with the seven other dimensions of relationships emergent in the context of consumers and their brands (for instance, voluntary versus imposed; positive versus negative; intense versus superficial). As scholarship that sought to better understand the integral characteristics of the basic construct of relationships, these additional dimensions are insightful in their own right. Yet Fournier further enhanced their value by drawing upon these seven dimensions to create a distinct but related prototypical grounded theory contribution: a typology, which we discuss below.

Typologies
Typologies tend to share the goal of illuminating the distinctions between varying elements in a set that together comprise a construct. Usually, elements of the set are differentiated by the constellation of properties or dimensions they may possess. So, for example, Fournier (1998) identifies 15 distinct relationship forms that she observed in her data, and that each exhibited a unique constellation of some or all of the dimensions of relationships she discerned. For example, 'casual buddies' is a relationship form that entails a friendship between the consumer and the brand that is characterized by low intimacy and affect, infrequent engagements and few expectations of reciprocity or reward. In contrast, 'committed partnership' is a relationship form characterized by a long-term bond, is voluntary, and is a socially supported union high in love, intimacy, trust and a commitment to stay together (Fournier, 1998).

While typologies are regarded by some as merely descriptive, they have been vigorously defended by Miller (1996). He argues that well-conceived and articulated typologies cluster together commonly co-occurring constellations of dimensions and/or properties and can accomplish many analytical tasks, including (a) drawing distinctions and identifying relationships; (b) invoking contrasts that facilitate empirical progress; and (c) succinctly capturing important conceptual implications (Miller, 1996, p. 507). Fournier (1998) demonstrates just such potential in her typology of relationships. She points out that distinguishing different relationship forms helps to identify the particular benefits, maintenance requirements and developmental trajectories that may be uniquely associated with each.

Conceptual frameworks
Conceptual frameworks are one form of theory often developed when research questions focus on the facilitators or implications of some construct of interest. Such frameworks can take the form of verbal statements about nomethetic networks (i.e. sets of constructs that influence/are influenced by one another). Frequently, however, they take the form of (in)famous boxes-and-arrows diagrams. It is in offering up such diagrams that grounded theorists most noticeably part company with their qualitative colleagues who adhere to other traditions and who (sometimes rightly) consider such frameworks reductionist. Grounded theorists accept and actively pursue the reduction of categories into a finite set of constructs and the clear expression of links between constructs, not because they view the world as simple, but because they see the value of simplification in order to bring neglected phenomena or linkages into view.

Furthermore, even if such boxes and arrows invoke adverse reactions among other qualitative scholars, they are often a communication device that speaks directly to those who rely mainly upon quantitative methods, and who are accustomed to, and expect, these types of visual representations. In depicting explicitly the ways constructs are linked, and in indicating the expected nature of such linkages, boxes-and-arrows diagrams succinctly convey the main thrust of a theoretical argument, even if that argument is explicitly conditional and limited in its claims of generalizability.

A fine example of a conceptual framework derived from a grounded theory approach can be found in Mick and Fournier (1998, p. 27). This framework, though it includes the dreaded (by some) boxes and arrows, is grand in sweep. Produced through a cyclical process of reading the literature and collecting and interpreting data, it incorporates components that range from Western world history and the industrial and modern periods through key paradoxes of technology. The frame links these paradoxes to a 'conflict/ambivalence' construct, which in turn produces 'anxiety/stress' and elicits the range of 'coping strategies' that contemporary individuals employ. Far from simplifying technology consumption to a narrow stimulus–response paradigm as might be feared by those who disavow boxes and arrows, this framework integrates the concepts of paradox, emotion and coping strategies within the domain of contemporary technology consumption, creating a provocative whole that challenges and complements prior notions of technology adoption, ownership and use.

Propositional statements
The other, closely related, type of theoretical contribution frequently offered by those who attempt to answer questions about the facilitators and/or implications of constructs is the

propositional statement. Propositional statements go one step beyond conceptual models that portray very general links between constructs (e.g. arrows that are unidirectional or bidirectional). Propositional statements speculate about direct, mediated or moderated relationships among constructs of interest that are likely to exist in certain contexts, and specify the nature (e.g. positive or negative) of the relationships under specific conditions.

Propositional statements can link constructs that are established or that emerge in the course of an investigation. They can specify previously unrecognized relationships, or modify existing assumptions about relationships. For example, Kirmani and Campbell (2004) elaborate on the construct of 'consumer reactions to persuasion knowledge'. They challenge previous conceptualizations of consumers as largely passive recipients or resisters of persuasion, and develop a rich typology of reactions, entailing a variety of both 'seeker' and 'sentry' strategies. They then highlight propositions that link the type of relationship between a persuasion agent and a consumer (thus connecting their work to earlier research that identifies the relationship construct as salient to persuasion attempts). They also introduce consumers' experience with persuasion (a construct not investigated previously in relationship to persuasion knowledge) as one that will mode-rate the extent to which the consumers' strategies help them achieve their goals in a per-suasion encounter. Thus, while they clearly integrate previous understandings of outcomes of persuasion knowledge, both the direct and moderator relationships they identify arise from their analysis of their data.

Furthermore, Kirmani and Campbell's paper illustrates how grounded theory can link to research in other traditions – in this case, experimentation. After developing proposi-tions, Kirmani and Campbell experimentally test whether (1) cooperative (competitive) relationships increase the use of seeker (sentry) strategies and (2), within competitive rela-tionships, whether more experienced consumers use more effective strategies (i.e., strate-gies that help goal attainment) than less experienced consumers. This example nicely illustrates both how grounded theory work can be motivated by research that has been undertaken from within a tradition reliant primarily on quantitative data (i.e. the prior research on persuasion knowledge) and how the results of a grounded theory investiga-tion can be conducive to further quantitative work.

We highlight this aspect of Kirmani and Campbell's study, not to suggest that theory testing represents the eventual goal of all grounded theorizing, nor to imply that all grounded theory is preliminary to quantitative investigation. In truth, not all grounded theory contributions are intended to be testable. Rather the contribution of grounded the-ories in whatever form they take is first and foremost to sensitize readers to the nature of constructs and links that may exist between them in certain contexts. Yin (1994) suggests that grounded theories should satisfy the criterion of being analytically generalizable: that is, they should stake their claims in the plausibility of their findings within the context at hand, and not in whether they are quantitatively verifiable and applicable to a larger population.

Key analytic strategies for developing grounded theory
Numerous works (e.g. Glaser and Strauss, 1967; Strauss and Corbin, 1998; Charmaz, 2002) have been written on the topic of how to analyze data so as to produce grounded theories. Our goal in this section is not to revisit all of these, but rather to highlight for students of marketing and consumer behavior three tactics for analyzing data. If the goal

of the researcher is to develop grounded theory in our field, the importance of developing proficiency in employing these tactics cannot be overstated.

Consulting the literature(s)
One now infamous aspect of the original advice given regarding the development of grounded theory was that researchers should put aside prior literature and start afresh in investigating contexts of interest. This practice (if ever prevalent) is no longer recommended. However, the point at which literature should be consulted in the research process remains open for debate. And the ideal that constructs and relationships should emerge from data persists in virtually all current guides to grounded theory development. However, it appears that every contemporary example of a paper published using a grounded theory approach consulted the literature well before data analysis was complete.

In some instances, the question of *what* literature should be consulted is an interesting and creative one. For example, in her study of invisible brands, Coupland (2005) found important insights not only from the prior literature on brands, but also from that on evolutionary biology. More common is immersion in the literature directly related to the focal constructs and relationships of interest. In their grounded inquiry that theorized new product development as knowledge management, for instance, Madhavan and Grover (1998) use the literature on organizational knowledge and distributed cognition as a starting point. Concepts in these literatures together with data from managers motivate their propositions.

Constant comparison
Comparing and categorizing are features of virtually every approach to qualitative data analysis. The practice of constant comparison refers in particular to a theoretical comparison of incidents, objects or actions, and is so integral to the grounded theory approach that grounded theory is sometimes called the 'constant comparative method' (Strauss and Corbin, 1994, p. 273). It involves the researcher's attempt to identify the dimensions or properties that lead him or her to classify entities as being alike or different, and eventually entails an effort to discern why particular instances are/are not alike. Constant comparison occurs in four distinct stages: comparing incidents in the context to the categories that emerge, synthesizing and integrating the categories, delimiting or bounding aspects of the emergent theory, and writing the theory (see Locke, 2001, for a succinct but thorough discussion of these stages).

The dimensions and properties that eventually are identified as distinguishing between elements in a set may emerge both from the literature and from close attention to the data (Strauss and Corbin, 1998, p. 80). Whatever the sources, these newly emergent properties and dimensions facilitate construct clarification and typology formation. For example, constant comparison enabled Schau and Gilly (2003) to identify both distinct types of motives that consumers have for creating personal websites and distinct self-presentation strategies deployed in personal web-spaces.

Negative case analysis
This practice consists of searching for instances where an incident, object or action that appears to share properties with other cases in the same category does not fit with others of its types in terms of the precursor, coexisting or antecedent constructs with which it

coincides. Negative case analysis enables researchers to identify new properties of a construct, or to specify hitherto unrecognized relationships.

Negative case analysis has been particularly useful for grounded theorists who attempt to challenge dominant understandings of a given phenomenon. For example, in confronting the dominant understanding of consumer satisfaction, Mick and Fournier (1998) state that 'Negative cases – those that did not clearly fit a priori satisfaction frameworks – played a critical role in the analysis, serving as springboards for the modification of existing, or instantiation of new, satisfaction paradigms, models, and modes' (ibid., p. 7). As one example, they identified instances when people had expectations of products that were negatively valenced (e.g. they thought the product would cause problems) that were underachieved (i.e. not experienced in use) and that resulted in satisfaction. Such cases did not fit the traditional model which posited that neutral or positively valenced expectations needed to be met in order for satisfaction to occur. Identification and analysis of such cases enables modification of existing theory. Indeed, researchers who work within the grounded theory tradition recognize that such cases may have the most potential to push theorizing into new directions.

Conclusion

Locke (2001) argues that the grounded theory approach is ideally suited for furthering knowledge in the field of management because it can (a) capture the complexity of 'the context in which the action unfolds' (p. 95), (b) link theory to occurrences in practitioners' everyday lives, because of its requirement of pragmatic usefulness, (c) support the building of theory in new substantive areas, especially in fast-paced contexts where change is a constant, and (d) 'enliven mature theorizing', (p. 97), or renovate and re-energize existing theoretical frameworks. As our concise review of studies in our own field has shown, Locke's statements hold true for grounded theory research in marketing as well. In short, the grounded-theory approach, when conceptualized and executed with care, holds great promise for challenging what we think we know about marketing, and helping to create new understandings of marketing and consumer behavior.

References

Bacharach, Samuel (1989), 'Organizational theories: some criteria for evaluation', *Academy of Management Review*, **14** (October), 496–515.

Charmaz, Kathy (2000), 'Grounded theory: objectivist and constructivist methods', in Norman Denzin and Yvonna Lincoln (eds), *Handbook of Qualitative Research*, Thousand Oaks, CA: Sage, pp. 509–35.

Charmaz, Kathy (2002), *Grounded Theory*, Thousand Oaks, CA: Sage.

Coupland, Jennifer Chang (2005), 'Invisible brands: an ethnography of households and the brands in their kitchen pantries', *Journal of Consumer Research*, **32** (March), 106–18.

Denzin, Norman K. and Yvonna S. Lincoln (1994), *Handbook of Qualitative Research*, Newbury Park, CA: Sage.

Denzin, Norman K. and Yvonna S. Lincoln (2000), 'The discipline and practice of qualitative research', in Norman Denzin and Yvonna Lincoln (eds), *Handbook of Qualitative Research*, Thousand Oaks, CA: Sage, pp. 1–28.

Drumwright, Minette (1994), 'Socially responsible organizational buying: environmental concern as a non-economic buying criterion', *Journal of Marketing*, **58** (July), 1–19.

Eisenhardt, Kathleen (1989), 'Building theories from case study research', *Academy of Management Review*, **14** (August), 532–50.

Flint, Daniel, Robert W. Woodruff and Sarah Fisher Gardial (2002), 'Exploring the phenomenon of customers' desired value change in a business-to-business context', *Journal of Marketing*, **66** (October), 102–17.

Fournier, Susan M. (1998), 'Consumers and their brands: developing relationship theory in consumer research', *Journal of Consumer Research*, **24** (March), 343–73.

Glaser, Barney (1978), *Theoretical Sensitivity*, Mill Valley, CA: Sociology Press.
Glaser, Barney (1992), *Basics of Grounded Theory: Emerge vs. Forcing*, Mill Valley, CA: Sociology Press.
Glaser, Barney and Anselm Strauss (1967), *The Discovery of Grounded Theory*, Chicago: Aldine.
Kirmani, Amna and Margaret C. Campbell (2004), 'Goal seeker and persuasion sentry: how consumer targets respond to interpersonal marketing persuasion', *Journal of Consumer Research*, **31** (December), 573–82.
Locke, Karen (2001), *Grounded Theory in Management Research*, London: Sage.
Madhavan, Ravindranath and Rajiv Grover (1998), 'From embedded knowledge to embodied knowledge: new product development as knowledge management', *Journal of Marketing*, **62** (October), 1–12.
Mick, David Glen and Susan Fournier (1998), 'Paradoxes of technology: consumer cognizance, emotions, and coping strategies', *Journal of Consumer Research*, **25** (June), 123–44.
Miller, Danny (1996), 'Configurations revisited', *Strategic Management Journal*, **17**, 505–12.
Schau, Hope Jensen and Mary C. Gilly (2003), 'We are what we post? Self-presentation in personal web space', *Journal of Consumer Research*, **30** (December), 385–404.
Strauss, Anselm and Juliet Corbin (1990), *Basics of Qualitative Research: Grounded Theory Procedures and Techniques*, Newbury Park, CA: Sage.
Strauss, Anselm and Juliet Corbin (1994), 'Grounded theory methodology: an overview', in Norman K. Denzin and Yvonna S. Lincoln (eds), *Handbook of Qualitative Research*, Newbury Park: Sage, pp. 273–85.
Strauss, Anselm and Juliet Corbin (1998), *Basics of Qualitative Research: Techniques and Procedures for Developing Grounded Theory*, 2nd edn, Thousand Oaks, CA: Sage.
Teagarden, Mary and Mary Ann von Glinow (1995), 'Toward a theory of comparative management research: an idiographic case study of the best international human resources management project', *Academy of Management Journal*, **38** (October), 1261–87.
Workman, Jr, John, Christian Homburg and Kjell Gruner (1998), 'Marketing organization: an integrative framework of dimensions and determinants', *Journal of Marketing*, **62** (July), 21–41.
Yin, Robert (1994), *Case Study Research: Design and Methods*, 2nd edn, Beverly Hills, CA: Sage.
Yin, Robert (2002), *Case Study Research, Design and Methods*, 3rd edn, Newbury Park, CA: Sage.

3 The semiotic paradigm on meaning in the marketplace
David Glen Mick and Laura R. Oswald[1]

The importance of understanding the nature and role of meaning in marketplace activities such as product design, branding, advertising and retailing is indisputable among marketing strategists and researchers today. Consumer culture is, in a sense, the product of the consumer's relationship to messages of all kinds, from advertising and the organization of retail space to the cultural cues internalized through group participation and ethnic identification.

One of the richest and oldest paradigms for understanding meaning is *semiotics*. The term itself originates from ancient Greece in relation to the study of signs, which were regarded in medical treatises as vital to the diagnoses of diseases. More generally, signs are regarded as anything that can stand for or communicate about something else (Eco, 1976, p. 7). As such, they permeate much of life in various ways: language, behavior, dwellings, clothing, artifacts, and so forth. During the Middle Ages and the Renaissance, scholars such as Saint Augustine and John Locke elaborated on the character and functions of signs, but it was not until the beginning of the twentieth century that semiotics was developed in detail by two intellectuals who were working independently on different sides of the Atlantic Ocean. They were the Swiss linguist F. de Saussure and American philosopher C.S. Peirce. Saussure (1913/1971/1983, pp. 100–101) envisioned a general science of signs modeled after linguistic science, which he named *la sémiologie*. Peirce (1955, p. 98) used the term 'semiotics' to describe the relation between signs and thought or logic. Today the paradigm as a whole is mostly widely called semiotics, reflecting a shift away from linguistics as a dominating frame of reference for understanding signs and sign processes.

Roland Barthes introduced semiotics to the marketing discipline almost 50 years ago (Barthes [1964] 1967). Semiotics and marketing spread throughout Europe in the 1970s and by the 1980s and 1990s had spread worldwide (Mick, 1986, 1997; Mick, Burroughs, Hetzel and Brannen, 2004; Oswald, 1996, 1999; Richins, 1994; Sherry and Camargo, 1987). Semiotics is now thriving internationally as an assortment of perspectives, concepts and tools for fostering new insights on communication and meaning in marketing and consumer behavior.

In this chapter we review advances in semiotic research within the traditions of Saussure and Peirce, and provide a range of illustrations to demonstrate how researchers have applied semiotics to a variety of strategic issues in marketing management. We conclude with a comparison of these two approaches and mention further resources for scholars looking to know more about semiotics and how to apply it in the service of marketing research.

The Saussurian tradition in marketing research

The Saussurian or European tradition in semiotics is grounded in the theory of structural linguistics developed by Ferdinand de Saussure. Saussure (1913/1971/1983) based the semiotic paradigm on the dialectical relationship between a phonetic signifier, such as the sound /tree/, and a mental image that the signifier represents (Figure 3.1). The linguistic sign, for Saussure, is arbitrary, inasmuch as the decision to associate certain sounds with certain concepts is based entirely on convention.

Though Saussure and his followers in the realm of linguistics focused on the relationship of sounds to meanings in linguistic signs, the two-dimensional Saussurian sign has become a model for analyzing the structure of meaning in a number of media, including poetic imagery (Jakobson, 1956/1990), myth (Levi-Strauss, 1967, 1983), cinema (Metz, 1974/1990; Oswald, 1986, 1994) and consumer behavior (Floch, 1990/2001). Such extrapolations are grounded in an understanding of non-linguistic signs, such as symbolism, rhetorical figures and rituals, as 'motivated' rather than arbitrary. In other words, the relationship between the signifier and signified for non-linguistic signs is driven by something intrinsic to the signified, rather than arbitrary or conventional, as in the relation between 'garden' and 'face' in the Shakespearean metaphor, 'There is a garden in her face.'

Theoretical developments in the twentieth century moved Saussurian or structural semiotics beyond the analysis of form to the implication of the speaking and spectating 'subject' in the construction of meaning (Benveniste, 1966/1971; Jakobson, 1956/1990; Lacan, 1971; Metz, 1981). For conciseness and the purposes of the present discussion, we will focus on the contributions of Roman Jakobson, who linked semiotic operations to innate cognitive processes that enable subjects to interpret and organize their reality and communicate with others. In a study of aphasics, he determined that humans divide along the lines of a propensity to favor associations by similarity, including paradigms and metaphor, or a propensity to favor associations by contiguity, including syntagms (linear alignment) and metonymy (such as representing the whole by a part). Thus the dramatic style of William Shakespeare can be distinguished by a metaphorical language that opens onto broad paradigmatic associations between multiple levels of human behavior and its meanings, such as good/evil, strong/weak, beautiful/plain and life/death, while the dramatic style of Samuel Beckett builds upon metonymical operations referencing absence, lack and logical implication between performance and off-stage reality (e.g., *Waiting for Godot*).

/tree/

Figure 3.1   The Saussurian sign

Illustrations of Saussurian semiotics in marketing research
Jakobson's research has important implications for brand strategy research. The very notion of brand equity – the value attached to a brand name or logo that supersedes product attributes and differentiates brands in the competitive arena – is testimony to the power of symbolic representation to capture the hearts and minds of consumers by means of visual, audio and verbal communication (see Aaker, 1991; Bouchet, 1991; Holt, 2004; Keller, 2002; Lannon, 1993; Sherry, 1998). Seen from this perspective, a brand can be defined as a system of signs and symbols that fulfill, in the imaginary/symbolic realm, consumer needs for intangibles such as an emotional experience, a relationship or a sense of belonging in an increasingly fragmented and confusing world (Oswald, 1996).

By accounting for relations between the form of meaning and mental operations in the speaker or spectator, Jakobson opened up the possibility of mapping semiotic relations between brand attributes and the satisfaction of unmet symbolic needs of consumers. For example, kids may buy Nike, not just shoes, and along with the acquisition of the brand goes participation in the Nike image and the Nike philosophy, 'Just Do It!' Brands enhance or even define use-value in terms of image value, with properties of significance that vary widely from status, playfulness, intelligence, masculinity and femininity, to refinement, frugality, defiance and sexiness.

Example: BMW
The symbolic function of brands is noteworthy in the automotive category, where drivers associate status, prestige and personality with the type of car they drive. For example, in a consumer study of luxury automotive brands (Oswald, 1991), respondents were put through a long interview involving projective tasks where they identified symbolic associations and personifications for luxury cars, including Mercedes, Volvo, BMW, Lexus, Audi and Cadillac. A 65-year-old male respondent reported that he had replaced his BMW with a Lexus several years before, when back pain made the sportier car too difficult to handle. However, when he retired from the business world, he bought a BMW 6-Series in order to soften the transition from work to retirement and the recognition of his advancing age. Table 3.1 maps the contrasts between the BMW and the Lexus brands in terms of paradigmatic differences stemming from the meanings and lifestyle experiences that consumers associated with the two brands in 1991.

This example highlights both the force and the limitations of symbolic consumption. After six months of back pain due to the sporty seats of the BMW, the man resigned himself to the more comfortable but stodgier car, and switched back to the Lexus.

Table 3.1 Two brands, two lifestyles

	BMW	Lexus
Style	Sports car	Sedan
Age	Young	Old
Personality	Radical	Conservative
Behavior	Risk-taking	Stodgy

Advertising rhetoric and symbolic consumption
By articulating meaning in terms of broad rhetorical operations, Jakobson provided means of accounting for the ability of non-linguistic discourse, such as imagery, to communicate without strict laws of grammar in the manner of language. Such developments beyond linguistics enabled scholars (see, for instance, Metz, 1990/1974; Wollen, 1973) to develop a structural model for producing and interpreting meaning in cinema. Visual communication operates along the lines of associations by similarity and contiguity. Associations of similarity operate on a rhetorical level in metaphorical figures, and on a discursive level in paradigms such as those mentioned above. Associations of contiguity operate on a rhetorical level in metonymical figures linking the part to the whole, for example, and on a discursive level in the alignment of elements in a sequence or syntagm.

The ability to create and read associations by similarity and contiguity enables marketers to communicate brand messages via photography. In the following advertisement for Nike Shox Turbo running shoes, an elaborate network of metaphorical and metonymical associations both creates associations of power and dexterity with the brand and implicates the reader/consumer in those associations (See Figure 3.2). By representing the Nike running shoe as a turbine driving an engine, the ad creates a chain of paradigmatic associations beginning with the metaphorical replacement of the turbine by the shoe. This substitution is then implicated in a metonymy of part for the whole, inasmuch as the turbine is a component of the engine. The turbine/shoe metaphor is implicated in another chain of metonymies associating the shoe with the foot, leg and body of the runner/consumer. Thus, by virtue of the metonymies linking the turbine and the shoe to the engine and runner respectively, the metaphor shoe = turbine takes on a persuasive force that would be absent from the metaphor standing alone, giving rise to the interpretation that, when the runner wears this shoe, they acquire the power of a turbine-driven engine. This chain of figures is condensed in the brand name for the shoe, the Nike Turbo Shox, designed to enhance the runner's performance.

To reinforce the associations between the turbine and the shoe, the image is inscribed with an extended verbal metaphor in fine print: 'This is a super-tuned blast of go-fast under the hood, a big breath of nitrous when you need it, with pure Nike Shox responsive cushioning technology to harness every last bit of horsepower. So be ready when you put your foot to the floor. The Nike Shox Turbo and other tools for better running at NIKERUNNING.COM.' Analysis of this semiotic system is summarized in the Table 3.2.

By linking the structure of signs to mental operations in the speaker or spectator, the work of Jakobson and other semioticians such as Benveniste (1966/1971) and Eco (1976) led to the intersection of semiotics, philosophy and the social sciences in the second half of the twentieth century (Bourdieu, 1977; Lacan, 1971; Levi-Strauss, 1967; Metz, 1981; Oswald, 1984, 1989, 1999), enabling marketing researchers to segment markets along the lines of the values, lifestyles and cultural imperatives, to position brands in terms of the symbolic associations they elicit in the marketplace, and to link brand meanings to advertising imagery.

Socio-semiotics: mapping consumer mythology
Though semiotics can be used to diagnose problems in visual communication, it can also be used strategically in consumer research to develop positioning, segmentation (Rose, 1995, 69–99) and advertising communication. European semioticians such as Floch

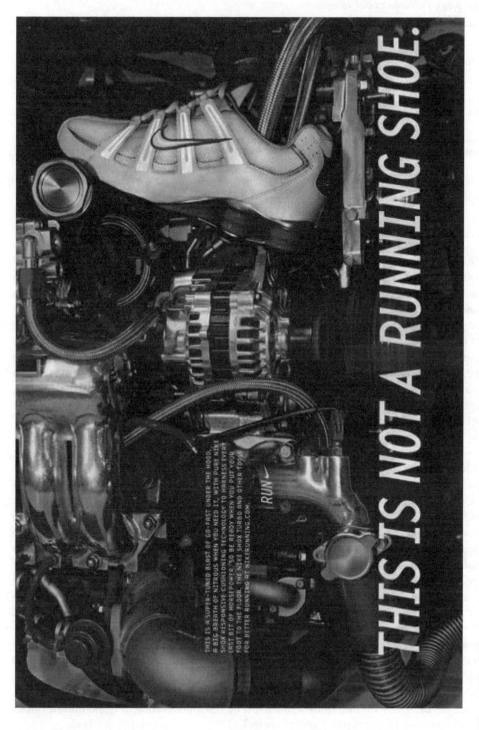

THIS IS NOT A RUNNING SHOE.

THIS IS A SUPER-TUNED BURST OF GO-FAST UNDER THE HOOD, A BIG BREATH OF NITROUS WHEN YOU NEED IT, WITH PURE NIKE SHOX RESPONSIVE CUSHIONING TECHNOLOGY TO HARNESS EVERY LAST BIT OF HORSEPOWER. SO BE READY WHEN YOU PUT YOUR FOOT TO THE FLOOR. THE NIKE SHOX TURBO AND OTHER 1900S FOR BETTER RUNNING AT NIKERUNNING.COM.

Figure 3.2   Nike

Table 3.2   Two aspects of language

	Similarity, metaphor	Contiguity, metonymy
Rhetoric	The Nike shoe is like a turbine (metaphor)	The shoe linked logically and spatially to the foot that would wear it, which is linked to the runner/consumer (metonymy)
	Paradigm	Syntagm
Discourse	The turbine is associated with engine power, force and drive in the automotive discourse The Nike shoe is associated with runner power, force and drive in the brand discourse	A turbine drives the engine A Nike shoe drives the runner

(1990/2001) use the semiotic square developed by Greimas (1966/1983) to map the brand world, as it is communicated in advertising, on the one hand, and as it is perceived by consumers, on the other. The semiotic square extends the binary models of Saussure and his followers, such as Claude Levi-Strauss (1983) in the realm of anthropology, by providing means of mapping semiotic dimensions in four rather than two dimensions. Beginning with the binary opposition of two values, such as male/female or 'for self'/'for others', the researcher can explore the gray areas between these extremes by introducing an operation of negation: 'not male/not female', 'not for self' and 'not for others'. By superimposing a plurality of binary oppositions including gender, relationships and emotional orientation, the semiotic square provides a more nuanced and refined grid for mapping consumer segments and brand meanings than the simple paradigmatic opposition of two dimensions.

Example: cosmetics for men
To illustrate how the semiotic square could be used to target consumer segments and position brands, the following case study examines the way cultural codes and myths influence both *perception* of masculinity and the *attitudes* of male consumers towards the men's cosmetics category. The market in cosmetics for men has grown by as much as 50 per cent in some sectors (Dano, Roux and Nyeck, 2003, pp. 1–3). The authors set out to articulate the semiotic dimensions of the men's cosmetics category, including an understanding of the ways cosmetics fulfilled unmet needs and wants among men, how the men's market could be segmented along the lines of personality, lifestyle and product usage, and how well brand messages met the needs of these segments. The researchers used a two-pronged approach including analysis of consumer data on the 'demand' side, and analysis of brand communication on the 'supply' side. By means of qualitative interviews with gay and straight men in France and Canada, they identified a spectrum of masculine identities, from the super male to effeminate. Second, they performed a semiotic analysis of codes communicating masculine identities in the advertising for 14 brands, Biotherm, Body Shop, Clarins, Clinique, Décléor, Lierac, J-P Gaultier, Aramis, Lancôme, Nickel, Nivea, Tim Robinn, Vichy and Zirh. The researchers then mapped findings from the two studies on a conceptual grid (Figure 3.3).

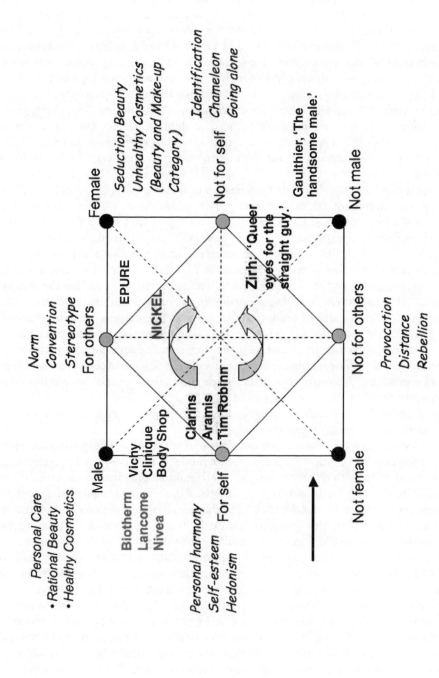

Female

Seduction Beauty
Unhealthy Cosmetics
(Beauty and Make-up
Category)

Identification
Chameleon
Going alone

Not for self

Not male

Gaulthier, 'The
handsome male.'

EPURE

NICKEL

Zirh: 'Queer
eyes for the
straight guy.'

Norm
Convention
Stereotype
For others

Not for others

Provocation
Distance
Rebellion

Male

Vichy
Clinique
Body Shop

Clarins
Aramis
Tim Robinn

For self

Not female

Personal Care
• Rational Beauty
• Healthy Cosmetics

Biotherm
Lancome
Nivea

Personal harmony
Self-esteem
Hedonism

37

Figure 3.3   Men's cosmetics

The qualitative study gauged relations between respondents' interpretations of masculinity (based on stereotypes ranging from the macho male to the effeminate male) and their perceptions and uses of cosmetics and cosmetic brands. Respondents were asked to respond to questions ranging from the choice and purchase of personal care products, to the importance of beauty and physical appearance in their own lives, and to express their feelings about the word 'cosmetics' generated by projective tasks such as free association.

The authors found that the use and perception of cosmetics among men divides along the lines of a central paradigmatic opposition, the masculine and feminine, each of which can be further articulated by means of lifestyle and psychological dimensions, including the degree to which self-care was subordinated to caring about or impressing others, men's emotional investment in cosmetics and their need or ability to deviate from the norm or stand out from the crowd. These dimensions translate into specific needs and wants relative to personal care products ranging from dermatological products to skin cream to makeup.

A multipart graphic model based on Greimas' semiotic square was then developed from analysis of two dominant codes that emerged from the interviews, one for gender, expressed in the binary opposition male/female, and the other relating to product use, expressed in the binary opposition for self/for others. Whether one used cosmetics for personal hygiene and comfort or to influence the perceptions and behavior of others was paradigmatically related to these primary oppositions, and these included reason/emotion, hygienic/cosmetic usage and self-care/seduction. The researchers found that the acceptance and use of cosmetics increase in proportion to the respondent's identification with more androgynous or feminine stereotypes that emphasize emotions, relationships and beauty. Above and beyond the important function of mapping the personal and cultural dimensions of the men's cosmetics category, the sociosemiotic approach by Dano *et al.* (2003) performs a key strategic function by tracing correlations between consumer types and brand symbolism, demonstrating trends in the competitive set, and identifying consumer segments that have not been a target at all. The semiotic square provided a virtual roadmap of the men's cosmetics category, enabling researchers later to map the various brands in terms of the kinds of men they targeted.

Figure 3.3 shows that most brands are concentrated in the upper left quadrant, targeting an unambiguous male type with personal care products for himself. They systematically elude association with either androgynous or feminine characteristics in the other quadrants. Alternatively, the brands that move away from the stereotypical male tend to target homosexual men who identify with feminine stereotypes for beauty and seduction (e.g., Gauthier, Zirh). Note that there are few or no brands in the lower left and upper right quadrants where the positions for masculinity are ambiguous. Those two quadrants point to an emerging male type represented in fashion magazines as the 'metrosexual', a heterosexual man whose consumer behavior betrays elements of seduction, performance for others, and personal embellishment traditionally associated with the feminine.

By introducing the element of negation to the traditional binary grid, the semiotic square enables the researcher to represent ambiguous realms of meaning in consumer behavior, such as the movement of male identity between the positions of masculine and feminine, between relatedness to self and to others, between reason and passion. In other words, male consumers of cosmetics need not be totally oriented to a masculine identity or a female identity, but may find themselves somewhere in between the two. They may be entirely focused neither on the role of cosmetics for personal satisfaction nor on the effects of cosmetic use on their appearance for others, but both, depending on the occasion. By positioning brands in the 'white spaces' between cultural stereotypes, marketers gain access to emerging realms of meaning that ultimately drive brand creativity, originality and innovation.

The Peircean tradition in marketing research
Peirce's semiotics (1931–58, 1955) is based on philosophy and the physical sciences. His model of signification involves three parts: the representamen (the sign), the object (physical or mental, which the representamen refers to) and the interpretant (which corresponds to a response, reaction or interpretation). Peirce developed an extensive taxonomy of different aspects of his three-part model, including the identification of numerous kinds of sign–object relations, for which many scholars use the label 'semantics'. He also delineated different types of interpretants, with one set of categories being the immediate, the dynamical and the final, and another set of categories being the emotional, the energetic and the logical. He also discussed different mental operations in processing signs, focusing on what he called 'firstness', 'secondness' and 'thirdness', in addition to the logical operations of induction, deduction and abduction.

Of the various sign–object or semantic relations that Peirce identified, there are three that he considered most important and that have since been widely applied in the humanities and social science. The first type is icons, which are sign–object relations based on similarity (e.g., a drawing of a well known person). Indexes are a second type that involve sign–object relations based on a causal connection (e.g., smoke and fire). Third are symbols, with sign–object relations based on convention or cultural rules (e.g., words and their core concepts; certain clothing and its meanings). These fundamental distinctions have been used across an array of marketing topics, and sometime crossed or combined in novel ways. In the subsections that follow, we focus on research within the Peircean paradigm that has emphasized the icon–index–symbol categories of semantic relations.

Illustrations of Peircean semiotics in marketing research

Product and logo design
Kawama (1987, 1990) has used Peirce's three main types of sign–object relations to identify and discuss how different product designs can potentiate intended key meanings. For example, he discusses a pure icon in the design of a camera where the camera is shaped like Mickey Mouse's face in order to suggest frivolity and its suitability for a particular target market (children). In more complex examples he discusses how iconic relations are merged with indexical relations, as when aircraft designs use adaptations of bird wings and when computer keyboards are formed according to hand and finger shapes.

The Finnish scholar Vihma (1992, 1995) shows, further, how on Peirce's three types of sign–object relations can assist in conceptualizing meaning and function in product design. Indexicality can include lights (e.g., yellow, red) and sounds (e.g., buzzes, beeps) that suggest when certain product operations are changing or completed. Symbolism can include logos and other graphics that differentiate one brand or model from another. Iconicity can include color (e.g., white suggests lightweight), materials (e.g., glassy suggests fragility) and shape (e.g., sleek and forward-leaning can suggest quickness). Given the importance of iconicity and meaning in product design, Vihma (1992) has further delineated six kinds of iconicity. For example, one form of iconicity is based on tradition (e.g., most paperclips look alike) and another form of iconicity is when products look as though they belong together in particular settings (e.g., kitchen appliances, office furniture). Together, Kawama (1987, 1990) and (Vihma, 1992, 1995) show convincingly that most product designs, even for mundane products like chopsticks and clothes irons, are a complex web of icons, indexes and symbols that serve to communicate a variety of meanings and goal-relevant procedures.

Looking more specifically at brand logos, Heilbrunn (1997, 1998) identified three variations founded on Peirce's sign–object relations. One is the alphanumeric type (e.g., IBM, 3M), a second is the iconic type (e.g., Shell Oil's yellow seashell), and a third is a mixture of the other two. Shell's logo, he argues, is an iconic and indexical sign–object relationship in regard to its corporate identity, including its genesis in maritime areas and activities, its name (with the similarity between seashells and the company's moniker), and its main business of mining oil that derives from fossilization. In a complementary analysis of logos based on Peirce's paradigm, Morgado (1993) showed how clothing trademarks that involve animals (e.g., Izod alligator) not only have obvious iconicities to real-world animals, but they also harbor indexical qualities (e.g., some emblems imply socioeconomic status due to higher costs of the clothes) and symbolic qualities (e.g., standing for a particular designer and other mythic associations about the specific animal).

Advertising
Peirce's sign–object distinctions have also been useful in theorizing and researching advertising. Zakia (1986) selected an evocative imagistic ad for Schnapple liquor that shows an attractive woman wearing a shiny evening dress and who is delicately holding a glass of liquor. The ad is saturated with meanings facilitated by several iconic, indexical and symbolic qualities. Moreover, to show that these Peircean distinctions can be linked insightfully to consumer responses – something that no one else had done up to that time – Zakia showed the ad to a small sample of consumers and had them supply immediate verbal reactions that expressed the overall meaning from their personal perspectives. He then codified the reactions into four themes, which he labeled sensual, sophisticated, exotic and femme fatale. Zakia next applied the notions of icon, index and symbol to the various ad elements to suggest which signs were evoking which themes in the minds of the respondents. His interpretive analysis suggested, for instance, that the sensuality theme was supported by iconic relations in which the woman's large pouting lips served as a genital echo. The sensuality theme was also reinforced by indexical relations (e.g., one of the woman's fingers pointed to a highlighted area of her breast) and symbolic relations (e.g., her tight dress and its snakeskin quality implied temptation and magnetism).

More recently, McQuarrie and Mick (1999) applied the same Peircean distinctions to establish their interpretative analyses for a set of visually oriented ads, which then served as the groundwork for manipulating key ad signs to examine the effects of rhetorical figures (e.g., rhyme, metaphor) on consumer attitudes, cognitions and memory. For instance, one of their ads was for a motion sickness remedy in which the product package appeared as the seat buckle on a car seat (with straps coming into each end, as with a true seat buckle). McQuarrie and Mick identified this type of rhetorical strategy as a visual metaphor in which different planes of reality (a cardboard product box and a metal buckle) are cross-stitched in an artfully crafted visual display. Further, they interpreted the ad and its meanings in terms of key (a) iconic relations (e.g., between the rectangular package shape and rectangular shape of a typical seat belt buckle), (b) indexical relations (e.g., between riding in a car and developing motion sickness) and (c) symbolic relations (between seat belts and what their use communicates about the user). To create a comparable control version of this ad (as they did for each target ad), the authors diminished the rhetoric and its meanings by substituting a real seat buckle for the product package, and moved the package to a position further back on the seat. This transition effectively deflated the metaphorical characteristics of the original ad without totally removing the package from its context or erasing the key brand meanings apparently intended by the advertiser. The experimental results revealed that subjects who saw the original visual metaphor for the motion sickness remedy invoked more meanings (had more elaborative thoughts) than those who saw the diminished rhetorical version. This same result held for three other rhetorical ads that were similarly manipulated. In a follow-up study, subjects who saw the original visual metaphor liked that ad more than subjects who saw the diminished version; this effect was particularly pronounced among American versus foreign students, apparently because the Americans were more acculturated to and more savvy about processing and appreciating such visually clever ads. In both Zakia's (1986) and McQuarrie and Mick's (1999) work, Peirce's distinctions among icons, indexes and symbols helped to highlight the potentialized meanings in select ads, and formed the foundations for understanding actual consumer responses.

Being there as a consumer
Peirce's paradigm has also been fruitfully applied to understanding experiences at various consumption sites. For instance, Umiker-Sebeok (1992) studied in depth 41 visitors to a Midwest museum, using a combination of observations, interviews and a survey. Based on Peirce, her analyses of the data suggested that the visitors first perceive the exhibits in terms of similar things seen before (iconic relations) and this initial stage of perception invites further involvement and interpretations. Then visitors note what is new or different in these particular exhibits, and they go about examining pertinent indexical relations, including how the exhibit qualities link to the world beyond the museum. In the third and final phase, visitors translate the exhibits as symbols, that is, drawing on the habits and proclivities of interpretation that are a function of the visitors' sociocultural background. Umiker-Sebeok concludes from her analysis that museum visitors are active participants in constructing meaning for exhibits according to their own needs and conditions. By implication, this insight likely holds for many other consumer settings as well, including malls, retail shops and Internet sites.

Everyday products and ownership
In a study focusing on understanding the nature of product ownership, Grayson and Shulman (2000) argued that the Saussurean paradigm is insufficient for explaining meaning and memory related to consumer possessions. To explore this proposition, they focused on special possessions as a case in point. The authors contend that memories are tangibly present in the many things that instigate those recollections, and this tangibility is clearly manifest in possessions that consumers consider irreplaceable (e.g., a wedding band from a now-deceased spouse). The authors argue that, if possessions had only

arbitrary symbolic meanings (which is the emphasis of the Saussurean paradigm), then any possession lost should be able to be replaced with an identical copy, without any loss of meaning or value. However, participants in Grayson and Shulman's (2000) research reported that precise substitutes for lost special possessions were not acceptable to them. The authors interpreted this finding to mean that irreplaceable possessions are causally linked to given people, places and activities, and thereby these possessions are more than symbolic in meaning. They are also indexical within the Peircean paradigm, insofar as they have a spatial–temporal quality of co-presence (meaning and memory) that cannot be replicated.

Discussion
As a research tool, semiotics provides means of examining how meanings in the marketplace are constructed at the intersection of marketing strategy and consumer behavior. In the narrow space of our chapter, we have sought to show how two major traditions of semiotics (Saussurian and Peircean) have led to descriptive and explanatory insights on marketplace meaning. Discussion of the European tradition in semiotics, beginning with Saussure, emphasized the formal similarity between the structure of language and the structure of non-linguistic sign systems such as consumer behavior and advertising imagery, and the potential to move beyond the description of meanings to the theoretical implication of the reader/spectator/consumer in the production of meaning. The European tradition in semiotics emphasizes the interface between semiotics and the social sciences of psychology, sociology and anthropology, enabling the researcher to draw inferences between the form of the message – be it advertising, consumer data or package design – and personal, cultural and social frames that shape the consumer's interpretation of meaning.

Our discussion of the Peircean tradition and its uses in marketing research revealed how just a few concepts from semiotics, such as index, icon and symbol, can be applied to an array of topics. Product designs and brand logos are replete with meanings from those tri-type semantic relations, triggered by the signs of varied textures, images, colors, lights, shapes, materials and so forth. Advertising can also be decomposed into indexes, icons and symbols, and the subtle manipulation of their characteristics exposes the rhetorical influence that these distinctions carry in the meanings set up and evoked. Attitudes and memories from processing the ads have been shown to be similarly affected. The concepts of index, icon and symbol also help to unpack experiences in consumption environments as a sequence of semantic events and to elucidate the meaningful spirit of product ownership and the valuation of special possessions. If one assumes, as Peirce did, that the universe is profused with signs, then by logical necessity all products, possessions and consumption are inexorably meaningful at their core. Adopting the viewpoint, concepts and analytical tools of semiotics extracts this core and helps to unpeel its layers of qualities and processes.

For purposes of marketing research, the semiotics of Saussure and Peirce offer equally valid but distinct tools for examining the structure and interpretation of meaning in the marketplace. However, it should be noted that these two approaches to semiotics stem from two distinct philosophical traditions, i.e. phenomenology and pragmatism, and imply two distinct ways of thinking about signs, meaning and reality. Peirce (e.g., 1955) sought to understand how a rational interpretation of the world is grounded in signs. His emphasis in semiotics is often related to logic, hence the name of his contribution to semiotics. He sought to classify signs in terms of their distinct formal properties, and to unpack the complex interrelationships among different types of sign in any instance of communication. Peirce's semiotics implies an interpretation of the world or 'reality' as a function of perception, inasmuch as perception is shaped by semiotic relationships, especially the indexical, the iconic and the symbolic.

Saussure, on the other hand, sought to identify a universal structure common to all kinds of signs. In line with a phenomenological interpretation of reality, the Saussurian sign consists of a dialectical relationship between a material *signifier*, such as a series of sounds, and a *signified*, an abstract concept in the mind of the speaker. In Saussure, signs do not operate in isolation , but create meanings in context with other signs in a semiotic system or discourse. It is only at the level of discourse that signs contribute to the formation of rhetorical figures or icons, indexes and symbols. Inasmuch as discourse is constructed by a conscious act, the Saussurian tradition is grounded in the phenomenological assumption of the origin and condition of possibility of meaning in the conscious Self. Thus the Saussurian tradition invited theoretical developments in European semiotics in the twentieth century that focused on the implication of self, society and culture in sign production or *semiosis*.

The goal of this chapter was to discuss the importance of meanings in marketing research and how semiotics can be used to understand consumers, advertising, possessions and brands. Furthermore, managing brand equity is tantamount to managing brand semiotics, since the semiotic dimension of brands is instrumental in building awareness, positive associations and long-term customer loyalty (Aaker, 1991). Semiotics provides the researcher with analytical and theoretical tools for explaining how brands mean: from the logo and packaging to the brand mythology generated by mass communications (Sherry and Camargo, 1987). Furthermore, semiotics includes a strategic function inasmuch as it provides means of clarifying the competitive differences between brands, identifying unmet emotional needs of their target segments and developing advertising that communicates the values and associations the brand represents.

Semiotics is broad in scope, variegated among its founders and subsequent contributors, and often technical in its vocabulary and applications. As a result, debates about the nature, labels and uses of semiotics are ongoing (Mick, 1997; Oswald, 1996, 1999). Nonetheless, many researchers continue to believe that semiotics is a discerning paradigm for effectively addressing the complex character and function of communication and meaning. More particularly, Mick et al.'s (2004) lengthy review demonstrates that there has been an unmistakable escalation and maturation of semiotic-oriented research and its value in marketing research.

The rewards of semiotic research outweigh the challenges encountered in learning and applying semiotic methods. The authors recommend several courses of action for the uninitiated. They include consulting distinguished compendiums (Barthes, 1964/1967; Bouissac, 1998; Nöth, 1990), attending seminars by knowledgeable scholars and practitioners, becoming acquainted with, and then emulating, some of the leading examples of semiotic marketing research, available in sources including but not limited to the following: Floch (1990/2001), Holbrook and Hirschman (1993), Pinson (1988), Solomon (1988), Umiker-Sebeok (1987) and a variety of other examples discussed in Hetzel and Marion (1995a, 1995b) and Mick et al. (2004).

Note

1. The authors' names are listed alphabetically; each contributed equally to this chapter.

References

Aaker, David A. (1991), *Managing Brand Equity*, New York: The Free Press.

Barthes, Roland (1964/1967), *Elements of Semiology*, trans. A. Lavers and C. Smith, New York: Hill and Lang.

Benveniste, Emile (1966/1971), *Problems in General Linguistics*, trans. Mary Elizabeth Meek Coral Gables, FL: University of Miami Press.

Bouchet, Dominique (1991), 'Marketing as a specific form for communication', in H.H. Larsen, D.G. Mick and C. Alsted (eds), *Marketing and Semiotics*, Copenhagen: Handelshøjskolens Forlag, pp. 31–51.

Bouissac, Paul (ed.) (1998), *Encyclopedia of Semiotics*, Oxford: Oxford University Press.

Bourdieu, Pierre (1977), *Outline for a Theory of Practice* (Cambridge Studies in Social and Cultural Anthropology), trans. Richard Nike, Cambridge: Cambridge University Press.

Dano, Florence, Elyette Roux and Simon Nyeck (2003), 'Les hommes, leur apparence et les cosmétiques: approche socio-sémiotique', *DM Decisions Marketing*, **29** (January–March), 7–18.

Eco, Umberto (1976), *A Theory of Semiotics*, Bloomington: Indiana University Press.

Floch, Jean-Marie (1990/2001), *Semiotics, Marketing, and Communication: Beneath the Signs, the Strategies*, trans. R.O. Bodkin, Houndmills, UK: Palgrave.

Grayson, Kent and David Shulman (2000), 'Indexicality and the verification function of irreplaceable possessions: a semiotic analysis', *Journal of Consumer Research*, **27** (June), 17–30.

Greimas, Algirdas Julien (1966/1983), *Structural Semantics: An Attempt at a Method*, trans. D. McDowell, R. Schleicher and A. Velie, Lincoln, NE: University of Nebraska Press.

Heilbrunn, Benoît (1997), 'Representation and legitimacy: a semiotic approach to the logo', in W. Nöth (ed.), *Semiotics of the Media: State of the Art, Projects, and Perspectives*, Berlin: Mouton de Gruyter, pp. 175–89.

—— (1998), 'My brand the hero? A semiotic analysis of the consumer–brand relationship', in M. Lambkin (ed.), *European Perspectives on Consumer Behavior*, Hemel Hempstead, UK: Prentice-Hall, pp. 1–43.

Hetzel, Patrick and Gilles Marion (1995a), 'Contributions of French semiotics to marketing research knowledge (Part I)', *Marketing and Research Today*, **23** (February), 25–34.

—— (1995b), 'Contributions of French semiotics to marketing research knowledge (Part II)', *Marketing and Research Today*, **23** (May), 75–84.

Holbrook, Morris B. and Elizabeth C. Hirschman (1993), *The Semiotics of Consumption: Interpreting Symbolic Consumer Behavior in Popular Culture and Works of Art*, Berlin: Mouton de Gruyter.

Holt, Douglas B. (2004), *How Brands Become Icons: The Principles of Cultural Branding*, Boston, MA: Harvard Business School Press.

Jakobson, Roman (1956/1990), in L. Waugh and M. Monville-Bruston (eds), *On Language*, Cambridge, MA: Harvard University Press.

Kawama, Tetsuo (1987), 'A semiotic approach to the design process', in J. Umiker-Sebeok (ed.), *Marketing and Semiotics: New Directions in the Study of Signs for Sale*, Berlin: Mouton de Gruyter, pp. 57–70.

—— (1990), 'A semiotic approach to product forms', in T.A Sebeok and J. Umiker-Sebeok (eds), *The Semiotic Web 1989*, Berlin: Mouton de Gruyter, pp. 625–38.

Keller, Kevin Lane (2002), *Strategic Brand Management*, New York: Prentice-Hall.

Lacan, Jacques (1971), 'Subversion du sujet et dialectique du désir dans l'inconscient Freudien', *Ecrits II*, Paris: Seuil, pp. 151–91.

Lannon, Julie (1993), 'Asking the right questions: what do people do with advertising?', in David A. Aaker and Alexander L. Biel (eds), *Brand Equity and Advertising*, pp. 163–76.

Levi-Strauss, Claude (1967), 'The structural study of myth', *Structural Anthropology*, New York: Doubleday-Ancor Books, pp. 202–28.

—— (1983), *The Raw and the Cooked*, trans. John and Doreen Weightman, Chicago: University Of Chicago Press.

McQuarrie, Edward F. and David Glen Mick (1999), 'Visual rhetoric in advertising: text-interpretive, experimental, and reader-response analyses', *Journal of Consumer Research*, **26** (June), 37–54.

Metz, Christian (1981), *The Imaginary Signifier: Psychoanalysis and the Cinema*, trans. Celia Briton, Anwyl Williams, Ben Brewster and Alfred Guzzetti, Bloomington, IN: Indiana University Press.

—— (1974/1990), *Language and Cinema: A Semiotics of the Cinema*, trans. Michael Taylor, Chicago: University of Chicago Press.

Mick, David Glen (1986), 'Consumer research and semiotics: exploring the morphology of signs, symbols, and significance', *Journal of Consumer Research*, **13** (2), 196–213.

—— (1997), 'Semiotics in marketing and consumer research: balderdash, verity, pleas', in S. Brown and D. Turley (eds), *Consumer Research: Postcards from the Edge*, London: Routledge, pp. 249–62.

Mick, David Glen, James E. Burroughs, Patrick Hetzel and Mary Yoko Brannen (2004), 'Pursuing the meaning of meaning in the commercial world: an international review of marketing and consumer research founded on semiotics', *Semiotica*, **152** (1/4), 1–74.

Morgado, Marcia A. (1993), 'Animal trademark emblems on fashion apparel: a semiotic interpretation', *Clothing and Textiles Research Journal*, **11** (3), 31–8.

Nöth, Winfried (1990), *Handbook of Semiotics*, Bloomington, IN: Indiana University Press.

Oswald, Laura (1984), 'The subject in question: new directions in semiotics and cinema', *Semiotica*, (3/4).

—— (1986), 'Semiotics and/or deconstruction: in quest of cinema', *Semiotica*, **60** (3/4).

—— (1989), *Jean Genet and the Semiotics of Performance*, Bloomington, IN: Indiana University Press.

—— (1991), 'Strategic branding study: the luxury car category', research conducted for D.D.B. Needham Advertising Agency, Chicago, Illinois.

—— (1994), 'Cinema-Graphia: Eisenstein, Derrida, and the Sign of Cinema', in Peter Brunette and David Wills (eds), *Deconstruction and the Visual Arts*, New York: Cambridge University Press, pp. 248–63.

—— (1996), 'The place and space of consumption in a material world', *Design Issues*, Spring, 48–62.

—— (1999), 'Culture swapping: the ethnogenesis of middle class Haitian–American immigrants', *Journal of Consumer Research*, **25**, March, 303–18.

Peirce, Charles Sanders (1931–58), *The Collected Papers of Charles Sanders Peirce*, vols 1–6, ed. Charles Hartshorne and Paul Weiss; vols 7–8, ed. Arthur Burks, Cambridge, MA: Harvard University Press.

Peirce, Charles Sanders (1955), 'Logic as semiotic', in Justus Buchler (ed.), *The Philosophical Writings of Charles Sanders Peirce*, New York: Dover Press, pp. 98–119.

Pinson, Christian (ed.) (1988), *The International Journal of Research on Marketing*, Special Issue on Semiotics and Marketing Communication Research, **4** (3 & 4).

Richins, Marsha (1994), 'Valuing things: the public and private meanings of possessions', *Journal of Consumer Research*, **21** (3), December, 504–21.

Rose, Dan (1995), 'Active ingredients', in J.F. Sherry (ed.), *Contemporary Marketing and Consumer Behavior*, Thousand Oaks, CA: Sage, pp. 51–85.

Saussure, Ferdinand de (1913/1971/1983), *Course in General Linguistics* (*Cours de linguistique générale*), Paris: Payot, trans. Roy Harris, London: G.Duckworth Publishers.

Sherry, John and Ednardo Camargo (1987), ' "May your life be marvelous" ', english language labeling and the semiotics of Japanese promotion', *Journal of Consumer Research*, **14**, 174–88.

—— (1998), 'The company store: Nike Town Chicago and the emplaced brandscape', in John F. Sherry (ed.), *Service Scapes: The Concept of Place in Contemporary Markets*, Chicago: NTC Business Books.

Solomon, Jack (1988), *The Signs of Our Time*, New York: Harper & Row.

Umiker-Sebeok, Jean (ed.) (1987), *Marketing and Semiotics: New Directions in the Study of Signs for Sale*, Berlin: Mouton de Gruyter.

—— (1992), 'Meaning construction in a cultural gallery: a sociosemiotic study of consumption experiences in a museum', in J.F. Sherry and B. Sternthal (eds), *Advances in Consumer Research*, vol. 19, Provo, UT: Association for Consumer Research, pp. 46–55.

Vihma, Susann (1992), 'Iconicity and other signs in the form of design products', in S. Vihma (ed.), *Objects and Images*, Helsinki: University of Industrial Arts, pp. 100–105.

—— (1995), *Products as Representation: A Semiotic and Aesthetic Study of Design Products*, Helsinki: University of Art and Design.

Wollen, Peter (1973), *Signs and Meaning in Cinema*, Bloomington, IN: Indiana University Press.

Zakia, Richard D. (1986), 'Adverteasement', *Semiotica*, **59** (1/2), 1–11.

4 Rethinking the critical imagination
Jeff B. Murray and Julie L. Ozanne

Introduction

As colleagues at Virginia Tech in the mid-1980s, we witnessed the beginning of interpretive consumer research. The emergence of this research tradition was gradual and involved heated debate. Twenty years later, interpretive research is an accepted and dynamic force in consumer behavior and marketing (Arnould and Thompson, 2005). Interpretive research is well represented at doctoral consortiums and national and international meetings of the Association for Consumer Research. The current web of social and cultural support includes the annual Heretical Consumer Research gathering of interpretive researchers, Eric Arnould's biennial interpretive methods workshop, and now this handbook of qualitative methods edited by Russ Belk.

The emergence of an interpretive tradition paved the way for the acceptance of critical theory in the *Journal of Consumer Research* (Murray and Ozanne, 1991). Although critical theory dates back to 1930 when the philosopher Max Horkheimer became director of the Society for Social Research in Frankfurt, Germany, for many consumer researchers this was their first exposure to the tradition (see Kilbourne, 1989; Rogers, 1987). Indeed, critical theory is philosophically different from interpretive research, although most consumer researchers interested in this area come from the interpretive community. It is puzzling to note that critical theory does not enjoy the same growth and support that we find with interpretive research. Given the hundreds of conversations with colleagues over the last 14 years, reasons for this slow growth are not lack of interest or motivation. Instead, confusion arises over the philosophy and method of critical theory. How exactly does one do critical theory?

The purpose of this chapter is to demystify critical theory and provide a clear and simple approach to the most important methodological issues. Doctoral students and researchers who would like to pursue a critical perspective may use this approach to orient them to critical work. This chapter is designed to get researchers excited about starting critical projects and beginning the research process (see references for additional reading). For experienced critical researchers, we hope to inspire critique and dialogue regarding critical theory and methodology. Admittedly, we accept a postmodern pragmatism that leaves many difficult philosophical issues unresolved. Our objective is to present a practical approach for doing critical research. We begin by articulating the ways in which critical theory differs from traditional social theory.

Critical versus traditional social theory

The phrase 'critical theory' lacks a definitive meaning. Since the early days of the Frankfurt School in the 1920s, this term was discussed in many different contexts and used in many different ways. Critical theorists intentionally avoided simple definitions, struggling to keep their perspective open-ended and mutable. For this reason, most critical theorists avoid definitions completely. Other theorists address this issue by positioning critical theory against or between other theoretical traditions. For example, Morrow and Brown (1994) suggest that critical theory exists in the tension between neo-Marxist theory on the political left and neo-Weberian conflict theory on the political right. More contemporary definitions describe critical theory as polycentric. Haraway (1997, p. 95), for instance, suggests, ' "critical" means evaluative, public, multi-actor, multi-agenda, oriented to equality and heterogeneous well-being'. Given this emphasis on broad ecumenical diversity, we identify six reference points to characterize critical theory and differentiate it from 'traditional' theory. These reference points include six concepts: normative, domination, history, reflection, dialectic and imagination.

Normative theory
Critical theory unites the empirical analysis of 'what is' with *normative* theorizing about 'what ought to be'. Empirically, critical theory analyzes how power relations constrain the realization of human potential (Murray and Ozanne, 1991). Human potential is understood in terms of human rights and fundamental values including justice, equality and liberty. The United Nations Charter (1945), the United Nations Universal Declaration of Human Rights (1948), the European Convention for the Protection of Human Rights and Fundamental Freedoms and Its Eight Protocols (1950), the African Charter on Human and People's Rights (1986) and the Beijing Declaration (1995) are all universal and detailed expressions of critical theory's foundation. This foundation cuts across cultures, helps to define human dignity and exists beyond mere words and language in the form of political practices and charters. Yet, justice, equality and liberty are also historical ideas since their interpretation is both culturally embedded and continually negotiated. Violations that contradict the cultural values in these charters and declarations open the door for critical analysis.

As is discussed next, power relations engender forms of distorted communication that result in self-deceptions by individuals with respect to their interests and needs (Morrow and Brown, 1994). Critical theory assumes that awareness, debate and participatory democracy may reduce self-deceptions or falsifying consciousness, ultimately leading to meaningful social change. Intellectuals play an important role as 'interpreters' of our complex and confusing culture. They are well positioned to raise awareness of social problems, articulate various positions and encourage public debate.

Domination
Critical theory assumes that all social relations and arrangements entail some form of domination and the critical–emancipatory interest seeks to change these relations of superordination and subordination. Even though social change may introduce new forms of domination, an overall evolutionary gain with respect to liberation is possible. Future social arrangements will be less constraining and more empowering than past social arrangements. Thus critical theory is committed to a belief in social progress.

Critical theory explores the cultural impact of three forms of domination. The first form of domination can emanate from above in a social hierarchy or from external exploitation. One example is the use of information technology and surveillance to collect information on individuals and the use of this information for social control. Another example is the outsourcing of work to Asian factories and the extraction of workers' surplus value as a form of external exploitation. The second form of domination occurs when people internalize the norms and values of their cultural context and, over time, make them their own (Agger, 1991). For instance, when we internalize the value of industriousness, socialization becomes a form of social control (i.e., we become workers 24 hours a day, seven days a week). Critical theorists seek to analyze widespread self-deceptions because this form of internal self-disciplining allows external exploitation to go unchecked (ibid.). The third form of domination is the emotional control that arises from superstition, cynicism, fear or fundamentalism. Given its historical roots in the Enlightenment, critical theorists believe that current contemporary struggles can be alleviated through the application of reason and they seek answers. What is reason? What are its historical effects? What are the limits and dangers of reason? Critical theorists believe that the Enlightenment project is not over – it is just unfinished.

History
Critical theorists study society as a historical construction. Social facts are not inevitable constraints on human potential but are pieces of history that are malleable (Agger, 1991; Durkheim, [1901] 1982). In other words, the society we live in is not natural; it is historical. Domination is most effective when people lose a sense of history and their potential to act in history. If people understand that society is a product of a specific set of interests, then they are better able to critique these interests and act to change society. Giddens (1982, p. 14) said it most poetically: 'social systems are like buildings that are at every moment constantly being reconstructed by the very bricks that compose them'.

Theoretical perspectives may be conserving in that they reinforce the status quo and therefore encourage the *reproduction* of the existing social system; or they may be critical in that they imagine an alternative social vision and therefore encourage the *transformation* of the existing social system. Denzin's (2001) seventh-moment research and Mick's (2006) transformational consumer research are best understood as approaches that seek social transformation. Every perspective contributes to either the reproduction or the transformation of society; no neutral Archimedean vantage point exists (Anderson, 1986). Critical theory's critique of positivism is that this perspective uses an elaborate language game designed to mask underlying interests and thereby claims to be value-free. But, in order to study society, all research adopts some social vision and thus embraces a substructure of assumptions, sentiments and values. The most untenable value position of all is to believe that one's perspective is value-free.

Reflection
If it is domination that makes the existing society appear natural and inevitable, then it is reflection that can restore a sense of history. Reflection is an important method used to challenge and contest domination. Critical theorists distinguish between two different types of reflection. First, one can reflect on the meta-theoretical meanings embedded in a theory. This type of reflection helps the researcher become aware of the underlying interests, sentiments and assumptions used in research. Critical theorists focus on relationships and connections. Specifically, which values are assumed by the theory and are therefore embedded in the research? What types of society do these values support or contradict? Since values are often masked, reflection is the process of excavation. Paul Anderson (1986) referred to this process as critical relativism:

A critical relativist demands to know a program's methodological, ontological, metaphysical, and axiological commitments before he or she is willing to grant epistemic authority to its knowledge products. Most importantly, critical relativists want to know a program's realizable cognitive (and social) aims before they are willing to give it serious consideration. (1986, pp. 167–8)

Anderson was trying to encourage reflection on the assumptions underlying a rigid and doctrinaire form of positivism that was, at the time, dominating marketing and consumer research. This type of reflection was necessary for the emergence of alternative ways of knowing such as critical theory.

The second type of reflection involves the thoughtful consideration and awareness of the cultural impact of social actions. For example, the relationships between individual lifestyles and forms of social organization might be considered. Ozanne and Murray (1995, p. 522) refer to this process as the reflectively defiant consumer:

> Thus a more radical notion of the informed consumer would involve consumers forming a different relationship to the marketplace in which they identify unquestioned assumptions, and challenge the status of existing structures as natural. Through reflection, the consumer may choose to defy or resist traditional notions of consumption, become more independent from acquisition and disposition systems, or define their own needs independent from the marketplace.

Craig Thompson's (2004) work on communities of reflexive doubt also examines consumers engaged in this form of reflection.

These types of reflection do not happen automatically. The purpose of critical education is to generate awareness and raise consciousness. Thus intellectuals are well equipped to launch theory-driven programs that focus attention on social problems, contradictions and injustices. This attention may lead to public debate, new ideas and potentially new social structures that may contribute to emancipation.

Dialectic
Rejecting both determinism and voluntarism, critical theorists assume that society is constructed on the basis of a *dialogue* between individuals acting in their own best interests and social structures that control or repress certain actions. Thus reflection is an important means of removing constraints such as self-deceptions. But democratic debate is an important way to explore the dialectical tension between people's ideas about society and the social ideas that get fixed in social structures and policies. Change often begins at the margins of society where people are most constrained. Creative ideas for change then diffuse to opinion leaders who encourage interpretation and public debate, and then, finally, the outcome of this debate might be a *new social movement* that is more strategic in advancing social change.

A good example of the dynamic interplay among individuals and social structure is Holt's (2002) dialectical theory of consumer culture and branding. He describes the way consumers continuously respond to and subvert the structural processes that attempt to influence and diffuse meaning. While marketers are using brands to engineer and package historical identities, consumers use them to speak back, pursuing personal sovereignty and individual life projects.

A second example is Murray's (2002) juxtaposition of sign experimentation and sign domination in the context of semiotic codes useful for individual expression. Here the struggle to control meaning involves a tug of war between structures and individuals. What often starts out as a personal creative expression, such as wearing vintage thrift shop clothes, may become commercialized and uncoupled from the life world of the individual, only to enter it later as an outside force. Given the colonizing tendencies of social systems, style becomes a dynamic project to maintain control of meanings that are important to the individual. Within this dialectical process, social change is possible.

Imagination
Critical theory consists of both a negative and a positive moment. The negative moment is the critique of actions that contradict fundamental values. The positive moment is the creative imagining of possible alternatives. It is the hopeful act of imagination that completes the critical paradigm bringing the six points of reference together as part of an interlocking perspective: *critical theory is a normative theory that prompts reflection on domination restoring a sense of history and the dialectical imagination*. The next section discusses the ways in which a critical method differs from more traditional research methods.

Critical versus traditional methods
The most important difference between critical and traditional methods is that a critical approach seeks to make social actors aware of domination or oppressive social structures. This awareness is used instrumentally as a necessary step towards social change. Murray and Ozanne (1991) extend the work of Comstock (1982) to present an organized and processual workbench method for critical theory. This approach puts the six reference concepts of critical theory into a progressive course of action that is consistent with how marketing and consumer researchers think about method as a step-by-step project. The method hinges on discovering contradictions between individuals' interpretations of social conditions and the actual social conditions. If these contradictions result in self-delusions or false consciousness that maintains a condition of repression, then this becomes the grounds for criticism, awareness and, eventually, social change.

Specifically, this method consists of seven distinct steps. First, the researcher needs to recognize a concrete practical problem. This involves developing a thoughtful and sympathetic understanding of a social problem related to consumption. For example, addiction, deception, pollution, globalization, obesity, overspending and product safety are all related to cultural practices that are linked to consumption. Second, the researcher seeks out all social groups that are, in some way, involved with this problem. For example, consumers, manufacturers, regulatory groups and activists may all be entangled in complex ways around a single social issue. Third, the researcher seeks an interpretive understanding of each of these groups. Since each group is involved in the problem in a different way, they will each have a different understanding of the causes and solutions of the problem. In addition, some groups may not perceive that a problem exists. Here the researcher is particularly interested in the interpretations of consumers. In the fourth step, the researcher builds an understanding of the historical–empirical conditions that exist separately from interpretations. For example, descriptive statistics might indicate that a product causes injury under certain circumstances, regardless of consumers' interpretations. Fifth, the researcher identifies contradictions between what consumers think and the actual situation. For example, consumers might believe that a product is safe or that a restaurant sells healthy food when the actual situation indicates otherwise. In the sixth step, the researcher helps consumers become aware of contradictions. Essentially, this involves becoming aware of the conditions and reproduction of oppression. This begins the process of social change and is discussed by a number of theorists as *critical pedagogy* (Freire, 1986; Kincheloe, 2004). The final step entails the development of a plan of action that will change society. It is assumed that the contradiction cannot be resolved under the current social arrangements. Thus social change is necessary to remove the contradiction and emancipate those people who are repressed.

Although this method is consistent with the six points of reference discussed in the previous section, a number of problems exist in its implementation. This seven-step critical research project is daunting and might require several difficult studies. Given the institutional demands for publications that are faced by researchers, the scale of this task is unreasonable within a single research project. In addition, it is difficult to identify every social group that has a stake in a social problem. This method also assumes that individual members of a group will all feel the same way regarding the problem, which is rarely the case.

Above and beyond the practical methodological issues lies a philosophical problem. The seven-step method assumes the articulation of an objective foundation from which interpretations are evaluated. This foundation may be difficult to defend and places critical theory directly in the path of the poststructural critique.

The poststructural critique of critical theory
In the critical method, the researcher identifies contradictions between what consumers think and the actual situation. Although complex interactions may arise between subject and object, the dialectical point of reference assumes that they are separate phenomena. In other words, this step assumes that an objective empirical reality exists outside of subjectivity, and that this *structure* has the power to dominate. Critical theory is based on this premise. If contradictions arise between the way that consumers are interpreting their world and the actual world, then consumers are falsely reading the world. From a Marxist perspective, this is false consciousness. From a critical theory perspective, these are self-deceptions. Note that the truth of things lies in the underlying structures of the world, not in our interpretations of the world. Here, the critical theorists are drawing on the enduring influences of Marx and Freud, who suggested that truths exist at the level of structure (i.e., *mode of production* or *unconscious drive*, respectively), but are camouflaged at the level of observable fact. This means that a critical perspective assumes 'realism', the view that a real world exists 'out there' that can be known by the human mind. In this context, 'mind' is understood as a receptacle for sense-data from which it constructs a picture of the world piece by piece. This assumes a correspondence theory of knowledge where words and concepts genuinely refer to material objects. The purpose of critical theory is to resolve the contradiction between subjects and objects so that people can begin to see the world as it really is. For example, what might appear to be education might actually be (thanks to the influence of the mode of production) socialization to accept the given life in a consumer culture. A critical pedagogy can be designed to help people begin to understand this contradiction.

But what if words and concepts refer only to other words in a linguistic system? In addition, what if these relations are negative, in the sense that meaning is derived from differences? Then meaning is derived not from a correspondence with things but from the context in which it is used. For example, what is the meaning of the word 'hot'? Well, it depends on the other words that are used in the linguistic system. If the word 'food' is combined with 'hot' one comprehends a very different meaning than if the word 'stove' is combined with 'hot'. Simply, it depends on the context. In this sense, meaning is not slowly accumulated by interacting with the world, meaning is derived through language. In fact, there is no *actual* world; there are only abstract interpretations of the world. Here we replace 'realism' with 'linguistic relativism'. From a critical perspective, this is problematic because no objective structures exist against which to measure our interpretations; we only have interpretations. Neither false consciousness nor self-deceptions exist.

This presents a very difficult philosophical problem for critical theory: how can critical theorists justify contradictions? If foundational concepts like 'domination', 'equality', 'justice' and 'reason' are merely words that refer to other words in a linguistic system, then they can be appropriated and used in a variety of ways by different groups. For example, both sides of the abortion debate root their claim in cognitive superiority based on *equality* and *justice*. Here, as with most situations, the meaning of these words depends on their use in context. This means that these concepts cannot be used as a foundation to adjudicate the debate. These problems have resulted in critical theory getting bogged down in difficult philosophical disputes that are probably irresolvable. The problem with these debates is that the original goal of making life better for consumers is lost. If critical theory is to survive, it needs to embrace a postmodern pragmatism that keeps the researcher close to the concrete problem. Emphasizing a postmodern pragmatism involves rethinking the critical imagination.

Rethinking the critical imagination
Contemporary theorists use critical theory as a mutable set of ideas that are instrumental in constructing critiques of current social problems (e.g., see Kellner's [2003] *From 9/11 to Terror War*). Thus critical theory should not be viewed as static or a finished project. Like all social theories, it was constructed in a specific historical context to help understand and explain cultural transitions and problems. The original interest of the Frankfurt School was to comprehend the appeal and spread of Nazism and fascism throughout Europe. Given that this problem shares some underlying characteristics with the success of chauvinistic and authoritarian movements such as the Fundamentalist Christian Right or White Separatists, it is still relevant today.

Essentially, critical theory springs from the assumption that we live amid a world of suffering and much can be done to alleviate this suffering (Poster, 1989; Prasad, 2005). Indeed, the poststructural critique comes off as elitist and Eurocentric when discussed relative to global poverty, genocide, ecological degradation and the AIDS epidemic (Prasad, 2005). At the same time, the poststructural and postmodern critiques force conventional social theories to confront their own blindspots and consider the need for greater plurality and diversity (ibid.). It is in this context that we can rethink the critical imagination, loosening and destabilizing some of its boundaries in hopes of encouraging a more useful and pragmatic critical theory that can remain close to concrete social problems.

In 'Postmodern Anxiety: The Politics of Epistemology' (1991) Steven Seidman claims that we should abandon metanarratives but retain local stories and situated narratives that can recount and explain events. Seidman's ideas are representative of a more general move toward a situated, local microemancipation. By emphasizing local emancipation, critical theory connects to interpretive research as theorists consider the phenomenology of situated, local 'free' spaces. This emphasis enables critical theory to take into account the fragmentation that characterizes the postmodern condition and welcome ideas dealing with plurality, identity politics and subject positions. Thus the term 'microemancipation(s)' reflects critical theorists' ability to adapt to contemporary contexts and respond to theoretical critiques. Researchers such as Best and Kellner (1997, 2001) and Laclau and Mouffe (1985) develop a critical vocabulary around key concepts such as pluralism, new social movements, identity politics, discursive formations, subject positions and decentering. In addition, they encourage critical theorists to think of resistance in a more decentralized, fragmented way. For example, the Internet introduces new possibilities for public intellectuals to reach broader audiences, coordinate with other activists and open up new avenues of critique. Rather than struggling to demonstrate contradictions between interpretations and actual social conditions, a greater emphasis is on interpretations in context. This expands critical theory to a wide range of domains such as critical hermeneutics, resistance postmodernism, cultural studies and critical ethnography (Kincheloe and McLaren, 2000).

The differences between critical theorists and poststructuralists may be partially bridged by realizing the wide range in scope and emphasis of change-oriented projects (see Table 4.1). Building on the work of Alvesson and Willmott (1992), we suggest that change-oriented projects can vary in their normative focus (i.e., identification of contradictions, localized change or generalized change) and in their historical and empirical analysis (i.e., consumer practices, power relations and interests). Both critical theorists and poststructuralists actively seek to question authority and reveal social tensions (see Table 4.1, col. 1). As Reynolds (1999) argues, we need to suspend our natural attitude about our everyday reality and problematize what seems self-evident, natural and true. For example, we might question consumer practices (i.e., means), such as the use of sweet flavored children's toothpaste, which is toxic when consumed in large quantities. Or we might challenge power relations that are imbalanced, such as the authority of a physician who is advocating the use of specific pharmaceuticals while receiving incentives from the manufacturer. We might also question interests and their priorities, such as whose 'interests in efficiency' is served with the proliferation of retailing self-checkout lines that appropriate the labor of consumers in order to 'save them time'.

Micro-imaginings focus on concrete practical activities that abound in our daily lives (see Table 4.1, col. 2). The same consumer practices, power relations and interests can both constrain and liberate. As Deetz (1992) argues, when constraints are placed on social action, a space of creative potential also opens. Acts of control can evoke skepticism and resistance as well as acceptance and conformity. For example, consumer practices might include the use of 'green' signifiers that could evoke the acceptance of the product as an environmentally safe product or the rejection of the product as a false choice when the better environmental solution is to avoid consumption. Micro-imaginings do suggest solutions to break temporarily the local constraints on human consciousness. These breaks are like the quick moves needed in a game of dodge ball. One must be ever vigilant, stepping to the left, ducking and forever moving. Space for critical reflection must be endlessly defended. Micro-imaginings involve many local projects and may or may not be integrated into a larger social change project. These localized social change projects

Table 4.1   The range of critical projects

	Normative Focus		
Historical-empirical focus	Reflections on contradictions	Micro-imaginings	Macro-imaginings
Consumer practices (means) Power relations Interests (ends)			

involve complex tradeoffs among many stakeholders; losses and gains will occur but in the long run social progress is anticipated.

At the same time, these local struggles exist within the larger social stage. While totalizing theoretical frameworks are appropriately criticized for being too grand and univocal, shortsightedness may arise when we limit the critical imagination to only local projects. Dangers arise when we focus exclusively on local struggles and leave unexamined the broader social systems within which we live, such as education, politics and laws. Macro-imaginings are driven by utopian visions that seek to resolve social contradictions (see Table 4.1, col. 3). These utopian visions, such as Habermas's ideal speech situation (see McCarthy, 1978, pp. 306–10) or feminists' dismantling of oppressive patriarchal structures, seek to remove constraints on human freedom by envisioning alternative social arrangements. Advocating a single correct solution would be antithetical to the anti-authoritarian impulses of both critical theory and poststructualism and, instead, the use of utopian ideals seeks to open up a range of solutions.[1] To the extent that affected stakeholders can engage in democratic debate over potential solutions, the constraining effects of new social arrangements can be minimized.

Summary and conclusion
The purpose of this chapter was to encourage consumer researchers to do critical theory. The first section discussed the differences between critical theory and traditional social theory. The second section discussed the differences between critical methods and traditional methods. The third section articulated the poststructural critique of critical theory. Understanding this critique is important since contemporary critical theorists are all rethinking critical theory on the basis of this critique. The last section presents some ideas on the way critical theory is changing and adapting to contemporary contexts. The typology discussed in this section provides an illustrative example of the way critical theorists are responding to new social conditions as well as various criticisms. This response is opening up the range of possibilities and therefore expanding the potential of critical theory in consumer research.

Note
1. This framework is offered as a heuristic device to organize critical reflection on what critical research could be. The boundaries between the cells are fuzzy. Clearly, reflection on social constraints could lead to macro social changes and utopian values are often implicit in the identification of contradictions. We envision that workbench critical research projects might emerge within a smaller subset of two or three cells as opposed to the nine cell illustrations provided.

References

Agger, Ben (1991), 'Critical theory, poststructuralism, postmodernism: their sociological relevance', *Annual Review of Sociology*, **17**, 105–31.

Alvesson, Mats and Hugh Willmott (1992), 'On the idea of emancipation in management and organizational studies', *The Academy of Management Review*, **17** (3) (July), 432–64.

Anderson, Paul F. (1986), 'On method in consumer research: a critical relativist perspective', *Journal of Consumer Research*, **13** (September), 155–73.

Arnould, Eric J. and Craig J. Thompson (2005), 'Consumer culture theory (CCT): twenty years of research', *Journal of Consumer Research*, **31** (March), 868–82.

Best, Steven and Douglas Kellner (1997), *The Postmodern Turn*, New York: Guilford Press.

Best, Steven and Douglas Kellner (2001), *The Postmodern Adventure*, New York: Guilford Press.

Comstock, Donald E. (1982), 'A method for critical research', in Eric Bredo and Walter Feinberg (eds), *Knowledge and Values in Social and Educational Research*, Philadelphia: Temple University Press, pp. 370–90.

Deetz, S. (1992), *Democracy in an Age of Corporate Colonization: Developments in Communication and the Politics of Everyday Life*, Albany: State University of New York Press.

Denzin, Norman K. (2001), 'The seventh moment: qualitative inquiry and the practices of a more radical consumer research', *Journal of Consumer Research*, **28** (September), 324–30.

Durkheim, Emile ([1901] 1982), *The Rules of the Sociological Method*, New York: The Free Press.

Freire, Paulo (1986), *The Pedagogy of the Oppressed*, New York: Herder & Herder.

Giddens, Anthony (1982), *Sociology: A Brief but Critical Introduction*, New York: Harcourt Brace Jovanovich, Inc.

Haraway, Donna (1997), *Modest Witness*, New York: Routledge.

Holt, Douglas B. (2002), 'Why do brands cause trouble? A dialectical theory of consumer culture and branding', *Journal of Consumer Research*, **29** (June), 70–90.

Kellner, Douglas (2003), *From 9/11 to Terror War*, New York: Rowan and Littlefield.

Kilbourne, William E. (1989), 'The critical theory of Herbert Marcuse and its relationship to consumption', in Richard Bagozzi and J. Paul Peter (eds), *Marketing Theory and Practice*, Chicago: American Marketing Association.

Kincheloe, Joe L. (2004), *Critical Pedagogy Primer*, New York: Peter Lang Publishing.

Kincheloe, Joe L. and Peter McLaren (2000), 'Rethinking critical theory and qualitative research', in Norman K. Denzin and Yvonna S. Lincoln (eds), *Handbook of Qualitative Research*, Thousand Oaks, CA: Sage, pp. 279–314.

Laclau, Ernesto and Chantal Mouffe (1985), *Hegemony and Socialist Strategy*, New York: Verso.

McCarthy, Thomas (1978), *The Critical Theory of Jürgen Habermas*, Cambridge, MA: The MIT Press.

Mick, David (2006), 'Meaning and mattering through transformative consumer research', Presidential Address, in vol. 33, Cornelia Pechmann and Linda L. Price (eds), *Advances in Consumer Research*, Provo, UT: Association for Consumer Research.

Morrow, Raymond A. and David D. Brown (1994), *Critical Theory and Methodology*, Thousand Oaks, CA: Sage Publications.

Murray, Jeff B. (2002), 'The politics of consumption: a re-inquiry on Thompson and Haytko's (1997) "Speaking of Fashion"', *Journal of Consumer Research*, **29** (December), 427–40.

Murray, Jeff B. and Julie L. Ozanne (1991), 'The critical imagination: emancipatory interests in consumer research', *Journal of Consumer Research*, **18** (September), 129–44.

Ozanne, Julie L. and Jeff B. Murray (1995), 'Uniting critical theory and public policy to create the reflexively defiant consumer', *American Behavioral Scientists*, **38** (February), 516–25.

Poster, Mark (1989), *Critical Theory and Poststructuralism: In Search of a Context*, Ithaca, NY: Cornell University Press.

Prasad, Pushkala (2005), *Crafting Qualitative Research: Working in the Postpositivist Traditions*, London: M.E. Sharpe.

Reynolds, Michael (1999), 'Critical reflections and management education: rehabilitating less hierarchical approaches', *Journal of Management Education*, **23** (5) (October), 537–53.

Rogers, Everett M. (1987), 'The critical school and consumer research', in Melanie Wallendorf and Paul Anderson (eds), *Advances in Consumer Research*, vol. 14, Provo, UT: Association for Consumer Research, pp. 7–11.

Seidman, Steven (1991), 'Postmodern anxiety: the politics of epistemology', *Sociological Theory*, **9** (2), 180–90.

Thompson, Craig J. (2004), 'Marketplace mythologies and discourses of power', *Journal of Consumer Research*, **31** (June), 162–80.

PART III

RESEARCH CONTEXTS

5 Qualitative research in advertising: twenty years in revolution
Linda M. Scott

An impressive body of qualitative research on the topic of advertising has emerged in marketing since the paradigm shift of the 1980s. Here, perhaps more clearly than elsewhere in the literature, we can see that the challenge to practice made in that decade was not just a matter of advocating new methods, but entailed questioning the purposes and interests that research in this field would serve.

Work on advertising was affected, as were other areas of marketing inquiry, by the shift in epistemology that attended the interpretive turn. In all areas, the notion of consumption as a meaning-based activity (as opposed to a more economistic, disembodied model of purchasing) had implications for research axiology, as well. Of particular import for advertising work, however, was the shift toward understanding the advertisement as a text and, thus, the consumer as a reader. By embracing the textuality of advertising experience, qualitative researchers opened the door to the indeterminacy of reading, to the reality of advertising as a cultural practice, and ultimately to the larger social questions that attend any purposive attempt to encourage consumption in post-industrial society.

The result has been a corpus of work too large and varied to be covered in a single chapter. My intention, therefore, is to discuss articles I have selected to represent the largest areas of inquiry. In assessing the scope of the literature to be covered, I have collected works published in *Journal of Consumer Research*, *Journal of Advertising*, *Journal of Marketing*, *Journal of Popular Culture*, *Journal of Advertising Research*, *Journal of Consumer Culture*, *Culture, Markets and Consumption*, and *Critical Studies in Mass Communications Research*. I have also followed up references that led to a range of sources from the *Journal of Business Ethics* to the *British Journal of Management*. I found that qualitative work in advertising was well represented in these journals by the end of the twentieth century, though there was certainly more in some than in others. I hope also to draw attention to the way that qualitative research in this area has circled back to engage with quantitative studies, as I believe that contribution to be important. Of particular import, though, is that late twentieth-century advertising research has occurred amidst a proliferation of book-length works coming from other fields – history, sociology, women's studies – and that many researchers in this area work in communications schools where cultural studies and critical theory were already well-established by 1985. Consequently, many of the influences on research in this area come from outside marketing, and these sources are so numerous that I will only be able to document them in a glancing manner.

The areas of interest that I will examine in this chapter are the responses of readers to advertisements, the practices of professionals in the creation of advertisements, the evolution of advertising as an art form and the theory and criticism of advertising as a social influence. These four areas encompass far and away the bulk of what has been published to date. I regretfully admit that this outline of topics will necessarily leave out some studies that did not fall neatly into the categories.

Responses of readers to advertisements

The 'textual turn' in advertising research has been fundamentally rhetorical in orientation even when the avowed theoretical orientation of researchers was elsewhere (e.g., post-structuralist, semiotic or formalist). I say this because, throughout this literature, there is a consistent emphasis on responses from and effects upon consumers, which is the feature that distinguishes rhetoric from other literary approaches. Even the formalist investigations and social criticism I will discuss later in this chapter can be said to fall under this rubric, as the final concern is virtually always with response or effect.

A fair number of articles appeared in the late 1980s and early 1990s that called for a text-based approach to advertising research. McCracken (1987) argued for a model of advertising based on culture and meaning, rather than information. Mick (1986) outlined an approach to both consumption and advertising as an investigation of signs; Stern (1988, 1989) called attention to the potential to analyze ads as literary texts. However, three articles in particular, Mick and Buhl (1992), Friestad and Wright (1994) and Scott (1994b), stand out as having spurred investigation into consumer response using qualitative methods. Scott (1994b) advocated the use of reader response theory to resituate the viewers of advertisements as thinking human beings immersed in and motivated by their own circumstances, who were as capable of rejecting a persuasive text as they might be of absorbing the advertiser's intention. Friestad and Wright (1994) outlined a folk knowledge of persuasion in which part of the ordinary wisdom of life was focused on learning to cope with persuasion attempts, including those of advertisers. Mick and Buhl (1992) was an empirical study of a small sample of readers interpreting advertisements. This study made very clear that consumers responded to ads in a very situated and skeptical manner – and, importantly, that ads affected consumers primarily in the context of their own life themes and projects. Usually citing Scott (1994b) and/or Friestad and Wright (1994) as the theoretical basis and Mick and Buhl as the research model, a string of new works made close investigations into the match between life projects or themes and the appeals of ads (e.g., Grier and Brumbaugh, 1999; Motley, Henderson and Baker, 2003; Parker, 1998; Stevens, Maclaren and Brown, 2003). Taken in sum, this body of research shows quite clearly the centrality of individual life projects, rather than manufacturers' intentions or formal tricks, in influencing the response to ads. Thus, when Douglas Holt published *How Brands Become Icons*, in which he says brands become 'cultural icons' only by speaking to the identity projects of large groups of consumers, his position was solidly underpinned by this body of research into the responses of readers (Holt, 2004).

The research into reader response, however, produced more than just a basis for understanding how viewers evaluated ads. This approach fundamentally changed the way the consumer was imagined: from being a passive recipient of advertiser intent (or an addled 'miscomprehender' of manufacturers' messages) to being an empowered, grounded, thoughtful human with better things to do than watch ads. From here, it is a short and logical jump to begin looking at consumers and their uses for ads in a social context. Ritson and Elliott (1999) accurately argued that the reader response approach as thus far practiced had continued the old paradigm tendency to characterize consumers as solitary creatures. So their study of British adolescents focused on the ways that consumers quoted, reinterpreted and reused ads as part of an ongoing local social discourse. In this study, the appearance of ads in conversation as phatic communication, shared jokes, ways of poking fun at teachers and friends, was a humbling reminder that humans consume to live, not live to consume – and that ads fall into a larger, complex 'text' of other media materials and actual face-to-face dialogue rather than being the isolated, privileged missives of information implied by the heretofore dominant model of research (see also Alperstein, 1990).

Throughout the reader response material, in fact, other cultural influences intermittently poke through. In spite of frequent charges that advertising has supplanted school, church and family as the dominant influence on behavior, this literature demonstrates that all three still have a strong influence on the particulars of the way ads are read and consumption is formed (for instance, see Parker, 1998). Thus, membership in certain subcultural communities, does, as initially articulated in the theoretical work (Scott, 1994b), have an effect on the way ads are read and evaluated. Grier and Brumbaugh (1999) showed, for instance, that the subcultural status of readers (by race and sexual preference) formed the reading strategy and ultimately had a strong impact on response to ads.

In cultural studies and critical theory, literary approaches had already become a primary vehicle for social analysis and criticism by the early 1980s. Thus it is not surprising that the textual turn in advertising research would be attended by a socially critical perspective. In some ways, however, the very rethinking of the consumer into a social setting in which persuasion attempts were resisted as often as accepted was bound to lead to questions about the power relationship between advertisers and consumers, the nature of control and resistance, and the relationship of research to the social structure.

One early study (Ahuvia, 1998), investigates the social uses of literary interpretation. Ahuvia questions the assertions of an established critic, who had already interpreted an ad for Airwalk shoes as carrying a message supporting a 'culture of rape' as well as racial stereotyping. Ahuvia's respondents shared some of the critic's interpretation, but not all of it. But, while Ahuvia's results supported the general trend toward understanding ads as polysemic texts subject to multiple interpretations by readers, the mismatch between a naïvely reader-oriented approach to studying ads and a more theoretically informed critical perspective emerged here. Specifically, the concept of 'ideology', a primary building block of the critical work in literary theory (see, for instance, Kavanaugh, 1995), refers to the way a text constructs social relations (class, gender, race) in such a way that they become 'natural' and therefore invisible to many, if not most, in the culture. With this perspective, researchers would not be surprised that readers did not articulate the same criticism that an ideologically sensitized critic would. At the same time, some of the verbatims from Ahuvia, as well as other studies, suggest the ability of respondents to see themselves as situated in oppressive social structures and to see the function of ads to support that configuration of relations. For instance, British women viewing spots for *Red* magazine expressed discomfort over the use of striptease, even if with a surprising 'twist' at the end: 'it's just, again, there we are – taking off our clothes to sell a magazine' (Stevens et al., 2003, p. 39). Further, Motley et al. (2003) argue that African-American respondents often interpreted offensive commercial racial memorabilia in a way that helped them confront, understand and work through their historical past, while not denying its oppressive and dehumanizing nature. The tension between seeing consumers as critical agents potentially engaged in change and seeing them as inextricably enmeshed in the ideology of their own social structure emerges as an unresolved question of the past 20 years, of particular concern in the arena of social theory and criticism discussed below.

Another factor complicating the general assessment of consumer sophistication is the increasing salience of postmodern form and style in advertisements themselves. The self-referential, dissembling and ironic stance of late twentieth century advertising tends to imply a jaded, even cynical, reader, yet the multiform, intertextual style of these same ads also implies a consumer who is increasingly imaginative, cognitively agile, full of whimsy and laughter, and able to consider (and reject) multiple propositions through image and music, as well as text.

Advertising as form
The early textual turn also highlighted advertising's formal properties in a way that the dominant paradigm did not recognize. The psycho-scientific orientation of the previous 20 years of research had tended to treat ads as assemblies of 'stimuli' or, at best, 'information' defined in a very limited way (see Levold, 2002). The new discourse of the late 1980s and early 1990s insisted instead on viewing ads as cultural artifacts (McCracken, 1986, 1987) or even as art (Stern, 1988, 1989), as well as expanding the scope of 'meaning' or 'information' to include visual and musical forms in addition to text or numbers (Scott, 1990, 1994a).

This approach drew impetus from the ready mismatch between ads running in the 1980s and 1990s – a genre period that has been concretely identified as a watershed in 'postmodern' signification (see, for instance, Goldman, 1992) – and the mock-ups or models that underpinned studies in the dominant stream of research. Spurred by the theoretical works that insisted on the 'fictive' or 'poetic' aspects of ads in contemporary discourse, some advertising researchers undertook to document the frequency of more sophisticated formal features, showing that, indeed, a major shift was under way (Callcott and Lee, 1994; Leigh, 1994; Phillips and McQuarrie, 2002).

At the same time, an important effort emerged to investigate the degree to which consumers understood and liked the new forms. Of particular interest is the work of Edward McQuarrie, David Mick and Barbara Phillips, who developed a robust stream that took the principles of rhetoric, applied them to visual messages and demonstrated, not only the ability of consumers to 'read' such texts, but their propensity to prefer those that were more figurative and thus 'deviant' from the kinds of predictable, straightforward messages presumed by the scientific, 'informational' research model (McQuarrie and Mick, 1992, 1996, 1999; Phillips, 1997). This research suggested strongly that treating pictures as mere 'stimuli' was wholly inadequate. This in turn had profound implications for the way the field should view a growing set of ads that was primarily imagistic.

Many attempted to build further on a literary/rhetorical premise by investigating other forms, such as drama, or other features, such as characterization (Deighton, Romer and McQueen, 1989; Hung, 2000, 2001; Frosh, 2002; Mulvey and Medina, 2003). One tactic that did not succeed was the notion that a particular genre or formal feature would necessarily always be preferred as a persuasive tool. As Deighton et al. wrote, 'As it happens, we can say that no one form of advertising consistently beat the other in our sample. And we cannot say from this study if there are contingencies under which one form would always dominate the other. In fact, given the inventiveness of advertising writers, we see little point in looking for such contingencies' (1989, p. 342).

One important feature of this area of research was the employment of quantitative methods to investigate claims made by theorists working out of humanistic traditions. Several teams made astute use of experimental methods to investigate theories that had been advanced directly from an arts perspective. The success of these researchers bodes well for the continued cross-pollination of qualitative and quantitative work, though such crossover efforts are still relatively rare. Note, too, that, while many of these studies were focused on the viability of certain forms, such as tropes, narratives or dramas, the tests used were almost invariably focused on the responses of readers; thus this category that I have labeled 'an investigation of form' is also an extension of investigating consumer response to ads.

The picture of the consumer emerging was very different from the one implicitly constructed by the scientific paradigm. This consumer is neither passive nor cognitively lazy, but instead is drawn toward more challenging textual forms, is more concerned with his/her own life experience than with learning brand attributes, can engage with the sociopolitical implications of ads despite the blinding force of ideology, and is adept at learning to read new meaning in unfamiliar forms. This view of the consumer is intrinsically more respectful than the one constructed by the field prior to the mid-1980s, but I must emphasize that this change is not a result of method, but rather one of theory. This radically different view of the reader/consumer has been substantially built and supported by researchers working in the qualitative tradition but using quantitative techniques.

If the concept of the consumer that held sway in the years from 1965 to 1985 is not a necessary outgrowth of scientific method, it must follow somehow from other influences on the way the field imagined and built itself in its earliest years. Prior to the interpretive turn, researchers in advertising often claimed that their purpose was to serve advertisers by showing them which advertising 'stimuli' worked best to persuade. This viewpoint has always been flawed on many levels, but we can certainly see at this point the way it ignored both the situatedness of formal features in a text and the situatedness of readers in their life projects and social settings. (Indeed, as Vakratsas and Ambler, 1999, exemplify, the old model can only be maintained now by ignoring the entire body of qualitative research.) As someone who entered the field from the advertising industry at the very moment of the interpretive turn, I felt the then prevailing view was marred by an amazingly misinformed speculation about how advertising professionals saw their work, imagined the consumer and understood the relationship between themselves as social actors and the academy as an independent intellectual force. Thus I am gratified to report that another large category of research emerging in the past 20 years has taken advertising professional practice as its object.

Studying advertising practice
The simplistic and manipulative agenda of advertising research prior to the mid-1980s takes on a very different cast when set in the context provided by researchers studying the production of advertising through qualitative methods in recent decades. Virtually all of the published research characterizes advertising practice as agonistic, fragmented, uncertain, fluid and stressful, suggesting further that the task of producing advertising itself is subject to multiple strategies, homilies, agendas and interpretations (Cronin, 2004a, 2004b; Hackley, 2002, 2003a, 2003b, 2003c; Kover, 1995; Kover and Goldberg, 1995; West, 1993). Though greater certainty of outcome would surely relieve much of the stress (a remark that could be made about most of life), the highest values consistently reported

for creative work include novelty, spontaneity and 'edginess' – especially 'something that has never been done before' – criteria that undercut the dominant paradigm's push for a one-from-column-A, one-from-column-B formula of advertising development.

To be sure, a constant refrain is the difficulty of demonstrating the effectiveness of advertising itself. This is not to say, as some old paradigm marketing researchers have inferred (e.g., Vakratsas and Ambler, 1999), that advertising is known not to work. On the contrary, the amount of time, money and effort that goes into producing ads suggests that industry people do believe it works, generally speaking. The problem is in tracing the effectiveness of particular ads with the specific goals and peculiar circumstances that are inevitably part of the campaign brief. Since advertising is *always* deployed into a market with an array of confounding influences and measured with, at best, flawed tools, the feasibility of evaluating a campaign's effectiveness in other than subjective terms is notoriously elusive. As a consequence, many in advertising are haunted by the fear that their work, rather than being the all-controlling social force that academicians elsewhere in the academy often pretend, is ultimately pointless (Schudson, 1984).

Given the real-life context of organizational struggle, complex markets, situated readers and morphing texts, the traditional marketing researcher's desire to codify reliable 'stimuli' that would consistently result in purchase seems a naïve attempt to try to introduce a rhetoric of certainty with which manufacturers could better control the efforts of their agencies, rather than any sincere belief in the existence of a formula that would sell in all times and places. Yet the circumstances of practice and the best judgments of advertising professionals tend to argue for a more situated, provisional, resilient, text-based approach – and now qualitative academic research in this area supports *them*. At this point, the evidence of multiple reading strategies being employed even by the same reader at different times and with different ads suggests that the old standard of producing a 100 per cent effective advertising toolbox through scientific method is nothing but a chimera.

Interestingly, the polarities discernible in the practice of research in marketing has a parallel in advertising practice. Chris Hackley, who has extensively studied (2003a, 2003b, 2003c) the efforts of advertising account planners to understand and articulate the views and voice of consumers, mostly through qualitative research, argues that advertising professionals have come to view consumer behavior 'as an imaginative activity realized through symbolic consumption as opposed to a merely instrumental activity driven by rational product evaluation' and thus an 'activity "inspired" by the beauty of persuasive and alluring images and ideas' (2003b, p. 2). Hackley suggests that agencies employ neopositivistic research methods primarily as a means to provide 'factual data' that will dress up their ideas enough for manufacturers to spend money on them. This is an agenda not dissimilar from the erstwhile goals of the marketing academy (Levold, 2002).

Tales of struggle for control over the final product of an ad campaign are, in fact, familiar to anyone who has worked in an agency or anyone who has read advertising histories and biographies with any breadth. Advertising practice, whether modern or postmodern, pre-direct mail or post-Internet, seems to be condemned to uncertainty of outcome, as a field that engages with the eternal instability of public reading might be expected to find itself. This aspect of the research on advertising practice enlightens and adds necessary balance to the analysis of ads-as-texts or consumers-as-readers, as one of these authors suggests: 'Whilst practitioners certainly cannot be said to determine viewers' reception of their texts, completely excluding practitioners from the analysis skews understanding of the significance of advertising practice and its textual products' (Cronin, 2004a, pp. 352–3). Nevertheless, I believe the long-term contribution of such studies ultimately lies in their ability to engage with and potentially challenge the burgeoning discourse of social criticism and cultural theory.

Advertising as an object for theory and criticism

Qualitative literature on advertising contains a number of essays that interpret one ad or a small group of ads in order to make larger accusations about the negative influence of advertising on society. There is a long tradition, after the manner of Williamson (1978), in which a handful of ads is used as the basis for exceedingly overblown social claims without attention or recourse to subtleties of probable reader response, plausible producer intent, possible product competition, or palliative price constraints (for instance, Delahoyde and Despenich,1994; Goldman, Heath and Smith, 1991; Covino, 2001).

The newer, more subtle, work attempts to theorize the effects of advertising in a way that accommodates the less-certain, destabilized vantages typical of a post-Marxist, post-Einstein, post-cultural relativist, and (of course) postmodern sensibility. Essays published in *Consumption, Markets and Culture* have been particularly sophisticated and offer a much-needed injection of both erudition and common sense to this often inflamed discourse. In this regard, the extensive experience within the advertising world that some scholars have can now provide a ballast that is lacking elsewhere, thus making it possible both to problematize the assumptions of cultural criticism and to mount a more compelling critique. For instance, Cronin, using her substantial experience with advertising professionals, raises multiple questions about the degree to which these people produce culture rather than 'siphon it off', the truth of nostalgic academic claims for a separation of economics and culture, and so on (Cronin, 2004a). In contrast, Chris Hackley, also working from a base of substantial experience, builds a case for the 'panopticon' properties of the advertising industry. The quiet understatement and frequent qualifications that clearly come from actual experience only serve to make Hackley's (2002) surveillance-for-control case more convincing, more compelling and, ultimately, more chilling, than less grounded, more flamboyant efforts at critique.

In the arena of theory, two issues seem to be emerging as potential flashpoints for contest and growth. Even the newer articulations of critical theory have a tendency to presuppose a certain kind of preindustrial past, a particular history for the emergence of consumer culture. Much of the rhetoric rests on a logic in which people *before* operated in such-and-such-a-way, *but now* they do things in a radically different thus-and-so manner. Some of these theoretical stances can, if one pauses to catch breath and think 'critically' in the commonly-used sense, be challenged even from a 'collective memories' sense of history. For instance, Clarke (1998) argues that before people defined themselves by their work but now they define themselves by their consumer goods. This statement is likely to fly brilliantly past any casual gathering of, say, regular readers of salon.com. Yet even a high school education in history suggests the argument that previous generations have defined themselves more by religion than either work or consumption. Further, other research tells us (e.g. Schor, 1991) that Americans, the citizens of the world's most advanced consumer society, are horribly overworked and tend to define themselves too much by occupation. So, in this case, the theorist has traded on a truism of our times, but not necessarily a factually based historical analysis.

Theory still tends to glamorize and sentimentalize preindustrial life, in the tradition of Marxist criticism. Yet my own work on the history of American women, feminism and the modern market has led me to believe, along with others who have studied feminism in world history, that there has been much about the industrial economy that was profoundly positive for women (Scott, 2000, 2005). Thinking a little further, it does not take much to see that African-American history might weigh the United States' agricultural period rather differently than some critical theorists' imagined past. And this is the crux of the problem: it *is* an imagined past. As my colleagues and I point out in another chapter in this volume, there has been painfully little written history on the emergence of consumer culture in America, let alone anywhere else. So there simply *is not* an evidentiary base to support these grandiose claims for the historical trajectory of the global consumer society. In the relative absence of written histories, ideology seems to take over: the contemporary critic's sentimental agricultural society is uncomfortably close to the 'agrarian myth' once identified by Richard Hofstadter (1955), the ideology manufactured by the disenfranchised agrarian gentlemen of post-Revolutionary America who saw the modern market eroding their power base. A challenge for future research *and* critique, then, would be to examine the whole question of the consumer past.

A further point of contention may emerge in the confrontation between theory and the growing number of studies documenting real readers' responses to ads. Contemporary theorists, though they sometimes vociferously reject the totalizing view of culture that once characterized social criticism, still often want to place consumers in an endless circle from which they cannot escape being duped by the forces of marketing. In a field now deluged with evidence of the intransigence and multiplicity of consumer viewpoints, this stance is beginning to look a little too much like the arrogant, derogatory view the old scientific paradigm once took of consumers.

Consequently, the 'vernacular theory' espoused by Thomas MacLaughlin (1998) may offer an interesting path toward reconciling a critical perspective with respect for our cultural compatriots. MacLaughlin reminds us that 'though Marx and Engels believed that *ideas* about revolutionary change had to be based on the proletarian *experience* of capitalism, they believed that those ideas were unlikely to come from the proletarians themselves. It was precisely the role of bourgeois intellectuals sympathetic to the proletariat to learn from that experience and articulate it intellectually for the masses, whom they considered too embedded in ideology to be able to understand their situation critically without the cognitive leadership of intellectuals trained in philosophical analysis and critique' (ibid., p. 208). This stance, which today we might be tempted to label 'paternalistic', has not only continued to infect critique, but leads to several problems: one is that 'it does a better job explaining why people fail to understand their society than why they succeed' (ibid., p. 209) and another is that it fails to encompass the historical record in which other oppressed groups (African-Americans and women are the examples MacLaughlin gives) manage to mount a substantial critique out of common experience and necessity: 'Groups defined by demeaning and dehumanizing mainstream values either do theory or die in spirit' (ibid., p. 221). MacLaughlin specifically invokes reader response theory for having overridden the Adorno/Horkheimer model of cultural control by 'teaching' that reading is an active process in which the readers themselves make meaning. Almost as if taking a page from an ad agency's handbook, he notes, 'It is the work of rhetoric to construct texts that maximize control over readers' responses, but the practice of rhetoric is based on the premise that there will *be* resistant readers, that control will never be total' (ibid., p. 217). He ends with a passionate recollection of his own working-class Philadelphia experience, insisting that this experience formed the basis for his own critical vision, and warns that 'not all the sharp minds get to go to college, and not all the theorists are in the academy' (ibid., p. 229). Such a spirited defense of vernacular criticism seems a fitting call for developing theory from our own group of scholars, who have now so well recognized the resistance among advertising readers.

Another common seam between qualitative and quantitative research on advertising presents itself, perhaps surprisingly, in the social criticism arena. Seemingly in response to criticism first mounted in the 1960s and 1970s by civil rights groups, Second Wave feminists and environmental activists, advertising researchers have often focused on trying to document, usually through content analysis, the incidence of imagery that political critics have found problematic: racial stereotyping, 'sexualizing' imagery of women, 'green' appeals, and so on (for instance, Bannerjee, Gulas and Iyer, 1995; Ferguson, Kreshel and Tinkham, 1990; Kolbe and Albanese, 1996; Stephenson and Stover, 1997). Others have tried to pick through, explain and synthesize the increasingly dense and often tangled arguments that characterize certain corners of social debate, most notably gender (Brown, Stevens and Maclaren, 1999; Kates and Shaw-Garlock, 1999; Schroeder and Borgerson, 1998; Stern, 1993). Over time the ability to document both the occurrence of these images or appeals and their interrelatedness to the discourse of criticism will ultimately add the kind of evidentiary ballast often lacking.

Conclusion

The first 20 years of advertising research using qualitative methods have upended many traditional assumptions and purposes formerly taken for granted in the field. In this way (and in others) this moment in scholarship has been revolutionary. It has led to a heartening proliferation of high quality research, appearing in a broad range of journals and showing the marks of influence from a variety of other disciplines. This stream has also led to a point where many of us may come to rethink our relationship to research and the interests we wish our work to serve, whether industry, consumers, government or some as-yet-unimagined world order. In that sense, the force of this work may also be turning the wheel.

References

Ahuvia, Aaron C. (1998), 'Social criticism of advertising', *Journal of Advertising*, **27** (1), 143–63.

Alperstein, Neil M. (1990), 'The verbal content of TV advertising and its circulation in everyday life', *Journal of Advertising*, **19** (2), 15–22.

Banerjee, Subhabrata, Charles S. Gulas and Easwar Iyer (1995), 'Shades of green', *Journal of Advertising*, **24** (2), 21–32.

Brown, Stephen, Lorna Stevens and Pauline Maclaren (1999), 'I can't believe it's not Bakhtin!', *Journal of Advertising*, **28** (1).

Callcott, Margaret F. and Wei-Na Lee (1994), 'A content analysis of animations and animated spokes-characters in television commercials', *Journal of Advertising*, **23** (4).

Clarke, David S. (1998), 'Consumption, identity, and space-time', *Consumption, Markets and Culture*, **2** (3), 233–58.

Covino, Deborah (2001), 'Outside-in', *Journal of Popular Culture*, **35** (3), 91–103.

Cronin, Anne (2004a), 'Regimes of mediation: advertising practitioners as cultural intermediaries?', *Consumption, Markets and Culture*, **7** (4), 349–69.

Cronin, Anne (2004b), 'Currencies of commercial exchange', *Journal of Consumer Culture*, **4** (3), 339–60.

Deighton, John, Daniel Romer and Josh McQueen (1989), 'Using drama to persuade', *Journal of Consumer Research*, **16** (Dec.), 335–43.

Delahoyde, Michael and Susan C. Despenich (1994), 'Games for girls', *Journal of Popular Culture*, **28** (1) Summer, 159–74.

Ferguson, Jill, Peggy Kreshel and Spencer Tinkham (1990), 'In the pages of *Ms.*', *Journal of Advertising*, **19** (1), 40–51.

Friestad, Marian and Peter Wright (1994), 'The persuasion knowledge model: how people cope with persuasion attempts', *Journal of Consumer Research*, **21** (June), 1–31.

Frosh, Paul (2002), 'Rhetorics of the overlooked', *Journal of Consumer Culture*, **2** (2), 171–6.

Goldman, Robert (1992), *Reading Ads Socially*, New York: Routledge.

Goldman, Robert, Deborah Heath and Sharon L. Smith (1991), 'Commodity feminism', *Critical Studies in Mass Communication*, **8**, 333–51.

Grier, Sonya A. and Anne M. Brumbaugh (1999), 'Noticing cultural differences: ad meanings created by target and non-target markets', *Journal of Advertising*, **28** (1).

Hackley, Christopher (2002), 'The panoptic role of advertising agencies in the production of consumer culture', *Consumption, Markets and Culture*, **5** (3), 211–29.

Hackley, Christopher E. (2003a), 'Divergent representation practices in advertising and consumer research', *Qualitative Market Research*, **6** (3), 175–84.

Hackley, Christopher E. (2003b), 'Accounting planning: a review of current practitioner perspectives from leading London and New York Agencies', *Journal of Advertising Research*, June, 1–11.

Hackley, Christopher E. (2003c), 'The implicit epistemological models underlying intra-account team conflict in international advertising agencies', *International Journal of Advertising*, **23**, 1–19.

Hofstadter, Richard J. (1955), *The Age of Reform*, New York: Vintage.

Holt, Douglas B. (2004), *How Brands Become Icons*, Boston: Harvard University Press.

Hung, Kineta (2000), 'Narrative music in congruent and incongruent TV advertising', *Journal of Advertising*, **29** (1).

Hung, Kineta (2001), 'Framing meaning perceptions with music: the case of teaser ads', *Journal of Advertising*, **30** (3).

Kates, Steven and Glenda Shaw-Garlock (1999), 'The ever-entangling web', *Journal of Advertising*, **28** (2).

Kavanaugh, James (1995), 'Ideology', *Critical Terms for Literary Study*, Chicago: University of Chicago Press.

Kolbe, Richard H. and Paul J. Albanese (1996), 'Man to man', *Journal of Advertising*, **25** (4), 1–20.

Kover, Arthur J. (1995), 'Copywriters' implicit theories of communication: an exploration', *Journal of Consumer Research*, **31** (March), 596–611.

Kover, Arthur J. and Stephen M. Goldberg (1995), 'The games copywriters play: conflict, quasi-control, a new proposal', *Journal of Advertising Research*, July/August, 52–62.

Leigh, James H. (1994), 'The use of figures of speech in print ad headlines', *Journal of Advertising*, **23** (2).

Levold, John (2002), 'Pictures and information theory in consumer research', dissertation, University of Illinois.

MacLaughlin, Thomas (1998), 'Theory outside the academy: street smarts and critical theory', *Consumption, Markets and Culture*, **2** (2), 105–231.

McCracken, Grant (1986), 'Culture and consumption: a theoretical account of the structure and movement of the cultural meaning of consumer goods', *Journal of Consumer Research*, **13** (1) (June), 71–84.

McCracken, Grant (1987), 'Advertising: meaning or information', *Advances in Consumer Research*, **14**, 121–4.

McQuarrie, Edward F. and David Glen Mick (1996), 'Figures of rhetoric in advertising language', *Journal of Consumer Research*, **22** (4), 424–38.

McQuarrie, Edward F. and David Glen Mick (1999), 'Visual rhetoric in advertising: text-interpretive, experimental, and reader-response analyses', *Journal of Consumer Research*, **26** (1), 37–54.

McQuarrie, Edward F. and David Glen Mick (1992), 'On resonance', *Journal of Consumer Research*, **19** (2), 180–97.

Mick, David Glen (1986), 'Consumer research and semiotics', *Journal of Consumer Research*, **16** (Dec.), 310–21.

Mick, David Glen and Claus Buhl (1992), 'A meaning-based model of advertising experiences', *Journal of Consumer Research*, **19** (3), 317–38.

Motley, Carol M., Geraldine R. Henderson and Stacey Menzel Baker (2003), 'Exploring collective memories associated with African-American advertising memorabilia', *Journal of Advertising*, **32** (1), 47–57.

Mulvey, Michael S. and Carmen Medina (2003), 'Invoking the rhetorical power of character to create identifications', in Linda Scott and Rajeev Batra (eds), *Persuasive Imagery: A Consumer Response Perspective*, Mahwah, NJ: Lawrence Erlbaum.

Parker, Betty J. (1998), 'Exploring life themes and myths in alcohol advertisements through a meaning-based model of advertising experiences', *Journal of Advertising*, **27** (1).

Phillips, Barbara J. (1997), 'Thinking into it: consumer interpretation of complex advertising images', *Journal of Advertising*, **26** (2), 77–87.

Phillips, Barbara J. and Edward F. McQuarrie (2002), 'The development, change, and transformation of rhetorical style in magazine advertisements, 1954–1999', *Journal of Advertising*, **31** (4), 1–13.

Ritson, Mark and Richard Elliott (1999), 'The social uses of advertising: an ethnographic study of adolescent advertising audiences', *Journal of Consumer Research*, **26** (3), 260–77.

Schor, Juliet (1991), *The Overworked American*, New York: Basic Books.

Schroeder, Jonathan and Janet Borgerson (1998), 'Marketing images of gender', *Consumption, Markets and Culture*, **2** (2), 165–202.

Schudson, Michael (1984), *Advertising, the Uneasy Persuasion*, New York: Basic Books.

Scott, Linda M. (1990), 'Understanding jingles and needledrop', *Journal of Consumer Research*.

Scott, Linda M. (1994a), 'Images in advertising: the need for a theory of visual rhetoric', *Journal of Consumer Research*, **21** (2), 252–73.

Scott, Linda M. (1994b), 'The bridge from text to mind: adapting reader-response theory to consumer research', *Journal of Consumer Research*, **21** (3), 461–80.

Scott, Linda M. (2000), 'Market feminism', *Marketing and Feminism*, London: Routledge.

Scott, Linda M. (2005), *Fresh Lipstick*, New York: Palgrave.

Stern, Barbara B. (1988), 'How does an ad mean?', *Journal of Advertising*, **17** (Summer).

Stern, Barbara B. (1989), 'Literary criticism and consumer research', *Journal of Consumer Research*, **16** (Dec.), 322–34.

Stern, Barbara B. (1993), 'Feminist literary criticism and the deconstruction of ads: a postmodern view of advertising and consumer response', *Journal of Consumer Research*, **19** (March), 556–66.

Stephenson, Theresa and William J. Stover (1997), 'Sell me some prestige!', *Journal of Popular Culture*, **30** (4), 255–77.

Stevens, Lorna, Pauline Maclaren and Stephen Brown (2003), '*Red* time is me time: advertising, ambivalence, and women's magazines', *Journal of Advertising*, **32** (1), 35–45.

Vakratsas, Demetrios and Tim Ambler (1999), 'How advertising works: what do we really know?', *Journal of Marketing*, **63** (January), 26–43.

West, Douglas C. (1993), 'Cross-national creative personalities, processes, and agency philosophies', *Journal of Advertising Research*, September/October, 53–62.

Williamson, Judith (1978), *Decoding Advertisements*, London: Boyars.

6 Qualitative historical research in marketing
Terrence H. Witkowski and D.G. Brian Jones

Introduction

Historians are generally disinclined to commit themselves to descriptions of their work, its goals and methods. A few notable exceptions among marketing historians have focused on scientific–quantitative methods of doing historical research (e.g. Savitt, 1980; Golder, 2000). Traditional western historians argue that their task is to trace and interpret the internal relations of human affairs (Collingwood, 1956). They describe the process as an imaginative reconstruction of the lives of people in other times (Dray, 1974) or as 'creatively thinking one's way a body of information' (Bailyn, 1963, p. 98). It is a process not easily reduced to description (Goodman and Kruger, 1988; Savitt, 2000).

This chapter describes qualitative historical research methods as applied to marketing. It is worthwhile at the outset to note that history is a subject, not a research method and, as just noted, not all historical research is conducted using qualitative methods. The fuzzy boundaries between different approaches and the different methodological assumptions of historians are perhaps captured by Abelson (1963) who described it as 'art and science, poetry and journalism, explanation, narration, and criticism; it is epochal and parochial, holistic and individualistic, materialistic and spiritualistic, objective and subjective, factual and normative, practical and theoretical' (p. 167). In this chapter we will describe some of those aspects of historical research in marketing.

The subject of history can be subdivided into many topics, including marketing history which has a parallel topic usually referred to as 'the history of marketing thought'. The academic study of marketing emerged in the late nineteenth century as a branch of applied economics and marketing historians have long followed the tradition of economic historians that divides their subject matter into more or less separate treatments of practice and of ideas (Jones and Shaw, 2002). Thus, as there are histories of economics and of economic thought, so are there histories of marketing and of marketing thought. Or, to follow the vernacular used by marketing historians, most historical research in marketing can be described as focusing either on *marketing history* or on the *history of marketing thought*. While they begin with a fairly common set of subcategories such as advertising, retailing, various other functional marketing activities, consumption behavior and so on, marketing history focuses on the history of the *activities or practices* themselves, whereas the history of marketing thought focuses on the *ideas* about those phenomena.

Of course, as Hollander once observed, 'practice is not entirely thoughtless and thought is often practice-driven' (1989, p. xx). Nevertheless, marketing scholars have studied history in this way since the beginning of the twentieth century. Marketing history (practices and activities) tends to be studied from the perspective of companies, industries, or societies (as in the case of consumption history). The history of marketing thought is approached at various levels such as ideas or concepts, theories and schools of thought. It also includes the perspective of individual contributors (biographical), educational institutions and organizations (e.g. the American Marketing Association), and bodies of literature (e.g. *Journal of Marketing*), to name a few. These various categories of topics within historical research in marketing are most evident in reviews of the field such as in Jones and Monieson (1990b) or in anthologies of works in the field such as in Hollander and Rassuli (1993). Regardless of category (marketing history or history of marketing thought), historical research in marketing can make use of either quantitative or qualitative research methods. Below we explain how qualitative historical research in marketing is carried out.

Overview of qualitative historical research methods
When historians do write about method, they are most likely to discuss things like source materials (much space is devoted herein to this important issue) or the principles which should guide the research process, principles such as accuracy, love of order, logic, honesty, self-awareness and imagination (Barzun and Graff, 2004, pp. 10–13) rather than the steps one goes through. Practically speaking and put quite simply, the steps include choosing a subject, gathering data, analyzing and interpreting the data, and writing the results (Jones, 1998; Lomask, 1986). Barzun and Graff's (2004) classic work on historical method expands on that somewhat, as follows:

1. Select a subject.
2. Consult secondary sources, otherwise known as the literature review.
3. Note taking and rewriting is analysis of thought.
4. Finding the facts involves collection of source material, primary data.
5. Verification of the facts is an ongoing process and relies on 'attention to detail, on commonsense reasoning, and on a developed "feel" for chronology and human affairs' (Barzun and Graff, 2004, p. 69).
6. Turning facts into ideas involves the search for probabilistic truth, for the types of causation that occur in a long chain of events or 'variously relevant conditions' (ibid., p. 148) and for a pattern which is most obviously demonstrated through periods in the chronology of ideas.
7. Organizing and writing the story is the final step.

The remainder of this chapter is loosely organized around this framework.

Selecting a topic
Because the selection of a topic is the first step in any research project, the reader might reasonably ask why this needs to be stated or why it is particularly important in historical research. The essence of topic selection is asking the right questions. Barzun and Graff (2004) describe this step as the prime difficulty in any historical study because if the topic is not carefully defined the researcher cannot know what questions to ask of the data or, therefore, what data to collect. The definition of subject is described as 'that group of associated facts and ideas which, when clearly presented in a prescribed amount of space, leave no questions unanswered within the presentation, even though many questions could be asked outside it' (ibid., p. 17). Closely related to the selection of a topic is the development of what is sometimes called a working hypothesis or hypotheses. They are working hypotheses because, as the historian develops a topic and begins to collect data, the questions that are asked will inevitably change as data are discovered. Smith and Lux

(1993) refer to this as 'question framing'; the historian develops iterations of research questions in response to answers discovered when questioning the data. The research questions, or working hypotheses, are refined as the data are collected.

Source material
After choosing a topic, framing questions and formulating working hypotheses, the marketing historian needs to gather source material. The quality of historical research depends largely upon the data sources selected. Indeed, the serendipitous discovery of a neglected lode of important historical evidence may sometimes be reason enough for launching a project. This section first considers the mix of primary and secondary sources and then describes four types of primary data, some of their strengths and weaknesses, and how to assemble them.

Primary v. secondary sources
Primary data sources are forms of evidence usually produced during the historical period under investigation. Oral history interviews are a special kind of primary data typically conducted many years after events have occurred, but based on memories created during the times in question. Secondary data sources are the literature about the period, such as books and articles, written at a later date. Some marketing historians (Jones and Monieson, 1990a; Savitt, 1983) favor heavy reliance on primary data; others (Fullerton, 1988; Hollander, 1986b) have made good use of both types; and still others (Dixon, 1995, 1998; Twede, 2002; Witkowski, 1989) have based their work upon fresh readings of existing literatures. The body of such secondary data, the literature of historical research in marketing, has grown dramatically during the past two decades. During that time over 400 papers were published in the proceedings of the Conferences on Historical Analysis and Research in Marketing (CHARM) and over 75 historical articles were published in the *Journal of Macromarketing*, to name just two venues.

The historical era being investigated will influence the mix of data sources. An enormous amount of primary material documents marketing practice and thought since the latter part of the nineteenth century. Much remains uninvestigated. For earlier periods, original evidence is often much less abundant, scattered across numerous records and sometimes quite difficult to locate. It may be redundant for marketing historians to reanalyze the same primary sources that others have combed. A great deal of historical research from fields as diverse as women's studies to material culture (Witkowski, 1990, 1994) begs to be read, reinterpreted and incorporated into the body of marketing history. For many years, scholars in marketing, advertising and consumer research have borrowed theoretical ideas and empirical findings from economics, psychology, sociology, anthropology and other fields. The large body of historical literature should also be mined for marketing insights. That said, researchers should familiarize themselves with the primary evidence from the earlier eras so that they can critically evaluate secondary sources.

Types of primary sources
Primary data sources can be divided into four groups: words, images, artifacts and memories elicited through oral history methods. Purely audio data, such as radio advertising or popular music, could be used as source material, but seldom is and then only as transcribed dialogue and lyrics. A particular piece of evidence can straddle more than one

category. Advertising, one of the most frequently consulted primary sources (see, for example, Belk and Pollay, 1985; Gross and Sheth, 1989; Pollay, 1985) and other ephemera (Neilson, 2005) often include both text and visuals. Paintings are images but also material objects, often with provenance, a history of sales and ownership (Witkowski, 2004). The type of project determines the kind and mix of primary sources. Whereas marketing and consumer histories draw from all kinds of data, biographies and histories of marketing thought are largely based upon written sources, although they too may be supplemented by oral history interviews.

Historians have consulted written documents for a very long time, but not until the invention of the printing press in the mid-fifteenth century, accompanied by growing rates of literacy, did texts proliferate enough to become the dominant data source. By the middle of the nineteenth century, many academic historians were basing their research solely on this material and, partly to give their emerging discipline an identity of its own, began espousing the written record as the only creditable evidence (Thompson, 1988). Today, written sources are used far more than any other type of primary data. Typical forms for marketing and consumer history, listed from the most public to the most personal, include the following.

1. Public records such as legal documents, governmental records and other institutional records such as those of universities and scholarly organizations.
2. Articles and letters in newspapers, magazines, trade publications and scholarly journals.
3. Print advertising, handbills, trade cards, trade catalogs and package labels.
4. Nonfiction travel accounts, cookbooks and housekeeping manuals.
5. Novels, poetry and other published fiction.
6. Private business records such as account books, letterheads and invoices.
7. Personal writing in the form of letters and diaries.

The books and articles of academic marketing are a primary source for biographies (Jones, 1998) and histories of marketing thought (Shaw and Jones, 2005; Wilkie and Moore, 2003), and even relatively recent publications have been used for consumption research. For example, Cohen (2003) cited *Journal of Marketing* articles from the 1950s and 1960s as evidence of increasing social segmentation in postwar America.

Written records of all types have their shortcomings. They are often incomplete, difficult to read if penned by hand, and not infrequently contradictory. More important, they should not be taken at face value. Documents have been faked. More likely, however, is selective perception and retention on the part of their creators. Documents frequently were (and still are) drafted to protect and embellish the reputations of certain individuals, organizations, social groups and political interests. Usually created by elite males, documents tend to underrepresent the experiences of the lower classes, minorities and women. Their survival rate is also problematic since preservation choices are often made deliberately, but subjectively. The researcher needs to guard against overgeneralizing from written sources and be alert to possible biases. 'Truth' is very elusive, and even so-called 'hard' demographic data can be untrustworthy. That is, social statistics are no more absolute facts than newspaper reports, private letters or published biographies. All represent, either from individual standpoints or aggregated, the *social perception* of facts; and all are in addition subject to social pressures from the context in which they are obtained. With these forms of evidence, what we receive is *social meaning*, and it is this which must be evaluated (Thompson, 1988, p. 106).

Images or visual data sources, which include paintings, prints, photographs, films and videos, can reveal things about past marketing and consumption that cannot be conveyed by written records (Belk, 1986; Witkowski, 1999, 2004). They can show what buyers and sellers and their merchandise and accoutrements actually looked like. They can depict color, form, movement and other details people once took for granted and failed to mention in texts (Burke, 2001). Through narrative content and allegory, art can express social attitudes and, hence, validate or challenge written sources such as diaries, letters, newspaper accounts or probate records (Witkowski, 1994). Burke (2001) points out that, unlike written evidence, where usually only the investigator has had an opportunity to visit an archive and read the material, when images are reproduced in research reports, both authors and readers have access to the data and can examine them together.

However, images too can be misleading, for their creators selected only certain subjects and rendered the world the way they personally perceived or remembered it, what Burke (2001) refers to as their 'painted opinion'. Visuals are often created within the expectations of patrons and audiences. Consequently they can sometimes be a better guide to past social attitudes and cultural conventions than to the exact nature of people, things and consumer behavior. American genre painters, for example, sometimes distorted actual behavior in order to instruct or entertain the viewer and drew upon stock social characters that fulfilled the expectations of their patrons (Witkowski, 1996, 2004). Works of art have aesthetic qualities and polemical content that can elicit powerful, possibly biased, emotional responses in the researcher. Art must be read carefully and the analyst needs to distinguish a contemporary reading from a historical or period reading. The challenge is to recreate what might be termed the 'period eye'.

Marketing historians have not very often consulted physical evidence, such as artifacts and architecture, although these alternative sources have potential for documenting the products actually sold, what they looked like, and how they may have been used (Witkowski, 1994, 2001). Material data can be classified as *found objects*, the bits and pieces archaeologists excavate at historical sites, or *preserved objects*, the antiques collected by private individuals and public institutions. Sometimes artifacts are all that remains of some goods deemed too trivial to be included in written records or captured in images. When they were used by a broad cross-section of the population, artifacts could be more representative data sources than texts. Moreover, objects are generally less self-conscious cultural expressions and, therefore, conceivably more truthful (Prown, 1982). Through their style, objects communicate tacit but fundamental values of a society (Prown, 1980).

On the other hand, artifacts do not reveal beliefs, attitudes, values and meanings as directly as written records. In addition, physical data sources suffer from their own problems in representativeness. Found objects are generally restricted to certain materials, such as ceramics, glass or precious metals, that can survive many years of burial on land or under water. Leather, wooden and base-metal consumer goods rarely last under these conditions and textiles hardly at all. Aside from pure chance, preserved objects were saved because they possessed special attributes. They may have been of the highest quality, particularly artistic or originally owned by distinguished people or affluent families. More common, often cruder artifacts experienced harder use, deteriorated more rapidly and were more likely to have been discarded as junk. Their survival rate is much less than that of high-style objects. Also preserved objects may have been altered over time, either innocently or with intent to deceive, and no longer are the evidence as they were when first produced and used. These historical accretions remind us that objects live in the present as well as the past.

Ritchie (1995) offers a succinct definition of our fourth primary source: 'Simply put, oral history collects spoken memories and personal commentaries of historical significance through recorded interviews' (p. 1). Today, these data are typically captured by audio/video equipment, although some situations still require note taking. Interview techniques can range from being very unstructured and free-flowing to obtaining open-ended answers to a specific list of questions. Sessions are then transcribed verbatim, save minor editing to clarify, to remove false starts or repetitions and to insert punctuation. Although time-consuming, transcription facilitates interpretation since most people can read and reread print faster than they can listen to and comprehend an audio or video recording. Further, given potential problems in accessing tape and/or digital storage media in the future, a written version helps preserve the findings.

A few historians have dismissed oral history as little more than the collection of sentimental memories from old people. Clearly 'some interviewees' remarks are self-serving; they remember selectively, recall only events that cast themselves in a good light, and seem to always get the better of opponents' (Ritchie, 1995, p. 92). Human memories start from different points of view and are fallible, although most forgetting takes place soon after an event has occurred. Oral history informants have been characterized as being 'special' people, survivors, more successful, and self-confident (Gluck, 1987). Oral historians frequently encounter informant nostalgia, the remembering of the past as better than it was lived, and thus need to press for more candid and critical responses (Ritchie, 1995).

All in all, however, interview data are probably no more subjective or less all representative than any other pieces of evidence and they have special advantages of their own. For one, respondents can be selected to ensure that many different points of view are being voiced. Oral history is democratic in its desire to gather information from a variety of social actors, including the more quiescent part of the population. Also oral interviews can elicit recollections of inner feelings and states of mind that are frequently absent from or disguised by written records. Finally, the interviewing process allows the astute investigator, in effect, to cross-examine informants and thereby reveal sources of bias. Thompson (1988) describes a phenomenon among the elderly known as a 'life review' – a sudden flood of memories, a desire to remember and a willingness to be candid and less concerned about fitting one's story to the expectations of an audience.

Oral interviews are especially useful for consumer history because they usually entail ordinary people recalling everyday experiences. The field of consumer research has made use of interview data for decades and, if anything, has seen a resurgence of interest over the past 20 years in more or less unstructured questioning and small samples. Interviews, in the sense of deliberately collected field data, have seldom been utilized by consumer historians. One exception is Hill, Hirschman and Bauman (1997) who based their account of Depression consumers on oral data originally collected by academics, journalists and writers between 1933 and 1935 under the direction of Harry Hopkins, director of the Federal Emergency Relief Administration. Witkowski and Hogan (1999) created new oral data by asking elderly California women to recall their consumer experiences during World War II.

Assembling primary sources
Two final points about primary evidence are in order. First, collecting different sources, both within and across categories, is highly desirable. Words, images, artifacts and oral histories can clarify, validate and sometimes dispute each other, leading to a deeper, more nuanced view of marketing history. Multiple methods are standard procedure in ethnography and other forms of qualitative marketing and consumer research. Second, researchers have fewer and fewer excuses for not using primary data. Numerous archival collections in museums contain sources to study marketing practice and many universities have collections relevant to the study of the history of marketing thought. Archives collect unpublished primary source materials, provide for their physical preservation, arrange and describe them for prospective users and usually provide reference service on their collections. Private records and personal (unpublished) writings are the bread and butter of archival collections, although photographic images and oral histories are also not uncommon forms of archival data. The effective use of archives including the importance of various types of finding aids, types of archives and so on is described in detail by Brooks (1969). Jones (1998) describes a sample of actual archival collections that are relevant to studying the history of marketing thought.

Although distant archives may pose a barrier to investigating some sources, many have been published and widely distributed. University libraries have long maintained good microfilm or microprint collections of newspapers, magazines and journals and have become better at fetching material from other libraries. All kinds of primary data, especially images, are increasingly available online from a tremendous variety of providers ranging from museums to eBay dealers. As just one example, the John W. Hartmann Center for Sales, Advertising, and Marketing History at Duke University has made accessible thousands of advertisements from its growing collections. Witkowski (2003) based his study of World War II posters largely on the online collection of the Northwestern University Library.

Analysis and writing
The analysis of qualitative historical data involves interpretation and synthesis. The data collected must be transformed into ideas, which involves the search for probabilistic truth, for the types of causation that occur in a long chain of events or 'variously relevant conditions' (Barzun and Graff 2004, p. 148), and for a pattern which is most obviously demonstrated through periods in the chronology of ideas.

The processes of qualitative analysis and of writing the results are interwoven. Narrative, telling the story of the past, is the most common structure for presenting historical findings (Hexter, 1971; Lavin and Archdeacon, 1989). Four basic elements, character, setting, action and happening, interact to produce narrative (Megill, 1989). Character and setting are called *existents*, whereas actions (taken by characters) and happenings (how settings impinge upon characters) are *events*. Although conventional wisdom identifies narration with the recounting of events, many historians emphasize existents. For example, Fernand Braudel's *Capitalism and Material Life, 1400–1800* (1967) focuses on setting: food and drink, housing and clothing, and technology and towns.

The *sine qua non* of historical writing is clarity. The dense jargon and convoluted phrasing of some social science prose, not to mention all too much critical writing in the humanities, is simply inappropriate. Some historians prefer a more dramatic and literary style than others who favor heavy documentation and elaborate presentation of empirical findings, but all must write in a straightforward and interesting to read manner. Good narrative depends upon a correct determination of historical tempo, the art of expanding and contracting the scale of time to establish the significance of events (Hexter, 1971). Narrative in historical writing needs to guard against being overly 'impressionistic' (Demos, 1970), where general statements are preceded or followed by a small number of illustrative examples. Dissatisfaction with this approach has increased the emphasis on cliometrics or 'scientific' history (Fogel and Elton, 1983), the use of quantitative models and measures and statistical analyses. Sometimes, however, a paucity of evidence leaves no alternative to the impressionistic approach. Marketing history needs to cover a topic adequately, but should also strive for economy in its written presentation.

Many scholars in the social and behavioral sciences, not to mention quite a few professional historians, view description as a less serious task than explanation. Explanation is deemed to be more scientific and generalizable than description of particulars. This position has been challenged, however, as evidenced by the debates between positivistic and interpretive consumer researchers (Hudson and Ozanne, 1988). Moreover, as Megill (1989) and Nevett (1991) point out, even nominally descriptive historical writing will have a large component of explanation. That is, the ordering of events chronologically implies (but does not prove) causality.

Organizing the narrative

The narration of marketing history can be arranged chronologically, topically, geographically, or in some combination of the three (Shafer, 1974). In argumentative or justificatory pieces the writer might limit the discussion to an analysis of sources or, in the case of Fullerton (1988) and Morris (1990), assemble and criticize evidence in order to evaluate alternative representations of the past. In historiographic essays or surveys of prior studies, narration of events is likely to be relatively less important than thematic issues. Whatever the organization, it should be synthesized through appropriate *linkages*, such as the comparative method, and it should be adequately *balanced* in its coverage (Daniels, 1981). Historical writing and data analysis are closely connected. How findings will be presented is implicit in the researcher's general questions and tentative hypotheses and so influence how data sources are interpreted.

Periodization is the process of dividing the chronological narrative into separately labeled sequential time periods with fairly distinct beginning and ending points. Periods are to the historian what acts and scenes are to the playwright. They summarize and structure historical narrative in a way that makes it more understandable. There are several different logics, or techniques, of periodization. The most common is to divide chronology into periods ending in '0' such as decades or centuries. As Hollander et al. (2005) point out, this system is inherently weak because 'human events rarely arrange themselves to fall evenly between years that end in the numeral zero' (p. 37). Other methods include context-driven periodization where the chronology is punctuated by the occurrence of some external event or events, justified when the event is likely to have precipitated a change in the direction of the material under study; and periodization by turning points in the events themselves. Hollander et al. (2005) advocate the latter approach as the most logical and acceptable. An example is Fullerton's (1988) revision of the history of modern marketing where his era of origins, beginning in mid-eighteenth-century Europe and mid-nineteenth-century America, relied on changes in political, religious and social forces that created a capitalist attitude as well as new production capabilities brought on by the Industrial Revolution. Periodization is essentially a way of compressing a stream of complex events into a single catchword or catchphrase, and that oversimplification or reductionism must be guarded against. This caution also applies to the choice of period duration. Shorter periods may induce greater volatility and variability in the data.

Narrative history that concentrates on character or setting does not require a chronological arrangement. John Demos (1970) organizes his highly regarded history of family life in the Plymouth Plantation (1620–1691) by subject matter. He begins with a discussion of physical setting, moves to household structure and then examines themes of individual development. Demos chose this approach not only because it seemed a better way to highlight analytical issues, but also because changes in family structure generally come very slowly and, hence, elements of stability and continuity loom unusually large. If spread over too long a period, however, a topical arrangement may 'seriously distort the objective reality of the past' and 'forfeit the fundamental historical essence of change through time' (Marwick, 1970, p. 145).

Preparing manuscripts for marketing journals

Publishing historical research in marketing journals entails much more than simply paying close attention to editors' pages, manuscript guidelines, acceptance criteria and statements of review philosophy. Marketing historians need to consider how closely their papers should adhere to existing models of marketing scholarship. How marketing history is packaged determines not only the likelihood of acceptance by top journals in the field, but ultimately its contribution to the advancement of marketing thought. Three topics of particular import are how to introduce the secondary literature, present the methodology and handle the issue of research implications.

The literature review

Unlike the typical article in marketing and consumer research, papers written by professional historians often proceed without a separate section integrating previous work on the subject into the body of the text. This is not to say that historians ignore prior findings and interpretive essays (secondary sources), but just that their narrative structures do not always lend themselves to the kind of presentation that first 'plugs into' existing literatures, theoretical perspectives or research traditions. When included, such material is usually placed in footnotes, a hallmark of the rhetoric of history. This lack of explicit 'positioning' can be frustrating to marketing journal editors and reviewers accustomed to the social science tradition. It makes historical research seem atheoretical, which it frequently is, and consequently irrelevant to the accumulation of knowledge, which it is not.

In order to be published in marketing journals, historical studies will usually need to make explicit mention of the secondary literature and sometimes provide a thorough review. This will be natural for papers taking a positivistic stance, such as theoretically driven content analyses (Belk and Pollay, 1985; Gross and Sheth, 1989), where finding loose theoretical ends precedes developing hypotheses. Essays and argumentative pieces also discuss relevant literature, sometimes in great detail. Incorporating prior research will probably be most difficult for the more qualitative narrative works, especially case studies that emphasize events.

Methods section

Professional historians are sometimes cavalier about explaining their data sources and analytical methods. For example, the following sentence from Roland Marchand's (1987) 'The Fitful Career of Advocacy Advertising' is as close as this article comes to a methods statement: 'A historical survey of some early advocacy campaigns will reveal both the variety of experiments within this advertising mode and the ways in which earlier practitioners tried to deal with the problems that still beset the genre' (p. 129). Marchand never explains what he means by the term 'a historical survey'. His text does not describe his sample of ads or say how they were interpreted, although his references do suggest he consulted several archival collections. Savitt (2000) describes Fernand Braudel as 'probably the most important economic historian of the twentieth century' (p. 89), but laments Braudel's failure to present a clear description of his historical reasoning and methodology. Other historians are more explicit, but often relegate their methodological statements to footnotes or bibliographic essays.

Historical writing for marketing journals needs to be transparent about methods. Data sources and their selection should be carefully described, along with the plan for their analysis. A good example of one such methods section can be found in Fullerton (1988), who first discusses the philosophical support for his historical approach, including the rationale for a cross-national investigation, and then describes his sample of primary and secondary sources. Note that Fullerton was not just writing a narrative history, but was scrutinizing a marketing theory, the so-called 'production era' concept inspired by Keith (1960).

Implications of historical research

Marketing journal editors and reviewers may insist that historical research either demonstrate some utilitarian purpose, such as relevance for marketing practice or public policy making, or contribute to marketing theory. To satisfy this expectation, marketing historians may need to write an 'implications' section. Nevett (1991) provides useful guidelines on ways that historical investigation can be applied to marketing practice as a supplement to positivistic thinking. Despite its 'scientific' pretensions, marketing management has much in common with history and historical methods can help managers evaluate the validity and interdependence of evidence, better exercise judgment to avoid marketing myopia and determine broad causal connections.

Historical research also can pay its way by formulating hypotheses and developing and appraising theories. The processes of assembling and analyzing the historical record can generate emergent themes just as readily as do ethnographic and other qualitative methods (Belk, Sherry and Wallendorf, 1988), yet historians disagree about the relationship between historical research and theory building. Continental European 'historicism', for example, stresses the development of 'historical laws, determining factors, and the meaning of the past as the source of the present' (Daniels, 1981, p. 96). The so-called 'cliometricians', who tend to focus more on collectivities of people and recurring events than on particulars (Fogel and Elton, 1983), are quantitative historians committed to the positivistic philosophy of building, testing and refining historical models.

Anglo-American historiography, on the other hand, generally approaches its work as an end in itself, an independent contribution to knowledge, rather than as a vehicle for building theories or making policy. The commitment is to the study of individual facts, the events, institutions and personalities that have historical significance, rather than to the discovery of broad conceptual constructs. These historians believe that each period contains its own reasons why events occurred and that these causes are usually not generalizable (Firat, 1987; Nevett, 1991). Although historians sometimes use theory as a means to specific ends, such as the application of psychology and psychoanalysis to explain the behavior of famous people, relatively few are willing to go very far in drawing implications. Historical research is a cumulative process and every generation builds upon and revises previous work.

Thoughtful presentations of the secondary literature, data sources and analysis, and research implications, should help historical studies survive the review process. Nevertheless, marketing historians will constantly need to continue their educational campaigns about the usefulness of their specialty (Hollander, 1986a; Jones and Monieson, 1990b; Nevett, 1991; Savitt, 1980).

References

Abelson, Raziel (1963), 'Cause and reason in history', in Sidney Hook (ed.), *Philosophy and History*, New York: New York University Press, pp. 167–73.

Bailyn, (1963), 'The problems of a working historian: a comment', in Sidney Hook (ed.), *Philosophy and History*, New York: New York University Press, pp. 92–101.

Barzun, Jacques and Henry F. Graff (2004), *The Modern Research*, 6th edn, Belmont, CA: Thomson-Wadsworth.

Belk, Russell W. (1986), 'Art versus science as ways of generating knowledge about materialism', in David Brinberg and Richard J. Lutz (eds), *Perspectives on Methodology in Consumer Research*, New York: Springer-Verlag, pp. 31–53.

Belk, Russell W. and Richard Pollay (1985), 'Images of ourselves: the good life in twentieth century advertising', *Journal of Consumer Research*, **11** (March), 887–97.

Belk, Russell W., John F. Sherry and Melanie Wallendorf (1988), 'A naturalistic inquiry into buyer and seller behavior at a swap meet', *Journal of Consumer Research*, **14** (March), 449–70.

Braudel, Fernand (1967), *Capitalism and Material Life, 1400–1800*, New York: Harper and Row.

Brooks, Philip C. (1969), *Research in the Archives*, Chicago: University of Chicago Press.

Burke, Peter (2001), *Eyewitnessing: The Uses of Images as Historical Evidence*, Ithaca, NY: Cornell University Press.

Cohen, Lizabeth (2003), *A Consumers' Republic: The Politics of Mass Consumption in Postwar America*, New York: Alfred A. Knopf.

Collingwood, R.G. (1956), *The Idea of History*, New York: Oxford University Press.

Daniels, Robert V. (1981), *Studying History: How and Why*, Englewood Cliffs, NJ: Prentice-Hall.

Demos, John (1970), *A Little Commonwealth: Family Life in Plymouth Colony*, New York: Oxford University Press.

Dixon, Donald F. (1995), 'Retailing in classical Athens: gleanings from contemporary literature and art', *Journal of Macromarketing*, **16** (1), 74–85.

Dixon, Donald F. (1998), 'Varangian-Rus warrior-merchants and the origin of the Russian state', *Journal of Macromarketing*, **18** (Spring), 50–61.

Dray, William (1974), 'The historical explanation of actions reconsidered', in Patrick Gardiner (ed.), *The Philosophy of History*, London: Oxford University Press, pp. 66–89.

Duke, Maurice and Edward N. Coffman (1993), 'Writing an accounting or business history: notes toward a methodology', *The Accounting Historians Journal*, **20** (2), 217–35.

Firat, A. Fuat (1987), 'Historiography, scientific method, and exceptional historical events', in Melanie Wallendorf and Paul Anderson (eds), *Advances in Consumer Research*, vol. 14, Provo, UT: Association for Consumer Research, pp. 435–8.

Floud, Roderick (1973), *An Introduction to Quantitative Methods for Historians*, Princeton: Princeton University Press.

Fogel, Robert William and G. R. Elton (1983), *Which Road to the Past?: Two Views of History*, New Haven, CT: Yale University Press.

Fullerton, Ronald A. (1988), 'How modern is modern marketing? Marketing's evolution and the myth of the "production era"', *Journal of Marketing*, **52** (January), 108–25.

Gluck, Sherna A. (1987), *Rosie the Riveter Revisited: Women, the War, and Social Change*, Boston: Twayne Publishers.

Golder, Peter (2000), 'Historical method in marketing research with new evidence on long-term market share stability', *Journal of Marketing Research*, **37** (May), 156–72.

Goodman, R.S. and E.J. Kruger (1988), 'Data dredging or legitimate research method? Historiography and its potential for management research', *Academy of Management Review*, **13**, 315–25.

Gross, Barbara L. and Jagdish N. Sheth (1989), 'Time-oriented advertising: a content analysis of United States magazine advertising, 1890–1988', *Journal of Marketing*, **53** (October), 76–83.

Hexter, Jack H. (1971), *Doing History*, Bloomington: Indiana University Press.

Hill, Ronald Paul, Elizabeth C. Hirschman and John F. Bauman (1997), 'Consumer survival during the Great Depression: reports from the field', *Journal of Macromarketing*, **17** (Spring), 107–27.

Hollander, Stanley C. (1986a), 'A rearview mirror might help us drive forward – a call for more historical studies in retailing', *Journal of Retailing*, **62** (Spring),7–10.

Hollander, Stanley C. (1986b), 'The marketing concept – a déjà vu', in George Fisk (ed.), *Marketing: Management Technology as Social Process*, New York: Praeger Publishers, pp. 3–29.

Hollander, Stanley C. (1989), 'Introduction', in Terence Nevett, Kathleen Whitney and Stanley C. Hollander (eds), *Marketing History: The Emerging Discipline*, Lansing: Michigan State University, pp. xix–xx.

Hollander, Stanley C. and Kathleen M. Rassuli (eds) (1993), *Marketing*, vols 1 and 2, Aldershot, UK and Brookfield, US: Edward Elgar Publishing.

Hollander, Stanley C., Kathleen M. Rassuli, D.G. Brian Jones and Laura Farlow Dix (2005), 'Periodization in marketing history', *Journal of Macromarketing*, **25** (June), 32–41.

Hudson, Laurel Anderson and Julie L. Ozanne (1988), 'Alternative ways of seeking knowledge in consumer research', *Journal of Consumer Research*, **14** (March), 508–21.

Jones, D.G. Brian (1998), 'Biography as a methodology for studying the history of marketing ideas', *Psychology and Marketing*, **15** (2), 161–73.

Jones, D.G. Brian and David D. Monieson (1990a), 'Early development of the philosophy of marketing thought', *Journal of Marketing*, **54** (January), 102–12.

Jones, D G. Brian and David D. Monieson (1990b), 'Historical research in marketing: retrospect and prospect', *Journal of the Academy of Marketing Science*, **18** (Fall), 269–78.

Jones, D.G. Brian and Eric H. Shaw (2002), 'History of marketing thought', in Robin Wensley and Barton Weitz (eds), *Handbook of Marketing*, London: Sage Publications, pp. 39–65.

Keith, Robert J. (1960), 'The marketing revolution', *Journal of Marketing*, **24** (January), 35–8.

Lavin, Marilyn (1995), 'Creating consumers in the 1930s: Irna Phillips and the radio soap opera', *Journal of Consumer Research*, **22** (June), 75–89.

Lavin, Marilyn and Thomas J. Archdeacon (1989), 'The relevance of historical method for marketing research', in Elizabeth C. Hirschman (ed.), *Interpretive Consumer Research*, Provo, UT: Association for Consumer Research, pp. 60–68.

Lawrence, Barbara S. (1984), 'Historical perspective: using the past to study the present', *Academy of Management Review*, **9** (2), 307–12.

Lomask, Milton (1986), *The Biographer's Craft*, New York: Harper and Row Publishing.

Marchand, Roland (1987), 'The fitful career of advocacy advertising: political protection, client cultivation, and corporate morale', *California Management Review*, **29** (Winter), 128–56.

Marwick, Arthur (1970), *The Nature of History*, London: Macmillan and Company.

Megill, Allan (1989), 'Recounting the past: description, explanation, and narration in historiography', *American Historical Review*, **94** (June), 627–53.

Merino, Barbara D. and Alan G. Mayper (1993), 'Accounting history and empirical research', *The Accounting Historians Journal*, **20** (2), 237–67.

Morris, David J. (1990), 'The railroad and movie industries: were they myopic?', *Journal of the Academy of Marketing Science*, **18** (Fall), 279–83.

Neilson, Leighann C. (2005), 'The remains of the day: a critical reflection on using ephemera in historical research', in Leighann C. Neilson (ed.), *The Future of Marketing's Past*, Long Beach, CA: Association for Historical Research in Marketing, pp. 351–2.

Nevett, Terence (1991), 'Historical investigation and the practice of marketing', *Journal of Marketing*, **55** (July), 13–23.

Pollay, Richard W. (1985), 'The subsiding sizzle: a descriptive history of print advertising, 1900–1980', *Journal of Marketing*, **50** (April), 18–36.

Previts, Gary John and Thomas R. Robinson (1996), 'A discourse on historical method in accountancy', in Alan J. Richardson (ed.), *Research Methods in Accounting: Issues and Debates*, Vancouver, BC: CGA-Canada Research Foundation, pp. 171–82.

Prown, Jules D. (1980), 'Style as evidence', *Winterthur Portfolio*, **15**, 197–210.
Prown, Jules D. (1982), 'Mind in matter: an introduction to material culture theory and method', *Winterthur Portfolio*, **17**,1–19.
Ritchie, Donald A. (1995), *Doing Oral History*, New York: Twayne Publishers.
Savitt, Ronald (1980), 'Historical research in marketing', *Journal of Marketing*, **44** (Fall), 52–8.
Savitt, Ronald (1983), 'A note on the varieties and vagaries of historical data', in Stanley Hollander and Ronald Savitt (eds), *First North American Workshop on Historical Research in Marketing*, East Lansing: Michigan State University, pp. 30–34.
Savitt, Ronald (2000), 'Fernand Braudel on historiography and its implications for marketing history', *Journal of Macromarketing*, **20** (1), 89–93.
Shafer, Robert Jones (ed.) (1974), *A Guide to Historical Method*, Homewood, IL: The Dorsey Press.
Shapiro, Stanley J. and Alton F. Doody (eds) (1968), *Readings in the History of American Marketing: Settlement to Civil War*, Homewood, IL: Richard D. Irwin.
Shaw, Eric H. and D.G. Brian Jones (2005), 'A history of marketing schools of thought', *Marketing Theory*, **5** (3) (September), 239–8.
Smith, Ruth Ann and David S. Lux (1993), 'Historical method in consumer research: developing causal explanations of change', *Journal of Consumer Research*, **19** (March), 595–610.
Thompson, Paul (1988), *The Voice of the Past: Oral History*, Oxford, UK: Oxford University Press.
Twede, Diana (2002), 'Commercial amphoras: the earliest consumer packages?', *Journal of Macromarketing*, **22** (Spring), 98–108.
Wilkie, William L. and Elizabeth S. Moore (2003), 'Scholarly research in marketing: exploring the "4 eras" of thought development', *Journal of Public Policy & Marketing*, **22** (Fall), 116–46.
Witkowski, Terrence H. (1989), 'Colonial consumers in revolt: buyer values and behavior during the Nonimportation Movement, 1764–1776', *Journal of Consumer Research*, **16** (September), 216–26.
Witkowski, Terrence H. (1990), 'Marketing thought in American decorative arts', *Journal of the Academy of Marketing Science*, **18** (Fall), 365–8.
Witkowski, Terrence H. (1994), 'Data sources for American consumption history: an introduction, analysis, and application', in Jagdish Sheth and Ronald A. Fullerton (eds), *Research in Marketing: Explorations in the History of Marketing* (Supplement 6), Greenwich, CT: JAI Press, Inc., pp. 167–82.
Witkowski, Terrence H. (1996), 'Farmers bargaining: buying and selling as a subject in American genre painting, 1835–1868', *Journal of Macromarketing*, **17** (Fall), 84–101.
Witkowski, Terrence H. (2001), 'The commercial building as a promotional tool in American marketing history, 1800–1940', in Terrence H. Witkowski (ed.), *Milestones in Marketing History*, Long Beach, CA: Association for Historical Research in Marketing, pp. 199–210.
Witkowski, Terrence H. (2003), 'World War II poster campaigns: preaching frugality to American consumers', *Journal of Advertising*, **32** (Spring), 69–82.
Witkowski, Terrence H. (2004), 'Re-gendering consumer agency in mid-nineteenth-century America: a visual understanding', *Consumption, Markets, and Culture*, **7** (September), 261–83.
Witkowski, Terrence H. and Ellen Hogan (1999), 'Home front consumers: an oral history of California women during World War II', in Peggy Cunningham and David Bussiere (eds), *Marketing History: The Total Package*, East Lansing: Michigan State University, pp. 151–64.
Wren, Daniel (1987), 'Management history: issues and ideas for teaching and research', *Journal of Management*, **13**, 339–50.

7 Researching the cultures of brands
Anders Bengtsson and Jacob Ostberg

Brands have emerged both as culturally important symbols that give ballast to consumers' identity projects and as devices that bring competitive advantages to their legal owners. In both these respects, the study of brands has become a matter of central concern to marketing scholars around the world. In standard brand management textbooks, brands are generally understood as devices that help companies achieve competitive advantages by offering added values to its customers (de Chernatony and McDonald, 2003), the so-called 'mind-share' approach (Holt, 2004). From this perspective, studying brands becomes a matter of analyzing and systematizing the strategies through which the brand was created and exploring the ways in which these strategies have the intended effects on consumers.

In contrast to this conventional way of doing brand research, there are other approaches that seek to capture the cultural richness of brand meanings in contemporary consumer culture. The view in this chapter is that a brand is a culturally constructed symbol, created by various types of authors who furnish it with symbolic content. This means that a brand is a co-constructed object whose meaning is closely bound to context and time. Many times, brand meaning is thought to be produced through a one-way communication process in which sets of neatly constructed brand identities are understood to be decoded into corresponding brand images. Rather than this overly simplified approach, we contend that the cultures of brands are dialectically constructed through iterative processes between various actors (Fournier, 1998; Holt, 2002). Consumers are one important group of actors and recent consumer research has shown that they have important co-creative roles in brand construction. This implies that different groups of consumers construct meanings around brands other than what sponsors may have intended (Bengtsson, Ostberg and Kjeldgaard, 2005; Kates, 2004; Kozinets, 2001; Muniz and O'Guinn, 2001).

What then is the reason why brands have become so important in our culture and hence so important for marketing scholars? Today, when we live in a consumer society, identity construction has moved from collective identities in the production realm to individual identities in the consumption realm (Slater, 1997). Identity construction has become a highly visual phenomenon (Schroeder, 2002) and products are valued as much for what they can do as for what they symbolize (cf. Gardner and Levy, 1955). A prime means of communication with consumption is brands, as they, through their high recognition, cut across the cluttered visual landscape. Therefore an understanding of brands and their functions as symbols is crucial for anyone wishing to study contemporary markets.

The widened view of looking at brands has some important implications for the ways brands must be studied. Many of the research methods described in the chapters of this book have previously been applied to research on brands. In this chapter we aim (1) to review briefly the main theoretical approaches used when studying brands (2) to look at the different methods that have been applied when researching the cultures of brands, and (3) point out some of the pitfalls in researching brands and how to avoid them.

What are brands and branding?
Since the chapter is dealing with approaches and perspectives for researching brands empirically, it seems pertinent to elaborate on what we mean when we use the term 'brand'. Formally, according to the American Marketing Association (AMA), a brand is defined as

> a name, term, design, symbol, or any other feature that identifies one seller's good or service as distinct from those of other sellers. The legal term for brand is trademark. A brand may identify one item, a family of items, or all items of that seller. If used for the firm as a whole, the preferred term is trade name (www.marketingpower.com).

This definition of a brand, adopted by standard marketing textbooks, covers the branding of most items offered on the market because even the 'no-name, no frills products' carry elements, such as a name or design, that distinguish them from other sellers' products. One should be careful, however, not to make the assumption that consumers understand the concept of brand in the same way as it is formally defined by marketing textbooks. Previous research on consumers and their notions about brands has shown that, when consumers are asked to explain what they think when they hear the word 'brand', oftentimes highly visible and omnipresent 'good' brands are mentioned (Bengtsson, 2002). So, although a symbol can formally be considered a brand, it is important to be sensitive to the way consumers understand the concept of 'brand', especially if one aims to research the cultural meanings of brands.

Brand management has developed into a management fashion where not only goods but entire companies, places, regions, universities, museums, help organizations, artists and even individuals are considered items it is possible to brand (see, e.g., Montoya and Vandehey, 2005, for a typical example of this genre). Generally, what is suggested is to use the same principles through which fast-moving consumer goods were branded throughout the last century. The great market success of the abundant variety of practical how-to branding books, written by brand consultants and retired marketers, furthermore illustrates that brand management is considered a key competence in contemporary businesses. With the increasing interest in corporate branding, the practice of branding is gradually changing from solely referring to marketing activities that add symbolic values to products, to a general management philosophy that permeates entire organizations (Olins, 2000).

One consequence of this diffusion of brands into all spheres of commercial and non-commercial life is that brands and branding appear in a wide variety of ways. Some brands are primarily signifiers for physical products whereas others are less tangible and signify processes or spaces. In addition, brands are often not just a mechanism that creates relationships between a company and consumers but involve many other stakeholders such as employees, investors, suppliers, partners, regulators, special interests and local communities (Hatch and Schultz, 2003). As a consequence, branding as phenomenon is more complex and requires attention both to the company's strategic vision, its corporate culture and its contemporary status in the consumer culture. Given that the application of brands and branding has evolved to include so many different aspects of the market, there are several perspectives – both conceptually and empirically – from which brands can be researched. But that is not the sole reason to widen the scope of the way we research brands. Brands have never been as simple as they have conventionally been thought to be. Over the last century, brands have developed into something far more important in contemporary culture than merely marketing tools.

Researching brand management

Much of existing research has focused on the strategies and tactics through which successful brands were built. The lion's share of this work is of the 'best practice' type where descriptions of successful brand building activities are presented and turned into normative accounts of how brand building should take place. The literature on brand management consists of a myriad of normative frameworks that provide managers with *the* prescription for the way to win and dominate markets with powerful value-added brands. Some of the dominant classical brand management frameworks or principles, such as brand equity (Aaker, 1991), brand identity (Aaker, 1996; Kapferer, 2004) and brand architecture (Aaker and Joachimsthaler, 2000) were developed through case studies of companies' branding strategies and provide guidance for brand-building work based on best practice. The emergent research stream focusing on corporate branding operates basically with the same approach, where case analyses of companies' corporate branding efforts are used to prove its effect (see, e.g., Hatch and Schultz, 2001; Schultz and Hatch, 2003). In this type of brand research, focus is directed towards the actions undertaken by companies, which means that empirical data about the strategies are gathered through collection of communication campaigns, interviews with managers and other employees in the company as well as the company's market communication agencies. In addition, a common source of empirical data is annual reports, newspapers and periodicals, where accounts of the brand's success and failure occur. In contemporary research on brand management it is often assumed that the brand owner exerts considerable control over the brand. From this perspective, successful brand management becomes a matter of finding the brand's true and timeless essence and carrying out brand-building activities that will translate the identity into a corresponding brand image (Csaba and Bengtsson, 2005). However, the metaphor of the brand manager as an alchemist who can mix and match components to achieve a desirable outcome relies on an overly simplified view of the culture in which brands exist.

The cultural production of the brand

Instead of the conventional view that a company communicates a certain brand identity that is more or less correctly interpreted by consumers as a brand image, we see the cultural meaning of a brand as constructed by various 'authors', as illustrated in Figure 7.1. According to this view, a brand's meaning is co-constructed by the brand owner, consumers, popular culture and other important stakeholders. The company which has given birth to the brand by making it available on the market is indeed a significant actor. Strategic, carefully tuned brand-building activities generate stories about the brand along with the everyday actions the company undertakes in order to run its business. The ultimate users of the brand, the consumers, or organizations if it is a brand that operates on industrial markets, are other significant actors that contribute to the cultures of the brand. Through consumption, the particular status, uses and meanings of brands are subject to social negotiation. In addition to these two actors, a brand's meanings are also produced

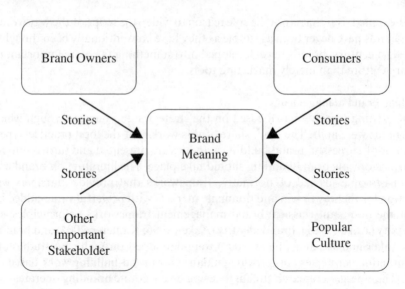

Source: Adapted from Holt (2004).

Figure 7.1   The authors of the brand

by popular culture such as TV programs, magazines, movies, books and so on. Finally, other important stakeholders include authors such as competitors, labor unions and retailers who frequently make statements through marketing communication or other actions.

Within each group of authors that produce stories about the brand, a particular culture of the brand emerges. The culture that develops within each group of authors is not homogenous but differs from that of other authors. It is in this sense that a brand can be understood as a multicultural entity whose peculiarities need to be examined from different perspectives. In the following, we will provide some examples of the way each of these cultures has been studied in prior research.

Brands and consumer culture theory

Conventional research on brand management as discussed above (e.g. Aaker, 1996; de Chernatony, 2001) oftentimes makes many assumptions about the way brand strategies will be received by the market. How consumers make sense of, acquire, use and dispose brands is discovered, however, in research on consumers and consumer culture. Research on consumer culture theory (a term recently suggested by Arnould and Thompson, 2005) focuses, among other things, on the 'desire-inducing marketing symbols' (p. 867), namely brands and advertising. There are four principal research programs within consumer culture theory that can all be adopted to focus on brands: consumer identity projects, marketplace cultures, the sociohistoric patterning of consumption, and mass-mediated marketplace ideologies and consumers' interpretive strategies. The first one, consumer identity projects, takes a micro perspective, whereas the other three take a macro perspective.

In past research, a micro perspective focusing on individual consumers, and hence studying the relationship in the upper-right corner of the figure, has been the most frequently employed in the study of *consumer identity projects and brands* (e.g. Fournier, 1998;

McCracken, 1993). In this type of research, in-depth interviewing with consumers, preferably in their everyday consumption context, is the most commonly used method. The general goal is to provide an understanding for how and in what ways brands become meaningful to consumers in their lives. The marketplace has become a source of mythic and symbolic resources through which people construct narratives of identity (Elliott and Wattanasuwan, 1998). In the view of Arnould and Thompson (2005, p. 871), the market produces certain kinds of consumer positions that consumers can choose to inhabit. Consequently, consumers are merely enacting and personalizing cultural scripts that align their identities with the structural imperatives of a consumer-driven global economy. Given such a view, the task for brand researchers becomes to uncover the available cultural scripts, which requires a more macro-oriented type of methodology, as well as to look into the way consumers behave in order to comply with, or resist, those scripts, which requires a more micro type of methodology.

The study of *marketplace cultures and brands* has been a thriving subject over the last decade. In this line of research, the tribal aspects of consumption (Maffesoli, 1996) are in focus and researchers try to grasp the linking values of certain brands (cf. Cova, 1997). Again, the principle means of doing research is through depth interviews but ethnographic methods of different kinds have increasingly been utilized (e.g. Kates, 2004; McAlexander, Schouten and Koenig, 2002; Schouten and McAlexander, 1995). In addition to interviews and ethnographic work, netnographic methods have proved successful for gathering empirical data on the communal aspects of brand consumption (e.g. Muniz and O'Guinn, 2001). Brown, Kozinets and Sherry's (2003) study of retro brand communities and Bengtsson, Ostberg and Kjeldgaard's (2005) research on the use of brands in tattooing illustrate how naturally occurring data gathered on the Internet can be used for such research projects.

Research on the *sociohistoric patterning of consumption*, i.e. research that addresses the institutional and social structures that systematically influence consumption, has been less directly focused on the consumption of brands. Still, this is a research venue that should hold much promise. A key element in structuring consumer society is class positions. Holt (1998) has studied how social class structures consumption. While this is not chiefly a study about brands, he does have some insights into the way consumers with different levels of cultural capital relate to branded goods (p. 21). These findings tease out some differences between social groups' relations to brands, more specifically decommodification, that have been overlooked by previous researchers that have not taken a class perspective (e.g. Wallendorf and Arnould, 1991). Another socializing structure that has traditionally been sorely lacking from consumer research is gender (Bristor and Fischer, 1993). Costa and Pavia (1993) and Olsen (1999) focus on how gender is influencing consumers' brand relationships, again tapping into the notion that there are many structural differences that should hinder us from painting a picture of consumer behavior in too broad strokes. An area that has taken this into consideration and indeed made it into the topic of investigation is multicultural or crosscultural studies. Typically, scholars in this field examine how brands can take on radically different meaning depending on the cultural context in which they are embedded (Eckhardt and Houston, 2002; Ger and Belk, 1996; Miller, 1998; Yan, 1997).

The last of the consumer culture theory research strands, *mass-mediated marketplace ideologies and consumers' interpretive strategies*, also holds potential for insightful brand-related research. Journalist Naomi Klein (1999) recently questioned the whole notion of a branded world and raised the debate about consumers' increasing skepticism towards the domination of symbols of the market in the public sphere. Studies investigating how consumers actively try to resist the market and the domination of brands include Thompson and Arsel's (2004) account of how consumers resist the dominant brandscapes of global companies, and Kozinets' (2002) research on how consumers try to escape the market. These two studies take a micro perspective, examining consumers directly through interviews and observation. Looking at marketplace ideologies from a macro perspective offers a different avenue for research. Instead of interviewing or observing consumers directly, this approach focuses on cultural analyses of the roles brand play in the culture. An example of this type of research is Askegaard and Csaba's (1999) study of the cultural resistance to the 'Coca-Colanization' of Denmark.

When doing cultural research on brands, historical methods can be a useful tool for collecting empirical data. Through analyses of archival accounts of a brand's management it is possible to achieve a more balanced understanding of what factors made the brand successful over time. Koehn's (2001) historical analysis of brands such as Wedgwood, Heinz and Estée Lauder, as well as Holt's (2004) genealogical brand studies, illustrate the usefulness of an historic approach to studying brand management processes. In Holt's (2004) case, for example, he showed that many companies were not as consistent in their brand management as contemporary theory suggests. A key aim in conventional brand management thinking is to streamline marketing communications so as always to communicate the same message. If a company stays true to its timeless essence over time it will, according to theory, achieve a clear, uncluttered image in the consumers' minds that is compelling because of its consistency and clarity. What Holt managed to show, through his genealogical brand research, was that many successful companies had not at all been consistent in their brand-building activities, but rather changed their branding over time to stay relevant in accordance with current social concerns. Without the historical perspective, however, Holt would only have captured the momentary brand-building activities which would, most likely, have led him to join the chorus singing the praises of consistency. When employing a historical approach, analysis of a brand's past advertising can be an interesting avenue for research. Methods for such an analysis can include approaches from art history, as suggested by Scott (1994) or literary criticism, as introduced by Stern (1989). A related stream of research stems from Schroeder (2002), who studies brand management from a visual perspective more broadly, e.g. by focusing on how classical architectural expressions in the banking sector are transferred to the Internet now that more banking activities are conducted online (Schroeder, 2003). While not directly focusing on brand management, this stream of visual research looks at the artifacts of companies' brand-building activities.

Methods and pitfalls for inquiries into the cultures of brands
Basically, as claimed by Dingwall (1997, p. 53), there are essentially only two ways of conducting studies within the social sciences: 'hanging out' or 'asking questions', or, as he puts it, 'interviewers construct data, observers find it' (p. 55). This should be supplemented by the study of artifacts, which is an extension of the observational venue. So, even though there might seem to be an endless number of different approaches to studying brands, it all comes down to essentially these two variations: either you hang out or you ask

questions. All the research mentioned in this chapter can be sorted into these groups, even though the different approaches are very frequently combined, at least to some degree.

Brand management research

As mentioned earlier, this line of research focuses on the strategies and tactics through which brands are built in the marketplace. In the case of brand management research, most studies are of the case-study type (Stake, 1994) where one, or a few, successful companies' branding strategies are described in detail. A panoply of different methods – including interviews with key persons at the particular company, the ad agency and/or consulting firms, document studies of company records and annual reports, media studies of the attention given to the company by the press and historic records from the stock market – are employed. The aim is to gain an overall understanding of a company's brand management activities. Case researchers usually seek out both what is common and what is particular about the case, but the end result regularly presents something unique (ibid., p. 238). Furthermore, this uniqueness is frequently portrayed as a key to success, that could, at least potentially, be copied by other companies. This movement, from the description typical of case studies to the production of normative accounts intended to be transferable to other companies, is highly problematic. Oftentimes, the normative accounts disregard the cultural uniqueness of the particular case and there is usually little scientific evidence that the findings would hold in another context. The explanations given for a brand's success or failure are usually only surface-level explanations. In order to achieve transferability of research findings, a more sensitive interpretation of the culture in which the brand operates is necessary. Providing a checklist that can be copied by other companies for successful brand building just does not work. The intended audience for much brand management research is managers, and managers do indeed seem to find the results of typical brand management research quite interesting and perhaps even useful. This fact should not, however, be confused with there being any scientific validity in much of traditional brand management research.

If one wants to establish an understanding of the strategies a company has used to develop a brand, it might seem reasonable to gather empirical data from sources within the company. Interviewing staff in the marketing department may be one way to achieve such information. However, it is important to interpret carefully the data gathered through such an approach. When brand managers are asked about the actions they have undertaken for a brand and the possible results these actions have generated, there is an obvious risk that the answers produced are highly simplified rationalizations. Hence the empirical accounts should not be taken at face value. Another aspect that might be especially important for students is access to data. Managers tend to view themselves as fairly busy people; this is especially true for successful managers. This means that they do not always find time in their agendas to meet researchers and students. The result is that students are given interviews with people lower down in the organization. These middle–managers might not always have access to companies' grand, overreaching brand management strategies. Whether they are willing to admit this shortcoming to inquiring students is an open question. Another access-related point is that many companies today view their brand strategies as their core competence and their main competitive advantage. Consequently they might not be too willing to share this information with students or researchers, fearing that their company's secrets will be spread to the public. An outcome of these difficulties of gaining access is that a large share of brand management research is conducted by academics that also work as consultants for the particular company under study. Such action research always runs the risk of glorifying the particular actions undertaken by the brand consultant doing the study. The researcher is sitting on two chairs, being both a consultant and a researcher, and it may be hard to separate these roles.

A final point regarding management research relates to the tendency for people working with brands to know how to talk brand-talk and use the pseudo-scientific lingo that is distributed through brand management texts (Melin, 2004). This should not be confused with their actually working in a highly scientific and structured manner. While other strands of management research have developed a much more critical approach (Alvesson and Deetz, 2000), conventional brand management research still sorely lacks a critical edge.

Consumer culture theory brand research
A critical awareness is also important when studying consumers' relationships to brands and brands' role in consumer culture. An integral part of individuals living in an advanced market economy is that they are savvy at navigating, and seeing through, the offerings made by companies (Holt, 2002). On a macro level, consumer culture and brand management strategies exist in a dialectical relationship where companies change strategies as consumers become better at decoding, and seeing through, their intentions. As researchers focusing on brands, we must be aware of this and realize that consumers constantly try to outsmart marketers. One way of doing this might be to emphasize or de-emphasize the importance of brands. Assuming a causal relationship between what people say they do and what they actually do is always dubious. When addressing an ideologically loaded issue like brands, it is likely that what is produced is merely a politically correct discourse about how that particular consumer believes one should relate to brands. Such information might indeed be highly interesting and relevant, but quite likely has, little to do with a consumer's actual behavior.

There is also a bias among many brand researchers to assume that brands are important to people. When a researcher enquires about a brand or schedules a meeting to do an interview about brands, the interviewee will most likely produce accounts about brands. The more the researcher questions and probes about brands, the more the consumer will speak about brands. This should not be confused with brands actually playing a significant role in the consumers' lives. Basic marketing textbooks (e.g. Kotler and Keller, 2004) usually tell us that, for some products, brands are important, while, for other products, they are less important or not important at all. This view builds on a false product ontology whereby the meaning of the branded product is placed in the product rather than in the relationship between the consumer and the product. Rather than taking this skewed essentialist standpoint, we propose that the importance of certain brands is always a matter of the individual subject. Some brands may be significant to one consumer whereas some other brands may be significant to another. And, even though this might seem shocking to a brand researcher, it is important to be open to the fact that some consumers may care very little about brands. A recent study by Chang Coupland (2005) investigates 'invisible brands', i.e. brands that blend into the household environment in an inconspicuous manner (p. 116), and suggests that households might not be as engaged in brand consumption as some previous research has suggested, but rather choose brands that lets them be disengaged and forget about the brands. This does not imply that all households would have the same invisible brands; instead, some households could have a meaningful relationship with, for instance, their washing powder, whereas other households might treat it as an invisible brand. The definition of the brand as significant or insignificant has little to do with the brand per se but is dependent upon the particular household.

In order to design and conduct exemplary brand research, it is crucial to keep these issues in mind. We might not be used to thinking about brand research as a sensitive topic where everything, from the initial contact with a presumptive research subject and onwards, is crucial to the results produced. Not paying close attention to the research topic is, in our view, a crucial mistake that might lead to fatal flaws in the results produced. When designing a qualitative study focusing on consumers, it is important to consider carefully the possible biases that the introduction of the study to the informants may generate. If the study is described as 'a research project addressing how people consume various brands' it is possible that the informant will produce stories reflecting a culturally accepted way of relating to brands. Unless one is interested in exploring this particular culturally accepted way, such a way to introduce the study may generate empirical data that may have little to do with consumers' actual thoughts and feelings. If the study is introduced instead as 'a research project addressing how people consume various household goods', one may avoid the problem that merely the cultural blueprint is reproduced. On the other hand, other biases may occur as consumers participating in the study might think that brands are not at all part of the study and keep from talking about brands.

Future brand research
In past qualitative research on brands, there has been a clear distinction between scholars who have studied the management of brands and scholars who have studied consumer culture and brands. This gulf between brand management research and brand culture research is unfortunate and has generated brand theories that are less potent in informing managers how to develop brands that are in tune with the market. If we acknowledge that a brand is a multicultural unit constructed by many different actors, it is necessary to design studies on the cultures of the brand accordingly. This might seem self-evident and unnecessary to comment on but it is surprising how researchers that for instance have studied a company's brand building activities often enter into a discussion of what the brand means to consumers when in fact no research on consumers was undertaken. Future qualitative research on brands should therefore seek to integrate the various perspectives from which the cultures of the brand can be studied. Overall, we can see that the main share of research on brands is focused on either companies or consumers. Studies on the relationships between popular culture and brands and other important stakeholders and their use of brands are far more scarce. Investigations into these relationships would most likely hold great potential in generating valuable knowledge about the cultural production of brand meaning. Another area of future interest is the study of brand cultures in emerging markets. Consumer researchers still debate whether or not global, mainly Western, brands homogenize local cultures and thus destroy cultural uniqueness. Further research into brand cultures across the globe will provide us with a better understanding of the roles brands play in contemporary consumption.

References

Aaker, David A. (1991), *Managing Brand Equity: Capitalizing on the Value of a Brand Name*, New York: Free Press.
—— (1996), *Building Strong Brands*, New York: Free Press.
Aaker, David A. and Erich Joachimsthaler (2000), *Brand Leadership*, New York: Free Press.
Alvesson, Mats and Stanley Deetz (2000), *Doing Critical Management Research*, London: Sage.
Arnould, Eric J. and Craig J. Thompson (2005), 'Consumer culture theory (CCT): twenty years of research', *Journal of Consumer Research*, **31** (March), 868–82.
Askegaard, Søren and Fabian F. Csaba (1999), 'The good, the bad, and the jolly. Taste, image, and the symbolic resistance to the Coca-Colonization of Denmark', in Stephen Brown and Anthony Patterson (eds), *Imagining Marketing*, London, Routledge, pp. 121–40.
Bengtsson, Anders (2002), *Consumers and Mixed-Brands: On the Polysemy of Brand Meaning*, Lund: Lund Business Press.
Bengtsson, Anders, Jacob Ostberg and Dannie Kjeldgaard (2005), 'Prisoners in paradise: subcultural resistance to the marketization of tattooing', *Consumption, Markets and Culture*, **8** (3), 261–74.
Bristor, Julia M. and Eileen Fischer (1993), 'Feminist thought: implications for consumer research', *Journal of Consumer Research*, **19** (March), 518–36.
Brown, Stephen, Robert V. Kozinets and John F. Sherry (2003), 'Teaching old brands new tricks: retro branding and the revival of brand meaning', *Journal of Marketing*, **67** (July), 19–33.
Chang Coupland, Jennifer (2005), 'Invisible brands: an ethnography of households and the brands in their kitchen pantries', *Journal of Consumer Research*, **32** (June), 106–18.
Costa, Janeen Arnold and Teresa M. Pavia (1993), 'Alpha-numeric brand names and gender stereotypes', in Janeen Arnold Costa and Russell W. Belk (eds), *Research in Consumer Behavior*, vol. 6, Greenwich, CT: JAI Press, pp. 85–112.
Cova, Bernard (1997), 'Community and consumption: towards a definition of the "linking value" of product or services', *European Journal of Marketing*, **31** (3/4), 297–316.
Csaba, Fabian F. and Anders Bengtsson (2005), 'Rethinking identity in brand management', in Jonathan E. Schroeder and Miriam Salzer-Mørling (eds), *Brand Culture*, London: Routledge.
de Chernatony, Leslie (2001), *From Brand Vision to Brand Evaluation*, Oxford: Butterworth-Heinemann.
de Chernatony, Leslie and Malcolm H.B. McDonald (2003), *Creating Powerful Brands*, 3rd edn, Oxford: Butterworth-Heinemann.
Dingwall, Robert (1997), 'Accounts, interviews and observations', in Jody Miller and Robert Dingwall (eds), *Method and Context in Qualitative Research*, London: Routledge, pp. 51–65.
Eckhardt, Giana M. and Michael J. Houston (2002), 'Cultural paradoxes reflected in brand meaning: McDonald's in Shanghai, China', *Journal of International Marketing*, **10** (2), 68–82.
Elliott, Richard and Kritsadarat Wattanasuwan (1998), 'Brands as symbolic resources for the construction of identity', *International Journal of Advertising*, **17** (2).
Fournier, Susan (1998), 'Consumers and their brands: developing relationship theory in consumer research', *Journal of Consumer Research*, **24** (March), 343–73.
Gardner, Burleigh B. and Sidney J. Levy (1955), 'The product and the brand', *Harvard Business Review*, March–April, 53–9.
Ger, Güliz and Russell W. Belk (1996), 'I'd like to buy the world a Coke: consumptionscapes of the "less affluent world"', *Journal of Consumer Policy*, **19**, 271–304.
Hatch, Mary Jo and Majken Schultz (2001), 'Are the strategic stars aligned for your corporate brand?', *Harvard Business Review*, February, 128–34.
—— (2003), 'Bringing the corporation into corporate branding', *European Journal of Marketing*, **37** (7/8), 1041–64.
Holt, Douglas B. (1998), 'Does cultural capital structure American consumption?', *Journal of Consumer Research*, **25** (June), 1–25.
—— (2002), 'Why do brands cause trouble? A dialectical theory of consumer culture and branding', *Journal of Consumer Research*, **29** (1), 70–90.
—— (2004), *How Brands Become Icons: The Principles of Cultural Branding*, Boston, MA: Harvard Business School Press.
Kapferer, Jean-Noël (2004), *The New Strategic Brand Management: Creating and Sustaining Brand Equity Long Term*, 3rd edn, London: Kogan Page.
Kates, Steven M. (2004), 'The dynamics of brand legitimacy: an interpretive study in the gay men's community', *Journal of Consumer Research*, **31** (September), 455–64.
Klein, Naomi (1999), *No Logo: Taking Aim at the Brand Bullies*, New York: Picador.
Koehn, Nancy F. (2001), *Brand New: How Entrepreneurs Earned Consumers' Trust from Wedgwood to Dell*, Boston, MA: Harvard Business School Press.

Kotler, Philip (2004), *Marketing Management*, 12th edn, Upper Saddle River, NJ: Pearson Prentice-Hall.
Kotler, Philip and Kevin L. Keller (2001), 'Utopian enterprise: articulating the meanings of star trek's culture of consumption', *Journal of Consumer Research*, **28** (December), 67–88.
Kozinets, Robert V. (2002), 'Can consumers escape the market? Emancipatory illuminations from burning man', *Journal of Consumer Research*, **29** (June), 20–38.
Maffesoli, Michel (1996), *The Time of the Tribes*, Thousand Oaks, CA: Sage.
McAlexander, James H., John Schouten and Harold F. Koenig (2002), 'Building brand community', *Journal of Marketing*, **66** (January), 38–54.
McCracken, Grant (1993), 'The value of the brand: an anthropological perspective', in David A. Aaker and Alexander L. Biel (eds), *Brand Equity and Advertising: Advertising's Role in Building Strong Brands*, Hillsdale, NJ: Erlbaum, pp. 125–39.
Melin, Lars (2004), *Corporate Bullshit: Om språket mitt i city*, Stockholm: Svenska Förlaget.
Miller, Daniel (1998), 'Coca-Cola: a black sweet drink from Trinidad', in Daniel Miller (ed.), *Material Cultures: Why Some Things Matter*, Chicago, IL: University of Chicago Press, pp. 169–87.
Montoya, Peter and Tim Vandehey (2005), *The Brand Called You: The Ultimate Brand-Building and Business Development Handbook to Transform Anyone into an Indispensable Personal Brand*, Tustin, CA Peter Montoya Publishing.
Muniz, Albert M. and Thomas C. O'Guinn (2001), 'Brand community', *Journal of Consumer Research*, **27** (March), 412–32.
Olins, Wally (2000), 'How brands are taking over the corporation', in Majken Schultz, Mary Jo Hatch and Mogens Holten Larsen (eds), *The Expressive Organization: Linking Identity, Reputation, and the Corporate Brand*, Oxford: Oxford University Press, pp. 51–65.
Olsen, Barbara (1999), 'Exploring women's brand relationships and enduring themes at mid-life', in Eric J. Arnould and Linda M. Scott (eds), *Advances in Consumer Research*, vol. 26, Provo, UT: Association for Consumer Research, pp. 615–20.
Schouten, John W. and James H. McAlexander (1995), 'Subcultures of consumption: an ethnography of the new bikers', *Journal of Consumer Research*, **22** (June), 43–61.
Schroeder, Jonathan E. (2002), *Visual Consumption*, London and New York Routledge.
—— (2003), 'Building brands: architectural expression in the electronic age', in Rajiv Batra and Linda Scott (eds), *Persuasive Imagery: A Consumer Response Perspective*, Mahwah, NJ: Lawrence Erlbaum, pp. 349–82.
Schultz, Majken and Mary Jo Hatch (2003), 'The cycles of corporate branding: the case of the Lego company', *California Management Review*, **46** (1), 6–26.
Scott, Linda M. (1994), 'Images in advertising: the need for a theory of visual rhetoric', *Journal of Consumer Research*, **21** (September), 252–73.
Slater, Don (1997), *Consumer Culture and Modernity*, Cambridge: Polity Press.
Stake, Robert E. (1994), 'Case studies', in Norman K. Denzin and S. Yvonna Lincoln (eds), *Handbook of Qualitative Research*, Thousand Oaks, CA: Sage, pp. 236–47.
Stern, Barbara B. (1989), 'Literary criticism and consumer research: overview and illustrative analysis', *Journal of Consumer Research*, **16** (December), 322–34.
Thompson, Craig J. and Zeynep Arsel (2004), 'The Starbucks brandscape and consumers' (anti-corporate) experiences of glocalization', *Journal of Consumer Research*, **31** (December), 631–42.
Wallendorf, Melanie and Eric J. Arnould (1991), ' "We gather together": consumption rituals of Thanksgiving Day', *Journal of Consumer Research*, **18** (June), 13–31.
Yan, Yunxiang (1997), 'McDonald's in Beijing: the localization of Americana', in James L. Watson (ed.), *Golden Arches East: McDonald's in East Asia*, Stanford, CA: Stanford University Press, pp. 39–76.

8 Researching brands ethnographically: an interpretive community approach
Steven M. Kates

Researching brands ethnographically

Brands are co-created by the efforts of both consumers and marketers, for consumers process brands and promotions for meaning as well as for information (Fournier, 1998; Kates and Shaw-Garlock, 1999; McCracken, 1987; Mick and Buhl, 1992; Ritson and Elliott, 1999; Scott, 1994). Yet, in postmodern conditions of fragmentation, decentering and ambiguity (see Firat and Venkatesh, 1995; Firat and Shultz, 1997), interpretation of brands and marketing promotions is a problematic issue for both consumers and marketers. Consumers construct different meanings from what brand sponsors may have intended, and different social types of consumers construct multiple meanings, depending on personal background, contexts of consumption and multiple frames of reference (e.g., see Elliot and Ritson, 1997; Grier and Brumbaugh, 1999; Kates and Shaw-Garlock, 1999; Ritson and Elliott, 1999).

This issue of brands possessing several potential meanings – what we might label the 'problem of polysemy' (see Gottdiener, 1995) – has significant implications for consumer theory. Traditionally, positioning has been conceptualized as a relatively stable set of intended consumer perceptions (or meanings) toward a brand, in relation to competitive alternatives. However, in postmodern social conditions characterized by a plenitude of meaning, and in everyday social practice, brands may often come to signify associations other than the dominant (or preferred) meaning or intended positioning desired by marketers (see Hall, 1980, 1997). Further, segmenting a market into non-overlapping groups of consumers vis-à-vis differential responses to promotional efforts becomes an increasingly problematic task in a commercial environment in which consumers are ironically aware of sponsors' intentions (Scott, 1994), may shift categories over time and indeed, depending on the context of consuming, actually straddle different segments.

In response to these questions, brand meaning may be understood in light of the structuring potential of interpretive communities and their associated interpretive conventions. In the section following, I briefly review the relevant literature on interpretive communities and link it to branding. Next, I review contributions recently introduced to the consumer literature, such as brand communities (Muniz and O'Guinn, 2001), subcultures of consumption (Schouten and McAlexander, 1995) and brand legitimacy (Kates, 2004) that raise a host of issues such as consumer opposition (Kozinets and Handelman, 2004), cultivating identity (Holt, 2002) and religiosity (Muniz and Schau, 2005). After that, I provide a demonstration using the interpretive community perspective when doing brand ethnographies in the field. Finally, I discuss avenues for future research.

Interpretive communities and co-creation of the brand

In the dialogic relationship between marketers and consumers, there is a decided need for cultural competency on the part of consumers; that is, the sociocultural knowledge that people in a particular society are thought to possess so that they may understand and act appropriately in the commercial environment (Peñaloza and Gilly, 1999; Scott, 1994). Meanings are not simply imposed by the textual aspects of advertising, direct mail or other brand stimuli; rather, meanings emerge between the texts of marketing communications and the bodies of cultural knowledge shared by consumers (Eco, 1972; Scott, 1994), co-creating the brand as a complex bundle of personal and sociocultural meanings. Traditionally, it has been argued that a broadly held or shared social consensus emerges and informs institutionalized meanings within a society (Schutz and Luckmann, 1973). Thus, when interpreting a form of marketing communication (such as an ad, coupon or even an interaction with a salesperson), consumers draw on various flexible sociocultural codes and construct meaning about the brand or sponsor (Hall, 1980, 1997; Kates and Shaw-Garlock, 1999). Use of the interpretive communities and convention concepts in the marketing and consumer research field may give considerable perspective to these consumer activities and provide much-needed structure for understanding brand meanings that contemporary consumers construct.

An interpretive community – a concept from reader response theory in the humanities (see Fish, 1976, 1980; Scott, 1994) – is a cultural formation with a shared social and historical context that delimits the potential of marketing communications. Although the boundaries of interpretive communities may be somewhat fuzzy and overlapping, the fundamental premises of the construct are that members of various audiences have significant connections to their social locations or positions and use broadly similar repertoires of interpretive strategies, resulting in similar interpretations of marketing communications (Hirschman, 1998; Scott, 1994). As Hirschman (1998, p. 303) notes, a condition of 'bounded diversity' characterizes interpretive communities as consumers construct individual meanings within the confines of an ideological structure (Radway, 1984). In other words, membership of an interpretive community is characterized by *structured polysemy* that allows for a limited range of readings relevant to the cultural identifications and social positionings of consumers (Hirschman, 1998; Ritson and Elliott, 1999). Critically, interpretation of brands may follow a discernible cultural logic that can be explored and mapped empirically with the use of interpretive communities and strategies (Scott, 1994).

Interpretive communities are associated with (indeed, are constituted by) a repertoire of commonly shared interpretive strategies among a group of consumers (Mailloux, 1982; Scott, 1994, p. 474). For the purposes of this chapter, interpretive strategies, 'include the manner of reading, the purpose of reading, the attitude toward the text, and the knowledge the reader may have (or lack) that is brought to the reading experience. Particular reading strategies . . . [are] typical of certain groups [called] "interpretive communities"' (Scott, 1994, p. 474). Interpretive conventions, as regularities in actions, beliefs and interpretation, prescribe the actions, beliefs and interpretive strategies that are the shared way of making sense of brands (Mailloux, 1982, pp. 10–11). Broadly speaking, consumers belong to the same interpretive community when they use similar interpretive strategies (Scott, 1994, p. 474). Examples of brand-related interpretive communities whose consumption patterns may be examined from the present analysis are gay men (Kates, 2004), Christian fundamentalists (O'Guinn and Belk, 1989), Star Trek enthusiasts (Kozinets, 2001) and devoted Apple users (Muniz and O'Guinn, 2001). Further, analysis from the perspective of interpretive communities and strategies may be useful for doing brand ethnographies of various social groupings that, to significant extents, revolve around and define themselves in relation to certain brands (e.g., Kozinets, 2001; Schouten and McAlexander, 1995). Thus interpretive strategies may reflect and construct a personal or shared social identity among consumers (e.g., Kozinets, 2001; Mick and Buhl, 1992; Scott, 1994), supported by brand meanings.

Brand-related interpretive communities in consumer research
The interpretive community and strategy constructs can assist researchers to do enhanced ethnographic or qualitative study of consumer–brand relationships and develop theory on the topic (see Fournier, 1998; Celsi, Rose and Leigh, 1993; Muniz and O'Guinn, 2001). Although a number of different types of social configurations have been studied recently, a number of common themes emerge, explored below: first, brands help negotiate a sense of social affiliation. Second, brand meaning that is relatively oppositional to others emerges in brand-related interpretive communities. Third, identity is negotiated and constructed in brand subcultures and communities. All of these means of relating to the brand help construct shared meaning, enabling brand co-creation between consumers and marketers.

Brands and social affiliation
Brands can foster a sense of social connection among consumers in informal social contexts or in more socially organized interpretive communities. While brands connect with consumers in consumer–brand relationships (Fournier, 1998), other studies support the view that brands have a 'linking value' or function (e.g., Cova, 1997) that connects consumers to each other through a set of common meanings or activities (see also McAlexander, Schouten and Koenig, 2002). For example, fashion discourses about brands allow consumers to create a style that is acceptable to self-relevant social cliques or help them fit in socially (Thompson and Haytko, 1997, p. 27). This linking value reaches its most organized expressions in brand configurations such as brand communities (Muniz and O'Guinn, 2001), subcultures of consumption (Schouten and McAlexander, 1995) and cultures of consumption (Kozinets, 2001).

   Different types of brand social configurations, all exhibiting linking value, have been previously studied in consumer research. Brand communities are usually focused on the enthusiastic use and promotion of a particular consumption object (such as a Saab, Apple Newton or Apple computer). Further, members of the brand communities studied by Muniz and O'Guinn feel somewhat marginalized (e.g., Apple users in relation to IBM users) and this point of difference promotes a sense of connection to the brand and among each other. The reflexivity or 'consciousness of kind' that characterizes many brand communities offers members a cachet from constructing difference or distinction from others, reinforced by traditions and rituals and enacted through acts that demonstrate social responsibility and moral obligation toward each other. These attributes are also shared, in part, by subcultures of consumption (Schouten and McAlexander, 1995), interpretive communities that share commitment to a brand or product and distinctive jargon, ethos, ways of expression and social structure. What appears to differentiate the former from the latter construct is the depth of commitment demonstrated by subculture members and the time invested in brand-related activities. Further, subcultures of consumption appear to possess and even thrive on a sense of social marginality (e.g., Hebdige, 1979) and reject aspects of mainstream culture's ideology. Cultures of consumption

(Kozinets, 2001), in turn, refer to brands, such as Star Trek, that revolve around extensive images, media texts and consumption objects, and which inspire fandom. Consumers in cultures of consumption perform the critical co-creative function of helping to institutionalize brand meanings, practices and acceptable means of demonstrating affiliation to the culture. All of these conceptualizations of sociocultural brand phenomena share the quality of allowing consumers to establish social bonds of various strength and meaningfulness among each other.

Brands and oppositionality

A brand-related interpretive community may reflexively view itself as apart from and even marginalized from mainstream culture. This raises the interesting issue of whether *every* interpretive community is marginalized or oppositional. While hippies, punks (Hebdige, 1979), mods, various youth subcultures, some Star Trek enthusiasts (Kozinets, 2001), ecofeminists, the deaf, Christian fundamentalists (O'Guinn and Belk, 1989), lesbian separatists and many other social groupings undoubtedly feel that they are marginalized from the mainstream and disadvantaged by the way they are treated by others, most brand-related members usually negotiate a significantly less stigmatized sense of otherness. Members of branded subcultures of consumption seem to revel in and enjoy the cachet of difference that their affiliation affords them, developing a unique set of values (Schouten and McAlexander, 1995, p. 50) that may actually be a source of social capital for the brand. The Apple loyalists observed by Muniz and O'Guinn (2001) feel the most aggrieved of the three brand communities studied, likely obtaining their sense of oppositionality and imminent threat from Apple's relatively low market share compared to Microsoft. In doing so, they construct a form of oppositional brand loyalty. Yet, of all branded social configurations studied, only the Star Trek enthusiasts studied by Kozinets (2001) negotiate an institutionalized safe place from the stigma and social isolation that many of them feel outside the culture of consumption, lending it the utopian quality that distinguishes it from other contributions.

Other interpretive communities rely on brands for expressing a sense of social discontent and marginality, but do not revolve around the consumption of brands per se. Local interpretive communities of gays and lesbians have traditionally inscribed 'campy' meanings on mainstream cultural icons or brands such as Judy Garland, Absolut Vodka, or Levi's jeans (see Chauncey, 1994; Kates, 2004). Kates's (2004) study of brands consumed in a gay men's community demonstrates that certain brands accomplish a sense of legitimacy (i.e., fit a community's key beliefs or values) when they pursue ostensibly pro-social agendas in the eyes of gay consumers. Thus brands can help support a type of community other than one whose focus is consumption, aiding in the public expression, enactment and even celebration of its key political values. Consumer movements such as those studied by Kozinets and Handelman (2004) consistently rely on companies and brands to act as adversaries, developing and propagating their stated ideologies and cultivating oppositional identities in relation to the more negative and institutionalized aspects of consumption. In accord with anti-corporate ideology, Thompson and Arsel (2004), in their study of consumers' associations of Starbucks and expressions of glocalization, conceptualize the 'hegemonic brandscape', a cultural model (or way of viewing) that situates brands and their structuring influence of consumers' activities and identities at the nexus of consumer capitalism. Thus brands may play key roles in the structuring of oppositional identities.

Brands and constructing identity
More generally, interpretive communities (or social groupings) play a role in the construction of identity. In Fournier's (1998) study of consumer–brand relationships, women
construct different types of gender identities (caring matriarch, working single mother
and young female university student) through consumer narratives, attesting to the structuring effects of gender on brand meaning. Brands also aid in the more active cultivation
of consumers' identities (Holt, 2002) in changing postmodern culture by providing a
wealth of cultural meaning.
    Participation in brand-related consumption cultures potentially adds more complexity
and nuance to consumers' identities. Those consumers that participate in Harley devotion
such as the outlaw bikers, the 'moms and pops', the lesbian Dykes on Bikes, and the
Rich Urban Bikers, etc. are separate interpretive communities that inscribe historically
bounded consumption meanings on Harley Davidson products. Moreover, the meanings
that Dykes on Bikes are likely to inscribe on Harley in practice (e.g., freedom from patriarchal society, lesbian separatism and other elements of feminist thought) are likely to be
quite distinct from the more mainstream, working-class cultural meanings that the more
traditional, socially conservative 'moms and pops' riders realize in consumer practice
(such as 'mom, baseball, and apple pie', patriotism, American heritage and machismo).
Indeed, these meanings may be oppositional and openly hostile to one another, constructing different social identities in relation to one another, an implication that Schouten
and McAlexander (1995) recognize when they explicitly note the unconscious tensions
between outlaw bikers and 'yuppie posers' (p. 58). Star Trek, a rich media brand, provides
a rich source of meaning for consumers' mattering maps (Kozinets, 2001, p. 78), offering
participants in the culture to incorporate strands of meanings into narratives of identity.
Kozinets (2001) also demonstrates the way that the Internet may be used by consumers to
engage in the culture of consumption and culture, and by researchers engaging in netnography, wishing to understand the context.
    An interpretive analysis of the Harley Davidson subculture of consumption from an
interpretive community/strategy perspective would note these social tensions and
differences, and would carefully explore and map the different interpretive strategies that
differentiate the outlaw bikers, Dykes on Bikes, moms and pops and the Rich Urban
Bikers. Indeed, an interpretation that focused on the *differences* among interpretive communities associated with the same brand would have value to researchers in identifying
and unpacking the different collective identities around the brand and might have significant commercial value to Harley Davidson itself in its promotional efforts to the
different segments of consumers that use its products. Thus it is plausible that both brand
communities and subcultures of consumption are composites of fragments of the
different interpretive communities. Critically, an attention to the differences among pre-
sumably homogeneous subcultures and communities may produce contextually sensitive
theory in consumer research that may map the structuring of meaning.

Doing interpretive strategy analysis of brands in the field: an application
Doing an analysis of the interpretive strategies (that in turn, comprise an interpretive community) during an ethnographic study requires identifying, exploring, tracking and unpacking the different cultural meanings inscribed on brands and products that arguably unite a
given interpretive community, distinguishing it from other interpretive communities and the

metaphoric 'mainstream'. After reviewing the relevant literature on the methods and inter-pretations of various ethnographies (Arnould and Wallendorf, 1994; Belk, Wallendorf and Sherry, 1989; Celsi, Rose and Leigh, 1993; Clifford and Marcus, 1986; Kates, 2000; Kozinets, 2001; Marcus and Fischer, 1986; Muniz and O'Guinn, 2001; Radway, 1984; Ritson and Elliott, 1999; Schouten and McAlexander, 1995) and the reader-response liter-ature (e.g., Culler, 1975; Fish, 1976, 1980; Iser, 1978; Mailloux, 1982; Scott, 1994; Tompkins, 1980) and integrating it with a passage of narrative from a consumer, the following per-spective on ethnographic technique is offered that may, in the future, assist others when exploring the structuring of commercial meaning in brand contexts.

Raymond (WM, 50s), a building manager and married father of two children, was interviewed during an investigation of the roles of brands in the household. During the interview, he revealed that he considered himself an active Christian who based many of his purchase decisions on his sense of religious and spiritual values. During analysis of the data, I interpreted the theme of 'cul-tivating spirituality through brand-related activities' such as purchase, use and rejection. This theme is supported by many of the meanings of consumption and practice in which Raymond engaged. Significantly, Raymond's was the only one of 30 households interviewed that did not have a television set. Almost 20 years ago, he began to discern the effects of television on the daily routines in his family. He was reading a book and found something interesting to tell the rest of his family; he was subsequently told to wait 20 minutes until a television show was over: 'I began to see how much television interrupted our lives because I thought to myself, "In twenty minutes' time, is the program that I want to watch going to be on?"' The family then had a two-week experimentation period in which they got rid of their television. After that period, they held a family vote and the majority ruled that the television would go permanently. Years later, he still believes that it was a positive decision not to own a television because his family is not exposed to 'all of the values that we have in a sense rejected . . . for all of that's pouring into the homes [of other people]'. Consumption and brand choices then are means of rejecting elements of pre-sumably damaging mainstream culture and cultivating spirituality through religious beliefs.

Raymond related the consumption decision not to own a television, among others, to his family's sense of 'values'. Values, in this context, refer both to his religious beliefs and to his con-victions of what is beneficial to his family's need for harmony and togetherness – that is, whether his family's social needs are satisfactorily met. The family reads a chapter of the Bible every day, and some household decisions are connected to an interpretation of scripture. Raymond offered an example of his values by giving an example of interpreting 'Blessed is the man who walks not in the council of the ungodly' from the First Psalm. He would then actively try to interpret what the passage means and its implication for daily living: 'What does "ungodly" mean? Is it someone who doesn't believe there is a God, or is it someone who doesn't take any notice of God's com-mandments, or doesn't go to church, or doesn't have a faith of some kind?' He would then seek guidance from other parts of the Bible in interpreting the line of scripture and the meaning of 'ungodly', attempting to figure out the best way for his family to live.

It may have been the psalm's unconscious influence that inspired his negative judgment of Magnum ice cream's 'Seven Deadly Sins' brand extension as ungodly and morally inappropriate for his family's continued loyalty. Magnum introduced a set of seven differently flavored ice cream bars, named after the seven deadly sins from Christian theology: Greed, Envy, Wrath, etc. (The bars were also appropriately flavored according to the sin; 'Envy', for example, was vanilla and mint-flavored.) Raymond was offended: 'it's just a sign of the promiscuity of our nation, our times, I suppose in a sense it's what the people want that they get, so the advertising campaign generally, I would think, is aiming at where the people are at. I would hope that that's not the case.' Raymond argued that advertising such as Magnum's encouraged 'irresponsible behaviors' of varying sorts. He then made a conscious decision that he would not buy the ice cream for his family, relating it to his religious values: 'there's a thing I read awhile back where it says "the Lord will give the people their heart's desire", and so I see that in a lot of the advertising . . . And how can you sort of say, "I'm eating an adulterous ice cream." I think it's a bit ridiculous.' Thus, according to Raymond's belief system, conscious choices of brands result in positive outcomes for his family, while those who indulge in negative decisions, presumably, get their just des(s)erts.

Researchers may also classify Raymond as a member of an interpretive community of 'conservative Christians' and deepen their interpretations of brands according to the recommendations given below.

Pay attention to the local politics
Given the 'consciousness of kind' that characterizes brand communities (e.g., Muniz and O'Guinn, 2001) or subcultures (Kates, 2002, 2004), it is likely that brand meanings may reflect the biases and loyalties of informants toward the brand and even hostilities toward others. For example, Muniz and O'Guinn (2001) noted that some Apple users were sensitive to the dominance of IBM products in the PC social world. These competitive rivalries and sentiments of 'otherness' are likely to inflect local brand meanings (see also Kates, 1998, 2000). Raymond's consumption can be seen as an historical and social reflection of the political organization among conservative Christians in the United States and other affluent countries that emerged during the late 1970s. Some interpretive communities of Christians consciously rejected certain aspects of mainstream society and demanded that the marketplace serve their needs and reflect their values (O'Guinn and Balk, 1989). Raymond demonstrated a high concern for interpretation of the Bible in influencing his values; other conservative Christian consumers, however, could prove to be more literal in their readings of scripture, placing them in different interpretive communities, from a branding perspective.

Understand how brands and marketing communications fit into consumers' daily lives
A key assumption of brand ethnography is that brand and product meanings are realized in the ordinary, mundane course of everyday life (see Fournier, 1998; Ritson and Elliott, 1999) and may go unnoticed and undisclosed. Thus immersion within the context of consuming brands and engaging relevant media for an extended period of time may allow researchers to understand the different shades of meaning consumers negotiate in their interpretations of brands and marketing communications. Raymond negotiated consumption meanings in relatively everyday decisions: what activities to engage in (e.g., reading instead of television) and which brands reflect his family's values (and which do not).

Be sensitive to emerging differences among informants
Individual informants may construct subtly different interpretations of brands and marketing communications within the overall structuring confines of the broad cultural meanings they appear to share. This observation raises the question of how market researchers 'know' that an interpretive community exists before they enter the field and investigate. The answer is: they don't. Interpretive communities arise in certain sociohistorical contexts and may change and even disperse over time. However, researchers may enter the field with sensible a priori assumptions about the existence of a somewhat cohesive community of consumers and modify these assumptions (often radically) once they begin to understand and track the shared practices of the group in question. For example, a researcher trying to understand hiphop culture might expect to find great diversity among its members. Research that includes field observations, interviews, media examination, archived historical documents and even quantitative surveys is likely to detect the

differences and similarities of these meanings and the ways they are inscribed in practice. In order to confirm that a number of interpretive communities of Christians exist, it would be necessary to interview other consumers who self-identify as Christian and interview them about their brand choices and meanings. Another strategy is doing historical analysis of archived materials.

Understand the ways brands, products and marketing communications are ritualized and institutionalized

In their ethnography of an interpretive community of teenaged consumers, Ritson and Elliott (1999) note that advertising meaning is transferred from the text to everyday life through repeated ritualistic exchange. It is very likely that brand communities and other brand-related groupings (like the generic community construct in sociology) have rather stable rituals and traditions that relate to commercial text. It is necessary to find the ones that appear to repeat, if in different forms. For example, Muniz and O'Guinn (2001) note the importance of storytelling among consumers in establishing shared meanings among brand communities. Raymond's family seems to ritualize daily Bible reading with the family, and this highly important activity may subsequently and unconsciously inform brand meanings and choices.

Learn the tropes that constitute interpretive strategies

Recent studies demonstrate that language is critical to human understanding (see Lakoff, 1980). Moreover, it is the tropes (poetic figures of speech) that simultaneously unite and differentiate interpretive communities. As Ritson and Elliott (1999, p. 272) found in their study of teenagers, metaphor is a key tropic manner of creatively transferring commercial meanings from text to life and brands, and of mocking authority figures. In other studies, the metaphoric glosses point to embedded consumption meanings that structure human interaction (see Arnould and Wallendorf, 1994). Irony and metaphor are characteristics of most people's interpretive repertoire (Lakoff, 1980), yet what distinguishes one interpretive community and its inscription of meaning on marketing communications and brands is the particularistic *ways* that consumers use figurative language. Thus knowledgeable application of the various branches of literary criticism (particularly reader-response criticism, but formalistic theories as well) is key to unpacking the cultural meanings and interpretive strategies that constitute brand-related social configurations. Raymond used the word 'conscious' a few times during his interview when referring to the way he chose brands or screened out external influences in order to protect his family. In this case, 'conscious' is a key trope that refers to his critical endeavor to scrutinize market offerings (including censoring all television shows and examining advertising and brands) in a fully aware manner, contemplate the implications of consuming them from a sacred set of values, and make a decision in accord with these values, and one that will result in spiritual outcomes that connects his family members.

Future research

The meanings of brands and marketing communications emerge from a complex interaction among text, social contexts and the bodies of cultural background knowledge with which consumers interact (Eco, 1972; Scott, 1994). The challenge for marketers and scholars is to find sets of local, institutionalized agreement of meanings inscribed on brands, consistent with a view of culture as a complex mélange of symbols, diverse practices and hybrids (Clifford and Marcus, 1986).

Research into consumption communities
The interpretive community and strategy concepts have implications for studying consumer–brand relationships (Fournier, 1998), yet brand relationships focus strictly on the psychological and clinical aspects of brands in consumers' lives. Ethnographic studies may extend our knowledge by demonstrating that *communal* relationships exist between brands and interpretive communities, ones that depend on past history with the brand and linguistic tropes that unite and divide consumers. More importantly, future work may identify the key social processes that communicate and institutionalize brand meanings among a localized set of consumers. For example, in the Muniz and O'Guinn (2001) study of brand community, storytelling among community members emerges as a key cultural and social process of meaning movement. Further, given the importance of Internet use among geographically dispersed, diverse consumers, future research is necessary to identify and unpack the institutionalized and ritualized cyber practices that create and sustain brand relationships between brands and interpretive communities over time (see Kozinets, 2001).

Further, the brand communities conceptualized and investigated by Muniz and O'Guinn (2001) are particular, specialized forms of interpretive communities that focus on specific brands (e.g., the Saab interpretive/brand community, the Apple interpretive/ brand community, etc.). However, it is entirely possible that the brand communities studied by Muniz and O'Guinn (2001) were constituted by undetected, *multiple* interpretive communities. Their key findings include an interpretation of the consciousness of kind, rituals and traditions, and moral obligations that characterize brand communities. Further research from an interpretive community perspective may detect that these three generic aspects of community are realized quite differently in actual practice by different interpretive communities that use the same brand. For example, one interpretive community of Apple users may maintain their social bonds through subtly different traditions and shared meanings than those of another interpretive community of Apple enthusiasts, depending on their respective physical location and social positioning. Studying brand communities from an interpretive community standpoint may reveal subtle (and perhaps dramatic) shades of meaning within the 'same' brand community, even as each different community embraces and celebrates a commercial and capitalist ethos (Muniz and O'Guinn, 2001). For example, the Apple users studied in Muniz and O'Guinn's study negotiate and inscribe different meanings compared to a group of left-wing, Marxist Apple users who, just for the sake of argument, ironically consume and enjoy Apple computers as they simultaneously advocate destruction of the capitalist system from which Apple emerged. In such a hypothetical scenario, the 'brand community' of Apple users is perhaps best conceptualized as composed of two radically different interpretive communities producing differences in meaning when their interpretive strategies are applied to the brand and consuming experiences.

Research into managers' branding practices
One underresearched area is marketing managers' and advertising creative staff's practices connected with branding. Kover (1995) has explored copywriters' implicit theories of

communication when inventing advertising, and Kates and Goh (2003) interviewed advertising strategists and creative staff, demonstrating that managerial and creative practices facilitate the 'morphing' of brand meaning among different interpretive communities of consumers. Brown, Kozinets and Sherry (2003), in a netnographic study of retro branding, demonstrate how the practice is a co-creative alliance between consumers and marketers. Yet more ethnographic investigation on the producer side, exploring the management of meaning from an interpretive community perspective, is needed to answer a host of unanswered questions: what do marketers do to fit brands into new foreign markets, given different cultural contexts? What brand executional elements are thought to structure consumers' experiences effectively and successfully? What kind of stories do brand managers try to create in order to connect with consumers from a variety of local and foreign markets? How do brand managers attempt to appeal to subcultural consumers such as gay men, lesbians, environmentalists etc.? These are all productive avenues for future ethnographic work in marketing and consumer research.

Broader issues and debate
As noted by previous research (Kates, 2004; Kozinets and Handelman, 2004), brands have greater implications for consumers and society as a whole. Are brand communities that are socially alienated from the rest of the society or from other communities beneficial for consumers and society? What are the consequences of alienated brand-related interpretive communities, such as the one described by Kozinets (2001)? Are there brand-related communities that practice forms of environmentally sustainable consumption, and what can other communities, governments and companies learn from their practices and ideologies? What beneficial, physiologically and psychologically healthy, and spiritual roles do brand-related interpretive communities play in the lives of consumers, considering the benefits of social connection, personal meaning and prosocial consumption goals? What are the conscious and unconscious differing motivations of those consumers who become involved in brand communities, subcultures of consumption, consumer activist groups, cultures of consumption and other related social configurations? How do consumers negotiate the sometimes conflicting values among different brand-related interpretive communities, if they belong to more than one, and what effects does this conflict have on their brand loyalty, health and well-being? Does involvement in these social configurations have effects on health and well-being and, if so, what are the positive and negative consequences? What brand interpretive communities have dialogic versus dialectical relationships with brands (see Holt, 2002; Thompson and Haytko, 1997) and what are the implications for brand meanings and practices?

Broader social implications are relevant to the study of brands from managers' perspectives as well. What are the managerial processes involved in designing a brand for different interpretive communities? Are there ethical concerns involved and, if so, what are they, and how do they influence brand managers' strategic planning and tactical activities? What are the benefits and drawbacks of having managers directly versus indirectly involved and participating in interpretive communities? Can valuable marketing research be obtained that way? What types of 'soft' market information can brand managers obtain through their personal involvement? Are there circumstances when company management should not be directly involved? These are all questions that can be addressed by future research from an interpretive community perspective.

References

Arnould, Eric J. and Melanie Wallendorf (1994), 'Market-oriented ethnography: interpretation building and marketing strategy formulation', *Journal of Marketing Research*, **31** (November), 484–504.

Belk, Russell, Melanie Wallendorf and John F. Sherry, Jr (1989), 'The sacred and the projane in consumer behavior: the odicy on the Odyssey', *Journal of Consumer Research*, **16** (June), 1–38.

Berger, Peter L. and Thomas Luckmann (1966), *The Social Construction of Reality*, New York: Anchor.

Brown, Stephen, Robert Kozinets and John F. Sherry (2003), 'Teaching old brands new tricks: retro branding and the revival of brand meaning', *Journal of Marketing*, **67** (July), 19–33.

Celsi, Richard L., Randall L. Rose and Thomas W. Leigh (1993), 'An exploration of high-risk leisure consumption through skydiving', *Journal of Consumer Research*, **20** (1), 1–23.

Clifford, James and George Marcus (1986), *Writing Culture: The Poetics and Politics of Ethnography*, Berkeley: University of California Press.

Cova, Bernard (1997), 'Community and consumption: towards a definition of the "linking value" of product or services', *European Journal of Marketing*, **31** (3/4), 297–316.

Culler, Jonathan (1975), *Structuralist Poetics*, Ithaca, NY: Cornell University Press.

Duncan, Tom and Sandra E. Moriarty (1998), 'A communication-based marketing model for managing relationships', *Journal of Marketing*, **62** (April), 1–13.

Eco, Umberto (1972), 'Towards a semiotic enquiry into the television message', paper presented at University of Birmingham, UK.

Elliott, Richard and Mark Ritson (1997), 'Post-structuralism and the dialectics of advertising discourse, ideology, resistance, in Stephen Brown and Darach Turley (eds), *Consumer Research: Postcards from the Edge*, London: Routledge, pp. 190–219.

Featherstone, Michael (1991), *Consumer Culture and Postmodernism*, London: Sage.

Firat, A. Fuat and Clifford J. Shultz (1997), 'From segmentation to fragmentation: markets and marketing strategy in the postmodern era', *European Journal of Marketing*, **31** (3/4), 183–207.

Firat, A. Fuat and Alladi Venkatesh (1995), 'Liberatory postmodernism and the reenchantment of consumption', *Journal of Consumer Research*, **22** (3), 239–67.

Fish, Stanley E. (1976), 'Interpreting the variorum', *Critical Inquiry*, **2** (Spring), 465–85.

—— (1980), *Is there a Text in this Class? The Authority of Interpretive Communities*, Cambridge, MA: Harvard University Press.

Fournier, Susan (1998), 'Consumers and their brands: developing relationship theory in consumer research', *Journal of Consumer Research*, **24** (March), 343–73.

Gottdiener, Mark (1995), *Post modern Semiotics: Material Culture and the Forms of Urban Life*, Oxford: Blackwell.

Grier, Sonya A. and Anne M. Brumbaugh (1999), 'Noticing cultural differences: ad meanings created by target and non-target markets', *Journal of Advertising*, **28** (1), 79–93.

Hall, Stuart (1980), 'Encoding and decoding', in Stuart Hall et al. (eds), *Culture, Media, Language*, London: Hutchinson.

—— (1997), 'The work of representation', in Stuart Hall (ed.) *Representation: Cultural Representations and Signifying Practices*, London: Sage.

Hebdige, Dick (1979), *Subculture: The Meaning of Style*, London: Methuen.

—— (1997), 'The Work of representation', in Stuart Hall (ed.), *Representation: Cultural Representations and Signifying Practices*, London: Sage.

Hirschman, Elizabeth C. (1998), 'When expert consumers interpret textual products: applying reader-response theory to television programs', *Consumption, Markets, and Culture*, **2** (3), 259–310.

Holt, Douglas B. (2002), 'Why do brands cause trouble? A dialectical theory of consumer culture and branding', *Journal of Consumer Research*, **29** (June), 70–90.

Iser, Wolfgang (1978), *The Act of Reading*, Baltimore: Johns Hopkins University Press.

Kates, Steven M. (1998), *Twenty Million New Customers! Understanding Gay Men's Consumer Behavior*, Binghamton, NY: Harrington Park Press.

—— (2000), 'Out of the closet and out on the street: gay men and their brand relationships', *Psychology & Marketing*, **17** (6), 493–513.

—— (2002), 'The protean quality of subcultural consumption: an ethnographic account of gay consumers', *Journal of Consumer Research*, **29** (December), 290–307.

—— (2004), 'The dynamics of brand legitimacy: an interpretive study in the gay men's community', *Journal of Consumer Research*, **31** (September), 455–64.

Kates, Steven M. and Charlene Goh (2003), 'The morphing brand: implications for advertising theory and practice', *Journal of Advertising*, **32** (10), 59–68.

Kates, Steven M. and Glenda Shaw-Garlock (1999), 'The ever entangling web: a study of ideologies and discourses in advertising to women', *Journal of Advertising*, **28** (2), 33–49.

Kover, Arthur (1995), 'Copywriters' implicit theories of communication: an exploration', *Journal of Consumer Research*, **21** (March), 596–611.

Kozinets, Robert (2001), 'Utopian enterprise: articulating the meanings of Star Trek's culture of consumption', *Journal of Consumer Research*, **28** (1), 67–88.

Kozinets, Robert V. and Jay M. Handelman (2004), 'Adversaries of consumption: consumer movements, activism and ideology', *Journal of Consumer Research*, **31** (December), 691–704.

Lakoff, George (1980), *Metaphors We Live By*, Chicago: University of Chicago Press.

Lukenbill, Grant (1995), *Untold Millions*, New York: Harper Business.

Mailloux, Steven (1982), *Interpretive Conventions: The Reader in the Study of American Fiction*, Ithaca, NY: Cornell University Press.

Marcus, George and Michael Fischer (1986), *Anthropology as Cultural Critique: An Experimental Moment in the Human Sciences*, Chicago, IL: University of Chicago Press.

McAlexander, James, John Schouten and Harold Koenig (2002), 'Building brand community', *Journal of Marketing*, **66** (January), 38–54.

McCracken, Grant (1987), 'Advertising: meaning or information?', in Paul F. Anderson and Melanie Wallendorf (eds), *Advances in Consumer Research*, vol. 14, Provo, UT: Association for Consumer Research, pp. 121–4.

Mick, David and Claus Buhl (1992), 'A meaning-based model of advertising experiences', *Journal of Consumer Research*, **19** (December), 317–38.

Muniz, Albert and Thomas C. O'Guinn (2001), 'Brand community', *Journal of Consumer Research*, **27** (4), 412–32.

Muniz, Albert and Hope Schau (2005), 'Religiosity in the abandoned apple newton brand community', *Journal of Consumer Research*, **31** (March), 737–47.

O'Guinn, Thomas C. and Russell W. Belk (1989), 'Heaven on earth: consumption at Heritage Village, USA', *Journal of Consumer Research*, **16** (September), 227–38.

Peñaloza, Lisa and Mary Gilly (1999), 'Marketer acculturation: the changer and the changed', *Journal of Marketing*, **63** (July), 84–104.

Radway, Janice (1984), *Reading the Romance: Women, Patriarchy, and Popular Literature*, Chapel Hill: The University of North Carolina Press.

Ritson, Mark and Richard Elliott (1999), 'The social uses of advertising: an ethnographic study of adolescent advertising audiences', *Journal of Consumer Research*, **26** (3), 260–77.

Schouten, John W. and James H. McAlexander (1995), 'Subcultures of consumption: an ethnography of the new bikers', *Journal of Consumer Research*, **22** (1), 43–61.

Schutz, Alfred and Thomas Luckmann (1973), *The Structures of the Life-World*, Evanston, IL: Northwestern University Press.

Scott, Linda M. (1994), 'The bridge from text to mind: adapting reader-response theory to consumer research', *Journal of Consumer Research*, **21**, 461–80.

Thompson, Craig J. and Zeynep Arsel (2004), 'The starbucks brandscope and consumers' (anticorporate) experiences of glocalization', *Journal of Consumer Research*, **31** (December), 631–42.

Thompson, Craig J. and Diana L. Haytko (1997), 'Speaking of fashion: consumers' uses of fashion discourses and the appropriation of countervailing cultural meanings', *Journal of Consumer Research*, **24** (June), 15–42.

Tompkins, Jane P. (1980), *Reader Response Criticism: From Formalism to Post-Structuralism*, Baltimore: Johns Hopkins University Press.

9 Making contexts matter: selecting research contexts for theoretical insights
Eric Arnould, Linda Price and Risto Moisio[1]

One of the most difficult tasks of any social scientist is to negotiate the links between abstract ideas and concrete instances of these ideas (Ellsworth, 1977; Alford, 1998). There is always a tension between our theoretical concepts and their empirical manifestations. As Alford notes, 'Abstract concepts never perfectly fit the complexity of reality. Evidence never contains its own explanation' (p. 29). There are numerous examples of researchers who cleverly devise experiments, select field settings or interpret contexts in ways that deftly traverse the divide between theory and data, but there are few guidelines for novice researchers attempting to pry understanding and explanation from the contexts they study, or struggling to align theories and contexts.

As social scientists who have warily and not always successfully traversed the divide between theory and data, the intent of our chapter is to encourage more systematic attention to the choice of context and to provide some suggestions for selecting contexts that have a high likelihood of impacting consumer and marketing theory. We restrict our attention to the problem of selecting contexts for interpretive research because context is a prominent characteristic of much interpretive consumer research, yet as a discipline we have devoted little discussion to the way to make research contexts matter theoretically. Looking at the carefully crafted thick descriptions used to unfold theoretical insights in the best interpretive research, the novice reader can come to believe that any context studied carefully will render new theory. In fact, the esteemed sociologist Howard Becker argues that every context is perfect for studying something, but the 'something' that should be studied often eludes us (Becker, 1998). The subtle nuances of sampling, domain parameters and timing and range of data collected that enabled the new insights often appear to the novice as lucky accidents of setting or observation rather than structured researcher choices. Certainly, serendipity and thoughtful observation play an instrumental role in interpretive work. Thick description of a context can help activate novel and useful insights about markets and consumers, but, as we argue, serendipity and thick description are rarely sufficient to trigger such insights. A compelling context, no matter how richly depicted, cannot substitute for theory. Moreover, we argue research contexts are likely to differ in the kinds of insights they generate, with some contexts more likely to spawn interesting insights. Surfacing theory is critical for both scholars and practitioners. For scholars, good theory always builds on prior theory; contexts are comprehended through theoretical lenses. For practitioners, surfacing implicit theory may suggest how to make sense of a data set in the service of improved strategy implementation, or the desirability of alternative theoretical perspectives that could drive alternative interpretations of data to suggest new strategic directions.

Our chapter consists of four sections. In the first two sections we briefly discuss the importance of context and some of the potential dangers of context for researchers employing qualitative data. In the third section, we discuss how to make context work for researchers in the area of consumer culture theory. Here we discuss how prior studies in CCT (Consumer Culture Theory) have used context and examine how theory and context come together in these studies. Through our discussion of interpretive research contributing to consumer culture theory over the past 20 years, we provide some guidelines for selecting contexts that pay off. Finally, we conclude by reflecting on the role of context in qualitative data analysis more generally.

The importance of context

Contexts are of fundamental importance to researchers in developing and testing theories. In simple terms, a theory is a story about why acts, events, structure and thoughts occur. The process of theorizing consists of activities such as abstracting, generalizing, relating, selecting, explaining, synthesizing and idealizing (Sutton and Staw, 1995). Contexts give theoretical stories veracity and texture. However, exactly how contexts enable and enrich theoretical insights often remains implicit. Sometimes we have difficulty articulating the crucial role of contexts in developing a better understanding of consumer behavior. At the most fundamental level, contexts engage our emotions and our senses, stimulate discovery, invite description and excite comparison.

Contexts engage our emotions and our senses

We find ourselves inspired, our passions inflamed by powerfully evocative contexts. Researchers have been visually stunned by Niketown (Peñaloza, 1998; Sherry, 1998); fascinated by the fervent commitments of X-Philes (Kozinets, 1997), organoleptically enthralled by skydiving (Celsi, Rose and Leigh, 1993), white water rafting (Arnould and Price, 1993) and the Burning Man Festival (Kozinets, 2002). Researchers have also been transformed into fantasy game avatars (Martin, 2004), moved to intervention by the poignancy of the plight of the homeless (Hill and Stamey, 1990) or the end-of-life decisions of the elderly (Price, Arnould and Curasi, 2000), converted into Apple Newton worshipers (Muñiz and Schau, 2005) or sucked into ardent neotribal brand and lifestyle communities (Cova, 1997). The power of contexts to engage our emotions and our senses also gives them the power to transform our lives and the lives of others.

Contexts stimulate discovery

In particular contexts, well-trained researchers grasp intuitively that there is a novel construct or relationship to be discovered (e.g., Becker, 1998; Wells, 1993). Simply paying attention to provocative natural occurrences is one of the most useful heuristics for generating research questions (McGuire, 1997). This involves 'cultivating habits of observation' that focus attention on productive aspects of experience including unexpected, non-obvious relations (ibid., p. 3). But it also involves analyzing one's own behavior in these settings, and role-playing behavior drawing on similar and opposite types of experiences (McGuire, 1997). Contexts and occurrences that seem puzzling or paradoxical move us to search for explanations or resolutions from our own unique combination of perspectives derived from our theoretical exposures: they stimulate discovery (Fiske, 2004).

Contexts that engage our emotions, imaginations and senses may be opportune for 'revelatory incidents' (Fernandez, 1986), locating 'negative cases' (Emigh, 1997) and 'dwelling in theory', (Burawoy, 1998). Of course, researchers' previous scholarship, or what Glaser and Strauss (1967) call 'theoretical sensitivity' informs this intuition. A prepared mind facilitates researchers' ability to absorb experiences from a context and translate them into insights that contribute to theory.

The consumer behavior Odyssey (Belk, Wallendorf and Sherry, 1989), a watershed event in academic consumer research in North America, was motivated by the conviction that the exploration of novel consumption venues such as swap meets or eclectic roadside attractions could spark new theoretical understanding, a proposition borne out in subsequent research (Belk, 1995; Sherry and Kozinets, 2001; Arnould and Thompson, 2005). While these researchers stress the value of thick description in obtaining these insights, equally important is the foundational training in anthropology, sociology and psychology that informed their scholarship (Belk et al., 1989). This foundational training is what provides researchers with the scholarly intuition needed to detect the theoretical interest of contexts (McCracken, 1988).

Contexts invite description and excite comparison
To communicate novel constructs or relationships we must characterize contexts in terms that are in some ways conventional to a community of researchers. We do this by approaching phenomena as cases of something already known (Walton, 1992). Part of the pleasure and fascination of contexts arises from our sense that they compare in some interesting way with things we already know (e.g., Burawoy, 1998). Contexts excite comparison. Commercial white water rafting is a service encounter but it differs from other service encounters in theoretically interesting ways. Raft trips are longer, more intimate, more hedonic, and take place in environments under minimal control of the service provider (Arnould and Price, 1993). One corollary of the invitation to comparison is that such comparisons also reframe difference and similarity in interesting ways. Thus, when framed appropriately by descriptive comparison, an individual's purchase of a treat becomes a self-gift (Mick and Demoss, 1990); brand loyalty becomes a brand relationship (Fournier, 1998); forgotten brands in the kitchen pantry become invisible brands (Coupland, 2005); heirlooms become inalienable wealth (Curasi, Price and Arnould, 2004); scruffy handicraft production in West Africa emerges as a regional market cluster of networked relationships (Arnould and Mohr, 2005). Notice that these scientific transformations are at the same time metaphorical ones; and it is often the case that thinking metaphorically about one's data can lead to theoretical insight (Lakoff and Johnson, 1980).

The dangers of context
Evocative, surprising, engrossing contexts are not unlike the taboo objects that inflamed the desire of Indiana Jones, his many nemeses and fans in the famous movie series (Smith et al., 2005). They are fraught with danger for researchers as well. Although contexts can be dangerous in other ways, we restrict attention to the dangers associated with researchers and readers becoming overabsorbed in contexts.

The researcher overabsorbed in contexts
One of the most important dangers is that the researcher will become overabsorbed in contexts. Such overabsorption may waste resources by keeping researchers in the field too long and may hinder theoretical insights because of an inability to manufacture distance from informants' lives (McCracken, 1988). The researcher walks a fine and nebulous line between absorption in the context that enables thick description and the analytical

distance needed to uncover theoretical contributions and get on with the crafting of science. Here researchers wrestle with the inevitable paradox between the need for intimate familiarity with and distance from context.

In some cases, informants' plights can overwhelm scientific goals, creating a tension between directly affecting consumer's lives through immediate assistance and improved understandings that can inform long-term marketing strategy and social policy. For example, researchers studying homelessness, juvenile delinquency, consumer literacy, race inequities, drug and alcohol abuse, access to health care and a host of other issues must balance empathy for their informants with scientific or policy goals.

At other times, the researcher is caught up in the emotional and sensory dimensions of a context and unable to attend to or sort out the dynamic elements and processes contributing to that experience. To imagine this overabsorption and how it might interfere with doing research, assume that you have been asked to do ethnography of a roller coaster ride. In this case, riding the roller coaster allows access to your own physical and emotional experience of the event but (at least in our case) is too absorbing to allow attention to anything else. Only by getting off the roller coaster and observing others can you distance yourself enough to trace the reactions of others and examine how the experience of a roller coaster ride is patterned and socially situated. Metaphorically, getting off the roller coaster enables the analytical distance to uncover how the experience is produced and unfolded within a social space.

Overabsorption in a context can also make it impossible to break free of taken-for-granted assumptions that parameterize and structure the context (Zaltman, 1983). The use of bi-gender, bi-racial and bi-disciplinary research teams is a tactic often used to get beyond taken-for-granted aspects of a single researcher's perspective that may constrain insight (Arnould and Price, 1993; Crockett and Wallendorf, 2004; Thompson and Haytko, 1997). Feminist and post-colonial scholars have demonstrated how Western male researchers often background gender and other power relationships that not so subtly color their results (Thompson, Stern and Arnould, 1998). Hirschman (1993) recognized this in her content analysis of the *Journal of Marketing*. Bristor and Fischer (1993) more specifically pointed out several specific areas where taken-for-granted influences of gender affect consumer research on emotions.

Anthropologists refer to the danger of compelling contexts in the myth of 'going native'. In this myth, the anthropologist is so beguiled by cultural context that he or she throws scientific commitments to the wind and throws him or herself wholeheartedly into his or her adopted culture. In short, he or she assimilates to the context, much as did Odysseus on Circe's island. The 'going native' problem in marketing may be better recognized as 'becoming a consultant' or 'becoming an empathetic social activist'. Absorbed by immediate managerial or social problems, the researcher can offer solutions but is unable to envision how these solutions refer to anything more general.

Contexts overabsorbing our readers
Contexts are dangerous not only for the way they threaten to swallow researchers, but for the way contexts can overabsorb our readers. Readers are prone to remember the context better than the theoretical insights rendered. Similarly, readers sometimes judge the context as worthy or unworthy of scientific inquiry rather than assessing what theoretical insights can be rendered through study of that particular context. For example, two of the

present authors were once advised by colleagues that a study of white water rafting would never be published in a major marketing journal: the river rafting market was too small and the wilderness setting too unusual. And indeed the critics were correct. However, they mistook the substantive context for the theoretical context; the theoretical context enabled top-tier publications modifying theories of service encounters, service satisfaction drivers and the tactical role of front line service personnel (Arnould and Price, 1993; Arnould, Price and Tierney, 1995, 1998). Many contexts for qualitative research are extreme. The extremities of these research contexts evoke critiques of 'generalizability', but often the extremity of variables and values enables researchers to derive theoretical insights. Going to extremes is at heart a defamiliarizing tactic that helps us transcend some of the assumptions we have in overly familiar contexts. Further defamiliarizing in extreme contexts helps theoretically interesting factors emerge more readily. For example, Holt (2002) interviews informants living at the fringe of consumer society to uncover how brands operate as cultural resources. Kozinets (2002) investigates how the anti-commercial Burning Man Festival reproduces notions of market and exchange that it sought to escape in the first place.

Mook (1983) persuasively argues the need to distinguish between population and theoretical generalizability (see also Stewart, 1998). Mook advocates using extraordinary contexts to examine how constructs operate at extremes or as venues where complex interactions between constructs surface. He views extraordinary contexts as opportunities for uncovering the boundaries of how, when, where and under what conditions our theories apply. For example, research in more mundane contexts has shown the unfolding and dynamic character of satisfaction, and the power of 'extras' even in brief, everyday service settings (Fournier and Mick, 1999; Price, Arnould and Deibler, 1995), both theoretical insights established in the extreme context of river rafting.

How to make context work for you

In applied marketing research, a focus on context has fueled something of a revolution in practice, including the propagation of qualitative research as a valued research tool. In the service of improved product design and positioning, and improved target marketing, applied researchers have conducted research in a vast array of purchase and consumption sites, ranging from grocery store aisles to stadium parking lots, teenagers' bedrooms, kitchens, TV rooms and even showers for a host of corporate sponsors (Belk and Kozinets, 2005; El Boghdady, 2002; Kottak, 2003; McCarthy, 1998; Sherry and Kozinets, 2001).

Research context choices foreground or background particular theoretical arguments (Alford, 1998). Some researchers highlight the features of a specific context to argue that it can make some constructs, construct relationships or processes salient to observation. They also leave latent aspects of contexts unexamined. An individualistic focus may background the role of social collectivities in shaping the consumption of Harley Davidson motorcycles (Holt, 1997), world systems theory may silence the gendered voices in descriptive participant observation (Thompson, Stern and Arnould, 1998), or a focus on rituals may background the role of myth in patterning commercialized celebration (Stern, 1995).

One role of foregrounding context in studies employing qualitative data has been to highlight bias in previous studies in terms of both the populations and the processes studied. Research foregrounding samples of homeless, illiterate, middle-class minority, women, European migrant and non Euro-American consumers has examined the boundaries of our knowledge by sampling understudied consumer groups. Research has also foregrounded neglected consumption processes through context selection such as gift giving, disposition, presumption, play, ritual and so on. In this section of the chapter we will focus selectively on research addressing sociocultural, experiential, symbolic and ideological aspects of consumption published in the *Journal of Consumer Research* to uncover how to make contexts work. This research primarily employs qualitative research methods and has been summarized by Arnould and Thompson (2005) under the thematic title 'Consumer Culture Theory' (CCT).

How consumer culture theory studies use context
We can begin by asking whether a CCT research project emphasizes variations in consumers or variations across spatial or temporal circumstances as the foundation for theory building. Of course, some CCT research varies both dimensions and other CCT research does neither. Figure 9.1 provides a few examples of CCT research characterized along these axes.

As illustrated in the figure, some CCT researchers foreground variations across spatial or temporal circumstances in their research questions. For example, the theoretical insights garnered by Kozinets (2002) from his exploration of the Burning Man Festival depend on a spatial and temporal environment that contrasts with everyday consumer life,

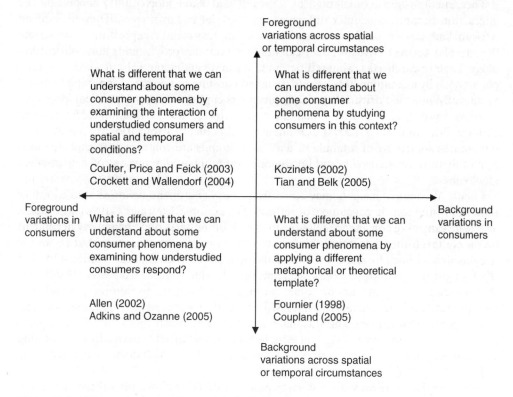

Figure 9.1 Theoretical contributions linked to variations in consumers and environments

not on variations in consumers. His research asks: what is different that we can understand about some consumer phenomena by studying consumers in this context? Specifically, what boundary conditions of consumer resistance and marketplace emancipation may we find at the Burning Man Festival? In another case, Tian and Belk (2005) study how work self and home self contend for dominance in the domain of the workplace. Researching valued possessions and the extended self in a novel spatial–temporal context (e.g., work) uncovers new theoretical insights.

By contrast, Allen's contributions (2002) do not depend on particular spatial or temporal circumstances. He could have studied choice contexts other than students' choices of higher education institutions. Instead, his research asks: what is different that we can understand about some consumer phenomena by examining how understudied consumers respond? Specifically, how does cultural capital influence the way consumers make choices? Here sampling consumers across levels of cultural capital helped to generate his theoretical contribution. In another paper, Adkins and Ozanne (2005) study low-literate consumers in order to understand the impact of literacy on buying behavior. Their implications derive from understanding how stigma linked to a consumer characteristic that varies among consumers is negotiated and mediated in market transactions. In a third study, Bernthal, Crockett and Rose (2005) reveal how individual differences in cultural capital resources pattern lifestyle regulation through credit cards and consumer debt.

Theoretical insights contributed by Crockett and Wallendorf (2004) depend on the interaction between consumer differences and spatial circumstances. They focused on African Americans in neighborhoods that varied in their racial composition to investigate the interplay between African-American families' everyday provisioning and political ideology. Their research asks: what is different that can we understand about some consumer phenomena by examining how an understudied consumer and spatial sampling interact? Specifically, how do African-American consumers employ normative political ideologies to make marketplace choices when their marketplace access is inhibited? Similarly, Coulter, Price and Feick (2003) examine a novel context (a transitional economy that represented something of a tabula rasa as far as brands are concerned) to explore variation in the way consumers' brand loyalty and commitment develop out of new political ideologies.

Finally, theoretical insights may come from the way a phenomenon is studied rather than from variations in consumers or settings. For example, Fournier's (1998) now classic article investigating consumers' relationships with brands was not particularly dependent on the context (other than North American) or the variation in consumers, but rather her insights were gleaned from the theoretical and metaphorical template of relationships that she brought to her study of consumers and brands. Her research asks: what is different that we can understand about some consumer phenomena by applying a different metaphorical and theoretical template? More recently, Coupland (2005) examines household practices that surround brands that we do not think much about but are just there – invisible brands. As with Fournier (1998), her theoretical insights derive from examining common customer activities with a new template that reveals hidden theoretical oversights.

Although the figure provides a starting point for thinking about what theoretical arguments to foreground in our selection of a sample and context, a more nuanced read of the way aspects of a context enable a theoretical payoff is required. In the next section, we select interpretive research examples corresponding to four different areas of theoretical contribution to consumer culture theory in order to uncover some of the particulars of the interplay between theory and context.

The interplay of theory and context

Table 9.1 provides a summary of some of the ways that choice of research contexts has enabled theoretical insights. The table follows Arnould and Thompson's (2005) framing and is organized around four categories of theoretical contributions associated with interpretive research in the *Journal of Consumer Research*, including consumer identity projects, marketplace cultures, sociohistoric patterning of consumption and mass-mediated marketplace ideologies and consumers' interpretive strategies. It is important to keep in mind that, although we have elaborated a particular point of contribution for the research represented, often this is not the only or even the most important contribution made by this piece of research. Moreover, this table is not intended to be all-inclusive. Much research that makes an equivalent or greater contribution to our understanding of consumer culture is not represented because of space constraints.

One thing that stands out in the table is that the value of contexts lies sometimes in its isolation of a group, process, variable or relationship that is critical for theoretical development. Moreover, across the four domains of theoretical contribution, a particular foregrounding strategy is often dominant, although multiple foregrounding strategies are present in each domain. In addition, many studies illustrate the theoretical value of selecting contexts that allow researchers to observe extreme values in domains of interest. These extreme values uncover and test our taken-for-granted assumptions about consumer beliefs and activities and help us identify the range over which particular patterns of behavior apply (Davis, 1971; Mook, 1983). Finally, examination of the table reveals that interpretive researchers often employ variants of quasi-experimental designs in order to uncover processes and differences among consumer responses.

Implicit in the table is that many perspectives are not yet represented (Fiske, 2004). For example, Adkins and Ozanne (2005), listed first in the table, make theoretical contributions to our understanding of consumer identity projects by studying illiterate consumers in a society where illiteracy is stigmatized. Further fruitful contributions might be made by exploring marketplace choices and behaviors of illiterate consumers in environments where illiteracy is not stigmatized, such as some third world contexts, or by exploring how consumers with other stigmas such as disabilities manage or negotiate those stigmas through marketplace choices (Baker and Kaufman-Scarborough, 2001; Kaufman-Scarborough, 2000). Alternatively, rather than isolating a group of consumers who are illiterate we might look for purchase contexts, such as gray markets or second-hand stores that may stigmatize consumers (Bardhi and Arnould, 2005) and examine how consumers negotiate and respond to that stigma. Hence, for each of the theoretical perspectives represented in the table, other fruitful theoretical perspectives are not represented, but could be.

Next we detail how isolating groups, processes and variables, going to extremes and drawing on some of the principles of experimental design in researcher choice of context, can facilitate theoretical payoffs.

Table 9.1 How interpretive research contexts enable theoretical contributions

Select interpretive research	Study	Contexts	Theory	Select theoretical payoff	Aspects of context that enable theoretical payoff
Consumer identity projects	Adkins and Ozanne (2005)	Illiterate consumers' marketplace behaviors	Stigma	Consumers manage their stigma through their marketplace choices and behaviors	Illiteracy is stigmatized in North America
	Bonsu and Belk (2003)	Funerals in Ghana	Identity construction	Post-mortem identity construction	Postmortem identity is a part of the life cycle in Asante
	Holt (2002)	Low income and disenfranchised consumers	Consumer resistance	While resisting marketing's cultural authority, consumers use brands as resources in identity construction	Consumer resistance to brands is evident in the socioeconomic margins in North America
	Hill and Stamey (1990)	Homeless consumers	Extended self	Consumers engage in a self-restoration process following the loss of possessions	Homeless consumers experience loss or have few possessions
	Martin (2004)	Fantasy card gamers	Consumer imagination	Consumers use multiple thematizing strategies for giving form to the evoked fantastic imaginary	Participant observation of imaginative play within a rule-governed game
	Mick and Buhl (1992)	Three brothers' interpretation of advertisements	Cultural theory of advertising	Consumers interpret advertisements through the lenses of individual life themes and projects	Siblings share sociocultural and family heritage, thus representing an internal control group
	Mick and DeMoss (1990)	Intra-personal gift giving	Gift giving theory	Self-gifts parallel dyadic gifts on three dimensions, but also develop and sustain self-concept	Gifts to the self in four circumstantial and motivational conditions
	Schau and Gilly (2003)	Personal websites	Presentation of self in everyday life	Consumers draw on virtual resources to construct and display novel selves to online publics	Self-presentation unconstrained by resources or standards of evidence
	Schouten (1991)	Consumers of aesthetic plastic surgery	Identity construction	Role transitions trigger consumers' reconstruction of their selves	Aesthetic surgery is an extreme case of identity reconstruction
	Tian and Belk (2005)	Workplace possessions	Extended self	Disconfirms the concentric spheres model of the consumer self	Work environment exposes conflicting aspects of self in North America

Marketplace cultures	Celsi, Rose and Leigh (1993)	Skydivers	Consumer risk	Consumers normalize perceptions of risk through process of risk acculturation	Regardless of level of experience, skydiving is a highly risky consumption activity
	Holt (1995)	Baseball spectators in Chicago Wrigley Field bleachers	Consumption practices	Consumers apply a range of action frameworks to their consumption encompassing play, integration, experience and classification	Consumption activity at baseball games is temporally, spatially and socially bound, exposing the variety of consumption practices
	Kates (2002)	Urban gay men	Subculture theory	Subcultural consumption is shaped by tensions internal to the subculture and contests over legitimacy	Gay subculture is a non-elective internally heterogeneous social collectivity
	Kates (2004)	Urban gay men and their brands	Cultural branding theory	Brand's social fit with a community alters the salience of brand attributes	The interplay of a non-brand community with high profile brands
	Kozinets (2001)	Star Trek fans	Subculture theory	Consumption practices are structured by mass media articulations between producers, microcultural and wider cultural meanings and practices	Star Trek is a commercial, mass media ideological product
	Kozinets (2002)	Burning Man Festival	Consumer resistance	Consumers emancipate from the marketplace through construction of a hypercommunity	The Burning Man Festival is an anti-consumption, temporary community
	Muñiz and O'Guinn (2001)	Consumers of Volvos, Macintosh and Ford Bronco	Community	Brands organize communal consumer relationships in both face-to-face and computer-mediated environments	Brands provide a resource for focalizing community sentiment
	Muñiz and Schau (2005)	Apple Newton users	Subculture theory	Brands energize mytho-religious narrative production in perpetuating the brand community, its values and beliefs	Deletion of a valued brand from a corporate portfolio threatens extinction
	Schouten and McAlexander (1995)	Harley Davidson consumers	Subculture theory	Subcultures form symbiotic relationships with marketplace institutions, expressing patriotism through their bikes	Selecting a subculture organized around a brand
Sociohistoric patterning of consumption	Allen (2002)	Students' higher education institution choices	Consumer choice theory	Identifies an embodied, intuitive and sociohistorically situated consumer choice process	Sampling extreme values along a continuum of cultural capital endowments

Table 9.1 (continued)

Select interpretive research				
Study	Contexts	Theory	Select theoretical payoff	Aspects of context that enable theoretical payoff
Arnould (1989)	Consumers in Niger	Theory of the diffusion of innovations	Reveals boundary conditions of the Eurocentric model of adoption of innovation	Tracing consumers' movement between local and global spheres of consumption uncovers processes
Askegaard, Arnould and Kjeldgaard (2005)	Greenlandic immigrants to mainland Denmark	Consumer acculturation	Transnational consumer culture represents a third acculturation agent in addition to host and home cultures	Cultural immigration without legal or political confounds found in other immigration studies
Bernthal, Crockett and Rose (2005)	Credit card usage	Practice theory	Credit card acquisition and utilization practices reveal the role of credit in the regulation of consumer lifestyles and their structuring by cultural capital	Sampling extreme values along a continuum of economic and cultural capital endowments
Commuri and Gentry (2005)	Households where women earn more than men	Household resource allocation theory	Multiple cultural models of resource allocation structure household pooling consumption decisions; separate gender ideology from economic resources	Households where women are the primary wage earners
Crockett and Wallendorf (2004)	African-American shoppers everyday provisioning	Ideology	Store patronage shapes and reshapes competing normative political ideologies	African Americans in racially homogeneous and heterogeneous neighborhoods
Curasi, Price and Arnould (2004)	Families' cherished possessions	Family (collective) identity	The role of inalienable wealth in the creation and preservation of family identity	Sample multiple generations at the family unit level
Henry (2005)	Financial management decisions	Cultural practice theory	Cultural capital resources structure marketplace empowerment, including perceptions of agency	Sampling extreme values on a continuum of cultural capital

	Author (year)	Context	Concept/theory	Description	Note
Mass-mediated marketplace ideologies and consumers' interpretive strategies	Holt (1997)	Consumer lifestyles in small town/rural setting	Consumer lifestyle	Critique of VALS; lifestyles are constructed in relation and opposition to other lifestyles	Sample lifestyle practices for varied collectivities within a bounded rural setting or shared market space
	Joy (2001)	Gift giving in Hong Kong	Social exchange theory	Gift giving practices constitute a continuum of social relationships	Comparison of gift giving practices across cultural contexts and social groups
	Joy and Sherry (2003)	Museum visitors in North America	Consumer judgment	Shows how consumers' aesthetic judgments are structured by somatic and corporeal processes	Museums are loci for practices of aesthetic consumption in the West
	Oswald (1999)	Haitian immigrant family in the United States	Consumer identity	The role of immigrant social class in ethnic identity construction through consumption	Immigrants from a single country across social class distinctions
	Coulter, Price and Feick (2003)	Eastern European women	Brand involvement	Differentiates involvement with brands from brand involvement, and changes in ideology have cascading effects on interpersonal relationships, consumption and brand involvement	Quasi-experimental before–after design allows observation of unfolding consumer brand involvement and commitment
	Holt and Thompson (2004)	Two US men	Masculinity	Through consumption choices middle- and working-class men accommodate competing ideological frameworks of masculinity in pursuit of a utopian ideal	Contrasting cases of men's prototypical consumption practices
	Kozinets et al. (2005)	American Girl Place, Chicago	Ideology	Via their interaction with the brand, families enact and reinterpret national ideologies and family history	Isolates intergenerational groups of female family members in a consumption process
	Maclaran and Brown (2005)	Powercourt, a Dublin shopping center	Utopia theory	Utopian processes structure consumer–marketer servicescape experiences accounting for divergence in satisfaction judgments before and after reconstruction of the mall	Quasi-experimental before–after design in an iconic, postmodern shopping mall

Table 9.1 (continued)

Select interpretive research	Study	Contexts	Theory	Select theoretical payoff	Aspects of context that enable theoretical payoff
	Peñaloza (2001)	Western Stock Show and rodeo	Servicescape theory	Marketers and consumers' cultural memories and multiple cultural representations reproduce the mythic tropes structuring the servicescape	The West evokes powerful mythic and historical associations for Americans
	Ritson and Elliott (1998)	Adolescents at English high schools	Cultural theory of advertising	Consumers use advertising as a cultural resource in their interpersonal interactions	Observing groups active in inter-personal identity formation and very involved in popular media
	Rose and Wood (2005)	Survivor II, Temptation Island, and the Mole TV show viewers	Authenticity	Authenticity depends on imaginative familiarity; paradoxical relationships between the exotic and the familiar	Reality TV represents itself as authentic
	Thompson (2004)	Natural health consumers	Cultural theory of advertising	Advertisements can be power discourses that allocate authority and animate constellations of consumer beliefs and behavior	Adversarial authority-based advertising about fundamental question of well-being
	Thompson and Arsel (2004)	Starbucks and local competitors	Cultural branding theory	Between-brand differentiation evolves via a dialectic between efforts to 'own' the category and consumer–marketer resistance	Hegemonic global brand and local competitors
	Thompson and Hirschman (1995)	Self narratives of 30 male and female consumers	Self concept theory	Demonstrates the role of ideology in self concept	The body is a fundamental site for the play of social, cultural and historical influences

Isolating groups

A large number of studies illustrate the value of isolating groups. Notice that such studies have made theoretical contributions in each of the four domains outlined in Arnould and Thompson (2005). For instance, studies of the homeless test the boundaries of theories of self-possession relationships contributing to our understanding of consumer identity projects (Hill and Stamey, 1990). Belk's (1988) theory suggests that homeless and other dispossessed groups are likely to seek self-restoration through objects, a pursuit that focuses on a more limited range of options than those of middle-class consumers.

Numerous interpretive studies isolate a group to enhance our understanding of marketplace cultures. For example, study of a non-elective (e.g., gay) consumer subculture contributes to our understanding of marketplace cultures by testing the boundaries of theory about subcultural values examined in other subculture research with elective subcultures (Kates, 2002). Kates (2004) argues this subculture provides a good case of an internally heterogeneous subculture given its 'rich oral and written histories that support a wide variety of dynamic contents, forms, and meanings' (p. 383). Examining emerging or dissolving subcultures also contending with internal heterogeneity might further advance our understanding.

Isolating groups is also used to enhance our understanding of the sociohistoric patterning of consumption. Studies of immigrant consumers outside of North America expose how North American consumer culture exerts an acculturating effect separate from home and host cultures (Askegaard, Arnould and Kjeldgaard, 2005), a fact concealed in studies of immigrants to North America (Peñaloza, 1994). Studies of immigrants varying in social classes test the boundaries of post-assimilationist theory developed primarily around lower class immigrants (Oswald, 1999). We could thus envision a re-inquiry of Peñaloza (1994) that sampled upper-class Mexican immigrants' acculturation in the US.

Finally, our understanding of mass-mediated marketplace ideologies and consumers' interpretive strategies is enhanced by research that isolates groups. For example, Thompson (2004) examines how advertising in the natural health marketplace deploys a Gnostic mythos that weds science and spiritualism. This mythic discourse is uncovered by isolating an interpretive community of marketers and consumers. Similarly, Ritson and Elliott (1998) enhance our understanding of advertising as a cultural resource by focusing on high school students who are both highly involved in popular media and active in interpersonal identity formation.

Isolating processes

Other interpretive studies isolate processes. Again, across all four areas of interpretive research we see examples of this theoretical foregrounding of processes. Mick and DeMoss (1990) contribute to our understanding of consumer identity projects by examining the process of intrapersonal gift giving over a range of circumstantial and motivational conditions. Our understanding of marketplace cultures is also enhanced through studies that foreground process. Holt (1995) is able to isolate a variety of consumption practices by focusing on an activity that is temporally, spatially and socially bound – in this case a baseball stadium event. An event at a racetrack, casino, soccer field, football arena or cricket pitch could perhaps have facilitated a similar theoretical contribution.

Numerous studies foreground processes as the keys to understanding the sociohistoric patterning of consumption. For example, Curasi, Price and Arnould (2004) examined cherished possessions within households and between generations, a focus that brought to light the interdependent roles of narrative, storage, use and display in intergenerational object transfers. Their design helped to reveal the process whereby alienable property is transformed into inalienable wealth.'Arnould's (1989) focus on the adoption of non-local consumer goods in Niger not only highlighted deviations from expectations based on Western models but brought to light competing acculturative globalization processes.

Finally, isolating processes aids research directed at understanding the interplay between mass-mediated marketplace ideologies and consumers' interpretive strategies. For example, multiperspectival ethnography of consumption among intergenerational groups of female family members at the American Girl Place reveals the deep involvement of the American Girl brand with both family history and national ideologies concerning gender, race, freedom and other issues (Kozinets et al., 2005).

Isolating variables or relationships
Sometimes authors use context to hold certain variables constant or relax them and examine a familiar process when they do so. Numerous examples of research that contributes to our understanding of consumer identity projects use some variant of this strategy. For example, Schau and Gilly (2003) looked at consumers' self-presentation tactics in on-line contexts where resource constraints are relaxed dramatically (cf. Solomon, 1983). Only imagination and technology access posed limitations on consumers' digital self-presentations. Mick and Buhl (1992) examined the emergence of variable life themes and projects via consumers' reception of advertisements, holding some potential influences of sociocultural and family heritage constant.

Others have informed our understanding of marketplace cultures by isolating, controlling or relaxing a variable through their choice of context. For example, brand community formation and reproduction processes in on-line environments relax the geographic criteria employed in classic community studies (Muñiz and O'Guinn, 2001). Temporary social collectivities organized around commercial brands such as Volvo or Ford Bronco illustrated the existence of a postmodern virtual community.

Our understanding of the sociohistoric patterning of consumption and the interplay of marketplace ideologies and consumers' interpretive strategy has been strengthened through research that isolates, controls or relaxes a particular variable. For example, examining reality TV has enabled intriguing insights into consumers' interpretation of authenticity (Rose and Wood, 2005). We may also delve into consumer authenticity by investigating simulated products or environments (Grayson and Martinec, 2004).

Going to extremes
As discussed earlier, the virtue of a particular context may be that it facilitates sampling of extreme values on dimensions of interest. Many of the examples we have already discussed use this foregrounding of extremes to test boundaries of our understanding or uncover processes otherwise undetectable. Cosmetic surgery and tattooing make profound and permanent marks upon the physical substrate of self-concept and image. Schouten (1991) found discussion of aesthetic surgery helped expose precipitating factors and consequences of consumers' role transitions. Bonsu and Belk (2003) found that study

of post-mortem identity in Asante led to new insights into consumer identity theory. The processes of post-mortem identity construction were more highly salient in Asante than in many cultures.

For the study of risk, Celsi, Ross and Leigh (1993) sought out a high-risk consumption subculture. The fact that the high levels of risk in skydiving do not vary significantly with experience enabled Celsi et al. (1993) to theorize novel insights into the way consumers acclimate to risk over time. Discontinuation of the focal brand of a product threatens extinction of a brand community. Muñiz and Schau (2005) found that this circumstance opened up a wealth of insights into quasi-religious narratives underlying the workings of this community, processes that would have been difficult to observe in a prospering brand community (Schouten and McAlexander, 1995).

Drawing on principles of experimental design
Table 9.1 also illustrates how drawing on the principles of experimental design in researcher selection of contexts foregrounds shifts in consumers' practices. For instance, some CCT research incorporates aspects of a before–after experimental design. Repeated probing of consumer experiences before and after renovation of an iconic shopping mall enabled Maclaran and Brown (2005) to isolate the impacts of a utopian ideological current evoked by the mall. In a study of the early diffusion of cosmetics brands in Eastern Europe, longitudinal study in a shifting cultural landscape provided a natural laboratory for study of emerging brand commitment and involvement (Coulter, Price and Feick, 2003). In particular, the use of branding strategies and large varieties of different brands were introduced to Hungary and Romania over the course of the research. Other contexts that might provide good opportunities for the study of the evolution of these constructs include Vietnam and China.

Much interpretive research resembles experiments in the way the contexts supply natural study boundaries. Many of the examples in Table 9.1 explore contexts with natural boundaries that parameterize what and who is included and not included in the study. For example, the Mountain Man Rendezvous took place in discrete locations and unfolded over a course of days (Belk and Costa, 1998). The same is true of the Burning Man Festival. Niketown, ESPNZone, Nature et Découvertes, Powerscourt, gift stores and American Girl Place share with other retail environments studied by interpretive researchers the convenience of enclosure in four walls. Similarly, a bus tour of Gettysburg, a Thanksgiving feast and a white water rafting trip exhibit convenient temporal boundaries that facilitate observation. Swap meet studies have documented a host of behavioral and symbolic processes within clearly bounded environments. On-line sites typically require participants to log in and out; behavioral rules may not cross these cyber boundaries. A semi-isolated population and market space in Pennsylvania allowed Holt (1997) to focus more clearly on between-group variations in lifestyle choices.

In summary, a discussion of Table 9.1 provides a number of guides for making decisions about context choices. A good context helps researchers isolate a group, process, variable or relationship that throws light on factors that are critical for theoretical development. Good contexts may also facilitate sampling of extreme values on dimensions of interest. Finally, certain contexts may usefully incorporate aspects of experimental design including where researchers can ask before–after types of questions or examine consumers within natural boundaries that constrain who and what is studied.

Conclusion

In this chapter we have argued that researchers can harness the potential of contexts by strategically using them to background or foreground particular theories, deciding theoretical issues to leave behind and those to invite in. Ultimately a thoughtful use of research contexts may contribute to a better understanding of our lives as human beings and consumers. We have suggested some specific guidelines for thinking about contexts, inviting researchers to select contexts that test the theoretical boundaries of constructs and relationships; contexts that are prototypical or exemplars of important consumer phenomena; and contexts that highlight responses at odds with prior research. Nevertheless, in closing, it is important to introduce two additional points.

First, what constitutes a good context in the abstract is not necessarily the same as the context that will engage *your* emotions and senses. A good context is not necessarily the same as one that will stimulate *your* sense of adventure and discovery. Neither is it one that does not converge with *your* own experience and *your* horizon of expectations. 'Good' contexts are those that fascinate the researcher and hopefully her audience as well. Ultimately contexts should fit researchers as much as they fit theoretical domains. Contexts that are readily accessible and exciting to one researcher may be inaccessible and/or unexciting to another. Holt (1995) sat in the bleachers at Chicago Cubs baseball games not just out of intellectual curiosity, but also out of an abiding affection for the Cubs. Kates (2002) mobilized shared demographics that enabled him to hang out with members of the gay community in Toronto, measuring his own responses against the responses of others. Martin (2004) lurked in an on-line gaming community in which he himself was involved. Peñaloza (1994) had to overcome class and linguistic barriers to gain acceptance from immigrant consumers although shared ethnic affiliation facilitated entrée. Researchers look for a match not only between a context and a theory, but also between a context and themselves.

Second, while we have argued for a more systematic examination of the relationship between context and theory in advance of selecting a context, contexts that are culturally significant and sociologically rich, intrinsically interesting some would say, have proved to support an array of theoretically compelling studies in part because they reflect great diversity and depth of significance for vast numbers of people. Harley Davidson rallies, baseball games or the Western Stock Show (Peñaloza, 2001) are locales in which diverse groups of people congeal around events and symbols that are powerfully resonant for North Americans. Similarly, Asante funerals play a very fundamental role in social ordering processes and their enactment draws in participants from all corners of the social spectrum (Bonsu and Belk, 2003). Selecting a consumer context that is significant in the lives of many people and that seems to have paradoxical or problematic elements in the researchers' own mind, when combined with careful study and thick description, is likely to result in a meaningful story with theoretical power.

Note

1.   The authors thank Russell W. Belk for extending our time line and providing multiple helpful suggestions for improving the manuscript.

References

Adkins, Natalie Ross and Julie L. Ozanne (2005), 'The low literate consumer', *Journal of Consumer Research*, **32** (June), 93–106.

Alford, Robert R. (1998), *The Craft of Inquiry: Theories, Methods and Evidence*, New York: Oxford University Press.

Allen, Douglas (2002), 'Toward a theory of consumer choice as sociohistorically shaped practical experience: the fits-like-a-glove (FLAG) framework', *Journal of Consumer Research*, **28** (March), 515–32.

Arnould, Eric J. (1989), 'Toward a broadened theory of preference formation and the diffusion of innovations: cases from Zinder-Province, Niger-Republic', *Journal of Consumer Research*, **16** (2), 239–67.

Arnould, Eric J. and Jakki J. Mohr (2005), 'Dynamic transformations of an indigenous market cluster: the leatherworking industry in Niger', *Journal of the Academy of Marketing Science*, **33** (Summer), 254–74.

Arnould Eric J. and Linda L. Price (1993), ' "River Magic": hedonic consumption and the extended service encounter', *Journal of Consumer Research*, **20** (June), 24–45.

Arnould, Eric J. and Craig J. Thompson (2005), 'Consumer culture theory (CCT): twenty years of research', *Journal of Consumer Research*, **31** (March), 868–83.

Arnould Eric J., Linda L. Price and Patrick Tierney (1998), 'Communicative staging of the wilderness servicescape', *Service Industries Journal*, **18** (3), 90–115.

Askegaard, Søren, Eric J. Arnould and Dannie Kjeldgaard (2005), 'Post-assimilationist ethnic consumer research: qualifications and extensions', *Journal of Consumer Research*, **31** (June), 160–71.

Baker, Stacey Menzel and Carol Kaufman-Scarborough (2001), 'Marketing and public accommodation: a retrospective on Title III of the Americans with Disabilities Act', *Journal of Public Policy & Marketing*, **20** (Fall), 297–305.

Bardhi, Fleura and Eric J. Arnould (2005), 'Thrift shopping: combining utilitarian thrift and hedonic treat benefits', *Journal of Consumer Behaviour*, **4** (4), 223–33.

Becker, Howard S. (1998), *Tricks of the Trade: How to Think About Your Research While You're Doing It*, Chicago: University of Chicago Press.

Belk, Russell W. (1988), 'Possessions and the extended self', *Journal of Consumer Research*, **15** (2), 139–68.

Belk, Russell W. (1995), 'Studies in the new consumer behaviour', in Daniel Miller (ed.), *Acknowledging Consumption*, New York: Routledge, pp. 58–95.

Belk, Russell W. and Janeen A. Costa (1998), 'The mountain man myth: a contemporary consuming fantasy', *Journal of Consumer Research*, **25** (3), 218–40.

Belk, Russell W. and Robert V. Kozinets (2005), 'Videography in marketing and consumer research', *Qualitative Market Research*, **8** (2), 128–42.

Belk, Russell W., Melanie Wallendorf and John F. Sherry (1989), 'The sacred and the profane in consumer behavior: theodicy on the Odyssey', *Journal of Consumer Research*, **16** (June), 1–38.

Bernthal, Matthew J., David Crockett and Randall L. Rose (2005), 'Credit cards as lifestyle facilitators', *Journal of Consumer Research*, **32** (June), 130–46.

Bonsu, Samuel K. and Russell W. Belk (2003), 'Do not go cheaply into that good night: death-ritual consumption in Asante, Ghana', *Journal of Consumer Research*, **30** (June), 41–55.

Bristor, Julia M. and Eileen Fischer (1993), 'Feminist thought: implications for consumer research', *Journal of Consumer Research*, **19** (March), 518–36.

Burawoy, Michael (1998), 'The extended case method', *Sociological Theory*, **16** (1), 4–33.

Celsi, Richard, Randall Rose and Thomas Leigh (1993), 'An exploration of high-risk leisure consumption through skydiving', *Journal of Consumer Research*, **20** (June), 1–21.

Commuri, Suraj and James W. Gentry (2005), 'Resource allocation in households with women as chief wage earners', *Journal of Consumer Research*, **32** (September), 185–96.

Coulter, Robin A., Linda L. Price and Lawrence Feick (2003), 'The origins of involvement and brand commitment: insights from postsocialist Central Europe', *Journal of Consumer Research*, **30** (September), 170–83.

Coupland, Jennifer Chang (2005), 'Invisible brands: an ethnography of households and the brands in their kitchen pantries', *Journal of Consumer Research*, **32** (1), 106–18.

Cova, Bernard (1997), 'Community and consumption: towards a definition of the "linking value" of product or services', *European Journal of Marketing*, **31** (3), 297–316.

Crockett, David and Melanie Wallendorf (2004), 'The role of normative political ideology in consumer behavior', *Journal of Consumer Research*, **31** (December), 511–29.

Curasi, Carolyn, Linda Price and Eric Arnould (2004), 'How individuals' cherished possessions become families' inalienable wealth', *Journal of Consumer Research*, **31** (December).

Davis, Murray S. (1971), 'That's interesting! Towards a phenomenology of sociology and a sociology of phenomenology', *Philosophy of the Social Sciences*, **1** (December), 309–44.

El Boghdady, D. (2002), 'Naked truth meets market research', *The Washington Post*, 24 February, H1, H4–H5.

Ellsworth, Phoebe C. (1977), 'From abstract ideas to concrete instances: some guidelines for choosing natural research settings', *American Psychologist* (August), 604–15.

Emigh, Rebecca J. (1997), 'The power of negative thinking: the use of negative case methodology in the development of sociological theory', *Theory and Society*, **26**, 649–84.

Fernandez, James W. (1986), *Persuasions and Performances: The Play of Tropes in Culture*, Bloomington: Indiana University Press.

Fiske, Susan T. (2004), 'Developing a program of research', in Carol Sansone, Carolyn C. Morf and A.T. Panter (eds), *Handbook of Methods in Social Psychology*, Thousand Oaks, CA: Sage Publications, pp. 71–90.

Fournier, Susan (1998), 'Consumers and their brands: developing relationship theory in consumer research', *Journal of Consumer Research*, **24** (4), 343–73.

Fournier, Susan and David Glen Mick (1999), 'Rediscovering satisfaction', *Journal of Marketing*, **63** (October), 5–23.

Glaser, Barney G. and Anselm L. Strauss (1967), *Discovery of Grounded Theory: Strategies for Qualitative Research*, New York: Aldine de Guyter.

Grayson, Kent and Radan Martinec (2004), 'Consumer perceptions of iconicity and indexicality and their influence on assessments of authentic market offerings', *Journal of Consumer Research*, **31** (September), 296–313.

Henry, Paul C. (2005), 'Social class, market situation, and consumers' metaphors of (dis)empowerment', *Journal of Consumer Research*, **31** (March), 766–79.

Hill, Ronald Paul and Mark Stamey (1990), 'The homeless in America: an examination of possessions and consumption behaviors', *Journal of Consumer Research*, **17** (3), 303–21.

Holt, Douglas B. (1995), 'How consumers consume: a typology of consumption practices', *Journal of Consumer Research*, **22** (June), 1–16.

Holt, Douglas B. (1997), 'Poststructuralist lifestyle analysis: conceptualizing the social patterning of consumption', *Journal of Consumer Research*, **23** (March), 326–50.

Holt, Douglas B. (2002), 'Why do brands cause trouble? A dialectical theory of consumer culture and branding', *Journal of Consumer Research*, **29** (June), 70–90.

Holt, Douglas B. and Craig J. Thompson (2004), 'Man-of-action heroes: the pursuit of heroic masculinity in everyday consumption', *Journal of Consumer Research*, **31** (September), 425–40.

Joy, Annamma S. (2001), 'Gift giving in Hong Kong and the continuum of social ties', *Journal of Consumer Research*, **28** (September), 239–56.

Joy, Annamma S. and John F. Sherry (2003), 'Speaking of art as embodied imagination: a multi-sensory approach to understanding aesthetic experience', *Journal of Consumer Research*, **30** (September), 259–82.

Kates, Steven M. (2002), 'The Protean quality of subcultural consumption: an ethnographic account of gay consumers', *Journal of Consumer Research*, **29** (December), 383–99.

Kates, Steven M. (2004), 'The dynamics of brand legitimacy: an interpretive study in the gay men's community', *Journal of Consumer Research*, **31** (September), 455–65.

Kaufman-Scarborough, Carol (2000), 'Seeing through the eyes of the color-deficient shopper: consumer issues for public policy', *Journal of Consumer Policy*, **23** (December), 461–93.

Kottak, N. (2003), 'A pilot market research study of the oasis tents & Jets tailgating, presentation to the New York Jets January 23, 2003', Ethnographic Solutions, LLC (retrieved April 28, 2005 from http://www.ethnographic-solutions.com/pages/nyjets.htm).

Kozinets, Robert V. (1997), '"I want to believe": a nethnography of the X-Philes' subculture of consumption', in Merrie Brucks and Debbie J. MacInnis (eds), *Advances in Consumer Research*, vol. 24, Provo, UT: Association for Consumer Research, pp. 470–75.

Kozinets, Robert V. (2001), 'Utopian enterprise: articulating the meaning of Star Trek's culture of consumption', *Journal of Consumer Research*, **28** (June), 67–89.

Kozinets, Robert V. (2002), 'Can consumers escape the market? Emancipatory illuminations from Burning Man', *Journal of Consumer Research*, **29** (June), 20–38.

Kozinets, Robert, John F. Sherry, Mary Ann McGrath, Stefania Borghini, Nina Diamond and Albert Muniz (2005), 'American Girl: the family brand', in Geeta Menon and Ashkary R. Rao (eds), *Advances in Consumer Research*, vol. 32, Valdosta, GA: Association for Consumer Research, pp. 10–11.

Lakoff, George and Mark Johnson (1980), *Metaphors We Live By*, Chicago: University of Chicago Press.

Maclaran, Pauline and Stephen Brown (2005), 'The center cannot hold: consuming the utopian marketplace', *Journal of Consumer Research*, **32** (September), 311–23.

Martin, Brett A.S. (2004), 'Using the imagination: consumer evoking and thematizing of the fantastic imaginary', *Journal of Consumer Research*, **31** (June), 136–50.

McCarthy, M. (1998), 'Stalking the elusive teenage trendsetter', *Wall Street Journal*, 19 November, B1: B10.

McCracken, Grant (1988), *The Long Interview*, Thousand Oaks: Sage University Press.

McGuire, William J. (1997), 'Creative hypothesis generating in psychology: some useful heuristics', *Annual Review of Psychology*, **48**, 1–30.

Mick, David Glen and Claus Buhl (1992), 'A meaning-based model of advertising experiences', *Journal of Consumer Research*, **19** (3), 317–38.

Mick, David Glen and Michelle Demoss (1990), 'Self-gifts: phenomenological insights from four contexts', *Journal of Consumer Research*, **17** (December), 322–32.

Mook, Douglas G. (1983), 'In defense of external invalidity', *American Psychologist* (April), 379–87.

Muñiz, Albert and Thomas C. O'Guinn (2001), 'Brand communities', *Journal of Consumer Research*, **27** (March), 412–32.
Muñiz, Albert and Hope Schau (2005), 'Religiosity in the abandoned Apple Newton brand community', *Journal of Consumer Research*, **31** (March), 737–48.
Oswald, Laura R. (1999), 'Culture swapping: consumption and the ethnogenesis of middle-class Haitian immigrants', *Journal of Consumer Research*, **25** (March), 303–18.
Peñaloza, Lisa (1994), 'Atravesando fronteras/border crossings: a critical ethnographic exploration of the consumer acculturation of Mexican immigrants', *Journal of Consumer Research*, **21** (June), 32–54.
Peñaloza, Lisa (1998), 'Just doing it: a visual ethnographic study of spectacular consumption behavior at Nike Town', *Consumption, Markets & Culture*, **2** (4), 337–400.
Peñaloza, Lisa (2001), 'Consuming the American West: animating cultural meaning at a stock show and Rodeo', *Journal of Consumer Research*, **28** (December), 369–98.
Price, Linda L., Eric J. Arnould and Carolyn Folkman Curasi (2000), 'Older consumers' disposition of special possessions', *Journal of Consumer Research*, **27** (2), 179–201.
Price, Linda L., Eric J. Arnould and Sheila L. Deibler (1995), 'Service provider influence on consumers' emotional response to service encounters', *International Journal of Service Industry Management*, **6** (3), 34–63.
Ritson, Mark and Richard Elliott (1998), 'The social uses of advertising: an ethnographic study of adolescent advertising audiences', *Journal of Consumer Research*, **26** (December), 260–77.
Rose, Randall L. and Stacy L. Wood (2005), 'Paradox and the consumption of authenticity through reality television', *Journal of Consumer Research*, **32** (September), 284–97.
Schau, Hope Jensen and Mary C. Gilly (2003), 'We are what we post? Self-presentation in personal web space', *Journal of Consumer Research*, **30** (December), 385–404.
Schouten, John W. (1991), 'Selves in transition: symbolic consumption in personal rites of passage and identity reconstruction', *Journal of Consumer Research*, **17** (March), 412–26.
Schouten, John and James H. McAlexander (1995), 'Subcultures of consumption: an ethnography of the new bikers', *Journal of Consumer Research*, **22** (June), 43–61.
Sherry, John F. (1998), 'The soul of the company store: Nike Town Chicago and the emplaced brandscape', in John F. Sherry (ed.), *ServiceScapes: The Concept of Place in Contemporary Markets*, Chicago, IL: NTC Business Books, pp. 109–46.
Sherry, John F. and Robert V. Kozinets (2001), 'Qualitative inquiry in marketing and consumer research', in Dawn Iacobucci and L. Krishnamurthi (eds), *Kellogg on Marketing*, New York: John Wiley & Sons, pp. 165–94.
Smith, Scott, S. Jason Cole, Dan Fisher, Jeff B. Murray and Molly Rapert (2005), 'Gearhead pilgrimage: the Queen Mary summit of Indiana Jones', film presented at the Annual Conference of the Association for Consumer Research, 31 September, San Antonio, TX.
Solomon, Michael R. (1983), 'The role of products as social stimuli: a symbolic interactionism perspective', *Journal of Consumer Research*, **10** (December), 319–29.
Stern, Barbara B. (1995), 'Consumer myths: Frye's taxonomy and the structural analysis of consumption text', *Journal of Consumer Research*, **22** (September), 165–85.
Stewart, Alex (1998), *The Ethnographer's Method*, Thousand Oaks, CA: Sage Publications.
Sutton, Robert I. and Barry M. Staw (1995), 'What theory is not', *Administrative Science Quarterly*, **40**, 371–84.
Thompson, Craig J. (2004), 'Marketplace mythology and discourses of power', *Journal of Consumer Research*, **31** (June), 162–81.
Thompson, Craig J. and Zeynep Arsel (2004), 'The Starbucks brandscape and consumers' (anticorporate) experiences of glocalization', *Journal of Consumer Research*, **31** (December), 631–43.
Thompson, Craig J. and Diana L. Haytko (1997), 'Speaking of fashion: consumers' uses of fashion discourses and the appropriation of countervailing cultural meanings', *Journal of Consumer Research*, **24** (1), 15–42.
Thompson, Craig J. and Elizabeth C. Hirschman (1995), 'Understanding the socialized body: a poststructuralist analysis of consumers' self-conceptions, body images, and self-care practices', *Journal of Consumer Research*, **22** (September), 139–53.
Thompson, Craig T., Barbara B. Stern and Eric J. Arnould (1998), 'Writing the differences: postmodern pluralism, retextualization, and the construction of reflexive ethnographic narratives in consumer research', *Consumption, Markets, and Culture*, **2** (September), 105–60.
Tian, Kelly and Russell W. Belk (2005), 'Extended self and possessions in the workplace', *Journal of Consumer Research*, **32** (September), 297–310.
Walton, John (1992), 'Making the theoretical case', in Charles C. Ragin and Howard S. Becker (eds), *What is a Case? Exploring the Foundations of Social Inquiry*, Cambridge: Cambridge University Press, pp. 121–37.
Wells, William D. (1993), 'Discovery-oriented consumer research', *Journal of Consumer Research*, **19** (4), 489–504.
Zaltman, Gerald (1983), 'Presidential address', in Richard P. Bagozzi and Alice M. Tybout (eds), *Advances in Consumer Research*, vol. 10, Provo, UT: Association for Consumer Research, pp. 1–5.

PART IV

DATA COLLECTION METHODS

10 Netnography 2.0
Robert V. Kozinets

Introduction

The world is changing. Maps are being redrawn, boundaries shifting, old ethnic groups re-merging, and new cultures proliferating. The multifarious and multiplicative nature of human culture is brought into high relief through even a cursory examination of the vast sphere of networked communications glossed in its glorious totality as the Internet. The Internet mutates on a second-by-second basis and in this chapter I take into consideration some recent mutations to update a methodology I initially developed at the beginning of the Internet's rise as a forum of consumer-to-consumer communications.

It is almost inconceivable to think that such a dominant and currently nearly indispensable innovation (Hoffman, Novak and Venkatesh, 2004) began as recently as 1969, the same year, incidentally, of the first manned moon landing. That year, four remote computers at UCLA, Stanford, UC-Santa Barbara and the University of Utah were linked together into the original ARPANET, a military–academic construction initially intended as a national defense project. As human networks tend to do, the (ARPA)net expanded, drawing in more of human society, building connections both obvious and sublime with corporate information technology structures and burgeoning home networks like AOL, Prodigy and CompuServe and eventually bursting forth in the mid-1990s as a full-blown mass commercial and cultural phenomenon.

The online, or virtual, communities of the Internet have expanded from small cloisters of academic–military personnel to encompass practically the entire range of human social behavior, everything from beading to bondage, political spoofing to terrorist-proofing, i-banking to e-dating. Seven years ago, I wrote about the many glorious varieties of netnographic experience, sketching the types of online community capable of being studied using an anthropological methodology adapted to the computer-mediated communication context.

For this chapter, I begin by overviewing the netnographic method and providing an abbreviated primer on netnographic methodology. In so doing I will also update the method and the field sites available to it, noting the many changes that have happened at lightning speed in the development of the Internet. I will also respond to some recent critiques of the netnographic procedures I advocated. In a final section, I will briefly explore the netnographic possibilities of blogs, one of the new communal forms, sketching their contours and mapping their exciting possibilities for further study. To close, I will suggest (with some more concrete examples) how marketers and market researchers might deploy netnography to keep pace with some trends and transformations in online community and communication.

Netnography revisited

Netnography, or online ethnography, certainly can be and has been applied to research questions concerning many interests of social scientists, from human sexual expression

(Correll, 1995; Hamman, 1997; Turkle, 1995) to game playing (McMahan, 2003) to disabled groups (Nelson, 1994). I originally developed and defined the technique during my thesis work on fan communities in 1995 as directed at what I then termed 'virtual communities of consumption' (Kozinets, 1997, 1998, 1999, 2002). The method was positioned as 'market-oriented': in truth it is of course agnostic as to application. The methodology adapts ethnographic research techniques to the study of cultures and communities emerging through computer-mediated communications and uses information publicly available in online forums. One of the main applications I have been interested in is the identification and understanding of the needs and decision influences of relevant online consumer groups.

In my central explication of the technique, I compared online ethnography with its offline variant and discussed the similarities and differences of their field procedures and methodological issues (Kozinets, 2002). These procedures include (1) making cultural entrée, (2) gathering and analyzing data, (3) conducting ethical research, and (4) providing opportunities for culture member feedback. Although I defer the most detailed elaboration of these techniques to that *Journal of Marketing Research* article, in keeping with the primer nature of this chapter, I will provide an updated overview of these procedures.

Entrée
As preparation for undertaking a netnography, I recommended that researchers initially have a set of specific marketing research topics or questions in which they are interested, and next that they identify particular online forums that might help to inform them about these topics and answer their questions. I also recommended that market researchers study the forums, groups and individual participants in them, and that online search engines would prove very valuable in this pursuit. As the Internet has grown and changed, so too have changed the search engines and the forums for undertaking consumer and marketing research. Search engines like google.com, MSN.com and Yahoo! currently have group search options that allow one to search newsgroup and blog archives. There are also a number of high-quality blog search engines available designed specifically for that space, including my current favorites Feedster.com, bloglines.com and Technorati.

In Kozinets (1999), I considered that there were five main forums for this communication: chat rooms, bulletin boards, playspace dungeons, lists and rings of interlinked webpages. As I consider them now, I would hypothesize that these forums varied in their communicative formats (e.g., WWW web-page, Bitnet board, Messenger chatroom), their central objectives (ludic, informational, social), their temporal orientations (synchronous/ real-time versus asynchronous/time-delayed) and their interpersonal modalities (individual broadcast, one-on-one, group, corporate). These categories tend to bleed into one another, and considerable overlap between them exists, as we find in all similar cultural categorization schemes.

To provide a broad-based recap, rooms are computer-mediated places in which two or more people gather together for primarily social objectives, interacting synchronously – in real time – usually without any fantasy role-playing (but often with a complex symbol system of acronyms, shortcuts and emoticons). Boards are distinct online communities organized around interest-specific electronic bulletin boards. People post messages, others reply and over time these messages (despite frequent digressions) form a reasonably coherent, traceable, asynchronous, conversational 'thread'. Dungeons (named from the original text-base game environment where players played Dungeons & Dragons) are any computer-generated environments where one or more people socially interact through the structured format of role- and game-playing. Lists are groups of people who gather together on a single e-mail mailing list in order to share information about a particular topic of mutual interest. Rings are organizations of related web-pages that are linked together and structured by interest.

I made some characterizations of these spaces that I believed were largely true at the time, such as that rooms are spaces populated principally by minglers and visitors, and that, in rooms, people primarily expressed relational and, secondarily, recreational inter-action modes. Similarly, I averred that the membership of boards contains a respectable concentration of insiders and devotees, and few minglers, and my netnographic writing thus far has tended to strongly favor boards as forums for the investigation of consumption and market-related issues and themes. Boards, I have stated, offer one of the best places to find consumption-related topics and the consumption-related communities of consumption that follow them, and my own netnographic research tends to focus on them (see Brown, Kozinets and Sherry, 2003a; Kozinets, 2001, 2002; Kozinets and Sherry, 2004; Kozinets and Handelman, 2004). Judging from their use in other consumer researcher's work (e.g., Langer and Beckman, 2005; Muñiz and O'Guinn, 2001; Muñiz and Schau, 2005; Schouten and McAlexander, 1995), this supposition seems supported.

Given the changing nature of the Internet, its expanding universe of forms and influences and the fluid migration of people between these forms, I do not believe that boards should enjoy a privileged status in our researching of online communities of consumption. Blogs, or web logs, in particular are ascendant right now as a forum for individual information that becomes a focus of communal response. As with all techno-fads, no doubt their popularity will wane. Instant messaging windows (chat, or rooms) have been used very effectively by Giesler (2006) in his study of the Napster community. I believe that they offer considerable potential as places where dyads and groups converse and share ideas (as I will detail later in this chapter). Finally, the playspaces I glossed as dungeons are coming of age as massively multiplayer online games (MMOGs) and environments.

Amazingly, at $135 million, the Sony Everquest game's local economy tops the GDP of the actual nation of Anguilla. These online environments are becoming more detailed and more commercialized. For instance, Massive Inc. is a new business dedicated currently to serving up dynamic ads to users of online games. After a decade, retail field sites online are reaching the maturity stage. The online universe has never been more populated or more filled with activity than it is this very moment.

Anywhere there is online consumer activity and interaction, there are interesting sources of data for consumer and marketing researchers and the potential for netnography to reveal insights about online communal consumer culture, practices and meanings. As the Internet continues to grow, these techniques become even more relevant to general audiences and contemporary understandings, and any changes made to adapt to transformations in its digital environment can only serve to make it more useful.

As recommended in Kozinets (2002), I still believe that researchers, whether they are studying online gaming groups, political blogs or book shoppers, need to favor studying online communities that (1) relate to their research question, (2) have more 'traffic' of different message posters (unless the focus seeks depth of understanding and willingly trades numbers for richness), (3) offer more detailed or descriptively rich data (as blogs and chat might), and (4) offer more social interactions.

Data collection and analysis
Data collection is directed at capturing three different types of data. The first is data that the researcher directly copies from the computer-mediated communications of online community members. The prodigious amount of this information and the ease of its downloading can make handling it daunting. The researcher may require a level or several levels of filtering for relevance. Second is data that the researcher inscribes regarding observations of the community, its members, interactions and meanings, and the researcher's own participation. Finally, netnographers may wish to approach individuals and interview them. E-mail is a common forum for this, but so too is chat or Instant Messaging. A caveat applies here. The current text-based IM tends to provide very different kinds of responses, as the communicative style of chat or IM-ing is much more distinct and abbreviated and far less like conventional written text. However, different does not necessarily mean worse or better. Over time, the chat style of text can offer many rich insights, but these insights may look less like the familiar textual verbatims that researchers are used to seeing. I write later in this chapter about some technological solutions that may alter the chat experience.

In a recent article, Langer and Beckman (2005) suggested that netnography should be considered to be more like content analysis, an established communication studies technique. My perspective is that netnography should never be tied too closely with any one particular method of data collection and analysis. As a form of ethnography, netnography encompasses multiple methods, approaches and analytic techniques. Experienced ethnographers are inevitably bricoleurs, and I would fully expect netnographers to deploy any of a number of techniques as they approach the rich lived worlds of cultural experience that people share and experience online. These techniques would include projective techniques, historical analysis, semiotic analysis, visual analysis, musical analysis, survey work, content analysis, kinesics and any of a world of specialties, as well as the more obvious observational, participative, and interview techniques. In a gender-based netnographic analysis, Pauline Maclaran, Miriam Caterall, Margaret Hogg and I have been adapting discourse analysis techniques to the netnographic datastream (some of our methodological thoughts are published in Maclaran et al., 2004).

I view netnography as necessarily multi-method. The methods that should be chosen depend on the research questions considered and the strengths of the researcher. The netnographic investigation undertaken by Langer and Beckman (2005), with Askegaard, which involved online bulletin boards, e-mail, face-to-face interviews, and literature and media archive research, stands as a good example of the type of multi-pronged multi-method study that characterizes ethnography and netnography. All that may be required for an investigation to be netnographic (and which would, for instance, differentiate a survey used as part of a netnography from an online survey that was not) is that the data collection be analyzed to understand consumers in the online communal and cultural context in which they are embedded, rather than that the analysis be conducted so as to strip out context and present consumers or their practices as more general representatives of a wider group or more universalized phenomenon.

Some of the confusion about linking netnography with appropriate methods may have come as a result of the lack of clarity regarding the different types of netnography that are possible. In particular, I would like to specify that the extent of research participation in an online community can definitely vary between netnographies. As Figure 10.1 illustrates,

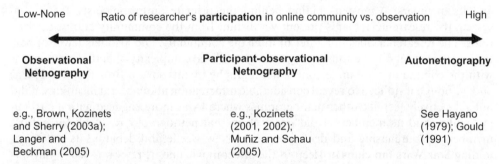

Figure 10.1   A spectrum of different types of netnography

there is a spectrum of researcher participation in online (and related offline) communities that includes participating in interactions, practices, exchanges and information. This can vary from a very distanced participation to one that is highly involved, and the representations of netnography that ensue from these approaches can diverge significantly.

My involvement in coffee connoisseur (Kozinets, 2002), Star Trek fan (2001) and X-Phile (1997) communities was high. I revealed myself to both groups, I participated and posted. For the coffee community, I traveled to different coffee retailers, bought and sampled different types of coffee. For Star Trek and X-Philes fans, I commented on television shows, joined fan clubs and the actual Board of Directors of a fan club and a Toronto Star Trek convention, and also attended conventions as a fan, buying paraphernalia, standing in line for autographs, meeting Star Trek stars. In Kozinets (2002), I advocated the participative element of netnography, as this form of close ethnography internalizes emic meanings and allows the netnographer to speak with authority as a member who represents other members of that culture. In these investigations, I moderated my participative online and offline role, balancing it with significant observation of online communities and embodied culture members and interviews with members.

However, the participative element could be taken to a logical extreme, and netnographies conducted following almost pure participation that become intensively introspective. Following the autoethnographic example of David Hayano (1979) or of Stephen Gould (1991), I can envision 'autonetnographies' where individuals reflect on their own online experiences and then use these field notes and observations to provide insights into online consumer practices and meanings. Indeed Bruce Weinberg initiated such a venture with his Internet 24/7 project (see http://www.internetshopping247.com/). After making a vow to do all of his shopping and make all of his purchases over the Internet, Weinberg kept a web-log (an early blog) about his experiences. Sidney Levy (2001), writing about Weinberg's blog, compared it to the famous seventeenth-century diary of Samuel Pepys. As he stated, 'Making use of a sample of one person is an old tradition. Individuals may be used as respondents who tell about themselves and as informants about other people as well. Samuel Pepys's diary tells us a lot about himself and about life in England in the middle of the seventeenth century, and Bruce Weinberg's diary tells us a lot about himself and modern life.'

At the other extreme from Weinberg's autobiographical/autonetnographic blog, and apparently far more commonplace, is the purely observational netnography. In this form of netnography, the researcher does not reveal him or herself to the online community and its members. Almost as hiding behind the primate anthropologist's traditional screen, the researcher remains present yet distant from the community and its interactions. The researcher does not enter or alter the community, and also has fewer opportunities to learn about the community through the lived complexity of actual interactions with the community. We undertook a netnography of this sort in Brown et al. (2003a) and, although it sufficed to reveal considerable information about brand meanings, it did not subjectively feel like other netnographies where I was more engaged with a particular culture and its members. I did not seek in that netnography to speak for culture members by purchasing and driving my own New Beetle and debating its merits, or joining Star Wars fan clubs or sleep-in-the-street movie lines (Przywara, 2001), but was content to describe their brand meanings and interactions from afar. Langer and Beckman (2005) assert that the more distanced form should be the norm for netnographies because it is unobtrusive. However, I argue here and elsewhere that this unobtrusiveness comes at a heavy cost. As with in-person ethnographies, the likelihood of changing behavior in many of these communities because of the presence of a careful and considerate researcher can actually be quite small, and the amount of understanding sacrificed can be quite large.

As Figure 10.1 illustrates, many netnographies, and the type that I have generally advocated, fall in the middle-range on the participation-observational axis. They seek to balance the obtrusiveness of introspecting, autobiographical researcher revelation with the distance of the purely observational mode. As inherent in the very nature of ethnography, the middle-range netnography seeks to tack back and forth between the emics of experientially close observation of online communities and cultures and the etics of experientially distant, theoretically focused representation of them. The standards for good ethnography, such as immersion, internalization, awareness of alterity and engagement, translate online, and translate into good netnography.

In terms of data analysis, I recommend the potential of a similar panoply of techniques. I see value in grounded theory approaches (see Fischer and Otnes, in this volume) and other approaches that take advantage of the online interaction's contextual richness. Although content analysis techniques and software have their place, I strongly suggest the use of penetrating metaphoric, hermeneutic and symbolic interpretation to reveal netnographic data's more profound insights, rather than relying solely upon the alleged 'rigor' of decontextualized classification of textual data.

Research ethics
A major area of interest has surrounded the netnographic procedures that I suggested to preserve good research ethics. Langer and Beckman (2005, p. 195) assert that these ethical guidelines are 'far too rigorous' and 'also endanger the unobtrusiveness of online communications studies'. I appreciate these pragmatic research concerns, and hope that expanding upon them here may contribute to the discussion and help to clarify the topic for other netnographers and for online researchers in general. As I asserted in Kozinets (2002), ethical concerns over netnography are based on two nontrivial, contestable and interrelated concerns: are the online sites used to be considered a private or a public site, and what constitutes informed consent in cyberspace? Although we have had five years to settle these issues, clear consensus has still not emerged. We are, however, much closer to an understanding of the first question.

Researchers in most online forums, upon making contact with the individuals posting to or interacting within them, can quickly ascertain whether the forum is consensually considered to be a public or private space. There are many of both, and determining this should be one of the netnographer's first concerns. If it is a private space, permission to post and to use posts is absolutely essential. If it is public, then I would still suggest that there is the need for informed consent in certain circumstances and for the use of certain kinds of information.

A confession: my standards may be more stringent than those of your Institutional Review Board. I would assert in my own defense that academics should be held to a higher standard, given the potential for netnography to do harm to communities or individuals, as numerous ethnographies have done. Sensitive information is present in chat rooms that, if overheard and shared, might lead to embarrassment or ostracism. The biggest question regards informed consent, and I believe that this should only be considered when using a direct quote from a consumer. Using contemporary search engines, many netnographic quotes and verbata are easily traceable to other identifiers of a contributor to the research; this is the reason for my stringency. In Langer and Beckman's (2005, p. 197) study of the sensitive topic of cosmetic surgery, they publish user names as posted on surgery-oriented newsgroups. They also tell us that, of the people posting, 43 posted personal mail addresses or phone numbers. It is thus possible to use the verbatim data in the article, to enter it into a search engine, and to have that search engine retrieve the connection to the entire message. From that information, any moderately motivated reader of the article might find the phone number of a particular 'participant' in the published research study and contact them, without that 'participant' even realizing that they had participated in Langer and Beckman's study.

To be fair to Langer and Beckman, they are using an established communication studies approach and its guiding metaphor to argue their point about netnographic research ethics. This approach treats all online postings as if they were published or broadcast works. Many published studies have taken this approach. The online community member is assumed to be analogous to someone who writes and signs a 'letter to the editor' in a newspaper (Langer and Beckman, 2005, p. 197). However letters to the editor offer an 'anonymous' category. Some posters have neither the time nor the technical knowledge to make their posting truly anonymous (and search technologies are quite sophisticated at identifying individual users).

Although there are similarities, online communications also have some important differences from published works. What are we to make of real-time conversations in, say, an online dating chat room? If we are studying the consumption of such spaces, are we entitled to report on the goings on, and provide identifying details like user names, without people's permission? Should researchers repeat some of the mistakes made by word-of-mouth marketers and go into chat rooms and deceive the consumers there, asking them questions as if we were fellow-consumers, without revealing our own identities and agendas? I firmly believe the answers here are no and no. We cannot act as if netnography is a study of professionally created and edited published texts and not a study of the captured interactive communications of real people. We are working with a new and unprecedented medium and are under some special obligations to treat it as such. That is why I continue to suggest the need to be careful and considerate of nethography's potential for harm.

In Kozinets (2002), I took the 'high road' and recommended that (1) the researcher should disclose his/her presence, affiliations and research intentions to online community members during any research, (2) the researcher should guarantee confidentiality and anonymity to informants by providing them with pseudonyms and not using their usernames, and (3) the researcher should seek and incorporate feedback from members of the online community being researched. My extra-cautious provision, which should be interpreted as my own personal preference, and not necessarily as a recommendation for the 'right' or 'appropriate' way to do ethnography, is to contact community members and obtain their permission (informed consent) to use any specific postings that are to be directly quoted in the research.

Member checks
Finally, I recommend that member checks be used. Member checks are a procedure whereby some or all of a final research report's findings are presented to the people who have been studied in order to solicit their comments. Good member checks prove valuable as a source of additional insights beyond the limitations of the material posted, downloaded, filtered and analyzed by the researcher. They also can be viewed as an ethical procedure whereby community members are given a voice in their own representation (their concerns may or may not make it into the final draft, as this is the determination of the researcher). Member checks can also help to establish an ongoing information exchange between marketing researchers and consumer groups. In netnography, this participation and partnership can be extensive.

Summary
In summary, I have overviewed and updated several procedures for conducting netnographic exploration of the world of online culture and community. These include: (1) making cultural entrée, (2) gathering and analyzing data, (3) conducting ethical research, and (4) providing opportunities for culture member feedback. I assert that the opportunities for making cultural investigations of cyberspace have never been greater or more varied. There is a range of methods for gathering and analyzing data. Netnographies can vary along a spectrum from being intensively participatory to being completely unobtrusive and observational. Although I contend that all of these should be considered netnographies, I do advocate a mix of participation and observation for best results (see Muñiz and Schau, 2005, for a good example of quality participant-observational netnography). There are pragmatic difficulties and challenges posed by informed consent procedures on the Internet, yet they are morally necessary. Finally, the inclusion of member checks creates more detailed, richer and more ethical netnographies, and also offers useful opportunities for further research.

In a recent article (Kozinets, 2005), I offered further advice and considerations based upon four trends in networked communications. These included taking advantage of the rise of instant messaging for the conduct of depth IMterviews, understanding and situating within the alternate realms of MMOGs and other digital playspaces, and utilizing the information in the ever-expanding blogosphere. In the following section, I will explore and briefly demonstrate a methodology for using archived blogs for qualitative Internet-based consumer research, a subcategory of netnographic technique that I somewhat mischievously term a 'netblography' (a more straightforward application would note that this is simply a netnography that uses blogs or web-pages). I then follow up this section with a brief series of sections that ruminates on some other changes and trends and how they might impact the conduct of 'Netnography 2.0'.

Netblography: applying netnographic methodology to blogs

From relatively humble beginnings in individuals' web-pages, blogs have gained considerable popularity as a form for individual self-expression and an alternative and addition to large media depictions of the news. Blogs are an abbreviation for 'web logs', a term referring to people's web-pages that usually contain detailed, archived postings of a current, time-sensitive (and usually personal) nature. A blog search engine reported that, as of August 2005, there were 14.5 million blogs, almost 9 million of them considered 'active' (http://www.pubsub.com/), an amount that had nearly doubled in a six-month period. According to Technorati, a blog measurement firm and search engine, 23 000 completely new weblogs are created every day, about one every three seconds. The entire world of blogs, often cross-networked through shared links and carefully measured and classified by a variety of dedicated and general search engines, is know as 'the blogosphere'.

On many of these web-pages, readers can respond to the individual or entity's blog entries and thus create a type of interaction very similar to that on corporate or personal web-pages. However, unlike more communal and democratic forums like newsgroups and mailing lists, the blog is a near-autocracy where the owner remains the undisputed star of his/her own page. Sidney Levy, describing Bruce Weinberg's Internet shopping blog, sounds a warning that is transferable both in its descriptions and in its implications: 'The venture is unnatural, as maintaining a Web site record of one's search and purchasing behavior is like living in a fish bowl. Weinberg has an audience who pay attention, who send examples of their own experiences and approving email. They come from the media and other organizations to hold interviews and invite talks, and they include research analysts in the wings. All this is exciting and adds a show business flavor to the enterprise. Bruce revels in all this as a performer as well as a shopper, conveying the tone of playing a game in which he is Master of the Universe, lordly dispensing his Brucies and Noosies of approval and chastisement' (Levy, 2001). Since Levy wrote these words, however, blogging has becoming increasingly 'natural' for literally millions of people, even though many of bloggers' practices are insular, narcissistic and ostensibly unnatural.

As an offshoot of the personal web-page, the blog remains acutely and exactly that: deeply personal. This is its greatest strength and its biggest limitation as a forum for the collection of data. Many interactions can be captured in the space of newsgroups, but these are far less present in individual blogs. One secret to their study – and it is still a new technique being mastered by very few – is to study and understand the network of relations between blogs, the way that information picks up and is simultaneously spread through cyber and social space. Blogpulse.com has a tool for tracking the spread of topics and ideas between blogs; pervasive memes are seen spreading like California wildfires. Private marketing research companies are developing much more sophisticated tools for their clients. There are numerous opportunities for us to follow the spread of ideas between bloggers, capturing and conceptualizing the entire blogosphere or major sections of it, rather than single blogs or web-pages, as the community of interest.

I find one of the most fascinating things about blogs to be the way that they have been able to seize attention from the conventional media, such as broadcast television and advertising (see Kozinets, 2005, for more details on the rise and impact of the blogosphere in politics, consumer resistance and corporate relations). As online communal forms capable of gathering millions of readers, and influencing the media, they are a new power on the block or perhaps a new gravitational force counterbalancing corporate-sponsored forms of communication. The largely consumer-created information on blogs also offers the same sorts of insights and influences that have previously been ascribed to bulletin boards: targeted, precise, influential comments and feedback on products and brands, sometimes with specific complaints and suggestions for their improvement. Although they are subject to the same vagaries and risks of much of the Internet world of publishing, blogs offer a sophisticated and often relevant source of consumer information and feedback that marketers and researchers can view as an important source of counterinformation that needs to be noted and sometimes countered. Blogs also provide another opportunity to enter the lifestreams of consumers and learn the role of products and services in them. They are a source of information that tends to offer rich, detailed, longitudinal data about individual consumers and their consumption practices, values, meanings and beliefs.

As a brief example, consider the 'Barq's – the blog with BITE!' blog. This blog was created by 'the BarqMan' Michael Marx (http://www.thebarqsman.com/). I encountered the page in my research and search for blogs and bloggers devoted to specific consumer products brands. There were surprisingly few. Although brands were often mentioned incidentally in the recounting of their days (e.g., 'we then found ourselves at Julie's Tea Room on 33rd and Main. Mmmm, I just love their Lemon-Mango Bubble Tea, way better than a Starbucks latte'), very few bloggers devoted the totality of their blog to a daily chronicle or collection centered exclusively upon particular consumption habits. If my cursory results hold to be true, this is an interesting finding, as there is considerably more material on the World Wide Web on these matters than there is in the blogosphere (but see Ralli, 2005).

Consider the depth of personal information provided by blogs such as this one, that *do* take an explicit consumption orientation. Marx begins with an introduction to his lifetime interest in Barq's Root Beer by telling us about the impactful moment that he first laid lips on the beverage.

> Finally back at school, after a nice Christmas break, I went down as usual to the vending machines to get a couple of A&W's for Sunday Night's Popcorn and Root Beer with my Cuz (Family tradition goes way back to the early 70s). The machines were full of something new called Barq's. There was no A&W to be found. So I grabbed a couple of Barq's. As I drank, I was expecting that smooth Frosty Mug Taste, and instead I got a sweet dark crisp bite in the lip. Barq's definitely had it's namesake BITE! Over the next few weeks I started to crave that BITE!, and I was hooked. It wasn't the caffeine that hooked me either, because the first Barq's I drank were bottled in Salt Lake and had NO CAFFEINE. For about 10 years I drank only Barq's and avoided most other root beers. (Posted on http://www.thebarqsman.com/?page_id=2; accessed 17 August 2005)

This is a tale of brand loyalty that most marketers would love to hear. BarqMan has also compiled, along with a number of other contributors, a very noteworthy scrapbook of Barq's meanings and associations. Although he never directly addresses the question of why he likes and is so loyal to the brand (other than its taste profile or 'bite'), his soliloquizing and choice of content for the blog offer many data points for an interpretive analysis that suggests an answer. The brand meaning portrait that Marx paints is colorful and complex. It draws on Mississippi roots and tradition. Taste differences between Americans and Europeans are analyzed for a sense of difference. Ingredients are pondered. The necessity of caffeine (Barq's bite, apparently) is a hot topic. There is poetry that idealizes the Barq's experience as classic Americana. There are sections of books and articles that nostalgically mention Barq's (often in its glass bottle) and in retro fashion link it to better, childhood days. There are drawings and painting of Barq's cans and bottles, pictures of stacks and stashes of Barq's, and large detailed scans of Barq's advertising and giveaways that cast it as art and artisinal. There are descriptions (and some commentary) on Barq's advertisements. As with Star Trek fans and other fans who are deeply involved in the management of the brand, there are sections of the blog in which BarqMan analyzes and critiques Coca Cola's management of the brand. At one point, BarqMan reveals his deep insider knowledge and calls out for an idealized past manager to return and manage the brand back to its glory days:

> If I worked for Coke, I would think it a worthy challenge to lift the Barq's brand above the stigma, opening the flood gates to millions of new customers. It's about time Coke brought on a visionary like Rick Hill, who in my opinion made Barq's the success it is today. The Barq's brand is still riding on the coattails of Rick's successful marketing in the 90s. Rick, where are you? (*actually I know where you are*) Come back! Barq's needs you to revitalize the brand strategy in the US and create one for Europe! (Posted on http://www.thebarqsman.com/?m=200507; accessed 17 August 2005)

This brief example serves to illustrate the deep and first-personal view of a consumption fascination that can be garnered from a blog. In my analysis of coffee connoisseurs (Kozinets, 2002), I recounted the many useful ways that a study of devoted online consumers interacting on a newsgroup can yield insights that can help in new product ideation and reveal trends that may eventually become mainstream consumer behavior. This quick study of the BarqMan's blog reveals another pragmatic possibility: netnographic brand meaning audits. The rich and multifaceted world of individualized brand meanings and brand practices is accessible through a deep analysis of individual brand stories, and the cultural worlds and communal connections that they incorporate and foster.

Netnographic data reveal cultural cachet, whether we are talking about automobiles and motion picture franchises (Brown et al., 2003a), personal web-page representations (Schau and Gilly, 2003), electronic goods (Muñiz and Schau, 2005), online food communities (de Valck, 2005), file-sharing programs (Giesler, 2006), breakfast cereals (Brown, Kozinets and Sherry, 2003b), television shows and their fan communities (Kozinets, 1997, 2001), boycotters and activists (Kozinets and Handelman, 1998, 2004), medical procedures (Langer and Beckman, 2005), coffee brands (Kozinets, 2002) or Barq's root beer. In consumers' stories, brands are related to history, location, social distinction, craftsmanship, personal involvement, emotion, childhood memories, authenticity and religious devotion, and the specific castings of these netnographic understandings are useful in articulating a range of positioning and branding strategies with wider appeal.

Netnographic modifications
In this final section, I will briefly mention some developments in the world of computer-mediated communications, and link them to netnography's inherent flexibility and its potential to embrace their study.

Instant messaging and the depth IMterviews
Instant messaging and the portable chat rooms that it creates and represents have reached a new maturity. According to a 2004 Pew Internet & American Life Project poll, over 40 per cent of all adult Internet users in the United States use instant messaging (or 'IM'). Instant messaging has become a standard aspect of many consumer's conversational repertoire, especially those under the age of 25. Recent studies suggest that instant messaging is replacing both phone calls and e-mail with a new modality that combines the two forms. The IM modality is quicker than e-mail and easily allows multitasking and real time multi-person online conversations.

Giesler (2006) has used Napter's instant messaging system (IMS) extensively in his netnography of file-sharing communities as he conducted 20 online interviews. As he notes, 'Although some of these informants could have been interviewed on the phone, using Napter's IMS kept that data in situ as much as possible' (ibid., p. 5). Informants in this tech-centered ethnography actually spoke through the systems as well as about it. And, thanks to technological improvements in hardware and software, IM is becoming even more interesting for netnographers.

With the addition of a small videocamera, currently available in the US for less than $50, the richness of facial expression and body language can be incorporated into online research. The coldness of the online interaction and the CMC interview is thawing. Online communities are gaining faces and places, and becoming naturalistic. Apple's newest OSX operating system, named Tiger, includes iChat AV3, which allows up to four users to communicate audiovisually on the same screen, as each user sees detailed visual information from the other three people with whom he or she is communicating. The online chat thus feels more and more like a face-to-face chat, and researchers incorporating this technology into their netnographies are likely to obtain interesting and more naturalistic results than they would with older text-based methods (whose limitations in terms of brevity and style I briefly mentioned above). In terms of textual communication, SMS or text messaging over cellular phones offers another possibility for the conduct of research and, given its own stylistic challenges (not unlike those of IM chat), netnographies of mobile communities and consumers might take advantage of its considerable possibilities.

No more playing around: fragging NetMMOGraphies
With the oft-noted ascendance of entertainment giants like videogame-maker EA (Electronic Arts), the entry of Microsoft in the game-making space with its Xbox, Xbox Live and Xbox 360, and the success of Sony's Everquest and LucasArts' Star Wars Galaxies online environments, it is clear that videogaming as a consumption practice has now reached a new, communally interactive level. Some experts estimate that the US MMOG industry (MMOG is short for massively multiplayer online games, games where large groups of people play together in the same virtual environment or world) will reach nearly $3 billion in subscriptions by 2006.

These virtual environments offer many opportunities for consumers to interact and to inform our knowledge of consumption both online and off. Consumers interact and create consumption practices with their digital environment and they also communicate and 'do' other things virtually with one another. Environments can be commercially sponsored as well. Consumers also often play communal online games like Halo2 while wearing headsets, and are as apt to discuss social matters such as restaurants, travel and music while they are on patrol and waiting for the sparks to fly as are actual soldiers. In 2002, McDonald's took an unprecedented sponsorship opportunity (and risk), sponsoring a functioning virtual McDonald's as a permanent part of The Sims Online's environment, where it still 'stands'. As consumption arenas, these virtual environments are rich fields worthy of netnographic exploration. They are not only marketplaces, but virtual third places where consumers build social ties and gather to consume place, experience and community, to build expertise and status.

Similar to SMS, games have also gone mobile, and this combination of online and offline play is another significant area that is ripe for investigation. And just as blogs are rewriting the laws of news broadcasting, podcasting is rewriting the rules of radio and creating new opportunities for specific segments to reach out, create content and communicate with each other about consumption habits, desires, gripes and dreams. Vlogs, flash mobs, net-conferences, micro-activism and other post-millennial phenomena are the initial offspring of the enormous organizational empowerment resulting from the intermingling of the physical world and its virtual variants. The possibilities leave ambitious netnographers giddy.

Conclusion

The world of online communal communication is constantly transforming itself. Consumer and marketing researchers and marketing practitioners are barely keeping up with these changes. Many of our tools and techniques are limited. The self-reports and laboratory limitations of surveys and experiments are patently unable to reveal the rich cultural worlds that are being created and experienced through online communications and systems. Researchers are dusting off their old surveys and posting them online, while marketers take their new television or print advertisements and paste them onto corporate blogs and web-pages. Such a lack of imagination never has been a source of valuable consumer insight, and never will be rewarded by the consumers that are constantly leading us and moving us into the new digital terrain. Instead, we must consider ourselves as true anthropologists, wearing digitally-wired pith helmets, braving bubbling hot cauldrons of zeros and ones, ever at risk of be(com)ing digital/ going native.

Netnographers, we think about the network, considering our tools. Hunters, we sniff digital air for clues. With different engines, we search pages upon pages. Bricoleurs extraordinaires, we adapt equipment and execution, taking off the shelf and building from scratch. In our kit bags, scraping light on our hard discs, we collect. We ask permission from the gods before we capture their souls, or we should, and we treat the disembodied natives with the respect and dignity they are rightly due. Poring over the entrails of our quarry, contemplating them in the light and in the darkness, we tell our tales until we are pleased with the way they sound, until the digital spirits themselves are pleased. We pursue again, to the brink, to the riverside, as they alter and change their paths – do they know we are following? Can they swim in this dark abyss yet? Now? How many jump in, and so quickly. As netnographers, we follow their charge. We tread in their wake and dive in. It is swirling, churning and frothing, strange at first and vigorous, transformative, but also welcoming and warm. Yes, the water's fine.

References

Brown, S., R.V. Kozinets and J.F. Sherry (2003a), 'Teaching old brands new tricks: retro branding and the revival of brand meaning', *Journal of Marketing*, **67** (July), 19–33.

Brown, S., R.V. Kozinets and J.F. Sherry (2003b), 'Sell me the old, old story: retromarketing management and the art of brand revival', *Journal of Customer Behavior*, **2** (1), 85–98.

Correll, S. (1995), 'The ethnography of an electronic bar: the lesbian café', *Journal of Contemporary Ethnography*, **24** (3), 270–98.

De Valck, Kristine (2005), 'Frames of discussion in virtual community forums: a netnographic analysis of consumer conversations', ESSEC/HEC/INSEAD Seminar, INSEAD, Fontainebleau, France.

Giesler, Markus (2006), 'Consumer gift system: netnographic insights from Napster', *Journal of Consumer Research*.

Gould, S.J. (1991), 'The self-manipulation of my pervasive, perceived vital energy through product use: an introspective-praxis perspective', *Journal of Consumer Research*, **18** (2), 194–207.

Hamman, R. (1997), 'The application of ethnographic methodology in the study of cybersex', *Cybersociology*, **1** (1), available online at http://www.socio.demon.co.uk/magazine/1/plummer.html.

Hayano, D.M. (1979), 'Auto-ethnography: paradigms, problems, and prospects', *Human Organization*, **38** (1), 99–104.

Hoffman, D.L., T.P. Novak and A. Venkatesh (2004), 'Has the Internet become indispensable?', *Communications of the ACM*, **47** (7), 37–42.

Kozinets, Robert V. (1997), 'I want to believe: a netnography of the X-Philes' subculture of consumption', in Merrie Brucks and Deborah J. MacInnis (eds), *Advances in Consumer Research*, vol. 24, Provo, UT: Association for Consumer Research, pp. 470–75.

Kozinets, Robert V. (1998), 'On netnography: initial reflections on consumer research investigations of cyberculture', in Joseph Alba and Wesley Hutchinson (eds), *Advances in Consumer Research*, vol. 25, Provo, UT: Association for Consumer Research, pp. 366–71.

Kozinets, R.V. (1999), 'E-tribalized marketing? the strategic implications of virtual communities of consumption', *European Management Journal*, **17** (3), 252–64.

Kozinets, R.V. (2001), 'Utopian enterprise: articulating the meanings of Star Trek's culture of consumption', *Journal of Consumer Research*, **28** (June), 67–88.

Kozinets, R.V. (2002), 'The field behind the screen: using netnography for marketing research in online communities', *Journal of Marketing Research*, **39** (February), 61–72.

Kozinets, R.V. (2005), 'Communal big bangs and the ever-expanding netnographic universe', *Thexis*, **3**, 38–41.

Kozinets, Robert V. and Jay M. Handelman (1998), 'Ensouling consumption: a netnographic exploration of the meaning of boycotting behavior', in Joseph Alba and Wesley Hutchinson (eds), *Advances in Consumer Research*, vol. 25, Provo, UT: Association for Consumer Research, pp. 475–80.

Kozinets, Robert V. and Jay M. Handelman (2004), 'Adversaries of consumption: consumer movements, activism, and ideology', *Journal of Consumer Research*, **31** (December), 691–704.

Kozinets, Robert V. and John F. Sherry (2004), 'Dancing on common ground: exploring the sacred at Burning Man', in Graham St. John (ed.), *Rave Culture and Religion*, New York and London: Routledge, pp. 287–303.

Langer R. and S.C. Beckman (2005), 'Sensitive research topics: netnography revisited', *Qualitative Market Research*, **8** (2), 189–203.

Levy, Sidney J. (2001), 'The psychology of an online shopping pioneer', in Joan Meyers-Levy and Mary Gilly (eds), *Advances in Consumer Research*, vol. 28, Provo, UT: Association for Consumer Research, pp. 222–6.

Maclaran, Pauline, Miriam Catterall, Margaret Hogg and Robert V. Kozinets (2004), 'Gender, technology and computer-mediated communications in consumption-related online communities', in Karin M. Ekström and Helene Brembeck (eds), *Elusive Consumption: Tracking New Research Perspectives*, Oxford: Berg, pp. 145–71.

McMahan, Alison (2003), 'Immersion, engagement and presence: a method for analyzing 3-D videogames', in Mark Wolf and Bernard Perron (eds), *The Video Game Theory Reader*, London and New York: Routledge, pp. 67–86.

Muñiz, A.M. and T.C. O'Guinn (2001), 'Brand community', *Journal of Consumer Research*, **27** (4), 412–31.

Muñiz, A.M. and H.J. Schau (2005), 'Religiosity in the abandoned Apple Newton brand community', *Journal of Consumer Research*, **31** (March), 737–47.

Nelson, J. (1994), 'The virtual community: a place for the no-longer disabled', *Proceedings of the Virtual Reality and Persons With Disabilities*, 2nd Annual Conference, Northridge, CA: CSUN Center on Disabilities, 98–102.

Przywara, Dennis (2001), *Starwoids*, feature documentary film, Ventura film distributors.

Ralli, Tania (2005), 'Brand blogs capture the attention of some companies', *New York Times*, 24 October, p. C6.

Schau, H.J. and M.C. Gilly (2003), 'We are what we post? self-presentation in personal web space', *Journal of Consumer Research*, **30** (December), 385–405.

Schouten, John W. and James H. McAlexander (1995), 'Subcultures of consumption: an ethnography of the new bikers', *Journal of Consumer Research*, **22** (June), 43–61.

Turkle, Sherry (1995), *Life on the Screen: Identity in the Age of the Internet*, New York: Touchstone.

11 Let's pretend: projective methods reconsidered
Dennis W. Rook

The rise, fall and revival of projective methods

A huge number of studies using projective research methods appeared in the behavioral science literature between 1940 and 1960, although their origins date back to the late nineteenth century. These studies proliferated in the clinical and developmental psychology fields, as well as in sociological and anthropological research. After World War II, projective techniques rapidly diffused from the behavioral sciences into advertising agencies and market research firms, where they were applied in numerous product development, advertising, media, retailing and consumer studies. Their migration into mainstream marketing was facilitated by several brilliant and charismatic individuals, particularly Ernest Dichter in New York, and the leadership of Social Research, Inc. in Chicago, which included the interdisciplinary team of Lloyd Warner, Burleigh Gardner, William Henry, Lee Rainwater and Sidney Levy. Publications by these and other projective researchers appeared regularly in both academic and trade publications. Two *Journal of Marketing* articles by Haire (1950) and Rogers and Beal (1958) are widely viewed as classics today. During their heyday, projective methods also featured prominently in several influential marketing academic and trade books about consumer motivation and research (Ferber and Wales, 1958; Henry, 1956; Leonhard, 1955; Newman, 1957; Smith, 1954).

Despite their contributions to marketing theory and practice, the popularity of projective research declined dramatically in the 1970s. Not surprisingly, many young researchers gravitated toward newly available computer-assisted analyses of large-scale survey and experimental data. By comparison, typically small-sample projective studies were vulnerable to being viewed as quaint, inefficient relics from the so-called 'motivation research' era of the 1950s. Accompanying this technology preference shift, projective research suffered more directly from increasingly severe criticism of its premises, procedures and findings (Kassarjian, 1974). Surprisingly, projective researchers generally failed to counter the often vitriolic and emotional published denunciations of their methods and findings (e.g., Yoell, 1974). As a result, the scientific status of projective methods plunged, and studies using them largely disappeared from the academic marketing literature. While business applications continued, they steadily lost ground to the focus group research. Overall, the cumulative effect of these developments was substantial, and by the mid-1980s projective methods were not even mentioned in mainstream marketing research textbooks; e.g., Lehmann (1985) and Boyd, Westfall and Stasch (1985). The decline was less severe in the UK and Europe, owing both to different philosophical paradigms there and to the strong reliance of advertising account planning systems on qualitative marketing research (Mostyn, 1978).

In the US, renewed interest in projective methods emerged from a general resurgence in qualitative methods of various kinds, particularly ethnography, but also individual depth interviewing, literary and semiotic analyses (Sherry, 1995). New users of projective methods were strongly influenced by Sidney Levy's enduring contributions, and by subsequent work of his Northwestern students and colleagues; e.g., Levy (1985), Rook (1988), Heisley and Levy (1991), McGrath, Sherry and Levy (1993), Belk, Ger and Askegaard (1997) and Zaltman (1997). Notably, four of these individuals are past Presidents of the Association for Consumer Research (ACR): Belk, Levy, Sherry and Zaltman. In addition to the impetus provided by individual scholars, projective methods were encouraged by a shift in topical and theoretical interests in consumers' emotions, desires, motivations and brand meanings and relationships. Such concerns are particularly well suited for projective techniques, thanks to their historical clinical psychological purpose, focus and design.

On the applied side, the trade press noted an increase in business applications of projective research, even characterizing them as 'hot' (Heath, 1996; Lieber, 1997). Noteworthy here is the work of Gerald Zaltman, at Harvard's Mind of the Market Lab, whose ZMET protocol has attracted widespread interest from both academic and managerial researchers, and received extensive coverage in the business and popular press (Eakin, 2002; Yin, 2001). Today, both consumer behavior and marketing research texts commonly have sections that explain and illustrate uses of projective techniques in various situations (Mariampolski, 2001; Sayre, 2001).

This recent revival occurs against a lingering historical backdrop of much methodological controversy and contention, none of which has ever been resolved satisfactorily. All the stinging criticisms aside, projective researchers themselves are often annoyingly vague about their research stimuli, procedures and analyses. This chapter will address some of these issues and seek to provide better understanding of why and when projective methods are particularly useful in marketing and consumer studies.

Projective methods: an extended family

Arguably, in comparison to other qualitative research methods, projectives exhibit more research design and task variety than even ethnographic fieldwork, and far more than typical focus groups or individual depth interviews. To illustrate this idea, Table 11.1 lists the most frequently used projective techniques in marketing research, based on their reported uses in published academic and managerial studies. The historical origins of the

Table 11.1   Projective techniques and their early marketing research origins

Projective technique	Early marketing research origins
Word association	Houghton (1936)
Sentence completion	Social Research (1953)
Symbol matching	Dichter (1960)
Cartoon tests	Masling (1952)
Object personification	Vicary (1951)
Shopping list analysis	Haire (1950)
Picture drawing	Krugman (1960)
Autodriving	Heisley and Levy (1991)
Thematic story telling	Henry (1956)
Dream exercises	Social Research (1953)
Collage construction	Havlena and Holak (1995)
	Zaltman and Coulter (1995)
Psychodrama	Dichter (1943)

techniques are cited, with an attempt to identify their earliest application in marketing research. For example, word association was used by Galton, Freud and others in the late nineteenth century, but its first published use in a marketing study appeared in 1936. Owing to much out-of-print source material, the cited studies should be viewed as early origins, since the historical first may be impossible to determine.

The very names of these techniques suggest substantial differences in the ideation, activities and creations of research participants. This methodological heterogeneity is quite long-standing, and it presents both research opportunities and challenges. On the one hand, as exemplified in Levy's (1963) protocol for evaluating business executives, projective studies often include a battery of different techniques that facilitate triangulation around a central topic. This approach capitalizes on the rich variety of data that different projective methods yield. Arguably, gathering consumer expressions that include verbal, visual, dramatic, artistic and imaginary material encourages highly nuanced behavioral analyses, and also gets closer to the actual ways that individuals think, feel and imagine (Zaltman, 1997).

At the same time, this diversity can be daunting. Remarkably few guidelines exist to help researchers select particular projective techniques, or construct a battery of them to investigate specific issues. The most prominent and enduring projective methods in psychology have matured largely within self-encapsulated research paradigms. Hundreds of studies have been reported that examine the reliability, validity and normative responses of the TAT, Rorschach and the Rosenzweig Picture-Frustration test, and many others. These scholarly achievements are impressive, but they rarely involve discussions across different projective paradigms. Consequently few guidelines exist to help researchers design studies that include a variety of projective techniques. This, as much as the ambivalence about their scientific respectability, may discourage researchers from using them. The following discussion builds on the psychological roots of projective techniques, but seeks to address key methodological issues in the context of consumer and marketing research perspectives and priorities.

Projective stimulus commonalities
Despite their apparent differences, there are distinctive and widely agreed-upon commonalities among members of the projective methods family. These similarities involve both the nature of the research stimuli and the type of data that they elicit. Compared to most survey and focus group research, projective techniques rely on *indirect questioning*. Rather than asking respondents directly about their purchase behavior and motivations, projective methods frame questions in terms of other people or imaginary situations. For example, a simple projective 'question' might ask a respondent to characterize 'the typical person who buys Cheese-Whiz', or to 'describe a dream involving Godiva chocolates'. A second common element is the reliance on relatively *ambiguous stimuli*. Most marketing research is fairly straightforward and 'upfront' in focus, and consumers generally know what the topic is, and what the researchers want. Projective research takes a less direct approach and relies on 'questions' whose ambiguous qualities reduce respondents' abilities to guess the topic. For example, they might be asked to match a brand with a type of bird or flower; or to draw a picture of someone in a new car showroom; or to make a speech, pretending to be Dr Pepper. A third feature of projective techniques is the high *degrees of freedom* they allow. The degrees of freedom in survey research are usually few in number, while projective techniques theoretically allow an infinite number of responses. Limitless variations

exist, for example, in the ways consumers might imagine dreams about a BMW, or construct collages that represent their thoughts and feelings about United Airlines.

Projective data commonalities
These stimulus similarities, inevitably, are linked to similarities in the type of data that projective techniques elicit. In the broadest sense, projective methods tend to generate data that originate in what neuroscientists characterize in lay terms as the *right brain*. They tend to encourage emotional, fanciful and visual expressions that materialize in consumer dreams, drawings and role-playing. They also tend to elicit data that are more symbolic, metaphorical and aesthetic. Such interests are clearly a direct concern of marketers with communication, product design and brand positioning responsibilities.

A related aspect of projective techniques is their ability to access *primary motivations* that arise from individuals' basic urges and instincts (Freud, 1911). Market research commonly targets only secondary thought processes that are typically expressed in consumers' rankings of attribute preferences, their like–dislike ratings of ads, and in relatively superficial explanations of their consumption behavior. Given their origins in clinical psychology, projective methods have historically looked at motivation with a harder, more realistic eye, conceptualizing it as involving competing psychological forces and as arising from different levels of consciousness.

Finally, a long and widely recognized common element is the ability of projective methods to generate data that are relatively free from *social desirability bias*. Early sociological studies report how projective techniques helped uncover individuals' actual feelings about religious and ethnic minorities, which failed to surface in prior survey research. Consumption often occurs in normatively charged environments that abound with notions of right and wrong, and the indirect and ambiguous nature of projective questions encourages consumers to stray from the party line, and more honestly express their 'true' feelings about spending money, eating and drinking, watching television, driving electric cars and using condoms. Data obtained in the Rogers and Beal (1958) study revealed farmers' strong (right brain) feelings about their land, which were often accompanied by fears that industrial chemicals might damage or destroy it. Many farmers might be reluctant to express their emotions openly, or to admit their fears and mistrust of science. The story-telling technique used in the research gave farmers 'permission' and the opportunity to surface their deeper level concerns. These common elements are a synthesized prototype, and any individual technique may vary considerably in the degree to which it exhibits one or another characteristic.

Situational dimensions of projective research
Decisions about the type of data desired, and the type of questions used, obviously depend on the particulars of any research project. Here we address the more basic question about which research situations invite the use of projective methods. Three contextual aspects of a research are proposed as suggesting their effectiveness: (1) consumer memory, communication and self-disclosure concerns, (2) the behavioral depth that a particular study seeks to achieve, and (3) the modality, form and quantity of data desired.

Consumer and market researchers rely to an extraordinary degree on consumers' verbal responses to direct questions. This approach is often reasonable and productive, but in many common situations it is more questionable. Focus group and survey research

sometimes assumes that consumers have extraordinary memories, profound and elaborate self-knowledge, strong motivations toward introspection and self-disclosure, and
high verbal expression skills. In fact, these traits are probably normally distributed. In
combination or alone, memory, articulation and privacy concerns may diminish the validity and productivity of direct verbal questioning. The following discussion looks at these
elements from the consumer side of the situation.

Consumer memory
This dimension affects consumers' basic self-report capabilities, and involves their capac-
ities to retrieve, access and accurately recall answers to the millions of questions that marketers ask them every year.

Memory retrieval: don't remember situations
Consumers know a lot of things, and readily inform researchers about their purchase
behavior, brand attitudes and product experiences. On the other hand, marketing research
sometimes pushes the limits of consumers' memories. A few years ago, United Airlines
surveyed a sample of its frequent flyers, and asked them to evaluate all their flight segments taken over the past year on 20 different criteria, using a 7-point response scale. It
is remarkable that United's research staff actually expected consumers to remember so
many relatively trivial details from months ago, and that such data would be taken seriously. In his classic work, *The Human Equation in Marketing Research*, Dietz Leonhard
(1967) reiterated Herman Ebbinghaus's (1885) findings about memory decay by reminding researchers that, 'within 24 hours, a man forgets about 75 percent of what he learned
the previous day' (p. 46). Undaunted by this, much modern survey research continues to
ask about things that very few consumers are likely to remember.

Knowledge structure: don't know situations
Researchers sometimes expect consumers not only to remember everything they do, but
also to have comprehensive awareness of their behaviors' causes, episodic details and consequences. In fact, consumption in many product categories is transitory and uninvolv-
ing, and consumers are likely to have both limited knowledge structures and limited
self-awareness regarding their consumption behavior. Projective methods are unlikely to
perform any better at obtaining factual recall, but they are more likely to elicit impressions of the emotionality and meaning of a consumer episode, as these elements are more
likely to be retained than individual facts. Also psychologists are long aware that memory
retrieval is enhanced when it is conducted in a context or state similar to the behavior's
original occurrence. As Zaltman (1997) observes, since most thought is image-based, its
recovery is facilitated with research tools that resonate with the images, metaphors and
emotions in which thought is imbedded. Projective techniques such as story telling, role-
playing, dream exercises and collage construction have the ability to induce state and
context elements that can improve consumer recall.

Memory access: can't know situations
This situation sometimes involves the operation of pre-conscious or unconscious influ-
ences on consumption behavior, a topic that is historically linked with much controversy.
On the other hand, most psychological thinking supports the view that there are different

levels of information processing. This idea permeates the Freudian distinction between 'primary' and 'secondary' thought processes; it is represented in cognitive psychological models of 'hot' and 'cool' cognitions; and it is central to emerging neuroscientific findings about the functioning of the left and right brain hemispheres. Zaltman's (1997) comprehensive review of this work provides overwhelming evidence that most mental life is tacit, unconscious and hidden in neurological substrates. Consumers will often need more than a pencil-and-paper survey to access such material.

Consumer communication
Regardless of consumers' memory and knowledge structure, their ability to communicate what they know will depend on at least two factors: their articulation skills and their verbosity.

Articulation skills: when consumers can't say
In some situations, consumers may actually possess the information that researchers want, but they lack the capacity to express their thinking verbally. Given the dependence of survey and focus group research on verbal responses to direct questions, the inability of consumers to articulate their answers is a serious problem in many common consumer research contexts. In some cases, the problem might lie in lower verbal abilities of either individuals or a particular consumer segment (e.g., young children). In others, the research topic may be the problem. Many key research priorities involve molar constructs: for example, consumer motivation, brand imagery, customer satisfaction. These are important issues for consumers, too, but their ideas about them are sometimes vague, even ineffable. Projective techniques that are particularly useful in these situations are those that rely on non-verbal expressions, such as picture drawing, symbol matching or collage construction.

Verbosity: when consumers can't say much
Individuals vary in their overall expressiveness, which is often viewed as an aspect of personality. Verbosity is one aspect of this, and some people are simply more talkative than others. Most qualitative marketing researchers have had the unpleasant experience of conducting a focus group with too many monosyllabic respondents, a situation that is aggravated in individual depth interviews. This issue undoubtedly also relates to individuals' literacy levels, which is a consumer characteristic that marketers rarely take into account (Wallendorf, 2001). Non-verbal projective techniques may help in such situations, by providing activities that involve drawing, construction or role-playing exercises. In addition to providing alternatives to asking verbal questions, these techniques increase the comfort level of respondents with limited verbal skills. Also they actually facilitate better verbal responses, in that they serve to anchor respondents' thinking and, also, provide tangible references for discussion.

Consumer's self-disclosure proclivities
In any particular consumption context, researchers may legitimately believe that consumers have adequate memory, knowledge and expressive capabilities to respond meaningfully to direct questions. If this is true, the use of projective techniques may seem not to offer much added value, yet there are many situations that consumers remember, understand and can explain, but simply won't.

Topic sensitivity: disclosure reluctance
Consumers vary in shyness, and sensitive consumption topics bring it out. Researcher shyness can also influence the situation and result in amusingly timid questioning about 'sensitive' topics. For example, a friend recently described a telephone interview he had with a researcher for a toilet tissue manufacturer. At one point, the interviewer asked him: 'How concerned are you about cleanliness *down there*?' He was instructed to reply using a 1-to-7 point scale, with 1 representing very concerned, and 7 indicating not at all concerned. My friend was somewhat taken aback by the reference to one's anus as 'down there' and he asked the interviewer if anyone had ever responded with a 7, indicating no concern whatsoever. She ignored his comment, and asked him for his number. Baby talk may help squeamish respondents cope with unpleasant topics, but the survey format avoids dealing with the sensitivity by merely asking for a summary number. The indirect and more lighthearted approach taken by projective techniques helps reduce respondents' reluctance to express themselves about sensitive topics that, however unpleasant, are often key marketing concerns.

Privacy concerns: disclosure refusal
Reluctance can be extreme, and result in a respondent's refusal to answer questions. Although survey research commonly codes respondent refusal rates, refusal actually materializes in more subtle ways. For example, telephone survey researchers often subtly or overtly discourage refusal behavior. Numerous anecdotes describe situations in which an individual expresses a non-response, but the interviewer ignores this and suggests (to paraphrase), 'Oh, just give me a number, and then we can move on.' Respondents are likely to comply, particularly if they are being paid, and what was really non-response/ refusal data makes its way into a study's findings. Projective techniques are sensitive to the likelihood that individuals are prone to avoid difficult, complex and painful topics, and they provide a means to cleverly and successfully circumvent respondents' refusal tendencies. The same individual who might resist direct questions about his or her alcohol consumption, for example, might freely provide stereotypes, drawings and associations about people who drink single-malt scotch, or wine coolers.

Social desirability biases: when consumers are inclined to lie
Behavioral researchers have long noted individuals' tendencies to provide responses that conform to social desirability factors. Consumer research is not immune to social distortions, and focus groups are particularly likely to stimulate self-presentational face issues, and encourage consciously modified responses designed to please, impress or intimidate fellow group members. Theoretically, consumers are less likely to distort their responses when research questions are framed indirectly in terms of other people, or nested in imaginary situations; and when questions are ambiguous and relatively playful. These common features of projective techniques help diminish social desirability influences on consumers' responses.

Research 'depth' priorities
Consumer capabilities and proclivities are one dimension of the research situation. Another aspect of situations that recommend projective research is the behavioral depth a particular study seeks to achieve. Projective techniques are historically viewed as having

the potential to go beyond consumers' surface-level explanations of their behavior to elicit data that reflect deeper levels of personality, motivation and meaning. Such concerns are not exclusively psychological, as marketers often need to obtain deeper levels of consumer understanding than statistical frequency reports typically provide. Unfortunately, there is not much explicit elaboration in the literature about what 'depth' actually is, with the notable exception of recent work from Zaltman (1997) and his colleagues (Zaltman and Coulter, 1995; Olson and Zaltman, 2001). Managers sometimes express their interests in digging deeper by requesting a study that is 'exploratory', 'broader' than usual, 'psychological' or 'touchy-feely'.

However well-intended such objectives are, their implementation is more difficult owing to a general vagueness at the levels of both research constructs and methods. Some constructs are clearly 'deeper' than others, not only in terms of their neurological structure and location, but also in terms of their relationship to consumers' lifestyle, self-image, personality and motivation. The broad marketing topic of 'brands' serves to illustrate this idea. The various measures of consumers' brand behaviors exist along a 'depth' continuum that ranges (low to high) from repeat purchase behavior frequencies, to attribute satisfaction levels, brand preferences, brand images, meanings and brand relationships (Fournier, 1998). The former two are measured with relative ease by UPC scanner data, or through survey research. Measuring images, meanings and relationships is not usually as simple. After all, from its inception, the concept of brand imagery identified the complex layers of symbols that constitute it (Gardner and Levy, 1955).

Data modality and quantity
The most prominent typology of projective methods typology relies on the 'nature' of the response gathered by a particular technique (Lindzey, 1959). This classification provides little assistance to consumer and marketing researchers, who are unlikely to care whether a particular technique involves 'expression' or 'association', for example. This discussion suggests that, rather than examine differences among projective techniques in terms of gross, abstract response qualities, it makes sense to consider their differences in terms of the quantity and modality of the data that different techniques elicit. Different marketing research and creative development situations vary in their needs for verbal versus visual information. For example, data generated through psychodrama exercises may be particularly useful for advertising creatives, as they materialize in units that are quite similar to the narratives they craft for broadcast and print media.

Or a packaging improvement project may have trouble getting consumers to explain verbally their ergonomic and aesthetic views about function and form, and might obtain more useful information by using visually dominant techniques, like picture drawing or collage construction. Other marketing projects (slogan generation) might logically require more verbal data. Understanding of more intimate and involving marketplace situations such as service encounters might benefit from research involving psychodrama and role-playing, or story-telling about pictures of people in service situations. Such an approach could yield rich understandings of customer satisfaction above and beyond the pervasive statistical measures of the degree to which a purchased service met customers' expectations. Table 11.2 provides a summary of the basic mode of data that the main projective techniques gather.

Market researchers who wish to use projective methods should also examine the menu of possible techniques in terms of the amount of data they tend to elicit. Relying only on

Table 11.2   Situational dimensions of projective research: consumer memory, communication and self-disclosure

Response modality	Prototypic projective technique(s)
Verbal/written response	Word association
	Sentence completion
	Cartoon tests
Verbal/written summary	Object personification
	Shopping list analysis
Verbal/written narrative	Thematic stories
	Dream exercises
	Autodriving
Visual association	Symbol matching
Visual construction	Picture drawing
	Collage construction
Physical/body language	Psychodrama

Table 11.3   Projective data modality and prototypic techniques

Low	Moderate	High
Word association	Object personification	Collage construction
Sentence completion	Shopping list analysis	Thematic stories
Cartoon tests	Picture drawing	Dream exercises
Symbol matching		Psychodrama
		Autodriving

word association or a cartoon test, for example, will tend to yield relatively little raw data. Table 11.3 identifies various projective techniques in terms of the amount of data they tend to yield.

In designing a research protocol that includes a battery of projectives, researchers increase their interpretive opportunities by including techniques that yield both varying types and amounts of material.

The scientific status of projective methods
Despite the unique analytic leverage that projective methods provide in common marketing research situations, their scientific status today remains largely unchanged from earlier years, and ranges from outright proscription to extreme ambivalence. A recent review of three prominent projective techniques (the Rorschach, TAT and human figure drawing) examined their psychometric properties (Lilienfeld, Wood and Garb, 2000). The authors found 'ample justification for skepticism concerning the most widely used projective techniques' (p. 53). As similar analyses have concluded for years, projective methods often exhibit low reliability and validity, fail to provide measurement norms, and often yield no incremental validity above and beyond that derived from psychometric survey measures. On the other hand, this review finds some empirical support for the validity of the Rorschach

and TAT on a small number of indices, and the authors conclude that 'dismissing in broad brush strokes all projective techniques as unreliable and invalid is unwarranted' (p. 53). However correct this suggestion might be, it seems unlikely to diminish the general and often scathing criticism of projective methods (Dawes, 1994; Lowenstein, 1987).

The net effect of more than 50 years of critical debate within psychology has resulted in 'generations of psychologists (who) have been trained with a deeply ingrained assumption that projective techniques are inherently invalid and unreliable' (Westen et al., 1990). The received view of psychologists has had a strong influence on how many marketing and consumer researchers evaluate projective methodology; similar concerns about their reliability and validity are fairly widespread (Kassarjian, 1974). Historically these concerns have caused more than a few marketers to recommend using projective methods only with 'extreme caution' (Bellenger, Bernhardt and Goldstucker, 1976) or, more sweepingly, to dismiss them entirely as 'scientifically illegal' (Yoell, 1974). The point here is not to question the findings about the often dismal psychometric properties of projective techniques. On the other hand, the basic logic of subjecting a qualitative paradigm to statistical criteria as the *sine qua non* of its scientific value is not particularly compelling (Holstein and Gubrium, 1995; Wallendorf and Belk, 1989). This difficult issue aside, one central concern about projective methods has been largely ignored: the *context* in which they are used. Clinical psychological uses of projective methods involve the diagnosis, treatment, prescription and, in some cases, the institutionalization of psychiatric patents. Within the legal system, projectives are used to inform judicial decisions in criminal sentencing and parole hearings and, increasingly, in child custody disputes. Clearly, these are grave matters that demand rigorous standards of evidence and analytic soundness.

In contrast, such concerns are rarely relevant to the typical needs and priorities of marketing managers and researchers. Commonly, projective research in management informs the front-end, developmental phases of a marketing campaign, where managers are trying to discover new ideas, broaden their customer understandings, and generate possibilities for new market offerings, brand positionings or communications. The psychometric properties of any particular idea or emergent theme are not a serious consideration. Similarly, academic research that relies on projective methods tends to be motivated by theory building rather than testing priorities. Owing to the dramatically different context in which projective techniques are used in consumer and marketing research, the historical albatross of invalidity and unreliability should be removed. Furthermore exclusive reliance on psychometric criteria assumes that convergence of measures is the critical evaluative issue. Given the behavioral complexities of marketing phenomena, a more realistic orientation would de-emphasize convergence in favor of the triangulation of different measures around a particular research issue. Given their data elicitation qualities, projective methods should generally be expected to yield findings that are substantively different, but still complementary to those obtained through direct questioning techniques in surveys or focus groups.

Projectives are also criticized because they require subjective interpretation. In a masterful essay in the *Journal of Consumer Research*, Sidney Levy (1996) suggests that the extensive and complex patterns of significance tests that emerge from statistical data analyses often require as much subjective interpretation as the analysis of a story or picture. Statistical work proceeds with more explicitness regarding analytic procedures and decision criteria, yet these rules primarily serve technical aspects of a study. They provide little help in resolving conflicting findings or failed hypotheses, or in naming and characterizing factors delivered via SPSS. These circumstances demand an interpretive synthesis of numerous data points, so projective techniques should not be singled out as uniquely or distressingly subjective.

Less frequently, projectives are admonished as intrusive procedures that trick respondents into giving information that they would otherwise not be inclined to provide. This criticism acknowledges the data elicitation strengths of projective methods, but it views them as ethically questionable. Contextual differences between marketing and clinical research, again, reduce the relevance of this point. Market researchers are not probing consumer psyches for clinical diagnoses, or to assist forensic analyses; and using a few projective techniques in a focus group or individual interview is unlikely to be experienced by respondents as unpleasantly intrusive. Rather respondents generally find projective exercises to be interesting, engaging and fun.

Summary and conclusion

'Science' is a big house, yet projective methods have found the welcome mat come and go over many years. The previous discussion suggests that the common criticisms of projective methods are largely irrelevant to the concerns of marketing researchers. This discussion alone is unlikely to resolve the longstanding controversies, but it will, hopefully, encourage the research community to distinguish between using projective methods in marketing and in clinical psychological and forensic contexts. On the more positive side, this chapter has sought to increase methodological explicitness about projective techniques by identifying common marketing situations in which they are particularly useful in overcoming consumers' knowledge structure limitations, self-expressive shortcomings and self-disclosure proclivities.

Given the pervasiveness of sensitive consumption topics, low category and brand involvement, and the influence of social desirability biases, the usage of projective techniques might be expected to increase, particularly when marketers hit the research wall. The classic marketing cases involving projective methods typically describe circumstances in which other research methods failed to explain why, for example, consumers do not buy instant coffee, despite positive taste test results (Haire, 1950), or when researchers cannot explain farmers' reluctance to purchase agrochemical products that enhance crop productivity (Rogers and Beal, 1958). These kinds of situations abound today, and the data elicitation strengths of projective methods remain unchanged from their heyday.

It is important to emphasize that projective techniques are rarely used exclusively in a given study, but are typically included with other questions in focus group and individual interviewing. This facilitates triangulation around a topic, and it also provides task variety for the respondents. A recent article in *Marketing News* describes how projective techniques can be used to provide an 'intervention' that 'breaks the monotony of nonstop (focus group) discussion' (Dalbec, 2001). Ethnographic research also has a long tradition of using story telling and other projective tools (Heisley and Levy, 1991). Projectives are rarely employed as components of quantitative studies, although they might provide incremental diagnostic value. For example, when concept testing reveals essentially similar purchase intent results, projective measures might help uncover underlying differences between a set of concepts that have otherwise identical scores. Similarly projective techniques might provide experimental researchers with additional interpretive leverage in situations where the results are statistically marginally significant, or when they go against well-grounded hypotheses.

Finally, given conjoint analysis's need to identify and incorporate all elements that influence product preferences, projective methods are likely to uncover in-depth motives and concerns that may not materialize from surveys or focus groups.

All this discussion derives from the thinking of a researcher who uses projective techniques regularly in both academic and managerial studies. Having also worked extensively with focus groups and survey research, I find that projective methods stand out as distinctly humanistic in their reliance on the enjoyment people derive from telling stories, drawing pictures and acting out dramas. The basic guiding premises of the projective pioneers of the 1950s appear strong today, and new support for them derives from the burgeoning literatures on imagery, metaphor and storytelling. Common sense also points to an enduring aspect and appeal of projective techniques: children universally love to play 'let's pretend' and more mature consumers do, too, if only we let them.

References

Bellenger, Danny, Kenneth Bernhardt and Jac Goldstucker (1976), *Qualitative Research in Marketing*, Chicago: American Marketing Association, Monograph Series #3, 33–41.

Belk, Russell, Guliz Ger and Soren Askegaard (1997), 'Consumer desire in three cultures: results of projective research', in Merrie Brucks and Debbie MacInnis (eds), *Advances in Consumer Research*, vol. 24, pp. 24–8.

Boyd, Harper, Ralph Westfall and Stanley Stasch (1985), *Marketing Research: Text and Cases*, Homewood, IL: Irwin.

Dalbec, Bill (2001), 'Stage an intervention for the focus group', *Marketing News*, 26 February, pp. 46–8.

Dawes, R.M. (1994), *House of Cards: Psychology and Psychotherapy Built on Myth*, New York: The Free Press.

Dichter, Ernest (1943), 'Raw material for the copywriter's imagination through modern psychology', *Printers' Ink*, 5 March, 63–8.

Dichter, Ernest (1960), *The Strategy of Desire*, Chicago: T.V. Broadman and Co. Ltd.

Eakin, Emily (2002), 'Penetrating the mind by metaphor', *New York Times*, 23 February.

Ebbinghaus, Herman ([1885] 1913), *Memory: A Contribution to Experimental Psychology*, trans. H.A. Rogers and C.E. Bussenius, New York: Columbia University Press.

Ferber, Robert and Hugh G. Wales (1958), *Motivation and Market Behavior*, Homewood, IL: Irwin.

Fournier, Susan (1998), 'Consumers and their brands: developing relationship theory in consumer research', *Journal of Consumer Research*, **24** (4) (March), 343–73.

Freud, Sigmund ([1911] 1956), 'Formulations on the two principles of mental functioning', in J. Strachey and A. Freud (eds), *The Standard Edition of the Complete Psychological Works of Sigmund Freud*, vol. 12, London: Hogarth.

Gardner, Burleigh B. and Sidney J. Levy (1955), 'The product and the brand', *Harvard Business Review*, March–April, 33–9.

Haire, Mason (1950), 'Projective techniques in marketing research', *Journal of Marketing*, **14**, April, 649–56.

Havlena, W.J. and S.L. Holak (1995), 'Exploring nostalgia imagery through the use of consumer collages', in Kim P. Corfman and John G. Lynch (eds), *Advances in Consumer Research*, vol. 23, Poro, UT: Association for Consumer Research, 35–42.

Heath, Rebecca P. (1996), 'The frontiers of psychographics', *American Demographics*, July, 38–43.

Heisley, Deborah D. and Sidney J. Levy (1991), 'Autodriving: a photoelicitation technique', *Journal of Consumer Research*, **18** (3), December, 257–72.

Henry, William E. (1956), *The Analysis of Fantasy*, New York: John Wiley & Sons, Inc.

Holstein, James A. and Jaber A. Gubrium (1995), *The Active Interview*, Thousand Oaks, CA: Sage Publications, Inc.

Houghton, Dale (1936), 'Methods of advertising evaluation', *Printers' Ink*, **32** (June), 18–20.

Kassarjian, Harold H. (1974), 'Projective methods', in Robert Ferber (ed.), *Handbook of Marketing Research*, New York: McGraw-Hill, pp. 85–100.

Krugman, H.E. (1960), 'The draw a supermarket technique', *Public Opinion Quarterly*, **24**, 148.

Lehmann, Donald R. (1985), *Market Research and Analysis*, Homewood, IL: Richard D. Irwin.

Leonhard, Dietz L. (1955), *Consumer Research with Projective Techniques*, Shenandoah, Iowa: AJAX Corporation.

—— (1967), *The Human Equation in Marketing Research*, New York: American Management Association.

Levy, Sidney J. (1963), 'Thematic assessment of executives', *California Management Review*, **5** (4), 3–8.

—— (1985), 'Dreams, fairy tales, animals, and cars', *Psychology and Marketing*, **2** (2), 67–81.

Levy, Sidney J. (1996), 'Stalking the amphisbaena', *Journal of Consumer Research*, **23** (3), December, 163–76.
Lieber, Ronald B. (1997), 'Storytelling: a new way to get close to your customer', *Fortune*, 3 February, 102–7.
Lilienfeld, Scott O., James M. Wood and Howard N. Garb (2000), 'The scientific status of projective techniques', *Psychological Science in the Public Interest*, **1** (2) (November).
Lindzey, Gardner (1959), 'On the classification of projective techniques', *Psychological Bulletin*, **56**, 158–68.
Lowenstein, L.F. (1987), 'Are projective techniques dead?', *British Journal of Projective Psychology*, **32**, 2–21.
Mariampolski, Hy (2001), *Qualitative Market Research*, Thousand Oaks, CA: Sage Publications.
Masling, Joseph M. (1952), 'The preparation of a projective test for assessing attitudes toward the International Motion Picture Service Film Program', Institute for Research in Human Relations, Philadelphia.
McGrath, Mary Ann, John F. Sherry and Sidney J. Levy (1993), 'Giving voice to the gift: the use of projective techniques to recover lost meanings', *Journal of Consumer Psychology*, **2**, 171–91.
Mostyn, Barbara J. (1978), *Handbook of Motivational and Attitude Research Techniques*, Bradford: MCB Publications.
Newman, Joseph W. (1957), *Motivation Research and Marketing Management*, Cambridge, MA: Harvard University Press.
Olson, Jerry and Gerald Zaltman (2001), 'Using projective methods to elicit deep meanings', in Mary Gilley and Joan Myers-Levy (eds), *Advances in Consumer Research*, vol. 28.
Rogers, Everett and G.M. Beal (1958), 'Projective techniques in interviewing farmers', *Journal of Marketing*, **23** (October), 177–83.
Rook, Dennis W. (1988), 'Researching consumer fantasy', in Elizabeth C. Hirschman and Jagdish N. Sheth (eds), *Research in Consumer Behavior*, vol. 3, Greenwich, CT: JAI Press, pp. 247–70.
Sayre, Shay (2001), *Qualitative Methods for Marketplace Research*, Thousand Oaks, CA: Sage Publications.
Sherry, John F. (ed.) (1995), *Contemporary Marketing and Consumer Behavior: An Anthropological Sourcebook*, Thousand Oaks, CA: Sage Publications.
Smith, George Horsley (1954), *Motivation Research in Advertising and Marketing*, New York: McGraw-Hill and the Advertising Research Foundation.
Social Research, Inc. (1953), *The Attitudes, Motives, and Behaviors of Subscribers to Better Homes & Gardens*, Des Moines, IA: Meredith Publishing.
Vicary, James M. (1951), 'How psychiatric methods can be applied to market research', *Printers' Ink*, 11 May, 39–40.
Wallendorf, Melanie (2001), 'Literally literacy', *Journal of Consumer Research*, **27** (4) (March), 505–11.
Wallendorf, Melanie and Russell W. Belk (1989), 'Assessing trustworthiness in naturalistic consumer research', in Elizabeth C. Hirschman (ed.), *Interpretive Consumer Research*, Provo, UT: Association for Consumer Research.
Westen, D., N. Lohr, K.R. Silk, L. Gold and K. Kerber (1990), 'Object relations and social cognition in borderlines, major depressives, and normals: a thematic apperception test analysis', *Psychological Assessment*, **2**, 355–64.
Yin, Sandra (2001), 'The power of images', *American Demographics*, November, 32–3.
Yoell, William A. (1974), 'The fallacy of projective techniques', *Journal of Advertising Research*, **3** (1), 33–6.
Zaltman, Gerald (1997), 'Rethinking market research: putting people back in', *Journal of Marketing Research*, **34**, 424–37.
Zaltman, Gerald and Robin Coulter (1995), 'Seeing the voice of the customer: metaphor-based advertising research', *Journal of Advertising Research*, **35** (4), 35–51.

12 Stories: how they are used and produced in market(ing) research

Gillian C. Hopkinson and Margaret K. Hogg

Stories . . . collecting them as data and telling them as theory. (Scott and Scott, 2000: 128)

Introduction

There is a growing interest in and use of stories in marketing research (e.g. Grayson, 1997a, 1997b; Thompson, 1997; Fournier, 1998; Escalas and Bettman, 2000; Hopkinson and Hogarth-Scott, 2001; Deighton and Das Narayandas, 2004). However, the diverse uses to which stories are put may bewilder marketing scholars wanting to use stories in their research or readers seeking to make use of story-based research. In writing this chapter we aim to introduce the reader to something of the breadth of feasible storied research approaches and to relate fundamental research issues to particular approaches to stories. We do not intend to limit the ways in which stories are used in marketing research or to establish one dominant approach. Rather we hope to highlight and discuss the critical decisions involved in the design of research in such a way as to assist researchers making decisions about using stories in their research designs, and also research audiences appraising research which flows from stories.

In the first part of our chapter we compare and contrast research presented in two recent articles, which we take as excellent exemplars of their type, within the field of consumer behaviour. These articles are Dahl, Honea and Manchanda (2003), 'The nature of self-reported guilt in consumption contexts', in *Marketing Letters*; and Susan Fournier's (1998) 'Consumers and their brands: developing relationship theory in consumer research', in *Journal of Consumer Research*. Both studies work with qualitative data in the form of stories told by consumers about their own consumption experiences. The authors diverge, however, in their respective positions in terms of the objectivist versus interpretivist debate or, to put it another way, in their ontological and epistemological underpinning assumptions. Consequently, the two studies differ with respect to the following four questions:

1. What type of stories are collected and how they are collected? (data collection)
2. What is then done with the stories? (data analysis)
3. How is the research reported? (research presentation)
4. What types of claims to knowledge are made? (theory building)

By considering two research papers in detail we are able to connect the critical methodological dimensions of these four questions to the ontological and epistemological stances of the respective researchers; to demonstrate how close reading of published text provides a more robust understanding of the research stance; and to demonstrate how these connections need to be incorporated and accounted for in designing research based on story.

From this comparison (and from Czarniaswska, 2004: 15) we derive a framework for incorporating stories into research (see Figure 12.1) which we present in the second part of our chapter. Here we consider the process of research reporting as itself a form of storytelling. In a reflexive turn we therefore scrutinize our own story as presented in this chapter, and we discuss what criteria might be applied to evaluate the way we have framed/told our story.

We have selected two papers which we consider provide a neat contrast in their use of stories. Both articles work with consumers' narrative accounts of themselves and their own actions. Both move towards knowledge creation, one via development of a typology (Dahl et al., 2003) and the other via refined conceptualization (Fournier, 1998), in order to build theory. We have chosen to work with these papers because, in our opinion, each demonstrates a high level of 'research integrity', by which we mean that the research is conducted and reported in a style that is consistent with the researchers' initial theoretical stance. Additionally, both papers, we believe, make a substantial and worthwhile contribution in areas of consumer behaviour that had previously been under theorized. Seeing the two pieces of research as comparable yet different, we seek to show what makes each legitimate research, rather than seeking to evaluate one against the other. Equally, in choosing to consider these two pieces we do not wish to imply that there are not other good papers based upon a narrative approach.

What is a story? The paradigm debate in research
What is a story? With the 'narrative turn' across the humanities (e.g. Stone, 1979; Hobsbawn, 1980), social sciences (Gergen and Gergen, 1988; Labov, 2001; Czarniaswska, 2004; Jokinen, 2004) and management sciences (Sherry, 1990; Czarniaswska, 1998), the potential power of stories has received increasing attention in marketing (Deighton and Narayandas, 2004[1]). Before detailed examination of the two papers, we briefly consider the wider paradigmatic context for stories and storytelling in research. Stories can take a variety of forms (see, for instance, Hopkinson and Hogarth-Scott, 2001) which means that they can be used in research designs which span the traditional paradigmatic divide. The different uses to which stories are put across this research spectrum are linked to different ontological ('what is', Crotty, 1998: 4) and epistemological ('what it means to know', ibid.) underpinning assumptions. The two, however, can be difficult to separate as 'ontological issues and epistemological issues tend to emerge together' (ibid.: 10–11). Paradigms represent a major area of debate, whose scope we cannot address here. We draw particularly on Crotty, who identified several theoretic perspectives (ibid.: 5–7), including positivist and interpretivist. We carry these two perspectives forward as contrasting positions for the purposes of this chapter since these perspectives align with the research papers that we explore.

The positivist theoretical perspective is associated with objectivism: 'the epistemological view that things exist as meaningful entities independently of consciousness and experience, that they have truth and meaning residing in them as objects ('objective' truth and meaning, therefore) and that careful (scientific?) research can attain that objective truth and meaning' (ibid.: 5–6). The interpretivist theoretical perspective includes several schools of thought with varying views of reality (e.g. constructionism, subjectivism) but which share a rejection of the view that behaviour is shaped by an objective reality available for discovery through scientific methods. The interpretivist concern is to understand a situation from the perspective of participants within that situation, and to explore the meanings through which they construct their reality. Positivist and interpretivist paradigms are widely associated with 'nomothetic' (positivist) and 'idiographic' (interpretivist) knowledge. Nomothetic knowledge seeks to identify rule-governed behaviour from which generalizations can be made (Belk, 1995) and therefore is in keeping with the positivist assumption of 'lawful' human behaviour (Deshpande, 1983). Idiographic knowledge seeks understanding of situated behaviour, linked to its social and cultural contexts (Belk, 1995).

Positivist and interpretivist theoretical perspectives embrace other important differentiating characteristics that we elaborate on further throughout our chapter. These characteristics include different views about the relationship between facts and values and thus truth claims; different conceptions of the relationship between the researcher and the researched; and differences in evaluating and presenting research. Underlining these differences are important and fundamental questions of power in research, relating particularly to issues such as whose views matter, whose voice is heard, who has the right to claim 'knowledge' and on what basis. We will return to these political issues in exploring the two articles that we have selected and also, finally, in reflexively questioning our own actions in writing this chapter, or, we could say, in telling this story.

Before concluding this section we wish to point out that positivist and interpretivist paradigms have been associated with quantitative (positivist) and qualitative (interpretivist) research methods. For example, Deshpande (1983) sees positivism as synonymous with quantitative research while admitting that this treatment is simplistic. We eschew this division given recent developments, and particularly fragmentation, within qualitative methods. The simplification of this divide is indeed illustrated in this chapter since we show that qualitative data, in the form of stories, is differently but appropriately used in both positivist and interpretivist studies.

So, what is a story? Whilst all researchers may view the story as a piece of qualitative data, the answer to this question will also relate to the paradigm from which it is answered. The positivist may answer that the story reflects events in the social world, it represents truth 'out there' and gives access to a nomothetic understanding of the world. For the interpretivist the story may represent experiences as understood by the storyteller and relate primarily to the ideographic. Additionally, we have introduced the idea, developed within the sociology of science (see, for example, Bruner, 1986, 1990), that the research endeavour is itself an act of storymaking and storytelling. We carry forward these diverse views of story by looking firstly at others' work and use of stories and then by questioning our own work and storytelling in this chapter.

Key differences across the two studies
We now move on to discuss and compare two studies. We provide a simplified account of the phases undertaken by these researchers in Table 12.1. Dahl, Honea and Manchanda (2003) look at guilt-inducing consumption, whilst Fournier (1998) explores brand relationships. Both studies are based on narrative material collected in interviews.

A key and obvious difference, shown in Table 12.1, is that between the number of 'story tellers', but of equal importance to us are the terms consistently used by the authors to describe these 'storytellers'. Dahl, Honea and Manchandra (2003) refer repeatedly to 'participants' or 'respondents'; Fournier (1998) refers instead to 'informants'. The

Table 12.1 Phases in data collection and analysis

Dahl, Honea and Manchandra (2003)	
Phase One Data collection and analysis	307 intercept interviews (286 usable) Deductive coding into three broad categories (2 research assistants) Inter-coder agreement testing (80%): resolution of disagreements by discussion Analytic induction coding: iterative (2 research assistants) Inter-coder agreement testing (90%): resolution by discussion Development of theory
Phase Two Data collection and analysis	Confirmatory research: 178 intercept interviews (173 usable) Deductive coding into previously developed categories (2 research assistants) Confirmation of theory Further theory development
Fournier (1998)	
Phase One Data collection	Purposive selection of informants (3 women) In-home interviewing (total 12–15 hours on 4–5 occasions over 3 months)
Phase Two Data analysis	Idiographic analysis of each informant Thick description of life histories and (112) brand stories
Phase Three Data analysis	Cross-case analysis by constant comparative method using axial and selective coding Conceptualization of consumer–brand relationships Development of relationship typology

latter term illustrates Fournier's interpretivist approach and her concern to understand the idiosyncratic and personal life worlds about which only the individual can inform. The term is bound up with ideas of gaining insight into a world of which the researcher is, initially, ignorant. By contrast the terms 'participants' and 'respondents' carry ideas of participation within the researchers' project, and of responding (more or less) precisely to the researchers' questioning. These differing views of the storyteller and of storytelling as an act have profound implications for research that we shall trace through four areas:

1.   What type of stories are collected and how they are collected (data collection).
2.   What is then done with the stories (data analysis).
3.   How the research is reported (research presentation).
4.   What types of claims to knowledge are made (theory building).

Data collection
Both studies commence with the collection of stories. Fournier interviews people in their homes and states that 'stories describing the genesis, evolution, and usage of brands in the informant's repertoire were elicited' (1998: 347) as they 'tell the story' behind the brands found in their cupboards. Dahl et al. approach people by intercept in public locations and they explain that 'the instrument first asked participants to recall, and describe in as much detail as possible, a recent situation where purchasing, using or disposing of a product/service involved feelings of guilt' (2003: 161). The development of the story differs across the two cases as they draw upon different research methods.

Fournier combines two established interview methods, the 'phenomenological interview' and the 'life story' interview. The phenomenological interview (see Thompson, Locander and Pollio, 1989) is largely unstructured, and develops through the active participation of both parties in what has the feel of a conversation. The conversational character of the interview, inevitably influenced by both parties, is shown as Fournier draws the reader's attention to her own role in the interviews, underlining the presence of the researcher in the research. The objective of the phenomenological interview is not to force into prominence the theoretic basis of the research but to give greater freedom, in setting the course of the conversation, to the interviewee. Through this technique, the phenomenological interview 'permits an understanding of the subjective meanings of consumers' lived experiences.' Fournier claims to have avoided any prompts or lines of questioning that used relationship concepts, thus giving prominence to the life worlds of the informants and avoiding setting the agenda according to her theoretic concerns.

Additionally, Fournier presents modified life-history cases which involved the blending of narratives concerning brands with participants' life stories. Life history methods and their heritage are reviewed in more detail elsewhere (see, for example, Goodson, 2001; Thompson, 2004). The use of life story involves a focus upon biography and background and demands that the participant make connections between historic past, present and future. In this way life stories, as told for example in interviews, are at a remove from lived experience and are 'lives interpreted and made textual' (Goodson, 2001: 138) thus forcing the researcher into what Goodson describes as possibly a 'messy' confrontation with other people's subjective perceptions. The prominence of life story in the interviews is therefore in keeping with Fournier's interpretivist objectives and with the intentions of the phenomenological interview.

Dahl et al. use the critical incident technique, a technique introduced and developed within a positivist framework by Flanagan (1954) who was very concerned to deal with 'fact' and to safeguard objectivity. The method has been considerably adapted by marketing scholars but continues to treat respondent stories as 'factual report' within the positivist tradition (Hopkinson and Hogarth-Scott, 2001; Gremler, 2004). Dahl et al.'s belief in the objectivity of story is seen in their data collection methods. In contrast to the conversational encounters sought by Fournier, storytelling is a more isolated, individual activity, demonstrated in the statement, 'the instrument first asked participants to recall, and describe in as much detail as possible . . .' (2003: 161). Here the instrument acts as the agent, thus avoiding the idiosyncratic and potentially contaminating influence of human interaction. The request for detail, but subsequent lack of questioning, prompting or probing, assumes that the storyteller will be able to give a full, accurate and realistic account of the events being told. While the stories are not developed in interaction, three questions that form the guilt construct are posed and answered, using Likert scales.

The different ways of generating story in these two studies are then consistent with the researchers' aims of exploring the subjective understandings of participants (in Fournier's case) or of collecting realistic accounts of the world (in Dahl et al.'s case). Decisions about the type of data to be collected also have important implications for the number of participants, for length of contact and for research recruitment.

As shown in Table 12.1, Fournier's study involves repeated and lengthy interviews with three informants. Dahl et al.'s 485 participants must have been involved in far briefer encounters (no timing is given). The shape of the sample also differs. Through purposive sampling, Fournier selects women in transitional life stages in order to 'maximise chances of uncovering insight on important brand relationship phenomena' (1998: 347). The level of interaction required indicates that these are eager participants with whom Fournier feels able to develop a rapport. Dahl et al. do not sample to ensure representativeness but are concerned to show a lack of systematic bias by reporting respondents' age and gender. Participants give less time and personal effort (in terms of explaining the self) to the research; and the issue of rapport is avoided as the personal role of the researcher is negated, as we have seen, with the instrument performing the action of story collection.

The relative importance of breadth to depth of participation and the representativeness of participants is in line with Fournier's concern with the particular, contextual and idiographic and Dahl et al.'s concern with generalisability and the production of context-free explanation, or the nomothetic. The latter researchers, therefore, seek to learn from many more people, in less depth and with an exclusive focus upon the topic of the study (consumer guilt).

It is often seen that the size of the sample and the depth of information collected are traded off in research. The two studies illustrate rather extreme positions in this trade-off and many intermediary positions can be envisaged. The important point we wish to make is that decisions relating to sample size and shape are driven by the ontology and epistemology of the research, and specifically by how these assumptions underpin a concern with the individual and particular or with the general.

Data analysis
Both studies are systematic in their analysis and, for both, the creation and use of categories that best describe the data is important. However, they approach the task of categorization, and of demonstrating its systematic character, in different ways.

Dahl et al. (2003: 162) use deductive categories derived from the literature as 'tentative broad categories' to place the stories initially into three categories, these being later refined though iterative movement between deductive (theoretically based) and inductive (data-derived) categories. The criteria used in category development are inclusiveness and inter-rater reliability. The former criterion demonstrates a concern with the 'normal' or 'widely experienced' above individual experience. The latter criterion demonstrates a concern with science and with objectivity. Two research assistants produce reliability statistics that rise from 80 per cent to 90 per cent agreement through the stages of the coding process. Disagreements are resolved through discussion. The reporting of these processes and their statistical results provides evidence of objectivity in a process that renders qualitative data into quantified categories, the relationships between which may then be statistically tested and subsequently confirmed through the second tranche of data collection.

Fournier draws upon the general procedures of grounded theory in an analysis that occurs in two broad phases. The procedures used initially are outlined as idiographic analysis, impressionistic reading and identification of recurrent behavioural and psychological tendencies mentioned. The initial objective of the analysis is to gain a broad understanding of the data by summarizing the identity issues and brand stories of each case. The biographical[2] and fragmented stories told by informants (life stories) are integrated within Fournier's 'life history cases' to portray a coherent sense of biography and its influence on consumption. Fournier comments that a 'holistic understanding of brand relationships within the context of the consumer emerged' (1998: 347) and this is reported through life histories using 'thick description' (we return later to look at this style of presentation).

The second level of interpretation draws upon the idiographic analysis; thus the credibility of the latter stage rests in large part upon that of the former. Constant comparative coding and comparison across cases (especially axial and selective coding following Strauss and Corbin, 1990) are used to discover patterns. A priori coding derived from the literature is constantly modified inductively as the analysis progresses. This process allows Fournier to propose both types of brand relationships and the dimensions along which they differ. The writing and presentation styles differ across the initial idiographic and later cross-case analyses, as we shall discuss in the next section.

The Fournier analytic method differs from that of Dahl et al. principally in its emphasis on interpretation rather than positivist science. Fournier, as the sole analyst, argues that her role as both collector and analyst of data 'permit(s) the holistic perspective sought through the method' (1998: 347). Thus Fournier is not concerned to prove objectivity either by distancing herself from the participants or by showing that others would reach the same conclusions. Rather she portrays an intimate and personal involvement with the informants and the data that is coupled with a systematic analysis demonstrated through detailed explanation of her procedures and discussion of the heritage of her methods. Thus Fournier seeks to show that her results are supportable and not casually derived, but do not represent an objective, complete account since 'others considering the same data will likely uncover additional themes in the analytic process' (1998: 361).

Research presentation
While we will focus principally upon the differences in presentation between the two papers, it is worth noting that they follow very similar writing strategies. Both broadly commence by claiming paucity of knowledge in their respective areas and review related literatures from other fields in order to highlight the importance and academic potential of the study. They then report on their methods of data collection, then analysis, present their findings and report on their contribution to the theory in this area and its relevance to practice. To this extent both follow rather well established and deeply embedded conventions of the genre for writing for academic journal publication: literature review, conceptualization, empirical (field) work, analysis and presentation of findings, interpretation and discussion of findings, contribution to theory building and knowledge generation.

The most obvious differences in writing style relate to the way in which the 'results', in Dahl et al.'s case), or the analysis (in Fournier's case), are/is written up. Indeed the use of these different terms sheds some anticipatory light upon this issue, one term being more oriented towards a product or outcome, the other to a process. In this way, 'results' are reified as a natural and objective outcome, a truth formed before the research took place that would have been found by anyone using the established methods. The focus upon process in 'analysis' is associated with a need to reveal far more of the author's thought development.

Fournier commences by idiographic analysis of each case in turn, pointing out the particular and unique that we would not expect to see replicated in the population. In these idiographic analyses we are offered the 'thick description' (1998: 344) associated with ethnographic work and described by Fournier as suited to a 'discovery-oriented task'; that is, 'exploratory and descriptive in flavour' (ibid.). The text is interspersed with numerous comments directly lifted from interview texts, many of which are lengthy. The informants' words are thus used as evidence of *their* view, or interpretation, of the world and of themselves. The interpretive act is extended as Fournier's text seeks to make sense of the informants' views and to identify the key life themes in each case. The ample quotation and discussion allow Fournier to support her developing interpretation. Further, she shows how these themes are negotiated and a self-concept is produced, in part, through brand relationships. The style of writing, with ample illustration and explanation, is an important feature of Fournier's attempt to convince the readership of the plausibility of her ultimate interpretation. Furthermore the extensive use of the informant's voice is appropriate given the idiographic character of the work. It is an exploration of the individual and the particular, and the individual is allowed to speak. At the same time the individuals who take part in the research are empowered as their voice is heard, a point to which we shall return later.

Dahl et al. report their results by presenting each category. More limited quotation from the data is used and these extracts are presented in order to illustrate 'the types of things said' in association with that category of story, rather than because of an intrinsic interest in what is being said. In this way the personal and particular (the idiographic) is not introduced. To illustrate this contrast, a quotation is used by Dahl et al. as an example of the kind of things categorized as guilt arising from actions in close relationships: 'one respondent described feeling guilty for "purchasing a $200 bowling ball without consulting my spouse who was unlikely to approve of such a purchase" ' (2003: 163). Though we both assumed the speaker to be male, we are told nothing about the speaker. In the context of Fournier's study the statement would need contextualizing in the life world of the speaker: for example, contextualized within their relationships with money and with their spouse. The speech in Dahl et al.'s study gets subsumed into the results, whilst speech is an important part of the material in the analysis and the development of thought for Fournier.

However, as discussed above, Fournier moves from idiographic analysis reliant upon thick description to a second-level analysis that draws more explicitly upon grounded theory methods. It is in the writing of this stage of analysis that Fournier refers to 'constant comparative method using axial and selective coding procedures (Strauss and Corbin, 1990)' (1998: 347). The difference in analysis – and the different intent of the two stages of analysis – are marked by a change in language. Fournier draws here repeatedly on the ideas of emergence and discovery: seven prominent dimensions were identified as emergent categories (1998: 361); 15 meaningful relationship forms emerge (1998: 361ff.). The second level of interpretation is used 'to discover patterns'. In this change of language Fournier conveys the idea that the results are now 'out there' and therefore available for discovery and to emerge ('out there' means, in her first-level analysis, the idiographic part). The earlier emphasis is on interpreting and making accessible the individual stories; this then moves to the more scientific emphasis of grounded theory as Fournier works with the 112 brand stories told by the three informants and seeks the more general within the particular. (She also talks of results in connection with this stage.) The changed vocabulary, then, is important in marking the difference between the interpretation that allows us to know (ken/*kennen*/*connaître*) the individual; and the scientific finding or discovery of facts now 'out there' and in the data so that we now know (*savoir*) something new.[3]

Theory building

The final stage is generation of theory from the research material represented by the stories; and the identification of the contribution to knowledge (always theoretical for the academic audience, and sometimes practical, for the potential managerial audience). Both papers identify theory building as their goal; and both talk of how the research can be useful, though there is a stronger focus on the managerial contribution in the Dahl et al. study compared with Fournier's study. Before stating their goals, they both follow the rhetorical convention of identifying significant gaps in existing research. Dahl et al. seek to address a significant theoretical gap arising from 'minimal attention' given to guilt in consumer behaviour research (2003: 159). They thus frame their goal for theory building as 'to identify a typology for consumption related guilt' from which flows an empirical goal 'to explore the relationship between categories of consumer guilt'. Fournier identified an empirical gap as her starting point: 'little empirical work has been conducted on relational phenomena in the consumer products domain, particularly at the level of the brand' (1998: 343). From here she argued that 'the field has leapt ahead to application of relationship ideas and the assumption of relationship benefits without proper development of the core construct involved'. Fournier's theoretical goal therefore centres on the development of 'a solid conceptual foundation from which brand relationship theory can be cultivated and to illustrate portions of this framework as a way of demonstrating utility of the consumer–brand relationship as a whole' (ibid.: 344).

At the end of their papers both Dahl et al. and Fournier discuss their contribution(s) to knowledge. Dahl et al. describe 'three broad categories of guilt' (2003:168) elicited from their stories; they identify 'unique implications for both marketers and consumers' (ibid.) and they discuss engineering, firstly, 'creative mechanisms that offer compensatory or rationalizations options to consumers' in order to reduce consumption guilt. Dahl et al. also identify the wider context for these findings, as their typology not only 'categorizes the types of consumer guilt but also provides a structure for distinguishing between "negative" and "positive" guilt in general' (ibid.: 169). Following the genre (and fitting their story back into the wider story – see Figure 12.1 below), Dahl et al. also call for further research wherein their taxonomy is suggested as a starting point to examine the antecedents and outcomes of guilt.

Fournier's conceptualization of consumer–brand relationships includes the delineation of 15 relationship types (1998: 361–3, including Table 1) and their trajectories (ibid.: 363–4, including Figure 1); and the 'development of an indicator of overall relationship quality, depth and strength' (ibid.: 363–5) from which Fournier proposes a preliminary model of brand relationship quality (ibid.: 365–6, Figure 2). This allows her to make some statements about relationship stability/durability. However, of equal importance is the weight which Fournier places on 'the *holistic* character of consumer–brand relationship phenomena' (ibid.: 366) (emphasis added), indicating the emphasis which Fournier continues to place on the 'life worlds' from which she has collected her stories, so that phenomena are not presented as 'context-less'. She contrasts this with the 'focus on fractionated concepts of self' (ibid.: 367) reported in earlier research. In discussing the contribution of her study, Fournier identifies 'two relevant domains': brand loyalty and brand personality, concentrating mainly on the linkages to existing academic research (ibid.) and only indicating very briefly the potential usefulness of her research to marketing practitioners (ibid.: 368).

In practice, the contributions each study claims to make only become such to the extent that the claims are accepted by readers and subsequent researchers. Therefore the 'genre' of academic research writing requires researchers to evaluate, and convince their readership of, the 'strength' of the material which they have collected, on which the interpretation and then subsequent theory building is based. The information (data, findings, results) generated via collecting, analysing and interpreting stories has to be evaluated against different sets of criteria depending upon the underpinning ontological and epistemological assumptions of the researcher(s).

The appropriate criteria for evaluation of interpretivist research are the subject of continuing debate. Some proposals are close to positivist-type criteria (see, for example, Lincoln and Guba, 1985, who include, inter alia, transferability and confirmability). Other researchers look away from the science domain and towards the humanities (see, for example, Golden-Biddle and Locke, 1993, who propose plausibility, authenticity and criticality). Fournier highlights trustworthiness as an important 'test' for her research. She uses member checks to gauge the credibility of her 'interpretative claims' (1998: 348). Colleagues also review her interview transcripts and interpretive summaries for the purposes of 'peer debriefing' (ibid.). This process leads to the 'reanalysis of the data on several occasions towards the goals of mutual comfort, objectivity and recognizability in interpretation' (ibid.). Fournier also employs triangulation across stories (e.g. collecting multiple stories from the same person); across interviews (e.g. a series of interviews with the same informant on a number of different occasions); and across information sources (e.g. grocery lists, shelf contents, stories of other household members) (ibid.). Fournier's purposive sampling enables 'transferability judgements of the insights obtained, as does the thick description offered therein' (ibid.). She does not claim to represent the only story or voice in this material and points out that she has not said all that can be said (e.g. there is 'evidence of multiplicity, incongruity, and instability . . . in the data' (ibid.: 361)). Nevertheless, Fournier argues that she has made 'tidy' connections which have captured regularity and consistency so that these are 'valid interpretations [whilst] . . . Transferability . . . remains an empirical, researchable question for consideration in future works' (ibid.). These checks contribute to the construction of 'trustworthiness' in an argument that convinces the reader and therefore supports the aim of theory building as set out in the paper.

By comparison, the criteria relating to positivist research are more clearly established and rarely debated: objectivity, reliability and internal and external validity. Dahl et al. (2003: 162) are therefore able to adopt a classic strategy to establish the credibility of their findings. These include, as discussed, the use of multiple coders, of statistical testing and of a confirmatory study. Therefore, having commenced with qualitative data in the form of stories, their argument in support of their findings can be made in terms most familiar in quantitative studies. Their argument in support of their credibility is therefore far briefer than that of Fournier since, in a sense, they are able to allow 'the numbers' to 'speak for themselves'.

Rounding off the story
So far in this chapter we have shown how stories may be used in research under different ontological and epistemological assumptions and traced the influences of these assumptions on key aspects of the research. We hope to have shown the consistency with which the authors whose work we have studied apply their assumptions. To round off our

discussion with respect to the two articles we will use them to explore some issues fundamental to 'the research project'. These are issues that we have raised but have left pending
throughout the text. In talking of the research project we refer to the role of research
within a broad societal context, and to the relations within and between the research community and the society that it researches. These issues were debated early on in consumer
behaviour research (e.g. Belk, 1991) and, before that, in van Maanen's (1988: 7) discussion of the epistemological and ontological issues surrounding different tales from the
field: realist, confessional and impressionist.

Power and voice: foregrounding and backgrounding
As attention has increasingly been paid to personal story, commentators across the disciplines have welcomed this as a movement that gives a voice to research participants, allowing them to provide an account and explanation. Thompson (2004) comments upon the
enthusiasm of his subjects to be named and included in the text. Hence it appears to place
power in the hands of the researched. Individual accounts count. The importance of
allowing subjects to speak is heightened when applied to marginal or neglected groups
(Hill and Stamey, 1990; Hill, 1991; Pavia, 1993) and with respect to sensitive topics
(Mason and Pavia, 1998; Pavia and Mason, 2004).

In the cases we have looked at we can see that participants have indeed told their own
story, but that the importance of the individual and the extent to which their story features in the research varies under the two treatments. For Dahl et al. individual stories are
collected but with the aim of subsequently quantifying the data so that the individual
story becomes part of the quantified explanation of society: the individual is backgrounded and the social is foregrounded (Crystal, 1985: 124).[4] In contrast, Fournier foregrounds the individual through her intense interest in the idiographic. Throughout the
analysis, and through an emphasis on holistic aspects rather than 'fractionated
approaches to the self', Fournier attempts to maintain, and present to the reader, the richness of the research context and of the stories she has heard. In effect, Fournier appears
to take the reader with her as she enters the world of the informants. That this is
convincingly achieved is, as we have pointed out, critical to our acceptance of the broader
theory of brand relationships that she subsequently develops, and in which the individuals move into the background. By comparison, Dahl et al. and their readers remain (intentionally) outside the world of the researched throughout their study. Their participants
remain anonymous throughout: what participants say is abstracted from the worlds they
inhabit and is interpreted within the scientific and theory-laden world of the researchers.

In survey research the researched may only respond within the framework developed
by the researcher and are absolutely constrained to their limited line of questioning.
Collecting stories from participants therefore always restores some freedom to the
researched who may include what they consider as relevant. However, participants' voices
feature to different extents and in different ways in the research text. As Foucault (1977:
27–8) argues, the presentation of voice in the production of knowledge is a political act
in that power and knowledge are mutually constituted. Therefore the extent to which
story-based research redresses power between researched and researcher, and may,
according to the research, give power especially to the marginalized and generally
silenced, demands a critical exploration of just whose voice is represented/reported.
Whose voice dominates or is privileged?

Dahl et al. are entirely privileged in their article; in Fournier's article the apparent power seems to move back and forth between the author and the storytellers. While individual voice does play a larger part in the idiographic analysis of Fournier's study, we can see various ways in which Fournier, inevitably, mediates that voice. Fournier is open about her role both in shaping (not leading) the conversations of the interview and in the analysis: both steps play a part in her mediation. The data comprise a collection of told stories but exclude other possible stories. These 'untold stories' include those that can never be told and those that would not be told in the particular context of these interviews and those that happened not to be told in these cases.[5] From the stories told, Fournier must necessarily select material to quote, however extensive this quotation is. Inevitably Fournier attends to some of the data more than others, and brings her own preferences to acceptance of the explanations her storytellers offer. In the second half, as Fournier's paper works to build theory, her voice and control become more explicit they organize the data (e.g. 1998: Table 1, Exhibit 1, Figure 1 and Figure 2). Here the 'language' of the researcher structures the presentation of the material as the 112 brand stories are amalgamated into different levels of abstraction (e.g. six faceted brand relationship quality construct, 1998: 363), which starts to create some distance from the 'phenomenological significance of the relationship pool'. The stories have now become a pool themselves, in that they have become a data set, so they have been distanced from their original storytellers, and absorbed into the theory building framework (1998: Figure 2). While we may question the mediated form of power that informants possess at the beginning of the paper, power later shifts explicitly towards Fournier as the storytellers become backgrounded and Fournier's voice is foregrounded with her story about the conceptualization of consumer–brand relationships.

Since the voice of the researcher is inevitably present in the text, albeit possibly intermingled with that of their participants, we can liken the task of research and its reporting to that of storytelling. According to narrative theory the narrator is selective in terms of what they attend to, and what theories they bring to bear, in providing a narrative about an event (Polkinghorne, 1987). Narration is similar to Weick's (1995) depiction of sense making as a process of attending, punctuating and bracketing. Thus we can regard the researcher as a storyteller as they attend to and theorize aspects of the world. Even when participants' voices are admitted or reported, they are overlaid with the voice of the researcher. We believe therefore that using a story method does not fully redress power issues between the researcher and the researched. Carefully handled, and we feel this to be the case in the Fournier paper, it goes some way to offering redress. Nevertheless we must recognize that the researcher has their own story to tell, recalling that the presentation of voice in the production of knowledge is a political act (Foucault, 1977), and telling and gaining an audience for that story is a political act.

However, we may also question the autonomous power of the researcher, and to what extent the researcher independently adopts a voice. Thompson (2002: 142) claims that 'a piece of research reveals as much about the research community as it does about the phenomenon being investigated'. Arguments about the situated nature of knowledge construction in the social sciences (Smith, 1998, Olsen, 2000) and in marketing (Sherry, 1990) point out that the researcher does not work in a vacuum and their studies are inevitably located within a broader scholastic community – and influenced, overtly or covertly, by that community. The community influences what the researcher attends to and what theories they draw upon in explanation. Equally that community is the audience without which the researcher's story remains unheard. The exercise of readership power is particularly pronounced in the journal review process where they (or their selected representatives) may intervene or the author may anticipate such intervention. We have alluded throughout our text to the conventions of the academic writing genre. We deal with this next.

The rhetoric of the research process

What we address briefly now is the rhetoric of research. Using and producing stories has to be undertaken within the context of research as recognized and accepted by the relevant community of scholars: in this case, marketing researchers.[6] How we write our stories has to fit in with the established genre for our field, and with our audience's expectations. Certain conventions and rules have to be followed. This brings us back to our starting point: the issue of the ontological and epistemological assumptions of our different audiences. The question then becomes how to maintain the integrity of the research process that we have followed in our respective research designs (and its affirmation of its own underlying epistemological and ontological assumptions) while meeting the needs of the journal audience as embodied by reviewers and their adherence to the rhetoric(s) of the genre, e.g. the formal organization of paper which usually flows from literature review to conceptualization; examination of key relationships in conceptualization via empirical data; writing up of the findings from the empirical study; an interpretation/discussion of the results in the light of the (pre-) existing state of knowledge; and some set of 'tests' which establish the credibility of the findings, and by which the findings can be evaluated, in order that the subsequent claims to knowledge can be clearly based on faith in the data set. Belk's arguments (1991: 237), revisited by Thompson (2002: 143), identified the subtle influences and constraints that positivistic narrative conventions exert on interpretivist consumer research, e.g. 'triangulation, audits, member checks, peer debriefings' (Belk, 1991: 237) which assume a singular, underlying objective reality, linked to a set of philosophical assumptions that may be antithetical to interpretivist research (ibid.). Thompson (2002: 144) also stressed the importance of identifying the underlying 'taken-for-granted assumptions, rhetorical conventions and social interests that shape the stories consumer researchers tell about consumers' and often necessarily shape the way we tell our interpretivist academic stories for journal publication.

Other rhetorics used to convince audiences of the logical soundness of research and arguments (Mingers, 2000) include different ways of writing, such as style, tone, vocabulary: 'Scientific writing is a stripped-down, cool style that avoids ornamentation . . . there is also a standardization of form – the theory–methods–findings–conclusion format – that is intended to limit rhetorical excess (Eisner, 1981). This absence of style turns out to actually be a rhetorical device in its own right (Frye, 1957)' (Firestone, 1987: 17). There are also different emphases in the 'plot'. Positivist studies which either draw on quantitative data or seek to quantify qualitative data tend to stress the careful application of a method in a well-designed study (cf. Dahl et al., above), whilst interpretivist studies (e.g. Fournier) concentrate much more on the unfolding process as the analysis of the findings from the qualitative dataset proceeds (Firestone, 1987). As we saw, from the comparisons which we drew above, stories can be collected, used and produced in different ways to meet various underlying ontological and epistemological assumptions, but then stories often have to be retold for the academic audience(s).

Discussion: telling our story

Story-based research has been welcomed across the disciplines as a means of giving voice to (and as a way of listening to the voice of) the researched. In the final part of this chapter we (re-) tell our story, framed[7] within Figure 12.1, which summarizes the key action stages in using and producing stories in marketing research.

- We chose two types of story (Fournier's life stories drawn from phenomenological and life history interviews; and Dahl et al.'s adaptation of critical incident technique) to show how stories can span the traditional positivist/non-positivist research divide.
- Our source of stories was published texts in mainstream academic journals, so that our primary informants were fellow academics, and our secondary informants were the participants in their studies. This just illustrated one of many potential sources for stories.
- Our context was a desk-based interrogation of our two data sets.[8]
- We evoked (rather than provoked) storytelling by trying to reconstruct the processes which had taken place in the generation of these two sets of stories.
- We analysed and interpreted the original stories, and also the academic stories in the two articles. We read back and forth between the articles, comparing and contrasting parts within each article (e.g. stated purposes for data collection; different reporting styles for data presentation; varying strategies for establishing the plausibility and trustworthiness of the research method and research findings), and wholes (e.g. the positioning of the papers within the debates about generating scientific knowledge) and we read across stories as well (e.g. the different approaches to the storytellers in each study).
- We wrote up our story, constructing it around four key issues: data collection, data analysis, research presentation and theory building.
- Much as Fournier moved from the ideographic to produce a general theory we extrapolated from our initial, intensive readings to comment more generally upon social research issues.
- We have argued that researchers become narrators in attending to particular aspects of their data, that they do so through the lenses of their preferred theories and that they adopt particular rhetorical strategies to tell their story to specific audiences.

We must see ourselves in this light and scrutinize our own storytelling activity and its role in the knowledge project.

Our voice, or should we say voices? (we return to this point) has dominated this text. We have selectively drawn upon the voices of Dahl et al. and Fournier and used fragments of their texts in support of the arguments we wished to pursue in this chapter. While we worked carefully with their texts and did not seek to silence or distort the voice of our participants, inevitably we have done so by privileging our own voice. Unlike Fournier, we did not undertake member checks. We have not corresponded with the authors and asked for their comments upon our interpretations. Perhaps worse still, we have not asked our participants for permission to use their work in ours. We set out with the view that published work becomes available to subsequent researchers. Nevertheless we recognize that we have co-opted the voices of our participants in our arguments, rather than giving them voice. Dahl et al. and Fournier are generally backgrounded here.

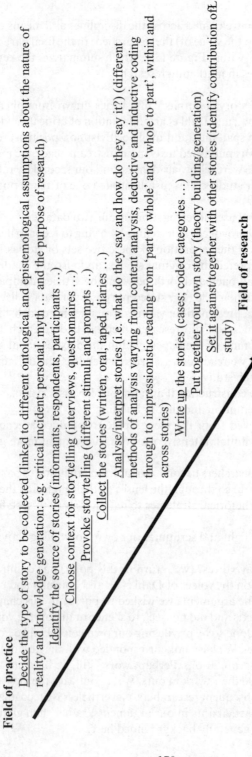

Field of practice

Decide the type of story to be collected (linked to different ontological and epistemological assumptions about the nature of reality and knowledge generation: e.g. critical incident; personal; myth … and the purpose of research)

    Identify the source of stories (informants, respondents, participants …)

        Choose context for storytelling (interviews, questionnaires …)

            Provoke storytelling (different stimuli and prompts …)

                Collect the stories (written, oral, taped, diaries …)

                    Analyse/interpret stories (i.e. what do they say and how do they say it?) (different methods of analysis varying from content analysis, deductive and inductive coding through to impressionistic reading from 'part to whole' and 'whole to part', within and across stories)

                        Write up the stories (cases; coded categories …)

                          Put together your own story (theory building/generation)

                            Set it against/together with other stories (identify contribution of study)

Field of research

Source: Derived from Czarniaswska (2004: 15).

Figure 12.1 Action stages in storied research: moving from the field of practice (empirical) to the field of research (theoretical) in using and producing stories for marketing research

Our storytelling has, then, been an act of power. In developing an argument and putting forward a claim to knowledge, we acknowledge the mutual constitution of power and knowledge. We have co-opted many voices from published research to show a heritage and to ground our line of thought. We anticipate that our work may subsequently be co-opted by others.

Finally, our story is a rhetorical act. 'We' have spoken; we have claimed a voice; we have co-opted other voices. 'We' have spoken in unison. Perhaps we have drawn upon the convention of inter-rater reliability to assert unwittingly inter-author reliability as assurance of the truth of what we write. Strangely, just as Dahl et al. achieved increasing inter-rater reliability scores through their study, we too seem to have become increasingly of one mind. We might argue that we have debated an agreed understanding of the intersection between the literature on stories (conceptual view) and the 'world of stories' (represented by the fields of practice and of research) as we tacked back and forth between these until 'understanding' emerged. Perhaps that understanding is pure; perhaps we have merely grasped a better understanding of each others' subjectivities?

But how might we justify our story to you, our readers? In terms of evaluating our story, and thus its contribution to knowledge creation and generation (rather than strictly theory building as we outline in Figure 12.1), we call on Golden-Biddle and Locke's (1993: 595) three dimensions in building our argument that we have a convincing story to tell: plausibility, authenticity and criticality. Authenticity is about convincing the readers that the interpretation is drawn from the data, about convincing readers that we, as researchers, have 'been present in the field and grasped how members understood their world' (ibid.) and that we have searched systematically and conscientiously through the material. We echo Golden-Biddle and Locke (1993) in the importance we have placed on 'depicting the disciplined pursuit and analysis of data, and qualifying personal biases' and also demonstrating clearly how all the points link back to some data point. Criticality and reflexivity are the two other key features. Criticality, for Golden-Biddle and Locke (ibid.: 595), incorporates reflexivity, searching for 'carving out room to reflect, provoking the recognition and examination of differences, and enabling readers to imagine new possibilities'; this we have sought to do along with achieving criticality by examining the underlying assumptions which researchers bring to their field of study, notably via 'scepticism towards rhetoric, tradition, authority and objectivity' (Mingers, 2000: 219).

In terms of the genre, we must address the limitations which surround our discussion about using and producing stories in marketing (research). We need to be careful to recognize that researchers can have two separate roles, firstly as story collectors and secondly as storytellers – sometimes aiming to allow the voice of the participant to come through clearly in the 'telling of tales from the field'; and in other cases coming close to appropriating the story for the purpose of theory building or theory generation. These two separate approaches to the relationship between the researcher and researched reflect somewhat the distinction which Crotty (1998) identified amongst interpretivist researchers in terms of social construction of reality (whereby the researcher explores with the researched in order to arrive at some view of the researched's reality) and subjectivism whereby the researcher imposes his or her categories upon the researched's world in order to generate meaning and understanding.

Another limitation of the story we have told relates to its concentration on consumer-generated stories, and here we need to fit our story back into the wider marketplace.

Stories are also generated elsewhere in the marketplace, sometimes purposefully: for instance, Twitchell's point (2004: 484), 'to me a brand is simply a story attached to a manufactured object'. Note that here the source of stories is identified in terms of anonymous actors within marketing communications, marketing management and brand management. This is a part of the 'marketplace/space' where stories circulate but this time they are managerially generated stories at the micro level of products and brands, but feeding into the 'meta narratives' about products and brands in the market place/space (e.g. brands as symbols, brands as heuristics of quality, for consumer decision making and choice). We have not dealt with any of these managerially generated stories.

On this note, dear readers, we must finish. We have told our story. We thank you for listening to us. We leave our story now to/for our various readers and audiences. We accept that our own story is now 'out there' and it (we) might well be incorporated into another story, over which we ourselves (like Dahl et al. and Fournier in our story) will have had little or no power, and therefore no control. By being incorporated into the wider world of stories, we will ourselves be (re)moved from the foreground to the background.

Notes

1. 'Stories can be read as illustrations of theory. . . . Stories can also be read as challenges to theory . . . telling stories is a tradition in anthropology, history, and some of the other interpretive social sciences, and if V & L [Vargo and Lusch, 2004] are correct that marketing scholarship must increasingly contend with value not frozen in objects but flowing in events, then, as anthropologists and historians do, marketing scholars may find that offering stories to one another to support or repudiate claims about the meaning of a sequence of events is a useful way to perform scholarship' (Deighton and Narayandas, 2004: 19).
2. We acknowledge our reviewer's points (from Heidegger and Husserl) about the role of memory in stories. We agree with Rosen's view that memory is 'an active social process'; and consider that parallels with storytelling can be drawn with Bearne's argument about oral history which 'raises complex and intriguing questions of truth and authenticity . . . about how the process of collecting oral evidence is itself a form of theorising about memory' (Bearne, 2000: 155–8).
3. These different treatments of the individual versus the social point to different types of 'knowledge' produced by the research. Many languages maintain a distinction between knowledge of a fact (e.g. *savoir*, *wissen*, *weten*, *sapere*) and knowledge of a person or a place with an implication of being acquainted with their particularities and character (e.g. *connaître*, *kennen* [German and Dutch], *conoscere*). For Dahl et al. the individual is backgrounded (see below for a discussion of backgrounding and foregrounding) and from this study the reader knows (*savoir*) social facts. For Fournier the individual is foregrounded and a key aspect of the study is allowing the reader to get to know or become acquainted with (*connaître*) the individuals. It seems to us critical that, just as when we speak of 'knowing' people in real life, we 'know' something but not everything about them, this applies equally to Fournier's study without in any way negating the idea of knowledge.
4. 'Foregrounding: A term used in stylistics . . . and sometimes in pragmatics and discourse analysis, to refer to any deviation from a linguistic or socially accepted norm; the analogy is of a figure seen against a background' (Crystal, 1985: 124). See also Hakemulder and van Peer (2004) for an extended discussion of the historical background and different theoretical applications of foregrounding whose origins can be traced to Russian Formalists (e.g. Shklovsky) and Prague Structuralists (e.g. Jan Mukarovsky) whose Czech term *aktualisace* was translated as 'foregrounding' and introduced by Garvin (1964) into linguistics. Foregrounding is found in stylistics, text linguistics and literary studies. 'Garvin's translation has rendered this temporal metaphor into a spatial one: that of a foreground and a background. This allows the term to be related to issues of perception psychology, such as figure/ground constellations' (Hakemulder and van Peer, 2004: section 1).
5. We thank our reviewer for reminding us of the importance of 'the untold stories'.
6. We recognize that researchers write (or present) for other audiences and in other media, each with their own conventions. We focus upon the academic media in which the papers we have analysed are situated, as is our own current contribution, and thus our own structure mirrors this genre; e.g. data collection, data analysis, research presentation and theory building. However we accept the important point made by our reviewer that, even within the academic media, alternative ways of presenting information are possible; e.g. the role of poetry (Sherry, 1998; Sherry and Schouten, 2002).

7. 'A story is a frame – a frame that emerges and is tried out, a frame that is developed and elaborated, or a frame that can easily absorb the new event. Boje's study [1991] shows that the line between "story making" and "story collecting" . . . is very fine if it exists at all' (Czarniaswska, 2004: 38).
8. 'One can ask: what are the reasons (motives) behind this text? Which are the causes that formed this text? How is this text read and by whom? Or how does this text say what it does? All are excellent questions and they all have in common one thing: they interrogate a text, which is the *raison d'être* of each enquiry' (Czarniaswska, 2004: 69).

References

Bearne, Eve (2000), 'Speaking from memory' (review of Harold Rosen's (1998) *Speaking from Memory*), *Cambridge Journal of Education*, **30** (1), March, 155–8.
Belk, Russell W. (1991), 'Epilogue: lessons learned', in R.W. Belk (ed.), *Highways and Buyways: Naturalistic Research from the Consumer Behavior Odyssey*, Provo, UT: Association for Consumer Research, pp. 234–8.
Belk, Russell (1995), 'Studies in the new consumer behaviour', in Daniel Miller (ed.), *Acknowledging Consumption*, London: Routledge, pp. 58–95.
Boje, David (1991), 'The story-telling organization: a study of story performance in an office-supply firm', *Administrative Science Quarterly*, **36**, 106–26 (cited in Czarniaswska, 2004).
Bruner, Jerome (1986), *Actual Minds, Possible Worlds*, Cambridge, MA: Harvard University Press.
Bruner, Jerome (1990), *Acts of Meaning*, Cambridge, MA: Harvard University Press.
Crotty, Michael (1998), *The Foundations of Social Research: Meaning and Perspective in the Research Process*, London: Sage.
Crystal, David (1985), *A Dictionary of Linguistics and Phonetics*, 2nd edn, Oxford: Basil Blackwell/André Deutsch.
Czarniaswska, Barbara (1998), *A Narrative Approach to Organization Studies*, Thousand Oaks, CA: Sage.
Czarniaswska, Barbara (2004), *Narratives in Social Science Research*, London: Sage.
Dahl, Darren W., Heather Honea and Rajesh V. Manchanda (2003), 'The nature of self-reported guilt in consumption contexts', *Marketing Letters*, **14** (3), 159–71.
Deighton, John and Das Narayandas (2004), 'Stories and theories', an invited commentary on 'Evolving to a new dominant logic for marketing', *Journal of Marketing*, **68** (1), January, 19–20.
Deshpande, Rohit (1983), 'Paradigms lost: on theory and method in research in marketing', *Journal of Marketing*, **47** (Fall), 101–10.
Eisner, E. (1981), 'On the differences between scientific and artistic approaches to qualitative research', *Educational Researcher*, **10** (4), 5–9 (cited in Firestone, 1987).
Escalas, Jennifer Edson and James R. Bettman (2000), 'Using narratives to discern self-identity-related consumer goals and motivations', in S. Ratneshwar and David Glen Mick (eds), *The Why of Consumption*, London: Routledge, pp. 237–58.
Firestone, William A. (1987), 'Meaning in method: the rhetoric of quantitative and qualitative Research', *Educational Researcher*, October, 16–21.
Flanagan, John C. (1954), 'The critical incident technique', *Psychological Bulletin*, **51** (4), 327–58.
Foucault, M. (1977), *Discipline and Punishment*, Harmondsworth: Penguin.
Fournier, Susan (1998), 'Consumers and their brands: developing relationship theory in consumer research', *Journal of Consumer Research*, **24** (March), 343–73.
Frye, N. (1957), *Anatomy of Criticism*, Princeton, NJ: Princeton University Press.
Garvin, P. (ed.) (1964), *A Prague School Reader on Esthetics, Literature Structure and Style*, Washington, DC: Georgetown University Press (cited in Hakemulder and van Peer, 2004).
Gergen, Kenneth J. and Mary M. Gergen (1988), 'Narrative and the self as relationship', *Advances in Experimental Social Psychology*, **21**, 17–56.
Golden-Biddle, Karen and Karen Locke (1993), 'Appealing work: an investigation of how ethnographic texts convince', *Organization Science*, **4** (4), November, 595–616.
Goodson, Ivor (2001), 'The story of life history: origins of the life history method in sociology', *Identity: An International Journal of Theory and Research*, **1** (2), 129–42.
Grayson, Kent (1997a), 'Narrative theory and consumer research: theoretical and methodological perspectives', Special Session Summary, *Advances in Consumer Research*, vol. 24, Provo, UT: Association for Consumer Research, p. 67.
Grayson, Kent (1997b), 'Stories and selling: the narrative strategies of direct sales agents', *Advances in Consumer Research*, vol. 24, Provo Utah: Association for Consumer Research, p. 68.
Gremler, Dwayne D. (2004), 'The critical incident technique in service research', *Journal of Service Research*, **7** (1) 65–90.
Hakemulder, Frank and Willie van Peer (2004), 'Foregrounding Research Development of Empirical Studies', (REDES.dehttp://www.redes.de/foregrounding/about.htm), accessed 20 July 2005.

Hill, Ronald Paul (1991), 'Homeless women, special possessions and the meanings of "home": an ethnographic case study', *Journal of Consumer Research*, **18** (December), 298–310.
Hill, Ronald Paul and Mark Stamey (1990), 'The homeless in America: an examination of possessions and consumption behaviors', *Journal of Consumer Research*, **17** (December), 303–21.
Hobsbawn, E.J. (1980), 'The revival of narrative: some comments', *Past and Present*, **86** (Feb.), 3–8.
Hopkinson, Gillian C. and Sandra Hogarth-Scott (2001), '"What happened was . . ." broadening the agenda from storied research', *Journal of Marketing Management*, **17**, 27–47.
Jokinen, Eeva (2004), 'The makings of mother in diary narratives', *Qualitative Inquiry*, **10** (3), 339–59.
Labov, William (2001), 'Uncovering the event structure of narrative', Georgetown University Round Table, Georgetown: Georgetown University Press (http://www.ling.upenn.edu/~wlabov/uesn.pdf).
Lincoln, Yvonna and Egon Guba (1985), *Naturalistic Inquiry*, Beverly Hills: Sage Publications.
Mason, Marlys and Teresa Pavia (1998), 'The disruption of the consumer life cycle by serious illness: the case of breast cancer', *Advances in Consumer Research*, vol. 25, Provo, UT: Association for Consumer Research, pp. 416–20.
Mingers, John (2000), 'What is it to be critical?', *Management Learning*, **31** (2), 219–37.
Mukarovsky, J. (1970), *Aesthetic Function: Norm and Value as Social Facts*, Department of Slavic Languages and Literature, Ann Arbor, MI: University of Michigan Press (cited in Hakemulder and van Peer, 2004).
Olsen, Wendy K. (2000), 'Originality or collective progress in the social sciences', *Feminist Economics*, available at (http://www.raggedclaws.com/criticalrealism/archive/wkolsen_ocpss.html).
Pavia, Teresa (1993), 'Dispossession and perceptions of self in late stage HIV infection', *Advances in Consumer Research*, vol. 20 Provo, UT: Association for Consumer Research, pp. 425–8.
Pavia, Teresa M. and Marlys J. Mason (2004), 'The reflexive relationship between consumer behavior and adaptive coping', *Journal of Consumer Research*, **31** (2), 441–54.
Polkinghorne, Donald E. (1987), *Narrative Knowing and the Human Sciences*, Albany, NY: State University of New York Press.
Rosen, Harold (1998), *Speaking from Memory: the Study of Autobiographical Discourse*, Stoke-on-Trent: Trentham Books.
Scott, Sara and Sue Scott (2000), 'Our mother's daughters', in Tess Cosslett, Celia Lury and Penny Summerfield (eds), *Feminism + autobiography*, London: Routledge, pp. 128–40.
Sherry, J.F. (1990), 'Postmodern alternatives: the interpretive turn', in H.H. Kassarjian and T.S. Robertson (eds), *Handbook of Consumer Research*, Englewood Cliffs, NJ: Prentice-Hall, pp. 549–91.
Sherry, John F. (1998), 'Nothing but net: consumption, poetry and research pluriculture (in the sixth moment)', presidential address, 26th Annual Conference of the Association for Consumer Research, Montreal.
Sherry, John F. and John W. Schouten (2002), 'A role for poetry in consumer research', *Journal of Consumer Research*, **29** (2), 218–34.
Smith, Mark J. (1998), *Social Science in Question*, London: Sage.
Stone, Lawrence (1979), 'The revival of narrative: reflections on a new old history', *Past and Present*, **85** (November), 3–24.
Strauss, Anselm and Juliet Corbin (1990), *Basics of Qualitative Research*, Newbury Park, CA: Sage.
Thompson, Craig J. (1997), 'Interpreting consumers: a hermeneutical framework for deriving marketing insights from the texts of consumers' consumption stories', *Journal of Marketing Research*, **XXXIV** (November), 438–55.
Thompson, Craig J. (2002), 'A re-inquiry on re-inquiries: a postmodern proposal for a critical–reflexive approach', *Journal of Consumer Research*, **29** (June), 142–5.
Thompson, Craig J., W. Locander and Howard R. Pollio (1989), 'Putting experience back into consumer research: the philosophy and method of existential phenomenology', *Journal of Consumer Research*, **16** (September), 133–46.
Thompson, Paul (2004), 'Pioneering the life story method', *International Journal of Social Research Methodology*, **7** (1), 81–4.
Twitchell, James B. (2004), 'An English teacher looks at branding', *Journal of Consumer Research*, **31**, 484–9.
Van Maanen, John (1988), *Tales of the Field: on Writing Ethnography*, Chicago: University of Chicago Press.
Vargo, Stephen L. and Robert F. Lusch (2004), 'Evolving to a new dominant logic for marketing', *Journal of Marketing*, **68** (1), Jan., 1–18.
Weick, Karl E. (1995), *Sensemaking in Organizations*, London: Sage.

13 The extended case method in consumer research
Steven M. Kates

The extended case method (ECM), a mode of data analysis and theory reconstruction, originates from sociological and social anthropological theory (Burawoy, 1991, 1998). It has made its appearance in recent consumer research studies and shows considerable promise to extend theory into relevant domains such as technology and satisfaction (Fournier and Mick, 1999), consumers' choices (Allen, 2002), brands (Holt, 1998) and institutionalized consumption settings (Holt, 1995). ECM, in contrast to its cousin, grounded theory (Strauss and Corbin, 1998), which seeks to develop invariant principles by abstracting from context, aids in the formulation of historically and contextually bound explanations of cases, social situations and particular consumption outcomes (see Burawoy, 1991, p. 280). Also in contrast to other interpretive, qualitatively oriented approaches such as grounded theory, ECM also seeks to understand the effects of macro social, cultural and contextual forces on situations, as reflected in micro observational and interview data. In the words of Michael Burawoy (ibid., p. 282), the method's chief proponent from sociology, ECM 'seeks to uncover the macro foundations of a micro sociology. It takes the social situation as the point of empirical examination and works with given general concepts and laws about states, economies, legal orders and the like to understand how those micro situations are shaped by wider structures'. The purpose of this chapter is to review the background of ECM, the ways it has been used in the consumer research discipline to further theory, give an example of its use and recommend avenues for further productive enquiry. I continue with a review on the background of ECM as developed outside of consumer research.

Background and defining attributes of the extended case method
ECM originates from the Manchester School of social anthropology, which sought to understand and create theoretical accounts of everyday practices, relating informants' actual practices to larger structures such as the intrusion of colonialism into African society (e.g., Gluckman, 1958; Mitchell, 1956; Van Velsen, 1960). More recently, the method has evolved into a means of building explanatory frameworks and understanding phenomena such as global markets' effects on local cultures (Burawoy, 2000), resistant cultural forms, such as the Radical Faeries, that undermine entrenched gender hegemony (Hennen, 2004), instances of violence in American schools (Sullivan, 2002) or the influence of consumer resistance on branding (Holt, 1998). What unites these disparate topics and analyses is the following elements that comprise the ECM: (1) an emphasis on a model of reflexive, rather than positivistic, science; (2) the selection of anomalous cases or contexts to reformulate (or reconstruct) pre-existing theory; (3) and engagement in a structuration stage of theory development in which the social forces that inform the ethnographic research context are mapped out and existing theory is

redeveloped in light of new findings. Each of these elements will be explored in turn, below.

Reflexive science

ECM's key philosophical tenet is that it seeks to explain social phenomena through the reflexive model of science: 'a model of science that embraces not detachment but engagement as the road to knowledge' (Burawoy, 1998, p. 5). In contrast, the model of positivistic science calls for the investigator to be appropriately distanced from the object of inquiry (reactivity) and to follow the rest of science's '4 R's' (Katz, 1983): reliability, reactivity, replicability and representativeness. In response, reflexive science embraces an orientation of active and creative engagement with the phenomenon under question. It advocates a productive dialogue and intersubjectivity between researchers and informants and even encourages interventions on the part of the researcher in order elucidate the 'secrets of the participant's world' (Burawoy, 1998, p. 14). ECM also calls for the researcher to understand the local knowledge and social processes that comprise the informant's world as reflected in the case scenario. For example, in Burawoy's (1972) own work on the decolonialization of the Zambian copper industry, he emphasizes that he was an actively engaged participant, not a non-intervening observer, in the African company in which he worked, rendering reactivity, problematic. Further, in such a context, the scientific criteria of reliability, reactivity, replicability and representativeness were all virtually impossible to attain owing to the unique and changing nature of the case.

Selection of anomalous cases

ECM's other key tenet is that researchers consciously select and problematize anomalous cases that are not satisfactorily explained and understood by extant theory and that promise to extend, reformulate and challenge theory, achieving *genetic* explanations of particular historical outcomes (Burawoy, 1991, pp. 280–81) rather than arriving at grounded theory's *generic* explanations for the similarities underlying several cases of a phenomenon. Burawoy (ibid., p. 273) provides an illuminating example of the value of anomalies in generating theory when he challenges Clifford Geertz's interpretation of the famous Balinese cockfight. Geertz (1973) interprets the cockfight as a key cultural exemplar, an event that demonstrates Balinese social organization, prestige and sense of national identity. Burawoy problematizes this interpretation by focusing on a key exception (i.e., an anomaly) that Geertz appears to dismiss – that the cockfight activities exclude women – and reformulates Geertz's interpretive theory. Hennen (2004), attempting to reconstruct Butler's (1990) postmodern theory on gender, chose the Radical Faeries, a group of 'self-described "country faggots" . . . devoted to undermining traditional masculinity' largely through drag, cross-dressing and other subversive cultural practices. The Faeries, as a marginal group that consciously rejects stereotypical gendered roles and understanding, qualifies as a worthwhile anomaly because its study promises to revise current theoretical formulations on gender. Sullivan (2002) studied one instance of extreme school violence in a middle-class neighborhood in order to theorize why violence would occur in a 'good' neighborhood with no previous history of violent crime. What unite these three research contexts are their unusual and exceptional natures compared to previous literature, and that previous theory could not fully account for them. Such unique cases, events and contexts may provide fruitful candidates for the use of the ECM, potentially yielding further insight into social reality and reconstruction of theory.

Structuration and reconstruction
ECM is also unique in that it requires researchers to explain social phenomena in light of both existing theory and the social forces that inform the research context selected, reconstructing existing theory and forging an understanding of the macro effects on the micro, interpersonal world. For example, in Burawoy's reconstruction of Geertz's interpretive theory, the cockfight is an exemplary of male domination in Balinese society in that it reinforces women's subordination and exclusion from the cash economy in the face of colonialization and foreign occupation (Burawoy, 1991, p. 279). Hennen reformulates Butler (1990) by arguing that the Radical Faeries, although undermining masculine hegemony with their various practices, do not provide any extreme examples of subversion of gender – a surprising finding because of the group's conscious rejection of heterosexual, normative masculinity and a testament to the enduring nature of dominant gendered cultural meanings. Sullivan (2002) explains school violence in a middle-class neighborhood with an analysis of family influence. All of these interpretations of new ethnographic or case contexts take previous theory as a springboard, demonstrate how the contexts are anomalous and, through analysis of interview and observational data, subsequently extend or reformulate previous theory.

This mode of interpretive explanation, along with the adoption of the model of reflexive science, addresses a key criticism of participant observation and most methods of qualitative data collection: that single case studies are not generalizable to other contexts (Burawoy, 1991, p. 272). In common with more conventional case analysis, the ECM achieves analytical generalization, not generalizations to populations (Yin, 2003). (That is, ECM seeks to build on theory by explaining a certain type of phenomenon or situation.)

Finally, distinct from conventional case analysis, but in common with much critical ethnography (e.g., Peñaloza, 1994), ECM incorporates the effects of power on the ethnographic context (Burawoy, 1998, pp. 22–4). The investigation of the research context is often jeopardized by the effects of domination, silencing objectification (i.e., assuming that social forces are external and natural) and normalization. In other words, like much methodology, ECM is prey to the effects of ideology (Hirschman, 1993). Burawoy offers the model of reflexive science in part to counter the effects of power and urges researchers to delve into the unconscious effects of gender, race, class and other structures of domination, promoting an understanding of who the research is intended to serve.

These previous studies demonstrate the way ECM has developed outside of consumer research, largely in sociology and anthropology. The next section shows how the methodology is used and has developed within the consumer research domain.

Use of the extended case method in consumer research
The ECM has been used to study various consumer phenomena including institutionalized leisure consumption (Holt, 1995), satisfaction with technology product (Fournier and Mick, 1999), choice of career colleges and universities (Allen, 2002), the ways consumers discursively escape market forces (Kozinets, 2002) and the link between brands and consumer culture (Holt, 1998). As above, what unites these studies is commitment to an interpretive, reflexive view of inquiry (i.e., engagement with the phenomena at hand),

choice of theoretically anomalous research contexts, reformulation of relatively mature bodies of theory in consumer research and the gathering of qualitative data from interview and observational sources. Four studies will be explored in depth (Allen, 2002; Fournier and Mick, 1999; Holt, 1998; Kozinets, 2002) to show the ways that the methodology is used and how it extends contributions to consumer theory.

Satisfaction models extended
Fournier and Mick (1999) employ the ECM to study the postpurchase consumption of technological products, thereby confirming, extending and challenging the dominant confirmation standards (CS) and related models of satisfaction in marketing. Technological products serve as a worthwhile anomalous context for a number of reasons: first, technological products are associated with important cultural meanings not previously studied; second, technology is often considered novel to many consumers, lending itself to productive theory development; and finally, the confirmation standards paradigm is a mature and developed body of theory in marketing that provides an excellent theoretical springboard, one that had not before incorporated consumers' firsthand experiences with technological products, for the authors to contrast their own findings and contributions. Overall, the Fournier and Mick (1999) study exemplifies a context in which the ECM may be used productively to generate new theoretical findings: well-developed pre-existing theory on satisfaction, a pronounced gap in knowledge in that consumers' accounts of postpurchase usage had not been studied and related to that body of theory, and an exceptional research context due to perceptions of newness and deeply embedded sociocultural meanings.

Fournier and Mick (1999) thoroughly elucidate what is new about their context, moving among data, memos and literature, systematically demonstrating that their interview cases confirm, extend and challenge the CS paradigm. Consistent with the CS paradigm, informants sometimes formed preconsumption expectations about products or benefits and had their expectations either confirmed or disconfirmed. Further, the authors demonstrate how the CS paradigm is moderately extended by their findings. For example, some consumers use an alternative comparison level (CLalt) to evaluate satisfaction outcomes, reflecting their dependency on technological products. The authors also extend theory by describing various new modes of satisfaction such as satisfaction-as-relief, satisfaction-as-awe and satisfaction-as-resignation. Moreover, particularly interesting about the study was the authors' identification of emergent anomalies of the CS paradigm: the way consumers' narratives appeared to violate fundamental tenets of the theory. For example, in some of the cases, consumers did not have apparent comparison standards, held unstable standards and revealed social and meaningful dimensions of satisfaction. Through systematic comparison of their data and previous literature, Fournier and Mick demonstrate the value that the ECM provides in terms of new insights. Their account also shows how the ECM is a very theory-driven mode of data analysis, in contrast to grounded theory. Each of their findings about technological consumption is made more meaningful by showing how it relates to prior theory but had not been previously incorporated by it.

The authors also develop a summarizing restructuration of technology consumption, another requirement of ECM, arriving at an expanded perspective of satisfaction. Technological consumption may be understood as balancing paradoxes, reflecting consumers' efforts to cope with the paradoxical nature of technology in their everyday lives.

In contrast to previous theoretical perspectives, technology is conceptualized as a domain in which consumers must handle basic tensions between freedom and enslavement, control and chaos, etc. in order to achieve satisfaction, and the authors link their findings with larger themes, such as quality of life. Although the authors do not link their analysis to larger historical and sociocultural forces – one requirement set forth by Burawoy (1998) – they do identify and explain anomalous cases that the current CS theory does not satisfactorily account for. Thus the ECM has evolved during its brief use in consumer research, suiting the needs of the research goals, not completely constrained by its original formulation.[1]

Choice models
The research goal of Allen's (2002) study of college and university choices was to develop a choice model named FLAG: 'Fits Like a Glove'. FLAG choice, in contrast to rational and constructive choice theories, is characterized by an emotional experience of instantaneous perfect fit with a choice object ('Aha! This is what I want!'), in situ encounter between an embodied consumer and a choice object, and shaping of the encounter by social and historical forces in the consumer and embedded in the choice object (Allen, 2002, p. 520). Allen (2002) faced a situation similar to the Fournier and Mick (1999) study: a well-developed body of theory (choice models) and an anomalous ethnographic context in which consumers made life-changing decisions (i.e., the choice of a career, college or university) emotionally and in the absence of clearly defined goals, weighted pros and cons, means–ends considerations and simplifying heuristics. FLAG choice of universities is set against a backdrop of rational choice theory and constructive choice theory, and Allen explicates how each element of FLAG is distinct from previous theoretical views in that it embodies experience of perfect fit with a consumption object, the importance of in situ context, and the social and historical shaping of the choice. These factors are also used to explain why such an important consumer choice is made instantly, in an impulsive and captivated manner, for a particular class of what was previously thought of as a high-involvement product.

Allen also critiques the ideology of choice that unconsciously informs other choice models. In the critical spirit of ECM, and as originally conceptualized by Burawoy (1991, 1998), Allen, in his account of the historical shaping involved in FLAG, shows how the effects of power and class were implicated in his informants' decisions. He contextualizes FLAG choice by describing how business and commercial education evolved in order to serve young women who, in the late nineteenth century, were displaced from rural areas and sought employment in large American cities. He also traces the related involvement of the Young Women's Christian Association (YWCA) in finding suitable employment for them, so they would not turn to prostitution. Allen broadens his critique by showing that traditionally, the working classes have been excluded from postsecondary university education and that commercial colleges stepped into this vacuum. Further, he concludes by critiquing the ideology of choice that informs much literature on consumer choices, arguing that the self and self-understandings are socially and historically embedded in context, and that his informants were subject to internalized and external inequalities that limited their life chances and opportunities to 'choose' the kinds of education and lives they might like. Thus, because the informants were unconsciously disposed with distaste for university education, their options were constrained without their fully appreciating it, and their choices are not illuminated by conventional paradigms such as rational or constructive choice theories.

Consumer emancipation/escaping the market

All consumers are constrained by the market – those discursive understandings and institutions that constitute postmodern capitalism. Kozinets (2002), in a participant observation study of the Burning Man arts festival, asks, 'How can consumers escape the market?' Although Kozinets' study on consumer emancipation does not explicitly acknowledge the ECM format, it does have the ordinary characteristics of research in this methodology: embrace of reflexivity, selection of an anomalous consumer context and reconstruction of pre-existing theory. Kozinets begins by reviewing the sources of cultural tensions between communal ideas ('caring and sharing') and market logics, and noting the problem of the market's constraining effects. The author assembles disparate strands of literature on brand communities, markets, subcultures of consumption and consumer emancipation, showing how past theory leaves unanswered questions about reconciling the isolating individualism of resistance with communality and about the undermining of community by markets (pp. 21–3). The Burning Man research context appears ideal to reconstruct past theory on community, markets and resistance, in that its members are determined to preserve a lived experience of caring and sharing community, by consciously distancing themselves from the market, physically by locating the festival in the middle of the desert and discursively by positioning their activities as diametrically opposed to the more negative aspects of commercial activity that characterize large corporations.

How then do consumers escape the seemingly omniscient and ubiquitous designs of the market? In rich ethnographic detail, Kozinets describes the ways the festival encourages all to participate, discourages commercial activity and explicitly disparages aspects of the market. Informants also alter conventional social relations by gift giving, sacralizing the notion of community and encouraging involvement, connection and personal disclosure at every possible opportunity. Art, as Burning Man's central institution, seems to replace the central role of consumption in the outside world, and participants use art as a means of individualistic self-expression, showing care for others, critiquing the negative aspects of the market and corporations and re-enchanting the world with creativity. Each of the ethnographic themes is developed in light of prior theory on markets and emancipation, while emphasizing the ways that (albeit temporary) communal social bonds are created among participants with sanctioned consumption practices. At every juncture, the author emphasizes that activities at Burning Man are positioned as creative and self-expressive, in opposition to the productivity and efficiency-obsessed preoccupations of the market, lying just outside the festival's boundaries. All of the artistic, critical and self-expressive practices help ensure creation of a contingent and temporary social space that is distanced from the market and yet reliant on market capitalism for its ideological grounding.

In typical ECM mode, Kozinets (2002, pp. 33–5) then reconstructs past theories on consumer communities and emancipation. Consumer communities may be viewed as means of counteracting the more disempowering aspects of consumer society, encouraging consumers to gather, express themselves and counter market tendencies toward attenuated social ties and bland self-expression. In recasting understandings of consumer emancipation, he also reconciles the sometimes alienating nature of individualistic self-expression, anathema to the communal ethos, by arguing that expression can be conceptualized as a gift to a community – often in the form of art. In conceptualizing the notion of 'hyper-community', Kozinets concludes that consumers may escape the market with an offering that is intense, short-lived and yet caring in its capacity to create social bonds. Indeed he opines that the impermanence, temporariness and speed of such a gathering may even help it evade the efforts of marketers to appropriate the experience into the corporate realm through sponsorships and the like. As Kozinets demonstrates, from the point of view of using the ECM, Burning Man serves as an excellent anomalous ethnographic context for theory development, largely because of its members' efforts to distance themselves from conventional corporate society, while depending on the influence of market logics to do so. Thus the cultural dialectics produced by the festival's social embeddedness lend itself very well to original and insightful theory development.

Brands and consumer culture
Dialectic tension is also central in Holt's (2002) theoretical analysis of branding and postmodern consumer culture. Holt, in attempting to explain the contemporary anti-branding movement, contrasts his theoretical perspective against two previously developed strands of thought: the Marxist critical tradition of the mass cultural industries developed by critical theorists in the 1950s, and the more recent theories of consumer emancipation and reflexive and creative resistance, as developed by Murray and Ozanne (1991) and by Firat and Venkatesh (1995). He argues that none of these theoretical perspectives describes postmodern consumer culture and branding and offers a dialectical model of a post-postmodern state of market affairs, depicting consumer culture as cultivating the self through brands and the dominant branding paradigm as the brand as citizen–artist enabling consumers' self-identity projects.

Holt bases his dialectical model on interviews with two consumers who exemplify anomalous resistant practices from the sociocultural mainstream. Consistent with the ECM methodology, he selected these informants from the periphery of American society, the sociocultural space in which consumer resistance might flourish. He identifies a number of themes that aid him in developing his model: reflexive resistance producing commodification of personal sovereignty, obtaining utility and useful cultural resources, filtering out propaganda and modes of creative self-production through brands. These themes serve as the basis for understanding brands as available cultural resources for identity construction, within a skeptical and ironic consumer culture. He then extrapolates from the findings of the two interviews to make predictions about the ways that consumer resistance will be co-opted to reproduce a new form of mainstream American consumer culture. He historicizes his theory by reviewing the developments in advertising agencies from the 1950s onward and by identifying the contradictions of postmodern culture that may move society toward an evolution toward post-postmodern culture: consumers' challenges of irony in advertising, sponsored market activities, claims to authenticity, violations of corporate values and the ability of brands to provide personal sovereignty. Holt concludes by describing how consumer resistance becomes a mode by which the market renews its cultural authority in providing consumers with original resources.

Summary
As described above, the ECM has helped make a number of important contributions to consumer theory in the areas of satisfaction, consumer choices, consumer emancipation

and branding. Its strength lies primarily in its capacity to identify contexts that appear unaccounted for by previous theories and allow original extensions and reformulations of pre-existing theoretical understandings. It also allows continued extension of theory, as will be demonstrated next.

An application of the extended case method
Holt's (1998) dialectical model of branding and consumer culture can be further refined and extended using the ECM. Arguably, consumer culture is quite fragmented and complex and his model of it – consumer culture as cultivation of identity through brands, and brands as cultural resources that act as citizens and artists – may be supplemented by alternative views of the role of brands in other consumers' lives. Consistent with the ECM, two informants were selected from the sociocultural margins of society: openly gay men whose consumer practices seem to challenge those of the dominant gendered mainstream, similar to Hennen (2004). Further, gay men's consumption is anomalous in a number of other ways: their subcultures allow for open discourse of sex, competition among men through consumption, and a critical view of consumer culture and homophobia (Kates, 2002, 2004). Further, gays in North American culture are culturally influential, socially visible and physically proximal to other communities, especially in large urban centers that have 'gay ghettos', making this population a prime candidate for investigation of their effects on consumer culture through the ECM.

For this illustration of the ECM, two interviews with gay men will be used. Stan (WM 25) and Clinton (BM 17) are two openly gay men whose consumption practices seem somewhat anomalous, even by the standards of other gay men. Both men offered numerous stories about producing alternative gendered selves through consumption, by using mainstream fashion, cosmetic and makeup brands. Interpretation of their interviews allows development of another theoretical view of consumer culture and brands, as below.

Constructing alternative gendered representations with brands
Both informants discussed activities such as wearing makeup, shopping for clothing at department stores and thrift shops, and hunting for unique items such as jewelry. Stan allowed that he wore makeup in order to 'look younger' and said that he was afraid of aging or showing his age. He also took pride in his ability to accessorize for every social occasion: 'If I was wearing a lot of green, I would smoke Craven A Menthol because it comes in a green and white package. I would have a green lighter to match the cigarettes, to match what I was wearing . . . If I was wearing burgundy or beige, it would usually be Avante with a beige or burgundy lighter.' Stan also liked to achieve an 'androgynous' look with his use of cosmetics, expressing pride that he was learning how to judge quality makeup: 'Clinique facial stuff, soaps, really good . . . then you go on to turnaround cream if it's during the day. And if it's the evening, I'll use the Clinique dramatic moisturizer, which gives you a glow [laughs] . . . for eyeshadows, either Shiseido or Lancome. And for men's colognes, would be Lancome or Calvin Klein Escape.' Brands are a means of expressing a form of gendered uniqueness, borrowing liberally from the stereotypically feminine domain. Nonetheless, Stan likes to put together 'his own look' by scouring department store displays and Salvation Army bins, negotiating a degree of masculine individuality (see Kates, 2002).

Gendered play and enacting strategic exhibitionism through brands

Clinton expressed a similar enthusiasm for shopping and wearing makeup, but his consumption practices assumed an additional nuance compared to Stan's: exhibitionism. He disclosed that he got his eyebrows waxed and then drew them on with eyeliner, wore a kilt, and wore other forms of makeup: 'I admit it, and I wear makeup . . . because I like to look good and I want to be hit on, specifically . . . I wear makeup which is considered a fag thing.' He clarified his stance on gender issues by stating: 'When you have guys going to the Body Shop, people normally think that's gay because the Body Shop sells perfumes and things like that. I think it's something that cares . . . once you care, you're gay. 'Cause guys don't care [about] anything. Stereotypically, men don't care. And if they do, this is the sensitive type that we're talking about here.' Wearing makeup and going to the Body Shop is connected to a key gender issue: men showing emotions and 'caring' about appearance, shopping and a host of personal concerns.

Clinton also enjoyed a form of gendered exhibitionism: 'I can then wear . . . my hoop earrings, a belt with a big metal buckle, some keys or something like that hanging out . . . I can walk and I can swish my ass from side to side or basically sashay down the street and then it's like "I'm gay! I'm gay! I'm gay!" It's how you wear it, not what you wear so much.' Gendered exhibitionism entails constructing a style that expresses difference from the heterosexual mainstream, calculated both to impress and to shock onlookers. It is also an ironic celebration of the ambiguities surrounding gender through consumption (Butler, 1990), a cultural theme in many gay communities (Kates, 2002).

The informants' practices also assume a broader sociocultural significance in light of Holt's (2002) dialectical theory of consumer culture and branding. Gay men, because of their social visibility and physical proximity to urban centers, are able to communicate their styles, consumption practices and preferences to the greater population through face-to-face contact, media and advertising (McCracken, 1986). And, historically, gay institutions such as drag, forms of camp and physical appearance standards developed in large urban centers in which they could be observed and could readily cross over through advertising and the fashion system (see Altman, 1982; Chauncey, 1994; Kates, 1998, 2002; Weeks, 1985). Based on their high visibility and social connections, consumer culture and the branding paradigm may assume other complexions, for some segments of consumers. Using Holt's (2002) methodology and theoretical framework, interpretation of informants' data suggests that postmodern consumer culture may be characterized by a strong and unconscious cultural meaning of 'homosexualization of mainstream consumer practices': that is, elements of mainstream and heterosexual society's adoption of various meanings and practices, culled from urban gay subcultures. Already we are beginning to see evidence of this crossover of consumer practices: young men are working out at the gym in greater numbers, showing anxiety about the muscularity of their physiques, and are even swapping beauty tips at the gym (Pope, 2000). Mainstream films such as *The Birdcage*, *Philadelphia* and *In & Out* feature both gay characters and plots and popular movie stars as they become box office successes. Fashions such as earrings, tattoos and shaved heads, popular among gay men, subsequently become popular among young heterosexual men. Mainstream culture is becoming very gay indeed!

The homosexualization of postmodern culture is accompanied by its supportive and corresponding branding paradigm principle: 'enablers of cultivating sexual and gender identities through brands, transforming masculinity'. This principle has been evident since the early 1990s. Mainstream marketers such as Ikea and Levi-Strauss target gay consumers and feature gay men and lesbians in their marketing communications. However, the branding principle goes beyond the niched strategy of courting gay consumers; marketers use ideas, meanings and practices drawn from gay culture and 'package' them along with their products. The recent success of the Nivea cosmetic line for men is an excellent example of the way gay men's commonly known concern for physical appearance has been transplanted from gay to mainstream context (see Kates, 2002). Calvin Klein targets many heterosexual male consumers with its sexually provocative, often homoerotic, imagery. Drag figures such as Dame Edna Everage are popular among both gay and heterosexual viewers. And finally, the success of the show *Queer Eye for Straight Guy* – featuring openly gay men showing heterosexual men how to eat, dress, shop and decorate – strongly attests to the crossover of gay customs and mores into the heterosexual cultural realm. (Tellingly, there's no show called *Straight Eye for the Queer Guy*!) The Queer Eye brand has recently branched out into other products such as books and videos. Thus studying a gay consumer context supplements Holt's (2002) dialectic theory of consumer culture and branding, suggesting that a rainbow of variation can coexist within each, informing consumers' and marketers' activities. Future research may investigate this proposition with the ECM.

Future research
Consumer research now has a well-developed and maturing body of theory informing many topics, including branding, choice, gift giving, consumer subculture, consumer emancipation and satisfaction. The ECM may enable researchers to confirm, challenge and extend this body of knowledge by investigating anomalous contexts. The ECM has not yet been extended into the study of gift giving (see Belk and Coon, 1993). For example, unusual gift-giving scenarios involving high levels of sacrifice by consumers may extend the vast body of work on gift-giving and further understandings of sacrifice. The method may also be employed to build on our developing understandings of gendered consumption (see Fischer and Arnold, 1990). For example, how do the consumption practices of men heavily involved in care of children extend our knowledge of gender and consumption? Different consumer and brand subcultures may challenge and extend our knowledge of social organization and consumption (see Muñiz and O'Guinn, 2001). In conclusion, the ECM, by seeking out challenging anomalies and unique contexts, has the potential to produce unique theory that challenges our current understandings.

Note
1. It should also be noted that, although Fournier and Mick (1999) identify, analyze and explain cogent anomalies and provide critique of the dominant CS model and related satisfaction theory, they do not *falsify* the CS model in Popperian fashion. The ECM is a reconstructionist, not a falsificationist, methodology in that it favors reconstructing theories in light of new observations/cases. A theory might eventually be rejected in light of many accumulated anomalies, in Kuhnian fashion, of course, but there seem to be certain sets of circumstances in which a theory might be wholesale rejected and falsified by a case or observation: when a case being investigated fits certain criteria in which the theory absolutely must predict a certain outcome in order to hold, such as virtually identical conditions under which the theory was developed.

References
Allen, Douglas E. (2002), 'Toward a theory of consumer choice as sociohistorically shaped practical experience: the fits-like-a-glove (FLAG) framework', *Journal of Consumer Research*, **28** (March).
Altman, Dennis (1982), *The Homosexualization of America, the Americanization of Homosexuality*, New York: St Martin's Press.

Belk, Russell W. and Gregory S. Coon (1993), 'Gift giving as agapic love: an alternative to the exchange paradigm based on dating experiences', *Journal of Consumer Research*, **20** (December), 393–413.

Burawoy, Michael (1972), *The Colour of Class: From African Advancement to Zambianization*, Manchester: Manchester University Press for the Rhodes–Livingstone Institute.

—— (1991), 'The extended case method', in Michael Burawoy et al. (eds), *Ethnography Unbound: Power and Resistance in the Modern Metropolis*, Los Angeles: University of California Press, pp. 271–87.

—— (1998), 'The extended case method', *Sociological Theory*, **16** (1), 4–33.

—— (2000), *Global Ethnography: Forces, Connections, and Imaginations in a Postmodern World*, Berkeley: University of California Press.

Butler, Judith (1990), *Gender Trouble: Feminism and the Subversion of Identity*, New York: Routledge.

Chauncey, George (1994), *Gay New York: Gender, Urban Culture, and the Making of the Gay Male World, 1890–1940*, New York: Basic Books.

Fischer, Eileen and Stephen Arnold (1990), 'More than a labor of love: gender roles and Christmas gift shopping', *Journal of Consumer Research*, **17** (December), 333–45.

Fournier, Susan M. and David G. Mick (1999), 'Rediscovering satisfaction', *Journal of Marketing*, **63** (October), 5–23.

Geertz, Clifford (1973), *The Interpretation of Cultures*, New York: Basic Books.

Gluckman, Max (1958), *Analysis of a Social Situation in Modern Zululand*, Manchester: Manchester University Press for the Rhodes–Livingstone Institute.

Hennen, Peter (2004), 'Fae spirits and gender trouble: resistance and compliance among the Radical Faeries', *Journal of Contemporary Ethnography*, **33** (5), 499–533.

Hirschman, Elizabeth C. (1993), 'Ideology in consumer research, 1980 and 1990: a Marxist and feminist critique', *Journal of Consumer Research*, **19** (March), 537–55.

Holt, Douglas B. (1995), 'How consumers consume: a typology of consumption practices', *Journal of Consumer Research*, **22** (June), 1–16.

—— (1998), 'Does cultural capital strective American consumption?', *Journal of Consumer Research*, **25** (1), 1–25.

—— (2002), 'Why do brands cause trouble? A dialectical theory of consumer culture and branding', *Journal of Consumer Research*, **29** (June), 70–90.

Firat, Fuat A. and Alladi Venkatesh (1995), 'Liberatory postmodernism and the reenchantment of consumption', *Journal of Consumer Research*, **22** (December), 239–67.

Kates, Steven M. (1998), *Twenty Million New Customers: Understanding Gay Men's Consumer Behavior*, New York: The Harrington Park Press.

—— (2002), 'The Protean quality of subcultural consumption: an ethnographic account of gay consumers', *Journal of Consumer Research*, **29** (December), 290–307.

—— (2004), 'The dynamics of brand legitimacy: an interpretive study in the gay men's community', *Journal of Consumer Research*, **31** (September), 455–64.

Katz, Jack (1983), 'A theory of qualitative methodology: the social system of analytical framework', in Robert Emerson (ed.), *Contemporary Field Research*, Prospect Heights, IL: Waveland Press, pp. 127–48.

Kozinets, Robert (2002), 'Can consumers escape the market? Emancipatory illuminations from Burning Man', *Journal of Consumer Research*, **29** (June), 20–38.

McCracken, Grant (1986), 'Culture and consumption: a theoretical account of the structure and movement of the cultural meaning of consumer goods', *Journal of Consumer Research*, **13** (June), 71–84.

Mitchell, Clyde (1956), *The Kalela Dance*, Manchester: Manchester University Press, for the Rhodes–Livingstone Institute.

Muñiz, Albert and Thomas C. O'Guinn (2001), 'Brand community', *Journal of Consumer Research*, **27** (March), 412–32.

Murray, Jeff and Julie Ozanne (1991), 'The critical imagination: emancipatory interests in consumer research', *Journal of Consumer Research*, **18** (September), 559–65.

Peñaloza, Lisa (1994), 'Atravesando fronteras/Border crossings: a critical ethnographic exploration of the consumer acculturation of Mexican immigrants', *Journal of Consumer Research*, **21** (June), 32–54.

Pope, Harrison (2000), *The Adonis Complex: The Secret Crisis of Male Body Obsession*, New York: Free Press.

Strauss, Anselm and Juliet Corbin (1998), *Basics of Qualitative Research*, 2nd edn, Newbury Park: Sage.

Sullivan, Mercer L. (2002), 'Exploring layers: extended case method as a tool for multilevel analysis of school violence', *Sociological Methods & Research*, **31** (2), 255–85.

Van Velsen, Japp (1960), 'Labour migration as a positive factor in the continuity of Tonga tribal society', *Economic Development and Cultural Change*, **8**, 265–78.

Weeks, Jeffrey (1985), *Sexuality and its Discontents: Meanings, Myths, and Modern Sexualities*, London: Routledge and Kegan Paul.

Yin, Robert K. (2003), *Case Study Research: Design and Methods*, 3rd edn, Thousand Oaks, CA: Sage Publications.

14 Unpacking the many faces of introspective consciousness: a metacognitive–poststructuralist exercise
Stephen J. Gould

Let us start with the idea that we are all introspectors. We assess all our experiences with the outer world reflexively in various forms and to varying degrees of introspection and self-consciousness. Moreover, intriguingly, we reflexively examine our own inner spaces to varying degrees and with varying sensitivities; that is, we engage in the practice of watching ourselves. While these issues tend to be psychological and cognitive, researchers taking a different orientation have also applied introspection especially in consumer research as embodying a subjective narrative about oneself. Some key elements of the psychological view of introspection drawn in part from current developments in metacognitive research (one's knowing about one's knowing) concern what we are or are not conscious of concerning ourselves, how we demarcate between I and other, how much and how deeply we penetrate our own consciousness, how motivated we are in this regard, and just how we understand our own mind and thought.

If we were to apply this understanding to a narrative point of view, the one largely followed in interpretive consumer research, we could consider how researchers and consumers construct these issues psychologically or use them to construct self stories. However the narrative approach does not, and generally might not even concern itself with such issues, instead focusing on the everyday story of one's life and consumption, generally within cultural theory contexts. All these parametric elements of introspection are defining, if not altogether reaching the level of a definition; we know introspection when we see it even if we cannot adequately define it. Perhaps it might be best to adopt a multilevel approach in which introspection is viewed from a wide range of perspectives, ranging from the micro psychological to the macro cultural (cf. Cacioppo et al., 2000). Here, in this chapter and informed by this multilevel approach, I offer the possibility of defining or at least comprehending introspection but only by relying more on you the reader's own experience of it through some proposed introspective exercises rather than depending on mere words.

Significantly in this regard, introspection can be seen to differ in the way various philosophical and research perspectives might approach it. Philosophically and historically the West has a tradition of self-examination which to varying degrees may be thought of as involving introspection and self-consciousness. Historically, the Greeks and specifically Socrates spoke of examining oneself. Descartes built on this approach with his 'I think, therefore I am' implying a noticing of one's inner being as central to one's existence. Asian cultures provide a fitting counterpoint to this perspective. In Asia (and I realize I am painting with a broad brush to make a point), self-examination and introspection have often taken the form of meditations in which consciousness is privileged not only in terms of thinking or the conceptual, but also in terms of the radical experience of the non-conceptual and non-self. For example, the state of emptiness focused upon in Buddhism is said to be recognized by the mind in a state of presence rather than conceptuality. Moreover, the idea of the non-self means that the self is a reified conceptual construction rather than something that is 'real'. Taken together, these broad cultural perspectives inform this chapter by suggesting that we need not only to consider both the cognitive and everyday narrative aspects of introspection, but also that both will be benchmarked against an experiential sensibility that embodies both the conceptual and non-conceptual without necessarily privileging the former.

Academic research perspectives on introspection have their own varieties, including psychology, ethnography in terms of researcher reflexivity and participant observation, autobiographical literature and consumer research, among others. Here we will consider psychological and consumer research. Psychology has focused on the cognitive aspects of introspection; however, where introspection emerged as a potential basis for research, controversy has reigned. Originally introspection was an approach to exploring the inner mind of individuals, but, as behaviorist viewpoints developed with the aim of taking a scientific approach and focusing on behavior, introspection was in effect censured. Later the ability to introspect successfully in terms of knowing things about one's mind and thought processes was overtly challenged. For example, in a very famous paper, Nisbett and Wilson (1977) reported that people relied on experientially derived rules rather than directly accessing their memories when asked about internal processes. Others sharply disagreed (e.g., Gould, 1995; Hixon and Swann, 1993; White, 1980).

In particular, I have argued (Gould, 1995) that putting people in the limiting circumstances of engaging in introspection in a lab setting for one single experiment does not allow for training in and practicing introspection, not to mention narrativity, that only comes to its utmost with time. To be sure, Nisbett and Wilson may have uncovered some limits on introspection that may reflect cultural limitations as much as they may reflect inherent capacity limitations for practicing it; certain introspective practices are simply bracketed out by individuals and cultures as unnecessary, epiphenomenal or not even recognized at all as being possible. Thus following the researcher-determined rules and contexts in the experimental setting Nisbett and Wilson created may have been the easy way for participants to get through the study. Different instructions and environmental settings, including more time and training, might have produced different results. A reverse bracketing is needed which seeks to penetrate beyond and bracket out the conventional or tacit rules of everyday suppression of many introspective processes so as to enable a more direct exploration of introspective processes.

In the continuous evolution of psychology, other research has emerged which could be said to involve introspection, though it is not called that. Self-consciousness (trait) and self-awareness (state) research evolved in which a person was said to focus on oneself or alternatively on one's environment. Interestingly for our concerns here, Fenigstein et al. (1975), who created the widely used self-consciousness scale, noted a connection to Asian meditative practices in their work; these types of practices will inform the introspective exercise approach to be developed later in this chapter. Later research which has concerned metacognition involving individuals' thinking about thinking or knowing about knowing would seem to be the latest incarnation of introspection though it is couched in other terms (cf. Alba and Hutchinson, 2000). Interestingly, one aspect of the metacognitive approach concerns the degree of confidence a person might have in what she is thinking about. Such an approach at least in part deals with the Nisbett and Wilson issue of whether introspection applies in personal thought process detection, though perhaps they would also argue that any confidence expressed is itself illusory.

In consumer research, introspection was born as a formal method within the larger paradigmatic context of qualitative or interpretive research versus so-called 'positivist' research. This division constituted a paradigm contest which has not altogether receded. Within this context, introspection came forth with such controversy that it divided not only positivist from interpretive researchers but also interpretive researchers from other interpretive researchers. Some of these interpretive opponents of introspection seemed to reflect a quasi-scientific point of view in which introspection as a case of one is seen to lack validity. A related issue concerns introspection as a process applied by anyone versus researcher introspection conducted by a researcher on herself (Wallendorf and Brucks, 1993; Gould, 1995). Wallendorf and Brucks in particular were concerned with the faults of a researcher writing about him or herself as exemplified in my earlier introspective paper (Gould, 1991) while I pointed (1995) to some of the advantages of doing so. Notably in this regard, Morris Holbrook (1988, 1995, 1996) richly focused on what he called subjective personal introspection which also drew on the researcher's own introspection without recourse to scientific method or thought. Perhaps at the least scientific-oriented extreme of the spectrum of thought, Stephen Brown (1998a, 1998b), reflecting autobiographical criticism, as well as more broadly various postmodern/poststructural perspectives, challenged any attempt to put the scientific into introspective approaches at all. Here I would suggest taking a poststructural site of meaning perspective with an emphasis on local meanings as opposed to universal ones so that various perspectives on introspection can be accommodated without being reduced to the others (cf. Holt, 1997). To show how this perspective can be applied I will propose some introspective exercises which you the readers can engage in and form your own opinions about the various facets and insights of introspection.

Introspective exercises or experiments
Based on the controversies and misunderstandings of prior introspective-related research, my own practice has evolved over the years to investigating what can and cannot be discerned or accessed by the individual in terms of conscious awareness. A major approach I have taken in this regard is to apply thought or meditational-type *introspective exercises* or *experiments* to point out the issues and let people investigate on their own the various perspectives. They also embody what people commonly refer to as thought experiments, though I conceive of them as encompassing a broader range of experience, including sensory perceptions, feelings and non-conceptuality while acknowledging that thought will still be a main driver in the conduct of these introspective exercises or experiments.

From a poststructural site of meaning perspective regarding the meanings and qualities of these exercises there may not be one universal set of introspective boundaries though, from other perspectives, such as cognitive psychology and cognitive neuroscience, there may be shared constraints or limits on what individuals can discern. Part of the issue concerns what is conscious versus unconscious and part concerns training to become conscious of what was formerly unconscious, ignored or epiphenomenal. Moreover there are various constraints, cultural and personal, that render some internal phenomena as phenomenal and some epiphenomenal. For example, the idea of lucid dreaming (being aware of one's dreams while actually dreaming) may seem epiphenomenal to those individuals or cultures who do not do it or who find dreams unimportant. To further illustrate in a consumer behavior context, researchers may fail to consider all the aspects of a consumption event, particularly those aspects which are private or otherwise hard to determine through research even though they may otherwise be salient. Thus there are some enduring introspective issues we can investigate.

The introspective exercises I am proposing stem from and are informed by a number of sources and roots, including meditation, various interpretive and research practices and various psychological perspectives. For meditation, I am informed mainly by Asian perspectives on meditation, though Western and other perspectives are also involved. Among interpretive research practices, such approaches as introspection, itself, phenomenology and literary–autobiographical approaches have been useful. Among psychological practices, many influence this perspective including again introspection, itself; self-consciousness, self-awareness and self-focus; exploring and manifesting variations in consciousness in terms of explicit, implicit and nonconscious perceptions; and metacognition, to name a few. Here I will use this exercise approach to stimulate, even incite, the reader to reach as far as possible in considering how research in terms of both process and content can be informed by such introspective exercises. You will note that my own introspection comes through in the creation of these exercises which I have constructed as processes for you to try and experiment with while leaving the content of your own thought as much as possible for you to watch on your own; that is, I am not attempting to substitute my particular thoughts for yours or to provide too many, which might bias your own processes. Of course there is a tradeoff between saying too much and too little since offering any suggestions to do something is necessarily suggestive but hopefully we can work with this potential source of bias by using the learnings we draw from any discoveries we might make.

The key exercise is just to follow one's thoughts. This method cuts across both academic disciplines and cultures and makes few if any assumptions about what thought is, or its contents. I say that because, whether thought is viewed more in micro-cognitive or macro-narrative terms, for instance, these descriptors and what they represent may be viewed as ornaments or aspects of thought rather than in the thoughts themselves. Let us see how all this works in Exercise 1. Exercise 1 is actually a series of exercises, conceived as being done in sequential order though, as almost everything I am saying here, much is left to the reader's discretion, including order of the exercises.

Exercise 1a   Thought watching
Sit quietly and watch your thoughts as they arise. At first, in particular, just try watching them without following them in the sense of paying attention to their content. This may seem hard to do since thinking is associated with its content and we do not typically view thought in this way. Get acquainted with this process and watch at various times. For instance, with some familiarity, you can try this exercise in active situations rather than just when sitting quietly.

Exercise 1b   Thought content watching
Alternate this process of not looking at the content of thought with periods of looking at the content. When we think of introspection as a research method or poststructural site of meaning or whatever, we are necessarily involved with its content.

Exercise 1c   Actively watching thought processes
Now also alternate not only with watching thought but also with taking a more active perspective. This means trying to think along some line of reasoning and then watching how that process proceeds. This is of course what consumers do when they pursue purchasing or using a product, that is they *consciously* pursue pertinent thoughts. At the same, notice how both pertinent and non-pertinent thoughts arise. Compare this to what is described in cognitive response research where non-salient thoughts are often isolated in favor of salient thoughts.

Exercise 1d   Watching senses and feelings
Beyond thoughts yet in conjunction with them focus on other aspects of your embodied and proprioceptive condition. Watch your senses and feelings in their ebb and flow. You could start with your breathing and see how that comes and goes. Watch how it changes in response to thoughts and feelings.

Exercise 1e   Watching and engaging watching
Next focus on watching your looking. Notice how you seem to select or focus on things, whether consciously or not. Try this with your other senses, one at a time. Be sure to include the proprioceptive sense which focuses on your sensing of your inner feelings. Later, try watching your senses in some conjunctive fashion, noticing how they may compete for attention. This can be related to emotional states as well so you can observe them separately and then in relation to the senses all together. You can focus on your emotions as they occur and even try inducing them as though acting to explore them more fully.

But a further element of this subject concerns the degree to which we focus on the actual workings of our minds versus just recalling or constructing something, as suggested by Nisbett and Wilson (1977). In some respects the thought here is to consider metacognitive elements of the issue in terms of how easily you introspect and how confident you are in the process or in your introspective skills.

Exercise 1f   What thinking can you watch?
Again watch your thoughts. But this time make an effort to really focus on them as a process. As with Nisbett and Wilson (1977) try focusing on a process such as multiplication and see if you can follow the process or are just constructing. Try several times over a period, noticing if your capacity for doing this changes. Then watch yourself as a consumer making a decision. Watch the process and see how it works. Can you really follow the process or are you really just reporting to yourself constructions from the past or the environment, etc.? Do a similar thing for your own research thought. Follow a research issue in your mind that your are dealing with and how you develop it. What can you detect about your own thought?

Now that we have this basis for engaging in introspective exercises we can engage in exploring a few vexing issues that have rendered introspection problematic for many researchers.

Extrospection versus introspection
One major issue to consider is that of extrospection versus introspection. Extrospection involves looking outward while introspection involves looking inward. The reason I have

posed this issue here is that consumer and other social science researchers are trained to focus extrospectively; their whole orientation is in that direction and this may cause them to miss a great deal in terms of understanding. In this regard, there is much that is paradoxical in this perspective which problematizes the meaning and experience of these two modes of perception. For instance, one can look inward at oneself extrospectively as though the watcher self is standing apart from the rest of the self. Or the opposite can also occur, namely that one views the outer world as a part or extension of oneself. As you might suspect from the foregoing in this chapter, one can experiment with these ideas through specific exercises.

Exercise 2a Extrospective focus
Deliberately try different ways to focus. First, focus outwardly and then consider where that focus goes. When you look outside, where is the boundary between that and any inner signaling you might make?

Exercise 2b Introspective focus
Then explicitly look inward while simultaneously retaining a consciousness of the external world. In that regard, consider the contrasts and borders between the two. When you think of yourself do you tend to do that with the external background prominent or not?

Subjectivity versus objectivity
Another issue concerns subjectivity versus objectivity. If objectivity is perhaps the *sine qua non* of scientific method in consumer and other social science research, subjectivity is anathema. However, introspection can connote, if not explain, what these concepts and practices of objectivity and subjectivity mean to us as sites of meaning, i.e., the focal conceptual locations where various meanings congregate both perserially and culturally. For instance, in my own personal understandings, I find that I am constantly exploring and negotiating within myself this Scylla and Charybdis of subjectivity and objectivity. Usually what we mean by objectivity involves an extrospective look at some outward standard. For example, we may feel cold and then look at a thermometer to confirm our feeling. Or we buy some clothes and ask others how we look in them. An equivalent in terms of mental states might be to experience a feeling and see how it correlates with a brain scan. Or we could have an experience such as drinking wine and checking with others whether it tasted the same to them or had the same bouquet. But if we look more metacognitively in terms of the watcher self, then objectivity and subjectivity deconstruct as useful concepts, as the following exercise shows.

Exercise 3 Subjective versus objective watching
We can pose the issue of objectively watching our thoughts and so on as an introspective version of extrospection; that is, we are watching almost as an outside observer our own mental states. Try such watching. Is this watcher self objective or subjective? For instance, how does it decide what to watch? Is it selective in what it attends to? Who watches that?

From a different perspective, experiment with subjectivity–objectivity in terms of the particular stance of the researcher through another introspective exercise.

Exercise 4a   Researcher objectivity versus subjectivity
Consider the idea that, when you hypothesize something, you are being subjective; that is, you already have an idea of what you are looking for and shade things accordingly. Conversely, consider that when you have no idea or do not hypothesize something you are being objective; that is, you have no preconceived idea of what to expect and this makes it more difficult to bias your thinking. How does this make you feel, since this perspective contradicts our usual training?

Exercise 4b   Considering a specific project subjectively or objectively
Now try taking something you are working on and form hypotheses (or a priori themes for qualitative research) about it. Think about how they guide your research as you think about it and watch with the watcher self how subjective or objective you seem to be. Then try again, perhaps with a different project, abandoning all preconceived ideas if possible. How can you think about this project? Even just to set it up may involve subjectivity, but remember you are trying to be objective without any preconceptions. Watch your mind as you engage in this process. Note how it makes you feel. Does it make you feel uncomfortable? Liberated? How might these feelings enter into your research?

As with any other conceptualizations, subjectivity and objectivity are social constructs that we tend to take for granted. These exercises informed by introspection might help you to view them in a new way, based on some experiential understanding.

Degrees of self-focus (consciousness)
A subtle and perhaps new issue to considering introspection in consumer research concerns the degree to which one focuses on the inner workings of the mind and the self during introspection. In psychology, there is research (e.g., Fenigstein et al., 1975) which concerns the degree to which one focuses on oneself, as opposed to externally. This echoes the introspective–extrospective aspects of introspection, but problematizes them. If we take introspection to concern a focus on one's internal processes, this may or may not involve the self. While much that involves introspection is also reflexive in the sense of one's referring to oneself in such terms as 'I' and 'me', especially in narrative introspection, introspection focusing on inner mental processes has the capacity to be less reflexive in terms of an 'I'. This is something we might see explicitly expressed in Asian thought, but which can be readily considered when people are asked to focus on their own mental processes. Various Buddhist exercises, for instance, deconstruct the self and yet do not obviate the continuation of mental processes.

Exercise 5   The introspective construction of self-focus
Once again, focus on your thoughts. Are you conscious of a self or not? Is that self even necessary? Play with focusing on the self and then not. When calling forth the self make sure it does not disappear and keep focusing on it. When trying not to focus on the self, block it when it arises. Notice how the self arises and in what form, 'I', 'me', your name or some other form. Even notice the voice or person that it arises in, first, second or third. Some people refer to themselves in their private inner speech if not in public in terms of 'you' or in such terms as 'this guy (gal)'.

All this should address what self-focus and reflexivity might mean and the forms it might take. Perhaps some discoveries can be made in terms of how consumers think about themselves and apply this in their consumption. As you experiment with these introspective exercises, consider what they mean for our understanding of both consumer behavior and research. How much can we say we understand what consumers and researchers are doing or think they are doing?

Narrative versus metacognitive introspection
Now, as researchers, consider what these perspectives might mean. As researchers, we generally tend to focus in an extrospective fashion on consumers as the 'subjects' of our gaze. In traditional social science research, this is the proper way to do it; that is, to disengage from our own self and its biases. But if the boundaries are not always that clear, such a perspective may be misleading at best. On the other hand, smearing all data with the self can be equally misleading. The idea here is to explore the range of the researcher's self-interventions in her research and develop ways to account for it. We might call that the Researcher Self which is a type of watcher self in which the researcher recognizes or at times even manipulates the effects of this self. Recognizing such a self leads not to excluding it in research and not to privileging it either. Rather awareness of it might be likened to a process of calibration where conclusions are drawn with understanding of its role and effects.

Verbalized introspection of any type takes the form of a narrative and text. The quick hitting, micro-level psychological study employing or making introspection salient in some aspect might be likened to a short story or even a poem, while the literary or auto-biographical approach is more like a novel. Thus there is a continuum of sorts. Sometimes it is forgotten that narrative and various related cultural appurtenances may emerge in the most micro as well as macro versions of introspection. For example, I have discussed cognitive response very much as an introspective technique in the sense of calling attention to one's own mind and reflecting the degree to which a person examines their own reasoning as opposed to external factors (Gould, 1999). Likewise I find phenomenological research to have similar effects. In all such research, I find a distinctive reflexive and introspective element in which informants relate virtually whatever they are discussing back to themselves in an explicit manner. This is not to say that such informants are necessarily watching their thoughts in some conscious manner but rather that, at least in some manner consistent with metacognitive perceptions, they consider what the particular things they are focusing on mean to themselves and in terms of themselves.

Moreover, when viewed in this way, the scientific versus non-scientific controversy is diluted if not entirely washed out to sea. This is not to sweep all such controversy under the rug, but instead is to lay out what for me is a far more cogent paradigm, namely that the various types, aspects and styles of introspection and therefore research in general when taken together constitute a vivid mapping of consumer research. Of course, each of the various introspective research approaches retains its integrity as a singularity and the contribution of each will vary according to some ideas of quality, originality, creativity, research and managerial implications and so on. Some readers of such research may seek out good *rich, thick* stories while others may seek out *valid* results. Insight can spring from anywhere and that is the key point here. Complementarities may be found if they exist, but at the same time nothing is reduced to anything else.

At this point it might be useful to consider and define further what I find to be the two major research and also everyday approaches to introspection to illuminate this point. One concerns what I call 'metacognitive introspection', which involves one investigating one's own mind and consciousness or some aspect of them in psychological and/or meditational terms by watching one's thoughts and feelings. The other is 'narrative introspection', which involves autobiographically thinking through and/or telling one's own story or various aspects of it. These two in their most extreme forms comprise the two ends of a continuum, as shown in Table 14.1, though often in practice both types may be present to varying degrees. When we view extant introspection in this way, we address a major issue as to why introspection is understood in such varying ways and why ownership and meaning of the term is somewhat confusing; polysemy and multiple introspections assert themselves. Some element of metacognitive introspection is involved in most if not all cognitive psychological research. On the other hand, narrative introspection permeates the domain of personal stories, autobiography and various other forms of interpretive research. It is exemplified in the work of Holbrook (1988, 1995), Earl (2001), Sayre (1999) and Brown (1998a, 1998b) who applied some form of what Holbrook has called 'subjective personal introspection'. So-called 'researcher introspection' has largely been embodied in narrative introspection though there is no necessity for that being the case.

Indeed my own work involving research introspection may be seen as a combination of approaches, though I may not have called them that at the time of my earlier work. In my 1991 article, I told aspects of my own story but applied them in terms of analyzing aspects of mind and, particularly, energy (cf. Gould, 1993, on consciousness). While my personal story was salient, my major aim was to draw on it to illustrate from what I now call a metacognitive approach the inner forces of consciousness and energy that I was and am primarily interested in. For example, I described (1991) very personal, even intimate experiences involving using products to maintain or enhance my own energy. I extended (1995) this idea of personal introspection by engaging the reader to try to some of the same introspective exercises herself. Thus while I naturally and unfailingly draw on my own experiences, I apply them to encourage others to see what they experience in similar contexts. What I had hoped and continue to pursue is the idea of people addressing these issues of consciousness, energy and inner states in ways that other research approaches do not permit.

This approach is now what I call 'metacognitive introspection', in that it involves introspecting about one's inner processes and engaging what in meditation circles is often called the Watcher Self. I merged that with what I now call 'narrative introspection', in telling about and applying my own particular experiences of watching the processes I applied. In this context, I would characterize what has been called 'subjective personal introspection'

Table 14.1   The continuum of narrative and metacognitive introspection

Metacognitive introspection (micro, watching thoughts, feelings in real time)	Narrative introspection (macro, telling stories, providing autobiographies)

as incorporating both metacognitive and narrative introspection, in that they both draw on subjectivity. I say this while recognizing the paradox of meta-cognition and the Watcher Self as also perhaps involving an effort to be objective and scientific. While this could be disconcerting to some, we need not be too concerned, but should play with this idea.

As we have discussed, a major contested issue in the domain of introspection concerns the seeming division of its processes into the watching and analysis of cognitive activity versus that of narrativity in which a person tells his or her own story. Here we need to explore this issue further in the form of a set of deconstructive exercises in which you can see what you, yourself, experience in this regard and what to make of it.

Exercise 6a   From metacognitive thought watching to narrative
While you can start anywhere, here, in describing this exercise, I will begin with thought watching. As before, watch your thoughts without trying to formulate any concepts or stories related to them. You might notice if and how they may nonetheless form a narrative line, if not a complete narrative. If that happens, notice it but then let it go. Do not get attached to these narrative lines or at least try not to. Notice how they arise and if there is an order you can discern or if they arise in some random fashion.

Exercise 6b   From narrative to metacognitive thought watching
Later, do the reverse. Think about a specific event in your life, perhaps one that is ongoing or one that occurred in the past. It might help to pick one you are particularly involved in so that its power captures your mind and holds its attention.

At the same notice how thoughts about it or other things arise as well. When deviating thoughts occur, bring your mind back to the story. Notice how easy or difficult that is to do and how you feel. What control do you have over these thoughts? Continuing, now purposefully disrupt the story. Notice what occurs and how that makes you feel. What life does the story have on its own and what say does your watching mind have in this process?

Exercise 6c   Narrative, thought and emotion
Experiment with the same story on different occasions as well as different versions or altogether different stories, perhaps some of different types. Again, the idea is to focus on the process of narrative construction and relate it to the thought process. Do different emotions or moods alter the process; for example do they produce more or less stability of a story line? Do more or less random thoughts occur at certain times, such as when you are calm or restive? How do thoughts get constructed into stories and, where relevant, how much or how little do these seem to correspond to something we might call 'external reality' for the lack of a better term? (Note: you might also explore whether external reality exists separately from your thought and, if so, how.)

You can tweak these exercises all you want and find your own permutations in terms of the process and content. The main thing is to explore thought and narrative and discover how they play or do not play together. Perhaps these introspective exercises can inform your research so that we can all better understand the process of narrative construction. How are consumer stories constructed, what 'thought' goes into them and what can we make of them? This might help us to understand better the research methods of cognitive response (protocol analysis) which I have previously argued is an introspective process (Gould, 1999), structured interviewing and the more unstructured approaches such as phenomenological interviewing (Thompson, Locander and Pollio, 1990). In terms of thought, cognitive response is seen to be more automatic and 'top of mind', while structured interviewing may be seen to create story lines that the researcher is interested in. Relatively unstructured approaches give more freedom to the informant's own story line.

You can further explore these aspects through your own elaborations of the exercises given here, as well as having informants placed in various situations and considering what emerges. Adapting a poststructual site of meaning perspective, each person is a site of meaning, each context socially and culturally is a site of meaning, each time is a site of meaning, each narrative research method is a site of meaning and ultimately each thought is a site of meaning. Taken altogether (and not to exclude any other aspects you might think of), they all constitute a constructed site of meaning, built of all these aspects. The perhaps infinite but not unmanageable topic of research is to dig more deeply into them in ways that are meaningful and relevant to you. As a discipline, we can collect these investigations into a further story or stories though not necessarily into some kind of overarching or choking metanarrative (Lyotard, 1979/1984).

Conclusion

Introspection is a central process of everyday life, albeit a culturally and scientifically contested one with many variations and understandings. Thus the meaning of this term is actually quite polysemic and ambiguous and laden with all sorts of charged connotations and ideological subtexts. Stepping back, as we have attempted here, we can interact with all these diverse meanings and parameters not to delimit them but rather to engage them as the rich expression of our human condition. Researchwise, we can choose to apply what we wish from this broad menu of understanding, ranging from the metacognitive to the narrative, depending on our particular applications, not to mention our own research personalities (cf. Hirschman, 1985). Thus the introspective exercise (thought experiment), while not typically thought about as a research method, may be used to inform these and other research choices by making us conscious of processes we already apply. It may turn out to be very useful to break down the barriers to our own self-understandings as we conduct research driven by those same understandings. Think about it.

References

Alba, Joseph W. and J. Wesley Hutchinson (2000), 'Knowledge calibration: what consumers know and what they think they know', *Journal of Consumer Research*, **27** (2), 123–56.
Brown, Stephen (1998a), 'The wind in the wallows: literary theory, autobiographical criticism and subjective personal introspection', in Joseph W. Alba and J. Wesley Hutchinson (eds), *Advances in Consumer Research*, Vol. 25, Provo, UT: Association for Consumer Research, pp. 25–30.
Brown, Stephen (1998b) (http://www.sfxbrown.com/on_marketplace_melodies.htm).
Cacioppo, John T., Gary G. Berntson, John F. Sheridan and Martha K. McClintock (2000), 'Multilevel integrative analyses of human behavior: social neuroscience and the complementing nature of social and biological approaches', *Psychological Bulletin*, **126** (6), 829–43.
Earl, Peter (2001), 'Simon's travel theorem and the demand for live music', *Journal of Economic Psychology*, **22** (3), 335–58.
Fenigstein, Allan, Michael F. Scheier and Arnold H. Buss (1975), 'Public and private self-consciousness: assessment and theory', *Journal of Consulting & Clinical Psychology*, **43** (4), 522–7.
Gould, Stephen J. (1991), 'The self-manipulation of my pervasive, perceived vital energy through product use: an introspective-praxis perspective', *Journal of Consumer Research*, **18** (September), 194–207.

Gould, Stephen J. (1993), 'The circle of projection and introjection: an introspective investigation of a proposed paradigm involving the mind as "consuming organ" ', in Janeen A. Costa and Russell W. Belk (eds), *Research in Consumer Behavior*, Vol. 6, Greenwich, CT: JAI, pp. 185–230.

Gould, Stephen J. (1995), 'Researcher introspection as a method in consumer research: applications, issues and implications', *Journal of Consumer Research*, **21** (March), 719–22.

Gould, Stephen J. (1999), 'Protocol and cognitive response analysis', in Peter E. Earl and Simon Kemp (eds), *The Elgar Companion to Consumer Research and Economic Psychology*, Cheltenham, UK and Northampton, MA, USA: Edward Elgar, pp. 468–72.

Hirschman, Elizabeth C. (1985), 'Scientific style and the conduct of consumer research', *Journal of Consumer Research*, **12** (September), 225–39.

Hixon, J. Gregory and William B. Swann (1993), 'When does introspection bear fruit? Self-reflection, self-insight, and interpersonal choices', *Journal of Personality and Social Psychology*, **64** (January), 35–43.

Holbrook, Morris B. (1988), 'Steps toward a psychoanalytic interpretation of consumption: a meta-meta-meta-analysis of some issues raised by the consumer behavior odyssey', in Michael J. Houston (ed.), *Advances in Consumer Research*, Vol. 15, Provo, UT: Association for Consumer Research, pp. 537–42.

Holbrook, Morris B. (1995), *Consumer Research: Introspective Essays on the Study of Consumption*, Thousand Oaks, CA: Sage.

Holbrook, Morris B. (1996), 'Romanticism, introspection, and the roots of experiential consumption: Morris the epicurean', in Russell W. Belk, Nikhilesh Dholakia and Alladi Venkatesh (eds), *Consumption and Marketing: Macro Dimensions*, Cincinnati, OH: South-Western College Publishing, pp. 20–82.

Holt, Douglas B. (1997), 'Poststructualist lifestyle analysis: conceptualizing the social patterning of consumption in postmodernity', *Journal of Consumer Research*, **23** (March), 326–50.

Lyotard, Jean François ([1979] 1984), *The Postmodern Condition: A Report on Knowledge*, trans. Geoff Bennington and Brian Massumi, Minneapolis: University of Minnesota Press.

Nisbett, Richard E. and Timothy DeCamp Wilson (1977), 'Telling more than we can know: verbal reports on mental processes', *Psychological Review*, **84** (May), 231–59.

Sayre, Shay (1999), 'Using introspective self-narrative to analyze consumption: experiencing plastic surgery', *Consumption, Markets and Culture*, **3** (2), 99–128.

Thompson, Craig, William B. Locander and Howard R. Pollio (1990), 'The lived meaning of free choice: an existential–phenomenological description of everyday consumer experiences of contemporary married women', *Journal of Consumer Research*, **17** (December), 346–61.

Wallendorf, Melanie and Merrie Brucks (1993), 'Introspection in consumer research: implementation and implications', *Journal of Consumer Research*, **20** (December), 339–59.

White, Peter (1980), 'Limitations on verbal reports of internal events: a refutation of Nisbett and Wilson and of Bem', *Psychological Review*, **87** (January), 105–12.

15 Mixed methods in interpretive research: an application to the study of the self concept
Shalini Bahl and George R. Milne

Introduction

Interpretive research by its very nature is multi-method, involving different forms of data collection, multiple studies, the use of triangulation, and so forth. Illustrative of a multi-methods approach in interpretive research is the study by Belk, Wallendorf and Sherry (1989), which used a combination of observation, field notes, interviews, photographs and video. Less common, however, in interpretive research, is the use of mixed methods, which we define as a research approach comprising qualitative and quantitative methodologies for both data collection and analysis.

The mixed methods approach is not frequently used in interpretive research owing in part to the paradigm wars, which have created artificial barriers that limit the use of methods across paradigms. In marketing, the positivist and interpretive paradigms have been profiled in terms of their ontological, axiological and epistemological assumptions (Hudson and Ozanne, 1988) that have been historically tied to the qualitative versus quantitative camps (Deshpande, 1983).

In the marketing literature most articles employing mixed methods have a positivist orientation. The philosophical assumptions guiding positivist research include an objective view of reality, which the research seeks to measure and explain. Consistent with its ontological and axiological assumptions, positivist research seeks the creation of knowledge that is generalizable across different people, times and situations and is, thus, time- and context-free. While the methods used in positivist research have primarily been quantitative, qualitative methods have been used but only to support the quantitative methods in the development of measures, in the development of theory using grounded theory approaches or clarifying existing quantitative results.

Examples of articles that use mixed methods in interpretive research are fewer in marketing. The philosophical underpinnings for interpretive research include the assumption of multiple realities that are socially constructed and the primary goal of understanding reality from the perspective of those experiencing it. In contrast to positivist research that seeks generalizations, interpretive research is typically time- and context-bound. Interestingly, the mixed method articles that ascribe to an interpretive approach in marketing tend to be more pragmatic, in that their primary focus is the research question, without being committed to a particular research approach and philosophy.

Despite the trend for most mixed methods research articles in marketing to be either positivist or pragmatic, we believe it is possible for interpretive research to use mixed methods, and remain true to their philosophical assumptions. Mixed methods may be avoided because interpretive researchers feel that the use of quantitative methods requires altering one's underlying assumptions. However, this is unnecessary since it is not the method but how it is used that needs to be consistent with the philosophical assumptions.

That is, the appropriateness and use of a method is determined by the researcher's orientation and the phenomena being studied (Morgan and Smircich, 1980). The flip side of this is that the methods do not define the type of study that is being conducted. As noted by Geertz (1973), methods do not define the research; rather, intellectual effort does. For example, qualitative methods can be and have been used successfully in positive studies. By the same logic, quantitative methods can be used in interpretive studies. In this chapter we demonstrate how quantitative methods can be used effectively in interpretive research.

Thus the purpose of this chapter is to illustrate the use of mixed methods in interpretive research. To this end, we present a mixed method approach that was used in a study of the self concept. The balance of this chapter is in four sections. We begin by reviewing the mixed methods approach. Next, we discuss the application of a mixed methods approach to study multiple selves. This is followed by an empirical demonstration of this approach. In the last section, we discuss the advantages and shortcomings of mixed methods, and comment on possibilities for other interpretive work to use this approach.

Mixed methods approach

Mixed methods is becoming a viable research approach that bridges the gap between quantitative and qualitative methodologies (Brewer and Hunter, 1989; Creswell, 2003; Tashakkori and Teddlie, 1998). Mixed methods are often seen as eclectic, pluralistic and rejecting traditional dualisms. Moreover they have been argued to be more pragmatic and driven by the research question rather than being constrained by paradigmatic assumptions (Johnson and Onwuegbuzie, 2004). Tashakkori and Teddlie (1998) outline the characteristics of pragmatism, where they feel that most mixed methods studies fit. The methods used are both quantitative and qualitative; the logic is both deductive and inductive. Moreover pragmatic research does not align itself with a single system of philosophy and reality (Creswell, 2003).

In marketing, a wide range of mixed methods studies can be found in the continuum between pure positivist and pure interpretive studies. Some studies tend to be closer to the positivist end of the continuum, in that they use qualitative methods to support quantitative methods that are used to measure and explain phenomena. Others tend to be more interpretive, in that both qualitative and quantitative methods are used to understand the meaning of an observed phenomenon from the perspective of the consumer. Interestingly, many of the mixed method studies do not explicitly state their philosophical assumptions and, based on criteria outlined by Tashakkori and Teddlie (1993) and Creswell (2003), these studies could be viewed as pragmatic (e.g. Price, Arnould and Tierney, 1995).

The classification of mixed method research has been undertaken by both Creswell (2003) and Tashakkori and Teddlie (1998). Creswell notes that mixed method research can be classified as having the quantitative and qualitative portions of the study, which can be conducted sequentially or simultaneously. Tashakkori and Teddlie (1998) emphasize that mixed methods influence multiple stages of the research, including type of inquiry, data collection/operations and analysis/inferences.

In Table 15.1 we present a 2×3 matrix to show the range of mixed methods approaches that are possible. The columns in the matrix represent the orientation of the research article (positivist or interpretive) and the rows represent the mixed methods strategy used in the article (independent, overlapping and fully integrated). We classify articles as having a positivist or interpretive orientation according to the philosophical underpinnings implicit

Table 15.1   Examples of mixed methods studies in marketing

Mixed methods research strategy	Research orientation	
	Overall positive	Overall interpretive
Independent	Milne, Iyer and Gooding-Williams (1996)	–
Overlapping	Hausman (2000)	O'Guinn and Faber (1989)
Fully integrated	McAlexander, Schouten and Koenig (2002)	Arnould and Price (1993)

in their study. Within each orientation, it is possible to employ either the independent, overlapping or fully integrated research strategy. We define the mixed research strategies based on two criteria. The first is whether the data from using a qualitative method serve as input to a quantitative method. (While rare, it is possible for data from quantitative methods to serve as input to qualitative methods.) The second is whether the quantitative and qualitative data are analyzed in an integrated manner. Articles are classified as independent if their methods do not meet either of these criteria, as overlapping if their methods meet one of the two criteria, and as fully integrated if their methods meet both of the criteria.

When compiling Table 15.1, there were many examples of positivist articles with mixed methods, but fewer examples for interpretive articles with mixed methods. We discuss the articles in this table next. Independent mixed methods research typically occurs with a study 1 – study 2 format, where data collection and analysis are done independently in the two studies. In the positivist realm, an example of an independent mixed method research is the article on green marketing alliances by Milne, Iyer and Gooding-Williams (1996). In their first study, they conducted a survey and used multivariate analysis to measure the relative effectiveness, formality, influence and political positions associated with different types of alliances. Because their research was only able to document differences across alliances and did not provide a well-rounded interpretation of results, they conducted study 2, which consisted of 24 in-depth telephone interviews based on organizations that participated in their survey. The purpose was to add to study 1's findings and help shape future research. Thus this article exemplifies the independent mixed methods strategy because the data collection and analysis in the two studies were conducted independently.

The occurrence of independent mixed method interpretive studies is unlikely. This is perhaps because interpretive studies combine various data sources as part of their research tradition. Thus we do not report any independent interpretive examples.

The next strategy of overlapping mixed methods has either data from one type of method serving as input to another, or the data from both quantitative and qualitative methods being analyzed jointly. Hausman's (2000) study of impulse buying provides an example of a positivist approach using the overlapping strategy. Sixty in-depth interviews were used to develop grounded theory and form hypotheses. These were, in turn, tested with the collection and analysis of survey data from 290 consumers. The hypotheses formed from the interviews were tested using survey data and analysis of variance. In this example of the overlapping strategy, data from the qualitative method were used as input for the quantitative method.

O'Guinn and Faber (1989) combine quantitative and qualitative data in a more inter-pretive manner. The purpose of their research was to provide a descriptive account of compulsive buyers. In their research they used in-depth qualitative interviews to contex-tualize descriptive survey data. This method included observing group therapy sessions, group and individual interviews and reading a thousand letters from compulsive buyers prior to fielding their survey. This was used to frame the study and form a sample for the mailing. In the study itself they used mixed methods. First, they used a mail survey to compare compulsive shoppers with other shoppers; second, they conducted five in-depth qualitative interviews with individual compulsive buyers to contextualize the quantitative findings. In this example of the overlapping strategy, data from both methods were ana-lyzed and interpreted jointly. However, this article was not considered fully integrated because data from one method did not serve as input to the other method.

The last strategy is fully integrated, in which data from one method serve as input for the other, and the data from both methods are analyzed together. McAlexander, Schouten and Koenig's (2002) study of the jeep brand community and customer relationships within the community is an example of a fully integrated mixed method strategy with a positivist orientation. This research strategy starts with an ethnography, which was used to develop themes. A pre-test/post-test quantitative survey tested conceptual relationships using structural modeling. The hypothesis tested and the constructs used in the model were derived from ethnographic data. The two sets of findings were then put together and the findings 'harmonized'. Since the ethnographic data were used to develop the survey and hypotheses and data from both methods were analyzed together, this article exempli-fies the fully integrated research strategy.

Arnould and Price's (1993) article on service encounters provides another excellent example of fully integrated mixed methods strategy. The Arnould and Price (1993) 'River Magic' article is an interpretive study that has data collection over two years, where data are gathered from multiple participants. Focus group data served as input to surveys conducted at two different time periods. Results from onsite depth interviews, participant observation (including field notes and photographs) and surveys (mail and drop-off) were analyzed together to understand the relationships between client expectations and satisfaction.

In the next section we describe an interpretive study (Bahl, 2005), that uses a fully inte-grated mixed methods strategy for exploring multiple selves. In contrast to the interpre-tive studies that use mixed method strategies to explore relationships across aggregates of people, this study combines narratives and different multivariate techniques in a more integrated manner to help understand the qualitative data at the individual level. Typically, in mixed methods studies, qualitative data are used to inform quantitative methods. However this study is novel in that the quantitative results are used to inform the qualitative methods. And because data from the mixed methods are also analyzed in an integrated manner, this study is an example of the fully integrated strategy.

Mixed methods approach for studying self concept
The self concept is a complex subject that has been studied using different paradigms and methodologies. Recent studies recognize the multiplicity of the self concept. As such, it has been studied as situational self (Hogg and Savolainen, 1998; Schenk and Holman, 1980), multiple self-concepts – actual, ideal and social (Belch and Landon, 1977; Sirgy, 1982), malleable self (Aaker, 1999), fragmented self (Firat and Shultz, 1997, 2001;

Firat and Venkatesh, 1995; Gould, 2001), role identities (Arnett et al., 2003; Kleine et al., 1993; Laverie et al., 2002) and so forth. Most of the aforementioned studies examine the relationship between multiple selves and specific consumption behaviors. Surprisingly little empirical work has been conducted to understand what multiple selves mean to consumers in their everyday lives. The study we describe in this chapter adds to this stream of literature by presenting an approach for identifying multiple selves in consumers that is based on the consumers' perspective and independent of market logic. Next we report the methodological steps taken in the self concept study.

Theoretical paradigm and assumptions
This study explores multiplicity of self concept using dialogical self theory, which is rooted in narrative psychology and amenable to an interpretive approach. Dialogical self theory uses the metaphor of the self as a polyphonic novel, which allows for a multiplicity of *I* positions among which dialogical relationships may emerge (Hermans, Kempen and Loon, 1992).

The ontological and epistemological assumptions guiding this study are as follows. First, people make sense of who they are through the psychosocial construction of life stories (Escalas and Bettman, 2000; Harré and Gillett, 1994; Hermans, Kempen and Loon, 1992; McAdams, 1996; Raggatt, 2002). Second, 'The life story is not a continuous, more-or-less integrated narrative' (Raggatt, 2002). Third, 'Any life story is a drama played out by different narrative voices' (ibid.). And fourth, the self can be understood by studying a person's most important symbolic valuations or attachments in the social (people), temporal (events), bodily, physical (objects and places) and moral (beliefs) spheres (Harré and Gillett, 1994; Raggatt, 2002).

Research strategy
This study used a fully integrated mixed methods strategy that included narratives, multidimensional scaling (MDS) and cluster analysis. The self was studied as a repertoire of narrative voices, wherein each voice has a unique web of affective attachments to people, events, beliefs and consumption experiences (Raggatt, 2002). Informants' narratives provided important attachments that were used as input for MDS and cluster analysis. The resulting MDS and cluster solutions were analyzed in combination with the informants' narratives in order to discern and understand multiple selves in the informants.

Purposive sampling
Sampling within the interpretive paradigm is mostly purposive or theoretical (Belk et al., 1989; Creswell, 2003; Denzin and Lincoln, 2000; Miles and Huberman, 1994). Purposive sampling seeks participants or sights that will best help understand the research problem (Creswell, 2003). Thus guided by the research questions or the conceptual framework, the sample may be pre-specified or emergent (Miles and Huberman, 1994). Consistent with our research goal of understanding the meaning of multiple selves we pre-specified a sample that represented people across different age groups in both genders in order to get multiple perspectives and a rich understanding. The sample is described in Table 15.2.

The informants were recruited using personal contacts and flyers in grocery shops in the area. They were given $200 in advance as a token of gratitude for four to five interviews of two to three hours' duration each. They were assured of confidentiality and

Table 15.2   Description of informants

Name	Age	Profession
Beth	54	Activist
Sam	57	Artist/writer
Dee	37	Project manager
Ari	38	Music instructor
Jessica	23	Student
Brad	26	Real estate agent

Table 15.3   Taxonomy of attachments

	Attachments		
People	Life events	Body orientations	Consumption
Three positive persons (personally known)	Childhood – peak experience – nadir experience	Two body parts liked most/ strongest	Three meaningful consumption experiences of products, brands or possessions
One positive public/fictitious figure	Adolescence – peak experience – nadir experience	Two body parts least liked/ weakest	Three meaningful consumption experiences of time
Two disliked figures	Adulthood – peak experience – nadir experience		Two negative consumption experiences

signed a consent form that explained the research process and their rights during the process. The interviews were audio-taped with the permission of the respondents and took place in quiet settings that were of respondents' choice.

The study was described to the informants as a research project that examined the relationship between consumers' self-concepts and their consumptions. The notion of multiple selves was not mentioned to the respondents throughout the study.

Data collection

Data were collected in two stages using multiple methods. A detailed protocol was developed, based on Raggatt's (2000, 2002) personality web protocol. Before the first meeting, the informants were given a written protocol to assist them in preparing for the first interview. They were asked to narrate stories with regard to people, life events, body orientations and consumption experiences that are important to them, hereafter called 'attachments'. The first interview lasted between two and four hours; it followed a semi-structured format and was audio-taped. Table 15.3 presents the taxonomy of attachments that were used to guide the informants in describing their life stories.

In order to evoke rich stories, the respondents were also asked to bring objects (for example, photographs, gifts and possessions) associated with the attachments they were going to describe in the interviews. The advantages of using such objects include opening dialogue with respondents, facilitating recall and spontaneous story telling (Collier and Collier, 1986).

In the second meeting, respondents were asked to think about the relationships among their attachments using quantitative and qualitative methods. Prior to the meeting the authors independently identified the important attachments in the narratives of the respondents and compared for inter-coder reliability. The differences were reconciled through discussions and the final sets of attachments were determined. Separate cards were also made for each of the attachments for a qualitative clustering task.

The second meeting involved two tasks. The first task involved getting respondents' proximity ratings between all possible pair-wise combinations of attachments on a nine-point scale. The respondents were asked to indicate the degree of association in their thoughts, feelings, actions and experience for all possible pairs of attachments.

After filling the matrix the respondents were given the cards with their attachments and asked to group them into separate clusters that reflected their self aspects. They were given extra cards in case they wanted to place an attachment in more than one cluster. After making the clusters they were asked to give a self-relevant descriptive label for each cluster. Table 15.4 illustrates the clusters created by Brad, along with the labels that described them.

A final task was given to the informants that required them to give proximity ratings between their attachments and self aspects.

Table 15.4   Qualitative clustering of Brad's selves

I Open self	IV Closed self
1. Camp director for soccer	1. Father
2. Helped people	2. Mother
3. Real estate	3. Stepfather
4. Peter	4. Mean grandmother
5. Gonzales	5. Harsh experiences in childhood
6. Scoring goal	6. Kids' lies
7. Strong legs	7. Communications book
8. Paul Atredies	8. High school soccer coach
9. Handsome face	9. Experience with drugs
10. Break dancing contest	10. Time spent worrying
11. Better communications with family	11. Peter
II Critical self	**V Spiritual self**
1. Hair	1. Holosync technology
2. Rogaine	2. Osho book
3. Time spent worrying	3. Book – spiritual materialism
4. Hurt ankle	4. Sedona method
	5. Meditation techniques
III Experience with Women	6. Communications book
1. Experience with women	
2. First girlfriend	
3. Ex-girlfriend	
4. Abortion	

Data recording

The audio-tapes of the first interviews were transcribed to yield 339 pages of single-spaced text. The respondents' descriptions of their clusters in the second meeting were also audio-taped but not transcribed as we had the card clusters and written notes describing the attachments that went into each cluster.

In addition to the transcribed text, proximity matrices and card clusters, the output from the two interviews included pictures of the informants' objects related to attachments and researcher notes made during and after the interviews.

Data analysis

Data were analyzed using the qualitative and quantitative inputs. The narratives were analyzed to determine important attachments that were then used to create the proximity rating matrix. The proximity ratings were used to explore relationships that were not initially described in the narratives. The pair-wise ratings data (attachments with attachments) for each respondent were input to the MDS program in SPSS (Statistical Package for the Social Sciences) in the form of a triangular similarity ratings matrix (the data was reverse coded to convert to dissimilar ratings matrix). The range of possible solutions was selected according to a reading of the scree plots of Kruskal's stress measure.

To finalize the dimensionality of the final solution in order to select the selves we clustered the acceptable solutions' MDS coordinates associated with the attachments using hierarchical cluster analysis. An initial range of solutions was selected, based on the agglomeration schedule. From these solutions we then compared the clusters formed by cluster analysis with the respondents' card clusters and narratives. The cluster solution that was most interpretable in terms of the respondents' card clusters and supporting narratives was selected. Respondents' selves were determined from this solution.

Next, to anchor the selves among the attachments and see the relative positions among the selves and attachments, the MDS program was rerun with the added pair-wise ratings between attachments and selves. The final dimensionality from the range of MDS solutions was selected based on scree plots.

The narratives were coded using the qualitative research software QSR NUD.IST 6. The attachments were coded according to the selves determined by the qualitative and quantitative clustering procedures. Finally, the coded narratives and MDS maps were jointly analyzed to help understand the creation, relative positioning and meaning of multiple selves in the respondents.

Member checks

Member checks involve sharing results with the respondents in order to ensure that the interpretations are valid (Belk et al., 1988). In this study, multiple methods were employed to discern multiple selves in the respondents. With the exception of two cases, the quantitative cluster analyses were mostly consistent with the qualitative clusters created by the respondents and their life stories. In Brad's case, however, the narratives and the cluster analysis highlighted an athletic self aspect that was not reflected in Brad's own qualitative clustering. He was subsequently asked if he felt that athleticism was an important aspect of his self. He not only agreed but said that he was impressed that the quantitative technique, about which he had been skeptical, actually worked. The other exception was Dee, whose two qualitative clusters comprising the strong self (physical self aspect) and focused/goal-oriented self (mental self aspect) merged into one cluster based on quantitative clustering. The result was a broader strong self cluster that included the mental and physical aspects.

Other checks involved clarifications from the respondents when certain relationships that they indicated in the proximities matrix were not consistent or substantiated elsewhere in their stories.

In the next section we illustrate the results of this study with the case of Brad.

The case of Brad

The case here illustrates the multiple selves in Brad who is an extremely aware and mature 26-year-old. He had a difficult childhood as his parents were divorced when he was four and the parental figures in his life were constantly degrading and making him feel that he was not good enough. He grew up with a strong need for acceptance, which he later sought to fulfill in his relationships with women. In his early years in college, he also used drugs to escape from the pain and insecurities related to his childhood. More recently, his thinning hair has been a cause of concern as it makes him feel less attractive to women. Despite the nadir experiences in his life, Brad has acquired wisdom and strength through insightful friends, books and contemplative practices to grow into a mature individual who is eager to help people in his personal life and in his career as a real estate agent. His passions are varied and include reading, soccer, music and contemplative techniques.

Analysis of Brad's narratives, qualitative clustering, multidimensional scaling and cluster analysis resulted in finding six selves, which he named as the 'closed self', 'open self', 'critical self', 'experience with women self', 'athletic self' and 'spiritual self'. Five of the selves were based on the qualitative methods and confirmed with subsequent quantitative methods. However, the athletic self emerged at the MDS and cluster analysis stage thanks to the close proximity of strong legs and scoring goal attachments. This self was subsequently confirmed by Brad, who felt he had inadvertently overlooked this important self. Table 15.5 lists the selves by the respective attachments that comprise the self and descriptive quotes taken from the narratives to exemplify the attachments.

Based on readings of the scree plot for Kruskal's stress, a three-dimensional solution was obtained (Kruskal's stress = 0.158, $R^2 = 0.828$). Figures 15.2, 15.3 and 15.4 depict the multidimensional maps, showing dimensions 1 and 2, 1 and 3, and 2 and 3, respectively. The multiple selves discerned in this study can be understood by looking at Table 15.4 in combination with Figure 15.1 of Brad's cluster analysis and Figures 15.2, 15.3 and 15.4.

The relative positioning of the attachments and the selves are depicted in the graphs of the final three dimensional MDS solution in Figures 15.2, 15.3 and 15.4. When viewing dimensions 1 and 2 (Figure 15.2), the closed and critical selves are positioned near the spiritual self; in contrast, the open, athletic and women experience selves are closer together. This suggests that the spiritual self is emerging to deal with some of his life's difficulties. In both maps denoted by dimensions 1 and 3 (Figure 15.3) and dimensions 2 and 3 (Figure 15.4), there is a pronounced separation between the positively viewed selves (spiritual, open and athletic) and the negatively viewed selves (closed, critical and women experience). The supporting narratives underlying the constellation of selves and attachments are presented next.

The 'closed self'

The closed self dates back to Brad's childhood which was full of harsh experiences, mostly related to the parental figures in his life. His Dad, who was divorced from his Mom, disappointed him with false promises. He recalls witnessing fights between his Mom and step Dad, and being hurt by degrading comments. Being 'caught in the middle of all this family turmoil' sometimes negatively affected other aspects of his life, such as soccer practices. He remembers feeling 'helpless' and 'betrayed' when his mother asked him to leave the house because he had disobeyed her and done what he believed was the right thing to do. As a result of the negative environment created by his family members, Brad closed down to them but sought acceptance from the women he dated in college. He also used drugs to forget the pain and to relax. In many ways he continued to recreate the drama that he had grown up with, until his friend Peter pointed out his insecurities and made him think about the way he lived his life and his beliefs. He describes his experiences with Peter as 'really painful' but 'very awakening'.

The 'open self'

The open self helped Brad make his own path, which resulted in his being more helpful and compassionate. The transformation in this self was through his friend Peter who made him confront his closed self. During his brief visit with Gonzales, an artist, he was introduced to new art and music, which helped him progress on this path. He describes this experience as 'meditative' and 'soulful'. It is evident that the traits that Brad admired in the fiction character Paul Atridies – 'intelligence, this awareness and charisma, leadership, the ability to overcome a challenge, extremely spiritual' – are the traits he is drawn to in friends and he aspires to in himself. While there is some evidence of these traits in his childhood, when he won the break-dancing contest, or scored a goal in a soccer match, Brad feels that today he is more open in his relationships. Now he is more open and capable of helping, be it his family, friends, his clients in finding the perfect home or as the camp director for soccer games.

The 'critical self'

While Brad's closed self is more a voice from the past, his critical self pertains to current insecurities, some of which have their origins in his childhood when he was made to feel he was 'never good enough'. His insecurities seep into many aspects of his life, such as 'stressing what does that person think about me? Am I good enough? Do they like me, don't they like me? Why don't they like me? Does she think I'm attractive? Did I play well enough? Did they get what they wanted house wise, did they like what they wanted, how did I come off?' More currently his thinning hair is of concern to him as it makes him feel that he will be less attractive to women. He says, 'It's really hard for me to look at mirror . . . I feel really insecure about my looks, it has everything to do with my hair.' He hesitatingly shared the hair product called Rogaine that he is using to deal with the problem.

The 'experience with women' self

Brad's stories abound in painful experiences with women. His first romantic relationship in high school was 'cool'. He was in love for one year, after which at some point he felt he 'was really just using her for sex'. He remembers, 'When I broke up with her

Table 15.5   Brad's attachments grouped into selves

---

1   Closed self

Father ('the first words that came to mind with my dad were pain, negativity,' 'guilt,' 'barbs,' 'lying, false promising,' 'it still hurts now,' 'in the past when I've tried it it's just like shut down mode, shut down defense mode.')

Mother ('my mom it was a tough experience,' 'I remember one time my mom sat me down and told me that I wasn't smart enough and I'd never be as smart as she was yeah just like yelling at me to my face,' 'she's like a time bomb in a lot of ways just exploding' felt 'helpless' and 'betrayed')

Mean grandmother ('her saying all that stuff was just creepy,' 'skin was crawling' 'the tone of it was just so dripping with jealousy dripping with kind of anger')

Harsh experiences in childhood ('most of my life going home was like walking on eggshells, just constant you know conflict constant horror')

Kids lies ('I was so mad,' 'most hurtful experience,' 'I didn't understand somebody could lie at that level,' 'I tried to explain to him (dad) that, what killed me the most is that he didn't believe me.')

Communications book ('just a beautiful book,' 'it's not bridges not walls to others it's bridges not walls to yourself,' 'if you open yourself up to somebody else, easier for you to open yourself up to yourself and back and forth same thing')

High school soccer coach ('my senior year and it was completely this conflict between the two of us,' 'I felt competitive towards him,' 'I felt like I wasn't good enough,' 'it's pretty horrible really I felt really scared I felt really picked')

Experience with drugs ('escape from reality,' 'it helped me relax and take off some of the pressure.')

Time spent worrying ('worrying thinking too much just worrying about the future, the past')

Peter ('he'd say things that point out my insecurities,' 'amazing it was really painful a lot of the time but it was very awakening.')

2   Athletic self

Scoring goal in soccer ('one of the main focuses of life was soccer,' 'I love soccer I love sports,' 'experience I can truly describe as a peak experience,' 'when the goal was scored it was like I was watching myself do it')

Strong legs ('legs um my legs are really strong,' 'fast,' 'I love just walking or running')

3   Critical self

Hair ('I've got a real hang up with my hair because it used to be really thick as you can see in the picture and now it's not and it like kills me,' 'it's really hard for me to look at mirror . . . I feel really insecure about my looks it has everything to do with my hair . . . ')

Rogaine ('I just that's it wish I didn't need it feel like wish I guess that's what it comes down to I wish I didn't feel like I needed it one way or the other.')

Time spent worrying ('people always think about the past, people often, I often think about the past and what's happened and how to plan for it not to happen in the future')

Hurt ankle ('I injured it playing soccer and it really hurt and I smoked a lot of weed did a lot of drugs and I worked as a waiter constantly working on it constantly working on it . . . and that kind of like ground it you know didn't really heal right,' 'it's in my head that it doesn't fit right because the symmetry's been thrown off.')

4   Open self

Peter ('there were teacher here and there but nobody kinda cracked my shell the way he did nobody . . . made me think about the way I live my life and my beliefs ever so much as he,' 'so much insight' 'he eventually was the person that kinda led me to really take my own path.')

Table 15.5 (continued)

Camp director for soccer ('then a peak experience recently was . . . I was the camp director six months later for summer.')

Helped people ('I can just help people so much more I can listen with so much more of my heart I can clear my mind and really find a way to . . . assist people . . . and so much of that I'd say Peter is the catalyst for.')

Real estate ('be able to like bring some kind of real joy and I can help them achieve a goal . . . he's dying to get a house and I'm helping him do that.')

Gonzales ('he was probably the most recent major force in my life,' 'he was really interesting . . . a lot of his like stuff was had a kind of meditative feel,' 'soulful')

Scoring goal ('when the goal was scored it was like I was watching myself do it')

Strong legs ('strong,' 'fast' 'I love just walking or running,' 'she (first girlfriend) was really cool to me she was a track runner I kind of ran track a couple times.')

Paul Atredies ('I just love that central character what he embodied was intelligence, this awareness and charisma, leadership um . . . the ability to overcome a challenge extremely spiritually guided he was omniscient in a sense.')

Handsome face ('I have a handsome face and I like that,' 'I think there's something to the eyes that speak a lot about a person,' 'it's a strong characteristic . . . it speaks a lot of me especially my eyes,' 'I think the eyes tell a lot about a person,' 'I look them in the eye and I think there's something very connective about that and in that sense it makes it genuine.')

Break dancing contest ('my god it was such a cool experience,' 'the coolest thing about it was there was big crowd there I didn't event think about the crowd I was totally just doing what I was doing you know.')

Better communications with family ('I just really tried to open up to them and to see them open up to me it's really beautiful,' 'I have one full sibling Page and I most recently spoke with her and we had a great opening experience,' 'I just love my siblings and I think they're awesome and I want that relationship with them no I won't say I that I want it, I'm allowing it to happen,' 'just extremely better relationships, my mother me and my father I can at least get along a little better.')

5   Experience with women

Experience with women ('so much of my identity through college had to do with girl . . . so much I took my self confidence had everything to do with that,' 'when I first came to college I had girlfriend in high school but I don't know what it was but a lot of girls really liked being involved with me I was just totally into that,' 'I just want approval I think a lot of that has to do with identifying with being attractive . . . a long time a lot of my identity is really a huge attachment for me is being attractive and the attractiveness that I got from women,' 'the attention that I got from that.')

First girlfriend ('experience um my first girlfriend that was pretty you know my first like real sexual relationship the first time that was really amazing experience, we were together for two years,' 'we were both kind of young and I was still going through all sorts of trouble but she was really cool to me,' 'it's funny because I was really in love with her for the first year and the second year I totally wasn't but I just kind of stayed in the relationship you know for like no good reason,' 'just remember so literally because it felt different it felt so warm it felt so genuine it felt so right,' 'I think at one point I was really just using her for sex I hate to say it but it's true and kind of all I really thought about,' 'when I broke up with her I cried so much because I felt so guilty.')

Ex-girlfriend ('it was probably the rockiest relationship I can imagine . . . she recently had an abortion and we broke up' 'it (having a baby) was really frightening but it was wonderful,' 'I just felt

Table 15.5   (continued)

---

like this was really unfair because it was as if saying ya know she was the like the sun . . . and I was like nothing . . . that my feelings and my thoughts were of no consequence to her . . . this was probably most one of the most effecting experiences of my life in a positive way because I learned so so much about myself,' 'it's very hard for me to look at her negative because despite the fact that we fought a lot ya know I really care about her,' 'funny,' 'laughed together,' 'enjoyed our sex life,' 'I found her extremely physically attractive.')

Abortion ('I didn't want to have the baby but every time I kinda like asked myself, my body was really thought it was good idea and it gave me a really soothing feel,' 'the procedure went two days and there were some complications and it was very painful just amazingly stressful experience.')

6   Spiritual self
Holosync technology ('it's good for health and healing just kind of reinforcing in a subconscious a potential for healing very important for me right now because I'm helping to heal my ankle . . . I carry it around with me I practice soccer with it on,' 'these waves are very therapeutic and healing.')

Osho cards ('you carry that card around with you for the week and you read the sutra . . . just kind of allow you to affect your life,' 'Deep,' 'Beautiful,' 'intelligent person lives life joyfully . . . thankfully gratefully.')

Book – spiritual materialism ('anybody whose at all on any sort of spiritual should read this,' 'it's more living and being aware of the moment which is a very moment to moment thing')

Sedona method ('it has everything to do with letting go of emotions and until I read that I didn't realize how simple it was,' 'you can apply it anywhere you can apply it to business I've applied it to relationships.')

Meditation techniques ('helps me be myself helps me focus . . . release all my stress and sink deeper into reality . . . to get out of my head and to really feel,' 'I got quite a few techniques at this point and I kind of go with whatever one I want sometimes I don't do any at all.')

Communications book ('just a beautiful book all about communication and I didn't how psychological communications was and how soulful communication was up to that point,' 'I found the path something I'm really passionate about.')

---

um . . . I cried so much because I felt so guilty . . . I felt like I was hurting her.' In college his self-confidence and need for acceptance were centered on his relationships with women, which were 'full of peaks and valleys, with no balance'. One of the most 'significant experiences' in his life was his relationship with his ex-girlfriend, which he describes as one of the 'rockiest relationships', but positive because he learnt from it. One of the most painful experiences that they shared was their second abortion decision. While he realized that this was not the relationship for him he was willing to support the child. He was disappointed when she decided to go through with the abortion. Despite painful experiences and many fights, he still cares for her and feels the positive aspect was the learning in it.

The 'spiritual self'
The spiritual self has helped Brad gain balance and perspective in life. Through books, music and attending classes, he has learnt different centering techniques, including yoga, tai-chi, Sudarshan Kriya (rhythmic breathing), Holosync technology and the

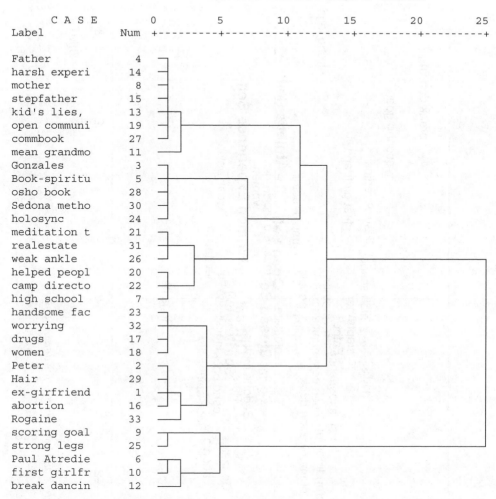

```
Dendrogram using Ward Method
                              Rescaled Distance Cluster Combine

          C A S E        0         5        10        15        20        25
        Label          Num  +---------+---------+---------+---------+---------+

        Father           4
        harsh experi    14
        mother           8
        stepfather      15
        kid's lies,     13
        open communi    19
        commbook        27
        mean grandmo    11
        Gonzales         3
        Book-spiritu     5
        osho book       28
        Sedona metho    30
        holosync        24
        meditation t    21
        realestate      31
        weak ankle      26
        helped peopl    20
        camp directo    22
        high school      7
        handsome fac    23
        worrying        32
        drugs           17
        women           18
        Peter            2
        Hair            29
        ex-girfriend     1
        abortion        16
        Rogaine         33
        scoring goal     9
        strong legs     25
        Paul Atredie     6
        first girlfr    10
        break dancin    12
```

*Figure 15.1   Cluster analysis dendrogram for Brad, based on three dimensional
          MDS coordinates*

Sedona method that have helped him in his everyday life. He feels that this
spiritual knowledge can be applied everywhere and he has personally applied it in his
relationships and work. Although Brad has used these books and techniques to grow,
he was made aware of how they can become harmful as they become part of the ego
when he read the book, *Spiritual Materialism*. While earlier he believed that he medi-
tated and therefore he was 'more enlightened' than those who do not, after reading the
book he realized that 'it's more living it, it's more living and being aware of the moment,
which is a very moment to moment thing; to act not even moment to moment, it's just
moment'.

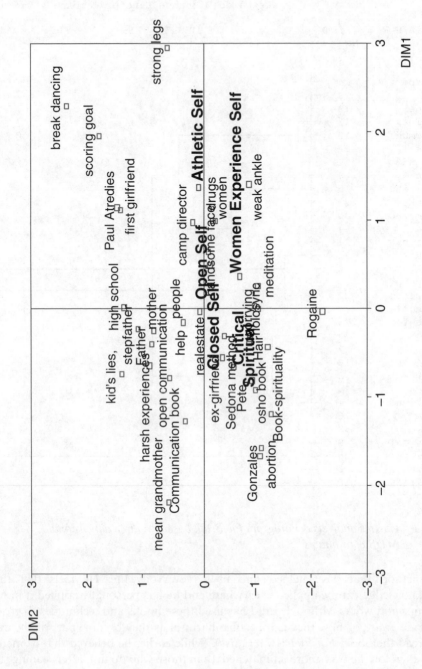

Figure 15.2   MDS map of Brad's selves and attachments for dimensions 1 and 2

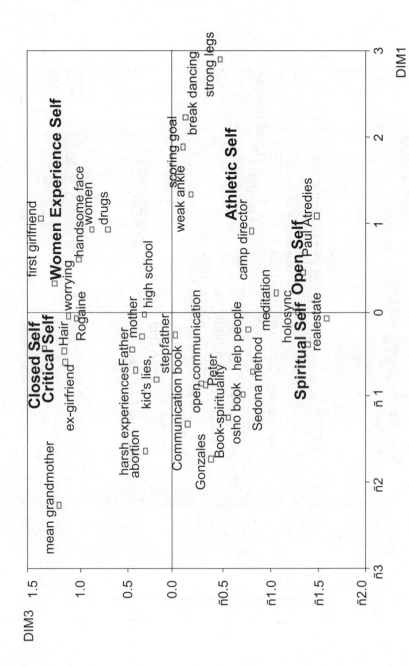

Figure 15.3   *MDS map of Brad's selves and attachments for dimensions 1 and 3*

213

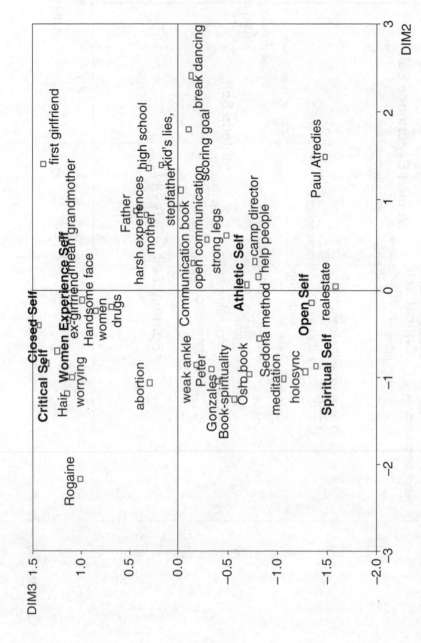

Figure 15.4   MDS map of Brad's selves and attachments for dimensions 2 and 3

The 'athletic self'

Brad's athletic self also dates back to his childhood when soccer was 'one of the main focuses' of his life. His peak experiences include his experience of scoring the perfect goal in a soccer match in school. 'Everything just clicked, clicked, clicked and then it was just like watching a movie.' Brad finds his legs strong and fast, which helps him in playing soccer, running and walking. He also describes many of his experiences while playing sports in very spiritual ways. He feels that playing sports is very meditative. The spiritual dimension in sports is also illustrated in his description of a soccer program that he has joined: 'the whole program is about love and enjoying the game and enjoying the ball and feeling yourself and just kind of finding yourself in that'.

Discussion

The selves discerned in this research approach were based on people's narratives and quantitative methods. There was the understanding of selves from the individual's perspective, which differs from previous self research. By capturing people's narratives, there were rich stories that showed how selves evolved into one another over time. There are bridges in Brad's stories that show how one self led to another. Brad's closed self, which was shaped by his tumultuous childhood, lead to his critical self and his negative experiences with women self. Guided by some key friends, Brad opened up as his open self came to the fore, along with his spiritual self. Currently the spiritual self is helping him grow and bring peace to his critical self. The narratives uncovered insights revealing the diachronic nature of selves, which might not have been possible through other data collection techniques.

The multidimensional scaling solution provided an approach for showing the relative positioning of both the attachments and the selves. Visual displays of the attachments were then used to understand the patterns within the narratives. As seen in Figure 15.2, the spiritual self is positioned near the critical and closed selves, while the experiences with women, open self and athletic self are farther away, depicting an inward versus outward positioning. Brad's spiritual self is helping in dealing with his closed and critical selves by going inwards. The athletic, open and experience with women selves reflect more of an external orientation. Figures 15.3 and 15.4 show the selves being arrayed according to positive selves (spiritual, open and athletic) and negative selves (closed, time with women and critical). The MDS maps illustrate the selves as a synchronic constellation of attachments that currently influence his life.

The quantitative approach also provided researchers with tools to discover relationships among the attachments that were not explained in the original narrative. Subsequent discussions with informants corroborated the discovered relationships with the supporting stories. For example, the relationship between spiritual book and Brad's ex-girl friend placed them far apart in Figure 15.3. During the narratives, Brad only spoke about how the books led to a spiritual path. After asking about the relationship, Brad indicated the books helped him move on from her, and other negative occurrences in his life.

The mixed methods approach helps offset the weaknesses of using quantitative and qualitative methods individually. The narratives provide depth and meanings to the attachments, and the MDS helps show spatially the relative attachments across multiple dimensions. The narratives and life stories, while providing rich data that can help determine selves, have the weakness that respondents may not describe all possible relationships among the attachments. It is possible that the informant may fail to discuss important stories related to the attachments. Moreover, at the time of qualitative clustering, the informant may also fail to put together a self from the attachments that are indeed significant. The pair-wise attachment ratings and subsequent MDS/cluster may help to discover selves based on groups of attachments, which were not identified in the informant's qualitative clusters. For example, Brad's cluster analysis (Figure 15.1) grouped the attachments of strong legs and scoring a first goal together, thus suggesting an athletic self.

The analysis of the narratives with the MDS and the cluster analysis provides a deeper understanding of multiple selves than if either the qualitative or quantitative method had been used separately. The relative positioning of attachments in the MDS maps were used to show the relationships among selves, which in turn helped in interpreting the narratives. At the same time, the narratives backed up the MDS maps and provided depth and meaning to the constellation of attachments.

Both the qualitative clustering and the quantitative approaches were used to arrive at a more complete and trustworthy solution than if either had been done separately. A limitation of qualitative clustering is that informants may overlook an important self. Quantitative clustering, on the other hand, is limited because it relies upon informants providing accurate inter-attachment proximity ratings. Having two separate but complementary methods to discern selves means that the results are more trustworthy through triangulation.

The use of multiple data collection approaches has the advantage of providing informants with different formats to respond to inquiries in case they have difficulty with one format or another. As mentioned earlier, different informants found the various tasks more or less difficult. For example, Brad spent four hours filling in the matrix but found it fairly easy to make and label the qualitative clusters. Sam, on the other hand, had few questions pertaining to the matrix but took a longer time in making his qualitative clusters. This further supports the strategy of employing multiple methods as people's capabilities to perform different tasks vary and by having them do different tasks it is possible to get multiple perspectives leading to rich insights.

Finally, while most methods encounter well documented problems such as social desirability and respondent fatigue, the mixed methods approaches can help limit the effects through the use of offsetting methods. If one method is limited by these shortcomings, there is a good chance the other method will not have this limitation.

The mixed method approach described, while having many advantages, does have limitations that need recognizing. The first is that the use of mixed methods is time-intensive. In the example described in this chapter, each informant spent a total of 10–12 hours, with single meetings lasting two to four hours. A second limitation with the use of mixed methods is that information overload may be a problem and it can be a challenge to understand and reconcile potentially conflicting data results. In this research we found that the number of selves identified varied by qualitative and quantitative clustering methods, and it required an examination of the narratives to resolve this conflict. A third limitation is that the use of mixed methods requires a diverse set of research skills in both qualitative and quantitative methodologies.

The fully integrated mixed methods example we presented illustrates how quantitative measures can be used to understand more fully the meaning of qualitative data. Unlike mixed methods approaches that use quantitative methods for survey data and estimating linear models, our employment of quantitative methods is more descriptive at the individual level. Further, with our approach, the input data for the quantitative methods were based on the attachments in the narratives, and the output of both the MDS and clustering were analyzed with the narratives in an integrated manner.

In conclusion, in this chapter we have argued that it is possible to conduct interpretive research that uses quantitative methods while remaining true to the philosophical underpinnings of interpretive research. We suggest that researchers should not see quantitative and qualitative methods as antagonistic. It is important to note that, while research orientations lie on a positivist–interpretivist continuum, methods are independent of the research orientation. Finally, while qualitative methods have traditionally been used to support quantitative methods, this study illustrates the use of quantitative methods to support qualitative methods.

References

Aaker, Jennifer (1999), 'The malleable self: the role of self-expression in persuasion', *Journal of Marketing Research*, **36** (February), 45–57.

Arnett, Dennis B., Steve D. German and Shelby D. Hunt, (2003), 'The identity salience model of relationship marketing success: the case of nonprofit marketing', *Journal of Marketing*, **67** (2), April, 89–106.

Arnould, Eric J. and Linda L. Price (1993), 'River magic, extraordinary experience and the extended service encounter', *Journal of Consumer Research*, **20** (June), 24–45.

Bahl, Shalini (2005), 'Multiple selves and the meanings they give to consumptions', unpublished dissertation, University of Massachusetts Amherst.

Belch, George E. and E. Laird Landon (1977), 'Discriminant validity of a product-anchored self-concept measure', *Journal of Marketing Research*, **14** (May), 252–6.

Belk, Russell W., John F. Sherry and Melanie Wallendorf (1988), 'A naturalistic inquiry into buyer and seller behavior at a swap meet', *Journal of Consumer Research*, **14** (March), 449–70.

Belk, Russell W., Melanie Wallendorf and John F. Sherry (1989), 'The sacred and the profane in consumer behavior: theodicy on the Odyssey', *Journal of Consumer Research*, **16** (1) (June), 1–38.

Brewer, John and Albert Hunter (1989), *Multimethod Research: A Synthesis of Styles*, Newbury Park: Sage Publications.

Collier, John and Malcolm Collier (1986), *Visual Anthropology: Photography as a Research Method*, revised and expanded edn, Albuquerque: University of New Mexico Press.

Creswell, John W. (2003), *Research Design: Qualitative, Quantitative, and Mixed Methods Approaches*, 2 edn, Thousand Oaks, CA: Sage Publications.

Denzin, Norman K. and Yvonna S. Lincoln (2000), *Handbook of Qualitative Research*, 2nd edn, Thousand Oaks, CA: Sage Publications.

Deshpande, Rohit (1983), 'Paradigms lost: on theory and method in research in marketing', *Journal of Marketing*, **47** (fall), 101–10.

Escalas, Jennifer Edson and James Bettman (2000), 'Using narratives to discern self-identity related goals and motivations', in S. Ratneshwar, David Glen Mick and Cynthia Huffman (eds), *The Why of Consumption: Contemporary Perspectives on Consumer Motives, Goals, and Desires*, London: Routledge.

Firat, Fuat A. and Clifford J. Shultz (1997), 'From segmentation to fragmentation: markets and marketing strategy in the postmodern era', *European Journal of Marketing*, **31** (3/4), 183–207.

Firat, Fuat A. and Clifford J. Shultz (2001), 'Preliminary metric investigations into the postmodern consumer', *Marketing Letters*, **12** (2), 189–203.

Firat, Fuat A. and Alladi Venkatesh (1995), 'Liberatory postmodernism and the reenchantment of consumption', *Journal of Consumer Research*, **22**, 239–67.

Geertz, Clifford (1973), *The Interpretation of Cultures*, New York: Basic Books.

Gould, Stephen J. (2001), 'O self, are thou one or many? An empirical study of how consumers construct and perceive the self', *Advances in Consumer Research*, **28**, 233–4.

Harré, Rom and Grant Gillett (1994), *The Discursive Mind*, Los Angeles: Sage.

Hausman, Angela (2000), 'A multimethod investigation of consumer motivation in impulse buying behavior', *Journal of Consumer Marketing*, **17** (4–5), 403–19.

Hermans, Hubert J.M., Harry J.G. Kempen and R.J.P. van Loon (1992), 'The dialogical self: beyond individualism and rationalism', *American Psychologist*, **47**, 23–33.

Hogg, Margaret K. and Maria H. Savolainen (1998), 'Symbolic consumption and the situational self', *European Advances in Consumer Research*, **3**, 11–16.

Hudson, Laurel Anderson and Julie L. Ozanne (1988), 'Alternative ways of seeking knowledge in consumer research', *Journal of Consumer Research*, **14** (4), 508–21.

Johnson, R. Burke and Anthony J. Onwuegbuzie (2004), 'Mixed methods research: a research paradigm whose time has come', *Educational Researcher*, **33** (7), 14–26.

Kleine, Robert E., Susan Schultz Kleine and Jerome B. Kernan (1993), 'Mundane consumption and the self: a social-identity perspective', *Journal of Consumer Psychology*, **2** (3), 209–35.

Laverie, Debra A., Robert E. Kleine and Susan Schultz Kleine (2002), 'Reexamination and extension of Kleine, Kleine, and Kernan's social identity model of mundane consumption: the mediating role of the appraisal process', *Journal of Consumer Research*, **28**, 659–69.

McAdams, D.P. (1996), 'Personality, modernity, and the storied self: a contemporary framework for studying persons', *Psychological Inquiry*, **7** (4), 295–321.

McAlexander, James H., John W. Schouten and Harold F. Koenig (2002), 'Building brand community', *Journal of Marketing*, **66** (Jan.) (1), 38–54.

Miles, Matthew B. and A. Michael Huberman (1994), *Qualitative Data Analysis*, 2nd edn, Thousand Oaks, CA: Sage Publications.

Milne, George R., Easwar S. Iyer and Sara Gooding-Williams (1996), 'Environmental organization alliance relationships within and across nonproft, business, and government sectors', *Journal of Public Policy and Marketing*, **15** (2), Fall, 203–15.

Morgan,Gareth and Linda Smircich (1980), 'The case for qualitative research', *Academy of Management Review*, **5**, 491–500.

O'Guinn, Thomas C. and Ronald J. Faber (1989), 'Compulsive buying: a phenomenological exploration', *Journal of Consumer Research*, **16** (2), 147–57.

Price, Linda L., Eric J. Arnould and Patrick Tierney (1995), 'Going to extremes: managing service encounters and assessing provider performance', *Journal of Marketing*, **59** (2), April, 83–97.

Raggatt, Peter T.F. (2000), 'Mapping the dialogical self: towards a rationale and method of assessment', *European Journal of Personality*, **14**, 65–90.

Raggatt, Peter T.F. (2002), 'The landscape of narrative and the plural self: exploring identity using the personality web protocol', *Narrative Inquiry*, **12**, 290–318.

Schenk, T.C. and R.H. Holman (1980), 'A sociological approach to brand choice: the concept of situational self image', in J. Olson (ed.), *Advances in Consumer Research*, Provo, UT: Association for Consumer Research, vol. 7, pp. 610–14.

Sirgy, Joseph M. (1983), 'Self-concept in consumer behavior: a critical review', *Journal of Consumer Research*, **9**, 287.

Tashakkori, Abbas and Charles Teddlie (1998), *Mixed Methodology: Combining Qualitative and Quantitative Approaches*, Applied Social Research Methods Series, vol. 46, Thousand Oaks, CA: Sage.

16 The Monticello correction: consumption in history

Linda M. Scott, Jason Chambers and Katherine Sredl

Thomas Jefferson's house at Monticello was preserved intact from the moment the states-man closed his eyes for the last time. A tourist visiting the home two hundred years later could see the residence as it was in use, just as the great leader and thinker lived in it. And yet that twentieth-century visitor got a false impression.

Monticello appears to be a home on a hill, an isolated haven perfect for study and thought, a quiet retreat for gentlemen of state to gather and discuss the key questions of a new republic. In Jefferson's time, however, the house was surrounded by a substantial collection of homes and shops, full of the bustle of many activities required to support the life of comfort that patricians required. Indeed, though the house itself rose slightly above the settlement of its servants, it was then surrounded by what amounted to a small village, rather than being the oasis of self-sufficiency it appears to be now. Thus the house on a hill created the false image of an imagined past for those who came to see it.

The docents, archivists and foundations that worked to preserve Jefferson's home did not think it necessary to maintain the places in which the ordinary folks, many of them African slaves, lived and worked to make Jefferson's exemplary life possible. So the small town that originally surrounded Monticello rotted, wasted and finally disappeared into the ground. It was not until about 15 years ago that efforts to excavate the places used by the commonfolk and slaves began.

The decision to restore the small town that supported Monticello coincided with a sharp turn in the path of those who write history. Much of history, not only in America but throughout the world, had been written to focus on the lives of 'Great Men' and the events in which they were involved, such as wars and the formation of governments. Virtually all history, until the late twentieth century, had a strong ruling-class male bias, not only because of selectivity about what (and who) was important to write about, but because of the pattern of preservation decisions such as those that made a misleading Monticello. Consider also that history is heavily dependent upon written sources – diaries and letters for instance – and it is easy to see that the literate segments of any population have an inordinate influence on the way history is told. Since literacy has been the province of the rich and male during most of the world's past, the stories of women, of slaves, of immigrants and of common people everywhere are badly underrepresented in the annals of the human experience.

The effort to correct this problem was manifest on many fronts, though it was particu-larly evident in women's studies, African-American studies and other areas of scholarly discourse founded on the study of disempowered groups. In the United States, the new focus produced a variety of fascinating new books taking a different view of the American past, beginning with Howard Zinn's *A People's History of the United States* (1980). The new spotlight on the lives of ordinary people also created fresh topics of interest, notably a growing fascination with the realities of material culture and the economic behavior of common citizens (for instance, Bushman, 1992; Hawke, 1989; Larkin, 1988). Thus, in the last 15 years of the millennium, an explosion of books appeared that focused on consumer culture, advertising, markets and everyday life (for instance, Hoy, 1995; Marchand, 1985; Vinikas, 1992).

As Daniel Miller and his colleagues have argued in *Acknowledging Consumption* (1995), the focus of history as a discipline on the phenomenon/institution of consumption is, as with other primary disciplines, long overdue. However the turn toward consumption in history is more clearly an outgrowth in the change of emphasis from documenting the lives of the powerful to narrating the experiences of the common and marginal than it is an epiphany about consumption. Though it is certainly true, as Paul Glennie has argued in Miller's book, that consumer culture seemed suddenly to take center stage as an explanation for a variety of social conditions at the end of the twentieth century, it is also the case that a shift in focus from the leaders of government or military to the people who keep house, plow fields and otherwise tend the fires of daily existence necessarily leads to a greater concern with material culture. This is important to acknowledge because the embryonic state of consumption history is inextricably tied to the status of its narrative characters: because commonfolk, especially women and servants, were so seldom literate and their belongings so rarely seen as the raw material from which history would be written, the relative paucity of evidence is a key reason for the late coming of this history – and it is the primary driver behind the sifting through unusual evidence that marks consumption historiography now.

Coincident with this sudden turn in the interests of historians was a cluster of efforts to bring history into consumer research. Articles by Russell Belk (1992), Terrence Witkowski (1989) and others gave examples of how history could enlighten the study of consumer behavior; Ruth Ann Smith and David Lux (1993) outlined the basics of historical method; Ronald Fullerton talked about the principles of an historicist perspective (1987). Smith and Lux (1993) claimed to have reviewed 31 historical articles appearing in five marketing journals between 1983 and 1990 (a number of these are classified as chronicles or presentations of trend data, which would not typically be considered history by historians, and a number are concerned with the history of the field rather than the history of consumption). The stage seemed set for history to become an important part of consumer research, much as consumer behavior was becoming a hot new topic in history. Yet, in the years since the first of these articles appeared, little more has been written about historical consumer behavior within this discipline. Indeed, of the approximately 930 articles published by the *Journal of Consumer Research* since 1987, only five of them have been historical.

In contrast, other areas of interpretive work in consumer behavior have grown (Arnould and Thompson, 2005). Explanations offered for the lag in historical work range from the difficulties that marketing academics have with the methods, objectives and writing style typical of history (see Witkowski in this volume) to the fact that journal-length articles do not allow historians enough space to do the theory building demanded by marketing journals (ibid.). Given that history is a far better established field than either marketing or consumer behavior, we feel it is incumbent upon marketing academics to come to grips with history's ways rather than vice versa, and we feel that such acceptance will be forthcoming if the discipline realizes the kinds of contributions that can be expected from historical research. In this chapter, therefore, we wish primarily to demonstrate the ways that histor-ical perspectives could be used in the future to bolster or challenge the theoretical per-spectives of other consumer behavior work.

The producer as elite

Popular books on commercial history, cultural studies analyses of consumer culture and historical articles appearing in the marketing literature show a pronounced tendency to overemphasize the producers of consumer culture: that is, most works focus on firms and their leaders (an example is Kreshel, 1990) or show a strong bias that attributes all control of the market to corporate actors (see Holt, 2002). In spite of growing evidence in both studies done in the present as well as research on the past that average people consume in support of their own agendas and gather product information from multiple sources (see Arnould and Thompson, 2005; Miller, 1995; Scott in this volume), the conceptual ten-dency is to put control of the market in the hands of producers: 'Marketing is a form of distorted communication in that marketers control the information that is exchange. Marketers organize the code, and we as consumers have no choice but to participate' (Holt, 2002, p. 72). In this way, market producers take the place of elites like the gentle-men statesmen who led the American Revolution. They are the focus of most of the work and they dominate the perspective from which the history and theories are written: to the extent that the enormous number of people who fought the battles or consumed the prod-ucts play a role at all, it is only as the masses at the beck of these leaders.

The bias of gender, class and race infects even the histories of corporations. For instance, in advertising histories, the focus on men in agencies is marked. Holt cites Stanley Resor of J. Walter Thompson in his 2002 article as one of the leaders who advo-cated a science-inspired, 'hard sell' approach to ads. Yet the evidence in the J. Walter Thompson Collection at Duke University suggests that Resor split agency responsibil-ities with his wife, Helen Lansdowne Resor: Stanley took care of the finances but it was Helen who led creative development (Fox, 1984; Scott, 2005). Helen Resor seldom appears in the histories, but she was one of the leaders of the 'image advertising' school in the early twentieth century (her childhood chum, James Webb Young, is given far more credit, even though Helen was his boss). Helen Resor's famous campaigns for Woodbury Soap, Pond's Creams, Cutex manicure treatments and other products are well docu-mented in the Duke collection. The testimony of others as to her influence is clear, but she herself was said to be 'publicity shy', so there are few interviews or photographs of her in the record of the trade. Helen Resor was also a feminist activist and a brilliant woman. It seems unlikely that she was actually a timid person; instead, her avoidance of personal publicity seems calculated to give her husband, Stanley, the limelight in the 'woman behind the man' way acceptable in her lifetime. Thus the record of Stanley's contribution (and Young's) versus Helen's is skewed by patriarchal prejudice, much as is the record of other history.

After women became more publicly prominent in advertising, the bias continued to be evident, even in source material. One book, *The Benevolent Dictators*, includes interviews with key figures from the mid-twentieth century, but none of them are women, even though the interview base from which the book is drawn included tapes (now decayed) of Shirley Polykoff, Rena Bartos and other well-known female advertising executives of the same period (Cummings, 1984). Steven Fox (1984) gives enormous credit to Bill Bernbach for the important campaigns of the 'Creative Revolution', as do most other historians. Scant attention anywhere is given to Mary Wells Lawrence, though she was famous in her own time as one of the key players of the Creative Revolution, the brains behind Alka-Seltzer, Braniff and other campaigns thought to mark the period. Her autobiography, *A Big Life*, was released in 2002, but by then Bernbach and others had dominated even the coffee table books for decades. Omitting women from the advertising histories underpins a frequent error in feminist commentary, in which critics regularly assume that the ads aimed at women are written by men, when, in fact, advertisements for products aimed at women, including especially beauty and fashion items, have traditionally been written by female creative groups (Scott, 2005).

A similar skew is discernible in matters of race. While books and articles have been devoted to the way the dominant culture stereotyped African Americans in ads and other marketing materials, there is not yet any work to document the considerable efforts of people like Claude Barnett, John Johnson, David Sullivan, Tom Burrell, Frank Mingo and Caroline Jones to market products, establish market research or even to wrest away the control of advertising campaigns from the 'dominant' agencies (Chambers, 2001, and forthcoming). Yet the inclination of ad agencies today to showcase the 'Urban Culture' mentioned by Holt (2002) and the efforts of 'mainstream' agencies to wrest back business from minority shops is testimony to the success of those entrepreneurs (Turow, 1997).

Particularly when looking at the earliest days of the consumer culture 'revolution', the matter of class also presents problems for the 'imagined history' of marketer-controlled culture. The modern market in America (and by this we are referring to the beginning of factory production, national distribution by mail and rail, and so-called 'mass media') emerged in the wake of the War for Independence, which substantially changed class relations by removing the monarchy as the primary point of hierarchical reference (Scott, 2005; Wood, 1992). The merchant class and the new middle class that were empowered by both the Revolution and the new economy were not of the leisured stratum that led the nation only a couple of decades earlier. Thus the market itself represented a challenge to an older order – the agrarian aristocracy as represented by men like Jefferson – and much of the critical commentary of the market and consumption that comprises the historical record (see Witkowski in this volume) expressed the status deprivation felt by these elites as their control of the culture began to slip away (Bushman, 1992; Scott, 2005; Wood, 1992).

Readers should remind themselves that most businesses in America were small enterprises until very recently. Owners of such businesses in the early 1800s were automatically defined as 'commonfolk' because they had to work for a living. In fact, a key marker of class status before the industrial and political revolution in the American colonies was the right to consume versus the obligation to produce: gentlemen were to consume, but commonfolk were to produce. Consumption by commonfolk was seen as immoral and a threat to the social order; the same behavior among gentry was seen as almost a kind of public service because it provided a market for the outputs of the common class (Wood, 1992). Thus the merchants of the preindustrial period were members of that class charged with supporting leisured men like Jefferson. To attribute the class dominance of today's corporate leaders to those early challengers is an example of what historians called 'presentism', the historical analogue to 'ethnocentrism'.

Presentism and the consumer

The error of presentism is even more evident in today's theoretical constructs of 'consumers' in the imagined past. Assumptions and agendas of the present are projected upon the buyers of the past, resulting in a consistent pattern that denies the existence of commodities before industrialization, that overlooks the participation in markets prior to mass production, that overly romanticizes earlier consumer behaviors as more 'rational' than today's consumers, or that, in contrast, overstates the gullibility of purchasers of the past (who are assumed not to have yet developed the irony and skepticism said to mark the generations of today).

Many, for instance, laud the 'self-sufficient' American of the preindustrial period, yet the histories emerging show, through analysis of wills and probate records, for instance, that few households had the means to produce everything they needed. Therefore most families traded what they produced – even unfinished goods – for the things they needed that they could not make (Hawke, 1989; Larkin, 1988). 'Self-sufficiency' could only be claimed by aristocrats like Jefferson who owned enough land and implements and employed enough people to produce everything at his own residence. In fact, the need to engage in trade in order to survive was a marker of common class status: this is probably the origin of the pejorative tone in the word 'consumer', as it comes down from similarly negative connotations in 'commerce' and 'trade' (Wood, 1992). Yet, here, too, there is an ideological sleight of hand: we can only say that Jefferson was 'self-sufficient' if we do not acknowledge his dependence on the village that once surrounded Monticello. But since history prior to 1980 used mostly the records of the literate and powerful and since our visits to national landmarks seldom exposed us to the daily lives of commonfolk, it was easy to assume that preindustrial Americans were 'self-sufficient' in the way that Jefferson appeared to have been.

Very early and even on the frontier, trading circles that spanned large geographic areas brought in items made by factories or craftsmen elsewhere (Dyer, Dalzell and Olegario, 2004; Scott, 2005). Manufactures imported from already industrialized nations like Britain showed up on the very edges of the wilderness, much as they did in Niger in the late 1970s, as documented by Eric Arnould (1989). Such trades occurred in both places and times despite the absence of local factories or advertising, though their distribution was hampered by long trade lines and a low supply of currency.

In America, small manufactured goods were brought to settlements (before rural free delivery and railroads) by itinerant peddlers. The Yankee peddler is, in fact, a repeating character in early American documents and literature (Benes, 1984; Wright, 1976). These peddlers were anxiously awaited and welcomed both for their goods and for their news, but they were also known for their ability to trick locals in trade. Thus the basis for a 'trickster' salesman in American literature was formed early, long before P.T. Barnum, whose nineteenth-century antics are usually used to mark the beginning of modern advertising (Twitchell, 2000; Wadlington, 1975).

Clever peddlers had to be careful of the local propensity to take advantage in trade, however. Historians of everyday life tell us that the ability to make a shrewd exchange was admired by early Americans, sometimes leading to outright deceptions even among neighbors. This is hardly surprising since the anthropological literature (especially Mauss, 1954) reveals that so-called 'gift societies' have consistently used the practice of gaining advantage through exchange (that is, profit taking). Thus the consumers of the past cannot be assumed to have been gullible, any more than we can assume they were self-sufficient.

Indeed one of the most salient prejudices of today's academic literature is the emphasis that is put on 'resisting the market' (Holt, 2002). Scholars often assume that the efforts of groups like Adbusters represent a newly-emergent ability to see through a market scam, but they also tend to overemphasize the importance of the institution of the market as a site of resistance as opposed to other institutions that have been more oppressive in the past. This oversight is a particular problem in the history of disadvantaged groups. For instance, while Jefferson and his kind were threatened by the emergence of the modern economy, the slaves who worked their plantations, having little interest in perpetuating the old agrarian order so romanticized by cultural critics today, pushed relentlessly toward a modern work and consumption ethic (Genovese, 1976). And, though the urban employments typical after the Great Migration offered little dignity, the consumption of the modern economy's products has frequently been an avenue for political expression in African-American culture. Eating lunch at a whites-only counter and riding at the front of the bus are just the most well known and recent of consumer actions that attacked the racial segregation system. Such acts of resistance have been observable since Emancipation, as African-Americans have displayed and used goods formerly reserved for whites in a bid for equal treatment. And, more recently, blacks have often demonstrated a preference for the chain stores compared to the local retailers – in a distinctive departure from the norms of leftist politics – because nationally owned stores were more likely to treat them well (Cohen, 2003). While it is easy to dismiss such politically motivated actions as 'mere consumption' or to discount them as 'still occurring within the market', such rejoinders fail to recognize that blacks have had restricted access to the 'normal' venues of politics (voting, membership in Congress), that material goods are a key site for bringing the social hierarchy to bear in all societies, and that the system of racial discrimination may understandably have had a higher priority on the African-American agenda than resistance to consumer culture.

Indeed the fact that restricted access to the market is often a marker of oppression is seldom recognized by today's literature, blinded as we are by a society in which 'free personal choice in the private sphere of everyday life' (Holt, 2002) is unfettered by anything except the availability of cash and in which the call to conform demands 'aggressive consumption' (Fullerton, 1987). In preindustrial societies such as Niger, as described by Arnould, and in America, as described by the scholars we have already cited here, family patriarchs and aristocrats have controlled the consumption and labor of entire communities. Further, laws regulating consumption – called 'sumptuary laws' – restricted goods ownership by class, as they did in Niger and have done in many other parts of the world. Indeed the original meaning of the word 'luxury' referred to those things that were rightly owned by aristocrats, but crimes if purchased by commoners (Tiger, 1992). It is remarkable that a field dedicated to consumption appears to have missed how frequently in history denying access to goods appears as a primary method used to humiliate, break and control large populations.

The freedom to consume is very often one of the first and most threatening acts taken by people who have broken the grip of dominance. The Revolution led by Jefferson and the other American 'patriots' upset the sumptuary customs that had originally been law in all of the American colonies. The newly equal citizens of the republic rushed to consume goods that were formerly off-limits, especially after factories made such products affordable and modern-economy jobs regularly put cash in the hands of ordinary people for the first time (Bushman, 1992; Scott, 2005). Similar behavior was frequently observed among freed blacks after the Civil War, and the contemporary commentary among whites shows the same discomfort with 'inappropriate' consumption among the formerly disenfranchised (Genovese, 1976; Hale, 1999). Throughout the history of race in America, in fact, blacks have recognized that consumption would not itself produce freedom, but that the restrictions on their consumption were an additional (and highly visible) marker of their social inferiority (Molnar and Lamont, 2002).

Because consumer goods are often used to enforce the hierarchy by making it visible (Douglas and Isherwood, 1996), the effect of sudden freedom to consume can actually cause the breakdown of the dominant order. In Arnould's account of Niger, those who had been controlled by the previous order – women, especially, but also slaves, workers and young people – caused the former system to 'disintegrate' quickly by exercising their new freedom to consume. Arnould remarks that, once this happened, there was 'no going back'. If you were advantaged by the old system, you might have viewed this outcome as a tragedy; if you were a member of the majority *dis*advantaged by the system, you might have seen the coming of the modern market in a much different light. And yet it is common to dismiss such examples as the illusions of people who *thought* they were breaking through a dominant system, but in fact were 'merely complicit with the market'. Again the presentist assumption that the social evil trumping all others is today's consumer culture ignores the vicious, totalizing institutions of the past. As histories and biographies coming out of postsocialist countries in the past 20 years attest, the neglect of consumption and 'consumer culture' by these regimes was understood by consumers as a tool for breaking the human spirit (Drakulic, 1991; Sredl, 2004a). Comparisons with preindustrial societies and socialist states, in fact, point to the increasingly problematic status of terms like 'market', 'commodity' and 'consumption'. Though much of the work in academia takes for granted that these terms apply unproblematically to the goods and systems of the here and now, historical work (and cross-cultural work) continues to produce counterexamples that muddy that certainty (Sredl, 2004b).

The rush to demonize the present often leads to generalizations, therefore, for which there is little evidentiary support. For instance, in an article in *Consumption, Markets and Culture*, David Clarke argues that people today define themselves by their consumption, as opposed to the past, where they defined themselves by work (1998). Yet, even in our own literature, evidence suggests that religion profoundly structured the lived experiences of the past, including both work and consumption, and that the connection of work to selfhood gave special status to implements of skill owned by our forebears, thus imbuing those objects with meaning beyond their utility (Belk, 1992). And, though present-day commentators continue to use the ability to distill goods to an inanimate 'use value' as the acid test of agency and autonomy (Holt, 2002), histories thus far suggest that consumption *was* used to constitute the self in the past, and that these acts of purchase, use, display and dispossession have always been complex, contentious, political and, above all, infused with meaning (Belk, 1992; Bushman, 1992; Scott, 2005; Witkowski, 1989). Finally anyone who wishes to argue that the sensibilities of the American 'forefathers' were somehow a more rationally 'utilitarian' approach to material culture should dig into the details of living under Puritan rule to see how thoroughly religion could control and pervert material life (for a particularly enlightening and unsettling account, see Earle, 1968).

When we delve deeply into the evidence and thinking of our ancestors, we often enter into a world very unlike what we imagine and find, instead, something quite alien. As one historian has remarked, 'the past is a foreign country' (Lowenthal, 1985). In a sense, then, history is much like ethnography, only it is a form of study that crosses the boundaries of time rather than space.

Archival bias
We began this chapter with the Monticello example in order to emphasize that class bias underpins the basis for history such that the evidence itself is profoundly skewed. This is true not only in the preservation of artifacts but in the archives of written material. It is common, for instance, to argue that the advertising and marketing materials of the past have been text-oriented and 'rational' in their approach, listing ingredients and prices, rather than making broad, imagistic allusions. Such generalizations are often based on little more than impressionistic projections, but they are sometimes supported by studies that have purported to analyze the historical record (e.g. Leiss, Klein and Jhally, 1990).

Yet what is the record? In every case, the data being used are an archive of magazines or newspapers in a university or public library. There are three problems here. One is that there is not much left of the image advertising of the early years of consumer culture. The print technology prior to 1875 did not allow much sophistication in the way of image reproduction at all, but other forms no longer available, such as painted signs and transit ads, did. We know that these forms were often fanciful and seldom full of text, because such forms then, as now, did not lend themselves to reading *and* because most of the population were not literate anyway. By 1900, new print technology produced a boom in image advertising, but nearly all of it was in posters and ephemera, little of which has survived to the present day. The newspapers of the early 'penny press' contained many illustrations, since those who looked at those papers were often not literate and many others did not speak English. These papers were not collected by libraries. The same can be said of the truly 'mass' magazines that came later (like *True Story* and *Physical Culture*). Deemed too 'common' to be collected by libraries even though their circulations were far larger than those of magazines used in studies (like the *Ladies Home Journal* or the *Saturday Evening Post*), these materials are now almost entirely unavailable to historians. So this is the second problem: the materials that *were* read by the common people (that is, those among them who were literate) are seldom available. Similar practices hold today: though *TV Guide* is one of the biggest circulation periodicals in the US, university libraries (and even public libraries) almost never collect it. The third problem is the common practice of binding periodicals through most of the twentieth century, in which the advertisements were removed to reduce the bulk by eliminating 'superfluous' material. In many cases, binders would insert a notice that an ad had been removed, but since that is not always true, we cannot even count how much of the record has been omitted, never mind comment on how 'imagistic' the missing matter was. Thus we cannot reasonably make the kinds of conclusions that have been drawn because the record is too incomplete and the known literacy rates of the past suggest that any theory of consumer consciousness (and rationality) built on an assumed ability to read is fundamentally biased by class (and race and gender).

Theory and antitheory

We would expect, in sum, that the work of history in consumer behavior would be much like the work of ethnography and would have similar applications to theory. The interaction between research questions and data (see Witkowski, this volume) is quite comparable. There may be somewhat more need for attention to absent data (that which has been destroyed or allowed to decay) in history than in ethnography. The limited ability to build theory from one example would be the same. Though the attention to the uniqueness of each social setting would be crucial, the summing of general notions – though perhaps not 'laws' – from many cases is, we think, possible (in contrast, see Fullerton, 1987; Smith and Lux, 1993). Though Smith and Lux argue that history cannot be used for theory testing because it is vulnerable to falsification from one case, we feel that this potential is actually history's strongest suit in research: as a kind of 'antitheory', history, with its infinite array of messy, alien particulars is a strong site for testing the generalizations built from present observations.

Let us offer some examples. Crockett and Wallendorf, for instance, have presented data to suggest that African-American consumers are influenced by political beliefs in their consumer behaviors (2004). The historical sources we have cited here support Crockett and Wallendorf in a very solid way, not only by showing additional cases within African-American culture where this has been true in the past, but by forming the basis for a potential argument that such behavior within that community is a long-standing *tradition* being brought to bear on the present. In trying to take Crockett and Wallendorf a little farther, we might add that the evidence presented by Witkowski (1989) showing the political basis for the nonimportation movement suggests that further research on politics as a frequent basis for consumer choices across many different times and groups would be a fruitful avenue for future research. Thompson and Arsel (2004) present evidence to suggest that coffeehouse consumers construct a critique of corporate capitalism. If we couple that argument with the historical record used by Hirschman, Scott and Wells (1998), we find that coffee has long been connected to insurgent thought and activity across a broad range of past cultures. Indeed Americans were big coffee drinkers at the time of the Revolution and several despots in world history have actually outlawed coffee because it was believed to lead to political unrest. Some have even suggested that consumption of coffee, which stimulates both cognition and sociability, does in fact lead to circumstances conducive to critical political thinking and conspiratorial conversation. So, while Thompson and Arsel's argument would also be consistent with the historical record. Douglas Holt's recent book, *How Brands Become Icons*, takes on a number of marketing shibboleths on branding, and ultimately destroys their credibility through painstaking historical research across several important historical counterexamples (2004). Scott, in her book, *Fresh Lipstick*, traces the feminist critique of the fashion and beauty industries in order to show its basis in class and race prejudice, and ends by smashing the critique's underlying theories. Thus history can be used cumulatively as a theory-building strategy, especially in connection with ethnography and in combination with other studies and methods, but it can also be especially strong at testing or countering theories, particularly those built on the false image of an imagined past.

Conclusion

The key points here are several. First, it is important to bear in mind that the extant history of ordinary life – that is, of consumption by most people of the past – is extremely thin. Generalizations about how things were 'then' versus how things are 'now' are, in many cases, based on an imagined past for the simple reason that there is not enough evidence saved or history written yet to make such remarks. Therefore it is important for consumer behavior researchers to be mentally vigilant about theories based on some implicit trajectory for which the starting point, in all honesty, cannot yet be reliably documented.

We tried to suggest that historical examples can be used both to support and to falsify theories as they are built on consumer behaviors. It is crucial, however, for researchers to respect the foreignness of their own past. Doing history is rather like doing fieldwork in another culture: even if you speak the language, you must be constantly vigilant against the presumption that your cultural precepts are shared by those you are studying. The values and viewpoints, as well as the material conditions and social restrictions, of the past are quite different from those of our own time and should be respected (but not romanticized) as we are attempting to piece together a coherent picture or narrative of consumption in earlier times.

Even in study and policy making that seems to focus exclusively on the present, there is often an implicit narrative of 'how we got where we are now' and, owing to the relatively new emergence of consumption history in the academy, these unspoken assumptions are often false – the projections of the present's agenda, a rhetorical history created by and for a particular argument. If our conclusions and decisions are to stand up to the test of time, it is important that they be founded on solid research into the habits and practices of the past, so we can be as informed as possible about the actual trajectory of events forming consumer culture. Therefore the astounding paucity of history on consumption is, we would argue, the most compelling reason that the field itself should begin to emphasize historical work.

References

Arnould, Eric (1989), 'Toward a broadened theory of preference formation and the diffusion of innovations: cases from Zinder Province, Niger Republic', *Journal of Consumer Research*, **16** (September), 239–67.
Arnould, Eric and Craig Thompson (2005), 'Consumer culture theory: twenty years of research', *Journal of Consumer Research*, **31** (March), 868–82.
Belk, Russell (1992), 'Moving possessions: an analysis based on personal documents from the 1847–1869 Mormon migration', *Journal of Consumer Research*, **19**, 339–61.
Benes, Peter (1984), *Itinerancy in New England and New York*, Boston: Boston University Press.
Bushman, Richard L. (1992), *The Refinement of America*, New York: Knopf.
Chambers, Jason P. (2001), 'Getting a job and changing an image: African Americans in the advertising industry, 1920–1975', PhD dissertation, The Ohio State University.
—— (forthcoming), *The Black Mirror Makers: African Americans in the Advertising Industry, 1920–2000*, University of Pennsylvania Press.
Clarke, David S. (1998), 'Consumption, identity, and space–time', *Consumption, Markets and Culture*, **2** (3), 233–58.
Cohen, Lizabeth (2003), *A Consumers' Republic: The Politics of Mass Consumption in Postwar America*, New York: Knopf.
Crockett, David and Melanie Wallendorf (2004), 'The role of normative political ideology in consumer behavior', *Journal of Consumer Research*, **31** (3), 511–28.
Cummings, Bart (1984), *The Benevolent Dictators*, Chicago: Crain.
Douglas, Mary and Baron Isherwood (1996), *The World of Goods: Towards an Anthropology of Consumption*, London: Routledge.
Drakulic, Slavenka (1991), *How We Survived Communism and Even Laughed*, New York: HarperPerennial.
Dyer, Davis, Frederick Dalzell and Rowena Olegario (2004), *Rising Tide: Lessons from 165 Years of Brand-building at Procter & Gamble*, Boston: Harvard Business School Press.
Earle, Alice Morse (1968), *Customs and Fashions in Old New England*, Detroit: Singing Tree Press.
Fox, Stephen (1984), *The Mirror-Makers*, New York: William Morrow.

Fullerton, Ronald A. (1987), 'Historicism: what it is, and what it means for consumer research', *Advances in Consumer Research*, vol. 14, Provo, UT: Association for Consumer Research, pp. 431–4.

Genovese, Eugene (1976), *Roll Jordan Roll: The World the Slaves Made*, New York: Vintage.

Hale, Grace (1999), *Making Whiteness: The Culture of Segregation in the South*, New York: Vintage.

Hawke, David Freeman (1989), *Everyday Life in Early America*, New York: Perennial Library.

Hirschman, Elizabeth C., Linda M. Scott and William D. Wells (1998), 'A model of product discourse: linking consumer practice to cultural texts', *Journal of Advertising*, **27** (Spring), 33–50.

Holt, Douglas B. (2002), 'Why do brands cause trouble? A dialectical theory of consumer culture and branding', *Journal of Consumer Research*, **29**, 70–90.

—— (2004), *How Brands Become Icons*, Boston: Harvard Business Press.

Hoy, Suellen (1995), *Chasing Dirt*, New York: Oxford University Press.

Kreshel, Peggy (1990), 'John B. Watson at J. Walter Thompson: the legitimation of "Science" in Advertising', *Journal of Advertising*, **19** (2).

Larkin, Jack (1988), *The Reshaping of Everyday Life, 1790–1840*, New York: Harper.

Lawrence, Mary Wells (2002), *A Big Life in Advertising*, New York: Knopf.

Leiss, W., S. Kline and S. Jhally (1990), *Social Communication in Advertising*, Scarborough, Canada: Nelson.

Lowenthal, David (1985), *The Past is a Foreign Country*, New York: Cambridge University Press.

Marchand, Roland (1985), *Advertising the American Dream*, Berkeley: University of California.

Mauss, Marcel (1954), *The Gift: The Form and Reason for Exchange in Archaic Societies*, Glencoe, IL: Free Press.

Miller, Daniel (ed.) (1995), *Acknowledging Consumption*, New York, Routledge.

Molnar, Virag and Michele Lamont (2002), 'Social Categorization and group identification: how African Americans shape their collective identity through consumption', in Andrew McMeekin, Ken Green, Mark Tomlinson and Vivien Walsh (eds), *Innovation by Demand*, Manchester: Manchester University Press, pp. 88–111.

Scott, Linda M. (2005), *Fresh Lipstick: Redressing Fashion and Feminism*, New York: Palgrave.

Smith, Ruth Ann and David S. Lux (1993), 'Historical method in consumer research: developing causal explanations of change', *Journal of Consumer Research*, **19**, 593–610.

Sredl, Katherine C. (2004a), 'Balkan Barbie: women and consumer culture in post-socialist Croatia', in Craig Thompson and Linda Scott (eds), *Association for Consumer Research Conference on Gender, Marketing and Consumer Behavior*, Valdosta, GA: Association for Consumer Research.

—— (2004b), ' "Why are we so stupid?": an historic approach to post-socialist consumer research', in Geeta Menon and Akshay Rao (eds), *Advances in Consumer Research*, vol. 32, Valdosta, GA: Association for Consumer Research.

Thompson, Craig and Zeynep Arsel (2004), 'The Starbucks brandscape and consumers' (anticorporate) experiences of glocalization', *Journal of Consumer Research*, **31** (3), 631–42.

Tiger, Lionel (1992), *The Pursuit of Pleasure*, New York: Little, Brown.

Turow, Joseph (1997), *Breaking up America*, Chicago: University of Chicago Press.

Twitchell, James (2000), *Twenty Ads that Shook the World*, New York: Crown.

Vinikas, Vincent (1992), *Soft Soap, Hard Sell*, Ames, IA: Iowa State University Press.

Wadlington, Warwick (1975), *The Confidence Game in American Literature*, Princeton: Princeton University Press.

Witkowski, Terrence H. (1989), 'Colonial consumers in revolt: buyer values and behavior during the nonimportation movement, 1764–1776', *Journal of Consumer Research*, **16**, 216–26.

Wood, Gordon S. (1992), *The Radicalism of the American Revolution*, New York: Knopf.

Wright, Richardson (1976), *Hawkers and Walkers in Early America*, New York: Arno.

Zinn, Howard (1980), *A People's History of the United States: 1492 to the Present*, New York: Harper and Row.

17 Using video-elicitation to research sensitive topics: understanding the purchase process following natural disaster

Shay Sayre

In the past, investigating sensitive behaviors was the equivalent of asking people to 'talk dirty to me' about topics such as HIV, sex, drug use, physical abuse, abortion and incest. Today, radio, television and advertising content have brought such topics to the forefront of socially acceptable discussion. Oprah invites bed-wetters and abortion survivors to tell all to viewers; Howard Stern's listeners join in on conversations from child abuse to sex change surgery; advertisers of Viagra portray newly functioning men as objects of a woman's adoration. In other words, few topics are considered to be 'media-sacred', as so many sensitive-topic barriers have been broken simply by offering people an opportunity to voice their opinions.

In preparation for their Depends commercials, a research company held focus groups on incontinence to discover that the stigma of wearing diapers was unbearable for older sufferers. Participants in photo sorts identified their favorite contemporary celebrities, and an advertising agency produced a television commercial where Jane Wyman endorsed the product with an admission that she was a Depends user. The results? Sales of Depends went through the roof.

Data on bodily dysfunction, as well as many other embarrassing maladies, have been collected successfully by advertising researchers through self-administered questionnaires, computer-assisted tools and neutral-site interviews. For instance, research on feminine hygiene with 18–24-year-old females revealed these consumers want straightforward pitches that are hip and edgy. In response, Ogilvy & Mather created a Kotex campaign that introduced a blaring red dot into its marketing and produced mural-size mall ads containing the slogan, 'Kotex fits. Period.' Account planners admit that few respondents refuse to discuss such subjects in private when they are compensated and when anonymity is guaranteed.

Still some topics remain taboo by virtue of the emotional trauma caused to respondents who recall life-changing events. One such event is natural disaster, which affects thousands of people and costs the insurance industry billions of dollars annually for destruction due to catastrophic loss. Dollars paid out in claim settlements to policyholders for replacing lost possessions warrants research into post-disaster buying behaviors to provide marketers with insight on how best to serve people who have lost everything. How survivors interpret these events and how researchers gather data without intrusive probing was a challenge of procedure, field relations and ethics.

Our research was stimulated by insurance company adjusters who were anxious to learn how to assist fire survivors and by retailers and service organizations (architects and builders in particular) that anticipated profitable associations with the disaster population. We approached our investigation ethnographically to answer two primary questions.

What can insurance companies expect to encounter from their clients following natural disasters? How would survivors go about the business of replacing lost possessions? Our academic interests pointed towards the loss of possessions and its impact on personal identity.

Disaster research is conducted with respondents who have personally gone through some degree of mass trauma. Disaster has provided an ideal setting for studying aspects of consumer behavior, communication, psychology and media influence (Sayre and Horne, 1996). Our research population were survivors of a firestorm that destroyed 350 homes.

Post-disaster conditions provide a unique opportunity for studying acquisitions that offer survivors an opportunity to redefine themselves (Belk, 1988) through the purchase of items from toothbrushes to refrigerators, faucets to fashion wardrobes, and carpets to roof shingles. An understanding of consumption following natural disaster is one instance where sensitive topic research techniques are not only necessary, they are essential. Victims of disaster are reluctant to discuss their traumas, and they refuse to engage in conversation with anyone outside their survivor community. Once private conversation is ruled out as an option, researchers are challenged to develop a user-friendly and anonymous means of gaining access to the disaster sample and eliciting information about the process of rebuilding through replacement purchases.

Like advertisers who use media to desensitize sensitive topics, we developed a mediated method to investigate loss and replacement based on the notion of parasocial relationships. Soap opera fans are known to form one-way relationships with stars who interact with their lives in real time. Such mediated relationships that occur between a star and viewer (Horton and Wohl, 1956) are key to producing access to a closed community by using the same principle: a mediated relationship developed with fellow disaster survivors for the purpose of mutual disclosure. If, as Cathcart and Gumpert (1983) assert, television personalities can approximate an ideal that is impossible in everyday life, using a video personality would make a difference in the length, depth and quality of a respondent's testimony.

Sensitive topics defined
This article predicates its definition of sensitive topics on a work by Sieber and Stanley (1988) who suggest that sensitive research applies to 'studies in which there are potential consequences or implications for the participants'. Disaster is not a topic ordinarily described as 'sensitive' because the consequences of participating in disaster research are still unknown. Potentially, however, disaster survivors may suffer mental anxieties from the reflection of events that were emotionally traumatic. While recovery is not an area of social life surrounded by taboo, the topic of surviving the loss of possessions and/or identity is sensitive to all those who have encountered either, from natural disasters such as fire, earthquake, tornados, hurricanes and flooding.

In a volume dedicated to disaster research, Sayre and Horne (1996) presented incidents where victims were reluctant to recall or relive their emotional reactions to catastrophic loss – not because the topic was defined as taboo, but because recollection of these events compromised their ability to move forward or their anonymity. According to respondents to the studies in this volume, the potential costs to those involved are emotionally, socially and monetarily significant.

Globally topics and activities regarded as private vary across cultures and situations. Traditionally, respondents record misgivings or unease about questions directed towards their finances or sexual behavior (Goyder, 1987). Other areas of personal experiences, such as bereavement or loss, are emotionally charged rather than private. In cases involving finances or sexual behavior, stress is not a factor; with victims of disaster, concerns about maintaining an appropriate demeanor in personal contact may be emotionally threatening and extremely stressful. And although disaster survivors have no threat of sanction or political threat, they may encounter threats of emotional devastation.

Institutional review boards have not identified disaster victims among their list of vulnerable subjects because, unlike minors, seniors and criminals, they are not likely victims of research effects or unintended consequences. And although disaster victims are not deviant populations requiring regulations, inquiry into disaster-related outcomes can be construed as physiologically and emotionally threatening.

Understanding the limitations of ethical inquiry, researchers must approach personally sacred topics as sensitive and design methods of data collection that allow anonymity while minimizing emotional trauma. Discussions of events following disaster, while useful, are seldom insightful. Rather than discussion, researchers must elicit intimate disclosure in order to understand the phenomenon of loss and identity reconfiguration.

Gated community syndrome: problems of access
Gaining access to special circumstance communities such as we encountered with disaster victims is fraught with politics of distrust. Once homeless, survivors huddled together against an onslaught of marketers eager to sell them products, of architects and builders lusting over potential contracts, and of insurance companies demanding itemized lists of all lost possessions. Fearful of unwanted advances, residents of our disaster community were unlikely to trust anyone from the outside.

The researchers' disaster community consisted of fire survivors from 350 homes that had burned to the ground from an arsonist prank during the dry Santa Ana wind conditions typical of California fall seasons. Forced to take refuge with relatives or in rental units, the community was dispersed and difficult to track down. And although my co-researcher acted as a *bridge* to the community, we needed additional legitimization in order to gain and maintain access.

Because sponsorships are closely tied to prestige, we approached the president of the survivor community organization (the group's gatekeeper) who agreed to cooperate if we met certain conditions for our research agenda. In exchange for access to ongoing field research, we agreed to share the results and to secure retailer discounts for fire victims. As our *sponsor*, the president served both as a *guide* through the unfamiliar territory of disaster survival and as a *patron* to help us secure the trust of the community.

Weekly meetings were organized and attended by the group who convened at a local church to discuss their mutual situations. As a result of attending these meetings with a survivor, I was able to convert my impersonal relationship into an interpersonal one in spite of the fact that I was not a community member. By 'fitting in', we could minimize the social distance between ourselves and the community under study. Such progressive entry minimized potential threats we might have posed by maintaining a sustained presence in the setting. We structured an approach strategy that began by telling the community what we wanted to do, explaining our purpose, describing our research timeline and asking for volunteers.

We guaranteed anonymity and circulated 400 surveys; 180 responses were received. Results revealed that most members had not progressed past the shock stage of recovery; some had compiled lists of lost items but few gave much thought to purchasing beyond their immediate needs. Survey respondents were asked to participate in a focus group to discuss their current concerns. Most were reluctant to talk freely about their insurance situation and voiced discomfort about sharing their plans with neighbors. Discarding the idea of a focus group, we set out to find a method of inquiry that would not compromise respondent privacy.

Intimacy for sale: self-disclosure defined
Self-disclosure refers to the process of telling another person about oneself, honestly sharing thoughts and feelings that may be very personal and private (Jourard, 1964). The distinction between self-disclosure and description lies in the nature of circumstances. Marketing and consumer research typically involves publicly shared stories about reactions to new products or advertising campaigns. Self-disclosure, on the other hand, is verbal behavior through which individuals truthfully and intentionally communicate private information about themselves (Fisher, 1984). Privacy is what distinguishes self-disclosure from descriptive narrative.[1]

Findings on self-disclosure are varied, but two consistent findings have emerged: disclosure tends to be reciprocal and disclosure tends to be liked by the recipient of the message (Archer and Earle, 1983). Research on self-disclosure is grounded in social penetration and exchange theories. The concept of exchange reciprocity (Erlich and Graven, 1971) depends on trust between teller and listener. In the presence of an 'intruder', reciprocity and disclosure is often reduced. During disclosure reciprocity – you tell me and I'll tell you – recipients disclose about themselves at a comparable level of intimacy. One explanation is trust liking, which holds that receiving intimate disclosure increases trust in and liking for the disclosure. Of course, most reciprocity is simply the result of modeling where the recipient of disclosure imitates the other discloser.

Disclosure is best experienced listening to radio talk shows or watching the Oprah genre on television. Here, intimate and typically embarrassing matters are discussed as if millions of people were not listening. Listeners, viewers and Internet chat room visitors regularly encounter cathartic disclosures of the most personal types. Perhaps such participants embrace Warhol's notion of 15 minutes of fame, using their experiences to cast them in the limelight. Unfortunately, similar disclosure is rarely forthcoming from victims of disaster.

To question or not to question: self-disclosure techniques
We surmised that, to be successful, our disclosure technique must foster reciprocity without the intrusion of a researcher and must also provide anonymity. To meet the challenge, we first evaluated existing disclosure techniques used to approach sensitive topics or with reluctant subjects: written narratives and surveys, focus groups, depth interviews and visual data gathering.

Surveys
We found surveys to be useful for assessing a situation and for validating information collected during fieldwork, but not effective as a primary data-gathering tool for vulnerable audiences. Internet surveys without computers made this technology mute for our population.

Written narratives
Diaries and logs, while assuring respondent privacy in sensitive situations, may not be appropriate for reluctant populations who are too emotionally distraught to write at length about their experiences. Alexander and Becker (1978) identified *vignettes* as a valuable technique for developing sensitive questions, and we liked the idea of using stories for depictions of disaster situations.

Focus groups
Advocated by marketers as ideal for eliciting information on sensitive topics, focus groups may not be appropriate for members of disaster populations who are reluctant to share their personal trauma in a group setting, for three reasons: first, group members may be hesitant to share openly feelings with someone they might directly or indirectly know; face-to-face interaction may be too compromising for emotionally sensitive participants. Second, partial or inaccurate disclosures might occur because of the 'halo effect' or group-think, where respondents try to please the interviewer or are influenced by other group members. Finally, an individual moderator's perceived empathy with victims would probably vary among respondents, and might even be seen as completely lacking by some of the subjects. We concluded that the dynamics of focus groups rendered them inappropriate for our purposes.

Depth interviews
Having been used successfully in a variety of sensitive situations, depth interviews have the potential to offer a more promising technique than focus groups for disaster survivors. However the more sensitive the topic, the more essential it becomes for researchers to establish their trustworthiness with subjects. Trust in research relationships has to do with the interaction between researcher and participant. Potential impediments to developing such a relationship may occur if a lack of alignment exists between researcher and informant (Lindloff, 1995). Speaking candidly to an outsider who had not experienced traumatic loss would be difficult for our disaster community members. And although Sykes and Collins (1988) reported that telephone interviews consistently elicit disclosure, such interviews would be interpreted as intrusive and marketing-oriented by our special population. In addition to problems of transference as described in psychoanalytic literature, depth interviews cause grief for respondents who are still sensitive about the trauma of the event. Using continual probing typical of depth interviewing may confine rather than expand the discussion in our case.

Visual techniques
Photographic images are often used for gathering information where visuals serve as the data set for analysis. Photography, film and video have been very successful in recording the subjects' point of view and for documenting social activity, but are rarely used to elicit information. Visual research is conducted by anthropologists in their studies of culture (Norman, 1984; Van der Does et al., 1992); visual sociologists use photoelicitation in their studies of group behavior (Harper, 1984); and psychologists use family photography for projective purposes in therapy (Wessels, 1985). Collier and Collier (1986) proposed photoelicitation as a projective technique appropriate for data generation in vulnerable settings. They suggested that photographic representations of familiar circumstances can

trigger deeply felt emotional replies that could be traumatic for subjects who are reluctant to revisit the painful circumstances surrounding catastrophic loss. Heisley and Levy (1991) developed *autodriving* to stimulate introspection and foster multiple layers of feelings from respondents through repetitive iterations about particular activity. This situation is less than ideal where subjects are reluctant to disclose. Also the issue of how to make this or any other projective technique appear empathetic remains problematic.

Ah ha! principal: discovery with pizzazz

After evaluating our disclosure technique options and considering the reluctance of our population and the emotional sensitivity of the situation, we decided to develop our own technique. The postmodern notion of combining bits of tradition with eclectic modernism led to the formulation of a technique combining historical foundation with practical application.

Named video-elicitation, our technique combines story vignettes with visual projectives to produce a talk-show format for depth interviewing. Our principles were simple: use actors to discuss their post-disaster concerns using videotaped vignettes that are designed to stimulate recollection and provide a platform for discussion.

Why would this work? In a mediated world where relationships are formed and developed electronically, viewers tend to identify with and trust many televised images. The notion of one member of a vulnerable population reacting to another member's self-disclosures intrigued us. We believed that trust could be established through a fictitious survivor's verbal and visual disclosure. If the actor–victim appeared genuine and his or her comments plausible, respondents could identify with that person and be forthcoming about their own experiences.

According to the psychology literature, instances where people identify and bond with video personalities may result in the development of *parasocial* relationships. Even though the relationship is mediated, it psychologically resembles face-to-face interaction; viewers come to feel they 'know' the people they 'meet' on television the same way they know their friends. For years, soap opera fans have coveted their afternoon friends, often blurring the line between real and fictitious personalities.

Countless media studies (Coughly, 1984; Rubin and McHugh, 1987; Sayre, 1987) suggest that parasocial relationships create a strong bond between viewer and video personality. If video models can affect behavior in viewers, we suspected that the notion of trading one secret for another secret might apply to video-elicited self-disclosure. After actors disclosed their post-disaster feelings, respondents could disclose theirs in the privacy of their own homes. By fostering and developing a parasocial relationship between the respondent and another actor as survivor, the researcher's role is greatly enhanced. If a researchers' role of empathizer is not plausible, trained actors can maintain empathy and eliminate interviewer bias from the disclosure process. We would develop synthetically personalized messages that would simulate solidarity and blur the social distance and distinctions between producers and receivers of the message-facilitating disclosure.

Television programs are sites for the popularized display of the 'talking cure' (Peck, 1995, p. 68) where the act of communicating is intended to lead to new information, insights and identities. Even disaster survivors are comfortable with disclosure-style narrative typical of popular talk shows. Video disclosure is successful because of viewer comfort with intimate topics in a mediated venue. Americans enjoy watching disclosure as well as participating in self-disclosure over the airwaves. This reality convinced us that video was a perfect forum for self-disclosing dialog without compromising subject privacy. Our technique would instigate response and generate intimate self-disclosure while establishing a reliable and consistent method of data gathering.

Virtual verbosity: ethics of elicitation
Disclosure should not be a painful process. To protect our participants, we invoked several safeguards into the production of our video vignettes.

Accurate portrayals
Character actors were selected to reflect the physical appearance, age and economic status of the couples affected by the fire. Their voices were moderated and their expressions were typical of couples engaged in reflection – serious but not syrupy.

A non-leading video script
Vignette discussions were peculiar to the victims' circumstances; respondents were asked about their own behaviors in comparison to the actors on screen.

Pre-testing
We interviewed 10 subjects for post hoc associations with scenarios presented in the video that could potentially trigger trauma. None of the test-sample subjects reported unpleasant associations.

Subject preparation
One week before viewing the tape, participants were asked to reflect on their purchasing experiences. Immediately prior to viewing, subjects were told that (a) the characters and their portrayals were fictitious; (b) the characters presented one of many possible reactions to repurchasing lost possessions; (c) there were no unacceptable responses to the questions posed by the video; and (d) all descriptions of personal experiences were appropriate for this study. The announcer on the videotape repeated the information during respondent viewing.

Private viewing
The video was intended to jog the interviewees' memories about different aspects of their experiences, and to provide rich insights into their attitudes and behavior. And because of the presence of realistic vignette scenarios provided by the video, interviewer's were absent during the information-gathering process to maintain the subject's privacy. Each respondent was delivered a combination TV–videotape player and audio-tape recorder. All responses to the video vignettes were audio recorded by the participants as they watched the videotape. Tapes and equipment were retrieved the following day.

Guaranteed anonymity
Tapes were labeled with an identifying number that corresponded with the names of the respondents that were kept by the group gatekeeper, who personally delivered and retrieved the recording devices.

Figure 17.1   Actors portraying firestorm victims talk about their experience to real victims participating in the video-elicitation study

Movie magic: producing a realistic videotape

Preliminary interviews provided researchers with post-fire stories and experiences that provided the basis of our vignette script. We crafted 20 vignettes and discarded four as inappropriate for probing what we needed to learn from respondents. The script was reviewed by four separate fire survivors and tweaked for language and phrasing.

Two actors who resembled our sample rehearsed their demeanor and mood to enhance respondent disclosure. A living room setting was designed to represent an environment familiar to the population, in this case the temporary residences of displaced disaster victims. Strobe lights and two cameras captured the action. We produced a musical score as background to put respondents at ease and to act as a transitional element between segments.

The tape opened with our actors, seated next to each other on a couch, looking at a magazine together. A voice-over explained, 'This video is designed to record the feelings and thoughts of fire survivors . . .' and continued to detail the procedure: 'After each vignette, stop the tape and respond to the questions on your screen. Take as long as you'd like. When you have finished, resume watching until you are again instructed to pause and respond.' Questions were read aloud and presented on the screen as well. When the session concluded, respondents were thanked, assured of their anonymous participation and given directions for returning the equipment.

Listening and learning: viewers tell all

Eighteen tapes of eight couples and two single adults provided our data for analysis. Theme-building software analyzed respondent transcripts, which contained varying levels of self-disclosure. We used Archer's (1980) system for rating self-disclosure based on two intimacy levels and similar-response disclosures. Transcripts were coded for the presence of *descriptive intimacy* (statements that contain revelations of fears, values or basic self-concepts and disclosures involving vulnerabilities and/or perceived inadequacies) and *evaluative intimacy* (statements of intense feeling expressed with loaded words, qualifying words, or an evaluative tone of joy or sympathy, statements concerning relationships using self-references, that is, 'I' statements).

Two judges used a sentence-oriented rating system (Morton, 1978). In the presence of either level of intimacy, judges rated respondent statements as HIGH when they contained one or more of the definitive traits. Judges also coded for the presence of *topical reciprocity* (similar themes and discussions appearing in both videotape and transcripts) and *reciprocal empathy* (respondents' references to sharing emotions with the actors on screen); 21 per cent of the total statements contained such references.

After the tapes were collected, we telephoned four of the respondents who described their viewing experience as positive. They suggested that the videotape allowed them to validate feelings, and commented on how much they liked the actors. Such strong empathy with the actors suggests that a parasocial relationship developed between viewer and viewed. One participant even inquired about the actors' well-being despite knowledge of their fictitiousness: 'The young woman [on tape] looks so worried . . . I hope they are doing OK. Do you know . . . are they doing OK?'

As the actors talked about their experiences, viewers mutually disclosed their own. And although there was clear evidence of disclosure reciprocity, no discernible pattern of agreement or disagreement with the actors was detected. And the more intimate the actors got, the more intimate were respondent testimonies. Occasionally respondents reacted to the actors' discussion with some wonder, allowing the video to become a valuable source of reciprocal disclosure.

Evidence of self-disclosure was present in participants' use of first person, their laughter, their cries and their anecdotes. Emotional outbursts, frustrations and sorrow, and periods of anger were recorded on audio-tape. Disclosures told of the survivor's struggle to reconstruct his/her life:

> It seems like, before the fire, I was all involved with my stuff – how many Prada bags I had, whether or not my rugs were from Turkey . . . that kind of thing. Now I see how silly, I mean how really superficial, it is. Not that I like shopping any less, but now I go about it differently . . . at least I like to think I do! (Female 34)

> [Shopping] is harder now. We have to fight with the insurance company and we have to spend hours driving around from store to store to find the right faucet, or the right door knob. It's really an overwhelming chore. (Male 52)

The stuff of life: meaning and merchandise
Using video-elicitation enabled us to learn about the meaning of possessions to people who now had none. If *having*, as suggested by Sartre (1947), is essential for defining personal identity, then who were these folks without their stuff? Research suggests that objects became less significant criteria for disaster survivors' self-definition. During such an absence of objects, many respondents thought that 'things' no longer assumed a significant role in their lives.Others were determined not to reinvest their emotional energy in material possessions, but to concentrate on relationships and self-actualizing activities. Such disclosures included the following:

> I had so much love tied up in my things. I can't go through that kind of loss again. What I'm buying now won't be as important to me. (Female 47)

> We got a Wolfe range instead of a Kenmore, and a Sub-Zero instead of a Hotpoint. Because we had the money. Not 'cause we care what people think. I guess we got quality conscious? (Female 33)

> Yea, we got better stuff, but it doesn't mean the same as our old things. It's just stuff. (Male 49)

One of the most significant findings from our respondents' testimonies is the extent to which reacquisition involved reconstruction of self-identity for these disaster survivors. Meanings inherent in possessions that were symbolic of accomplishments, events or relationships were destroyed with the material objects. One man wondered if, by losing his golf trophy, he also lost the accomplishment of winning. If there were no photographs to record events, did they really happen? So, for many survivors, meaning could be created through the shopping experience. Stories of acquisition provided meaning for the material objects collected after the fire.

After a traumatic experience, people often feel the need to reward themselves for surviving. Our population disclosed similar feelings, and three themes of self-gifting and impulse buying emerged: *bigger is better*, *cash is king* and *just desserts*. Given the opportunity to improve their personal lifestyles, respondents viewed *rebuilding a bigger home* as a well-deserved gift:

> We decided to go for it. After all, we deserve it, going through the fire and all. Bigger will be better. (Female 45)

> We always wanted a bigger bedroom . . . maybe an office . . . certainly a hot tub. So after the fire we said, 'Why not?' After all, we will never get another chance like this. (Male 41)

> Hey, our family is growing and the insurance company is paying, so for sure we're building bigger. (Male 29)

If you've got it, spend it. Respondents seemed to feel that having a full wallet made buying things much more fun. Recipients of significant insurance settlements, survivors were prone to engage in cash and carry:

> I never used to shop, but now that we have the cash, it's fun! (Male 42)

> [After I got the money] my sister came to town and we went down to the store and bought everything at once. We just picked out one of this and one of that. Only took a few hours. (Female 81)

> We are so used to buying that our lifestyles have gotten to a new level. We're sort of nervous about what will happen when the money dries up. Can we go back to just living on our salaries? (Male 44)

> No buyer's remorse for us, right honey? We just go around spending like kids in a candy store. (Female 32)

Impulse buying resulted from *feelings of deserving*. Respondents felt that the trauma and hardships endured after the loss of their homes and possessions were ample justification for rewarding themselves. Some bought things out of their normal price range; others upgraded their cars and appliances. Most rationalized their spending:

> . . . so we decided to splurge on a Porsche. What the hell, we deserve it. (Male 52)

> After all we've been through, why should we deny ourselves the best? We buy whatever catches our eye. (Female 41)

> We're going to Paris for our anniversary. It's our treat to ourselves, for our pain. (Female 33)

Professional shoppers: combing the aisles for replacements
We were surprised at the amount of anecdotal material provided about the nature and enormity of the shopping experience. Transcripts were filled with remarks about the huge amount of time survivors were allocating to the shopping process. Everyone, without exception, described shopping as a 'task' that took too much of their time:

> Shopping became my full-time job. I quit work just so I could attend to all the details. You just don't realize how much work there is in getting all new stuff. From your shoes to the door knobs, you know. Everything has to be picked out. (Female 42)

If I have to make one more decision I'll scream. This is too much for any person to do alone. (Male 55)

Disclosure outcomes: mutually beneficial programs

Video-elicited disclosures benefited both fire survivors and service providers. Respondents suggested that the nature of the shopping experience was crucial to developing attachment to objects and infusing meaning into new possessions. This information translated into *retail programs*, such as providing shopping assistants, delivering instructional seminars on choosing appliances and other major acquisitions, and offering discounts and free delivery for fire survivors. We learned from our subjects that architects and builders were primary sources of information for selecting most of the household fixtures, interior coverings and exterior materials. Such knowledge stimulated these professionals to develop *shopping aids* for evaluating and selecting building-related purchases. Finally, disclosures showed insurances companies that *periodic allocations* of cash might be a better strategy for fund distribution to survivors than single disbursement checks, which had led to irrational buying behaviors.

Process, not panacea: video-elicitation evaluated

Sensitive topics and reluctant respondents tax the ingenuity of researchers, stimulating methodological innovation. Useful borrowing from other disciplines and subfields open a variety of research strategies and data collection opportunities. Because the context of research is constantly changing, eclectic, imaginative and non-traditional research designs are being developed to respond to situational variations.

Populations can be labeled as 'special circumstance' when self-disclosure is difficult because of the presence of emotional trauma and/or unusual logistics, or where cultural and/or language barriers are present. Since our first video-elicited study, we have invoked the technique for research on other types of sensitive topics and special populations, with very satisfying results. We advocate this method for a variety of situations where such special circumstances prevail. In the plus column are the following:

- a high degree of reciprocal exchange between subjects and actors, which fosters lengthy, free-flowing dialog;
- unencumbered interviews that do not rely on or become biased by an interviewer;
- reliability created by using the same stimulus for every participant;
- maintenance of respondent anonymity to legitimate the research process;
- in-home interviewing that results in a comfortable and secure environment for respondents.

As with all techniques, there are also mitigating factors:

- cost and expertise needed to produce the videotape;
- time involved in developing scenarios and vignettes in script form;
- reliance on skill and empathy of actors to stimulate disclosure.

We believe that video-elicitation offers researchers a reliable, affordable and flexible data collection technique when special circumstances or special populations require a non-intrusive environment. Our subjects seem more willing to talk in the presence of a non-threatening parasocial relationship than with strangers who might compromise their privacy.

For sensitive topics where populations have access to the Internet, video-elicitation may be useful for gathering interviews via the web. With the ability to cross physical and geographical boundaries, web-based video-elicitation may be appropriate for incarcerated prisoners, hospitalized or quarantined patients, hearing impaired using dialog subtitles, non-English speakers using native language actors, or groups of voters, activists, warring populations and a myriad of others who are not reachable using traditional methods. In an era of technological innovation, researchers are now able to minimize risk and maximize private self-disclosure for all populations who are victims of special circumstances.

Note

1. For a comprehensive review of self-disclosure literature, see Derlega et al. (1993).

References

Alexander, C.S. and H.J. Becker (1978), 'The use of vignettes in survey research', *Public Opinion Quarterly*, **42**, 93–104.

Archer, R.L. (1980), 'Self-disclosure', in D. Wagner and R. Vallocher (eds), *The Self in Social Psychology*, London: Oxford University Press, pp. 298–310.

Archer, R.L. and W.B. Earle (1983), 'The interpersonal orientations of disclosure', *Basic Group Processes*, New York: Springer Verlag.

Belk, Russell (1988), 'Possessions and the extended self', *Journal of Consumer Research*, **15** (September), 139–68.

Cathcart, R. and G. Gumpert (1983), 'Mediated interpersonal communication: toward a new Typology', *Communication*, **2**, 1–22.

Collier, J. Jr and M. Collier (1986), *Visual Anthropology*, Albuquerque: University of New Mexico Press.

Coughly, J.L. (1984), *Imaginary Social Worlds: A Cultural Approach*, Lincoln, NB: University of Nebraska Press.

Derlega, V.J., S. Metts, S. Petronio and S.T. Margulis (1993), *Self-disclosure*, Thousand Oaks, CA: Sage.

Erlich, H.J. and D.B. Graven (1971), 'Reciprocal self-disclosure in a dyad', *Journal of Experimental Social Psychology*, **7**, 389–400.

Fisher, D.V. (1984), 'A conceptual analysis of self-disclosure', *Journal for the Theory of Social Behavior*, **14** (3), 277–96.

Goyder, J. (1987), *The Silent Minority: Non-respondents on Sample Surveys*, Cambridge: Polity Press.

Harper, D. (1987), *Working Knowledge: Skill and Community in a Small Shop*, Chicago: University of Chicago Press.

Heisley, D.D. and S.J. Levy (1991), 'Autodriving: a photoelicitation technique', *Journal of Consumer Research*, **18**, 257–72.

Horton, D.D. and P.R. Wohl (1956), 'Mass communication and para-social interaction: observations on intimacy at a distance', *Psychiatry*, **19**, 215–29.

Jourard, S. (1964), *The Transparent Self*, Princeton, NJ: Van Nostrand.

Lindloff, T.R. (1995), *Qualitative Communication Research Methods*, Thousand Oaks, CA: Sage.

Morton, B. (1978), 'Conversational strategies and performative policies', in J. Grimes (ed.), *Papers on Discourse*, Dallas, TX: Summer Institute of Linguistic Publications, pp. 298–310.

Norman, W.R. (1984), 'An examination of centenary: United Methodist Church using the photograph as artifact', unpublished dissertation, Department of Anthropology, Ohio State University.

Peck, J. (1995), 'Talk shows as therapeutic discourse: the ideological labor of televised talking curse' *Communication Theory*, **5** (1), 58–81.

Rubin, R. and M.P. McHugh (1987), 'Development of para-social relationships', *Journal of Broadcast Media*, **31** (3), 279–92.

Sartre, J.P. (1947), *Being and Nothingness*, New York: Philosophical Library.

Sayre, S. (1987), 'Gender and prime time TV: who are our role Models?', paper presented to the Western Communication Educators' Conference, Fresno, CA (November).

—— (1996), 'I shop, therefore I am: the role of possessions for self definition', *Advances in Consumer Research*, vol. 23, Provo, UT: Association for Consumer Research, pp. 323–8.

Sayre, S. and D.A. Horne (eds) (1992), *Earth, Wind, Fire and Water: Approaching Natural Disaster*, Pamona, CA: Open Door Press.

Sieber, J. and B. Stanley (1988), 'Ethical and professional dimensions of socially sensitive research', *American Psychologist*, **43**, 49–55.

Sykes, W. and M. Collins (1988), 'Effects of modes of interview: experiments in the UK', in R.M. Groves, P.P. Biemer, L.E. Lyberg, J.T. Massey, W.L. Nichols and J. Waksberg (eds), *Telephone Survey Methodology*, New York: Wiley.

Van der Does, S., S. Edelaar, I. Gaskins, M. Leifting and M. Van Mierlo (1992), 'Reading images: study of a dated neighborhood', *Visual Sociology*, **7** (1), 4–68.

Wessels, D.T. Jr (1985), 'Using family photographs in the treatment of eating disorders', *Psychotherapy in Professional Practice*, **3**, 95–105.

18 Using oral history methods in consumer research
Richard Elliott and Andrea Davies

This chapter introduces oral history methods and positions oral history as a useful but neglected approach and demonstrates how oral history can provide consumer researchers with a means to examine critically their theories, knowledge and assumptions about consumers and their consumption. As an example of the method in use, we present a case study of oral history applied to the evolution of brand consciousness in 1918–65. Both are characteristic of consumer culture and are deeply implicated in our theories of symbolic consumption, branding and brand theory.

Perhaps understandably, empirical evidence of early mass-consumer culture is limited principally to documents of production flows, shopping inventories and other market technologies such as advertisements of branded goods. These form the basis of an analysis which largely omits the voice of the consumer. Oral history brings back to our analysis of early mass-consumer culture the voices of ordinary consumers. Focused on generating and archiving consumer (life) histories this approach takes the ordinary and everyday remembered experiences of shopping to collate consumption biographies that can be used to inform a critical (re-)analysis of the development of consumer culture. Oral history identifies the meaning ordinary people have given to brands and brand choices throughout their lives. It also records the impacts and influence of brand consciousness on their lives in terms of their changing expectations, desires and behaviours.

While historical methods have been used in consumer research, Smith and Lux (1993) gave only brief mention to the literary roots and narrative practices of ancient and contemporary historiography to concentrate instead on the possible contributions of history developed on a scientific model. As a consequence, the voice of the consumer has been largely absent. Most studies, with the exception of Olsen (1995), fail to record the viewpoints of consumers in their own words. This is where oral history has a significant contribution to offer. Not only does oral history record consumers' voices but it also has a remit to record oral consumer evidence for posterity (Lummis, 1987). This has produced a methodological focus within oral history on the breadth of interview topic and appropriate forms of archiving and consent to ensure that oral data are captured for the use of future researchers to examine the past (Jones, 1994). This is an interesting proposition that has been mostly neglected by consumer researchers to date: to create archives of consumer oral testimonies to enable future historical research.

Oral research tools have formed the bedrock of empirical knowledge in consumer research yet in terms of historical methods they are conspicuous by their absence. To recognize that oral history methods have been neglected in consumer research reveals an interesting methodological paradox for a discipline where it is commonplace to talk to consumers, capture their speech and ask for their opinions, attitudes and experiences as part of depth interviews, focus groups, questionnaire responses and/or as experimental subjects. A further aim of this chapter is to also explore this paradox. By doing so our analysis makes explicit the working assumptions that we often unquestioningly accept in consumer research.

As a worked example of the method, we present a case of oral life history. This research is located in the United Kingdom. It seeks to understand further the development of mass-consumer culture in the United Kingdom by collecting consumer voices on when and how brand consciousness developed. Life history analysis enables us to locate and describe the beginnings of brand consciousness in the United Kingdom when brands were used as functional markers of quality and performance by the working-class population. We then trace the development of brand consciousness through time to show when and how brands became the important symbolic, emotional and cultural resources we recognize today. By presenting our oral history we endeavour to show how oral history methods offer one way to examine critically the origins, developments and possible future(s) of consumer culture.

Approaching oral history

Oral history is located with the micro-history tradition (Iggers, 1997). The term was first introduced by Allan Nevins in 1947 in his work on elite American social groups. In Europe, oral history has a very different background. It emerged in projects focused on working-class lives and experiences and was politically committed to 'history from below' (Perks, 1998; Trapp-Fallon, 2002). By the late 1960s, American oral history was also concentrated on non-elite groups, and now shares the main focus of European oral history (e.g. Gluck, 1987).

Oral history was conceived as a tool for recovering hitherto undocumented facts, but has now developed into a 'significant, theoretically dense, and diverse sub-set of historical and social scientific enquiry' (Godrey and Richardson, 2004, p. 144). There is consensus that oral history offers the potential to look behind the public representation of a particular time to seek out private memories, which include everyday talk, comparisons and narratives (Johnson and Dawson, 1998; Mallinson et al., 2003). It partly achieves this by seeking to redress in history studies the balance of experience against artefacts (Lummis, 1987), to bring back 'the human' and subjective account (Iggers, 1997), but also does so by acknowledging the dynamic nature of people's memories and experiences as they weave together the past and present. This provides the 'opportunity to explore what people did, what they thought at the time, what they wanted to do and what they think about it now' (Mallinson et al., 2003, p. 775). Oral history is also the only historical method that allows the historical researcher to intervene directly in the generation of historical evidence relating to the recent past. It is as such much more than, and should not be confused with, personal biography (Lummis, 1987). At a theoretical level oral history has much in common with an interpretive consumer research approach. There is not a strict subject–object split. The researcher and interviewees are seen to co-create the oral transcript, which has much in common with interactive introspection (Ellis, 1991) and the more recent introduction of co-operative inquiry (Heron, 1996) to consumer research (Edwards et al., 2005). Differences between ontology and epistemology are collapsed and this is seen as a strength rather than as a weakness (Arnold and Fisher, 1994; Shankar et al., 2001).

Individual life narratives are the building blocks of oral history where people's memories are used as data. The use of life narratives was popularized as a basis for academic study by Freud and psychoanalysis but have a much longer tradition as a primary methodology in anthropological fieldwork (Atkinson, 1998; Trapp-Fallon, 2002). Life narratives allow researchers to hear people's memories about their past and its impact on their present. It is linked with narrative theory and the 'narrativization of experience' (Mishler, 1995) which recognizes that we are socially and culturally (Gergen and Gergen, 1988), or perhaps genetically (Bruner, 1986) conditioned to use stories to structure, make sense and create meaning of our lives and past experiences. Narrative has had an important but relatively limited use in marketing management and consumer research (for a review, see Shankar et al., 2001). Although narrative has been recognized as ideally suited for longitudinal studies of consumption behaviour and consumer researchers have been asked to embrace the narrative perspective as ontological rather than analytical (Shankar et al., 2001), narrative has not been a useful historical method to better locate and understand consumer history. Narrative theory has an undisputed ontological place in oral history.

Generating life narratives is achieved through in-depth interviews and relies on retrospective recall. The role of the interviewer is to stimulate personal recall and the narration of first-hand experience. The interviewee narrates for historical purposes stories about their involvement with and meaning given to a particular topic structured by life events and changes. These must be preserved on a system of reproducible sound for others to use (Lummis, 1987). Whether recorded 'in-time' or 'retrospectively', experiences narrated by an interviewee and interpreted by researchers are contextualized by personal, social, cultural, economic and political circumstance (Godrey and Richardson, 2004; Mallinson et al., 2003). There is no 'objective' reality to record. Oral historians, like interpretive consumer researchers, recognize that the history they generate is ideographic and time and context-dependent. Not only do they recognize that oral history developed from retrospective interviews represents a history that is time and context-dependent but the discipline is charged with archiving the oral transcripts so that they can be used in a future time to generate a different history or re-inquiry of history based on the theoretical and empirical preoccupations and pre-understandings that exist at this other period. Oral history has the potential to contribute in a prospective as well as retrospective way to the call for theoretically diverse re-inquiry in consumer research (Wilk, 2002; Wells, 2002; Hunter, 2002; Thompson, 2002).

Oral history has challenged the boundaries and traditions of the history profession and the theoretical basis detailed above for oral history presents a contemporary view of historiography that neglects the uncertain and often hostile position of oral history in the last century. During this period the factual veracity of archival sources, particularly those of an 'official', 'statistical' or factual nature, led some authors to suggest that the written archive may be 'festished' as the only means by which an accurate narrative of the past can be constructed (Samuel, 1994; Thompson, 1988; Lummis, 1987; Harvey and Riley, 2005). Owing to uncertainties surrounding the mechanics of memory, for example, the ability of interviewees to reconstruct past lived experiences as facts by telling life narratives (Lummis, 1987; Iggers, 1997) and sensitivities over both the creation and distortion of popular memory discourses or public myths (Heehs, 1994; Tonkin, 1992), oral narratives as a way of recording the past have often been overlooked or devalued. Anthropologists have been successful in their attempts to bridge the distance between memory and history (e.g. Larson, 1999) and recent attention in the history profession has sought empirical exploration of these tensions (Clark, 2002). Oral history has gained a respectable status in a discipline that has reorganized in the light of contention and debate occasioned by from postmodernism and the linguistic turn to reorganize, not as a new paradigm, but as a discipline of 'expanded pluralism' (Iggers, 1997, p. 140). Oral history offers a unique data contribution. Insight can be gained when people recount their experiences divorced in time from the emotional intensity and popular ideologies of the past and this is used together with other historical data which have also been 'set down at different times and were subject to different personal biases, contemporary pressure and social conventions' (Lummis, 1987, p. 155). Issues of memory are now recognized as insurmountable epistemological problems relevant to most historical sources and the subjective and literary basis of history and history making are recognized and even embraced. There are some parallels in the genealogy of oral history and debates on theoretical approaches in consumer research. The foundations of oral history make it seem compatible with interpretive approaches in consumer research, and we aim in the next section to demonstrate by case study example the overlooked contribution oral history can play as a further theoretical perspective to build the consumer research canon.

An oral history of the evolution of brand consciousness in the UK

The emergence of mass-consumer culture in Europe can be considered a postwar phenomenon (Usherwood, 2000) and it became the dominant ideology in the 1970s and 1980s (Bocock, 1993). The development of consumer culture in the UK through the twentieth century has been studied from a number of standpoints, including a focus on the department store (Nava, 1996) and on the crucial role of women (Winship, 2000). Other approaches have studied food shopping and the change from small local counter-service shops to large supermarkets (Adburgham, 1989; Davis, 1996). Various forms of documentary evidence have been used to trace the origins of consumer culture, but what is missing is the voice of the consumer. While consumers' personal experiences can be used to inform a critical analysis of the development of consumer culture (Strasser, 2003) the use of brands in symbolic consumption has largely been a research topic of the late twentieth century (Coulter et al., 2003). To further understand the development of consumer culture we seek to add the consumers' perspective by writing an oral history on when and indeed how brand consciousness developed. Because of space constraints what we present here is only a small part of a larger oral history. The excerpts we present demonstrate how oral history can be a useful tool to inform critically our understanding of early consumer culture, symbolic brands and the explosion in brand choice through the growth of self-service retailing.

Using oral history techniques allows the capture of rich and varied experiences and interpretations of retail change and developing brand consciousness as memories (Atkinson, 1998; Rubin, 1995; Roberts, 1995; Thompson, 1988). There are very few previous studies that have focused on an oral history of the shopping experience. Mullins and Stockdale's (1994) oral history of retail change provides experiential data but this is only from the retailer's perspective. The consumer experience of retailing during wartime rationing has been explored by drawing on Mass Observation accounts (Alexander, 2002; Zweiniger-Bargielowska, 2000) and through oral history in California by Witkowski and Hogan (1999). Recently Olechnowicz (2002) proposed oral history as a way to improve the analyses of wartime rationing that rely on Mass Observation accounts.

Our oral history was developed from the reported memories of 22 women. The sample was based on prewar and postwar age cohorts. Women born between 1910 and 1935 became active consumers in what we may think of as a pre-consumer society and women born between 1940 and 1950 made their consumption choices as teenagers and young adults against a rapidly developing consumer culture (Hebdige, 1979; Bedarida, 1991; Benson, 1994). Our informants have lived in a wide diversity of locations and the childhoods and early adulthood experiences captured in this study record life in large urban cities and smaller rural towns and villages.

Extended life story interviews of one to three hours took place in the informants' homes, surrounded by their personal possessions and memory cues (Atkinson, 1998; Gunter, 1998; Rubin, 1995). The interviews adopted a biographical approach beginning with early childhood, when our ladies had little responsibility for choosing goods purchased for the household and accompanied their mothers' shopping activities, or ran errands for grocery provisions, to early adulthood and marriage, where they bore the primary responsibility for household purchases and where entry into the labour market, often as store assistants or with involvement in the manufacture of consumer goods, brought them into contact with the market and market media. Our interviewees held clear and detailed memories of shopping with their mothers, going back as early as 1918 and shopping alone from the early 1920s. The interviews were tape-recorded and later transcribed verbatim. Respondents' life stories were analysed, drawing on the principles of narrative theory (Shankar et al., 2001; McAdams, 1996) where the data were analysed for interpretive themes using pattern-coding methods (Coffey and Atkinson, 1996). The first level of analysis was idiographic and hermeneutic (Arnold and Fisher, 1994) and involved the identification of recurrent behavioural and psychological tendencies. The second level of interpretation involved 'across-person' analysis to identify patterns across situations and individuals that helped to structure an understanding of consumer behaviour over time and place, and across families. Although interpretation is an important part of communicating the consumers' voice, we believe it is vital to retain as much as possible of the original verbatims and not to reduce the data through excessive analysis in pursuit of an illusory positivistic objectivity. In the words of Clifford (1985, p. 7), 'Ethnographic truths are thus inherently *partial*'; at a later stage we will compare the findings with other data sources (e.g. Mass Observation) but we favour storytelling over analysis.

Frugality as a way of life
Frugality was a way of life up to the 1960s, when self-sufficiency divorced individuals from the market and wartime rationing precluded free and full consumer choice. Wartime rationing was at a sustained period where choice was absent for clothing, food, items and household products. Brands were absent from consumer consciousness and people were content to have what was available:

> You just couldn't go and buy it when you made up your mind, it was a case of when you were lucky, on the spot when it came in, you dived for it, because a limited number came in and if you were lucky you were lucky. That was for saucepans, bowls, buckets, anything in that line. Clothes were on coupons. I can't remember how many coupons you used to have, but you were allowed so many coupons. When I was getting married it was a case of grab a coupon here and grab a coupon there from anybody who'd like to give you one, to get enough clothes together. Meat, that was on ration. I can't remember how much meat anybody had. I know I used to go in the butcher's and order a joint of pork or something for about half a crown, and my mum had to do that for six of us, make a meal with whatever she was lucky enough to get. (Informant 17, born 1926)

While rationing limited consumption and choice, the depression also meant people could only buy what they could afford and our informants born before the late 1930s told us how they and their mothers maintained households by growing their own food, preserving vegetables and fruits for the winter months, and making clothes and other forms of self-sufficiency.

> We made a lot of our own clothes. My mother used to cut down my father's pyjamas and trousers for the younger boys and for her grandchildren, because we couldn't afford new clothes. I remember having a coat made for me by a lady who was a dressmaker and I was very proud of that, it had to last a long time. It was a mustard coloured cloth with a brown, velvet collar. We even knitted swimsuits, if you can believe it, which sagged dreadfully when we went in the water. During the war there was some material made available from parachutes that had come down and they were like nylon. I suppose it was our first introduction to nylon. And my mother made me a bikini to swim in, but horror of horrors, when you get in the water they become transparent, so I came home with a red face and said, 'Mum, will you line it with something', so she got some old blue material out and put a lining in it. (Informant 10, born 1934)

There were generally few choices to be made. In local shops goods were not pre-packaged and their source was not identified or displayed by retailers. Counter-service distanced the consumer from the pre-purchase examination of products. It was also quite usual for customers to be seated on a chair by the counter. Women would read out their list of grocery provisions to the attendant grocer who would then move between the various jars, drawers and cabinets behind the counter to collate the grocery basket.

> And there would always be bacon slicers in the shops, so there'd be great flitches of bacon hanging up and bits would be hacked off this and then it would be put into this bacon slicer and you'd get whatever thickness you'd want and they would then slice the bacon, rather like they slice ham and stuff now. But in those days it was hand turned . . . I can remember seeing them tapping it out on brown paper, and they would sort of tap it out like this. I can remember seeing them. And they were very neatly folded at the top and folded over, and perhaps a bit of string put round. You don't get that now. And sugar would be in blue bags. Butter and cheese would be on a big block and a hunk would be cut off with butter patters, the wooden butter patters, and then on a marble slab it would be cut into the amounts you wanted, shaped, and plonked on the scale, taken off, a little bit more cut off and a little bit more. And, of course, during the war paper was short, so mostly you did your own basket or something to put the things in. (Informant 8, born 1928)

Prior to the introduction of the National Health Service, visits to the doctor were prohibitively expensive and buying medicines over the counter from chemists was commonplace. For the majority of our informants they only associated buying brands with sickness and ill health at home. Brands were outside the experience of most Cohort 1 women, and when they were used it was to provide emotional reassurance.

> You only had Ovaltine if you were a bit poorly or something. Mother would say, 'I'd better make you some Ovaltine.' Gruel we had when we were young, made with fine oatmeal, and that was a good standby, because you didn't get all the cereals for breakfast – porridge or gruel is all I remember. And if you had a poorly chest, you had a cough, more often than having any cough mixture – although at a young age I drank the cough mixture – we would have what was called Thermogene wool. Oh, it was so tickly, it wasn't nice, and it was thick and it was orange coloured, and mother would cut a square off the Thermogene wool and put it on our chest before our vests went on, and that was supposed to ease your chest and your cough. Or we'd be rubbed with hen's

fat. When you had a chicken you saved the fat that came out of it when you cooked it and kept it in a jar, covered . . . Oh, the thing you bought if you were poorly, right from when I was young – and I was still buying it when Janet was a baby – was Fennings's Fever Cure. Thinking about it now, it was a little bit bitter – not bitter bitter, but it was a little bit sharp, and you only had to give a weeny little bit in a teaspoon and that was to reduce the fever if you had a temperature with a baby or a child or anything. (Informant 1, born 1911)

Taking responsibility for choosing: retail innovation

The move from loose to pre-packaged goods which started in the UK in the 1880s with tea, coffee, spices, soap and sugar established the still-familiar brands of Cadbury, Bovril, Oxo and Rowntree. Usherwood (2000) locates changes towards a mass-consumer society as occurring in the early 1950s. At this time economic conditions started to improve, and the lifting of building restrictions meant that larger supermarkets could be built. The change to self-service brought about the need for the pre-packaging and pre-selling of goods. This in turn led to retailers stocking more than one brand, and with the advent of commercial television in 1955 advertising could be used to 'turn the relaxed viewer of yesterday evening into this morning's purposeful and brand-conscious customer' (Sales Appeal, 1955). The development of brand consciousness can be seen as producer-initiated.

Retail process innovations, including the self-service format and large supermarkets, increased choice but required women to take responsibility for their consumption choices. They changed the shopping practices of women and broadened their brand knowledge. Women's reactions and interpretations of self-service were varied. All our informants remarked that choice increased but that initially they felt ill-equipped to manage the transition from retailer-defined choice to choosing for themselves. The proliferation of choice experienced by women marked a significant change: women had to learn how to shop.

> But there was a big event in Croydon [a London suburb] in that the Sainsburys at West Croydon suddenly decided to show us how to do self-service . . . I remember queuing up outside and a sort of commissionaire type standing in the door saying 'Right, let's have another five' and we'd go in with our baskets. And because of the choice and the different ways of doing things I remember being bewildered and thinking what do I need to buy? . . . and it was bewildering. You stood and looked at all these things, and all you had to do was put your hand out and get hold of it and put it in your basket. And that was extraordinary at the time, quite extraordinary. And I think of people much older that I was at the time – because I'm talking of me being in my late 20s – but people middle-aged and older would have found it totally confusing because they were used to going and saying, 'Right Mr Smith, I want a pound of this, or a quarter of that', and having it given to them. But after a bit we realized we could choose not only the variety we wanted but also the price we wanted to pay. (Informant 20, born 1930, talking about the mid-1950s)

> It seemed very funny, of course, picking up a basket and helping yourself. Well, it felt very strange at first to have to do that. You just walked around and you got what you had to get really. It doesn't stay in my memory really for very long, what we did used to do. (Informant 18, born 1930, talking about 1958)

In dealing with the freedom of choice offered by the self-service environment, respondents began to rely on brands and to pay premium prices. For our informants, brand choice was no longer based solely on functional performance criteria.

> I like Heinz tomato soup . . . I don't like the home brands. I can remember his dad once went to a factory where they made jellies and he said all the jellies come off conveyor belts and they're all

exactly the same, he said one lot go and they get wrapped in Marks, and another lot go and they get wrapped in Tesco's, and another lot get wrapped in another label, and he said they're all the same jellies. But I wouldn't have it, I like particular . . . And he said it's the same with everything. But I do, I think Heinz tomato soup is different from everybody else's. (Informant 22, born 1950)

Symbolic brand consciousness

Today consumers are faced with an infinite diversity of brand semiology from which to construct a coherent narrative of self-identity (Elliott and Wattanasuwan, 1998; Sarup, 1996). Before the 'affluent society' and the 1960s (Bedarida, 1991; Benson, 1994), some branded goods such as cigarettes were used to signify social status:

> Of course everybody smoked cigarettes in those days. You were very, very upmarket if you smoked Passing Clouds. They're an oval one and it was very upmarket to have an oval cigarette in your handbag. Most of us used to smoke Players and Woodbines. Senior Service was another one, which was slightly upmarket from anything else. (Informant 9, born 1926)

In the late postwar period we begin to see the beginnings of consumer sophistication and the symbolic importance of branded goods. Our informants, and particularly Cohort 2 women born after 1940, were knowledgeable about brands and, although they had limited means to acquire brands, had the desire to do so. This led to new forms of lifestyle and social stratification, group membership and exclusion:

> And at one stage early on we managed to buy a radiogram, with the radio at the top and the record thing underneath. And it cost us a lot of money. But we had got what (the radiogram) I think possibly some of the gang hadn't, where they had had something else that we hadn't been able to buy. It was a Pye. We bought it because it was a Pye, knowing that it was a good name. (Informant 20, born 1930, referring to the early 1960s)

Concluding an oral history

From the recollections and stories told by our 22 women we have begun to write an oral history that shows the development of brand consciousness to be associated with a movement from the community-located consumer with little sense of choice in many aspects of life, to the individual/family decision maker for whom consumption is a major arena for lifestyle choices. Tracing the change from frugality and rational choice to symbolic consumption has shown how the brand has been redefined from a trademark of functional quality to become an important symbolic resource for lifestyle choices and social stratification. Retail innovation, and in particular self-service, was a major catalyst for this development. Self-service and large supermarkets have led to a significant change in the lives of women. It gave women (often for the first time) the opportunity to choose and to take responsibility for that choice. It also changed the way they managed their households as exemplified by the introduction of branded convenience and frozen foods. Brands were quickly adopted as a means by which to negotiate the explosion of choice on the supermarket shelf and later became an important resource for the construction of self-identity. Our oral history also highlights that, for ordinary people, mass-consumer culture was far from mature in the 1960s, as has been suggested by studies that have not included consumers' recollected phenomenological experience (Usherwood, 2000; Bocock, 1993). Consumer culture would be more appropriately characterized as infantile, where the skills needed to participate in consumer culture were being learnt through self-sufficiency enterprise.

Increased choice and responsibility for consumption was not always easy or welcomed by our ladies. A commonly held assumption in consumer choice is that consumers will perceive any increase in choice (i.e. control in the market place) as a benefit (Wathieu et al., 2002; Schwartz, 2004). The roots for this assumption lie in classical economic theory. Having more choice and helping consumers make choices (often by providing information) is presumed to maximize consumer utilities and hence benefits (e.g. Kreps, 1979). Our oral data provide some initial empirical support for Wathieu et al. (2002) and Schwartz (2004), who have suggested that consumer sovereignty and choice at a phenomenological level is not always straightforward. There may be difficulties and concerns before any benefits are truly realized.

Concluding comments on consumer history
Studies in the consumer research discipline that have incorporated an historical focus have been limited but important, but in this chapter we have shown that these studies have concentrated on using traditional historical evidence (i.e. documents and other archive materials) and neglected to represent the voices and memories of consumers. In this chapter we have introduced oral history, locating it as a humanities discipline and describing its position in twenty-first-century historiography (Iggers, 1997). By charting the political and ontological base or genealogy of oral history we have also shown that oral history is resonant with a broad body of consumer research, namely studies that hold an interpretive perspective, and those that explicitly or implicitly rest on narrative theory.

Our work once again draws attention to the importance and strength of multidisciplinary work, which is characteristic of the consumer research canon. By introducing and working with a related humanities discipline (history) it makes us as consumer researchers look into a mirror at ourselves. By doing this we see our research practices through another's gaze and this can help us become more sensitive and reflexive in our research practice. In history there has been significant theoretical debate concerning memory and recollection that is inescapable when oral evidence forms the basis of empirical data. This debate has not been public in consumer research. For history the micro-history tradition (of which oral history forms a part) has been significant in redressing the balance between experience and material artefact. The use of life narratives in oral history does not reject or stand in opposition to macro or scientific historiographies but rather is intended to bring to them (or grounds them) with personal experience and meaning (Harvey and Riley, 2005). This has been perhaps less problematic in consumer research where there has been significant attention to phenomenological understanding. Introducing oral history to consumer research has the impetus to put on permanent record historical experience and to recognize that the only limitation to future consumer history is that of living memory (Lummis, 1987). Oral history suggests to consumer research that it is important to archive consumer voices to enable future historical re-inquiries of our theories.

References
Adburgham, Alison (1989), *Shops and Shopping 1800–1914*, London: Barrie and Jenkins.
Alexander, A. (2002), 'Retailing and consumption: evidence from war time Britain', *International Review of Retail, Distribution and Consumer Research*, **12** (1), 39–57.
Arnold S. and E. Fisher (1994), 'Hermeneutics and consumer research', *Journal of Consumer Research*, **21** (June), 55–70.
Atkinson, Robert (1998), *The Life Story Interview*, London: Sage.

Bedarida, François (1991), *A Social History of England 1851–1990*, London: Routledge.

Benson, John (1994), *The Rise of Consumer Society in Britain 1880–1980*, London: Longman.

Bocock, Robert (1993), *Consumption*, London: Routledge.

Bruner, Jerome S. (1986), *Actual Minds, Possible Worlds*, Cambridge, MA: Harvard University Press.

Clark, M.M. (2002), 'The September 11, 2001, oral history narrative and memory project: first report', *Journal of American History*, Sep., 569–78.

Clifford. J. (1985), 'Introduction: partial truths', in James Clifford and George Marcus (eds), *Writing Culture: The Poetics and Politics of Ethnography*, Berkeley: University of California Press.

Coffey, Amanda and Paul Atkinson (1996), *Making Sense of Qualitative Data: Complementary Research Designs*, London: Sage.

Coulter, R.A, L.L. Price and L. Feick (2003), 'Rethinking the origins of involvement and brand commitment: insights from post socialist central Europe', *Journal of Consumer Research*, **30** (Sep.), 151–69.

Davis, Dorothy (1996), *A History of Shopping*, London: Routledge.

Edwards H., A. Davies and R. Elliott (2005), 'United we understand: co-operative inquiry in consumer research', EIASM Interpretive Consumer Research Workshop, Copenhagen Business School, May.

Elliott, R. and K. Wattanasuwan (1998), 'Brands as resources for the symbolic construction of identity', *International Journal of Advertising*, **17** (2), 131–44.

Ellis, C. (1991), 'Sociological introspection and emotional experience', *Symbolic Interaction*, **14** (1), 23–50.

Finley, M.I. (1965), 'Myth, memory and history', *History and Theory*, **4** (3), 281–302.

Gergen K. and M. Gergen (1988), 'Narrative and the self as relationship', *Advances in Experimental Social Psychology*, **21**, 17–56.

Gluck, Sherna Berger (1987), *Rosie the Riveter Revisited: Women, the War and Social Change*, New York: Meridian.

Godrey, B.S. and J.C. Richardson (2004), 'Loss, collective memory and transcripted oral histories', *International Journal of Social Research Methodology*, **7** (2), 143–55.

Gunter, B. (1998), *Understanding the Older Consumer*, London: Routledge.

Harvey, D. and M. Riley (2005), 'Country stories: the use of oral histories of the countryside to challenge the sciences of the past and future', *Interdisciplinary Science Reviews*, **30** (1), 19–32.

Hebdige, D. (1979), *Subculture: the Meaning of Style*, Routledge: London.

Heehs, P. (1994), 'Myth, history and theory', *History and Theory*, **33**, 1–19.

Heron, John (1996), *Co-operative Inquiry: Research into the Human Condition*, London: Sage.

Hunter, J.E. (2002), 'The desperate need for replication', *Journal of Consumer Research*, **28**, 149–54.

Iggers, Georg G. (1997), *Historiography in the Twentieth Century*, London: Routledge.

Johnson R. and G. Dawson (1998), 'Popular memory: theory politics and method', in Richard Perks and Alan Thomson (eds), *The Oral History Reader*, London: Routledge, pp. 75–86.

Jones, R. (1994), 'Blended voices: crafting a narrative from oral history interviews', *The Oral History Review*, **31** (1), 23–42.

Kreps, D. (1979), 'A representation theorem for preference and for flexibility', *Econometrica*, **47**, 565–77.

Larson, P.M. (1999), *Becoming Merina in Highland Madagascar: History and Memory in the Age of Enslavement, 1770–1822*, London: Heinemann.

Lummis, Trevor (1987), *Listening to History: The Authenticity of Oral Evidence*, London: Hutchinson Education.

Mallinson, S., J. Poppy, E. Elliott, S. Bennett, L. Botock, A. Gatrell, C. Thomas and G. Williams (2003), 'Historical data in health inequalities research: a research note', *Sociology*, **37** (4), 771–81.

McAdams, D. (1996), 'Personality, modernity and the storied self: a contemporary framework for studying persons', *Psychological Inquiry*, **7** (4), 295–321.

Mishler, E. (1995), 'Models of narrative analysis: a typology', *Journal of Narrative and Life History*, **5** (2), 87–123.

Mullins, Sam and David Stockdale (1994), *Talking Shop; An Oral History of Retailing in the Market Harborough Area During the 20th Century*, Stroud: Alan Sutton Publishing.

Nava, M. (1996), 'Modernity's disavowal: women, the city and the department store', in Pasi Falk and Colin Campbell (eds), *The Shopping Experience*, London: Sage.

Olechnowicz, A. (2002), 'Review: austerity in Britain: rationing, control and consumption, 1939–1955', *Twentieth Century British History*, **13** (4), 449–57.

Olsen, Barbara (1995), 'Brand loyalty and consumption patterns: a lineage factor', in John F. Sherry (ed.), *Contemporary Marketing and Consumer Research. An Anthropological Sourcebook*, Thousand Oaks, CA: Sage, pp. 245–81.

Perks, Robert (1998), *Oral History: An Annotated Reader*, London: Routledge.

Roberts, Elizabeth (1995), *Women and Families: An Oral History 1940–1970*, Oxford: Blackwell.

Rubin, David C. (1995), *Remembering Our Past: Studies in Autobiographical Memory*, Cambridge: Cambridge University Press.

Sales Appeal (1955), 'Find the link', September/October, pp. 26–32.

Samuel, Raphael (1994), *Theatres of Memory*, London: Verso.

Sarup, Madan (1996), *Identity, Culture and the Postmodern World*, Edinburgh: Edinburgh University Press.

Schwartz, Barry (2004), *The Paradox of Choice: Why More Is Less*, New York: Harper Collins.

Shankar, A., R. Elliott and C. Goulding (2001), 'Understanding consumption from a narrative perspective', *Journal of Marketing Management*, **17**, 429–53.

Smith, R.A. and D.S. Lux (1993), 'Historical method in consumer research: developing causal explanations of change', *Journal of Consumer Research*, **19** (March), 595–610.

Strasser, S. (2003), 'The alien past: consumer culture in historical perspective', *Journal of Consumer Policy*, **26**, 375–93.

Thompson, C. (2002), 'A re-inquiry on re-inquiries: a postmodern proposal for a critical–reflexive approach', *Journal of Consumer Research*, **28** (1), 142–6.

Thompson, Paul (1988), *The Voice of the Past: Oral History*, Oxford: Oxford University Press.

Tonkin, Elizabeth (1992), *Narrating Our Pasts: The Social Construction of Oral History*, Cambridge: Cambridge University Press.

Trapp-Fallon, T.M. (2002), 'Searching for rich narratives of tourism and leisure experience: how oral history could provide the answer', *Tourism and Hospitality Research*, **4** (4), 297–305.

Usherwood, B. (2000). ' "Mrs housewife and her grocer": the advent of self-service food shopping in Britain', in Maggie Andrews and Mary Talbot (eds), *All the World and Her Husband: Women in Twentieth-Century Consumer Culture*, London: Cassell, pp. 113–30.

Wathieu, L., L. Brenner, Z. Carmon, A. Drolet, J. Gournville, A.V. Muthukrishnan, N. Novemsky, R. Ratner and G. Wu (2002), 'Consumer control and empowerment', *Marketing Letters*, **13** (3), 297–305.

Wells, W.D. (2002), 'The perils of n=1', *Journal of Consumer Research*, **28** (3), 494–8.

Wilk, R. (2002), 'The impossible necessity of re-inquiry: finding middle ground in social science', *Journal of Consumer Research*, **28** (2), 308–12.

Winship, J. (2000), 'New disciplines for women and the rise of the chain store in the 1930s', in Maggie Andrews and Mary Talbot (eds), *All the World and Her Husband: Women in Twentieth-Century Consumer Culture*, London: Cassell.

Witkowski, Terrence and Helen Hogan (1999), 'Home Front consumers: an oral history of California women during World War II', in Peggy Cunningham and David Bussiere (eds), *Marketing History: The Total Package*, East Lansing: Michigan State University.

Zweiniger-Bargielowska, Ina (2000), *Austerity in Britain: Rationing, Controls and Consumption, 1939–1955*, Oxford: Oxford University Press.

19 Focus groups in marketing research
Miriam Catterall and Pauline Maclaran

Introduction

Qualitative marketing research and academic marketing and consumer research have grown in parallel with little contact between the two (Catterall and Clarke, 2000). This lack of communication between commercial and academic consumer research has meant that, overall, commercial qualitative research practices have often been disparaged and judged as lacking theoretical and methodological depth. As the most popular commercial qualitative marketing research technique, the focus group has borne the brunt of such criticisms (Achenbaum, 1995). More recently, it has become something of an unfashionable technique, overshadowed by the current search for ethnographic 'insights', and is generally overlooked in the academic literature. Thus as academic marketing and consumer researchers our main, or only, model of focus group research is drawn from the extensive practitioner literature on the subject.

In this chapter we revisit the market research focus group. We discuss the three key issues in undertaking focus group research, namely the role of group dynamics, the theories that inform focus group research approaches, and focus group implementation practices. In doing so we argue that there is far more variety, innovation and creativity in focus group research than is generally assumed. However we begin by placing this discussion in a wider historical context.

The origins and rise of the focus group

The focus group is believed to have originated in the USA and patrimony is most usually attributed to the sociologist Robert Merton. The term 'focus group' is generally assumed to have derived from the focused interview developed by Merton and his colleagues at Columbia University during the 1940s, when investigating audience reactions to radio programmes (MacGregor and Morrison, 1995). However it is more likely that the focus group emerged in a number of different geographic and disciplinary locations over a period of 30 years. Between the 1920s and 1950s various permutations of the focus group method emerged in Britain (Abrams, 1949), France (Adam, 1951), Germany (Banks, 1956), Italy (Arvidsson, 2000) and the USA (Bogardus, 1926). Additionally, the focus group emerged from a number of different disciplinary locations including anthropology (Wilson and Wilson, 1945), sociology (Merton and Kendall, 1946), psychology (Bogardus, 1926), education (Edmiston, 1944) and advertising (Smith, 1954), all of which provide different theoretical perspectives on focus group research today.

The emergence of the focus group in the advertising industry seems to have been a chance discovery (Goldman and McDonald, 1987). In Britain, Mark Abrams (1949) was one of the first market researchers (anywhere) to publish a detailed account of the group discussion method and how it could be usefully employed for testing advertising copy and illustrations. Meanwhile, in the USA, Ted Nowak of Alderson and Sessions undertook his first group interview in 1949 with the aim of informing subsequent survey work.

Nowak's second group interview was undertaken for a client who did not have sufficient budget to finance a survey. Similarly, George Horsley Smith undertook his first group interview in 1951 for a client that needed information on consumer behaviour within a few days. Since a survey could not be completed within the time available, the group interview was devised as a solution. Herbert Ableson, of Opinion Research Corporation, discovered the group by accident in 1957, when some respondents recruited for individual interviews turned up early and others late. Rather than interview them one at a time, he interviewed them collectively (Goldman and McDonald, 1987).

Thus one of the enduring criticisms of the market research focus group (that it is largely used as a quick and cheap alternative to 'proper' survey or interview research) seems to have some justification. It was also the case that the focus group/group discussion was not taken particularly seriously by motivation researchers, the predecessors of today's qualitative marketing researchers (Smith, 1954). The individual depth interview was their method of choice and had been since the origins of motivation research in the late 1920s. However, by the end of the 1960s, individual depth interviews had been comprehensively superseded by focus groups (Bellenger, Bernhardt and Goldstucker, 1976). This remarkable turnaround in the fortunes of the individual interview appears to have been due to its time and cost disadvantages when compared with focus groups. A project that involved a programme of individual interviews would require a number of suitably qualified interviewers, then in short supply, whereas a single moderator could undertake all of the focus groups necessary to complete a project. Additionally the individual interview project would take longer to complete and eat up costly researcher time.

Thus the individual depth interview lost its once pre-eminent position in qualitative market research because it was too difficult and expensive to implement and not because the focus group was considered to be the more desirable technique. Indeed there was little discussion in the early market research literature on the theoretical underpinnings or methodological justification for the technique. An exception to this was the assumption that group dynamics would have a positive impact on the data generated in groups. In other words the primary methodological justification for the focus group is the role that group dynamics plays in generating data that would not be accessible if respondents were interviewed individually (Morgan and Krueger, 1997). In the discussion that follows we explore this methodological justification for focus groups.

Group dynamics at the heart of focus group methodology
One of the most consistent findings from the small group research literature in psychology is that all groups, no matter how temporary, will be subject to group processes or dynamics. These group dynamics are of benefit in focus groups in that the group environment provides greater security and anonymity for its members, encourages participants to speak out in front of others, and is also supportive and exciting. Simultaneously group dynamics are considered to be the main drawback of focus groups (Bristol and Fern, 1993). Participants may alter their opinions in groups, leaving the researcher in doubt as to which opinion to take as the 'real' one (ibid.). The discussion in the group may be dominated by one or two forceful individuals who suppress or unduly influence the views of other participants. As a result, individual attitudes and opinions can be contaminated or polluted by group interaction (ibid.).

Thus the only distinctive methodological feature of the focus group is represented as its primary strength as well as its main weakness. Market researcher practitioners have appealed to the group literature in psychology to justify the benefits of group interaction in generating data. By contrast, marketing academics have argued that insights from this literature cast serious doubt on these benefits. This paradox can be explained by the fact that each party calls upon different theories from the group literature to support their arguments, as we now explain.

Market research practitioners and focus group interaction
Practitioners have tended to draw heavily from the group therapy literature to inform their understanding of how focus groups work. The origins of group therapy can be traced back to the early years of the twentieth century, however the Second World War provided a major boost to the spread of group therapy when military psychiatrists were forced by the sheer number of psychiatric casualties to adopt group rather than individual approaches to treatment. After the war a diverse range of group therapy practice models or approaches emerged. Some of these approaches gave little attention to group dynamics, viewing group therapy as 'treatment of individuals in a group', whilst others focused on 'treatment in and through a group' (Scheidlinger, 2000). It was these latter approaches that were to influence British focus group research (Gordon and Langmaid, 1988; Robson and Foster, 1989).

Wilfred Bion (1961) argued that a group has two agendas. First, there is the overt conscious purpose of the group, a work task for example. Secondly, there is a hidden agenda that participants are not consciously aware of. This is an unconscious concern for the life of the group itself. It is as if two groups are operating in parallel; the conscious group concerned with the overt group task and a second, unconscious, group concerned with the emotional needs of the group (Morgan and Thomas, 1996). This second, unconscious, group has been described in various terms, for example, 'group as a whole', 'group as group' and 'group mind'. The focus group moderator needs to work with the group as a group (its unconscious agenda) in order to maximize group performance. The group therapy literature provides insights on how this might be achieved by describing the trajectory or life of a group from its start to its finish.

Market researchers have described two very similar focus group trajectories. Drawing on the concept of hierarchic integration, Goldman and McDonald (1987) identified the three stages in group development as, globality, differentiation and hierarchic integration. Initially group members are undifferentiated, without any social structure to organize interaction, the globality stage. During the differentiation stage group members identify themselves on the basis, say, of levels of experience in buying the product under study, or on the basis of personal characteristics, such as submissiveness or aggressiveness. After this stage a 'true' group emerges whereby the group members interact according to some social structure. It is at this hierarchic integration stage that the group begins to 'work', attitudes and feelings are revealed and the social processes that shape these become public. Group members assume different roles as hierarchical integration develops during the group session, including surrogate leader, moderator's ally, authoritative figure, diversionary, and so on. Recognition of these roles can help the group moderator manage the group to ensure maximum productivity (ibid., 1987).

The importance of individual participants performing as a group has also been recognized by Chrzanowska (2002). People come to focus groups with the intention of keeping things light, free of conflict, safe and comfortable. In order to maximize group productivity the moderator needs to move the group beyond this light conversation. Tuckman's (1965) linear model of group development is widely cited by British market researchers (Gordon, 1999; Chrzanowska, 2002). Tuckman argued that groups followed the stages of forming, storming, norming, performing and ending (or mourning). This model can help moderators identify which stage the group is in and what is happening at each stage so they can manage these in ways that will benefit data production (see Table 19.1).

In summary then, the group therapy literature distinguishes between the individuals who participate in groups and the group, which is more than the combination of its

Table 19.1   Stages of a focus group

Stage	Underlying processes	What happens	Moderator task
Forming	Participants feel separate, dependent, anxious, relatively powerless	Awkwardness, caution, light social chit-chat, testing behaviours	Empower and make safe by explaining the task, behave as you would want them to, encourage interaction
Storming	Share of voice, demanding attention, challenges to moderator and others, opting out or rebelling	Challenge moderator or each other, question the task, emphasize individuality, dominant and passive participants emerge	Signal all opinions are equally valued, accept negative views but look also for positive, stop potentially dominant respondents becoming overbearing
Norming	Sense of harmony, cohesion and support, norms emerge and group takes off	People take turns to speak without moderator having to ask, the energy feels more positive and harmonious	Notice and enforce norms, deal with any implicit rule breaking; time to make plans and set agendas, keep communication channels flexible
Performing	Individuals are subservient to the group, roles are flexible and task-oriented	Sense of concentration and flow, everything seems easy, high energy, group works without being asked	Time to introduce difficult issues, stimulus material, projective techniques
Re-adjustment: performing uses energy so after a while the group slips back into one of the other stages before it can perform again			
Mourning	Completion of task and disbanding the group; may be sense of loss and anxiety, need for closure	If task is incomplete people may not want to leave	Signal that the end is coming, summarize to give sense of achievement, ask if there is anything else they want to say, thank everyone

Source: Chrzanowska (2002, p. 52).

individual participants. The moderator needs to aid the transformation of the collection of individuals that come to the group into a functioning group. This offers a direct challenge to those moderators who assume a good group is one in which each participant receives equal time and weight and where the focus group can be more like a set of individual interviews. Additionally the group therapy literature is important because it does not make a clear distinction between the individual and the social. This is a very different model from the one most usually associated with small group research in psychology where the individual and the social are considered as distinct and separate entities and the idea of a group mind or group unconscious is rejected. Marketing academics who argue that focus group interaction results in contaminated or polluted data have drawn extensively from this latter model, as we now go on to explain.

Academic perspectives on group interaction

Marketing academics have tended to question the positive effects of group interaction on the data produced in focus groups. Edward Fern and Terry Bristol (Fern, 1982; Bristol and Fern, 1993, 1996; Bristol, 1999), individually and in jointly authored work, have consistently challenged qualitative market researchers' 'naïve' theories about focus group research. Fern's study (1982) challenged the belief that focus groups are more useful than individual interviews for the generation of ideas thanks to the positive benefits of interaction amongst participants. He found that individuals performed better than groups in the quantity and the quality of ideas they generated. Similarly a study by Bristol and Fern (1996) challenged the belief that group interaction creates an open, relaxed and anonymous atmosphere that is conducive to generating data that are not obtainable by other research methods. Focus group participants were found to be less confident and relaxed than survey participants.

   Bristol and Fern's studies are in the tradition of research on small groups in experimental social psychology. Most of the theory and research on small groups has emerged from the experimental social psychology tradition. Although it is defined by the methodology it employs, experimental social psychology assumes a particular perspective on groups and the individuals that comprise them. The focus is on the individual and how individual psychology is transformed in group situations and, more specifically, how individual reasoning and thinking processes are transformed in a group (Wetherell, 1996). Classic topics of study in this tradition have included the emergence of group norms (Sherif, 1936), group pressure towards conformity (Asch, 1955) and compliance under pressure (Milgram, 1974). Other research in this tradition has identified the concepts of polarization, compliance and groupthink, all of which cast doubts on the efficacy of group interaction.

Attitude polarization

This refers to individuals in groups adopting a more extreme attitudinal position than the one that they held on being interviewed prior to the group. Polarization represents a shift in degree but not in direction (Allison and Messick, 1987). It is suggested that the presence of others in the group increases the individual's self-awareness and thoughts about his or her own attitudes and feelings (Carver, 1979). Given the exchange of information between group participants, group members may be exposed to and led to consider information that they had not thought about when forming their attitudes, leading to attitude polarization (Allison and Messick, 1987).

Compliance
Albrecht, Johnson and Walther (1993) pointed out that social interaction affects not only opinion formation but also its articulation. Compliance or responding in ways that one believes are expected by a questioner occurs in anticipation of some immediate reward. This can lead to socially desirable or company-flattering responses. Of course compliance is not unique to focus groups and can occur in individual interviews.

Groupthink
The concept of groupthink has also been employed to explain the compliance that can occur in focus groups. Janis (1982) argued that highly cohesive groups would try and maintain consensus on key issues and ignore challenges to this consensus; this was termed 'groupthink'.

Different theories of group interaction
The discussion above illustrates that those who suggest that group dynamics have a positive impact on data generation in focus groups and those who argue that group dynamics have a negative impact may be drawing from entirely different theories of group processes to justify their positions. The group therapy literature focuses on the ways that the individual and the group or the individual and the social merge. Researchers in this tradition have explicated the idea of the group mind or group unconscious. By contrast, experimental social psychologists take the view that psychological processes reside in individuals and there is no such thing as a group mind.

Wetherell (1996) suggests that experimental social psychology has been particularly predominant in North America. By contrast, therapeutic group psychology is more commonly accepted in Europe. This may also account for the reported differences between focus group research approaches in the USA and in Europe (Goodyear, 1996). Focus groups in the USA are portrayed as question and answer sessions whereby each individual in the group is expected to provide opinions and moderators are expected to ensure that time to speak out is shared amongst group participants (Goodyear, 1996). By contrast, British focus group moderators find this approach problematic since it seems to ignore the 'group as a group' characteristic of the focus group (Gordon, 1999; Chrzanowska, 2002).

Focus group theories
The idea that there are quite different approaches to undertaking focus groups in market research is not a new idea. The most widely cited classification of focus group research approaches, and the nearest there is to a theory of focus groups in market research, was developed nearly three decades ago by Bobby Calder (1977) and remains widely cited in the marketing (McDonald, 1993; Fern, 2001) and social science literature (Puchta and Potter, 2004). In the discussion that follows we will briefly explain Calder's classification and then go on to discuss a more recent classification from the market research practitioner literature.

Calder (1977) represented focus group research as a variety of different philosophically and theoretically informed approaches. He identified three different approaches to focus groups, the exploratory, phenomenological and clinical approaches, each of which differed on the type of knowledge that was generated, the research purposes for which it was suitable, and on the ways it would be implemented.

The *exploratory* approach is based on the underlying assumption that people can explain their attitudes and behaviour when asked to do so. Researchers that subscribe to this approach will generate data from participants at the individual cognitive level and then summarize and report these data as everyday knowledge. Exploratory focus groups would usually be undertaken as a precursor to survey work to check understanding of questionnaire items and to identify or select ideas or hypotheses for later testing in survey work.

The *clinical* approach is based on the assumption that people's everyday explanations of their behaviour are often misleading and that they will conceal or may not be consciously aware of the real reasons for their behaviour and attitudes. The purpose of the clinical approach is to reveal these hidden reasons. The clinical approach employs psychoanalytic theory as a problem-solving framework.

The *phenomenological* approach embodies the assumption that attitudes and behaviour are contextual, formed in the wider social and cultural worlds. Drawing largely from the work of sociologists, the purpose of this approach is to experience consumers, to see things from their point of view and describe experiences in consumers' own terms. This may result in a report that simply provides consumers' own descriptions and language or the researcher may apply an existing body of theory or theoretical concepts to the interpretation of data (Calder and Tybout, 1987).

During the late 1980s, Chandler and Owen identified three distinctive focus group approaches prevailing at the time, which they subsequently updated (Chandler and Owen, 2002). Unlike Calder, they do not assume that each approach is suitable to a particular research purpose or, unlike Goodyear (1996), representative of prevailing practice in a particular regional marketplace.

Discursive or cognitive approach
The discursive or cognitive approach is based on the assumption that, if the researcher wishes to discover how consumers think, act and feel, the best way to achieve this is to question them. Responses are taken largely at face value, classified, summarized and reported to the client. Chandler and Owen (1989) argued that the real value of this approach was its simplicity: the group moderator needs to ensure that all group participants have their say and does not become involved in 'subjective' interpretation. Implicated in this approach is a model of consumer behaviour that assumes the individual consumer is a rational decision maker.

Psychodynamic–humanistic approach
This approach is broadly equivalent to Calder's clinical approach (1977). It is informed by psychodynamic and humanistic psychology theories. It is most unlikely that this represents a single unified approach to focus group research as Calder implied. Specifically, some approaches could be classified as psychodynamic whilst others were more consistent with various theories and concepts from humanistic psychology (Imms and Ereaut, 2002).

Researchers employing these approaches have argued that it is too simplistic to assume that individuals can express their attitudes or discuss their behaviour in response to direct questioning. They are either too inhibited or may simply be unable to express themselves because the real determinants of attitudes and behaviour are often locked beyond the cognitive conscious mind (Cooper, 1989). In order to gain access to these data researchers need to employ more indirect methods of questioning, such as projective and enabling techniques. Managing group dynamics is essential to ensure a functioning productive group.

This is a more sophisticated and complex model of the consumer than that embraced by cognitive researchers. However, according to Chandler and Owen (1989), they still tend to conceptualize the individual as the target of marketing action and the consumer as passive. In other words if the marketer can gain an understanding of both the overt and the covert or deep influences on consumer behaviour, marketing action can be devised and applied appropriately.

Analytic or cultural and linguistic approaches
In this approach the research focus is on consumer culture and consumption and not the individual consumer. The basic assumptions that underpin this approach are that culture is the frame in which individual action takes place and that people share cultural meaning systems and the researcher's task is to identify the meaning systems that shape behaviour (Valentine and Evans, 1993). Since these meaning systems are taken for granted in everyday life, such as rules of turn taking in conversation, they can be inaccessible to questioning and probing whether this is at the rational or the deep psychological level (Chandler and Owen, 2002). These meaning systems are like codes that need to be cracked by the researcher (Valentine, 1996). By listening to what respondents have to say about a topic, the researcher is provided with the cues and clues to crack these cultural codes. Thus the attitudes and experiences of the individual respondent or groups of respondents are primarily of interest insofar as they provide clues to shared meaning systems. The interaction that occurs in the focus group is a useful way of gaining access to shared meanings such as shared language, what is taken for granted and what other participants in groups challenge.

This approach is also gaining considerable ground amongst British market research practitioners who previously favoured psychodynamic/humanistic approaches. Many sociologists favour this approach also, claiming the knowledge gained can short-cut weeks of participant observation in the field (Bloor et al., 2001).

In summary, then, the theories that market research practitioners bring to and that inform their focus group research have not stood still. For many years the cognitive and psychodynamic/humanistic approaches were implicit and taken for granted within the industry and, thus, rarely subjected to critical reflection and scrutiny (Imms and Ereaut, 2002). This situation altered during the 1980s as researchers faced new challenges, including more informed and active consumers and client demands for research that would provide input into more creative marketing, branding and advertising strategies.

Focus group implementation
It might be expected that the variety in focus group approaches would be reflected in the ways that focus group research is implemented in practice. Calder (1977) argued that the implementation of focus group research would vary under each approach, resulting in differences in group composition, the moderator's training and skills, and so on. However there is a marked degree of consistency in some practices, such as group recruitment and

the duration of a focus group regardless of the approach adopted and these vary little across national boundaries (Goodyear, 1996). Some of these practices have been in place since focus groups were first widely used in market research (Bellenger, Bernhardt and Goldstucker, 1976) and seem to be sustained largely for commercial rather than methodological reasons, as the following examples illustrate.

Focus groups usually last for one and a half hours
This enhances moderator productivity, and profitability, allowing the moderator to undertake two groups in a single working shift, usually in the evening, at a single location.

Focus groups should consist of up to eight participants
Focus groups in Europe tend to be smaller than their USA counterparts, with up to eight and 12 participants, respectively, although USA groups have been reducing in size (Langer, 2001; Mariampolski, 2001). Fern (1983) argued that as group size increased the time for each participant to speak would be at a premium. Implicit in this argument is the view that all participants in a focus group are expected to contribute, more or less equally, to the discussion. As we noted earlier, this viewpoint is not consistent with maximizing the benefits that can be achieved from group dynamics. It is also clear that group size is important in a commercial environment. As Gordon (1999) points out, the addition of two or more participants to group size can have an impact on profits.

Focus groups participants should be homogeneous in personal characteristics
Participants are more likely to disclose information when they are similar on key demographic and socioeconomic characteristics (exogenous homogeneity) and on their knowledge and experience of the subject matter (issue homogeneity). Corfman (1995) found that homogeneity was not as vital to data quality in groups as is commonly assumed, even in situations where the sensitive issues are discussed. An exception might be mixed gender groups; Schlosser (1997) found that minority gender members in such groups selectively tailored their responses during the discussion. As with other focus group 'givens', practices in terms of participant homogeneity have been resistant to change owing to client expectations and the management of recruitment within the industry (Spenser and Wells, 2000).

Focus groups should consist of strangers rather than acquaintances
There is little inter-country variation in this practice (Rose, 1996). It is argued that acquaintances might disrupt group dynamics and participants will reveal more in the presence of strangers than friends (Feldwick and Winstanley, 1986). Two studies designed to test the effect of acquaintanceship suggested that it does not have an adverse effect on the data generated (Fern, 1982; Nelson and Frontczak, 1988). Bristol (1999), in his work with Fern and Mandrik, found that the intimacy and number of self-disclosures made by males were greater in groups composed of strangers. By contrast, females disclosed more amongst acquaintances. In the face of this evidence, it can be difficult to justify a blanket policy of strangers only on methodological grounds alone. The policy is largely client-driven: clients become suspicious of recruitment practices if they find groups composed of acquaintances and any decision to recruit acquaintances needs to be justified to the client (Gordon, 1999).

While some practices seem rather resistant to change, others demonstrate considerable variety, innovation and creativity that keep focus group research fresh and relevant, as the following examples illustrate:

Friendship groups   Frequently associated (but not exclusively) with young consumers and youth markets whereby small groups or even pairs of friends are recruited to overcome any shyness that might occur if they were recruited as strangers (Collier and Fuller, 1998). They also offer a supportive setting with one's peer group which encourages self-disclosure. For example, Stevens (2003) found this a successful means of interviewing networks of women readers in her study of women's experiential consumption of magazines.

Mini-groups   Involve fewer participants (usually three to six) and are used where individual participants have specialist knowledge or experience and might be expected to contribute a great deal to the discussion (Goodyear, 1998). O'Donohoe (2001) used small groups to explore young adult responses to advertising.

Conflict groups   Participants who have opposing views on a subject are deliberately recruited so that the discussion can highlight core issues, differences and, perhaps, ways to resolve these differences. Participants are explicitly informed of the nature and purpose of the group at recruitment.

Creativity groups   These are longer than the standard one-and-a-half hour group. The workshop format is gaining in popularity; here larger groups of participants break up into subgroups, and then come together in a larger discussion and feedback session. Longer sessions running to half a day or even over two or more days allow the use of more creative projective research techniques (Desai, 2002).

Leading edge groups   Groups designed to explore new territory and develop groundbreaking ideas. They are a response to the criticism that qualitative research is poor at developing truly new ideas. Participants tend not to be members of the target market for the product or service but bring special insight to it. To explore new packaging designs, for example, participants may be identified and recruited via word of mouth from a design-articulate population that includes web-site designers, photographers and people involved in film production (Collier and Fuller, 1998).

Brand obsessives groups   These are recruited because of their high levels of interest or enthusiasm for brands (or product category). They are of course atypical consumers, but it is because of this that they can bring new insights to a problem and identify potential and ideas for the future.

Pre-tasking groups   Here group participants may be asked to perform various activities or tasks before they come to the group. Desai (2002) undertook a research project on army recruitment offices whereby participants were given instamatic cameras to take photographs during visits to these offices that represented the 'brand' for them prior to the group discussion.

Reconvened groups   A group is recruited for two sessions separated, say, by a week. In the intervening period the participants are asked to engage in some activity or activities. For example, they might be asked to cease using a product, such as meat, for a week. These activities focus their thinking on the product or service in preparation for the second group session. Group participants are usually much more involved in the second group; they have more to say and raise new issues. An innovative variant of this type of group was when Jump Associates conducted research to learn more about student life for discount retailer Target. Jump developed a board game about going to college and recruited students to join in a number of games nights. As students played the game and answered the questions it entailed, they shared their experiences of college life (Wellner, 2003). This research resulted in the development of new products aimed at students, for example, a laundry bag with instructions on how to do the laundry printed on it.

Consumer–client dialogue groups   David Spenser (Spenser and Wells, 2000) is one of the pioneers of client–consumer work sessions in which the two groups are brought together to work on a specific project or task. Interestingly he notes that client company executives have more initial difficulty with this concept than consumers; the latter tend to respond very positively to such dialogue.

In summary, then, the strictures in the literature regarding focus group implementation and practices are difficult to justify on methodological grounds alone. We have shown that many of these remain in place as a result of client expectations as to what a focus group comprises and market researchers' concerns with productivity and profitability. When clients can be persuaded to increase their budgets, focus group research designs can exhibit considerable creativity and innovation in group design, size, composition, recruitment practice, nature of data generated, and so on. It is in these variations on the 'standard' focus group that academic marketing and consumer researchers can find new ideas for focus group research, and use them in combination with other methods such as observation or ethnography (see Chapters 8 and 21) and projective or enabling techniques (see Chapter 11).

Conclusion

In this chapter we have traced the history of the focus group and discussed the different theoretical and methodological influences that underpin its use. Whilst some argue that focus group research is best used for exploratory research purposes only, others have drawn variously from psychodynamic theory, humanistic psychology and cultural and linguistic theories to provide rich insights into marketplace phenomena. Despite the various criticisms that have been levelled against it, therefore, we believe that the focus group is a dynamic and highly versatile technique that still has much to offer researchers, as a stand-alone method or in tandem with other marketing research techniques.

References

Abrams, Mark (1949), 'Possibilities and problems of group interviewing', *Public Opinion Quarterly*, **13** (Fall), 502–6.

Achenbaum, Alvin A. (1995), 'The future challenge to market research', *Marketing Research: a Magazine of Management and Applications*, **5** (2), 12–15.

Adam, Louis (1951), 'A psychoanalytical method as an aid to selling', *Travail et Méthodes*, **47** (November), 25–9.

Albrecht, Terence L., Gerianne M. Johnson and Joseph B. Walther (1993), 'Understanding communication processes in focus groups', in David L. Morgan (ed.), *Successful Focus Groups: Advancing the State of the Art*, Newbury Park, CA: Sage, pp. 51–63.

Allison, Scott T. and David M. Messick (1987), 'From individual inputs to group outputs, and back again', in C. Hendrick (ed.), *Group Processes and Intergroup Relations*, Newbury Park, CA: Sage, pp. 111–43.

Arvidsson, Adam (2000), 'The theory of consumption motivation research and the new Italian housewife, 1958–62', *Journal of Material Culture*, **5** (3), 251–74.

Asch, Solomon E. (1955), 'Opinions and social pressures', *Scientific American*, **193** (November), 31–55.

Banks, John A. (1956), 'The group discussion as an interview technique', *Sociological Review*, **5**, 75–84.

Bellenger, Danny N., Kenneth L. Bernhardt and Jac L. Goldstucker (1976), *Qualitative Marketing Research*, Chicago: American Marketing Association.

Bion, Wilfred (1961), *Experiences in Groups and Other Papers*, London: Tavistock Publications.

Bloor, Michael, Jane Frankland, Michelle Thomas and Kate Robson (2001), *Focus Groups in Social Research*, London: Sage.

Bogardus, Emory S. (1926), 'The group interview', *Journal of Applied Sociology*, **10**, 372–82.

Bristol, Terry (1999), 'Enhancing focus group productivity: new research and insights', in Eric J. Arnould and Linda M. Scott (eds), *Advances in Consumer Research*, vol. 26, Provo, UT: Association for Consumer Research, pp. 479–82.

Bristol, Terry and Edward F. Fern (1993), 'Using qualitative techniques to explore consumer attitudes: insights from group process theories', in Leigh McAlister and Michael L. Rothschild (eds), *Advances in Consumer Research*, vol. 20, Provo, UT: Association for Consumer Research, pp. 444–8.

Bristol, Terry and Edward F. Fern (1996), 'Exploring the atmosphere created in focus group interviews: comparing consumers' feelings across qualitative techniques', *Journal of The Market Research Society*, **38** (2), 185–95.

Calder, Bobby J. (1977), 'Focus groups and the nature of qualitative marketing research', *Journal of Marketing Research*, **14** (August), 353–64.

Calder, Bobby J. and Alice Tybout (1987), 'What consumer research is . . .', *Journal of Consumer Research*, **14** (June), 136–40.

Carver, Charles S. (1979), 'A cybernetic model of self-attention processes', *Journal of Personality and Social Psychology*, **37** (August), 1251–81.

Catterall, Miriam and William Clarke (2000), 'Improving the interface between the profession and the university', *International Journal of Market Research*, **42** (1), 3–16.

Chandler, John and Mike Owen (1989), 'Genesis to revelations: the evolution of qualitative philosophy', *Proceedings of the Market Research Society Conference*, London: The Market Research Society, pp. 295–305.

Chandler, Jon and Mike Owen (2002), *Developing Brands with Qualitative Market Research*, London: Sage.

Chrzanowska, Joanna (2002), *Interviewing Groups and Individuals in Qualitative Market Research*, London: Sage.

Collier, Maggie and Kirstie Fuller (1998), 'Choose change: forward-looking research at its best', AQRP Trends Day presentation.

Cooper, Peter (1989), 'Comparison between the UK and the US: the qualitative dimension', *Journal of the Market Research Society*, **31** (4), 509–20.

Corfman, Kim P. (1995), 'The importance of member homogeneity to focus group quality', in Fred R. Kardes and Mita Sujan (eds), *Advances in Consumer Research*, vol. 22, Provo, UT: Association for Consumer Research, pp. 354–9.

Desai, Philly (2002), *Methods Beyond Interviewing in Qualitative Market Research*, London: Sage.

Edmiston, V. (1944), 'The group interview', *Journal of Educational Research*, **37** (April), 593–601.

Feldwick, Paul and Lorna Winstanley (1986), 'Qualitative recruitment: policy and practice', *Proceedings of the Market Research Society Conference*, London: The Market Research Society, pp. 57–72.

Fern, Edward F. (1982), 'The use of focus groups for idea generation: the effects of group size, acquaintanceship, and moderator on response quantity and quality', *Journal of Marketing Research*, **26** (February), 1–13.

Fern, Edward F. (1983), 'Focus groups: a review of some contradictory evidence; implications and suggestions for further research', in Richard R. Bagozzi and Alice M. Tybout (eds), *Advances in Consumer Research*, vol. 10, Provo, UT: Association for Consumer Research, pp. 121–26.

Fern, Edward F. (2001), *Advanced Focus Group Research*, Thousand Oaks, CA: Sage.

Goldman, Alfred E. and Susan S. McDonald (1987), *The Group Depth Interview: Principles and Practice*, Englewood Cliffs, NJ: Prentice-Hall.

Goodyear, Mary (1996), 'Divided by a common language: diversity and deception in the world of global marketing', *Journal of the Market Research Society*, **38** (2), 105–22.

Goodyear, Mary (1998), 'Qualitative research', in C. McDonald and P. Vangelder (eds), *ESOMAR Handbook of Market and Opinion Research*, Amsterdam: ESOMAR, pp. 177–239.

Gordon, Wendy (1999), *Goodthinking: A Guide to Qualitative Research*, Henley-on-Thames: Admap Publications.

Gordon, Wendy and Roy Langmaid (1988), *Qualitative Market Research: A Practitioner's and Buyer's Guide*, London: Gower.

Imms, Mike and Gill Ereaut (2002), *An Introduction to Qualitative Market Research*, London: Sage.

Janis, Irving L. (1982), *Groupthink: Psychological Studies of Policy Decisions and Fiascos*, 2nd edn, Boston: Houghton Mifflin.

Langer, Judith (2001), *The Mirrored Window: Focus Groups from a Moderator's Point of View*, Ithaca, NY: Paramount Market Publishing.

MacGregor, B. and D.E. Morrison (1995), 'From focus groups to editing groups: a new method of reception analysis', *Media Culture and Society*, **17** (1), 141–50.

Mariampolski, Hy (2001), *Qualitative Market Research. A Comprehensive Guide*, Thousand Oaks, CA: Sage.

McDonald, William J. (1993), 'Focus group research dynamics and reporting: an examination of research objectives and moderator influence', *Journal of the Academy of Marketing Science*, **21** (2), 161–8.

Merton, Robert K. and Patricia L. Kendall (1946), 'The focused interview', *American Journal of Sociology*, **51**, 541–57.

Milgram, Stanley (1974), *Obedience to Authority*, London: The Tavistock Institute.

Morgan, David L. and Richard A. Krueger (1997), *The Focus Group Kit, Volumes 1–6*, Thousand Oaks, CA: Sage.

Morgan, Helen and Kerry Thomas (1996), 'A psychodynamic perspective on group processes', in Margaret Wetherell (ed.), *Identities, Groups and Social Issues*, London: Open University/Sage, pp. 63–117.

Nelson, James E. and Nancy T. Frontczak (1988), 'How acquaintanceship and analyst can influence focus group results', *Journal of Advertising*, **17** (1), 41–8.

O'Donohoe, Stephanie (2001), 'Living with ambivalence: attitudes to advertising in postmodern times', *Marketing Theory*, **1** (1), 91–108.

Puchta, Claudia and Jonathan Potter (2004), *Focus Group Practice*, London: Sage.

Robson, Sue and Angela Foster (eds) (1989), *Qualitative Research in Action*, London: Edward Arnold.

Rose, John (ed.) (1996), 'Qualitative recruitment. Report of the industry working party', *Journal of the Market Research Society*, **38** (2), 135–43.

Scheidlinger, Saul (2000), 'The group psychotherapy movement at the millennium: some historical perspectives', *International Journal of Group Psychotherapy*, **50** (3), 315–39.

Schlosser, Ann E. (1997), 'Examining the instrumentality of attitudes: the interactive effect of social context, medium and product type on product thoughts and evaluations', PhD thesis, University of Illinois–Urbana-Champaign.

Sherif, Muzafur (1936), *The Psychology of Social Norms*, New York: Harper and Row.

Smith, George Horsley (1954), *Motivation Research in Advertising and Marketing*, Westport: CT.: Greenwood Press.

Spenser, David and Stephen Wells (2000), 'Qualitative research and innovation', in Laura Marks (ed.), *Qualitative Research in Context*, Henley-on-Thames: Admap, pp. 233–52.

Stevens, Lorna (2003), 'The joys of text: women's experiential consumption of magazines', PhD thesis, University of Ulster.

Tuckman, B.W. (1965), 'Developmental sequences in small groups', *Psychological Bulletin*, **63**, 384–99.

Valentine, Virginia (1996), 'Opening up the black box: switching the paradigm of qualitative research', *Marketing and Research Today*, **24** (2), 95–106.

Valentine, Virginia and Malcolm Evans (1993), 'The dark side of the onion: rethinking the meanings of "rational" and "emotional" responses', *Journal of the Market Research Society*, **35** (2), 125–44.

Wellner, A.S. (2003), 'The new science of focus groups', *American Demographics*, **25** (2), 29.

Wetherell, Margaret (1996), *Identities, Groups and Social Issues*, London: Open University/Sage.

Wilson, Godfrey and Wilson, Morica (1945), *The Analysis of Social Change Based on Observations in Central Africa*, Cambridge: The University Press.

20 Fielding ethnographic teams: strategy, implementation and evaluation

John F. Sherry

Despite the heroic view of ethnography as the solitary pursuit of the maverick scholar, the enterprise has long been conducted as an extreme team sport. The holism espoused in data collection and analysis is often most effectively achieved by a group, rather than an individual. Arguably, even individual fieldwork and interpretation are best served by a multiphrenic, extended self in constant conversation with that internal voice comprising the portfolio of literatures that guides the hermeneutic tacking that is the ethnographic quest. Remember, *pace* Whitman, we contain multitudes, and this introjection of mentors and nemeses disposes us by nature to be team players. How much more interesting, productive and challenging to shift from psychodrama to actual teamwork in contemplation of consumer behavior.

I have written this chapter as an essay rather than as a more conventional academic tract, to reflect my personal experience of ethnographic teamwork and to offer some avuncular advice to readers capable on their own of sourcing material on ethnographic methods and perspectives. While I have appended a few references to this chapter, my intent in these few pages is practical rather than philosophical.

I have worked in ethnographic teams for over three decades across a range of marketplaces, industries, categories and households. I have developed some strong preferences and biases in the conduct of this work, many of which I share in the balance of this text. Principal among these, beyond the achievement of substantive understanding and the sheer enjoyment of the lived experience of fieldwork, is that the goal of any ethnographic undertaking is the acquisition and honing of portable skills. Insofar as ethnographic success is dependent upon the efficacy of the researcher as instrument, the cultivation and refinement of intraceptive intuition as well as the expansion and deepening of the clinical repertoire are opportunities and obligations resident in any field setting. Team-mates are a powerful catalyst for such professional and personal growth. Thus every team outing is a peripatetic seminar, whatever else it may accomplish.

In the following pages, I describe ways of selecting, building and maintaining an ethnographic team. I also discuss the intricacies of managing group fieldwork. I develop a template for the interstitial strategy sessions that inform the ongoing ethnography. I propose a framework for orchestrating interpretation as it emerges over the course of a project. I offer suggestions for crafting the written accounts that capture the team's understanding of focal phenomena. Finally, I consider options for using the current team project as a platform for future endeavors. For convenience's sake, I write from the perspective of the Principal Investigator, the coach whose task it is to lead by example, and who is an integral member of the team in both the field and the library.

Selecting, building and maintaining a team

Clearly the success of any team ethnography depends upon the capabilities that group members both bring with them and develop during the course of a project. On successful teams, these capabilities quickly become synergistic, inspiring group members to ever-greater technical precision and ever more nuanced interpretation. For example, a team-mate using an ethnic lens and an interest in social class in conversation with another team-mate using a sportsman's lens and an interest in racial 'stacking' in professional sports produce a more dimensional account of sales floor behavior in a postmodern sports bar than either researcher alone might accomplish. Properly motivated, each team member becomes a coach in his or her own right, steadily raising the ante for contribution as the project progresses. A healthy competition informs any vital collaboration.

I recruit team members on the basis of several criteria. While most of these criteria are functional in nature, there are several that might be more appropriately described as expressive in character. I begin this recruitment discussion with a consideration of the latter, to emphasize the importance of what might otherwise seem to be fairly trivial issues.

As I believe social scientific research to be at base a self-indulgent hedonic undertaking, the lived experience of the *doing* of research is important to me. I prefer to work with people whose company in the field I enjoy for more than the mere clinical expertise it provides, and whose engagement in hermeneutic discourse I enjoy more for the intellectual playfulness it liberates in me than in the mere idiosyncratically brilliant insight it brings to bear upon a problem. Thus a sense of humour, an appreciation of the ambiguities of social life, a willingness to achieve (in Burke's phrase) perspectives by incongruity, a work hard/play hard ethic, a tolerance for quirkiness and a deep commitment to a common goal I find essential in a congenial team-mate. Team ethnography is as much about family dynamics as it is about corporate dynamics. Researchers are not just a work group, they are a play group as well. Insight often arises from the ability to play well with others. The playful aspect of collaboration is one of the joys and strengths of ethnographic writing.

Clinically I select team members on several dimensions. Chief among these is problem-focused expertise. I find it helpful for at least one team member to have research experience grounded in the nominal focal phenomenon. This helps the team come up to speed more quickly in the literature search and evaluation, and facilitates access to informants earlier in the game. This particular team member may actually be a 'nonprofessional' key informant discovered in the prospecting phase of the inquiry, whose 'research', however informal or nonsystematic, may be so thoroughgoing as to provide an anchor in the beginning, and a sounding board throughout the project. As we reposition the role of informant to one of consultant, such cross-sectional collaboration will become increasingly common. Ethnographers have always employed natives as researchers in their own right, whether in the collection of aboriginal oral literary texts or of photo/video documentation of contemporary New Age rituals. I have been asked by citizens of Burning Man's Black Rock City to produce my anthropological union card (my AAA membership credential) before they would consent to an interview, in which subsequently they would hold forth on topics and literatures as competently as an Oxford don, enriching my understanding of the phenomenon and its hermeneutic context, before referring me on to other prospective occasions of enlightenment.

Methodological complementarity is another important recruitment consideration. While most ethnographers imagine themselves to be generalists, many likely rely on those 'go-to' techniques with which they feel most comfortable. Keen observers, game partici-pants, flexible moderators, subtle and tenacious interviewers, precise surveyors, sensitive projective analysts, accomplished photographers and videographers, and vigilant project managers should all be represented on the team, if not instantiated in individuals. Techniques more orthogonal to traditional ethnography – experiment, LISREL model-ing, CAT scanning and the like – are more commonly being brought into the tent. Others will surely follow. Complementary skills abet the partnering of team-mates to greater effectiveness.

Disciplinary diversity is a fellow traveler of methodological complementarity. An inter-disciplinary perspective of the focal phenomenon leads to a deeper interpretation and a proliferation of managerial implications. Anthropologists, sociologists, political scien-tists, educational specialists, psychologists, ergonomicists, narrative analysts, historians, religious studies scholars and a host of other specialized disciplines have long incorpo-rated ethnography into their folds. Other disciplines, which have either not yet or only recently embraced ethnographic method are usefully involved in the interpretation and analysis phase of team projects. A devotion to holism, however, can devolve quickly from synergy to faction fighting, if the negotiation of interpretations becomes a zero sum game. Confrontation is an expected byproduct of high-energy analysis, and must be managed to help integration triumph over schism, as Victor Turner might imagine it. Keeping a team agenda foregrounded, emphasizing the prospect of multiple papers and charging all researchers with stewardship of the stream are ways of encouraging cohesion.

Demographic heterogeneity is a final criterion I invoke during recruitment. I have found it most helpful to assemble teams whose members vary by age, gender and culture (national, ethnic, regional, etc.). This variance encourages greater diversity in sampling in the field, and produces a wider array of insight in the analysis and interpretation phases of a project. Properly motivated, diverse team-mates inquire into one another's perspec-tives, intuitions, assertions and assumptions, treating their collaboration much like a field site and mirroring techniques employed in the current project.

Team building requires the Principal Investigator to pitch the project to his or her prospects in a way that highlights the opportunities for both distinctive and holistic con-tributions, and holds out the promise of an almost acephalous governance structure of project management. Each team-mate is apprised of everyone's indispensability, collegial equality and reciprocal obligation; the PI assumes the role of player–coach. Unlike the legendary herding of cats and confederacy of dunces, the team is a committee everyone has enthusiastically joined, and is ostensibly amenable to the wise counsel and unstinting example of the PI.

Obligations, expectations, timetables and deliverables are negotiated at the outset, and revisited throughout the project, given the emergent nature of ethnographic research. I try to assume the role of focus group moderator throughout the project, building con-sensus and commitment by constantly polling and clarifying team-mates' positions, and catalyzing forward movement by continually exploring the implications of current find-ings for future fieldwork. Helping each group member achieve greater 'instrumentality' (in the sense of intraceptive intuition) throughout the project, and thus potentiating team-mates' growth as well, is the key to group maintenance. Like creating a sustained nuclear chain reaction, the coach encourages the released energy of each individual to energize the group. Project beginnings and endings can sometimes be arbitrary and mechanical, sometimes reasoned and organic. I imagine such demarcations to be clinal zones in the polyvocal conversation researchers conduct with one another, but when tenure clocks and client deadlines are winding down, the team has got to make the trains run on time.

Managing group fieldwork

Fielding an ethnographic team is both an antecedent to and consequence of recruitment. Before I begin a group project, I request that each of my prospective team-mates visits the field site on a solo reconnaissance exercise. A preliminary walk-through (or series of initial visits) contextualizes the problem for group members and gives each an initial, tangible sense of the contribution he or she stands to make, and of the fun likely to be had. Once the team is recruited and mutually introduced, I encourage another preliminary solo walk-through, to allow for projective fantasies of collaboration and grist for the marketing imagination that will be engaged at the next team meeting.

At the initial group assembly, I facilitate some open-ended discussion of first impressions of the context, the problem, preliminary minimal parameters, potential sources of theorizing and prospective managerial implications. This discussion is all by way of generating enthusiasm and camaraderie, rather than systematic, comprehensive insight. Teammates introduce themselves, and speak briefly of their backgrounds and motivations for involvement in the project. Then I turn directly to a logistical overview of the project, a template I expect the group to modify as the project unfolds.

I project a schedule of the enterprise that identifies key dates for obtaining IRB (Institutional Review Board) clearance, arranging permissions to inhabit proprietary sites, completion of sampling objectives, data archiving and sharing, progress reports, strategy sessions, draft writing, member checking and final document and/or presentation preparation, again allowing for the emergent character of ethnographic research. I encourage the team to inhabit the fieldsite with an immersive blanketing Geertz has described as 'deep hanging out'. I set up a timetable to achieve pervasive coverage of the phenomenon to the extent possible, with team-mates committing to particular times and dates of participation. Schedules are set so that everyone logs field time as individuals and as members of dyads and triads (and on rare occasions, population density permitting, even larger groups). Awareness of this schedule makes it possible for individuals to undertake additional ad hoc fieldwork without impacting the habitat.

I work rotations with everyone on the team, so I am able to assess core competencies and deficiencies, monitor potential conflicts and suggest compatible group pairings. I request each team member to work a rotation with every other team member, to help insure complementarity, redundancy and state-dependent learning. By project's end, everyone has worked a site with everyone else, and reaped the benefit of procedural and clinical instruction from everyone as a result. Polishing diamonds with diamond dust, as my own mentor advocated, the team teaches itself.

Interspersed with scheduled fieldwork days are days devoted to strategy sessions. As ethnography involves constant tacking between field and library, and constant comparison such that data collection and analysis are inextricably intertwined, it is imperative that team-mates discuss findings on a timely and regular basis. This requires preparation of epic proportions, since team-mates must be familiar not only with their own fieldnotes, but with those of everyone else as well. Early strategy meetings involve data sharing and the workshopping of methods and techniques, as well as habituation of team-mates to one another's work styles. In initial meetings, I both elicit and model tentative interpretations of current findings, laying down the template for the negotiation of understanding that will ensue in later weeks. Early sessions contribute primarily to team building and maintenance, so it is important to engage all team members in discussions, as tentative as contributions may be.

As the project evolves, strategy sessions deepen as well as broaden in their scope. A division of labor is negotiated that involves player-controlled environmental scanning, information brokerage and selective sharing of external readings. That is, each group member identifies a literature (both scholarly and managerial) of prospective theorizing, digests it for relevance and brings a summary to the attention of the group. Simultaneously, each group member searches for compelling linkage to current and traditional disciplinary concerns. Because ethnography is a grounded theory enterprise, researchers can only sift a literature for potential relevance, bracketing their insight as they return each time to the field. By apprising team-mates of relevant insights from various disciplines throughout the project, everyone's cognitive peripheral vision (in Jerry Zaltman's delightful phrasing) is enhanced. Thus a retail spectacle focus may morph from an emphasis on cultural construction and ludic agency into a concern with kinship dynamics, and thence into a treatment of heroic feminism, as team-mates blanket American Girl Place (flagship store for the American girl brand) over the course of several editions of the *Journal of Consumer Research*.

Hand in hand with this literature sharing goes a protracted discussion of cumulative findings. I model the proposing of interpretive themes from data, elicit contributions from the group, and work on constructing an exhaustive inventory of themes as the project emerges. The group quickly learns to negotiate interpretations, challenging and supporting views from data collected individually and communally. Early strategy sessions conclude with interpretive summaries of procedural and substantive learning, and a set of action steps to be accomplished prior to the next meeting.

Orchestrating interpretation
Then, as the shampoo label advises, 'Lather, rinse and repeat.' Group members revolve from field to library, with past learning modifying current findings, which in turn guide future inquiry, until the team either achieves saturation and redundancy in its results or encounters the limits of its clinical ability to elicit additional insight. At this point, the current project is tentatively concluded, and becomes a platform from which additional projects may be launched. Pending the discovery of holes in the archive during the final rounds of analysis and interpretation that might require additional data collection, fieldwork is suspended and the team convenes in the library for the winnowing work of interpretation.

Throughout the strategy sessions, I revisit the inventory of emergent themes, soliciting both champions and devil's advocates for each of them, so that every team member is engaged in a constant contestation of our principal findings. This contestation produces penetrating and systematic discussion, which greatly enhances the coding process. I have used Spradley's diagnostic research sequence and Strauss' and Corbin's open/axial/selective process, both in isolation and in hybrid formats, to guide coding, but any coding scheme selected will only be as good as the processed data upon which it is overlaid. That is why the contestation during strategy sessions must be so vigorously encouraged. This hermeneutic cycling of insight within the group sets the stage for the ultimate coding.

Once the team is comfortable that all the major themes have been identified, we begin the process of segregating, aggregating and integrating the themes into the story lines that will eventually become manuscripts. This winnowing process mirrors the fieldwork enterprise, insofar as we work as individuals, dyads, triads and complete group, in part to whole fashion, in the reduction of our findings to manageable and compelling proportions. I have found it useful to work in conference rooms where the team has access to chalk-boards and whiteboards, VCRs and computers, easels and post-it notes, and all of its data simultaneously, so that the built environment facilitates group process. When the group has thus tangibilized its understanding by getting its knowledge into the world, it can return to the field with discrete insights and elicit commentary on them by key informants. This member checking may or may not add additional grist for analysis, but it serves both as a reality check of sorts and as an ethical debriefing for participants in the study. Then the serious work of writing is ready to be undertaken.

Writing, representation and voice

Even (or especially) after 30 years of fieldwork, I find the parsing of findings to be the most difficult challenge I face as a consumer researcher. Ethnographers understand the fabric of their focal phenomenon to be of a piece, and chafe at the notion of a jpu (the infinitesimally incremental 'just publishable unit'). As an anthropologist, my inclination has always been monographic. My preference is to write up my analysis as comprehensively as possible, to capture the phenomenon as holistically as I am able, in one fell swoop. This tendency is dysfunctional in a field that values concise journal articles to the exclusion of other formats. I struggle mightily as a writer to produce accounts of my work that amount to a mere 60 pages, which I find unbearably concise.

Imagine collaborating with other like-minded souls on a common project. A team ethnography might easily be expected to yield a document running to several hundred pages. Such a product would be fit to export to contiguous disciplines that value books, but, for junior professors, it is merely a white elephant impeding their progress toward tenure. Cognate articles are the Holy Grail of team ethnography.

Once a project has been running long enough to provide a glimmer of the focal phenomenon's minimal parameters, I ask group members to think about the kinds of outlets that would be amenable to prospective findings. Given the distinctive positionings of journals in our discipline, it is convenient to imagine the kinds of stories that might be told for particular audiences. Compartmentalizing findings by streaming during the research process also makes it simple to avoid idioplagiarizing during the write-up phase, as the data set will be large and distinctive enough to be parsed over several publications with no duplication. As a PI with a big picture perspective, I find it most helpful to work with team-mates who have a more granular view and an appreciation of the discrete contributions to be made by particular components of the larger project. This interplay of perspectives makes it possible to plan for a series of articles fairly early in the fieldwork process.

Armed with a sense of what the group thinks is possible and reasonable, I outline briefly the projected contribution by journal, and elicit ramrods for each manuscript (or sections thereof), whose charge it is to develop the nucleus around which the article will eventually be written. As drafts emerge, they circulate within the group for discussion, elaboration, clarification and, sometimes, outright argument. As in other stages of the research, each group member brings particular skills – eloquence, theoretical sophistication, concision, diplomacy, etc – to the crafting of documents that ultimately result in a manuscript draft ready for final editing.

Penultimate drafts face rigorous internal peer review from the team, as well as more informal external peer review (via invisible colleges in which team members participate), before the decision is made to submit the manuscript to a journal. To prevent the draft from reading like it was written by a committee, team-mates delegate an editor or editors to harmonize the voices as closely as possible. In some cases, the voices may actually be amplified, if discordant notes serve a representational purpose.

Diplomacy and grace must be cultivated and practiced among team-mates at this stage of the process, as everyone has a large stake in the outcome. It is one thing for official journal reviewers to call your baby ugly; it is quite another when you are encouraged to take one for the team by sidelining your own individually brilliant ideas or prose. Here the willingness of the PI to sacrifice as an exemplar is most effective. Equally effective is the practice of cultivating a team *bricoleur*, who tries to insure that anything left on the cutting room floor is recycled into yet another manuscript (or the stimulus for a new project). A team study of ESPN Zone Chicago foregrounding gender as its initial issue of interest produced more theoretically compelling possibilities as it emerged, pushing a systematic treatment of gender to the periphery of early manuscripts; insights eventually were culled from these textual backwaters to create a stand-alone account of an issue the team was reluctant to abandon all together. Finally, the negotiation of authorship order on the final manuscript should be public and decided by consensus. My rule of thumb has been to use alphabetical order in the case of equal contribution, and to rank authors by ramrod status in cases of unbalanced contribution. Order may often be readjusted during the revision process.

Once formal peer reviews are received and a revision is requested by the journal editor, the team handles the rewrite in the same manner as it negotiated the strategy sessions. Changes are agreed upon, additional data may be collected, theorizing may be reconfigured, and a ramrod shepherds the process to a revised manuscript. Outtakes and promising but unaccommodated reviewer suggestions are managed by the *bricoleur*, in the event that additional manuscripts might be produced.

Whither the regime?
One of the pleasures of team ethnography, once all hands are rowing in the same direction, is the realization that everyone has a roving eye and is prone to sighting exotic new islands of research just off the main course. The lone ethnographer is accustomed to thinking of his or her own research regime in terms of rhizome or walkabout, and of following emergent interests as they present themselves. Amplify this nomadic questing by the current number of team-mates and imagine how many side projects might delay progress on the focal group project.

I find it helpful to think of the current project as a platform for future research, whose outlines are dimly discernible at the moment, but promising nevertheless. Prospecting forays into this new geography are inevitable, but comprehensive exploration must await another day. I encourage team-mates to keep a journal of these interesting prospects against the day that we get the band back together, or until fission and fusion among our ranks produce new coalitions of researchers and other teams. In this manner, research streams can be advanced ever more rapidly, and researcher enthusiasm can be greatly prolonged.

Conclusion

Conducting ethnography in teams conveys some benefits that the lone ethnographer will find more difficult to reap. Teamwork allows for more ambitious projects to be undertaken. More comprehensive coverage of a phenomenon is possible with a group. Efficiency is an important benefit, with economies of scale and scope to be realized. Arguably teamwork leads to more and deeper insights, in the field and in the library. For continuing education and constant updating of clinical and analytic skills, group ethnography is a powerful motivator. Finally, for the lived experience of collegiality, the sense of dwelling in a scholarly community, team ethnography delivers a communitas of the road that is difficult to replicate.

Graduate students in marketing are accustomed to working on solitary projects, often one-off exercises that flow from their advisor's research stream, the published result often co-authored with that mentor. This is a tag-team tradition at best, and does little to promote the rhizomatic, synergistic impulse of truly collaborative research. It is easy to imagine a joint project pursued by a team of doctoral students, whose output would be a set of dissertations comprising a mosaic of monographic proportion, reduced in turn to a discrete set of solo- and co-authored journal articles. Such an approach would deliver a learning experience to doctoral students of much greater power, intimacy and satisfaction than they are currently receiving. It would provide junior faculty aspiring to tenure with a multidimensional coping mechanism, increasing their productive capacity and their resilience. The teamwork ethos is best laid down during graduate school. It is a challenge I hope some doctoral program will accept, and an opportunity I wish some academic department would extend.

Selected bibliography

General ethnographic sources
Bernard, H. Russell (2001), *Research Methods in Anthropology: Qualitative and Quantitative Approaches*, Lanham, MD: Altamira Press.
Emerson, Robert, Rachel Fretz and Linda Shaw (1995), *Writing Ethnographic Fieldnotes*, Chicago: University of Chicago Press.
Erickson, Ken and Donald Stull (1995), *Doing Team Ethnography: Warnings and Advice*, Thousand Oaks, CA: Sage.
Lofland, John and Lyn Lofland (1994), *Analyzing Social Settings*, Belmont, CA: Wadsworth.
Miles, Matthew and Michael Huberman (1994), *Qualitative Data Analysis*, Thousand Oaks: Sage.
Schensul, Jean (1999), *Ethnographer's Toolkit*, 7 vols, Thousand Oaks, CA: Altamira Press.
Sherry, John F. (1995), *Contemporary Marketing and Consumer Behavior: An Anthropological Sourcebook*, Thousand Oaks, CA: Sage.
—— (1998), *Servicescapes: The Concept of Place in Contemporary Markets*, Lincolnwood, IL: NTC Business Press.
Sherry, John F. and Robert V. Kozinets (2001), 'Qualitative inquiry in marketing and consumer research', in Dawn Iacobucci (ed.), *Kellogg on Marketing*, NY: Wiley, pp. 165–94.
Spradley, James (1997), *The Ethnographic Interview*, Belmont, CA: Wadsworth.
Strauss, Anselm and Juliet Corbin (1998), *Basics of Qualitative Research*, Thousand Oaks, CA: Sage.

Ethnographic teamwork in marketing and consumer behavior Odyssey
Belk, Russell (1999), *Highways and Buyways: Naturalistic Inquiry from the Consumer Behavior Odyssey*, Provo, UT: Association of Consumer Behavior.
Belk, Russell, John F. Sherry and Melanie Wallendorf (1988), 'A naturalistic inquiry into consumer behavior at a swap meet', *Journal of Consumer Research*, **14** (4), 449–70.
Belk, Russell, Melanie Wallendorf and John F. Sherry (1989), 'The sacred and profane in consumer behavior: theory on the Odyssey', *Journal of Consumer Research*, **16** (1), 1–38.

ESPN Zone Chicago

Duhachek, Adam (2003), 'Exploring ethnography at ESPNZone Chicago', *Kellogg Marketing Case*, Northwestern University, Evanston, IL, USA.

Kozinets, Robert, John F. Sherry, Diana Storm, Adam Duhachek, Krittinee Nuttavuthisit and Benét DeBerry-Spence (2002), 'Themed flagship brand stores in the new millennium: theory, practice, prospects', *Journal of Retailing*, **78**, 17–29.

—— (2004), 'Ludic agency and retail spectacle', *Journal of Consumer Research*, **31** (3), 658–72.

Sherry, John F., Robert Kozinets, Diana Storm, Adam Duhachek, Krittinee Nuttavuthisit and Benét DeBerry-Spence (2001), 'Being in the Zone: staging retail theatre at ESPNZone Chicago', *Journal of Contemporary Ethnography*, **30** (4), 465–510.

—— (2004), 'Gendered behavior in a male preserve: role playing at ESPNZone Chicago', *Journal of Consumer Psychology*, **14** (1&2), 151–8.

River rafting

Arnould, Eric and Cele Otnes (1999), 'Making consumption magic: a study of white water river', *Journal of Contemporary Ethnography*, **28** (1), 33–68.

Arnould, Eric and Linda Price (1993), 'River magic: extraordinary experience and the extended service encounter', *Journal of Consumer Research*, **20** (1), 25–45.

Arnould, Eric and Patrick Tierney (1998), 'The wilderness servicescape: an ironic commercial landscape', in *Servicescapes: The Concept of Place in Contemporary Markets*, John F. Sherry (ed.), Chicago: NTC Business, pp. 403–38.

Periodic markets

Heisley, Deborah, Mary Ann McGrath and John F. Sherry (1980), *Participant Observation*, Belmont, CA: Wadsworth.

Heisley, Deborah, Mary Ann McGrath and John F. Sherry (1991), 'To everything there is a season', *Journal of American Culture*, **14** (3), 53–79.

—— (1993), 'An ethnographic study of an urban periodic marketplace: lessons from the Midville farmers' market', *Journal of Retailing*, **69** (3), 280–319.

Thanksgiving

Wallendorf, Melanie and Eric Arnould (1991), ' "We gather together": consumption rituals of Thanksgiving Day', *Journal of Consumer Research*, **18** (1), 13–31.

PART V

DATA ANALYSIS METHODS

21 Writing pictures/taking fieldnotes: towards a more visual and material ethnographic consumer research
Lisa Peñaloza and Julien Cayla

Introduction

> Nothing is less real than realism. Details are confusing. It is only by selection, by elimination, by emphasis, that we get at the real meaning of things. (Georgia O'Keeffe)

Ethnographic methods are especially well suited to capturing and analyzing consumption behavior. From the multisensorial consumption Mecca of Mall of America (Csaba, 1999) to passengers traveling in Parisian subway trains (Floch, 1989), shoppers strolling in a farmer's market (Heisley et al., 1991b) or tourists wandering through the streets of an unfamiliar town (Ladwein, 2002a), ethnographic studies of visual images and material artifacts allow us to draw meanings from the experiential and kinesthetic aspects of consumption: people moving their bodies through consumption spaces, interacting with artifacts in those spaces and forging their identities and social worlds. They help us go beyond talk and text about what consumers do to provide a more holistic account of consumption behavior.

We focus here on two ethnographic methods, recording and analyzing field observations in fieldnotes and photography. The writing of fieldnotes is a standard activity in ethnography. The researcher enters a social setting, participates in the daily routines of that setting and regularly writes down what s/he observes and learns. Virtually every anthropologist uses fieldnotes to record their observations, insights and analysis. They try to get close to the people they are studying and describe their ways of life in detail. Geertz (1973) talks of a commitment to 'microscopic' detail that allows thick description of a social setting (p. 20).

Taking photographs in the field is also common practice in anthropology. As soon as the technologies were available, anthropologists brought cameras to the field, producing records of alien cultures to be stored in archives (Edwards, 1992). By opening another information channel, that of images, photographs encapsulate still more information, enriching textual representation of a culture with records of lived experience and contexts in rich detail.

Visual ethnographic methods and those used to study material artifacts are widely used in social sciences such as sociology (Becker, 1981), architecture (Tilley, 1992; Hodder, 1990), semiotics (Floch, 1989) and, of course, cultural anthropology (Harper, 1987). In one of the classic examples of visual ethnography, Bateson and Mead (1942) used sequences of photographs of the Balinese performing rituals and engaged in everyday behavior as a research tool to generate theory. In an example of ethnographic study of material culture, Price and Price (1992) demonstrated complex interfaces of cultural tradition, commerce and museum collections in wood carvings. In these ways, ethnographers have studied images and artifacts as empirical data to excavate cultural meanings within and across social groups (Halle, 1993) and to document social change (Rieger, 1996). In addition to being a research tool for recording cultural patterns, fieldnotes and photographs help ethnographers recall experience – theirs and those they study. Fieldnotes and photographs have the power to evoke the times and places of fieldwork, acting as *aide-mémoire* enabling ethnographers to reconstruct field experience.

In contrast, consumer research has entailed a much more limited use of visual images and material artifacts as data on consumption, at least in the US and in the *Journal of Consumer Research*. Here experimental consumer researchers tend to use visuals more commonly as experimental stimuli (Mitchell, 1986), while interpretivists tend to use them in elaborating interview responses (Heisley and Levy, 1991a; Wallendorf and Belk, 1987) and illustrating findings (Peñaloza, 2001; Belk, Sherry and Wallendorf, 1988). Material studies have largely been centered on what consumers do with consumption artifacts, such as advertisements (Ritson and Elliott, 1999) and clothing (Thompson and Hirschman, 1995), rather than focus on the artifacts themselves (Schroeder, 2002; Scott, 1994). The predominant use of visual images and material artifacts in generating other forms of data or communicating results belies their potential contributions in generating theory with ethnographic consumer research.

The purposes of this chapter are twofold: (1) to discuss the properties and potential contributions of photographs and fieldnotes, and (2) to address ontological and epistemological challenges in using them to a greater degree in ethnographic consumer research. In highlighting the characteristics, strengths and weaknesses of fieldnotes and photographs, we draw from a range of literature combined with selections from our own ethnographic work and that of others. Our work features a range of consumption places, organizations and advertisements: a Latino marketplace, a city, a Niketown store, a western stock show and rodeo in the US, and ad agencies, multinational corporations and the rapidly changing urban landscape of Mumbai, India, to name a few.

We end by detailing the implications of a more visual approach for research in marketing. We call for research analyzing the nuances of place, the richly textured, sensory elements of bodily movement, and intricacies of researcher subjectivity in taking pictures and writing fieldnotes. In expanding upon recording, analyzing and interpreting activities that we playfully redesignate as *writing* pictures and *taking* fieldnotes, we challenge the dominance of word over deed, mind over body and subject over object that has resulted in a fetish of the narrative in contemporary consumer research. Taking a cue from the 'differences that make a difference' (Deetz, 1996), we imagine consumer research from the perspective of a more visual, material ethnography that restores a more balanced approach to consumption behavior.

Visualizing and materializing studies of consumption behavior
In making space for more visual and material approaches to the study of consumption behavior, it is useful first to review the place of less visual and material approaches. Consumer *behavior* is, after all, the name of our field, although this is easy to overlook in its current emphasis on consumer decision making, information processing and narrative that characterizes the literature.

Dominated by psychology and economics (Cochoy, 1998), our field has come to emphasize what people *say* over what they *do*. This is not surprising, given the more general tradition in western metaphysics that values the spoken word over its written forms and over nonverbal actions (Derrida, 1978). Consumers' reasoning and intentions are the building blocks forming a canon of motives, beliefs and attitudes – constructs one does not *see* – that explain consumption behavior. Yet even interpretive work shares with survey and experimental work the logic of science operationalized via consumer narratives. That is, researchers turn to consumers, recording diligently their responses to experiments, surveys and depth interviews to access their conscious will and, as importantly, maintain their agency, or so the story goes.

Or does it? As Deetz (1996) noted, remaining within the positivist paradigm inherently limits appreciation of alternative research approaches and stymies their critique of positivist work. Only by reversing the research gaze, by examining interpretive work on its terms, and by re-examining positivist work from the interpretive paradigm, can we make the 'differences that make a difference'.

Viewed from the dominant positivist research paradigm, visual and material ethnographic studies may be seen to fall short. A common concern is that the researcher's ability to capture consumer will and agency is compromised because s/he takes pictures and writes footnotes. This challenge is not insurmountable, as we will show in applying insights and directives from visual and material studies to ethnographic consumer research. Conversely, viewed from the tenets of the interpretive paradigm, experimental and survey work may be seen to fall short. Consumers' conscious will and agency merit consideration in designs that either disguise or refuse to mention the purpose of the study.

Researcher activity is inescapable. All research has limitations, and thus the pragmatic issue becomes leveraging its strengths and working with its limitations in advancing knowledge within our field. The limitations of work based primarily on what consumers say become even more problematic when the subject matter of interest concerns physical consumption environments, consumption objects and bodily aspects of consumer behavior. These are all critically important elements in advancing the study of consumer behavior. They are either ignored or not well dealt with in the consumer-mediated episteme, but fall well within the purview of visual and material cultural research approaches (Schroeder, 2002; Taylor, 1994; Miller and Tilley, 1996).

In the following we examine fieldnotes and photographs as form and mode of social representation (Rabinow, 1986). By form of social representation, we refer to their structural properties as a record of social phenomena; by mode of social representation, we refer to the dynamic research processes in which these records are utilized. All too often, detractors of the use of visuals and material data focus on its limitations, overlooking what it strives to accomplish, and masking those of their own data. We adapt the research objectives of detail, comprehensiveness, contextualization and transparency from visual/material studies in striving for a greater range of opportunities for study. We compare the roles of the researcher as author/photographer and his/her instruments of pen or keyboard/camera in the combined activities of observer, recorder and social contemplator/commenter in dealing with researcher constructions and selectivity.

As a record, photographs generally provide much more detailed observation, while fieldnotes combine the thoughts, feelings and reason of the researcher with what s/he observes in less detail. Given that the two records capture different aspects of consumption phenomena, we emphasize leveraging their strengths in tandem. Thus writing pictures and taking fieldnotes can extend the range and depth of ethnographic work to transcend dualities of subject/object and synchronic/diachronic perspectives by examining interconnections between subjects and objects and shifting attention back and forth from each across various sites and across time (Miller and Tilley, 1996).

Regarding attention to the process of research, fieldnotes and photographs differ markedly in the way they are written/taken and read/viewed. Sontag (1977) noted 30 years ago that photographs are presumed to be measures of veracity even as they are recognized to idealize in their way of seeing and in the substantive content they represent. Photographs both certify and refuse experience, she continued, describing how they communicate on the basis of a visual code, altering and enlarging 'notions of what is worth looking at and what we have a right to observe' (p. 3). As a part of culturally informed observation, photographs provide more detailed and complete physical records, enabling access to 'aspects of culture never successfully recorded by the scientist, although often caught by the artist' (Bateson and Mead, 1942, p. xi).

These qualities of veracity and idealized representation in what we take notice of and what we see in photographs are opportunities for consumer researchers. With prolonged, meticulous study of photographs, consumer researchers can become more conscious of our ways of seeing and how they affect our ways of thinking. In comparing photographs with elements of the social realities from which they are drawn, from others, and from the literature, we are better able to document, analyze and contextualize consumption venues, artifacts and phenomena, and to build theory.

In contrast, fieldnotes raise different issues of representation as a function of their use in recording events, impressions, and interpretations of consumers and their behavior. Because of the central, indeed formative, role that fieldnotes have played in ethnography in anthropology and sociology, their form, content, uses and confidentiality have come under greater scrutiny in these fields over the years (Sanjek, 1990). Fieldnotes can help us become more conscious in our thinking and more transparent in our writing as consumer researchers because they entail a record of what we hold to be going on in social life in regard to consumption behavior. The challenge here is separating our ways of thinking from those stemming from those whom we study and from the literature, all the while diligently tacking between the two in learning from the field.

Issues of representation diverge for fieldnotes and photographs as a research process as well, as the result of the ways in which each is understood to represent reality. Both fieldnotes and photographs are social representations constructed by researchers in learning about particular consumption phenomena. As such, among the most serious challenges in using fieldnotes and photographs are researchers' selective perception and intentionality (Collier and Collier, 1986; Harper, 1994). Rigor in taking fieldnotes and writing pictures requires that the researcher capture the range of phenomena in the field. As useful is becoming aware of his/her way of approaching, accessing and recording social phenomena to yield greater depth in representations.

Like Bateson and Mead (1942), we both have gained new insights through the use of photographs as forms of representation and as the means of data collection. In the first author's work with Mexican immigrants, for example, photographs of stacked grocery carts stimulated further inquiry into shared uses of automobiles by several families within particular dwellings and in neighborhoods (Peñaloza, 1994). Similarly, photographs of adults twirling a rope at a western stock show and rodeo initiated further inquiry into the combination of play and didactic history lessons by adults and children, cityslickers and ranchers (Peñaloza, 2001).

In work by the second author, comparisons of pictures and fieldnotes in various social settings brought into stark relief dramatic disjunctures and differences in the ways Indian consumers are represented. Cayla (2003) tracked *consumer representations* (i.e., the symbols and language used in meetings and everyday talk to imagine consumers) in theorizing advertising and marketing managers' joint processes of learning about Indian consumers and developing marketing strategies. Consumer representations vary in authorship and may be found in many places, pointing to important theoretical issues regarding consumer subjectivity and agency: consumers representing themselves when using products and services to enact identities (Firat and Dholakia, 1998) and when asked to participate in consumer research (Applbaum, 1998, 2000); advertisers and marketers representing consumers in advertisements, in meetings, and in strategic discussions; and consumer researchers representing consumers in journal articles, conferences and classes.

Putting fieldnotes and visuals side by side allows ethnographers to follow consumer representations at different moments of the 'circuit of culture' (du Gay et al., 1997). For example, the second author placed pictures of consumers in the streets of Bombay next to fieldnotes about consumers in meetings between ad agencies and MNCs (Cayla, 2003). He then compared these representations to those on billboards, in magazines and on television. Instead of following the commodity and tracing the social life of things (Appadurai, 1986), this ethnographic project traces trajectories of consumer representations across various cultural intermediaries such as ad executives, marketing managers, consultants and academics, and across different moments in this process. Here photographs of Bombay street scenes displayed the large religious and social class heterogeneity of the city, while everyday talk in marketing organizations tended to suppress that heterogeneity and replace it with a prototypical middle-class Hindu representation that has become widely accepted in India, and thus hegemonic in its power to represent Indians.

Discussion

> If we think physically rather than metaphysically, if we think the mind–body split through the body, it becomes an image of shocking violence. (Jane Gallop, 1988)

In the previous section we suggested that photographs and fieldnotes can be used for much more than framing or illustrating the study. In thinking through them, we are able to situate consumers and consumption phenomena within their social times and spaces, and consider the ways in which we mediate both as consumer researcher(s). In this section we elaborate a few methodological points on the study of consumption venues, artifacts, bodily aspects of consumption and researcher reflexivity.

Consumption places

Further work is necessary to establish the importance of studying place in consumer research. Interpretive and non-interpretive researchers have worked in different ways to establish more socially embedded conventions of consumer research (Peñaloza, 2001; Frenzen and Davis, 1990). Interpretive work tends to emphasize consumption behavior as constituted within, and therefore inseparable from, its social and historical locations; non-interpretive work focuses on how the environment influences individual emotional states and, subsequently, consumption behavior (Lynch, 1982). Remnants of the view of place as an *influence on* consumption behavior (Belk, 1975) remain strong across both paradigms; the positivist tenets upon which it depends render consumers at worst passive or at best reactionary in their relation to space.

The currency of this view among interpretive researchers is illustrated in an often-repeated phrase: we do not study *consumption venues*, we study what consumers do *in* them. This distinction has proved useful in articulating the fascinating ways in which consumers use market spaces to forge cultural meanings related to identity (Miller et al., 1998), religion (Belk and O'Guinn, 1989), national history (Peñaloza, 2001) and nature (Arnould and Price, 1993), to name a few. Yet it is lamentable, in eclipsing the ways in which material places create people and cultural worlds, in facilitating and constraining who we are and who we can become (Miller and Tilley, 1996).

We argue for rephrasing this edict as follows: we study consumption venues *and* what consumers do in them. This we believe will yield greater knowledge and understanding of consumption places and the way consumers behave within them. An example is Creighton's (1992) study of products and services, layout and architecture in major Japanese department stores to document changes over time from domestic to foreign and back, and generating insights into the way shifts in national policy impinge upon consumption environments and, in turn, consumption and consumers.

In working towards more visual and material approaches to consumption places, it is important to consider individual and social levels of analysis and change. Sack's (1992) relational approach to place is especially helpful in going beyond an individual view to feature various groups at a place, with particular attention to relations between them and how they are situated there. In the same vein, Noschis's (1984) study of a neighborhood in Venice shows how service places such as the pub and shop serve a social function for the community and act as extensions of private space in the public domain.

Photographs of social scenes in pubs, malls and public squares help us elaborate social structure, cultural identity and psychological expression. Contrasting what people say with what they do is invaluable to overcoming limitations of social posturing and goes beyond primary symbolic functions to feature social interactions of consumers and tensions across their subject positions, in addressing who speaks to whom, when, where and from what position (Hodder, 1994).

Several consumer researchers have attempted to grasp social phenomena by attending to changes in places over time. Heisley and her colleagues (1991b) used observation and picture taking to analyze seasonal consumer behavior in a farmer's market. Other researchers have recorded practices of appropriation of place: bank clients hiding to avoid the gaze of the personnel (Aubert-Gamet, 1997) and vacationers appropriating space at a 'club hotel' by laying their towels on lounge chairs (Ladwein, 2002b). Importantly, this body of research looks at consumers as active producers of their experience of place and as constrained by it.

Consumption artifacts
Further work is also necessary to establish the importance of studying consumption artifacts. Material consumption artifacts include product logos, designs, packages, advertise-

ments and web sites, to name but a few. Probably because we have given emphasis to consumer *behavior* in our field, artifacts tend to be viewed as props to the main event, that is, what consumers *do* with them.

We suggest that the field would benefit from putting consumption artifacts more fully under the research gaze as ends in themselves, going well beyond content analyses (Kassarjian, 1977) to document their characteristic dimensions and properties. Dan Rose's work is a step in this direction. Rose (1995) elaborates a package of shampoo in detail, using a photograph to bring us along with him in reflecting upon using the contents in washing his hair. This type of work is more common in design studies, in familiarizing designers with past successful and unsuccessful prototypes in the product class under consideration and in related areas. For example, Salvador et al. (1999) describe the process of ethnographic design for kitchen utensils, going into detail regarding those used in an Italian kitchen in expanding upon conceptions of meals, mealtimes and family.

It is ironic that, in our effort to emulate the sciences, we have left off the important step of inventorying and cataloging. The field of consumer research can take lessons from anthropology and material culture in paying more attention to artifacts and building theory from the analysis of these artifacts. For example, Marcoux and Legoux's (2005) videography of souvenirs at Ground Zero draws keen insights regarding the trauma of terrorist attacks and their impacts on cultural memory and national identity by comparing them with artifacts at other tourist sites, and by contrasting the views and activities of various agents.

Material studies of consumption artifacts are more common in Europe, and scholars in the US can learn much, both theoretically and methodologically, from their work. For example, anthropologist Danny Miller (1987) provides a wealth of social theoretical grounding for material culture studies of consumption artifacts. His work with Tilley in the *Journal of Material Culture* (Miller and Tilley, 1996) outlines a number of valuable avenues for cutting-edge theoretical and epistemological work in developing taxonomies of objects and relating them to cultural categories and schemes of perception.

Bodily aspects of consumption

As troublesome as the focus of our field on narrative over behavior is the predominant focus on mind over body. We take inspiration from anthropological and feminist work examining bodily aspects of consumer behavior, arguing that constructs of the body are badly needed to complement those of the mind currently dominating our field. Early examples of anthropological studies of movement include E.B. Tylor's search for a universal 'gesture language' that could transcend cultures (1865), and Franz Boas's (1888) studies of dance as emotional and symbolic expression. Based on universal assumptions, this early work removed bodily movement from the very social and linguistic contexts so fundamental to its meanings. Acknowledging that the meanings of physical acts vary widely across cultures, and that movement is fundamental to social phenomena (Clifford, 1997), anthropologists have moved away from definitions of human movement as 'physical behavior'. Instead, subsequent work emphasizes people as embodied, meaning-making creatures, whose 'culturally and semantically laden actions are couched in indigenous models of organization and meaning' (Williams, 1982, p. 15).

In an insightful work by the same title, feminist Jane Gallop (1988) speaks of 'thinking through the body', in working to redeploy the focus on mental activities so common in the social sciences to a middle ground that better encompasses rich, sensorial, bodily experience. Gallop is concerned particularly with women's physicality in its relation to ways of seeing and knowing, and how it differs from stereotypically masculine episte-mologies emphasizing thought and reason. Consumer researchers Joy and Sherry (2003) stress links between embodiment and aesthetic experiences informing our logic about art. In doing so, they elaborate the affective and biological foundations of our social con-structions of reality.

What this suggests for consumer research is a more holistic approach to the body that studies dynamic, embodied action within structured semantic spaces. Also called for is work studying the body in movement, and recognizing that movement is a fundamen-tal characteristic of much consumption phenomena, in expanding consumer research beyond discourses of the body and bodily practices (e.g., Thompson and Hirschman, 1995). For example, the first author's study of Niketown (1999) employs visual and mater-ial cultural approaches in attending to the design, architecture and accoutrements of the market spectacle in relation to cultural meanings regarding the body. She generated insights regarding how the arrangement of detailed personal stories of athletes tran-scending physical and mental challenges, in combination with strikingly beautiful images, stimulate not just feeling but acting and thinking by consumers as they move through the place and relate personal stories of bodily shape, beauty and sexuality.

Regarding methodologies, this work would feature a range of participation and obser-vation, using fieldnotes and photographs to immerse researchers in the social setting in which consumer movements take place. For example, the first author used photographs in examining types of people and their patterns of movement and other activities at a western stock show and rodeo, and fieldnotes in reflecting upon what it felt like to be there (Peñaloza, 2001). While a very different topic and setting than Gallop's pregnancy, the stock show provided parallel challenges in moving across time, space and mind in analyz-ing how ranchers and cityslickers interacted with each other and with the various animals throughout the site. That is, reviewing the photographs ushered in a flood of memories of going to the Heart of Texas Fair and Rodeo as a kid growing up in central Texas, which she recorded in the fieldnotes, and from which she developed questions for further inter-views and field study regarding relations between humans and animals and the place of ranching in consumers' imagination regarding markets, national culture and memory.

Further, while some of this work on consumers' physical movement and sensorial activ-ities flows from an individual unit of analysis, other work is more social in nature, in studying interpersonal proxemics and relations. For example, Schroeder (2002) uses art and historical research conventions to study depictions of women and people of color in advertising. Methodologically, he compares structural features of subject matter, form, media, style, vantage point and depth of field across other art forms and across time, and situates the visuals within contemporary race and gender conventions and discourses to argue that including black and gay references in these ways does not normalize them, but rather contributes to their exoticization.

Researcher subjectivity
A final area of discussion is researcher subjectivity. Notably, not all interpretive researchers explicitly incorporate their subject position into their work. Perhaps this omission is due to a reluctance to undermine the authority of the researcher, or to a concern with potential

bias that is the legacy of positivist thought. If so, the recognition that all work is limited in perspective and scope may help shift the discussion from bias in the abstract, to developing a methodology of concrete steps that acknowledges one's own subject position and use it in considering more explicitly our relation to the topics and people we study (Foley, 2002). This is another important part of calibration, crucial in recognizing that the relatively upscale consumer groups and market settings which most consumer researchers study, and within which most consumer researchers reside, leave vast gaps from other nations and peoples in the US that we must deal with.

Building from previous elaboration of how fieldnotes and photographs can be used to render more conscious our ways of seeing and thinking, we suggest that both can be employed to a greater degree in doing more reflexive ethnographic consumer research and writing more reflexive ethnographic texts. First, photographs taken early in the research can be canvassed in bringing forward what we notice initially in consumption places, artifacts and consumers, and for consumption phenomena, as they tend to mark what is most different from our experience and our literature. In turn, using fieldnotes to work through and document where we were initially in our thinking and how it changes over time and in relation to extant theory is crucial in retaining points of difference so fundamental to building theory. Further, using the two in combination is vital in situating ourselves within the previously mentioned circuits of cultural production, from the particular social positions of our backgrounds, to field site and phenomena, and to academic discourses, as we collect and analyze our data and write our ethnographies. Integrating these activities into our writing more explicitly takes advantage of writing as a rich activity in building theory (Richardson, 1994). Finally, questions for further research may be mined in the gaps between our constructions of consumer representations in fieldnotes and articles, as they compare to the phenomena we draw from in developing them.

Conclusions
Consumer researchers deserve more than serving as mere reporters of social phenomena. It is our opportunity, dare we say obligation, to utilize to a greater extent all the tools at our disposal and unleash our full faculties of reason and imagination as we examine consumption places, objects, consumers and ourselves in writing and knowing each. While we do well in continuing to document what is, we can do so much better in suggesting what consumer behavior might be, and analyzing where it falls short and why.

In moving towards more visual and material studies of consumption, we must go beyond the fetish of the narrative as the ultimate measure of consumption behavior. While what consumers say and what they say they do remain important, we must work from the recognition that consumption narratives paradoxically are limited in accessing consumer subjectivity and agency as a function of social posturing, who we speak to and what we discuss, and relations between the researcher and the researched.

Our field needs to demystify the fetishism that equates narratives of consumption and consumer behavior. Eliciting reasons and intentions from consumers can only approximate an understanding of their behavior. Yet these measures reign supreme in our field. Behavior is what matters, and we can approach its study more strategically by broadening the field to include more studies of characteristic properties and dimensions of consumption settings (households, marketplaces, neighborhoods, cities) and consumption objects (e.g., brand logos, packaging, advertisements) as ends in themselves and as the means to better understanding patterns of consumers' use of them. Further, with more concerted use of fieldnotes and photographs, researchers can capture consumers' dynamic processes of bodily movement in places, and interactions with consumption objects and people over time.

We call for greater balance in incorporating photographs and fieldnotes with informant testimony in doing more reflexive ethnographic research and writing more reflexive ethnographic texts. Using the two in combination can render our research process more transparent by attending more explicitly to our ways of seeing and thinking as we construct consumer representations and write our ethnographies.

Work on reflexivity tends to be relegated to interpretive work and, while this is our main focus, because all research is interpreted, we suggest that it is just as relevant to positivist researchers. We can use developments from the use of photographs and fieldnotes in ethnographic work to draw in stark relief what often goes unexamined in experimental and survey work: researchers' selection of questions asked, their phrasing and the number of experimental designs reported versus those employed. Further, issues of selectivity and accuracy tend to be sidelined to matters of sampling and statistical significance, respectively. Positivist researchers can benefit from interpretivists' development of techniques to render more transparent the research process in working towards more explicit acknowledgment of researchers' views and assumptions regarding consumers, and incorporation of the perspectives and issues of those studied in the work.

Finally, we call for greater creativity in using photographs and fieldnotes in writing ethnographic texts about consumers and consumption. As an example, Taussig (1987) used montage to disrupt the imagery of the natural order reproduced in realist ethnographic accounts. By more explicitly incorporating the writing of our photos and taking of our fieldnotes, we can contribute to knowledge regarding marketplace sites, the things consumers do in them, and what researchers do as we learn about consumption behavior.

References

Applbaum, Kalman (1998), 'The sweetness of salvation: consumer marketing and the liberal–bourgeois theory of needs', *Current Anthropology*, **39** (3), 323–50.
—— (2000), 'Crossing borders: globalization as myth and charter in American transnational consumer marketing', *American Ethnologist*, **27** (2), 257–82.
Appadurai, Arjun (1986), *The Social Life of Things: Commodities in Cultural Perspective*, Cambridge: Cambridge University Press.
Arnould, Eric J. and Linda Price (1993), 'River magic: extraordinary experience and the extended service encounter', *Journal of Consumer Research*, **20** (June), 24–45.
Aubert-Gamet, V. (1997), 'Twisting servicescapes: diversion of the physical environment in a re-appropriation process', *International Journal of the Service Industry Management*, **8** (1), 26–41.
Bateson, Gregory and Margaret Mead (1942), *Balinese Character: A Photographic Analysis*, New York: New York Academy of Sciences.
Becker, Howard S. (ed.) (1981), *Exploring Society Photographically*, Chicago, IL: University of Chicago Press.
Belk, Russell, W. (1975), 'Situational variables and consumer behavior', *Journal of Consumer Research*, **2** (December), 157–64.
—— and Thomas O'Guinn (1989), 'Heaven on earth: consumption at heritage village', *Journal of Consumer Research*, **16** (September), 227–38.
——, John Sherry and Melanie Wallendorf (1988), 'A naturalist inquiry into buyer and seller behavior at a swap meet', *Journal of Consumer Research*, **14** (March), 449–70.
Boas, Franz (1888), 'On certain songs and dances of the Kwakiutl of British Columbia', *Journal of American Folklore*, **1**, 49–64.
Cayla, Julien (2003), 'A passage to India: an ethnographic study of the advertising agency's role in mediating the cultural learning and adaptation of multinational corporations', unpublished doctoral dissertation, University of Colorado.

Clifford, James (1997), *Routes: Travel and Translation in the Late Twentieth Century*, Cambridge, MA: Harvard University Press.

Cochoy, Franck (1998), 'Another discipline for the market economy: marketing as a performative knowledge and know-how for capitalism', in Michel Callon (ed.), *The Laws of the Markets*, Oxford: Blackwell, pp. 194–221.

Collier, John and Malcolm Collier (1986), *Visual Anthropology: Photography as a Research Method*, Albuquerque, NM: University of New Mexico Press.

Creighton, Millie (1992), 'The Depato: merchandising the west while selling Japaneseness', in Joseph Tobin (ed.), *ReMade in Japan*, New Haven, CT: Yale University Press, pp. 42–57.

Csaba, Fabian (1999), 'Designs of the retail entertainment complex. Marketing, space, and the mall of America', doctoral thesis, Syddansk Universitet.

Deetz, Stanley (1996), 'Describing differences in approaches to organization science: rethinking Burrell and Morgan and their legacy', *Organization Science*, **7** (2),190–207.

Derrida, Jacques (1978), *Writing and Difference*, Alan Bass, trans, Chicago: University of Chicago Press.

du Gay, Paul, Stuart Hall, Linda Janes, Hugh Mackay and Keith Negus (1997), *Doing Cultural Studies: The Story of the Sony Walkman*, London: Sage/The Open University.

Edwards, Elizabeth (ed.) (1992), *Anthropology and Photography: 1860–1920*, New Haven, CT: Yale University Press.

Firat, Fuak and Nikhilesh Dholakia (1998), Consuming People: From Political Economy to Theaters of Consumption, London: Routledge.

Floch, J.-M. (1989), 'Etes-vous arpenteur ou somnambule? L'élaboration d'une typologie comportementale des voyageurs du métro', *Sémiotique, Marketing et Communication*, Paris: PUF, pp. 19–48.

Foley, Douglas (2002), 'Critical ethnography: the reflexive turn', *Qualitative Studies in Education*, **15** (5), 469–90.

Frenzen, Jonathan K. and Harry L. Davis (1990), 'Purchasing behavior in embedded markets', *Journal of Consumer Research*, **17** (1), 1–12.

Gallop, Jane (1988), *Thinking Through the Body*, New York: Columbia University Press.

Geertz, Clifford (1973), *The Interpretation of Cultures*, New York: Basic Books.

Halle, David (1993), *Inside Culture: Art and Class in the American Home*, Chicago, IL: University of Chicago Press.

Harper, Douglas (1987), *Working Knowledge: Skill and Community in a Small Shop*, Chicago, IL: University of Chicago Press.

—— (1994), 'On the authority of the image: visual methods at the crossroads', in Norman Denzin and Yvonna Lincoln (eds), *Handbook of Qualitative Research*, Thousand Oaks, CA: Sage, pp. 403–12.

Heisley, Deborah and Sidney Levy (1991a), 'Autodriving: a photoelicitation technique', *Journal of Consumer Research*, **18** (December), 257–72.

——, Mary Ann McGrath and John F. Sherry (1991b), 'To everything there is a season: a photoessay of a farmers' market', *Journal of American Culture*, **14** (Fall), 53–79.

Hodder, Ian (1990), *Theory and Practice in Archeology*, London: Routledge.

—— (1994), 'The interpretation of documents and material culture', in Norman K. Denzin and Yvonna S. Lincoln (eds), *Handbook of Qualitative Research*, Thousand Oaks, CA: Sage, pp. 393–402.

Joy, Annamma and John Sherry (2003), 'Speaking of art as embodied imagination: a multi-sensory approach to understanding aesthetic experience', *Journal of Consumer Research*, **30** (2), 259–82.

Kassarjian, Harold (1977), 'Content analysis in consumer research', *Journal of Consumer Research*, **4** (June), 8–18.

Ladwein, Richard (2002a), 'Les modalités de l'appropriation de l'expérience de consommation: le cas du tourisme urbain', in E. Remy, I. Garubuau-Moussaoui, D. Desjeux and M. Filser (eds), *Sociétés, consommations et consommateurs*, Paris: L'Harmattan, pp. 85–98.

—— (2002b), 'Voyage à Tikidad: de l'accès à l'expérience de consommation', *Décisions Marketing*, **28** (Octobre–Décembre), 53–63.

Lynch, John (1982), 'On the external validity of experiments in consumer research', *Journal of Consumer Research*, **9** (December), 225–39.

MacDougall, David (1994), 'Whose story is it?', in Lucien Taylor (ed.), *Visualizing Theory*, New York: Routledge, pp. 27–36.

Marcoux, Jean-Sebastien and Renaud Legoux (2005), 'Selling tragedy: the commodification of Ground Zero', *European Association for Consumer Research*, Gothenburg, 15–18 June.

Miller, Daniel (1987), *Material Culture and Mass Consumption*, Oxford, New York: Basil Blackwell.

—— (2000), 'The fame of trinis: websites as traps', *Journal of Material Culture*, **5** (1), 5–24.

—— and Christopher Tilley (1996), 'Editorial', *Journal of Material Culture*, **1**, 5–14.

——, Peter Jackson, Nigel Thrift, Beverley Holbrook and Michael Rowlands (1998), *Shopping, Place, and Identity*, London: Routledge.

Mitchell, Andrew (1986), 'The effects of verbal and visual components of advertisements on brand attitudes and attitude toward the advertisement', *Journal of Consumer Research*, **13** (June), 12–24.

Noschis, Kaj (1984), *Signification Affective du Quartier*, Paris: Méridiens Klincksieck.
Peñaloza, Lisa (1994), 'Atravesando Fronteras/Border Crossings: A Critical Ethnographic Exploration of the Consumer Acculturation of Mexican Immigrants', *Journal of Consumer Research*, **21** (June), 32–54.
—— (1999), 'Just doing it: a visual ethnographic study of spectacular consumption behavior at Niketown', *Consumption, Markets, Culture*, **2** (4), 337–400.
—— (2001), 'The consumption of the American West: animating cultural meaning and memory at a stock show and rodeo', *Journal of Consumer Research*, **28** (December), 369–98.
Price, Sally and Richard Price (1992), *Equatoria*, London: Routledge.
Rabinow, Paul (1986), 'Representations are social facts: modernity and postmodernity in anthropology', in James Clifford and George Marcus (eds), *Writing Culture: The Poetics and Politics of Ethnography*, Berkeley: University of California Press, pp. 234–61.
Richardson, Laurel (1994), 'Writing: a method of inquiry', in Norman K. Denzin and Yvonna S. Lincoln (eds), *Handbook of Qualitative Research*, Thousand Oaks, CA: Sage, pp. 516–29.
Rieger, Jon (1996), 'Photographing social change', *Visual Sociology*, **11** (1), 5–49.
Ritson, Mark and Richard Elliott (1999), 'The social uses of advertising: an ethnographic study of adolescent advertising audiences', *Journal of Consumer Research*, **26** (December), 260–77.
Rose, Dan (1995), 'Active ingredients', in J.F. Sherry (ed.), *Contemporary Marketing and Consumer Behavior*, Thousand Oaks, CA: Sage, pp. 51–85.
Sack, Richard (1992), *Place, Modernity and the Consumer's World: A Relational Framework for Geographic Analysis*, Baltimore, MD: Johns Hopkins University Press.
Salvador, Tony, Genevieve Bell and Ken Anderson (1999), 'Design ethnography', *Design Management Journal*, **10** (Fall), 35–41.
Sanjek, Roger (ed.) (1990), *Fieldnotes: The Makings of Anthropology*, Ithaca, NY: Cornell University Press.
Schroeder, Jonathan (2002), 'Marketing identity, consumer difference', in J. Schroeder, *Visual Consumption*, London: Routledge, pp. 115–40.
Scott, Linda (1994), 'Images in advertising: the need for a theory of visual rhetoric', *Journal of Consumer Research*, **21** (September), 252–74.
Sontag, Susan (1977), *On Photography*, New York: The Noonday Press.
Spradley, James (1980), *Participant Observation*, New York: Holt, Rinehart and Winston.
Taussig, Michael (1987), *Shamanism, Colonialism, and the Wild Man: A Study in Terror and Healing*, Chicago, IL: University of Chicago Press.
Taylor, Lucien (ed.) (1994), *Visualizing Theory: Selected Essays from V.A.R. 1990–1994*, London: Routledge.
Thompson, Craig J. and Elizabeth Hirschman (1995), 'Understanding the socialized body: a poststructuralist analysis of consumers' self-conceptions, body images and self care practices', *Journal of Consumer Research*, **22** (September), 139–54.
Tilley, Christopher (1992), *Reading Material Culture*, Oxford: Basil Blackwell.
Tylor, Edward B. (1865), *Researches into the Early History of Mankind and the Development of Civilization*, London: Murray.
Wallendorf, Melanie and Russell Belk (1987), *Deep Meaning in Possessions: Qualitative Research from the Consumer Behavior Odyssey*, video, Cambridge, MA: Marketing Science Institute.
—— and Merrie Brucks (1993), 'Introspection in consumer research: implementation and implications', *Journal of Consumer Research*, **20** (December), 339–59.
Weinberger, Eliot (1994), 'The camera people', in Lucien Taylor (ed.), *Visualizing Theory*, New York: Routledge, pp. 3–26.
Williams, Drid (1982), 'Semasiology: a semantic anthropologist's view of human movements and actions', in David Parkin (ed.), *Semantic Anthropology*, London: Academic.

22 Metaphors, needs and new product ideation
Jeffrey F. Durgee and Manli Chen

Background
Marketers have been using metaphors for many years in marketing and marketing research in all three stages of the marketing process: need finding (Zaltman, 2003; Rapaille, 2001), new product idea generation (VanGundy, 1988; Cougar, 1995; Schon, 1979; Dahl and Moreau, 2002) and marketing actions including advertising (Mick and McQuarrie, 1999), product naming (Durgee and Stuart, 1987) and new product design (Dumas, 1994). In each phase, marketers, consumers and new product development people use metaphors to understand each other better, and they use them to see needs, new product concepts and other marketing actions from fresh perspectives, perspectives which help marketers and product developers conceive new variations on these needs and products.

Looking across the range of marketing activities, there is particular pressure for marketers of goods and services to answer the question, 'what's next?' Inevitably, they face a lot of pressure to come up with the next version or definition of that good or service that will fire consumer imagination and generate sales.

Consequently, in this chapter, we are concerned with the question of how marketers can creatively redefine or reconceive their offerings. We review the metaphor concept as well as literature dealing with the way market needs and metaphors are used to generate new product ideas. We also describe a series of exploratory projects aimed at improving the effectiveness of metaphor usage in new product ideation, in particular how needs might be incorporated more directly in the metaphor-seeking process.

Metaphors
Hunt and Menon (1995) define metaphor as 'a literally false, declarative assertion of existential equivalence that compares two concepts or things, where one concept, called the primary concept, is claimed to be another, the secondary concept' (p. 82). A metaphor depends upon the drawing of implications grounded in perceived analogies of structure between two subjects belonging to different domains (Black, 1962, 1979; Ortony, 1979), but it needs to be recognized that a metaphor also stretches beyond a declaration of similarity in order to be a heuristic device of value. As Bacharach (1989) describes it, 'the imagery contained in the metaphor must assist the theorist in deriving specific propositions and/or hypotheses about the phenomenon being studied' (p. 497). In order further to understand the role of metaphors and their significance in qualitative marketing research, Cornelissen (2003) argues that 'in drawing implications grounded in perceived analogies of structure between two subjects, belonging to different domains, a metaphor always implies a statement of similarity as well as a hypothesis of comparison between disparate concepts' (p. 209). When a metaphor is generated, similar attributes of phenomena, subjects or domains are actually identified to form an analogy (the implied simile), whereas dissimilar attributes of the referents are identified to produce semantic

anomaly (Mac Cormac, 1985). However, these dissimilar attributes, while being semantically anomalous or grammatically deviant when taken literally (Mac Cormac, 1985; Stern, 2000), might nevertheless provide fresh and previously nonexistent insights into the reality of marketing by offering a hypothesis of the dynamics and identity of a marketing phenomenon (Cornelissen, 2003). As Kaplan (1964) maintains, the use of analogies and metaphors to point out the awareness of resemblances serves 'the purpose of science', and it is his recognition of using metaphors that led to the increased attention in the marketing domain to the role of metaphor in theory and research (Hunt and Menon, 1995). After Nataraajan and Bagozzi (1999) reviewed the introduction of new metaphors and terms to understand marketing phenomena, they viewed them as plausible progress 'as new terms not only add to the existing explanatory power in marketing, but also revamp the discipline with a sense of excitement' (p. 634). Despite the increasing enthusiasm and attention for the potentials and development of metaphors within the marketing arena, Weick (1989) states that, with a few exceptions (Hunt and Menon, 1995; Zaltman, 1997), there has been little in the way of prescriptions or methods to aid theorists in being 'more deliberate in the formation of these images and more respectful of representations and efforts to improve them' (p. 517).

Nowadays, with the increasing recognition of significant usefulness of metaphors, we can see a lot more examples of metaphors in qualitative marketing research. In projective methods (see the Rook chapter in this volume), respondents are asked to describe some category A in terms of non-related categories B, C and D. In consumer research, categorization studies examine how consumers understand new product introductions by interpreting them in terms of categories of objects they already know (Moreau, Markman and Lehmann, 2001), and interpretive research uses metaphors to capture and explain consumer behaviors and lifestyles (Mick et al., 2004).

Good qualitative marketing research is research that is creative, that facilitates new, exciting understandings, theories and interpretations. Creativity is about banging two previously unrelated things together (Csikszentmihalyi, 1996) to bring new meanings into the world, so the study of metaphor fits perfectly with creative and qualitative marketing efforts.

Using metaphors in new product ideation

Designers and planners use metaphors in a variety of ways to come up with new product ideas. At one extreme are the approaches that involve totally random metaphors, trigger words or 'random objects' (Leith, 2004). A designer simply starts with the product category, takes a random word off of a trigger word list and asks, 'Would it be useful if X (the starting category) was more like Y (the trigger word)?' For instance, if the starting category was toothpaste, the designer might pull the word 'parachute' from the trigger word list, and then might start thinking of ways that soft fabric might be used to protect teeth. This is generally a good method for opening up the creative process to maximize creative possibilities.

More common methods (e.g., VanGundy, 1988; Cougar, 1995) are the ones that involve generating a list of objects, persons, situations or actions that are similar but unrelated to the starting category. If the starting category was vacuum cleaners and we want ideas for new vacuum cleaner products, for example, the list might include things like brooms, waste baskets, garbage disposals and fish that suck on pond bottoms. The designer then selects an individual item from this list, and breaks it into separate properties, anticipating that each property might suggest a way to redesign the original category. A garbage disposal unit, for example, breaks up garbage. Would it be helpful if the vacuum cleaner broke down dirt into smaller particles? The garbage disposal can also accommodate a lot of different food (and nonfood) items. Would it be useful to have a vacuum cleaner that could suck up a wide range of small and large things?

More interesting approaches tie metaphor usage more directly to consumer needs. Michalko (1991), for instance, suggests phrasing the starting problem as a challenge, then using a key word in the challenge to help search among 'parallel worlds'. If the challenge is to 'make a vacuum cleaner quieter', the key word or need might be 'quiet'. Michalko provides a list of 150 parallel worlds; for example, biology, library, cemetery, finance, flying, cartoons, fishing, Germany, calculus, ballet and grocery stores. The researcher scans through the list of worlds, and selects four or five that relate to the 'key' word above. Suppose, for example, the parallel worlds included ballet, library and cemetery. Next, the researcher examines each of the parallel worlds individually for properties which might apply to the starting category. The next task is to scan one of these for all of its properties, which might suggest improvements to vacuum cleaners. Thus ballet dancers dance on padded feet. Would vacuum cleaners be quieter if they had padded wheels? Ballet is also all about movement. Could the movement of the vacuum cleaner be designed in a way so that it is more efficient and needs less time – and therefore makes noise for a shorter time period?

Schon (1979) argues that, in the case of generative metaphors, designers start with a product design problem then suddenly see a metaphor for it which suggests new product ideas. He claims that, in these cases, product planners are not focusing on relevant needs but rather on sudden epiphany-like similarities they see between the starter object and some metaphor. One example he describes is a story about some product developers who wanted to redesign a new paint brush, which had synthetic bristles. As it turned out, the bristles would not bend and would not spread the paint like a regular brush. Apparently one of the designers suddenly said 'a paint brush is sort of like a pump'. This led the team to look for pump-like attributes in paintbrushes, and they reasoned that the channels between the bristles can act as channels to carry paint if the bristles would 'pump' the paint. In short, Schon argues that, when developers have a problem, they should look for a metaphor which directs their attention to new design ideas. They start with the problem, come up with a metaphor, and *then* see the connecting attributes or needs.

Dahl and Moreau (2002) conducted an interesting study in which they used two samples of student designers to understand the use of metaphors to create new car-based products, which would make it possible for people to eat while driving. The first sample was specifically instructed to use metaphors, the second, standard brainstorming. Note that, although the metaphor group was told to use metaphors – and that the new product should meet certain criteria, including 'practical and effective, safe, reusable, portable, and easy to assemble and use' – respondents were given no specific instructions on how to use metaphors in new product ideation. In one wave of the tests, samples were enjoined to use 'far' metaphors (seemingly unrelated to the starting category, as car is to truck, as opposed to car is to monkey), but received few step-by-step directions in terms of using metaphors in the ideation sequence. The resulting ideas were rated in terms of originality by a panel of three design experts and were rated in terms of product value by a panel of consumers. (Value was judged in terms of how much money these consumers said they would spend on the product.) Product ideas from the metaphor group scored significantly higher than those from the brainstorm group in terms of originality and product value. Also originality bore a statistically significant relationship to product value. The use of far analogies was statistically related to originality and value.

Needs and metaphors in new product ideation
While all of these approaches have value, we most agree with Michalko (1991). Like Michalko, we suggest that needs should play more of an initiator role in the new product ideation process. To augment the strengths of metaphorical approaches in new product ideation, it should be possible to use customer needs 'up front' to facilitate the metaphor-seeking process.

Usually needs are well-known for most categories, and research and development people work on developing new technologies which address those needs. There is a general need for everything to be faster today, for example, so microwave technology provided a huge leap forward for the kitchen ovens category. Other common needs today are for products to be more personal, more environmentally sensitive, more powerful, more mobile and more convenient (e.g. SUVs/hybrid cars, GPS, PCs/laptops, MP3 players 'iPod', sub-zero refrigerators, customized gifts, 'Things Remembered' [notes to oneself] and mobile phones etc.).

Often needs have pointed to metaphors which shaped the development of the new technologies (Crawford and Di Benedetto, 2000; Cougar, 1995; Gordon, 1961; Goel, 1997). Most people know the story about the need for a better, easier fastener – and a researcher's problem with burrs on his clothes on coming out of a field – leading to the idea of Velcro.

There are many examples of the way needs and metaphors might have been used over the years to come up with many products that we take for granted today. For example, imagine that it was 50 years ago, and we were looking for new offerings in a range of categories including retail banking, potato chips and bicycles. The first step would be to ask consumers for properties that they would like to see in these categories. These properties would include top-of-mind ones such as lower interest rates from the bank, and great taste for the potato chips. It might also include secondary needs such as neatness for the chips.

Then, if we find metaphors which have those properties and combine the metaphors with the original categories, we would see how the new products might have come about. Just as Goldenberg, Mazursky and Solomon (1999) did, we can review a list of past new products and look for patterns which might explain how they may have been conceived. We identify a popular product or product design and think of how a combination of needs and metaphors might have been used to conceive it.

In Table 22.1, for example, a metaphor which represents accessibility is the vending machine. If it was 40 years ago, and we combined retail banking with vending machines, we conceived the ATM. If it was 40 years ago, and we combined potato chips with the neatly stacked Ritz crackers, we conceived Pringles potato chips.

In Table 22.1, note in the 'Need' column that most of the needs are focused on ease, convenience and accessibility. As indicated above, these seem to be driving a lot of new product development in many categories. Even today it is possible to see the evolution of current new products in terms of desired attributes and metaphors. In the automotive industry, for example, tire manufacturers (and car companies) are searching for ways to make tires and wheels much more stylish. Stylishness and appearance have become much more important car buyer wants in general (Nesbitt, 2002). Thus one tire company

Table 22.1   How metaphors and consumer wants might have been used to create many of today's products?

Product category	Need	Metaphor	New product idea
Retail Banking	*accessibility*	*vending machine*	*ATM*
Guitar	louder	amplified voice	electric guitar
Videos	accessibility	library	video library
Phone	go anywhere	walkie talkie	cell phone
Potato chips	*neater*	*Ritz crackers*	*Pringles*
Bicycle	go anywhere	dirt bike motorcycle	off-road bike
Diapers	easier to use	band aids	Pampers
Coffee	easy, fast to make	powdered milk	Instant coffee
Car	carry more	truck, van	mini-van
Bandage	stick to wound	Scotch tape	band aids
Black and white TV	color	colorized movies	color TV
Motorboat	personal	snowmobile	jet ski
TV news	more available	round clock radio	CNN

seeking stylishness has chosen the metaphor of running shoes, and is introducing a co-branded line, which will be called the Nike Tire Line.

Also note in Table 22.1 that the metaphors that seem close to the category of interest are 'close' metaphors. A generative metaphor which might have been used to redevelop the phone (and invented the cell phone) might have been the walkie-talkie. A metaphor which might have been used to redevelop the potato chip (into Pringles) might have been the Ritz cracker.

Given the importance of needs in the metaphor-seeking process in new product ideation, how could this process occur?

The needs–metaphor–ideation process
Needs or wants can be gathered by any number of research approaches, such as focus groups, depth interviews, adjective checklists or ethnographic research. Many of the chapters in this book describe methods for identifying both overt and latent needs and opportunities. The next step is to find metaphors which address those needs.

Metaphors come from brainstorming or lists of words in a thesaurus, or lists in books like *Word Menu* by Glazier (1992) or the list of 'parallel worlds' of Michalko (1991). The *Word Menu* book contains lists of thousands of items in different categories: arts, nature, cooking, sports, home goods, etc. Jensen (1978) claims that most metaphors used in new product ideation fall into one of five categories: restoration, journey, unification, creation or nature. Restoration involves examples such as cleaning, medical (such as reconstructive surgery) or theft. Journeys are about barriers or clogged channels. Unification is about teams, home or family. Creational metaphors fall into areas such as edifice, fabric or music. And nature metaphors involve biological items, light or darkness.

In addition to brainstorming and books, another good source of metaphors consists of some new computer programs. For example, IdeaFisher is a powerful computerized brainstorming software package with a word-linking base to help generate creative ideas and business solutions. It was also developed to help designers come up with many interesting metaphors. In this dynamic system, each word and phrase is included for its relevance to a topic and for its power to trigger associations. With IdeaFisher, the user types in the desired adjective or attribute, and IdeaFisher extracts a list of words and phrases called Key Concepts that have the property for the user. 'From the Key Concepts, the user then selects those ideas, which he/she likes the most or which seem to have the greatest potentials. The ultimate goal of the questions and idea associations is to trigger new perspectives and spark new ideas in a person's mind.'[1]

An exploratory study

Phase one
To assess the needs-metaphor approach, we decided to try it in a small-scale new product ideation project with two groups of university marketing and design students. The students worked in teams of two. All students were asked to come up with new ideas for 'a new shower or bathing product for the home'. All teams were given 30 minutes to complete the project.

The first group, which consisted of 34 students, was asked simply to brainstorm and submit two of their best ideas. The second group, which consisted of 32 students, was asked first to list at least 10 needs, which the bathing/shower experience might address. After they wrote these needs down, they were instructed to think up metaphors for each need or property. This last group of students was then asked to look at the metaphors and use them to come up with their new product ideas and submit their best two ideas.

Results
This research has many obvious flaws and was just an attempt to get some initial experience in the metaphor research area. There was no way to control how hard each team worked, and more work needs to be done to develop more thorough instructions for the metaphor teams.

The list of the brainstorm ideas is shown below in Table 22.2. There were only 19 ideas because many of the ideas were duplicates of other team ideas. The list of ideas submitted by teams using metaphors is in Table 22.3. This group submitted 29 unduplicated ideas in total. The needs that the metaphor students came up with for bathing products were not particularly creative or unusual (Table 22.3). A lot of the bathing needs that they generated were to bathe faster, to feel relaxed and be more comfortable. A few felt that bathing should be more 'multi-purpose', 'entertaining' and 'exciting'.

Some of the connections between category, need and metaphor were rather direct. A team that wanted showering to be more productive, like a PDA (Personal Digital Assistant), came up with the idea of a shower with a PDA. Other teams used more imagination. The team, for example, that wanted their bathing experience to be more satisfying said that they like the satisfying feeling a person gets after a good haircut, reasoning that a good haircut is easily seen and assessed. This led them to the idea of a cleanliness gauge for body and hair.

Next, all ideas from brainstorm and metaphor groups were mixed together in a long list, which was administered to a convenience sample of 37 male and female adults ages 22 to 55. These adults were asked to rate the ideas in terms of originality, from 1, which reflected the lowest originality, to 7, the highest originality.

Table 22.2   Ideas submitted by brainstorm teams and their ratings in terms of originality and unwillingness to give up

Idea	Originality	Unwillingness to give up
Controlled temperature/Memory temperature for bath/shower water	3.3	5.2
Water pressure control shower	3.5	5.1
Heated tub	3.5	4.5
Air filtration removes condensation from air	3.8	4.4
Vent built into shower to take steam away	3.8	4.4
Special feet washer in shower	5.2	4.1
Automatic soap-dispensing shower head	4.4	3.8
Soap foam available at the push of a bottom	3.1	3.8
Sensor shower: the shower head can sense where you are and moves with you	5.9	3.7
Lie down shower: lie on flat surface, and water jets and soap are sprayed on you	5.1	3.7
Sink in shower for shaving and brushing teeth	4.5	3.7
Automatic tub cleaner	4.9	3.4
Motion sensor; if no motion, shower stops	5.2	3.3
Antibacterial soap to use without water	2.9	3.1
Deodorant spray dispenser	4.4	3.0
Ultrasonic shower: uses no water	5.5	2.6
Shower brews coffee	4.9	2.2
Shower in the middle of a large empty room	3.7	2.1
Black light shower	4.5	1.7
Average rating	4.32	3.57

Note: The product ideas in Table 22.1 are arranged from the highest rating of 'unwillingness to give up' to the lowest rating of the category.

The sample was also asked to rate the items in terms of 'willingness to give them up after they had used them on a daily basis for six months'. The scores ranged from 1, which meant 'very willing to give up', to 7, which meant 'very unwilling to give up'. This latter question is important because many of the ideas sound at first bizarre, outside of the comfort zone of most consumers. Respondents tend to give low liking ratings to products that sound a little unusual or 'too original/unconventional' to them. So, instead of only evaluating the liking ratings in this study, we asked respondents to imagine that they used the item on a regular basis for six months and suddenly had to give it up. It was felt that this might give a more accurate sense of how attached they might become to these products, even if the initial impression about these ideas may not be very positive. A good example of a similar case would be, in the 1950s, if people were asked how they would like heating food by zapping it with radio waves: they would have thought the researcher was crazy. If they were asked how they would feel about using (and then losing) a new technology which heats their food in one-tenth the normal time (e.g. Microwave), they would probably say they had become quite attached to it and would not like to give it up.

As the above tables indicate, students in both groups came up with a wide range of interesting product ideas. Interestingly both groups of students came up with the idea of brewing

Table 22.3   Ideas submitted by metaphor teams including bathing needs, metaphors, and new product ideas as well as their ratings in terms of originality and unwillingness to give up

Need	Metaphor	New product idea	Originality	Unwillingness to give up
Fast	Steam cleaner	Push-button shower that releases relaxing steam jet	3.9	4.0
Exciting	Surfing	Wave pool in the bath tub	3.6	3.9
Multi-purpose	Microwave oven	Shower that washes body and clothes	4.9	3.8
Comfortable	Leather seat	Soft floor bath tub	4.7	3.6
Safer	Airbags	Airbags to protect seniors and children from slipping or falling	5.7	3.5
Fuzzy	Fleece blanket	Soft brushes spinning on wall shower	5.1	3.5
Relaxing	Being on beach	Heat lamp like being on a beach	3.7	3.5
Fast	Hair dryer	Blow dryer for body and hair	3.1	3.5
Easier	Massage	Mechanical arms to wash you	5.3	3.4
Timely/Informed	TV	TV in shower behind glass	4.0	3.4
Satisfying	Good haircut	Shower with cleanliness gauge for body and hair	5.7	3.3
Energy-free	Pedal generator	Walk-in-service conveyor to pump water for camps, if no pressure	5.2	3.3
Efficient	Oil change	Soap dispenser on long hose to soap various body parts	4.0	3.3
Musical	Concert	Surround sound music shower	3.5	3.2
Relaxed	Massage	Reclining lounge chair in shower	4.2	3.1
Pleasant	Spring meadow	Scented shower	4.6	2.8
Invigorating	Waterfall	Gushing sheet of water shower	4.2	2.8
Fun	Toys and games	Water games enticing kids to the tub	3.9	2.8
Lively	Circus	Water jets from floor, like water slides in an amusement park	3.3	2.8
Like swimming	Pool	Raised bathtub like a swimming pool	3.2	2.8
Exotic	Tropical island	Fish tank in bath walls, bath with fish	4.9	2.7
Clean	Fountain	Re-circulating water in bath	4.6	2.7
Helpful	PDA	PDA in shower for daily briefing	4.8	2.6
Modular	Train set	Mini-waterslide kit for children in bath	4.7	2.5
Relaxing	Hot tub	Coffee maker in shower	4.8	2.3
Touching & sense	Bubbles, foam	Bubble generator	3.7	2.3
Transparent	Aquarium	Large transparent aquarium-like tub	4.7	2.2
Entertaining	Club	Flashing lights and music, like disco	4.4	1.9

Table 22.3   (continued)

Need	Metaphor	New product idea	Originality	Unwillingness to give up
Colorful	Rainbow	Soap that changes color as you use it	4.4	1.9
Mobility		Sensor shower – shower head senses your location, moves with you	5.9	3.7
Average rating			4.57	3.14

coffee in the shower. Therefore this idea was actually tested twice for 'originality' and 'willingness to give up' and the ratings are very similar (4.9 v. 4.8 and 2.2 v. 2.3, respectively).

Some of the brainstormed ideas that gained high originality scores included a system to wash feet in the shower and a sensor that stops the shower if the bather stops moving. The top brainstormed ideas that received the highest ratings for originality included sensor shower (5.9), ultrasonic shower (5.5), special feet washer (5.2) and motion shower (5.2). Among the metaphor group, the ideas that got the highest originality scores included a shower with a cleanliness gauge for hair and body (5.7) and a system of airbags in the shower (5.7) to protect senior citizens and children from slipping and falling as well as the mechanical-hand body washer (5.3).

Among the brainstormed ideas the products that the respondents felt the most unwilling to give up were a control temperature for the shower water (5.2) and a device to adjust the water pressure in the shower (5.1). Respondents indicated generally low attachment to most of the metaphor-generated ideas, with the highest rating given to the idea of a steam cleaner that releases relaxing steam jets with a push of a button.

In order to further understand the ratings, we used a paired samples t-test to compare the respondents' evaluation of the originality of the ideas developed by the two teams. The result indicates that the ratings of the metaphor ideas (M = 4.46) were slightly higher than those of the brainstorm ideas (M = 4.27), as indicated by a significant t-test [t (36) = 2.02, $p < 0.05$]. In other words, the metaphor approach did not yield much stronger or more creative ideas in the eyes of the consumer respondents. They felt that the two sets of ideas were almost equally original, and that the brainstormed ideas would be a little harder to give up. A correlation test was also conducted and the result was not significant, with p = 0.185. Therefore, from this exploratory project, we would conclude that there is no significant association between 'originality of products' and consumers' 'unwillingness to give up the products'.

Phase two
Since the metaphor approach did not yield higher-scoring ideas in terms of respondents' willingness to give up the ideas than those of brainstorming, we turned back to the lists in Table 22.1 to try to understand why metaphors might have produced successful product concepts in these cases (e.g., retail banking plus metaphor of vending machine yields ATM) but not in ours. The needs looked similar to the needs our students listed. Needs in each case were quite standard needs for the respective product categories. Most needs

Table 22.4   Needs for bathing and showering products, associated metaphors and new product ideas as well as scores for idea creativity and unwillingness to give up

Need	Metaphor	New product idea	Originality	Unwillingness to give up
Fast	Car wash	Very strong warm air blower dries you instantly after shower	5.6	4.7
Helpful	Waterproof control panel in speedboat	In-shower waterproof control panel, so the bather can turn on coffee maker, news, curlers, TV, kitchen lights, toaster and other household items	5.2	4.2
Satisfying	Sauna	Sauna/shower combo unit. Sit for sauna while in the shower	4.2	3.7
Invigorating swimming	Water aerobics	Tub is deep enough for water aerobics	5.2	3.5
Exotic	Tropical island	Round tub is surrounded by bright alternating images of exotic beaches	5.2	2.5
Average rating			5.1	3.7

Note: The product ideas in Table 22.3 are arranged from the highest rating of 'unwillingness to give up' to the lowest rating of the category.

reflected general expectations that people have for these products, including being faster, easier, more accessible, more entertaining, satisfying and relaxing.

As indicated earlier, many researchers and planners (Dahl and Moreau, 2002; Michalko, 1991) suggest using distant metaphors. Dahl and Moreau argue that distant metaphors extend creative thinking farther, and inspire more creative ideas. This may be true, but the metaphors in Table 22.1 tend to be close metaphors. The progression of new products in a category seems to move in a stepping stone pattern, like a hiker hopping sideways and forward on stones scattered up a stream. The bicycle comes first, then the motorcycle and dirt bike (off-road motorcycle), which in turn inspires a sideways step ahead into the dirt bicycle. In short, it might be best to look for close metaphors for new product ideas' especially in the categories in which an incremental pattern seems to make better sense and be better received by consumers (e.g. products used on daily basis, kitchen appliances, bathing products or breakfast products etc.). It would be more difficult to convince people to change their habits dramatically and get used to something that is very different from what they normally use or do in their daily lives.

Hence we took several needs from the metaphor group, and identified close metaphors for bathing and showering (i.e. items relating to water, cleaning products and hygiene), and then came up with new product ideas ourselves (Table 22.4). We tested each idea among a sample of 10 men aged between 22 and 45 and nine women aged between 30 and 55, again for ratings of 'originality' and 'unwillingness to give up' for those ideas.

This time, the ideas were felt to be more creative, yet the scores for unwillingness to give up were not much higher than those of the brainstorming groups. The average score in this study for idea creativity was 5.1, which is higher than the results of the previous two groups. For the last group, however, the unwillingness to give up score was only 3.7.

Analysis and conclusion
These were quick, small studies and, as a result, have many design flaws. There were very few controls on sample design, for example, so this limits the appeal of many new and relatively radical concepts. After the surveys were administered, some people said that the idea of a round tub surrounded by tropical island scenery was very creative, but that they 'never take baths'. While water aerobics are popular with many women respondents, the male respondents could not be expected to be very excited about the idea of an aerobics tub.

At the same time, if we go back to the original list of new products and possible generative metaphors in Table 22.1, there might be some answers to the question why the concepts in Table 22.4 did not score as expected in terms of unwillingness to give up. Even though we used close metaphors we still did not get a high rating of unwillingness to give up.

The highest appeal in all tables seems to be associated with concepts which are based on needs that are strong and ongoing. Needs for an exotic bathing experience or for a satisfying sauna experience in Table 22.4 might simply not resonate with what consumers really need for a good bath or shower experience. The ideas may sound creative and fancy, but they may not be effective in addressing the 'necessary needs' for a bath/shower. On the other hand, after completing the surveys, many respondents said that they would really like the speed and convenience of the hot air blast and high speed dryer because they did not like the cumbersomeness and moldiness of towels and the time they have to spend in drying themselves. Another good example of the need for accessibility was the presumably strong need that drove the rapid acceptance of ATMs. Likewise, strong needs for practicality undoubtedly drove the rapid diffusion of the minivan.

In an earlier project, Durgee (in Just and Salvador, 2003) labeled these needs CNNs or 'Constant nagging needs'. Potato chips are always messy, so Pringles stackable chips were a brilliant innovation. Cloth diapers were a constant nuisance, so Pampers became widely popular. In the brainstormed ideas in Table 22.2, products that respondents were unwilling to give up were directed at common, ongoing problems with showers: changes in water pressure and water temperature, dealing with condensation and clouds of steam in the shower. In the metaphor groups (Table 22.3), concepts that scored the highest were based on metaphors which reflected needs for fast showers (steam cleaner and multi-purpose shower to wash both body and clothes), convenience and safety (protecting children and seniors from falls).

Metaphors can suggest novel solutions to consumer needs, but it is more likely that the needs themselves are what drive acceptance of new products and services. It is possible that, for given needs, a wide range of metaphors (and new product ideas which they inspired) might find favor with consumers. The main objective is that the needs driving the metaphors are truly significant.

Note
1. *IdeaFisher 6.0 Pro User's Guide*, 2003.

References

Bacharach, S.B. (1989), 'Organizational theories: some criteria for evaluation', *Academy of Management Review*, **14**, 496–515.

Black, Matthew (1962), *Models and Metaphors*, Ithaca, NY: Cornell University Press.

Black, Matthew (1979), 'More about Metaphor', in Andrew Ortony (ed.), *Metaphor and Thought*, Cambridge: Cambridge University Press, pp. 19–43.

Cornelissen, J.P. (2003), 'Metaphor as a method in the domain of marketing', *Psychology & Marketing*, **20** (3), 209–25.

Cougar, J. Daniel (1995), *Creative Problem Solving and Opportunity Finding*, New York: Boyd and Fraser.

Csikszentmihalyi, Mihaly (1996), *Creativity: Flow and the Psychology of Discovery and Invention*, New York: HarperCollins.

Dahl, D.W. and P. Moreau (2002), 'The influence and value of analogical thinking during new product ideation', *Journal of Marketing Research*, **34** (February), 47–60.

Dumas, A. (1994), 'Building totems: metaphor-making in product development', *Design Management Journal*, **5** (Winter), 71–82.

Durgee, J. and R. Stuart (1987), 'Advertising symbols and brand names that best represent key product meanings', *Journal of Consumer Marketing*, **4** (Summer), 15–24.

Glazier, Stephen (1992), *Word Menu*, New York: Random House.

Goldenberg, J., D. Mazursky and S. Solomon (1999), 'Toward identifying the inventive templates of new products: a channeled ideation approach', *Journal of Marketing Research*, **36** (May), 200–210.

Hunt, S.D. and A. Menon (1995), 'Metaphors and competitive advantages: evaluating the use of metaphors in theories of competitive strategy', *Journal of Business Research*, **33**, 81–90.

Jensen, J. (1978), 'A heuristic for the analysis of the nature and extent of a problem', *Journal of Creative Behavior*, **12**, 168–80.

Just, L.A. and R. Salvador (2003), 'Marketing meets design', *MSI Reports*, Issue One, Marketing Science Institute, Boston.

Kaplan, Abraham (1964), *The Conduct of Inquiry*, San Francisco, CA: Chandler.

Leith, Martin (2004), 'A taxonomy of idea generation methods', retrieved 23 June, 2005 (http://www.ideaflow.com/ideagen.htm).

MacCormac, Earl R. (1985), *A Cognitive Theory of Metaphor*, Cambridge, MA: MIT Press.

Michalko, Michael (1991), *Thinkertoys: A Handbook of Business Creativity for the 90s*, Berkeley, CA: Ten Speed Press.

Mick, D.G. and E. McQuarrie (1999), 'Visual rhetoric in advertising: text-interpretive, experimental, and reader-response analyses', *Journal of Consumer Research*, **26** (June), 37–54.

Mick, D.G., J. Cotte and S. Ratneshwar (2004), 'The times of their lives: phenomenological and metaphorical characteristics of consumer timestyles', *Journal of Consumer Research*, **31** (2), 333–45.

Moreau, C., A. Markman and D. Lehmann (2001), ' "What is it?" Categorization flexibility and consumers' responses to really new products', *Journal of Consumer Research*, **27** (March), 489–98.

Nataraajan, R. and R.P. Bagozzi (1999), 'The year 2000: looking back', *Psychology and Marketing*, **16**, 631–42.

Nesbitt, B. (2002), Conversation with Mr. Nesbitt, Chief of Design, General Motors.

Ortony, A. (1979), 'The role of similarity in similes and metaphors', in Andrew Ortony (ed.), *Metaphor and Thought*, Cambridge: Cambridge University Press, pp. 186–201.

Rapaille, Clotaire G. (2001), *7 Secrets of Marketing in a Multi-cultural World*, Provo, UT: Executive Excellence.

Schon, D. (1979), 'Generative metaphor: a perspective on problem-setting in social policy', in Andrew Ortony (ed.), *Metaphor and Thought*, Cambridge: Cambridge University Press, pp. 254–83.

Stern, Josef (2000), *Metaphor in Context*, Cambridge, MA: MIT Press.

VanGundy, A. (1988), *Techniques of Structured Problem Solving*, New York: Van Nostrand Reinhold.

Weick, K.E. (1989), 'Theory construction as disciplined imagination', *Academy of Management Review*, **14**, 516–31.

Zaltman, Gerald (1997), 'Rethinking market research: putting people back in', *Journal of Marketing Research*, **34**, 424–37.

Zaltman, Gerald (2003), *How Customers Think: Essential Insights into the Mind of the Market*, Boston, MA: Harvard Business School Press.

23 Critical visual analysis
Jonathan E. Schroeder

Marketing often relies on strong visual identity. Products and services are promoted via images, corporate image commands increasing attention and images of identity pulse through marketing communication, consumer households and mass media. Many battles of the brands take place in the visual domain. Furthermore, the Web mandates visualizing almost every aspect of corporate strategy, operations and communication, bringing visual issues into the mainstream of strategic thinking, and spurring research and thinking about perception and preference of visual displays.

Critical visual analysis offers researchers an interdisciplinary method for understanding and contextualizing images – crucial concerns, given the cultural centrality of vision. If marketing depends upon images, including brand images, corporate images, product images and images of identity, then research methods in marketing must be capable of addressing issues that such images signify. By connecting images to the cultural context of consumption, researchers gain a more thorough (yet never complete) understanding of how images embody and express cultural values and contradictions.

This chapter presents qualitative methods for researching images, including advertising images, websites, film and photographs. I draw on a theory of visual consumption to show how cultural codes and representational conventions inform contemporary marketing images, infusing them with visual, historical and rhetorical presence and power. To illustrate how theory informs critical visual methods, I invoke an analytical concept of *consuming difference* to describe a relational framework of contemporary branding campaigns. I discuss how marketing communication draws upon the *ideology of the group portrait* as a visual technique for representing identity. I treat advertising imagery in much the way an art historian treats pictures as I analyse illustrative examples through the classic art historical techniques of formal analysis, compare and contrast, and interpretation, framed within representation understood as a cultural practice.

Identity, and how it functions within visual consumption, is a key concern in my analysis. In discussing identity issues such as gender, race and sexual orientation, I open up consideration of the ways in which advertising functions as representation within the social contexts of cultural difference (Borgerson and Schroeder, 2002). I offer a short tutorial on the basic issues of criticism and then apply these to several iconic images. One such image, a CK One ad, photographed by Steven Meisel for Calvin Klein, that profoundly influenced recent advertising photography, illustrates how CK One draws upon several distinctive visual genres, including group portraiture and fashion photography. For example, group portraits, genealogically linked to the golden era of Dutch art, are a masculine genre: historically, men inhabited most portraits of groups such as guilds, corporate boards and sports teams. In contrast, fashion photography can be considered a feminine genre, more closely associated with images of women than men, although men dominate the scene behind the lens. By juxtaposing and superimposing these two gendered genres – the group portrait and the fashion photograph – the CK One image creates an androgynous atmosphere, subtly supporting its brand identity of genderless cologne. Thus genre delineation provides a powerful theoretical insight into the way CK One works as an image, a brand strategy and a visual icon.

This interdisciplinary analysis illuminates key tensions within the politics of representation, identity and marketing. Humanities provide theoretical tools to understand image genres, content and narrative, whereas social science affords methods for discussing context, effects and strategic implications (cf. Phillips and McQuarrie, 2004; Stern and Schroeder, 1994).

To be clear, the approach introduced here need not rely on 'structural' understandings of semiotics; rather, critical visual analysis remains open to consumer response and post-structural notions of image production and consumption (see Borgerson and Schroeder, 2005; Schroeder and Zwick, 2004). Questions appropriate to critical visual analysis include the following. How do images communicate strategically? How do images circulate in consumer culture? How do consumers understand advertising images? How do images relate to brand meaning? What does the World Wide Web mean for visual consumption? What are some ethical and social implications for the reliance on images in marketing communication?

Researching visual consumption
Visual representations in marketing can be considered sociopolitical artifacts, creating meaning within the circuit of culture beyond strategic intention, invoking a range of issues formerly reserved for the political sphere and widely circulating information about the social world. Cultural codes, ideological discourse, consumers' background knowledge and rhetorical processes have been cited as influences in branding and in consumers' relationships to advertising, brands and mass media. Consumers are seen to construct and perform identities and self-concepts, trying out new roles and creating their identity within, and in collaboration with, brand culture. Largely missing from these insights, however, is an awareness of basic cultural processes that affect contemporary brands, including historical context, ethical concerns and consumer response. In other words, neither managers nor consumers completely control branding processes: cultural codes constrain how brands work to produce meaning (see Holt, 2004; Schroeder and Salzer-Mörling, 2005).

Analytic categories for critical visual analysis
There are many ways to begin an analysis of a work of art, a photograph or an advertisement, but most critics agree that interpretation begins with description. Basic descriptive work requires articulation of form, subject matter, genre, medium, color, light, line, and size – the building blocks of images. Some art historical knowledge is helpful for identifying form and genre and making art historical comparisons. When working with photographs, for example, relevant descriptive variables include production qualities, the photographer's vantage point, focus and depth of field; each constitutes aesthetic, ideological and strategic choices (Barrett, 2005). The relationship between description and interpretation is intricate but, ideally, interpretations emerge from descriptive details. Researchers may also benefit from one of the many guides to visual methods (e.g., van Leeuwen and Jewitt, 2001), as well as related chapters in this volume. In the following section, I present key variables for critical visual analysis: description, subject matter, form, medium, style, genre and comparison.

Description

The first step in critical visual analysis is to describe the image, pointing out features contained within it, such as formal properties of composition, color, tone and contrast. This level of analysis will be most uniform among observers, varying in terms of visual knowledge, language and jargon. A basic descriptive technique involves placing the image within a genre, or type, largely dependent upon subject and medium. Genre categories are not wholly separate, and it is often impossible to prevent interpretation from seeping into description (cf. Baxandall, 1987; Roskill, 1989). A key step concerns placing images within context. In this example, this involves a brief case study of the company's marketing communication strategy.

Calvin Klein's marketing campaigns have sparked controversy and comment for over 20 years (e.g., Churcher and Gaines, 1994; Lippert, 1996; Schroeder, 2002). Sensationalized sex appeal usually infuses Klein's ads, creating his company's fame and ensuing brand equity and generating media attention via what I call 'the strategic use of scandal' (Schroeder, 2000). Introduced by Calvin Klein in 1994, CK One is a fragrance marketed to both sexes. 'For a man or a woman', reads the ad copy, noteworthy within the fragrance product category that is closely linked with gender identity and sexual allure (see Figures 23.1 and 23.2). CK One is marketed through unusual channels, as well: it is sold in Tower Records music stores, packaged in an aluminium military-type water bottle. The jasmine, papaya and pineapple scented fragrance was a success and its ads became well known among teenagers and 'twenty-somethings'.

As an advertising exemplar, CK One provides a compelling image for critical visual analysis. The CK One ads seem to play on and subvert gender norms, and they have generated much attention and controversy (e.g., Schroeder, 2000). As an influential icon of 1990s visual culture, they have been cited, referenced and parodied by many other brands. The multi-million dollar CK One campaign was the first to garner the Fragrance Foundation's top awards in both men and women's fragrance categories (Campbell, 1995). Examples from the campaign were displayed in the Whitney Museum of American Art in New York as part of the art exhibition 'The Warhol Look' (Francis and King, 1997). Dozens of websites feature CK One images, versions of the ad are sold as posters and the original campaign remains a staple point of purchase display items in cosmetics counters (see, for example, Images de Parfum website, 2005). The trend-setting style of the 1990s CK One campaign has been carried throughout the brand's history; the 2005 relaunch mimics the original, casting 40 unknown models in a series of ads reminiscent of the 1994 image discussed here.

Like so many image-based ads, CK One ads make no mention of the product's physical attributes, but instead promote a highly abstract connection between the photographer's models and the brand (Stern and Schroeder, 1994). We are asked to transfer meaning from the identity of the people in the ad – their image, lifestyle and physical appearance – and the ad's visual style, onto the product. Therefore it is critical to understand how meaning is visually constructed in this ad.

Subject matter

A useful starting point for descriptive analysis is to identify and describe persons, objects, places or events in a photograph (Barrett, 2005). The CK One ad under scrutiny appeared across six pages in the September 1994 *Glamour* magazine. There are many versions of the

Figure 23.1   CK One advertisement, 1994 (2 covering pages of 6 page spread)

Figure 23.2   CK One advertisement, 1994 (overleaf foldout)

basic ad; all consist of a stark black and white image of several people standing, most facing the camera. In certain CK One images, several separate photographs seem to be joined together, resulting in a jarring, disjointed look that resembles a collage.

Kate Moss, the highly recognizable British supermodel, dominates the scene. She 'hails' us, the viewer, through her fame, her roles in other Calvin Klein ads, and her image as a white, heterosexual woman informed by her well-publicized romantic liaisons with male stars. She gives viewers a hook into the ad, providing a visual anchor, and guiding its interpretation (Berger, 1972). Moss's status overwhelms the other figures in the ad, making them supporting players in the icon-driven world of celebrity, glamour and global brand management.

However the physical appearance of the models contributes to the ad's character. As a group, they appear different, multicultural and not often seen (at the time) in major ad campaigns. In the version of the ad analysed here, the image folds out to reveal further CK One images. Closed, the ad pages are covered by a picture of Kate Moss and another white women facing each other, turned profile to the camera, gazing into each other's eyes. In the first image, Moss, hands in her back pocket, head thrown back, dressed in a black bra and black cutoff shorts, is grasped at the belt loops by the other women's fingers. This opens out to reveal the four pages of photographs depicting a small group of people against a white background. Upon unfolding this image, Moss no longer interacts with the other woman, who seems to have disappeared.

The models appear to be posed together, not really displaying characteristics of friends or a familiar group. At first glance, the models seem grungy, unkempt. All, except one woman, are wearing jeans, CK's undoubtedly; five of the men are bare-chested, two revealing their (Calvin Klein?) underwear. Excluding Kate Moss, the women are not particularly feminine in the traditional sense of being made-up, petite and well groomed. One black woman, in particular, has an angry expression on her face, and a group of two white men and a white woman seem to be engaged in a heated argument.

Form refers to the way the subject matter is presented. The CK One ad features stark black and white photographs of people who seemed – at the time – out of place in advertising's pantheon of perfect people. Skinheads mingle incongruously with tough-looking black women. Feminine men are posed next to Moss. Long-haired men appear next to a short-haired woman with large tattoos on her arm. The CK One image plays to several audiences, and appears to subvert visual advertising conventions while simultaneously reinforcing stereotypical concepts of identity, sexuality and difference.

An additional formal element is the 'centerfold' format of the ad; it swings open to reveal four photographs spread out over four magazine pages. This form resembles a *polyptych*, a work of art composed of four or more panels, often hinged together (West, 1996). Altarpieces are frequently polyptychs, and commonly open up to reveal hidden images of their sacred subjects. Renaissance altarpieces traditionally showed four saints, one for each panel of the polyptych. These panels open up to reveal an image of Christ, or the Madonna enthroned, and the particular saint associated with the church or parish. This altarpiece aspect gives the ad additional art historical resonance, and may contribute to the 'worship' of the CK One icons.

Medium refers to the material form of object or image: canvas, wood, paper, bronze and so forth. The medium of the CK One ad is a black and white photograph, specifically an advertising photograph that appears as a slick woman's magazine reproduction. The use of black and white film makes this image somewhat gritty in contrast to many of the glossy cosmetics advertisements of the era. The medium also imbues the image with fine art status: most art photographs are black and white. Black and white signifies a step toward signness; that is, it often makes the photograph look more like a photograph than a brilliant color image does. Black and white advertising photographs need something else to activate their rhetorical power – graphic devices, graphic signs or words (Triggs, 1995). The ad's copy – CK One in small type – is sufficient to remind viewers that this image speaks for Calvin Klein cologne.

Style 'indicates a resemblance among diverse art objects from an artist, movement, time period, or geographic location and is recognized by a characteristic handling of subject matter and formal elements' (Barrett, 2005, pp. 35–6). Well known advertising photographer Steven Meisel, known for singular, artistic portraits and routinely sampling other photographers' work (Daly and Wice, 1995), photographed the CK One ads in the style of photographer Richard Avedon. Like many Avedon photographs, Meisel's CK One image shows a plain white background that serves to decenter the subjects, decontextualize them and help to undefine the portrait. Avedon is arguably the world's most influential modern fashion photographer. Renowned for his stark, icon-making black and white portraits of the famous and not-so-famous, Avedon broke away from fashion poses in favour of more naturalistic shots of people moving about, gesticulating, talking and generally not appearing posed (Solomon, 1994). Moreover, Avedon photographed one of Calvin Klein's groundbreaking images, Brooke Shields breathlessly proclaiming that 'nothing comes between her and her Calvins' (see Schroeder, 2000).

The CK One image emulates Avedon's work, echoing his use of multiple shots of the same group (see Avedon, 2004). Specifically, the CK One ad quotes Avedon's famous 1960s photograph of Andy Warhol's factory crowd (Francis and King, 1997). This photograph of Warhol and various friends and assistants comprises four separate images placed together and appears strikingly similar to the CK One ad. Indeed Warhol was well known for his entourage of 'downtown' models, artists, and hangers-on, and the Factory came to represent a way of life outside the mainstream uptown world of established art galleries and museums. By photographing the CK One ad in the style of Avedon's Warhol gang photograph, Meisel superimposed one icon – Andy Warhol – onto another, CK One (see Schroeder, 1997, 2002).

Genre refers to a type or category. This step in critical visual analysis requires interdisciplinary sources, and often a good introductory book from a relevant field offers a useful start: for example, Sylvan Barnet's wonderfully informative *A Short Guide to Writing About Art* (2002). A key genre reference for the CK One ad concerns the group portrait, which became an established painting type in the Golden Age painting of Holland, when Dutch painters moved beyond pure description to idealize their subjects and to portray a glimpse of their personalities. Group portraiture of guild members was a particularly Dutch forte (Stokstad, 2004). A well-known example is the 'Dutch Masters' portrait that appears in packages and advertisements for a popular brand of cigars. The Dutch group portrait genre usually represented private guild commissions who wished to celebrate solidarity and good fortune. The basic requirement of group portraiture 'was to organize a number of portraits of equal individual distinction into a coherent whole. One solution was to portray the group in one single row, unevenly spaced and further differentiated by agitated gesticulation and a variety of different and occasionally *rather weird poses*'

(Fuchs, 1978, p. 95, my emphasis). The poses in the CK One ad are also oddly spaced: the group is lined up in a row; several pictures are placed together, producing an odd montage of bodies. One visual theorist offers a clue by arguing that the elements in an ad need to signal something different from a mere photograph: 'the disposition of each sign-value on the page must not be normal, rather, the positions must be other than ordinary, and be such that an interaction of their visual and conceptual aspect occurs' (Triggs, 1995, p. 86). Thus the CK One ad's rather weird poses directly contribute to the conceptual meaning: the consumers shown are 'different'; they use CK One.

From a critical visual analysis perspective, pictures of groups in ads 'are not random collections of persons but deliberate constructions of the significant relationships among them' (Brilliant, 1991, pp. 92–3). Group portraits, for all their seeming spontaneity, reflected and inscribed a strict social hierarchy, within the ideology of the group portrait (Schroeder, 2002). Dutch art is art of the here and now, anchored in daily actives of the middle class, preserving and recording the manners and mores of an entire society (Schama, 1988). For our purposes, a particularly relevant example of Dutch group portraiture is Cornelius Ketel's dramatic group composition *The Militia Company of Captain Dirck Jacobsz, Roosecrans*, c.1588, which hangs in Amsterdam's Riksmuseum, credited as the earliest known group portrait that depicts its subjects full length, rather than sitting down or in close-up (Rijksmuseum website, 2005) (see Figure 23.3). Comparable to the CK One ad, we see a jumbled group posing for a picture, arrayed in apparent random order, presenting a mixed social tableau. The men, in this case, are portrayed at odd angles, lacking uniformity, and bring a dynamic composition to what is largely a static image. Each man has an assigned place within the portrait, based on rank, favor and, often, payment to the artist (Schama, 1988). Guild membership unites the subjects: they represent a group linked by common membership in a militia company. As in most portraits, closer inspection reveals a mannered series of poses, calculated and scripted for a particular effect.

I find these two images, one from sixteenth-century Holland, the other from twentieth-century America, to be strikingly similar, disparate as they are in time, place and purpose. Each represents group identity through visual conventions. In the Dutch example, production constitutes membership: the guild produces something in common. In the CK One ad, consumption implies membership; we assume that the group shares use of the promoted fragrance. This is not to suggest that Calvin Klein (consciously or unconsciously) set out to imitate Ketel's painting, although CRK, their in-house ad agency, certainly knows something about Dutch art. Rather I suggest a resonance between the images (cf. McQuarrie and Mick, 1992) and point to an important antecedent in CK One's visual genealogy.

Art historical conventions influence contemporary images directly and indirectly: directly through their impact on pictorial conventions, artistic and photographic training, and cultural capital of specific images; indirectly through its power as a cultural process, that, over time, produces a mode of representing and seeing the world. CK One ads build on the visual past, reminding us of a tradition of artistic expression, and re-present images that are celebrated and valued (see Schroeder and Borgerson, 2002). For, in the Netherlands of the past, like today, 'the visual culture was central to the life of society. One might say that the eye was a central means of self-representation and visual experience a central mode of self-consciousness' (Alpers, 1984, p. xxv).

Figure 23.3 The Militia Company of Captain Dirck Jacobsz, Roosecrans, *c.1588, Cornelius Ketel, Rijksmuseum, Amsterdam*

Comparison: the rationale for comparison 'is to call attention to the unique features of something by holding it up against something similar but significantly different' (Barnet, 2002, p. 92). Several comparisons to the CK One ad will be made in the following section. The blank background group portrait motif recurs in Calvin Klein marketing, with the 2005 campaign strikingly similar to the iconic mid-1990s efforts (see Figure 23.4). Furthermore the group theme recurs in many contemporary ads, reminding us of the basic structure of social interaction, brand communities and representational conventions (Borgerson and Schroeder, 2005). For example, the Italian brand Dolce and Gabbana often groups like-minded consumers in their eye-catching campaigns (see Figure 23.5).

Interpretation and evaluation
Gender, race and class have emerged as three crucial contextual issues for interpretive work (e.g., Bloom, 1999; Borgerson and Schroeder, 2005; Schroeder and Borgerson, 2003). To formulate interpretive conclusions about the CK One ad's meanings, I turn to several cultural critics who write about identity and images, including sociologist Erving Goffman's brilliant work on gender advertisements, Henry Giroux's trenchant analyses of the pedagogical role of popular culture and bell hooks' critical perspective on race and class. I conclude by placing CK One within a frame of consuming difference.

Gender is a 'social concept referring to psychologically, sociologically or culturally rooted traits, attitudes, beliefs, and behavioral tendencies. Because gender is a filter through which individuals experience their social world, consumption activities are fundamentally gendered' (Bristor and Fischer, 1993, p. 519). Gender also marks a critical issue in art history and art criticism (e.g., Davis, 1996). Goffman turned to advertising to demonstrate how gender roles are inscribed in what appear to be natural expressions, situations and poses (Goffman, 1979; Lemert and Branaman, 1997).

Like painted portraits, ads are carefully constructed for rhetorical effects. Goffman argued that ads are part of the real world and a powerful influence on our self-concepts, how we view right and wrong, and how we conceive of living a good life, and how subjects perform gender (Goffman, 1979). Gender critically marks difference: 'gender . . . means knowledge about sexual difference. I use knowledge, following Foucault, to mean the understanding produced by cultures and societies of human relationships, in the case of those between men and women. Such knowledge is not absolute or true, but always relative' (Scott, 1988, p. 2). Goffman, in analysing advertisements, as well as social interaction, showed that 'every physical surround, every box for social gatherings, necessarily provides materials than can be used in the display of gender and the affirmation of gender identity' (Goffman, in Lemert and Branaman, 1997, p. 207).

Most fragrances and colognes are marketing to either men or women, as an integral part of gender identity and sexual attraction (cf. Stern and Schroeder, 1994). CK One seemed to deconstruct this connection: it is for both a man and a woman, after all. However, Calvin Klein's other well-known scents, such as Obsession, are still marketed to women *or* men, although a percentage of each is used by the non-target gender, and certainly have not been discontinued in a revelatory wake of recognition that fragrance could be gender-neutral. CK One remains well within the target marketed realm; it represents only one more market segment, which arguably does little to disrupt or question entrenched gender roles and gender segmentation.

Figure 23.4   CK One advertisement, 2005 (foldout from 4 page spread)

Figure 23.5   Dolce & Gabbana advertisement, 2004

Race: a crucial contextual issue concerns how racial identity has been depicted in the history of art as well as advertising. One might argue that CK One breaks down racial barriers via its multicultural milieu. A relevant comparison is Benetton's ads, which have also captured the attention of critics and consumers alike through their use of provocative, racially charged imagery. Indeed one commentator claims that, within the trend of shock advertising, the positioning of CK One resembles Benetton's graphic images of violence and social injustice (Teather, 1995). In one Benetton ad, a black female torso appears, breasts exposed, holding a naked white baby, nursing on the women's breast. The woman wears only a cardigan, unbuttoned and pulled back, displaying her breasts for the baby as well as the viewer.

Social historian and prolific cultural critic Henry Giroux exposed potential racist and colonialist meanings pulsing through this image (Giroux, 1994). Giroux argues that, whereas Benetton claims to be promoting racial harmony and world peace, by deploying this loaded image it ends up reinforcing racial prejudice. Perhaps the CK One images are not quite as alarming as the Benetton campaigns, but it may be that, by including images of marginalized segments of society, some of the same stereotyping processes are at work (see Borgerson and Schroeder, 2002; Ramamurthy, 2000).

A critical essay by cultural theorist bell hooks about CK One photographer Meisel's work provides a contextual comparison to illuminate CK One's racial and sexual stereotyping (hooks, 1994). hooks discusses the pop superstar Madonna's sensational book *Sex* (1992), which features photographs by Meisel. The photographs that accompanied writing about various eroticized scenarios – ostensibly directly from Madonna's imagination – have several features in common with CK One images. In many of the scenes, Madonna interacts with black men and women in images reminiscent of the CK One ad's racial mixing, although far more sexually explicit. The photographs are reproduced in crisp black and white, and many have a plain background. hooks' analysis of how Meisel's images work in the *Sex* book shows how consideration of matters beyond what photographs show contributes to an interpretive stance.

Class: Madonna, white, affluent, 'beautiful', experiences various sexual encounters, emerging unchanged, still Madonna. hooks writes: 'increasingly, Madonna occupies the space of the white cultural imperialist, talking on the mantle of the white colonial adventurer moving into the wilderness of black culture (gay and straight), of white gay subculture. Within these new and different realms of experience she never divests herself of white privilege. She maintains both the purity of her representation and her dominance' (1994, p. 20). Thus Madonna serves as a kind of tour guide through a Disneyland of difference, assuring mainstream viewers that their own identities are not at risk.

I believe Kate Moss serves the same tour guide function in the CK One series. Madonna consumes difference in her *Sex* pictures: she experiences black lovers, uses them, but remains unaffected by the experience, contends hooks. She does not become black, or lose white status; rather she serves as a guide for us, the viewer, to experience the stereotyped exotic erotic pleasures of an ethnic subculture. Steven Meisel's Madonna pictures inevitably exploit many clichés about blacks – oversexed, sexual experts, animal-like – and do nothing to assess, counter or interrogate these notions. These images may work to reproduce cultural differences: 'though *Sex* appears to be culturally diverse, people of color are strategically located, always and only in a subordinate position. Our images and culture appear always in a context that mirrors racist hierarchies. We are always present to white desire' (hooks, 1994, p. 21). Thus the rich white pop star Madonna consumes race and alternative sexuality, according to hooks.

Theoretical insights: consuming difference
In the CK One ad, Kate Moss serves as a visual anchor. Well-known, non-threatening (especially when compared to others in the ad), a famous supermodel, she represents the world of cosmetics, fashion and celebrity. Moss's expression indicates that she does not belong in this world of difference; she seems bored and unaffected by the others in the ad. She is with them but not of them, she emerges as a voyeur, she looks and asks that we look at her looking. I do not mean to imply that Kate Moss herself is somehow responsible for the ad's effects, the ad scenario or the cosmetics industry's practices. Men, largely, still retain control of the image-producing industries (Ohmann, 1996). However, as a spokesperson and icon of alternative fashion, her image contributes to much of CK One's meaning construction.

Moss, as supermodel, can fit in anywhere. She has entered this world of difference for a mainstream audience, and is able to maintain her identity in the midst of difference. Thus those normally outside the 'different' segment are given access to a world suggested by this ad, yet can feel safe and unchanged by the experience. They do not risk actually becoming different, racially, sexually or in a class hierarchy. It is unclear why white skin-heads, who are associated with intolerance in popular discourse, are lumped in with others, especially black women. What are they doing in this group, and why are they so angry? The lesbian-tinged image from the foldout disappears, along with the promise (threat) of homosexual activity. In the world of major brand advertising, gay and lesbian consumers are largely absent (until fairly recently), reflecting a culture of homophobia and heterosexism (see Borgerson, Isla, Schroeder and Thorssén, 2006; Frye, 1983). In the CK One ad, homosexuality is also sublimated to heterosexual pleasure, and becomes merely an exploration for Moss's (assumed heterosexual) experience. Her image usurps the others through her fame, her sexual identity (inscribed by her presence in Calvin Klein's more heterosexual-appearing advertisements) and her feminine demeanour, diminutive, thin and submissive. The image teases with a potential lesbian encounter, then retreats, leaving us unsatisfied, discontented. Moss's control over her body – demonstrated here in her aloof pose – is paramount to her fame and success.

In comparison to most advertisements of the mid-1990s, the world of CK One appears to be an unhappy place, populated by dissatisfied, angry people. In the words of one of my students, 'it looks like a freak show, as if the only thing these people have in common is that they look strange'. This echoes an art historian's claim about representations of difference in fine art: 'the rhetorical traditions of Western painting have long traded in the coin of social class and racial difference as a means of marking human value. Thus there is a radical distinction between portraits . . . and scenes from everyday life, especially those involving the lower social orders, representing not individuals, but types – simply "people" defined en masse' (Leppert, 1997, pp. 173). The CK One imagery signalled a shift in advertising representation toward grungy looking models – a short-lived trend, but one that paved the way for shock advertising and provides a visual vocabulary for contemporary brand repositioning campaigns such as Burberry's highly successful move into a hip market segment, via the use of Kate Moss and group portraits reminiscent of CK One images (see Figure 23.6).

Figure 23.6   Burberry advertisement, 2002

317

By using stereotyped models, CK One draws on cultural codes of appearance influenced by social relations, the media and prejudice (cf. Jhally, 1987). In a variation of the CK One ad, we see a big, burly white guy with a shaved head (coded 'skinhead') talking to a black woman. Given no other information to contradict cultural representations, we may assume that they are not having a lively conversation about a mutual friend. Within the media, 'skinhead' is a codeword for racist, neo-nazi and intolerance, iconographic functions rooted in representational practice. This is not to say that all white men with shaved heads are in fact racist, only that the overpowering image of the skinhead is associated with violent fanaticism. In the absence of disrupting information within the ad, the reading of this image may be overdetermined (Goldman, 1992). In addition, until recently, advertising showed very few individuals who looked like this. This fact accentuates his difference: he is pitted against traditional male models that populate fragrance ads. In showing these two figures engaged in what appears to be a heated discussion, the ad further draws on stereotyped conventions of race and gender. Imagine these two as lovers, smiling, arms draped around one another, or perhaps both laughing together, bodies engaged in mutual pleasure. These images *might* serve to disrupt stereotypical notions of gender, race and ideology. But this is not what is represented. Instead, we see a white skinhead arguing with a black woman, physically engaging with her space, using his mass to make his point. They are portrayed as natural antagonists, playing into cultural stereotypes of racial and gender relations (see Davis, 1981). Given the skinhead's large size, and aggressive in-your-face gesture grounded in the social reality of the historical and current oppression of black women, it is not difficult to interpret this image as racial oppression. Given the history of white men's exploitation of black women, for slave labor, for sex, for wet nurse, for nannies, the meaning of this image, contextualized within a racist world, must be read as reflecting, not challenging, the status quo (cf. Gordon, 1997).

Visual genealogy, critical analysis and research insights
Many insights emerge from critical visual analysis that would be difficult to generate with traditional social science approaches. Links to the tradition of fine art serve to remind us that advertisements have a visual and historical genealogy. For example, the CK One ad can be understood within the art genre of the portrait, particularly guild portraits associated with the 'Dutch masters', mainly a masculine tradition. The form of the ad is, of course, situated within the world of fashion, specifically fashion photography, which is largely a feminine realm; that is, women's fashion dominates the fashion scene. I argue that recognizing and analysing the juxtaposition of these gendered genres affords new insights to the representation – and commingling – of gender within the CK One ad.

Genre analysis produces generalizable insights into contemporary marketing images. Quoting or mimicking an art historical tradition helps ground it for the viewer, drawing associations to the visual tradition. By noting and investigating the links between a new image with an old tradition, we generate clues into the way CK One establishes itself through visual representations that transcend the here and now.

Drawing upon aspects of the group portrait contributed to understanding the perceptual categorization of people pictured within a frame as *belonging to a group*, or having something in common, what I call the ideology of the group portrait. In other words, there is nothing 'natural' that tells us that people who appear together in a frame share some essential identity characteristic. Rather we have built up this cultural association to the point where it now underlies perceptual and cognitive processes of group attribution: when we see people together in a picture, we assume that they belong to some group. So, in the CK One image, this perceptual effect contributes to the underlying assumption that the models pictured share something, their use of CK One. Once again, as sophisticated ad viewers, we should realize that they may or may not actually use the endorsed product, and that their group membership lasted only a day or two for the shoot. Thus engaging critical visual analysis reminds the viewer and researcher alike that the CK One group is constituted via their appearance in the image, and the group did not exist prior to or after the photographic session. In contrast, we assume that the Militia companies and guilds in Dutch portraits constituted a group before, during and after the portrait making. The CK One group is identified by *consumption*, the Dutch group by *production*, visually expressing a complex cultural transformation of the past several centuries.

Finally, critical visual analysis points out limitations in an information-processing model of consumption, one in which culture, history and style are attenuated. For example, the 'white space' of the CK One images – the studio backdrop – does not neatly fit into cognitive models; from a strictly 'decision making' or 'persuasion' perspective, this white space carries no 'information', it is 'lost' amidst persuasive or rhetorical devices. In contrast, critical visual analysis points out how white space imbues images with meaning. In other words, white space is not 'nothing', it helps to situate subjects within images, and its use links images to a broader cultural world of aesthetics, luxury and value.

Critical visual analysis points to the cultural and visual context of ads within the flow of mass culture, underscoring the powerful role marketing plays both in the political economy and in the constitution of consuming subjects. A key element of critical visual analysis often entails constructing a visual genealogy of contemporary images, to contextualize and historicize them, and point to the cultural domain of contemporary visual consumption (see Schroeder and Zwick, 2004). I have argued that CK One ads exemplify a spectacular combination of old and new representational systems. An important issue to consider is how the art historical antecedents and connections discussed affect viewers' perceptions. Most consumers are not necessarily visually literate, and art historical references and conventions may not consciously inform their viewing of an ad. Likewise, most language speakers have a limited awareness of the linguistic horizon that shapes their use of vocabulary, grammar and syntax; nor do they have a well developed sense of how language developed over time. However historical conventions shape communication. In this way, even if the target market for CK One has no experience of Dutch group portraiture, the representational conventions of portraiture, fashion and advertising photography impart influence on contemporary visual expression, and the art directors and photographers responsible for producing the ad certainly were aware of art historical referents discussed here. Furthermore the renewed popularity of Dutch Art, spurred by the success of books, exhibitions and films such as of *The Girl with the Pearl Earring*, demonstrate how Dutch images recirculate through culture.

Conclusion
The interactions of identity, consumption and image represent one of the critical imperatives of contemporary consumer culture. Critical visual analysis affords new perspectives for investigating specific cultural and historical references in contemporary images. Researchers can take advantage of useful tools developed in art history and cultural studies

to investigate the poetics and politics of images as a representational system. Constructing a visual genealogy of contemporary images helps illuminate how marketing acts as a representational system that produces meaning beyond the realm of the advertised product, service or brand, connecting images to broader cultural codes that help create meaning.

Acknowledgments

Thanks to Janet Borgerson, Laurie Meamber, Craig Thompson, Barbara Stern, Karin Becker, Tom O'Guinn and Elizabeth Milroy for comments and insights on this chapter, and to Russ Belk for supporting the visual turn in consumer research.

References

Alpers, Svetlana (1984), *The Art of Describing: Dutch Art in the Seventeenth Century*, Chicago: University of Chicago Press.
Avedon, Richard (2004), *Richard Avedon Portraits*, New York: Harry Abrams.
Barnet, Sylvan (2002), *A Short Guide to Writing About Art*, 7th edn, New York: Longman.
Barrett, Terry (2005), *Criticizing Photographs: An Introduction to Understanding Images*, New York: McGraw-Hill.
Baxandall, Michael (1987), *Patterns of Intention: On the Historical Explanation of Pictures*, New Haven, CT: Yale University Press.
Berger, John (1972), *Ways of Seeing*, London: Penguin/BBC.
Bloom, Lisa (1999), *With Other Eyes: Looking at Race and Gender in Visual Culture*, Bloomington: University of Minnesota Press.
Borgerson, Janet L. and Jonathan E. Schroeder (2002), 'Ethical issues of global marketing: avoiding bad faith in visual representation', *European Journal of Marketing*, **36** (5/6), 570–94.
—— and Jonathan E. Schroeder (2005), 'Identity in marketing communications: an ethics of visual representation', in Allan J. Kimmel (ed.), *Marketing Communication: New Approaches, Technologies, and Styles*, Oxford: Oxford University Press, pp. 256–77.
——, Britta Isla, Jonathan E. Schroeder and Erika Thorssén (2006), 'The representation of gay families in advertising: consumer responses to an emergent target group', in Karin M. Ekström and Helene Brembeck (eds), *European Advances in Consumer Research*, vol. 7, Duluth, MN: Association for Consumer Research.
Brilliant, Richard (1991), *Portraiture*, London: Reaktion.
Bristor, Julia M. and Eileen Fischer (1993), 'Feminist thought: implications for consumer research', *Journal of Consumer Research*, **19** (1), 518–36.
Campbell, Roy H. (1995), 'CK One takes top awards', *Houston Chronicle*, 29 June, Fashion Section, p. 8.
Churcher, Sharon and Steven S. Gaines (1994), *Obsession: The Lives and Times of Calvin Klein*, New York: Carol Publishing Group.
Clarke, Graham (1997), *The Photograph*, Oxford: Oxford University Press.
Daly, Steven and Nathaniel Wice (1995), *alt.culture: An A-to-Z Guide to the '90s – Underground, Online, and Over-the-counter*, New York: HarperPerennial.
Davis, Angela Y. (1981), *Women, Race and Class*, New York: Vintage.
Davis, Whitney (1996), 'Gender', in R.S. Nelson and R. Schiff (eds), *Critical Terms for Art History*, Chicago: University of Chicago Press, pp. 220–33.
Francis, Mark and Margery King (1997), *The Warhol Look: Glamour, Style, Fashion*, Boston: Bulfinch Press.
Frye, Marilyn (1983), *The Politics of Reality: Essays in Feminist Theory*, Freedom, CA: The Crossing Press.
Fuchs, R.H. (1978), *Dutch Painting*, London: Thames and Hudson.
Giroux, Henry A. (1994), *Disturbing Pleasures: Learning Popular Culture*, New York: Routledge.
Goffman, Erving (1979), *Gender Advertisements: Studies in the Anthropology of Visual Communication*, New York: Harper & Row.
Goldman, Robert (1992), *Reading Ads Socially*, New York: Routledge.
—— and Stephen Papson (1996), *Sign Wars: The Cluttered Landscape of Advertising*, New York: Guilford.
Gordon, Lewis R. (1997), *Her Majesty's Other Children: Sketches of Racism from a Neocolonial Age*, Lanham, MD: Rowman and Littlefield.
Hall, Stuart (ed.) (1997), *Representation: Cultural Representations and Signifying Practices*, London: Open University Press/Sage.
Holt, Douglas B. (2004), *How Brands Become Icons: The Principles of Cultural Branding*, Boston: Harvard Business School Press.
hooks, bell (1994), *Outlaw Culture: Resisting Representations*, New York: Routledge.
Images de Parfum website (2005) (http://imagesdeparfums.perso.wanadoo.fr/), accessed 2/10/05.

Jhally, Sut (1987), *The Codes of Advertising*, New York: St Martin's Press.
Lears, T. and J. Jackson (1994), *Fables of Abundance: A Cultural History of Advertising in America*, New York: Basic Books.
Lemert, Charles and Ann Branaman (eds) (1997), *The Goffman Reader*, Cambridge: Blackwell.
Leppert, Richard (1997), *Art and the Committed Eye: The Cultural Functions of Imagery*, Boulder, CO: Westview/HarperCollins.
Lippert, Barbara (1996), 'Sex: both sides now', *Adweek*, **37**, 18 March, pp. 26–8.
Madonna (1992), *Sex*, New York: Warner Books, photographs by Steven Meisel .
McQuarrie, Edward F. and David Glen Mick (1992), 'On resonance: a critical pluralistic inquiry into advertising rhetoric', *Journal of Consumer Research*, **19** (2), 180–97.
Ohmann, Richard (1996), *Selling Culture*, London: Verso.
Phillips, Barbara J. and Edward F. McQuarrie (2004), 'Beyond visual metaphor: a new typology of visual rhetoric in advertising', *Marketing Theory*, **4** (1/2), 111–34.
Ramamurthy, Anandi (2000), 'Constructions of illusion: photography and commodity culture', in Liz Wells (ed.), *Photography: A Critical Introduction*, London: Routledge, pp. 165–216.
Rijksmuseum website (2005), 'Company of Captain Roosecrans', available at http://www.rijksmuseum.nl, accessed 1/07/05.
Roskill, Mark (1989), *The Interpretation of Pictures*, Amherst: University of Massachusetts Press.
Schama, Simon (1988), *The Embarrassment of Riches: An Interpretation of Dutch Culture in the Golden Age*, Berkeley: University of California Press.
Schroeder, Jonathan E. (1997), 'Andy Warhol: consumer researcher', in Merrie Brucks and Deborah MacInnis (eds), *Advances in Consumer Research*, vol. 24, Provo, UT: Association for Consumer Research, pp. 476–82.
—— (1998), 'Consuming representation: a visual approach to consumer research', in Barbara B. Stern (ed.), *Representing Consumers: Voices, Views, and Visions*, London: Routledge, pp. 193–230.
—— (2000), 'Édouard Manet, Calvin Klein and the strategic use of scandal', in Stephen Brown and Anthony Patterson (eds), *Imagining Marketing: Art, Aesthetics, and the Avant-Garde*, London: Routledge, pp. 36–51.
—— (2002), *Visual Consumption*, London and New York: Routledge.
—— (2003), 'Visual methodologies and analysis', *Visual Anthropology*, **16** (1), 81–8.
—— and Janet L. Borgerson (1998), 'Marketing images of gender: a visual analysis', *Consumption Markets & Culture*, **2** (2), 161–201.
—— and Janet L. Borgerson (2002), 'Innovations in information technology: insights into consumer culture from Italian Renaissance Art', *Consumption, Markets and Culture*, **5** (2) 153–69.
—— and Janet L. Borgerson (2003), 'Dark desires: fetishism, ontology and representation in contemporary advertising', in Tom Reichert and Jacqueline Lambiase (eds), *Sex in Advertising: Perspectives on the Erotic Appeal*, Mahwah, NJ: Lawrence Erlbaum Associates, pp. 56–89.
—— and Miriam Salzer-Mörling (eds) (2005), *Brand Culture*, London: Routledge.
—— and Detlev Zwick (2004), 'Mirrors of masculinity: representation and identity in marketing communication', *Consumption Markets & Culture*, **7**, 21–52.
Scott, Joan Wallach (1988), *Gender and the Politics of History*, New York: Columbia University Press.
Solomon, Deborah (1994), 'A career behind the camera', *Wall Street Journal*, 25 March, p. 31.
Stern, Barbara B. and Jonathan E. Schroeder (1994), 'Interpretive methodology from art and literary criticism: a humanistic approach to advertising imagery', *European Journal of Marketing*, **28** (3), 114–32.
Stokstad, Marilyn (2004), *Art History*, Upper Saddle River, NJ: Prentice-Hall.
Sullivan, Robert (1995), 'Denim and desire', *Vogue* (US edn), November, pp. 166–70.
Teather, David (1995), 'Hidden gender: androgyny in advertising', *Marketing*, 30 November, p. 18.
Triggs, Edward (1995), 'Visual rhetoric and semiotics', in Teal Triggs (ed.), *Communicating Design: Essays in Visual Communication*, London: Batsford, pp. 81–6.
van Leeuwen, Theo and Carey Jewitt (eds) (2001), *Handbook of Visual Analysis*, London: Sage.
West, Shearer (ed.) (1996), *The Bulfinch Guide to Art History*, Boston: Bulfinch Press.

24 Framing the research and avoiding harm: representing the vulnerability of consumers

Stacey Menzel Baker and James W. Gentry

Researchers who work with qualitative data, like photographers, are instruments of data collection and at the center of the interpretive process (Patton, 1990). When a photographer prepares to take a picture, he/she examines the context through the camera's viewfinder and focuses on the subject so that the context does not overwhelm the desired theme of the photograph. If the picture is to document and preserve the story, the focal subject must be illuminated and viewers must regard the picture as a credible representation of the central theme. Similarly the way a researcher focuses on and experiences data has a profound impact on the story the data tell and the meaning readers derive from that story.

Like a photograph, documentary film or slice-of-life painting, the interpretation presented in the write-up of a contextual inquiry represents the perspective and creativity of the researcher who follows the conventions of the research paradigm or perspective within which he/she is working. Thus the researcher's bias limits data analysis and interpretation, as do the biases inherent in the audience to whom the story is presented (Joy, 1991; Sherry, 1991; Stern, 1998a). Specifically, a bias is a predisposition or preconceived notion about the way that research should be framed in terms of theory, paradigm, method or perspective. If a researcher's bias is recognized by readers, it may weigh heavily on the readers' willingness to accept research findings. If a researcher's bias is not recognized by readers, it may be because the research frame is deeply ingrained in academic and/or popular discourse.

Though this chapter focuses on interpretation of qualitative data, it is no less important to those who interpret quantitative data. When researchers interpret data, their job is to tell a story about why the data say what they say. This chapter addresses the importance of data framing and the potential impact of bias. We acknowledge that all research is biased, because all researchers have a predisposition to certain paradigms (positivist, critical) or perspectives (feminist, ethnic models). A concrete example of research on consumer vulnerability shows how critically important data framing is to avoid harming those people being researched. The chapter shows how projecting vulnerability when vulnerability does not exist is a data frame that may unintentionally cause harm by denigrating aspects of one's social identity (Baker, Gentry and Rittenburg, 2005). For instance, suggesting that all women or all people with disabilities are vulnerable all the time is a data frame that can impact the group of consumers being researched and the readers who perceive the interpretation as a representation of truth.

The chapter begins by discussing the concept of bias, including contrasting examples that help to illustrate how a researcher's frame of reference influences data interpretation. Next, the chapter sheds light on the process of data framing and potential harmful biases within the context of consumer vulnerability. The chapter concludes with some specific recommendations for data framing and for interpreting research related to consumers' vulnerabilities.

Bias
It is generally agreed that to make a claim of contribution researchers have to provide support for their claim or make a causal statement (Miles and Huberman, 1994). Support for a contribution claim is generally based within a set of theories upon which researchers draw. That is, all researchers have a predisposition to certain paradigms (positivist, post-positivist, constructivist, critical) or certain perspectives (feminist, ethnic models, cultural studies) (Denzin, 1994). Thus bias in framing and interpreting data is inevitable, with the interpretation representing a perspective, not absolute truth (Denzin, 1994; Hirschman and Holbrook, 1992; Patton, 1990). In fact, Denzin (1994, p. 507) suggests, 'All texts are biased, reflecting the play of class, gender, race, ethnicity, and culture, suggesting that so-called objective interpretations are impossible.'

Contrasting examples of data framing (bias)
Debates over paradigms or perspectives almost always focus on the bias inherent in the opposing camp. Though these debates often focus on method of data collection, they can also focus on how research questions are framed and how data are subsequently repre-sented (Joy, 1991; Stern, 1998a). Three brief examples emphasize how perspective influ-ences framing and data interpretation.

Disease versus health model in psychology In the last decade, a movement within the American Psychological Association has attempted to shift the focus from a disease model (psychology focused on what is wrong with people) to a health model (helping people develop what is right with them) (Ruark, 1999). Mainstream psychology for years examined constructs like anxiety, fear and selfishness (e.g., Festinger, 1965; Freud, 1938), then 'positive psychologists' began talking about what is right with people, focusing on constructs such as flow, creativity and happiness (e.g., Csikszentmihalyi, 1996, 1997; Seligman, 2002). The positive psychologists believe disease model researchers have repre-sented individual and societal ills instead of presenting evidence of 'the good life'. That is, positive psychologists suggest the qualities posed and addressed by disease model researchers are negatively framed and thus biased.

Medical versus social model in disabilities studies Traditionally studies in the disabilities field used the medical/disease model approach, which begins with the premise that an indi-vidual's mental or physical impairment makes participation in everyday life difficult, if not impossible. According to this perspective, if the person cannot be 'fixed', then isola-tion from society is likely (Johnston, 1996; Oliver, 1990). In contrast, the social model focuses on the limitations in society that restrict participation of people with disabilities. The social model views disability as socially constructed, resulting in part from a failure to provide appropriate services to meet adequately the needs of people with disabilities (Oliver, 1996). Social model researchers see the medical model as inherently biased in not recognizing that factors external to the individual can contribute to the isolation of people with disabilities. In both instances, researchers base their charge of bias on the way research questions are framed. Kaufman-Scarborough and Baker (2005) argue that both models are inherently biased, and develop an alternative consumer response model (adapted from Baker, Stephens and Hill, 2001), which takes both the characteristics of the individual and the environment into account.

Focal versus field   Research has shown that individuals have a tendency to orient them-selves toward, or process information from, only one part of the environment to the exclusion of others (Chun, 2005; Goldstone and Steyvers, 2001; Nosofsky, 1987). Thus selective attention involves differential cognitive processing (e.g. knowledge activation and inference) regarding different features of a stimulus event (see, Taylor and Fiske, 1978). Cognitive processing may focus either on figure or on ground: salient *focal* objects or the *field* where the objects occur.

Empirical research reveals consistent differences in processing across cultures. Several studies have found that East Asians tend to attend more to the field than European Americans, who are more likely to attend to a salient target object (Ishii, Reyes and Kitayama, 2003; Ji, Peng and Nisbett, 2000; Kitayama et al., 2003; Masuda and Nisbett, 2001). For example, when observing another person making a statement, North Americans automatically attend to the content of that statement. In contrast, Asians focus more on contextual factors, such as the tone of voice in which the statement was made (Ishii et al., 2003). Kitayama et al. (2003) showed that, whereas Americans are more capable than Japanese of ignoring contextual information (when a task requires them to do so), Japanese are more capable than Americans of incorporating contextual information (when that is required). In some Asian cultures, those with physical disabilities may be virtually shunned. An emphasis on field versus focal may facilitate such processes. Attending to only the focal aspects of a situation is a bias, but so too is attending to only the contextual aspects of a situation. That is, both perspectives are inherently biased and the perspective used affects the conclusions drawn.

Researchers are usually trained in or drift toward a perspective, such as one of those in the examples above. These perspectives are used to frame and interpret the data with which the researcher is working. Debates over the contrasting perspectives illustrate how research communities negotiate bias inherent in any perspective.

Bias in research on consumer vulnerability
Research seeks to classify, represent and evaluate social events and phenomena. In the process, some representations or perspectives are more dominant than others. For instance, the disease model has dominated psychology at least since the conclusion of World War II, when pragmatic concerns for treating mental illness became a growing social concern (Ruark, 1999). Researchers could easily get grants to pursue mental illness and the frenzy ensued for 50 years, until researchers, including Csikszentmihalyi and Seligman, looked critically at the way this perspective (bias) was affecting their field.

Many consumer researchers have been similarly motivated to study social problems. For instance, in the 1970s, customer satisfaction came to the forefront, Ralph Nader and other consumer activists exposed the failings of business and, in an effort to be useful and relevant to public policies, consumer researchers responded by examining the social consequences of marketing in a variety of contexts from within a variety of populations.

Andreasen's (1975) book, *The Disadvantaged Consumer*, stimulated research on the social consequences of marketing. His book stated three basic hypotheses: the problems disadvantaged consumers face are (1) largely attributable to their personal characteristics, (2) attributable to market structure and (3) attributable to unscrupulous business prac-tices. He further defined disadvantaged consumers as those 'who are particularly handi-capped in achieving adequate value for their consumer dollar in the urban marketplace because of their severely restricted incomes, their minority racial status, their old age, and/or their difficulties with the language' (ibid., p. 6). That is, disadvantaged consumers are 'disadvantaged' because of their personal characteristics. This perspective has been dominant in social marketing for many years, and often consumer disadvantage and consumer vulnerability have been treated as synonymous. For instance, Smith and Cooper-Martin (1997, p. 4) built on previous research to develop their definition of who vulnerable consumers are: 'those who are more susceptible to economic, physical, or psychological harm in, or as a result of, economic transactions because of characteristics that limit their ability to maximize their utility and well-being'.

Hill and Stamey (1990) helped to dispel the myth that the homeless are responsible for their existence, explored how structural and societal problems contributed to their existence and painted a picture of consumers as active agents in meeting their own needs. Consumer research, using qualitative methods conducted among the homeless (Hill, 1991; Hill and Stamey, 1990) and immigrant consumers (Peñaloza, 1994), research on feminist thought (Bristor and Fischer, 1993; Hirschman, 1993) and other qualitative research that also explored the life worlds of consumers in underrepresented groups *as they live it* has served as a catalyst for many researchers interested in social issues and the social consequences of marketing. The term 'consumer vulnerability' provides a unifying label for this body of work, but heretofore consumer researchers have lacked consensus on what this term means (Baker et al., 2005; Ringold, 1995; Smith and Cooper-Martin, 1997). This lack of consensus is most likely because researchers with different perspectives and different biases have been engaged in the dialogue.

Because of the lack of clarity, consumer vulnerability has been treated as a status, not a state (Baker et al., 2005). Consumer researchers and social marketers have primarily defined *who* is vulnerable, implying that some categories of people, because of their membership in a defined class, are always vulnerable (ibid.). Assuming that consumer vulnerability is a steady-state condition is a bias. What are the effects of defining classes of people as vulnerable? How has this perspective impacted the consumer research field? How does this view harm, or have the potential to harm, groups of consumers?

Creating harm
All people eventually experience vulnerability when they face the death of a loved one (Gentry et al., 1995a) or face other difficult experiences in their lives; thus defining vulnerability on the basis of *who* experiences it lacks clarity (Baker et al., 2005). Harm is created when groups are labeled as vulnerable. Vulnerable means liable to be injured or victimized, incompetent, incapable and weak. Thus when people in a group defined by race, disability, sex or any other classification variable are characterized as vulnerable, this characterization has the potential to denigrate aspects of individuals' social identities.

Much of the harm created has come from efforts to classify, sort and represent consumers into social categories. In striving for relevance and usefulness, tidy categories that represent market segments have been formed. All in all, the process of market segmentation may be one of the most beneficial strategic tools that the marketing field offers. Clearly all consumers are not the same. However, because of the way the information can be and has been interpreted, harm has come from the process of segmenting consumers according to demographic characteristics (race, age, gender, income). Demographic characteristics describe who engages in a behavior; they do not explain why they engage in a behavior. For example, when we take a complex phenomenon such as vulnerability and boil it down to a single dimension (i.e., who is vulnerable), harm may be created. In other words, readers' interpretations could be that entire classes of people are not capable of taking care of themselves so 'the privileged' need to take care of them.

Smith (1999) articulates some of the harm this sort of frame/bias creates. To indigenous peoples (groups regarded as part of the 'other'), the term 'research' brings bad memories and distrust because of a belief that their voices are silenced and a belief that the underlying meaning of most research is that people in indigenous groups are not fully human (i.e., not unique and competent individuals). The indigenous are blamed for failure and are told that failure is their fault.

Avoiding harm
Researchers (including ourselves) who have engaged in research which they thought would be labeled as investigating consumer vulnerability often express surprise when they do not find any vulnerability, or find that vulnerability is not associated with the expected variables. When researchers are engaged enough to get past prior beliefs and preconceptions, they exhibit *experiential knowing* (Reason, 1994) and they are able to avoid doing harm.

Experiential knowing requires that researchers be able to understand and articulate the point of view of those who live the behavior (ibid.). The understanding does not come from sympathy or even empathy (putting one's self in another's shoes); the understanding unfolds as one observes and begins to understand the symbolizing activities of the way people represent themselves (Geertz, 1983; Schwandt, 1994). As the researcher writes, he/she plays the role of a *bricoleur* who 'fashions meaning and interpretation out of ongoing experience' (Denzin, 1994, p. 501; see also Lévi-Strauss, 1966). In consumer research, the symbolizing activities are observed in consumer acquisition, consumption and disposition processes, processes which a consumer uses to define the self, both for one's self and for others (Belk, 1988).

People define themselves using their own variables of identification, not those ascribed to them (Baker, 2006; McCracken, 1986; Schouten and McAlexander, 1995). For example, Baker (2006) shows how, when consumers shop, they try on and affirm their identities by employing the characteristics they use in their own self-definition processes. However, when symbolic elements in the shopping environment indicate they should use alternative personal characteristics for self-definition, they feel unnatural and not normal. Baker's (2006) informants who have visual impairments see themselves as people with visual impairments, not people defined by visual impairments. When a person is labeled or evaluated as 'visually impaired' or 'disabled', then the person is viewed from a single perspective (Langer and Chanowitz, 1987). In reality, there are multiple layers to identities that allow the person to experience personal control (Langer, 2000; Smith, 1999). To avoid harm, researchers must discover the variables that consumers use in their own self-definition processes by exploring the 'activities, objects, and relationships that give their lives meaning . . . and substantiate their place in the social world' (Schouten and McAlexander, 1995, p. 59).

Listening to the voices
The majority of empirical research in marketing and consumer behavior has focused on able-bodied, middle-class Caucasian consumers (Baker et al., 2005). Researchers have

questioned the effect of the silenced voices (Denzin, 1994; Smith, 1999; Stern, 1998b), encouraged researchers 'to be more aware of, and articulate, the ways in which the questions asked and the research conducted promote the interests of some and ignore those of others' (Bristor and Fischer, 1996, p. 27) and highlighted the social consequences of portrayals (or lack thereof) of consumer groups in research studies (Hill, 1995). Researchers are increasingly becoming interested in sharing the stories of the consumers who have traditionally been absent from consumer studies.

Baker et al. (2005) provide a review of research on or related to consumer vulnerability and uncover three key themes in the research: (1) factors that increase the incidence of vulnerability, (2) the actual experience of vulnerability which is characterized by lack of control, and (3) consumer responses to vulnerability including coping mechanisms and impacts on the self. Internal characteristics, internal states and external conditions are all contributing factors that increase the likelihood of a consumer experiencing vulnerability (Baker et al., 2005). Individual characteristics including biophysical characteristics (e.g., addiction, age, appearance, functional ability, gender, health, race/ethnicity, sexual orientation) and psychosocial characteristics (e.g., cognitive capacity, cognitive development, felt ethnicity, education/learning, self-concept, socioeconomic status); individual states (e.g., grief, mobility, mood, life transitions, motivation and goals); and external factors beyond a person's immediate control (e.g., discrimination, repression, stigmatization, the distribution of resources, physical elements, logistical elements and other environmental conditions) contribute to the way a consumer experiences a consumption context and affect the likelihood of his/her experiencing vulnerability. For example, Peñaloza (1995) discovered that the vulnerability of her immigrant consumer informants is created because of low language ability, literacy and market experience and savvy, and because of their consumer aspirations; additionally, as immigrants, they are 'stigmatized, subordinated, and segregated' (p. 92).

The experience of vulnerability is ultimately an experience of loss of control. Consumption adds meaning to life when individuals can control the meaning (Belk, 1988), but when consumers are vulnerable, they are not in control of their life meanings. For example, when Appalachian poor consumers are treated as disempowered victims and unable to control their surroundings, they experience vulnerability (Lee, Ozanne and Hill, 1999). When women are faced with a choice of abortion, their biggest regret after the decision is finalized, regardless of the decision, has to do with capitulating to the wishes of others, i.e., not being able to make decisions for themselves (Patterson, Hill and Maloy, 1995). As well-meaning as most researchers are, there is danger in inferring vulnerability. Careful listening enlightens us as to when vulnerability is experienced and, just as important, as to when it is not.

Consumers do not just passively accept their circumstances; instead, they negotiate and fight for their identities. People who are homeless seek work in nontraditional ways, scavenge and share possessions with other members of the homeless community (Hill and Stamey, 1990). Consumers living in a racially segregated city do not just passively accept the economic, social and cultural forces that marginalize their existence. Instead, they develop political ideologies about what is acceptable and unacceptable, and in the process they form their own choices about where to shop and what to buy (Crockett and Wallendorf, 2004). Captives at Buchenwald concentration camp created their own hedonic, spiritual and intellectual consumption experiences to resist being 'consumed' by their captors and to help them maintain their sense of self (Hirschman and Hill, 2000). In other words, consumers do not just passively accept their vulnerability as an equilibrium condition, they fight to regain control.

When the voices of consumers who experience vulnerability are interpreted and their voices are heard, we discover that a multitude of factors contribute to vulnerability. Baker et al. (2005) define consumer vulnerability as a state of powerlessness arising from the consumption of marketing products and messages or an imbalance in marketplace interactions. This definition was developed from the lived experiences of informants documented in numerous studies in consumer research. Because it comes from informants' experiences, this definition does not focus on who is vulnerable; instead, it focuses on the experience of vulnerability which is multidimensional in nature (ibid.). Unfortunately all of us may face conditions where we are incapable of (or uninterested in) protecting ourselves from the occurrence of intentional or unintentional inequities in marketplace transactions.

Recommendations
Though there are many research studies that serve as notable exceptions, in general, consumer researchers have created a great deal of noise and confusion in explaining consumer behavior because people within consumer groups have been treated as though they were homogeneous. We know from our own experiences that we are not exactly like other people with our same demographic characteristics, so why have we been so persistent in creating these social categories? The answer seems to be that this view may have been deeply ingrained in our perspectives as researchers.

When the central construct of study is not a customer type, qualitative researchers should not be asked to explain how women are different from men, blacks are different from whites or people with disabilities are different from people without disabilities. Creating these dichotomies may be detrimental. A methodological characteristic of qualitative studies is that they are context-bound. In contextual inquiry, we can generalize the framework, but we cannot generalize the findings (Peñaloza, 1994; Schouten, 1991). When we deny that people within groups are different, we are denying their uniqueness and their self-determination (Smith, 1999). The question then becomes, what can we do about it?

For data collection
There is no a priori reason to assume vulnerability going into an interview. There are individual characteristics, individual states and external conditions that increase the likelihood of observing vulnerability (Baker et al., 2005). Just because any one or a combination of those factors is present does not mean a researcher will find vulnerability. All people experience vulnerability on occasions (Gentry et al., 1995a). Projecting vulnerability onto informants in all situations could be detrimental to their identity by ascribing to them a social stigma inherently wrought with lack of control (Baker et al., 2005).

For interpretation
In the interpretive process, it is the researcher's job to make sense of patterns in the data, apply insights and take interpretive leaps (Arnould and Wallendorf, 1994; Spiggle, 1994). In writing, 'researchers represent consumers by transforming data into a research narrative'

(Spiggle, 1998, p. 156). The framing of the problem is important; treating such things as homelessness, race, or disability as 'the problem' is a frame that harms people within consumer groups (Crockett and Wallendorf, 2004; Hill, 1995; Hill and Stamey, 1990; Lee et al., 1999; Smith, 1999).

Qualitative researchers conduct research *among* consumers, not *on* consumers (following Wolcott, 1990). When research is conducted *on* consumers, people are lumped into categories and not recognized for their uniqueness; they may not be recognized as fully human. When research is conducted *among* consumers, the tremendous variation of people, abilities, perceptions and needs within a subculture or social group is recognized (Bristor and Fischer, 1996; Smith, 1999). Because consumer researchers have spent time interviewing and observing people with disabilities and people who are homeless, we have begun to understand more about consumer vulnerability, but much of this research has been conducted *among* consumers, rather than *on* consumers. In other words, just because consumer vulnerability has been examined within the context of people with disabilities or homelessness, we cannot conclude that all people in these categories are the same and vulnerable all the time.

Exploring the vulnerability of consumers has helped illuminate important consumer phenomena including consumer ideologies and resistance (Crockett and Wallendorf, 2004; Hirschman and Hill, 2000; Kates and Belk, 2001; Peñaloza, 1995), consumer adaptation (Baker et al., 2001; Hill and Stamey, 1990; Lee et al., 1999), consumer transitions (Gentry et al., 1995a, 1995b), identity projects and transformations (Baker, 2006; Bonsu and Belk, 2003; Hill, 2001) and symbolic contamination (Stephens, Hill and Gentry, 2005). The development of these concepts exemplifies the value of contextual inquiry where a researcher studies a unique context and/or an underrepresented population. One caveat to contextual inquiry is that readers may walk away from it believing the study was about the unique context or understudied population (e.g., white-water rafting, consumers with visual impairments, or people in grief) and not about what these particular contexts or consumers have taught us about important consumer behavior concepts such as the extended service encounter, consumer independence, transition and so forth. Also, when the research is grounded in the consumer vulnerability literature, readers may infer that all consumers with a particular personal characteristic (e.g., visual impairment) are vulnerable all the time, and this is not the case. It is important that researchers clearly articulate the manner in which context influences how vulnerability is experienced and why certain situations create vulnerability (Baker et al., 2005).

For policy and practice
In developing implications for policy and practice, it is important to articulate that multiple segments within different social categories exist – not all women are alike, not all Native Americans are alike, etc. (Bristor and Fischer, 1996; Smith, 1999). One should not define segments in too aggregate a nature in terms of policy. Also a balanced approach that examines internal and external conditions that increase the likelihood of experiencing vulnerability is more likely to have an impact on policy makers than one which plants the blame solely on one of those perspectives (Hill, 1995).

Most importantly, people for whom policies are supposedly developed need to be involved in decisions that affect their lives. As an example, the first author often recalls how several of her informants with visual impairments who lived in the same city were extremely upset with the city's decision to spend thousands of dollars to put in a 'talking walkway'. The talking walkway was placed at one of the busiest intersections in town, and the supposed effect was to help people with visual impairments. But many of the informants interpreted the action as condescending, because (1) no one in the blind community was involved in the decision and (2) if a person with a visual impairment could cross all the other, almost equally busy intersections, before he/she got to that one, then why could she/he not cross this one? The first author also heard people with vision in the community questioning how much the talking walkway cost and one unfeeling person even wondered, 'Why don't "they" just stay home?' Obviously this sort of decision did not help the informants cross the street, nor did it engender positive feelings toward people with visual impairments in the community.

Conclusion

The point of this chapter has not been to explain the philosophical underpinnings of any one particular approach to collecting and interpreting qualitative data; rather the point has been to discuss the critical importance of data framing and interpretation, particularly as consumer vulnerability is discussed within different social groups. Other consumer researchers have argued for well over a decade the perspective that is advocated here: the behavior of consumers cannot be explained by neat and tidy social categorization schemes (e.g., McCracken, 1986; Schouten and McAlexander, 1995). However, the potential for harm in this context, attributing vulnerability when vulnerability does not exist, is especially great because this type of misattribution devalues at least a portion of one's identity and has the potential to denigrate and suppress groups of consumers.

References

Andreasen, Alan R. (1975), *The Disadvantaged Consumer*, New York: The Free Press.

Arnould, Eric J. and Melanie Wallendorf (1994), 'Market-oriented ethnography: interpretation building and marketing strategy formulation', *Journal of Marketing Research*, **31** (November), 484–504.

Baker, Stacey Menzel (2006), 'Consumer normalcy: understanding the value of shopping through narratives of consumers with visual impairments', *Journal of Retailing*, **82** (1), 37–50.

——, James W. Gentry and Terri L. Rittenburg (2005), 'Building understanding of the domain of consumer vulnerability', *Journal of Macromarketing*, special issue on consumer vulnerability, ed. Ronald Paul Hill, **25** (2), 128–39.

——, Debra Lynn Stephens and Ronald Paul Hill (2001), 'Marketplace experiences of consumers with visual impairments: beyond the Americans with Disabilities Act', *Journal of Public Policy and Marketing*, **20** (Fall), 215–24.

Belk, Russell W. (1988), 'Possessions and the extended self', *Journal of Consumer Research*, **15** (September), 139–68.

Bonsu, Samuel K. and Russell W. Belk (2003), 'Do not go cheaply into that good night: death-ritual consumption in Assante, Ghana', *Journal of Consumer Research*, **30** (June), 41–55.

Bristor, Julia and Eileen Fischer (1993), 'Feminist thought: implications for consumer research', *Journal of Consumer Research*, **19** (March), 518–36.

—— and Eileen Fischer (1996), 'Exploring simultaneous oppressions: toward the development of consumer research in the interest of diverse women', in Ronald Paul Hill (ed.), *Surviving in a Material World: The Lived Experience of People in Poverty*, Notre Dame, IN: University of Notre Dame Press, pp. 17–30.

Chun, Seungwoo (2005), 'Cultural differences in fan ritual learning: a cross-cultural study of the fan ritual learning process of Americans and East Asians', unpublished PhD dissertation, University of Nebraska-Lincoln.

Crockett, David and Melanie Wallendorf (2004), 'The role of normative political ideology in consumer behavior', *Journal of Consumer Research*, **31** (December), 511–28.

Csikszentmihalyi, Mihaly (1996), *Creativity: Flow and the Psychology of Discovery and Invention*, New York: HarperPerennial.

—— (1997), *Finding Flow: The Psychology of Engagement with Everyday Life*, New York: Basic Books.

Denzin, Norman (1994), 'The art and politics of interpretation', in Norman K. Denzin and Yvonna S. Lincoln (eds), *Handbook of Qualitative Research*, Thousand Oaks, CA: Sage, pp. 500–515.

Festinger, Leon (1965), *A Theory of Cognitive Dissonance*, Stanford, CA: Stanford University Press.

Freud, Sigmund (1938), *The Basic Writings of Sigmund Freud*, New York: The Modern Library.

Geertz, Clifford (1983), *Local Knowledge: Further Essays in Interpretive Anthropology*, New York: Basic Books.

Gentry, James W., Patricia F. Kennedy, Katherine Paul and Ronald Paul Hill (1995a), 'The vulnerability of those grieving the death of a loved one: implications for public policy', *Journal of Public Policy & Marketing*, **14** (Spring), 128–42.

—— (1995b), 'Family transitions during grief: discontinuities in household consumption patterns', *Journal of Business Research*, **34** (September), 67–79.

Goldstone, Robert L. and Mark Steyvers (2001), 'The sensitization and differentiation of dimensions during category learning', *Journal of Experimental Psychology: General*, **130** (1), 116–39.

Hill, Ronald Paul (1991), 'Homeless women, special possessions, and the meaning of "Home": an ethnographic case study', *Journal of Consumer Research*, **18** (December), 298–310.

—— (1995), 'Researching sensitive topics in marketing: the special case of vulnerable populations', *Journal of Public Policy & Marketing*, **14** (1), 143–8.

—— (2001), 'Surviving in a material world: evidence from ethnographic consumer research on people in poverty', *Journal of Contemporary Ethnography*, **30** (August), 364–91.

—— and Mark Stamey (1990), 'The homeless in America: an examination of possessions and consumption behaviors', *Journal of Consumer Research*, **17** (December), 303–21.

Hirschman, Elizabeth C. (1993), 'Ideology in consumer research, 1980 and 1990: a Marxist and feminist critique', *Journal of Consumer Research*, **19** (March), 537–55.

—— and Ronald Paul Hill (2000), 'On human commoditization and resistance: a model based upon Buchenwald concentration camp', *Psychology & Marketing*, **17** (6), 469–91.

—— and Morris B. Holbrook (1992), *Postmodern Consumer Research: The Study of Consumption as Text*, Newbury Park, CA: Sage.

Ishii, Keiko, Jose Alberto Reyes and Shinobu Kitayama (2003), 'Spontaneous attention to world content versus emotional tone: differences among three cultures', *Psychological Science*, **14** (January), 39–47.

Ji, Li-Jun, Kaiping Peng and Richard E. Nisbett (2000), 'Culture, control and perception of relationships in the environment', *Journal of Personality and Social Psychology*, **78** (5), 943–55.

Johnston, Marie (1996), 'Models of disability', *The Psychologist*, **9** (May), 205–12.

Joy, Annamma (1991), 'Beyond Odyssey: interpretations of ethnographic writing in consumer behavior', in Russell W. Belk (ed.), *Highways and Buyways: Naturalistic Research from the Consumer Behavior Odyssey*, Provo, UT: Association for Consumer Research, pp. 216–33.

Kates, Steven M. and Russell W. Belk (2001), 'The meanings of Lesbian and Gay Pride Day: resistance through consumption and resistance to consumption', *Journal of Contemporary Ethnography*, **30** (August), 392–429.

Kaufman-Scarborough, Carol and Stacey Menzel Baker (2005), 'Do people with disabilities believe the ADA has served their consumer interests?', *Journal of Consumer Affairs*, **39** (Summer), 1–26.

Kitayama, Shinobu, Sean Duffy, Tadashi Kawamura and Jeff T. Larsen (2003), 'Perceiving an object and its context in different cultures: a cultural look at new look', *Psychological Science*, **14** (3), 201–6.

Langer, Ellen J. (2000), 'Mindful learning', *Current Directions in Psychological Science*, **9** (December), 220–23.

—— and Benzion Chanowitz (1987), 'A new perspective for the study of disability', in Harold E. Yuker (ed.), *Attitudes toward Persons with Disabilities*, New York: Springer, pp. 68–81.

Lee, Renee Gravois, Julie L. Ozanne and Ronald Paul Hill (1999), 'Improving service encounters through resource sensitivity: the case of health care delivery in an Appalachian community', *Journal of Public Policy & Marketing*, **18** (Fall), 230–48.

Lévi-Strauss, Claude (1966), *The Savage Mind*, 2nd edn, Chicago, IL: University of Chicago Press.

Masuda, Takahiko and Richard E. Nisbett (2001), 'Attending holistically versus analytically: comparing the context sensitivity of Japanese and Americans', *Journal of Personality & Social Psychology*, **81** (5), 922–34.

McCracken, Grant (1986), 'Culture and consumption: a theoretical account of the structure and movement of the cultural meaning of consumer goods', *Journal of Consumer Research*, **13** (June), 71–84.

Miles Matthew B. and A. Michael Huberman (1994), *Qualitative Data Analysis*, 2nd edn, Thousand Oaks, CA: Sage.

Nosofsky, Robert M. (1987), 'Attention and learning processes in the identification and categorization of integral stimuli', *Journal of Experimental Psychology: Learning, Memory, & Cognition*, **13** (1), 87–108.

Oliver, Michael (1990), *The Politics of Disablement: A Sociological Approach*, New York: St Martin's Press.

—— (1996), *Understanding Disability: From Theory to Practice*, London: Macmillan Press.

Patterson, Maggie Jones, Ronald Paul Hill and Kate Maloy (1995), 'Abortion in America: a consumer behavior perspective', *Journal of Consumer Research*, **1** (March), 677–94.

Patton, Michael Quinn (1990), *Qualitative Evaluation and Research Methods*, 2nd edn, Newbury Park, CA: Sage.

Peñaloza, Lisa (1994), '*Atravesando fronteras* / border crossings: a critical ethnographic exploration of the consumer acculturation of Mexican immigrants', *Journal of Consumer Research*, **21** (June), 32–54.

Peñaloza, Lisa (1995), 'Immigrant consumers: marketing and public policy considerations in the global economy', *Journal of Public Policy & Marketing*, **14** (Fall), 83–94.

Reason, Peter (1994), 'Three approaches to participative inquiry', in Norman K. Denzin and Yvonna S. Lincoln (eds), *Handbook of Qualitative Research*, pp. 324–39.

Ringold, Debra J. (1995), 'Social criticisms of target marketing: process or product', *American Behavioral Scientist*, **38** (February), 578–92.

Ruark, Jennifer K. (1999), 'Redefining the good life: a new focus in the social sciences', *The Chronicle of Higher Education*, 12 February, A13–A15.

Schouten, John W. (1991), 'Selves in transition: symbolic consumption in personal rites of passage and identity constructions', *Journal of Consumer Research*, **17** (March), 412–25.

—— and James H. McAlexander (1995), 'Subcultures of consumption: an ethnography of the new bikers', *Journal of Consumer Research*, **22** (June), 43–61.

Schwandt, Thomas A. (1994), 'Constructivist, interpretivist approaches to human inquiry', in Norman K. Denzin and Yvonna S. Lincoln (eds), *Handbook of Qualitative Research*, pp. 118–37.

Seligman, Martin E.P. (2002), *Authentic Happiness: Using the New Positive Psychology to Realize Your Potential for Lasting Fulfillment*, New York: Free Press.

Sherry, John F. (1991), 'Post-modern alternatives: the interpretive turn in consumer research', in Thomas S. Robertson and Harold H. Kassarjian (eds), *Handbook of Consumer Behavior*, Englewood Cliffs, NJ: Prentice-Hall, pp. 548–91.

Smith, Linda Tuhiwai (1999), *Decolonizing Methodologies: Research and Indigenous Peoples*, Dunedin: University of Otago Press.

Smith, N. Craig and Elizabeth Cooper-Martin (1997), 'Ethics and target marketing: the role of product harm and consumer vulnerability', *Journal of Marketing*, **61** (July), 1–20.

Spiggle, Susan (1994), 'Analysis and interpretation of qualitative data in consumer research', *Journal of Consumer Research*, **21** (December), 491–503.

—— (1998), 'Creating the frame and the narrative', in Barbara B. Stern (ed.), *Representing Consumers: Voices, Views, and Visions*, London: Routledge, pp. 156–90.

Stephens, Debra Lynn, Ronald Paul Hill and James W. Gentry (2005), 'A consumer-behavior perspective on intimate partner violence', *Journal of Contemporary Ethnography*, **34** (February), 36–67.

Stern, Barbara B. (1998a), 'The problematics of representation', in Barbara B. Stern (ed.), *Representing Consumers: Voices, Views, and Visions*, London: Routledge, pp. 1–23.

—— (1998b), 'Narratological analysis of consumer voices in postmodern research accounts', in Barbara B. Stern (ed.), *Representing Consumers: Voices, Views, and Visions*, London: Routledge, pp. 55–82.

Taylor, Shelly E. and Susan T. Fiske (1978), 'Salience, attention, and attribution: top of the head phenomena', in L. Berkowitz (ed.), *Advances in Experimental Social Psychology*, vol. 11, New York: Academic Press, pp. 249–88.

Wolcott, Harry F. (1990), *Writing Up Qualitative Research*, Newbury Park, CA: Sage.

PART VI

PRESENTING QUALITATIVE RESEARCH

25 Camcorder society: quality videography in consumer and marketing research
Robert V. Kozinets and Russell W. Belk

Imagine taking a trip to your local supermarket, your local shopping mall or the home of a neighbor without the benefit of the accompanying sights and sounds. Clearly our lives as consumers are distinguished not merely by thoughts, attitudes and concepts, but by the colors, shapes, noises, motions and sounds of people and things in constant interaction. Although we might hit the mute button on our computer as we shop on-line for something other than music, if the screen goes dark, our shopping is brought to an abrupt end. The dancing colors, images and sounds from our TVs, the sparking glow of neon signs, the murmuring self-talk of a hypervigilant consumer roaming the aisles of a clothing store: all of these make it obvious that consumer culture is bright and noisy – it is an aspect of life that we tend to experience primarily using our eyes and our ears: audio-visually. Technology may add the inputs and change their pace and vibrancy, but buying and consuming were no less audiovisual in the ancient agora and bazaar. Yet, with some notable exceptions such as Heisley and Levy (1991), Meamber (1999), Schroeder (2002), Scott (1994), McGrath, Sherry and Heisley (1993), the visual aspect of consumer experience has been largely ignored by our research representations. And with even fewer exceptions it has been silent.

In the past, consumer researchers have tended to play down or ignore the importance of visual and audio literacy in their own works and thus to underrepresent the lived visual and auditory aspects of the experience of living within a consumer culture. This is a loss not only in terms of representing the world of consumers, but also in terms of conveying the vision and melodies that comprise the researcher's potential conceptual contribution. John Debes included in his influential definition of visual literacy (1968, p. 27) that these skills allow 'a visually literate person to discriminate and interpret the visible actions, objects, symbols, natural or man-made' and to use these competencies creatively in order to 'communicate with others'. There is no question that the communicative function of consumer research is crucial, as scholars seek to communicate the importance of findings and implications to fellow scholars, to students, to policy makers, and to members of the general public.

We live in a mass-mediated world where rich, colorful, multilayered, sound effects-laden, quick-moving, quick-cutting, audio-visual information is increasingly the norm. Advertising, the news, the Internet, the profusion of *Blade Runner*-esque street signs increasingly come in the form of audiovisual representations. In the interest of *audiovisual literacy* in consumer research, we have both been working to develop examples of audio-visually literate consumer research, and to encourage and assist other interested scholars in the production of works of videographic consumer research that represent (through the medium of edited videotape) the audiovisual aspect of the lived experience of contemporary consumption. As of this writing, we have hosted four Association for

Consumer Research Film Festivals and will host three more scheduled in the next year, including our first ever ACR-Pacific and ACR-Latin American Film Festivals. Between us, we have conducted videographic workshops in North America, Europe, Australia and Asia. Over the past 20 years, we have also both produced and edited a variety of video-based research projects, with the second author pioneering these methods in this field during the influential Consumer Behavior Odyssey.

In this chapter we seek to provide an introductory overview of the use of audiovisual research methods in contemporary consumer research. We first briefly overview the technological developments that have made it possible for individual consumer researchers with limited budgets to create and present works of video ethnography, and then move into a discussion of the different types of consumer research videography that are possible. Third, and perhaps most importantly, we discuss some of the standards for judging the quality of videographic consumer research, referring especially to our experiences over the last four years as co-chairs of the Association for Consumer Research film festival. Finally, we discuss some of the institutional forces that affect the production and distribution of videographic consumer and marketing research.

The video revolution
Today's digital revolution in video technology has affected everyone from the home photographer documenting their child's Communion to professional documentarians like Michael Moore and Morgan Spurlock. With the advent of digital camcorder and cameras, and inexpensive microprocessors to handle their complex data streams, the cost of broadcast-quality video has plummeted while the technological possibilities have expanded. Currently, with high definition digital video cameras coming on-stream at very affordable prices, equipment to shoot and produce high-quality digital video has never been smaller, better or more accessible.

Not only have cameras become smaller and more affordable, but so too have computers and the digital editing software to run on them. Apple Computer has supported and upgraded its renowned Final Cut Pro video editing suite, which now handles high definition video and DVD production. SoundForge's excellent programs were acquired by Sony, which turned them into the acclaimed 'Vegas' suite of products for Wintel Windows users. Long the standard in broadcasting, Avid is now available for both Windows and Apple operating systems. All of this technology has made it possible for the 'prosumer' (a market with needs that exists somewhere in-between professional broadcasters and consumer camcorder hobbyists) to become a powerfully equipped digital documentarian. Combining a digital camcorder, a couple of extra microphones and a home desktop or laptop computer, the digital documentarian can shoot and edit their own video, add narration, titles and transitions, and prepare finished products for distribution via videotapes, DVDs, the Internet and perhaps via broadcast television, film festivals and even theatrical release. A new, digital world of possibilities has opened to those who are interested in creating and communicating videographic consumer and marketing research.

As videography has become more affordable, it has also become more accepted by corporations as the gold standard for conveying consumer experience. As we mentioned elsewhere (Belk and Kozinets, 2005b), Nissan recently hired two prominent consumer researchers to conduct research on brand community among owners of its vehicles. To represent their findings, the corporation insisted that the finished product be video only, with no accompanying written material. A recent *New York Times* article suggested that a film studies degree might be 'the new MBA' (Van Ness, 2005). As this article details, the hunger for videographic work is increasing, and requests for videographic presentations are now commonplace. In the boardroom as well as the classroom, those who wish to make a powerful impact on an audience are learning to rely on the vivid power and detail of screened audiovisual materials rather than blackboards, whiteboards and staid slideshows. And with the democratization of video production, creating and distributing video is no longer limited to those in traditional positions of power. Even street gangs and terrorist organizations have seized the public attention by making their own videos and DVDs. What are the main options and formats used by consumer and marketing researchers interested in deploying videography in their work? Our next section outlines some of these formats and also conveys a sense of the possibilities inherent in the method.

Varieties of videography
Over the course of our combined quarter-century of experience with consumer research-based videography, we have used and observed a variety of audiovisual data collection methods. In this section, we discuss some of the most basic uses of video in marketing and consumer research – individual or group interviews, naturalistic observation and autovideography – and also discuss some hybrid and emerging techniques.

We begin with an overview of some of the methodological varieties of videography in consumer research. Some of these forms are (1) videotaped interviews, (2) observational videography, (3) autovideography, (4) collaborative, (5) retrospective and (6) impressionistic.

The most basic and still most commonly used videographic technique is filmed interviews. In this case, the researcher directs and videotapes (usually with an assistant) individual or group interviews. Much happens in an interview in terms of body language, proxemics, kinesics and other time-bound and spatial aspects of human behavior that communicate meaning. These are captured by video. Similarly, the immediate context of an interview can be conveyed through video work in a way that is more immediate, more intimate and more accessible to an audience. The heightened impact of even seemingly action-less 'talking heads' has been made evident to us numerous times when someone who has seen the resulting video subsequently describes or mimics the words, posture and mannerisms of a memorable informant. This is not unlike a film buff imitating a favorite cinematic performance, but it says something about the increase in potential emotional impact in lifting printed words from the page and placing them back into the mouths and bodies of those who uttered them.

Interviews can be conducted in a research facility or in the richness of a field setting. If informants are observed in a naturalistic setting instead of (or in addition to) being interviewed, the result is an observational videography. Unobtrusive observation of consumers in the field is also possible, and may use concealed video equipment. Good quality, ultra-small CMOS 'spy' cameras are now available for under $30, making the world of high-tech surveillance open to almost everyone. It is important to note that the use of concealed camera techniques raises the very important topic of research ethics protocols in videographic research. We do not advocate these techniques, and highly recommend subjecting any research plan that includes them to a thorough, formal ethics review.

Another technique is autovideography. Based on autobiographical techniques, audio-videography has people capture their own lived experience on videotape. Oftentimes, this capture includes the videographer's own first-person narration. This technique tends to be perceived as less intrusive, more active and less directed by researcher motives and needs than participant-observational methods. Autovideography is the basis for Morgan Spurlock's *Supersize Me* video critique of McDonald's Fast Foods as well as being a signature part of Michael Moore films like *Roger and Me*, *Bowling for Columbine* and *Fahrenheit 911*. A middle-ground application between the etic-like distance of an observational videography and the intense emic-like closeness of an autovideography is offered by collaborative videographic research techniques. Collaborative videography has researchers and informants jointly negotiating the end product. Both are involved in the filming of the project, and both make editorial decisions about the final content of the videography; this technique has been used successfully in anthropological films such as those of Jean Rouch, Sol Worth and John Adair.

Retrospective applications are also possible, using, for example, home movies. This archival footage can be combined with subsequent elicitation of verbal informant data, and the archival footage would act as a projective stimulus for eliciting other videographic data. Retrospective applications would also include historical treatments such as Ken Burns' series on the American Civil War using still images very creatively. Finally, impressionistic techniques can be employed that employ a pastiche of videographic materials. For example, a film could combine stop motion animation, captured screen shots of television screens, captured television commercials, interviews, re-enactments and observations of consumers. The impressionistic consumer videography might involve staging or even special effects to illustrate particular points about consumption and consumers. Of course, these six formats for videography – interviews, observation, autovideography, collaborative, retrospective and impressionistic – are merely intended as suggestive archetypes. Many submissions to the film festival combined a number of these techniques, and still others may emerge from creative film-makers in the future. For example, if the film-maker constructs them to allow it, interactive CDs, DVDs and web sites can allow the audience to choose the material, sequencing, language and presentation format for what would otherwise be invariant linear presentations.

With all of these options, videography offers considerable latitude for researchers to exhibit and expand their own creativity. The resulting representations can be resonant, moving and intellectually stimulating. However, our field is dominated by the research text: the written representation of consumer research. In a recent introduction to a special 'Resonant Representations' DVD issue of the journal *Consumption, Markets and Culture* (Belk and Kozinets, 2005a), we wrote about the differences between written and audio-visual consumer research. We asked and wondered whether audiovisual representations were best thought of as accompaniments to written material that treated its research topic in a more conventional fashion. Does audiovisual material depend upon written material to gain credibility or acceptability? Or should it be treated as a different and entirely independent medium? Do audiovisual and written works provide different types of understanding and, if so, should one type of understanding be considered more valid or valuable than the other? These are significant questions, and they deserve a significant answer. In the following section, we discuss videographic consumer research and its relation to theory and representation as we attempt to outline some criteria for judging the quality of this work.

Judging videographic quality

The judgment of qualitative, interpretive, postmodern or 'Consumer Culture Theory' work is a topic that has occupied the consumer research field for over two decades. From initially dismissive answers that questioned qualitative works' ability to be judged valid, we have evolved through a stage that builds on the positivistically based trustworthiness criteria developed in Guba (1981) and presented in Lincoln and Guba (1985).[1] As the field matured in the wake of anthropology's paradigm-shifting crisis of representation and the influential rise of postmodern thought, more criteria were included (e.g., 'rhizomatic' validity) and influential volumes written on the conduct and multifaceted judgment of quality interpretive and ethnographic work (see, e.g., Lincoln and Denzin, 1994). Guba and Lincoln (1994, p. 114) later stated that 'although these [trustworthiness] criteria have been well-received, their parallelism to positivist criteria makes them suspect'. A recent *Journal of Consumer Research* (JCR) article by Sherry and Schouten (2002) exemplified the latest thinking on the topic, propounding the view that the emotional resonance of a given piece of consumer research was a higher standard (cf. Thompson, 1991).

This debate on quality standards in interpretive or qualitative research is certainly far from being settled. An ongoing aspect of the debate concerns the proper ratio of descriptive elements to more abstract theoretical elements, regardless of the mode of representation. It is possible that videography could be in the very thick of this debate. As a rich representational form, videography tends to be perceived as far closer to data than theory. Indeed videographic data can be analyzed in order to develop and test abstract theories, so how could a representation of it, itself, be considered valid or trustworthy research? According to this line of thought, videography is inherently at a disadvantage to text because it cannot adequately represent existing literature and portray theoretical extensions. In fact, one of the greatest strengths of videographic work – its accessibility – is turned into a weakness by stating that the medium is so comprehensible and grounded in commonplace experience that it cannot be scientific except at the level of description.

It would be unwise to dismiss such a critique out of hand. If we consider scientific works to be rigorous works of theory which provide abstract and general ideas that are subject to rules of organization, then we can see that videographic work apparently is different from other, more abstract, representations. As a grounded reality, videography could be thought to be much more like the real world, and less like the theoretical system that 'floats, as it were, above the plane of observation, and is anchored to it by roles of interpretation', as it is for Hempel (1952, p. 36).

However these arguments tend to mistake videographic simulation for reality. Although their lingua franca is audiovisual, videographies are narratives just as surely as are written texts. It is important to realize the layers of interpretation and constructedness underlying even the simplest videography. That videographic work tends to come across as so very emic is part of the spell that it can weave, but it is important that it not be confused with Reality and Truth. Although the camera may not lie, the videographer unavoidably 'lies' all the time; for example, in what we choose to film, how we film it, how we select and edit material together, and how we embellish it with titles, subtitles, music and narration. These and countless other choices, together with the added dramatic presentation possibilities of film and video, make it fully as susceptible to manipulation as the written word, if not more so. Furthermore, there are film-makers who embrace these possibilities, escape the confines of simple objectivity and intentionally take up a particular position or cause that they passionately seek to advance (again think Michael Moore or Morgan Spurlock, as well as the makers of *The Corporation*, Achbar, Abbott and Bakan, 2005).

Because videographic representations can be resonant, emotional, vibrant and humanizing, they have been viewed as offering compelling advantages over extant forms of interpretive (especially ethnographic) research. Videographies can provide audiences with a vicarious sense of experience that deepens understanding and fosters empathy. They have also enriched a number of fields, from medical field studies of hospital care, to oceanic studies of whale behavior, to studies of criminal behavior in public places. However, until now, the standards for judging the quality of videographic work have been sketchy at best. In our work as co-chairs of the Association for Consumer Research Film Festival, we have carefully considered the criteria for quality consumer research videography.

In this chapter, we suggest four important criteria for judging the quality of consumer videography. These four sets of judgmental criteria are the topical, theoretical, theatrical and technical standards, or the Four Ts of Videography.

The topical criterion

The first criterion distinguishes a consumer or marketing videography from any other type of videography. Essentially the topicality criterion focuses on questions such as whether the videography is centered on a topic that is of interest to consumer research and consumer researchers. Is there a good choice of field or filming site, and has the field site yielded good quality data and informants? This criterion suggests that the consumer or marketing videography should be directly related to the topics and problematics of the consumer research or marketing research community. Does the videography deal with a topic that is recognizable, related to theories and topics of consumers, marketing and consumption? Suitable topics that have been presented in the ACR film festivals thus far include the globalization of holidays, anti-consumption festivals, media fan gatherings, the consumption of comfort through homes, the practice of cell phone picture taking, the practice of touristic picture taking, the practice of brand-oriented tattooing, the relationship between religion and capitalism in churches in Ghana, the marketing and consumption of addictive drugs, the brand community of Macintosh users and the use by families of American Girl products and brands. Unsuitable topics are political or social explorations or exposés with no consumption context, filmed marketing conferences or meetings, and how-to marketing films. We have rejected some otherwise very good films because they lacked topical relevance.

The theoretical criterion

The second criterion concerns whether the videography contributes in a compelling way to our understanding of the consumption phenomenon it treats. As our statement above indicates, the theoretical criterion is often the most difficult criterion for a videographer to negotiate. How can films convey the world of theory? How much theory is too much? How do I present theory cinematographically in a dramatically compelling manner? The exact nature of the theory-driven videographic enterprise is still very much in a state of flux. We have considered the theory-driven research filmic enterprise to be an experimental one and encourage a wide berth of creativity in this area. While some film-makers prefer to include theory by means of citations from other researchers (or their pictures), others merely hint at or offer homages to theorists. It is, however, important that film-makers position their research film in a body of work that relates to other research (not just other films) in its topical domain: this is a research film and not simply a documentary.

Thus it is not enough to expose a problem, introduce a phenomenon or document a behavior. The audience should be helped or challenged to think about broader principles than the concrete instance that the film depicts. This may seem an overly narrow criterion and it is possible to think of some provocative films that make no theoretical contribution. But in challenging film-makers to think abstractly, conceptually and theoretically, we are suggesting that every consumer research film should potentially and ideally make a lasting contribution to our understanding of consumption. To take a hypothetical example, suppose a film-maker wants to study how a family buys an automobile. An expository treatment that follows the family or certain of its members to an automobile dealership and records the behavior and transaction that occurs there has gathered some potentially valuable data. But if the film stops there the viewer learns little more than might be gathered from perusing an anonymous family album. That is, we might recognize some familiar rituals and behaviors (in this case, parts of the auto shopping and buying process), but, without knowing more about what the film-maker has chosen to show us and why, we learn precious little. If the film goes on to talk about how the behaviors and rituals depicted represent role behavior within the firm, adversarial customer–client relationships, use of choice support networks or enactment of consumer fantasies, then we may appreciate a theoretical or conceptual vantage point that allows us not only to better understand the focal behavior, but also potentially to apply this framework more broadly. Metaphors can be especially helpful, not just verbal metaphors, but visual metaphors as well.

The theatricality criterion
The theoretical criterion is counterbalanced and, in practice, often can present a trade-off against the next criterion, that of theatricality. The theatrical criterion asks if the videography is dramatically compelling. Is there some sort of 'story' that unfolds in the filmic representation? Is there a sense of mystery, of unknown questions that gradually become answered to provide a sense of satisfaction? Theatricality is a challenge, but there are many good guidelines available for creating compellingly dramatic video representations. Good documentaries must follow scripts and have a sense of unfolding, tension and dénouement. It is through theatricality that a research film stresses that it is a film, and conforms to filmic conventions and standards. When judging theatricality, the judges or critics will often rely upon their intuition and ask whether the film moved them emotionally, whether it seemed true, whether they were on the edge of their seats with excitement and whether it was resonant.

Theatricality does not mean that every film needs to be a BIG film of *Starwars* proportions. There is ample opportunity for small films that instead aim at less epic, but nevertheless interesting and important, goals. How can we better understand a meal, photo taking or pet ownership? What do cars really mean to consumers? What are the material rituals of dating, marriage and divorce? And how can the way we craft any of these videographies help the film have greater impact on its audience?

The technical criterion
Finally, the technical criterion is considered. The technical criterion asks whether sufficiently high 'production values' of the film are evident. That is, did the film-maker

show some mastery of the craft of film-making. First, there is the quality of the camera work. Was the camera work still, or relatively steady? Were the events and persons recorded in frame, or posed interestingly against their background? Was the lighting sufficient, or even interesting, or was the video over- or underexposed? Next is the sound quality, almost always a problem area for videographers and documentarians. Was the sound during interviews audible? Was background noise a problem? Were microphones used when appropriate? Next is the quality of the editing, which encompasses a panoply of concerns, from the length of the film, the way that images are positioned and the color correction, to the titling to transitions and other effects, and even including use of appropriate editing techniques to create continuity and tension, contributing to the criterion of theatricality. Is narration used? Is it adequate? Is music used? Is it appropriate and successful in creating the desired mood for the videography? All of this and more is part of the technical criterion.

We consider these four criteria – the topical, theoretical, theatrical and technical aspects of consumer videography – to be the starting point of discussions about quality videographic work, rather than some sort of final say. We do believe that they begin to capture some of the complex technological nature of the work and to draw our attention to relevance to the field and to the film's relation to emotions and resonance that seem to be increasingly playing a part in the human elements of our work.

Challenges and opportunities in videographic research

The many avenues of videography open up to a highway of possibilities, but the method has drawbacks as well as challenges. Certainly videography's resonance is powerful and cutting-edge, but is also double-edged. As it seems to present 'reality', videography can seem to be evidential and taken as 'truth'. Skillful consumer videography is also rather difficult, in that videographers seek (with rather limited means) to enchant an audience of experienced screen watchers with rather high expectations about what it takes to please them. Another problem with videography is that the presence of a camera can definitely interfere with the conduct of interviews, and add complications that range from reduced disclosure to a more lengthy and involved IRB/ethics review procedures. Videography can also be used fairly easily to manipulate audiences, using imagery, emotional appeals, music and other editorial techniques. And there are additional ethical questions when informants cannot be promised anonymity because they will appear in the video.

Consumer and marketing videography offers many exciting possibilities to engage the minds and imaginations of various constituents: fellow researchers, policy makers, practitioners, students, media outlets and others. In digital forms, distributing our research over the World Wide Web could turn out to be an opportunity to bridge the gap between theory and practice that academics in business schools have been struggling with since the inceptions of the professional managerial school. With a touch of irony to match its market orientation, videography appeals to the screen age and Nintendo generation in times when book and newspaper reading are sharply on the decline.

Yet the tendency of video viewers to be less critical of what they see represented on screen equates to an added responsibility for consumer videographers to use video ethically and efficaciously. This efficaciousness means balancing the four criteria, rather than seeking to maximize all of them. Too much topicality and the videography might be so narrow and specific that its audience would consist of only a dozen people worldwide (perhaps like some of our written articles). Too much theory and the message will likely be obscure or inaccessible. Too much theatricality and the very purpose of the academic enterprise might be submerged by the tow of entertainment. Similarly, technical wizardry should be present behind the scenes, in creating a seamless narrative flow, one that is not heavy handed, but is almost invisible. Overly intrusive narrators or 'talking heads', overzealous zooming in and out and too obtrusive transitions between scenes are examples of distracting uses of nonlinear filming and editing that can draw too much attention to the medium, and take it away from the message.[2]

Although textually bound consumer research papers link themselves firmly to the abstract realm of 'science', consumer videographies are also almost inescapably bound to the realm of 'art'. For those who love the humanities, and for researchers who see their research representations as largely rhetorical affairs, this should come as no surprise. In fact, seeing research as equal parts art and science can be extremely liberating.

The major difficulty here is in the positioning of videography as a legitimate form of 'scientific' research representation within our own field. After hard-fought battles to have interpretive work recognized as legitimate, are researchers willing and ready to have another such debate thrust upon them? Somehow, the association with art deprivileges and delegitimizes videography, making it seem more entertainment than knowledge (see Belk, 1998).

So, one might ask, what is required for videography to become legitimized and institutionalized in consumer research and theory? We believe that we have taken an important first step with this chapter, by starting the open discussion about the judgmental standards for assessing quality videographic work. Using these standards, editors and reviewers can begin to discuss the strengths and deficiencies of any particular work. In addition, the history of videography in our field, along with the ACR Film Festival and special issue of *Consumption, Markets and Culture* (CMC), mean that we have a decent-sized and growing library of videographic works to hold up as exemplars, and against which to compare particular new works. As academic journals and conferences draw on this body of work, refining and negotiating these quality standards, we will begin to see consumer videography treated as a more legitimate form of research presentation. Whether it will ever be able to stand alone as a representational form is something highly dependent on the field and the skills and abilities of individual consumer videographers. Perhaps last of all will come acceptance in the reward structure for academics, where quality videographic work is recognized as a contribution equivalent to a journal article or a book. These are matters that will likely take years to decide, with numerous difficult test cases being established. However we know of at least one videographic thesis dissertation currently being undertaken by a consumer research scholar, and the growth of the film festivals and the workshops bodes well for a 'strength in numbers' approach to finding legitimacy and institutionalization. The strong demand for videographies in commercial consumer research is further evidence of its relevance.

Notes

1. These criteria were later denounced by their authors. Lincoln and Guba completely revised their position in Guba and Lincoln (1994). Belk challenged the criteria of Wallendorf and Belk (1989) in Belk (1991).
2. However, as a 'postmodern' technique that draws attention to the videographic form of representation, these techniques can be used and already have been used very effectively.

References

Achbar, Mark, Jennifer Abbott and Joel Bakan (2005), *The Corporation*, New York: Zeitgeist Films.
Belk, Russell W. (1991), 'Epilogue: lessons learned', in Russell W. Belk (ed.), *Highways and Buyways: Naturalistic Research From the Consumer Behavior Odyssey*, Provo, UT: Association for Consumer Research, pp. 234–8.
Belk, Russell W. (1998), 'Multimedia consumer research', in Barbara Stern (ed), *Representation in Consumer Research*, London: Routledge, pp. 308–38.
Belk, Russell W. and Robert V. Kozinets (2005a), 'Introduction to resonant representations issue of *Consumption, Markets and Culture*', *Consumption, Markets and Culture*, **8** (September), 195–203.
Belk, Russell W. and Robert V. Kozinets (2005b), 'Videography in marketing and consumer research', *Qualitative Market Research*, **8** (2), 128–41.
Debes, John (1968), 'Some foundations for visual literacy', *Audiovisual Instruction*, **13**, 961–4.
Guba, Egon G. (1981), 'Criteria for assessing the trustworthiness of naturalistic inquiries', *Educational Communications and Technology Journal*, **29** (2), 75–92.
Guba, Egon G. and Yvonna S. Lincoln (1994), 'Competing paradigms in qualitative research', in Norman K. Denzin and Yvonna S. Lincoln (eds), *Handbook of Qualitative Research*, Thousand Oaks, CA: Sage, pp. 105–17.
Heisley, Deborah and Sidney Levy (1991), 'Autodriving: a photo-elicitation technique', *Journal of Consumer Research*, **18** (2), 257–72.
Hempel, Carl Gustav (1952), *Fundamentals of Concept Formation in Empirical Science*, Chicago, IL: University of Chicago Press.
Lincoln, Yvonna S. and Norman K. Denzin (1994), *Handbook of Qualitative Research*, Thousand Oaks, CA: Sage.
Lincoln, Yvonna S. and Egon G. Guba (1985), *Naturalistic Inquiry*, Beverly Hills, CA: Sage.
McGrath, Mary Ann, John F. Sherry and Deborah D. Heisley (1993), 'An ethnographic study of an urban periodic marketplace: lessons from the Midville farmers' market', *Journal of Retailing*, **63** (Fall), 280–319.
Meamber, Laurie A. (1999), 'Art as life–life as art: the embeddedness of art in life and life in art in postmodernity', ed. Richard A. Goodman (ed.), *Modern Organizations and Emerging Conundrums*, Lanham, MD: Lexington Books, pp. 184–99.
Schroeder, Jonathan (2002), *Visual Consumption*, London: Routledge.
Scott, Linda (1994), 'Images in advertising: the need for a theory of visual rhetoric', *Journal of Consumer Research*, **21** (September), 252–73.
Sherry, John F. and John W. Schouten (2002), 'A role for poetry in consumer research', *Journal of Consumer Research*, **29** (2), 218–34.
Thompson, Craig (1991), 'Eureka and other tests of significance: a new look at evaluating interpretive research', in G. Gorn M. Goldberg and R. Pollay (eds), *Advance in Consumer Research*, vol. 17, Provo, UT: Association for Consumer Research, pp. 25–30.
Van Ness, Elizabeth (2005), 'Is a cinema studies degree the new M.B.A.?', *New York Times*, 6 (March) (http://interactive.usc.edu/archives/003968.html).
Wallendorf, Melanie and Russell W. Belk (1989), 'Assessing trustworthiness in naturalistic consumer research', in Elizabeth Hirschman (ed.), *Interpretive Consumer Research*, Provo, UT: Association for Consumer Research, pp. 69–84.

26 Writing it up, writing it down: being reflexive in accounts of consumer behavior
Annamma Joy, John F. Sherry, Gabriele Troilo and Jonathan Deschenes

The purpose of this chapter is to rethink the concept of reflexivity within consumer research and to highlight the complexities and various levels of reflexive thought. In doing so, we were inspired by the work of Kristen Campbell, in particular her article, 'The promise of feminist reflexivities: developing Donna Haraway's project for feminist science studies', in which she expands on Haraway's ideas of diffraction and situated knowledge. We are indebted to her. Our title, 'Writing it up, writing it down', we owe to Clifford Geertz (1988).

The turn to reflexivity
Reflexivity is the act of turning backward, the act of mirroring the self. It is a human undertaking and, as the neurologist Ramachandaran (2003) notes, our reflective self-consciousness – the possibility of contemplating the consequences of our actions – is what is special about us humans. While it is a theory about epistemology, in current anthropological contexts it is also viewed as an embodied activity, a process and method for conducting fieldwork and constructing ethnographies. Reflexivity allows for the revelation and contemplation of one's own biases, theoretical predispositions, preferences, the researcher's place in the setting and the context of the social phenomenon being studied (Foley, 2002). It is a means for a critical and ethical consideration of the entire research process.

Reflexive thinking as a corrective mode to contemporary ethnographic writing was introduced more than a couple of decades ago. Foley (2002) identifies three streams within anthropology: first, auto-ethnography with its emphasis on a more intuitive and experiential type of knowledge which emphasizes metaphor, parody and irony over scientific discourse; second, sociological reflexivity as espoused by Bourdieu and Wacquant (1992). It does not reduce the self and subjectivity to mere effects of discourse as the poststructuralists do but recognizes the historical and disciplinary context that shapes thinking and requires a constant disciplined abductive (that is, a deductive and inductive way of knowing through ethno practices) process of theory development within and against the discursive traditions within the discipline. The third stream is intertextual reflexivity that focuses on rhetorical practices (Folay, 2002, pp. 477–8). We will take up some of these issues a little later in the text. Suffice it to say that initially an ethnography was a factual text followed by confessional accounts of fieldwork. Reflexivity in writing was proposed as a corrective to the omniscient authority of the author, to the power of the person who represented the exotic 'other' without addressing the effect of the observer on those being studied and their effect on the observer (Fabian, 1983; Marcus and Fischer, 1986; Said, 1979). This led to a great deal of experimentation in creating texts. Van Maanen (1988) identifies the different styles of textualization available to ethnographers.

That we drive research projects with our values, histories and interests is central to the understanding of any interpretation in the social sciences, including consumer research (Bristor and Fischer, 1993; Firat and Venkatesh, 1995; Thompson, 1997). Researchers create the text. As researchers we also assume that the research is an interaction between a historically produced text and a historically produced reader (Allen, 1995, p. 176). Hermeneutics affirms the position of the researcher in the hermeneutic circle. Within this tradition, the researcher and the researched move between a background of shared meaning and a finite foreground of experience within it (Gadamer, 1976).

Reflexivity in writing is only one aspect of this process; reflexivity embraces all aspects of the research process. It is the turning back of an inquiry on to its own formative possibilities (Hopkinson and Hogg, 2005). Agar (1982) recognizes four major components of the reflexive process: the researcher, the informant, the text and the audience. Its roots are in critical theory, standpoint theory and textual deconstruction, as well as in anthropology, or more generally a sociology of knowledge, power and meaning. Three strands of reflexivity have been proposed: radical reflexivity, infrareflexivity and diffraction (initiated through a discussion on situated knowledge and standpoint theory). In consumer research, the work of Bristor and Fischer (1993), Costa (1994), Hirschman (1993) and Joy and Venkatesh (1994) are early attempts to broker these concepts into the field of consumer behavior.

The landmark event in the turn of consumer research to reflexivity was a 1986 study by a group of consumer researchers who criss-crossed the United States in a 27-foot recreation vehicle conducting qualitative studies with the express goal of revitalizing research into consumer behavior. (It was financed by a seed grant from the Marketing Science Institute.) As these early pioneers were moving physically from the west to the east coast, metaphorically they were moving away from existing definitions of consumer concepts in an attempt to enlarge the contexts and meanings associated with consumption. Russ Belk (1991, p. 11) summarizes the journey: 'We have made a brave leap when we didn't know how to jump and found that it brought us joy. Through this research and through each other we have encountered something of the fullness of life.' The number of researchers with a similar interest has grown. A March 2005 article in the *Journal of Consumer Research* by Eric Arnould and Craig Thompson ('Consumer culture theory') summarizes their overall contributions over the last 20 years.

We believe the time has come to assess critically some of the assumptions inherent in the consumer research work reported by Arnould and Thompson and to do this by invoking reflexivity. In a 1991 article, Joy discussed some of the issues related to reflexivity in writing and textualization – an extension of the notion of ethical representation of the individuals studied. Thompson, Stern and Arnould (1998) take this one step further and suggest that critical pluralism can move beyond what is provided by a unified narrative voice. Both ethnographic understandings and feminist critiques can be mutually enriching. Gould's (1991) article on introspection, and Wallendorf and Brucks's (1993) response, tested epistemic boundaries and called for renewed reflection on the relationships between the knower and the known. More recently, Sherry and Schouten (2002) explored and celebrated the use of poetry as an alternate mode of representation. While rhetoric and discourse remain critical elements in the process of reflexivity, in this paper we embrace a broader definition of reflexivity, one that focuses on what Haraway (1997) calls 'articulation', a term we prefer to 'representation'. Articulation connotes a certain level of indeterminacy, perhaps even a form of informality (much like the term 'conversation') rather than the finality connoted by 'representation'. In Haraway's words (1992, p. 318), 'To articulate is to signify. It is to put things together, scary things, risky things, contingent things . . . we articulate, therefore we are.' Earlier, Dorothy Smith (1987) had observed that the articulation of knowledge is both situated and reflexive, embodied and relational. We do realize, however, that journal articles and books continue in some sense the process of representation: stories of other places, other people, other times.

Knowledge is always partial, embodied, constructed and situated (Marcus, 1994). For Haraway, a situated knowledge reflects the 'particular and specific embodiment' of the knower (1991, p. 190). For Latour (1993,1999), knowledge is also always partial, fictitious and embodied, but the latter two argue that neither bodies nor materialities can be taken as pre-given.

In studies in anthropology, the writing of field notes and field diaries has always been treated as an essential component of research. Not only is being in the field transformative (Agar, 1982) but, importantly, there is a difference between knowledge creation in the field and the final text that is the product of such knowledge. Fabian (1983) argues that there is a suppression of dialogical realities that leads to anthropological insights. In sociology, Gouldner (1970) (in his discussion of the sociology of sociology) and Bourdieu (2000) (in his critique of the institutions that produced him) have both drawn attention to the importance of epistemological reflexivity. We extend Agar's (1982) four components (researcher, informants, text and readers) to include the research community within which the researcher is situated (Bourdieu, 2000), and the reader/audience (academics, activists who might also be researchers, and policy makers) (personal communication with Lisa Peñaloza, 2005). Depending on who is being addressed, different types of reflexivity are invoked.

Science is a sociocultural and textual construct; as soon as we recognize this, there are options for different definitions of reflexivity. As Campbell (2004) notes, the question is, while recognizing the constructed nature of knowledge, how can we imagine and implement new models of scientific practice?

In what follows we outline and weave together three strands of reflexivity: radical reflexivity as espoused by anthropologists Marcus and Fischer (1986), infrareflexivity as described by Latour (1988) and diffraction as proposed by Haraway (1991, 1992, 1997). Among the valuable discussions on reflexivity are Anderson (1986), Bristor and Fischer (1993), Hirschman (1993), Harding (2004), Murray and Ozanne (1991), Firat and Venkatesh (1995), Peñaloza (2005) and Stern (1993). We acknowledge their contributions but our focus remains on three connected categories of reflexivity: radical reflexivity, infrareflexivity and diffraction.

There is agreement that some regulatory standards exist within any discipline; these standards collectively and individually affect all researchers and the knowledge they produce. The three are constructivist in nature. Practice of course creates its own context and this is where the three types differ.

In Lynch and Woolgar's (1990) proposal for a radical reflexivity the problematization of meaning, value, knowledge and representation is clear. They espouse constructivist and relativist approaches to the creation of knowledge. Latour (1988) proposed a corrective to what he calls a naïve belief in the creation of 'truer texts' (p. 168) in his discussion of infrareflexivity. He argues that, although radical reflexivity recognizes the importance of the problem, it is too narrow and in the end too sterile (p. 175). Within feminist studies, there were also concerns over how we document the lives and activities of women, to understand this from their standpoint and to conceptualize it as an expression of specific historical and social contexts.

We begin by identifying three forms of reflexivity and then outline possible directions. Table 26.1 outlines the similarities and differences between the three positions.

Radical reflexivity in anthropology

Part of the problem of the way we conceptualize reflexivity has its origins in the issues that have concerned ethnographers from the very beginning. Fieldwork, as Rosaldo (1993) notes, is probably inherently confrontational: it is the purposeful disruption of other people's lives, however much they permit one to enter it. Other anthropologists have argued that exploitation and even betrayal are endemic to field work. It has even been described as a form of violence, albeit symbolic violence (Crapanzano, 1977). Agar (1982) argues that research is not conducted in the unmediated world of the people studied, but on the borders between the researcher and the researched. At the same time, this 'between-ness' is shaped by the researcher's biography and position. The 'self' should not be identified as merely analogous to the researcher but must take into consideration other aspects such as gender, ethnicity and class that are not shared with those being studied. Agar's insights into the reflexive process are more complete. He identifies the four components as the researcher, the informant, the text and the audience. But, as noted earlier, the research community and its various audiences must be included in that list.

In the early 1970s, at the time when reflexivity became a central concern of anthropology, Ricoeur's idea (1970, p. 530) that 'the world is the ensemble of references opened up by the texts' (exemplified also in the writings of Geertz, 1973) had become well accepted. This led to a focus on the writing rather than on the substance of these texts. This conflation of style with substance led Marcus and Cushman (1982) to note that 'the way of saying' is not only the 'what of saying', it is all there is. In retrospect, the lowly field studies that have been rejected for publication because they 'have little to say that advances the march of theory' are as important as the grand or meso theories that have been identified as making profound contributions to the field (see Arnould and, Thompson, 2005).

Reflexivity surfaced in anthropology in a number of ways; we identify a few that are typical. First, anthropological discourse has historically sought to study the 'exotic other' as a way to study the self (Marcus and Fischer, 1986; Said, 1979). It has served to denaturalize the reality of local rather than central institutions, thereby frustrating the original critique. Dove (1999) argues that anthropologists are more likely to study local organizations of resistance rather than central organizations of oppression. Laura Nader (1972, p. 286) describes this as a fascination with studying 'down, out and far', rather than 'up, near and in'.

Michalowski (1996), who studied Cuban communities, considers how anxieties became part of reflexive routines in the field and served to shape his interpretations. He argues that reflexivity is not to be confined to the standpoint embedded in the field worker's biography but also to address the ways in which macropolitical processes enter into the biographies of field workers, their informants and their audiences and influence the interactions between them.

For others like Stoller (1997) the crisis in anthropology is not just one of representation, as Marcus and Fischer (1986) argue, but one of epistemology. He is sensitive to issues of understanding and representing the cultures that ethnographers are studying. Stoller

Table 26.1   Similarities and differences between the three types of reflexivity

	Radical reflexivity	Infrareflexivity	Diffraction
Reflexivity objectives	*Find a way to account better for the otherness of those being studied in order to understand one's own society * Provide a richer problematization of meaning, value, knowledge and representation	* A material, semiotic and political practice that should help the researcher study her society in the same way she studies others *Infrareflexivity is a process of telling stories the way novelists and journalists do	*How we document the lives and activities of women, to understand from their standpoint, and to conceptualize them as an expression of historical and social contexts * Standpoint theory and postmodernist views enrich this form of reflexivity
Nature of knowledge	*Constructivist/relativistic view * All work is incomplete and requires a response from others positioned differently	*Constructivist/relativistic view *Research should generate explanations that create unexpected differences *Emphasizes ontic relationality	*Constructivist/relativistic view combined with realism *Certain social positions will produce more accurate descriptions of the world *Standpoint theory is a cognitive, psychological and political tool for constructing more adequate knowledge
Nature of accounts	* Focus is on representations	*Considers articulation over representation *Keeps the discussion open	*Considers articulation over representation *Importance of diffraction: articulation implies multiple readings. However, the emphasis is on interferences that would affect the creation of what is 'real'
Nature of the world	* Dualist view *There are different groups involved: researcher v. informant, local v. exotic culture *Fieldwork is inherently confrontational *Researcher's biography affects the fieldwork	*Non-dualist view *No separation of social sciences from the natural sciences. No separation of culture from nature *Objects are quasi-objects (composed of both natural and cultural elements) *Both humans and non-humans play a role within networks	*Non-dualist version of science and the world *Interrelationality in all things *Dichotomies are tools of power and oppression *Winners and losers are identified and studied: the field is perceived as not neutral and participants as not equal

Table 26.1 (continued)

	Radical reflexivity	Infrareflexivity	Diffraction
Nature of the world (continued)	*Macropolitical processes affect fieldwork, informants and audiences *Researcher's self (gender, ethnicity, class) can greatly differ from that of those studied		
Nature of writing	*The text is ultimately what matters *Use depth, respect and poetic evocation to tell informants' stories (i.e. to strengthen epistemology) *Ethnographers write within a matrix of existing representations and incorporate critical power and insight into their ethnographies	*Effort placed on writing better 'fictions' *Including the author and identifying the method do not make the story more believable *Avoidance of meta-language (i.e. not to subsume information under new terms) *The right cut is one that will distinguish inarticulate from well articulated propositions *Make research articulations relevant to other disciplines through interdisciplinary co-authorship	*Gives voice to the subjugated and leverages emancipatory possibilities *Negotiation and argumentation are necessary mechanisms by which a collectivity accepts one or another story
Political involvement	*Ethnographer is often neutral in the causes and issues of the locals	*Argues for politically involved writing but not for direct political action *The assumption is that ontic relationality is inherently political	*Emphasis is placed on political action *Feminist standpoint values accountability and commitment to ideals such as freedom and justice
Critique of approach	*Naïve belief in the creation of 'truer texts' *Emphasis on the process of knowing and not enough on the known *Leads to semiotic hierarchy of texts	*Unclear as to criteria for evaluating the quality of a research account (deflation of methodology, improvement in style, providing accounts of the known rather than the knower, refusing macro-theories and meta-language, and refusing disciplinary boundaries)	*Feminist practices are splintered because of the multiplicity of definitions of gender and other factors (postmodern point of view) *Feminist researchers have to convince others that they provide a *more accurate rendering* of the world than other accounts

| | | *Feminists have a political orientation that may not be shared by other women |
| *Leads to misleading and sterile self-referencing system | *Most of these methods have been used by feminists | *No accurate theorization of the multiple axes of oppression |

Notes: Standpoint theory is probably one of the most controversial theories in feminist studies. I summarize below some of the issues raised by Harding (2004). Its origins can be traced to a period when women felt that they had been treated primarily as the object and not the subject of knowledge projects studied by others. Haraway uses the term 'God trick' to refer to the ways in which scientific studies spoke authoritatively about what was studied but from no particular social location or human perspective (1991). Public policy and disciplinary knowledge standpoint, theorists argue, were also advanced with little consideration of the interests of women. The outcomes of such inquiries marginalized not only women but men as well. The identifying features of this theory are (1) the goal to 'study up', i.e. using a bottom-up approach, (2) providing a distinctive insight about how a hierarchical social structure works located in material or political forms of oppression, (3) creating a nuanced understanding of oppressed groups, through data that are historically recorded, written and/or empirically gathered, and (4) focusing on the creation of group consciousness rather than on individual consciousness.

Harding's argument is that standpoint theory (contentious as it is), does raise critical issues for a philosophy of knowledge production. The three considerations that she deems important are (1) epistemological issues (a rethinking of conceptual practices that shape what situations or conditions get identified as scientific problems and researched); standpoint theory questions the domain of scientific method and takes it back to the context of discovery; (2) the role of group consciousness in the production of knowledge (standpoint theorists propose the notion of a subject that is different from that constructed under liberal individualism or structuralist and poststructuralist alternatives to it); and (3) reasonable constructionism (to maneuver between excessive constructionism and therefore relativism).

argues that not only must ethnographers try to contribute to social theory, but they must also tell the story of a people with depth, respect and poetic evocation.

Wasserfall (1993) raises the ethical question, what happens when the anthropologist does not like or identify with the communities being studied? She was a Jewish woman studying the problems faced by Palestinian women. When the researcher finds herself in profound opposition to the beliefs and actions of her informants, what are the commitments of a feminist scholar to her informants?

Marcus (1994) identifies four levels of reflexivity in ethnographic writing. The first recognizes the inevitability of reflexivity in human action and exposes previous accounts to discussion and criticism. Although this did not challenge the existing research paradigm it produced an unsettled view in the field. Marcus's second type is positional reflexivity, which some feminists espoused. Positioning assumes that all work is incomplete and requires a response from others positioned differently. He identifies a third type as experimental ethnography; ethnographers are keenly aware that they write within a matrix of existing representations and incorporate critical power and insight into their ethnographies. While he (inspired by feminist critiques) offers a critique of authority, he does not place much significance on political action. Feminist experiential reflexivity (also linked to positional reflexivity) is the fourth type. Feminist standpoint theory is an example of this, where the objective is not just to give voice to the subjugated but also to leverage emancipatory possibilities.

To summarize, Marcus and Fischer (1986), Marcus (1994) and Lynch and Woolgar (1990) all argue that, if we accept that scientific knowledge is a semiotic practice, then we need to recognize that our knowledge of science utilizes practices of representation and is therefore relative. Constitutive reflexivity (the interrogation of the practices that we use to deploy our accounts) is the key here and not just the self-reflection of the knower. There are two considerations: practices that we are engaged in and the ideology of representation that we share (Campbell, 2004). But we are still left with the question of what is 'radical' about the radical reflexivity espoused above.

Infrareflexivity and Latour's corrective in science and technology studies

Latour (1988) critiques the position of radical reflexivity because it proposes the creation of a 'truer text'. Nevertheless, Latour's (1987, 1993, 1999) general philosophical position on the nature of scientific research is also important in our argument. First, he argues against the separation of the social sciences from the natural sciences, and the study of the social as separate from the material aspects of the world we live in. He defines reflexivity as a material, semiotic and political practice, Although he pays less attention to the political aspects of such constitutive practices, what he suggests when he says that we should not close off the discussion by prematurely identifying naturalized objectified fact is profoundly political.

He argues that the radical reflexivists err on the side of emphasizing the process of knowing and not enough on the known. By inserting themselves in the text, they try to show how they are positioned within the account. In Latour's terms there is only text democracy, and not a hierarchy of texts in a semiotic sense.

He argues that metareflexivity, as evidenced in experimental ethnographies with their self-referencing system, is sterile and misleading. Worse yet, it is unbelievable. Instead, he suggests infrareflexivity, a process of simply telling a story pretty much as novelists and journalists do. This would necessarily mean a reduction in methodological detail and a greater focus on style. The aim is to write better stories (1988, p. 172). No privilege is asked for the account at hand. Reliance on the world and not the word is encouraged. Ultimately, since no quantity of words and literary devices will make our stories into non-stories, it is better to focus on writing better fictions. Latour argues that including the author in a text and identifying how the story was constructed do not make it any more believable.

Another element in the process of being infrareflexive is to avoid metalanguage. It is important not to subsume information under a new term; this defeats the purpose of providing the explanation. A final component of infrareflexivity is hybridization and making research articulations relevant for other disciplines. This can be achieved, he argues, among other strategies, through co-authorship with scientists from other disciplines. Latour, like Haraway, prefers the term 'articulation' to single overarching explanations that close off all possibility of further discussion. The advantage of articulation, he says, is that there is no end to it.

His view of science is non-dualistic and is outlined in what he calls 'actor-network theory'. In this theory, actors are entities that do things (1993, p. 241) and can include humans and non-human actants. The term 'network' is defined as a 'group of unspecified relationships among entities'. A network ties together two systems of alliances: people (everyone who is involved one way or the other with the artifact) and things (all the pieces that had to be brought together to connect people).

Nevertheless, while they are analytically distinct, one cannot be studied without the other. An actor cannot act without a network and vice versa. Thus the power of actors depends on their position within the network and the number of alliances that can be generated. Translating is what actant networks do (they are also known as translation networks (Callon, 1986, p. 90). Latour argues that nothing is by itself either knowable or unknowable, sayable or unsayable, near or far. Everything is translated (1988, p. 167).

This theory differs greatly from the theory that specifies a subject, an object and an intermediary (language that mediates between the two). Borgerson (2005) provides another stance on this topic, but through a critical examination of the work of Daniel Miller. Articulation in this sense is about being affected by differences. It is an ongoing process; one proceeds from less articulate to more articulate proposals, thereby generating explanations that create unexpected differences. The advantage, Latour argues, of such an enlargement of propositions is that it undercuts the premature closure of discussion. There is no sure ground for criticism, although the critique we offer may not be all that different from that of the conspiracy theorists, except that it is clothed in elevated language and causes such as discourse, knowledge/power and fields of force (Latour, 1993).

However, if we ask which fictions are more persuasive than others and how one arrives at such a judgment, there is no answer except by the use of the following criteria: a deflation of methodology, an improvement in style, providing accounts of the known rather than the knower, refusing macrotheories and metalanguage, and refusing disciplinary boundaries (Latour, 1988, p. 160). In his view, the right cut 'is not the one that will distinguish science from politics [read natural sciences versus the social sciences] but the one that will distinguish inarticulate from well articulated propositions' (1993, p. 8).

Feminist critical reflexivities and practice
The feminist epistemologies that we discuss here have generally developed from the perspectives of standpoint theory and postmodernism. Traditional standpoint theory

privileges knowledge that is unitary, whereas postmodernism undercuts this form of knowledge and emphasizes different standpoints based on the positions of various sub-alterns on the basis of color, class, ethnicity and sexual orientation (Anderson, 2004; Bristor and Fischer, 1993; Joy and Venkatesh, 1994). The problem with an undue emphasis on the decentering of the subject in postmodern theory is that feminist practice becomes splintered because of the multiplicity of definitions of gender and other factors. Feminists who see the value of both perspectives have negotiated their way by insisting on taking 'responsibility in one's construction of one's representations' as well as through the process of 'mobile imagination' – literally putting themselves in the shoes of another woman (Campbell, 2004). Haraway (1991, 1992, 1997) is conscious of the possibilities in such an approach. She identifies it in her work through two concepts: 'situated knowledge' and 'diffraction'. Campbell (2004, p. 165) asks, 'How can feminist scientific studies (FSS) recognize the social construction of knowledge claims while also insisting upon a feminist critical practice?'

Historically, feminist accounts have been seen as weak and unscientific, and hence have been discounted. Second, and perhaps more importantly, feminist studies must demonstrate why they provide a more accurate rendering of the world than other accounts (read 'sexist'). Insofar as the choice of narratives is based on the political act of persuasion, negotiation and argumentation are the necessary mechanisms by which a collectivity accepts one or another of these stories. Latour (2003a) agrees and acknowledges that 'we should undertake moral judgments in terms of strategies of negotiation and compromise that permit new arrangements and combinations of networks' (p. 45). He provides some insights into how this could be done in a half-joking (but perhaps deadly serious) way in one of his popular articles, 'Dialogue prepared for a volume in honor of Donna Haraway'. An excerpt follows.

The two protagonists ('He' refers to Latour, 'She' to Haraway) acknowledge that she is more interested in 'dialectics' and he is concerned about 'difference'. This passage conveys Latour's position with perhaps greater clarity despite the profound overlaps:

> *She*: Except that without a critical stance this inquiry can go on indefinitely without modifying the initial positions an iota.
> *He*: Except if it ends up rendering the issue itself critical.
> *She*: But you have deprived yourself of any critical edge.
> *He*: Critical is also the name of a state, in case you forgot your physics. Make sure that issues reach criticity, would that not be a better slogan?
> *She*: Do you by any chance claim to increase the temperature of an issue without yourself being in any way critical?
> *He*: Do you by any chance believe that you increase the temperature by simply feeling indignation and sharing this indignation with your buddies? You are confusing the subjective definition of critique with its objective one. It is the object itself, the issue at stake that has to be rendered critical.
> *She*: And that could be carried out in any emotional state? Including quiet indifference to the solution?
> *He*: Not indifference no, rather, passionate interest for an uncertain and surprising solution, yes. And only that, but I am tempted to say that it's just the critically minded people, because they are so sure of who should win and who should lose and why, who actually cool down the issues to the point that they manage to decrease the temperature under them . . . they prefer to feel critical than to induce criticality. And you know what? It's because they leave out the little details.

Latour's (1993) solution has been what he calls 'the parliament of things'. Everything is provisional, although there might be a constitutional settlement. The issues he raises are what gets rights to representation and how do these things with rights arrange relations between themselves in order to live well together. Haraway is not too impressed with constitutional arrangements. Instead she worries that some things are endlessly produced and are real but others are not. How can one intervene through speech and action in the configurations of the real? For Haraway, what is real is also 'other' (for example, dogs are not furry children). They have their own partially different specificities and these deserve respect. For her, then, natures (they are plural – there is no one reality out there) are partially connected to humans and they are only partially made together. To this extent the relation between humans and nature is linked. The other cannot be totally known. It is in relation to the Same and it needs to be accorded this respect.

Thus, despite Latour's laments about the desire of the critically minded to win, feminists are indeed concerned with who wins and who loses and why. In Campbell's words this includes asking, 'Which accounts have which resources with which to compete? Who is prevented from competing?' (2004, p. 178). These questions suggest that a politics of power (defined in pragmatic terms) is involved. The field is not neutral and the participants not equal. Haraway underscores the importance of interferences in the definitions of what is 'real'. What is missing from radical reflexive accounts and to a certain extent from infra-reflexive accounts is any acknowledgment of political practice. So now the question, very much like the one Woolgar asked in the 1980s, is 'Where do we go from here?'

Haraway (1997) provides a partial answer by introducing the concept of 'diffraction', a term she coined to reflect the articulation process; it implies a multiple reading. Nevertheless she does offer new directions through her concept. According to her, diffraction is composed of 'interference patterns, not reflecting images. This concept will produce effects of connection, embodiment and of responsibility for an imagined elsewhere' (Haraway, 1992, p. 295). This model depends on a model not of representation but of articulation.

But to discover why this concept is a useful one we have to begin with her concept of 'situated knowledge'. Haraway (1991, 1997) has always espoused a non-dualist version of science and the world. She stresses interrelationality in all things and is very suspicious of binary categories and distinctions (including the distinctions between nature and culture and, by extension, between male and female), identifying them as tools of power and oppression. In this sense, her approach is close to Latour's. She argues that 'human societies do not exist except in so far as they are produced by and in mutual dialogue with the eco systems of which they are a part . . . No science should imagine that it observes the natural world unimpaired by cultural bias, because this implies too simplistic a distinction between the two' (1991, p. 187).

Situated knowledge combines insights and elements of both constructivism and feminism. It takes into account location, partial embodiment and partial perspective (1991, p. 191). Insofar as it allows recognition of how accounts are constructed it is deconstructive in orientation and intent. For Haraway, certain social positions will produce more accurate descriptions of the world. Her words are evocative of her beliefs: 'The knowing self is partial in all its guises, never finished, whole, simply there and original: it is always constructed and stitched together imperfectly, and therefore able to join with another, to see together without claiming to be another' (ibid., p. 7). It is not identity that she is seeking but partial connections. Feminism, she adds, 'loves another science: the sciences and politics of interpretation, translation, stuttering, and the partly understood. Translation is always interpretative, critical and partial. Location is about vulnerability and resists the politics of closure . . . So science becomes the paradigmatic model not of closure but that which is contestable and contested'. She finds her way through the concepts of ontic relationality (similar to Latour) and poststructuralism through a form of partial embodiment and materialism. The poststructuralist text becomes written in and on the body, and through the practices of everyday life.

But Haraway's position, says Campbell (2004), is not without flaws. For instance, she does not make the distinction between the standpoint of a feminist scholar and that of any other woman in a society. Feminists have a political orientation that may or may not be shared by other women. Although feminism's critical knowledge may be different from womens' subjugated knowledge, Haraway does not seem to distinguish between the two. Second, while she acknowledges the multiple axes of oppression, she does not adequately theorize them except to imply that oppression is an effect of concrete social structure. She does not offer an account of the sociality that produces subject positions other than a general description of white capitalist patriarchy (ibid., p. 176). A third problem is the tension between constructivism and empiricism. Either practices construct knowledge (constructivism), in which case there is no possibility of critical knowledge, or they do not, in which case there is a possibility of critical knowledge (feminism) (ibid., p. 177). Haraway seems to vacillate between the constructivist nature of all knowledge while at the same time positing feminist standpoint theory claims as accurate descriptions of reality and thereby not relativist. Woolgar (1988, p. 98) calls this 'ontological gerrymandering'.

Therefore 'knowing becomes a way of engaging with the world, and to understand it we must study the patterns created by interactions' (Haraway, quoted in Campbell, 2004, p. 174). Diffraction engages with the different possible patterns that interactions with others create. This interference pattern makes it possible to shift existing meanings.

Haraway (1997, p. 198) describes diffraction as an oppositional practice in which we learn to rethink our political aims from the analytical and imaginative standpoint of those existing in different networks to those of domination. She argues that a standpoint is a cognitive, psychological and political tool for more adequate knowledge. In feminist standpoint theory there is accountability and a commitment to ideals such as freedom and justice (p. 199). However, she falls short of describing how such practices should occur, although she encourages other women to participate in the imagination of the future of feminist practice.

Campbell takes on the challenge to continue Haraway's line of emancipatory thought. She recognizes three elements in the new feminist studies: the type of analytic knowledge produced is not unitary but dependent on ethnicity, class and gender; putting oneself in the shoes of other women requires imaginative knowledge; and finally, such knowledge is based on the political commitments of the feminist knower (p. 176).

She further suggests that FSS produce regulatory standards to govern their practices. This means asking hard questions. What material resources are necessary and available? Who has access to them? Who is excluded? Next, women should reconsider the networks through which feminist knowledge is constructed. If actor network theory (reworked by Haraway) is appropriate, then questions about who are the actors and which actants are central become important. Because of the possibility of falling into a deconstructive mode, such processes must be guided by the explicit feminist political goals of freedom and justice.

Although neither Haraway nor Campbell specifies who is left out and who is included in this process, we suggest that responsibility and accountability must translate into a commitment to negotiate from the position of difference: gender, ethnicity, sexual orientation and class.

Where do we go from here?
The purpose of this chapter has been to present three types of reflexivities and to demonstrate the complexities of reflexive thinking. We suggest that radical reflexivity is primarily centered on a reliance on rhetorical devices that yield 'truer' texts. We agree with Latour, however, that it is better to accept that some fictions are better than others. But which are the better stories? What criteria can we use to make such decisions without closing off the lines of discussion prematurely, as Latour contends? For him, what is 'other' in one kind of constitutional settlement might have rights to being taken into consideration the next time around. This is an ongoing and endless process; any premature closure might be antithetical to the goals of freedom and truth. Haraway's concept of situated knowledge and diffraction promises a new stance on this subject because of its emphasis on political practice and pragmatism, absent from the proposals offered by Latour. Both recognize the political practices involved, but the feminist position insists on responsibility, accountability and commitment to principles of freedom and justice in the definition of the real.

Although we do not explicitly outline an agenda for reflexivity in marketing and consumer research, we highlight a few directions. First, if, as Latour says, we should be concerned about hybridization in our research endeavors, an interdisciplinary approach would lead to the writing of much better stories. To accomplish this requires an emphasis on style, rhetoric and detail. Poetry, fiction, films and journalistic writing are some of the possibilities. Examples have already appeared in the *Journal of Consumer Research* and *Consumption, Markets and Culture*.

In line with Haraway's argument, we suggest that situated knowledge requires a deeper understanding of consumers, their contexts, their networks of interactions and their different points of view. Holt (1995) uses the umbrella term of 'consumer practices'. We argue that it is in these practices that consumer knowledge is situated. Pragmatism is also a concern raised by feminists. Perhaps we should begin to focus on issues that may help consumers live better and more satisfactory lives. Casting light on their needs, fears, desires, dreams and even rights through the telling of their stories might help achieve this goal, particularly if we widen the audience for our writing to include consumers themselves as well as our academic colleagues. Peñaloza's (2001) study of ranchers tries to do just this, working with communities with the goal of writing public policy implications.

We end by articulating some of the issues raised by Sandra Harding (2004) on the value of feminist standpoint theory to a philosophy of science. Standpoint theory has been the most vexing feminist theory when it comes to a postpositivist philosophy of science or even to science studies. Situated knowledge and positionality in the creation of knowledge seems to have touched a raw nerve and has managed to keep the discussion of how science is constructed very much alive in all disciplines, not just feminist ones. As long as the discussion continues and the issues at stake are on the table, the process is precisely what Latour has called for – no premature foreclosure of issues.

Here is Harding's (2004, p. 32) summary of the value of the critique of discovery in science espoused by standpoint theory: 'It focuses not on the choice of individual rational thinkers as does mainstream philosophy of science constrained by its epistemological lenses, but on the collective consciousness of an age that selects interesting hypotheses for us outside the range, beyond the horizon, of the kinds of critical thought that disciplinary conceptual frameworks easily generate.' It is in this context that Campbell's questions, such as what resources are deployed? and who has access to them?, become central to feminist practice.

Standpoint theory has tried to avoid the excessive constructivism and the attendant relativism of postpositivist science. For Haraway (1991, p. 187), this necessitates the recognition of scientific activities as historically constructed. She notes, 'The problem for feminists is how to have simultaneously an account of radical historical contingency for all knowledge claims and knowing subjects, a critical practice for recognizing our own semiotic technologies for making meanings, and a non-nonsense commitment to faithful accounts of a real world.' This thinking, which posits a world 'where truth and power do not issue from the same social locations' (Harding, 2004, p. 34), requires new ways of doing scientific research.

It is here that we can begin to design and implement relevant and purposeful consumer research – writing it up and writing it down as we go.

Acknowledgments

We acknowledge a grant from the Social Sciences and Humanities Research Council No: 410-2004-1497. We would like to thank all our reviewers, especially Lisa Peñaloza, Eric Arnould, Eileen Fischer, Jean-Sebastien Marcoux and Russ Belk, who took the time to help us refine our thoughts. We regret that we could not incorporate a number of issues raised by our reviewers because of space and time constraints.

References

Agar, Michael (1982), 'Toward an ethnographic language', *American Anthropologist*, **84** (4), 779–85.
Allen, D. (1995), 'Hermeneutics: philosophical traditions and nursing practice research', *Nursing Science Quarterly*, **8** (4), 174–82.
Anderson, Elizabeth (2004), 'Feminist epistemology and philosophy of science', *Stanford Encyclopedia of Philosophy*, (summer), p. 1–36. (http://plato.stanford-edu/archives/sum2004/entries/feminism-epistemology/).
Anderson, Paul F. (1986), 'On method in consumer research: a critical relativist perspective', *Journal of Consumer Research*, **13** (September), 155–73.
Arnould, Eric and Craig Thompson (2005), 'Consumer culture theory', *Journal of Consumer Research*, (March) **31** (4), 868–93.
Belk, Russ (1991), 'The history and development of the consumer behavior odyssey', in Russell W. Belk (ed.), *Highways and Buyways: Naturalistic Research from the Consumer Behavior Odyssey*, Association for Consumer Research, Provo, UT: pp. 1–12.
Borgerson, Janet (2005), 'Materiality, agency, and the constitution of consuming subjects: insights for consumer research', *Advances in Consumer Research*, **32**, 439–43.
Bourdieu, Pierre (2000), *Pascalian Meditations*, trans. Richard Nice, Cambridge: Polity (originally published 1997).
Bourdieu, Pierre and L.J.D. Wacquant (1992), *An Invitation to Reflexive Sociology*, Chicago: University of Chicago Press.
Bristor, Julia and Eileen Fischer (1993), 'Feminist thought: implications for consumer research', *Journal of Consumer Research*, **19** (March), 518–36.
Callon, Michael (1986), Some elements of a sociology of translation: domestication of the scallops and the fisherman of St. Brieuc Bay', in J. Law (ed.), *Power, Action and Belief: A New Sociology of Knowledge*, London: Routledge & Kegan Paul, pp. 196–233.
Campbell, Kristin (2004), 'The promise of feminist reflexivities: developing Donna Haraway's project for feminist science studies', *Hypatia*, **19** (1), 162–82.
Costa, Janeen (ed.) (1994), *Gender Issues and Consumer Behavior*, Thousand Oaks, CA: Sage.
Crapanzano, Vincent (ed.) (1977), *Case Studies in Spirit Possession*, New York: Wiley.

Dove, Michael R. (1999), 'Writing for, versus about, the ethnographic other: issues of engagement and reflexivity in working with a tribal NGO in Indonesia', *Identities*, **6** (2–3), 225–53.
Fabian, Johannes (1983), *Time and the Other: How Anthropology Makes its Objects*, New York: Columbia University Press.
Firat, Fuat and Alladi Venkatesh (1995), 'Liberatory postmodernism and the re-enchantment of consumption', *Journal of Consumer Research*, **22** (December), 239–67.
Foley, Doug (2002), 'Critical ethnography: the reflexive turn', *Qualitative Studies in Education*, **15** (5), 469–90.
Gadamer, Hans-George (1976), *Philosophical Hermeneutics*, trans and ed. David Linge, Berkeley: Berkeley University Press.
Geertz, Clifford (1973), *Interpreting Cultures*, New York: Basic Books.
Geertz, Clifford (1988), *Works and Lives*, Stanford: Stanford University Press.
Gould, Stephen J. (1991), 'The self-manipulation of my pervasive, perceived vital energy through product use: an introspective praxis perspective', *Journal of Consumer Research*, **18** (September), 194–207.
Gouldner, Alwin W. (1970), *The Coming Crisis of Western Sociology*, London: Heineman.
Haraway, Donna (1991), 'Situated knowledge: the science question in feminism and the privilege of partial perspectives', *Simians, Cyborgs and Women*, New York: Routledge.
Haraway, Donna (1992), 'The promise of monsters: a regenerative politics for inappropriate/d others', in Lawrence Grossberg, Cary Nelson and Paula Triechler (eds), *Culture Studies*, New York: Routledge.
Haraway, Donna (1997), *Modest_Witness @ Second_ Millennium: Femaleman Meets_ Oncomouse*, New York: Routledge.
Harding, Sandra (2004), 'A socially relevant philosophy of science?', *Hypatia*, **19** (1), 25–47.
Hirschman, Elizabeth (1993), 'Ideology in consumer research, 1980 and 1990: a Marxist and feminist critique', *Journal of Consumer Research*, **19** (March), 537–55.
Holt, Doug (1995), 'How consumers consume: a typology of consumption practices', *Journal of Consumer Research*, **22** (June), 1–16.
Hopkinson Gillian, C. and Margaret K. Hogg (2005), 'Stories: how they are used and produced in market(ing) research', in Russ Belk (ed.), *Handbook of Qualitative Methods in Marketing*, Cheltenham, UK and Northampton, MA, USA: Edward Elgar Publications.
Joy, Annamma (1991), 'Beyond the Odyssey: interpretations of ethnographic research in consumer behavior', Russell W. Belk (ed.), *Highways and Buyways: Naturalistic Research from the Consumer Behavior Odyssey*, Provo, UT: Association for Consumer Research, pp. 216–233.
Joy Annamma and Alladi Venkatesh (1994), 'Postmodernism, feminism and the body: implications for consumer research', *International Journal of Research in Marketing*, **11**, 333–57.
Latour, Bruno (1987), *Science in Action: How to follow Scientists and Engineers through Society*, Cambridge: Harvard University Press.
Latour, Bruno (1988), 'The politics of explanation', in Steve Woolgar (ed.), *Knowledge and Reflexivity: New Frontiers in the Sociology of Knowledge*, London: Sage.
Latour, Bruno (1993), *We Have Never Been Modern*, trans. Catherine Potter, Cambridge: Harvard University Press.
Latour, Bruno (1999) 'How to talk about the body? The normative dimension of science studies' (http://www.ensmp.fr/~latour/articles).
Latour, Bruno (2003a) (pop articles), 'Dialogue prepared for a volume in honor of Donna Haraway, edited by Sharon Ghamari' (http://www.ensmp.fr/~latour/poparticles).
Latour, Bruno (2003b), 'Why has critique run out of steam? From matters of fact to matters of concern', *Critical Inquiry*, **30** (2), 1–11.
Lynch, Michael and Steve Woolgar (1990), 'Introduction: sociological orientations to representational practice in science', in Michael Lynch and Steve Woolgar (eds), *Representations in Scientific Practice*, Cambridge: MIT Press.
Marcus, George (1994), 'What comes (just) after post? The case of ethnography', in Norman Denzin and Y. Lincoln (eds), *Handbook of Qualitative Research*, London: Sage, pp. 563–74.
Marcus, George and Dick Cushman (1982), 'Ethnographies as texts', *Annual Review of Anthropology*, **11**, 25–69.
Marcus, George E. and Michael M.J. Fischer (eds) (1986), *Anthropology as Cultural Critique: An Experimental Moment in the Human Sciences*, Chicago: University of Chicago Press.
Michalowski, Raymond (1996), 'Ethnography and anxiety: field work and reflexivity in the vortex of U.S.–Cuban relations', *Qualitative Sociology*, **19** (1), 59–82.
Murray Jeff and Julie Ozanne (1991), 'The critical imagination: emancipatory interests in consumer research', *Journal of Consumer Research*, **18** (September), 129–44.
Nader, Laura (1972), 'Up the anthropologist: perspectives gained from studying up', in Dell Hymes (ed.), *Reinventing Anthropology*, pp. 284–311.
Peñaloza, Lisa (2005), 'Have we come a long way baby? Negotiating a more multicultural feminism in the marketing academy in the U.S.', in Miriam Catterall, Pauline McLaran and Lorna Stevens (eds), *Marketing and Feminism*, London: Routledge.

Ramachandaran, Vilanayur (2003), 'Neuro science: the new philosophy', *BBC Radio 4–Reith Lectures* (http://www.bbc.co.uk/radio4/reith2003/).

Ricouer, Paul (1970), *Freud and Philosophy: An Essay on Interpretation*, New Have: Yale University Press.

Rosaldo, Renato (1993), *Culture and Truth: The Remaking of Social Analysis*, London: Routledge and Boston: Beacon Press.

Said, Edward (1979), *Orientalism*, New York: Vintage Books

Sherry, John F. and John W. Schouten (2002), 'A role for poetry in consumer research', *Journal of Consumer Research*, **29** (September), 218–34.

Smith, Dorothy (1987), *The Everyday World as Problematic*, Boston: North Eastern University Press.

Stern, Barbara B. (1993), Feminist literary criticism and the deconstructionism of ads: overview and illustrative analysis', *Journal of Consumer Research*, **19** (March), 556–66.

Stoller, Paul (1997), *Sensuous Scholarship*, Philadelphia, PA: University of Pennsylvania Press.

Thomspon, Craig J. (1997), 'Interpreting consumers: a hermeneutical framework for deriving marketing insights from the texts of consumers' consumption stories', *Journal of Marketing Research*, **34** (4), 438–56.

Thompson, Craig, Barbara Stern and Eric Arnould (1998), 'Writing the differences: poststructural pluralism, retextualization, and the construction of reflexive ethnographic narratives in consumption and market research', *Consumption, Markets and Culture*, **2** (2), 105–61.

Van Maanen, John (1988), *Tales of the Field: On Writing Ethnography*, Chicago: University of Chicago Press.

Wallendorf, Melanie and Merrie Brucks (1993), 'Introspection in consumer research: implementation and implications', *Journal of Consumer Research*, **20** (December), 339–59.

Wasserfall, R. (1993), 'Reflexivity, feminism and difference', *Qualitative Sociology*, **16**, 23–41.

Woolgar, Steve (1988), 'Reflexivity is the ethnographer of the text', in Steve Woolgar (ed.), *Knowledge and Reflexivity: New Frontiers in the Sociology of Knowledge*, London: Sage.

27 Reporting ethnographic research: bringing segments to life through movie making and metaphor

Diane M. Martin, John W. Schouten and
James H. McAlexander

Introduction

Marketing managers responsible for functions such as advanced product planning, product design and product positioning can benefit greatly from an intuitive and empathic understanding of their target customers. The surest way to empathize with the textures, rhythms and challenges of customers' lives would be for marketing managers to live with them, socialize with them and participate in activities that involve their product usage. In fact we have worked with firms that have sent their own teams into the homes and workplaces of target customers for days at a time to do just that. However immersion in customers' lives is impractical for most marketing strategists or product designers, especially if the target customer is a Boston executive and the manager is a designer based in Tokyo. Short of complete immersion in customers' lives, the most effective means of developing deep customer understanding or 'bringing segments to life' is market ethnography.

Marketers who understand ethnographic methods do not dispute their ability to develop rich, empathic and highly contextual knowledge of consumer behaviors, motivations and unmet needs. However, many marketers question ethnographers' ability to transfer that knowledge meaningfully to a manager who is separated from the original research experience by multiple layers of people, culture and reporting media.

Ethnographic research often plays to tough crowds. For a research report to have broad impact, especially within a multinational organization, it must communicate clearly to a wide range of decision makers, including people with limited or stereotypical views of customers' sociocultural environments, people with inherent biases against qualitative research and even people (like many product designers and advertising creatives) who mistrust or depreciate the value of customer research altogether. Academic abstractions are often lost on such audiences, and they may regard the findings of qualitative research as too obvious to be of any real value.

For any given research project there is typically one person in the client organization with ultimate responsibility for the choice of vendors and for the usefulness and impact of the research outcomes among various internal audiences. These research liaisons within the client organization often stake career advancement on the performance of their research vendors. They face a dilemma of agency and responsibility, expected on the one hand to manage creatively complex research that relies on the expertise of others while, on the other hand, being mindful of the organizational culture and personalities that inevitably will color interpretations and affect acceptance or rejection of the research results.

Like Scheherazade, whose life for a thousand and one nights depended on the quality of the stories she told, the ethnographic research firm stakes its viability on the quality of its story telling. The risk of mediocre research or lackluster reporting is born not only by the researchers but also by the client liaison who hired them. However a research firm that helps clients to look good may also help itself toward becoming a preferred vendor, thus smoothing out the obstacle-ridden road of modern procurement processes. Excellent research well reported can also develop legs within the client organization. The research report that gets passed around rather than finding a narrow slot of shelf space for its first and final resting place builds the credibility of the client research liaison and the reputation of the research firm. For example, we recently learned that one of our research reports from over five years ago still occupies a place on the desk top of a corporate Vice-President and functions as his 'bible' when making decisions about a particular market segment.

In this chapter we discuss methods that we have developed in conjunction with key clients to bridge the culture gap that too often impedes the effective communication of ethnographic findings from the market place to high-level marketing decision makers.

Bringing market segments to life: a communication challenge

Market place ethnography uses a robust set of methods with many powerful applications. Our most common research objective involves the task of 'bringing segments to life'. Segment-to-life research, as we practice it, typically follows a quantitative market segmentation study. Although the segmentation study provides many details about the nature and size of market segments, planners, designers and marketers often feel a need to understand more intimately the consumers they are trying to serve. Market segmentation research locates a client's market segments on a map, but ethnography goes into the neighborhood and experiences how the people in those segments live. As explained by one client research liaison, 'Segment-to-life research provides a face to the story. It makes [our] people more interested. . . . People just don't get that passionate about [quantitative] data.'

The biggest challenge in segment-to-life research is not gaining a nuanced understanding of the target segment's lives, motivations and product usage behaviors. It lies in communicating that nuanced understanding accurately and effectively to a diverse audience within the client organization. One way to enhance the effectiveness of a research report is to invoke multiple communication modalities. The field of neurolinguistic programming describes the basis for understanding in terms of three modalities: visual, auditory and kinesthetic (LaBorde, 1983). While any given individual will have preferred communication modalities, the most effective communication involves all three.

Savvy researchers include multiple modalities in their presentations. For example, Dennis Stefani, a senior executive at Diagnostic Research, described an especially creative approach. His firm had been engaged by a manufacturer and marketer of products for young people to conduct a psychographic segmentation study. Their quantitative research yielded seven viable market segments. As part of their reporting they had created caricature-like renderings of the segments and vivid literary descriptions. Even so, the client felt too removed from the real people in the segment. After some extensive brainstorming the research team decided to produce a theatrical performance. They employed actors, wrote scripts and created costumes. The production was unveiled as part of a formal research presentation at the client's offices. At what the client believed to be the conclusion of the formal presentation the research team shared their observation that it would be very valuable if they could, somehow, bring members of the segment to the meeting. Just then, there was a knock on the door, and in came the performers. From

Stefani's description this presentation was a tremendous success. In one dramatic production the research team had presented their results orally, visually and kinesthetically, truly bringing the segment to life.

While a play with live actors may not always be feasible, as a general premise creative, multimodal reporting offers great value to audiences of ethnographic work. In our work with large, culturally complex client organizations we have discovered several keys to powerful research reporting. The first key is to organize and deliver the main themes of the research in the form of a strong guiding metaphor. The second is to engage the client in dramatic, multimodal story telling. The third is to involve the client research liaison as an active partner throughout the research process.

We now begin with a discussion of the guiding metaphor and its core usefulness in ethnographic research reporting. We then discuss our process of conducting and reporting segment-to-life research, which we describe both literally and metaphorically as 'making movies'. Finally, throughout the research process, we emphasize the importance of involving the client research liaison.

Making meaning: the hard-working metaphor

Metaphors help us to understand unfamiliar things in terms of things that are more familiar (Aristotle, 1954). According to many theorists (e.g., Nietsche, 1911; Osborn, 1967) metaphors are the doorways to understanding reality because phenomena in the world only become accessible to us through the metaphors or symbols that we attach to them. Metaphors in an ethnographic research report can convey deeper insights and enhanced understanding of the lived experiences of consumers than can mere description.

The problem of communicating the findings of segment-to-life research is precisely the one described by Aristotle: making unfamiliar things familiar. Metaphors can serve as maps (Lakoff and Johnson, 1980) or patterns by which we understand and communicate how customers' reality occurs. As ethnographers we strive to make customers' unfamiliar lifestyles, emotional responses and ways of understanding seem familiar and readily accessible to members of our client organizations by linking them to concepts the client understands. One client describes the benefits of metaphor for her advance planning and strategy team:

> A metaphor is so much easier for people to recall later. There is so much arguing and negotiating that other noise will occur. Metaphors, they strike a chord with people. It is a common understanding – when there is some kind of metaphor – people already have some sort of thing to draw reference to.

Dennis Stefani of Diagnostic Research similarly states that metaphors 'make something very complicated come to life. The client is elated. They now have an easy way to explain to their people what the research is about in a very easy to understand form.'

The choice of a metaphor shapes our understanding of a phenomenon (Osborn, 1967). For example, the saying that 'time is money' helps us understand something intangible in terms of something tangible; however, more than that, it fosters an understanding of time as 'something that can be spent, budgeted, wasted, and saved' (Foss, 1996, p. 359). In this case 'time is money' is a guiding or deep metaphor that serves as the underlying logic for other surface-level metaphors (Gozzi, 1999) such as 'time-saving devices' or 'squandering one's life'.

The sources of metaphor in segment-to-life research originate from the ethnographic data, that is, from customers' words, behaviors and assembled belongings (cf. Denny and Sunderland, 2005). For example, in research with automobile owners the guiding metaphor, 'my car is a human helper', is uncovered as owners refer to attributes of their vehicles in embodied human terms. A woman whose arms are loaded with shopping bags refers to her remote door opener as 'a helping hand'. A man negotiating a tight parallel parking space refers to the distance sensors in the rear bumper as 'an extra set of eyes'.

Beyond merely shaping our understanding, metaphors can govern our behaviors as individuals and societies. For example, Schon (1979) discusses the public policy imperatives suggested by the metaphor of an urban neighborhood as a 'blighted area' as opposed to a 'folk community'. One metaphor demands a cure or the eradication of disease whereas the other argues implicitly for appreciation and the preservation of cultural uniqueness. In the world of automotive design the metaphor 'my car is a sanctuary' suggests different design imperatives than 'my car is a warrior' or 'my car is a rolling family room'.

One way to bring a segment to life, according to Dennis Stefani, is to 'find the archetype of the segment, a real person that embodies the qualities of the segment'. Some clients prefer to focus their planning and design efforts on one individual who serves as the 'face' of the market segment. The guiding metaphor in such a case is 'Person X is the target market.' The field of semiotics, through the analysis of signs, symbols and their functions, provides additional insight into the usefulness of this application of metaphor in segment-to-life research. Semiotics refers to a sign as something that includes both a representation and an object represented. In this case the image of the individual customer (Person X) functions like an icon that evokes or conjures the characteristics of the segment which it represents. To have sign value for a market segment the customer displayed in the report must be seen as a classic example of the segment. However, a segment archetype need not be an accurate representation of an individual customer. It can also be a composite drawn from attributes of several customers in the study. In our segment-to-life research reports we often include mini-biographies or character sketches of individual informants that serve as emblems of different facets of the target segment.

Seeking the right metaphor

Gozzi (1999) suggests a process of metaphor analysis that we find very useful. It begins with identifying the surface-level metaphors that arise from the text in question, in our case the ethnographic data. For example, a segment of hard-core freeway commuters may emphasize the desire to shut out the outside world, to retreat into their music or books on tape, and to unwind from work stress on the way home. Attending to themes among the surface metaphors may reveal the deeper, guiding metaphors that organize customers' meaning-making processes. In the case of our hypothetical commuters we may conclude that the 'car is a sanctuary'.

The next step is to tease out the implications of the guiding metaphor and to question the conclusions that flow from it. What, for example, are the implications of the 'car is a sanctuary' metaphor? Interior attributes such as quiet and coziness may well be implied. What about exterior attributes? Is a sanctuary flashy and attention grabbing, or does it tend toward anonymity? Which of these tendencies best reflects the preferences of the hard-core commuter segment? If exterior flashiness is a desired attribute, maybe the sanctuary metaphor needs rethinking.

The third step is to suggest alternate metaphors. This is similar to the practice of 'devil's advocacy' (cf. Schouten and McAlexander, 1995) in that it forces a higher level of scrutiny of our conclusions. What other guiding metaphors might also account for the emerging system of surface metaphors? A den? A library? A concert hall? Finally Gozzi recommends studying the source and usage of the guiding metaphor to better understand its political agenda or position. Some metaphors serve certain philosophies or dogmas better than others. We should ask ourselves, is the guiding metaphor we have identified for the target segment representative of their moral and emotional reality?

The metaphor as persuasion: rhetoric illuminates reality
As market ethnographers we enjoy the privilege of luxuriating in a deep understanding of customer's lives. However, we also face the difficult task of conveying the essence of complicated consumption experiences to our clients. The segment-to-life report is more than a compendium of our research activities and findings. It also serves as a rhetorical text. It must persuade the client audience to accept the meaning of our analysis. Ideally it will also help to protect the integrity of the analysis by reducing the chance of its being misinterpreted. The guiding metaphor that frames the report must therefore serve accurately as a signifier of the deeper meaning in the data, and it must also function as a rhetorical device.

The persuasive ability of a metaphor relies on its verisimilitude. As a comparison of two unrelated terms or classes of experience (e.g., automobile and sanctuary) the metaphor juxtaposes two sets of characteristics (Black, 1962). The verisimilitude of the metaphor rests on the audience accepting the appropriateness of the comparison. If the attributes of a commuter car and the attributes of a sanctuary seem sufficiently comparable, the metaphor works. Well-crafted ethnographic research builds plausible findings on a corpus of data and on carefully developed themes. Likewise a well-crafted metaphor is a result of harmonious comparisons. For this reason the guiding metaphor for a research report should emerge from the data. The data form the foundation of the metaphor and the metaphor helps to carry the meaning intended by the researcher.

We believe the process of selecting a guiding metaphor should involve client research liaisons, drawing on their insights and understanding of their organizations. Client liaisons are likely to have a better understanding of the kinds of metaphors or phraseology that have already circulated in their realm. They also will be more sensitive to potential misunderstandings that may arise from cultural differences within the firm. On many occasions we have been dissuaded by client research liaisons from using terms or phrases in our research reports because of a belief that they would spark misconceptions among certain internal audiences and possibly bring about the rejection of our conclusions.

Making movies: the segment-to-life research process
Our preference for a final report of segment-to-life research takes the form of a documentary-style video accompanied by a multimedia presentation with embedded photographs, video clips, in-depth prose notes and written character sketches of customers that embody important facets of the target segment. Both the video and the multimedia presentation are built around a central guiding metaphor. We may use the same metaphor for both reports, or we may choose different metaphors for each report, depending on the message we desire to communicate with each. We find that this combination of forms and media provides the necessary multi-modality to reach diverse audiences.

We have discussed the role of metaphor in our research and reporting. We now turn our attention to the overall research process. In the spirit of the foregoing discussion we have chosen to describe the ethnographic process of bringing segments to life in terms of its own guiding metaphor: movie making. The metaphor works whether or not we actually include a documentary-style video as part of the final report product.

Pre-production planning: fine-tuning the research objectives
Client research liaisons are the executive producers of segment-to-life research. Client involvement starts with the request for proposals and continues throughout the research process. We want client liaisons to feel ownership of the project. We want them to be defenders and promoters within their organizations. As executive producers they have commissioned the project, they are responsible for the budget and they should be kept informed of progress. If problems arise in any aspect of the project, they should be informed and consulted. When the time comes to begin data collection, the client liaisons or their agents should be encouraged to join the field research team.

Once awarded a research project, we assume the role of production manager working closely with the client liaison in pre-production arrangements. We concentrate on refining the research objectives and the interview guide, which functions as a set of stage directions for the actual production of the ethnographic field work. Clients' insight on their firm's organizational culture and climate is invaluable as we carefully craft objectives and interview guides that encompass the interests of disparate audiences within the firm. For example, what may be of primary importance to the product design team is of less consequence to the marketing department. Client liaisons can bring this insider knowledge to light during pre-production. Client liaisons are also instrumental in location scouting or choosing cities for interviews so that regional representation objectives are met. Eventually the production schedule, a timeline for data collection and reporting, is ironed out and we go into the next phase of pre-production.

Casting and scripting: planning the field work
Next we move to the casting decision, that is, correctly identifying and recruiting informants from the target market. Based on the traditions of qualitative research, segment-to-life research does not require large casts of players (Miles and Huberman, 1994). We often find that a purposive sample (e.g. Potter, 1996) of 12 to 18 informants from varied geographic regions is sufficient to generate thematic saturation and capture the important differences that nuance a market segment. The easy part of the informant screening process involves procuring a list of customers that meet target criteria for demographic and product usage characteristics. From there, informants should be further screened for key segmentation (most often psychographic) variables, generally using a reduced battery of measures from the study that yielded the segmentation. Final screening should ensure that informants are also articulate. One way to ensure good verbal skills is to ask recruits to answer an unexpected question requiring a measure of thought and creativity. For example, a recruiter might ask, 'If you could invite any historical figure to dinner, who would it be? And why?'

Assembling a solid production team is critical to the segment-to-life project. We typically use dual-interviewer teams, most often consisting of one male and one female interviewer. Multiple sets of ears, eyes and brains help the team to glean the maximum amount of information from the interview situation, something that is especially important in cases of small sample research. While one interviewer pursues a particular line of inquiry the other one can observe and reflect on where to explore next.

Finally, the production team needs a skilled videographer, preferably one with feature film or other creative experience. Videographers need to be able to manage cameras, microphones and lights, setting up and taking down equipment rapidly and as unobtrusively as possible. More importantly, they need to be perceptive, sensitive and creative in the gathering of B-roll material (i.e., non-interview footage that captures interesting contextualizing images such as possessions in use, art on display and activities unfolding) and interesting camera angles that will add life to the final video product.

Ethnographic interviews do not adhere strictly to scripted dialogue. The actual dialogue emerges as gently guided ad libs by the actors. However a general script is still necessary. In this case it is a semi-structured interview guide (e.g. Kvale, 1996) consisting of general discussion topics with possible probe questions, and a set of basic stage directions (such as 'begin home tour', 'move to vehicle for ride-along' or 'shoot B-roll of neighborhood and home exterior').

The shoot: field work and data collection
The shoot begins when the field team rolls up in front of the first set, or research site, with the camera rolling to begin capturing the scene, which will be situated in some combination of the informant's home, vehicle, workplace or some other relevant consumption venue. At this point it becomes very important that the recruiters have made it quite clear to informants that the interview involves multiple researchers and videotaping.

Data collection proceeds as a semi-structured interview, akin to what Zaltman and Coulter (1995) call 'guided conversation', with the primary purpose of eliciting informant narratives or stories. The importance of the venue cannot be overstated. By conducting the research in the places where consumption occurs we are able to ground the informants' narratives in the sensory and symbolic fullness of their lives as lived and displayed through their own possessions. In the course of an interview we invite (and videotape) informant commentary on such items as art objects, family photos, music CDs, recreational gear, collections, wardrobe and accessories, and the contents of kitchen cabinets and refrigerators. We pay attention not only to the existence of such items but also to nuances of their brands, their condition and their placement. We have also found success in asking informants to create day-in-the-life photographic journals. Using the informants' own possessions and images as projective stimuli we achieve a richly illustrated story replete with visual and verbal descriptions (and metaphors) of the informants' own construction.

The goal of segment-to-life research is not merely to tell and illustrate individual informants' stories. Rather it is to craft a single story of a target market as enacted by multiple actors in multiple situations. Cinematically the product is analogous to a film like Robert Altman's *Short Cuts*, which weaves numerous personal micro-stories into a single meta-story of which the real star and subject is the city of Los Angeles. Between shooting individual informant scenes, the field team begins the process of crafting the meta-story. Through field debriefs with the client and a version of constant comparative analysis we examine similarities and differences among the subplots and characters with the end goal of a guiding metaphor that will serve as the premise of the larger story of the target market. Ideally a client liaison will have joined the field team as an observer. Client participation in the data collection and analysis greatly enhances buy-in and smooths the process of approval for the final product.

The editing room: post-production and report preparation
By the time shooting is finished it is usually possible and desirable to provide a top-line report (preliminary executive summary) for the client liaison for purposes of early feedback and pre-approval for the intended creative direction. At this stage of the project, the work becomes almost as much a creative endeavor as an analytical one. In fact, to find the guiding metaphor that will give unity and power to the meta-story requires a synergy between creativity and analysis. Several tools, both literary and analytical, are useful in bringing it off.

One tool we use routinely is the creation of character sketches of individual informants. We begin with actual data regarding such issues as lifestyles and motivations, and from there we craft short biographies leading to plausible hypotheses. We try to understand each informant as a well-rounded, fully contextualized character, complete with driving motivations and human conflict and contradictions.

In the course of reviewing data tapes, we create rough time-coded transcriptions. In the transcriptions we make special note of quotes, images and observational data (e.g., CDs that were in the informant's car at the time) that capture particular themes or sentiments we might wish to highlight in the finished documentary or multimedia presentation. We also remain vigilant to informant-created metaphors that help to capture important themes. In effect more than in actual techniques, this identification of metaphors resembles the ZMET methodology described by Zaltman and Coulter (1995). The primary difference is that the ethnographic method of bringing the segment to life draws the metaphors organically from the lived contexts of informant experience.

In the spirit of what Potter (1996) calls 'horizontal collaboration', members of the research team distribute their own transcriptions and character sketches, after which we begin a think-tank style analysis to finish the job that began in the field, namely of identifying the higher-level themes that best subsume or account for the various subthemes emergent from the data. We sift through and discuss various metaphors for the major themes. We play them out on a kind of story board until we decide on a single, guiding metaphor with the power and freshness to drive the story of the target market.

The next step in reporting is to prepare a multimedia presentation. The CD-based presentation is intended to stand alone as a self-guided exercise. In it we embed photos and video clips from the data to provide visual context and to feature the 'voice of the customer'. In the 'notes pages' format we create an in-depth written report that fleshes out and provides examples of concepts captured in the bulleted slides. This portion of the final report is useful in many ways. First, it delivers findings quickly and in a fashion that is easily revised, based on feedback from the client representative. Keeping the client close during the report production phase of the project is valuable. It is the client that best understands the internal audience for the report, including their biases, filters and potential strong reactions. Second, the presentation format allows the client to edit it, adapt it for specific internal audiences or incorporate it at will into larger-scale presentations. Third, it serves as a template or storyboard for a documentary video report.

Producing the documentary video requires script writing, voice-over recording, video clip selection, music selection, on-screen graphics creation and hours of editing. Much of the work is already done in the course of producing the multimedia presentation. The flow of the script is suggested by the structure and content of the presentation, which in turn is influenced by the guiding metaphor. Video clip selection is abetted by the time-coded interview transcripts. Music selection is made easier by attending to the musical preferences observed among the target customers. Pulling it all together into a documentary quality video that captivates the client and delivers the desired conclusions in an emotionally powerful way is an art. For that reason we prefer to collaborate with a video professional with feature film experience.

The advent of mediated communication in the forms of visual display, photography and embedded video provides a richness of multidimensionality to the meaning signified by a fresh, creative, data-grounded guiding metaphor. Carefully crafted and inventive metaphors can launch new ways of thinking about customer realities and product concepts.

Conclusion

Our use of the metaphor of movie making emphasizes the artistic aspect of the research endeavor as well as its analytical side. It also emphasizes collaborative effort over individual effort, making it more appropriate than metaphors such as novel writing, painting or music composing. A group musical performance metaphor might have come close, except that Linda Price and Eric Arnould (1998) have already used that metaphor to perfection. The movie-making metaphor serves as a symbol of the actual process as well as an archetype of multimodal research reporting. Our experience in the field provides evidence supportive of the power of metaphor to convey complex ideas in an approachable manner that is both meaningful and memorable. Further we observed that careful attention to oral, visual and kinesthetic communication modalities adds to the dynamic nature of the research report, metaphorically bringing the market research to life for many and varied audiences.

There is a long history of using metaphors to communicate ideas in marketing theory and practice (e.g. Zaltman and Coulter, 1995). This chapter has explored the theoretical foundations that at least partially explain the success of metaphors in marketing research. Ultimately the documentary video, multimedia presentation and written 'character sketches' of customers provide clients with deep insights that, when artfully presented, are inherently useful for communicating with client audiences that have diverse responsibilities and experiences.

Acknowledgments

The authors wish to thank Patti Sunderland of the Practica Group, LLC, for her insightful feedback on an earlier draft of this chapter. We also thank Dennis Stefani and Heather Blankenhorn for their input to this chapter and for their friendship over the years.

References

Aristotle (1954), *The Rhetoric and Poetics of Aristotle*, New York: Modern Library.
Black, Max (1962), *Models and Metaphors: Studies in Language and Philosophy*, Ithaca, NY: Cornell University Press.
Denny, Rita M. and Patricia L. Sunderland (2005), 'Researching cultural metaphors in action: metaphors of computing technology in contemporary U.S. life', *Journal of Business Research*, **58** (October), 1456–63.
Foss, Sonja K. (1996), *Rhetorical Criticism: Exploration and Practice*, 2nd edn, Prospect Heights: Waveland Press.

Gozzi, Raymond (1999), *The Power of Metaphor in the Age of Electronic Media*, Cresskill, NJ: Hampton Press.
Kvale, Steinar (1996), *InterViews: An Introduction to Qualitative Research Interviewing*, Thousand Oaks, CA: Sage.
LaBorde, Genie (1983), *Influencing With Integrity*, Palo Alto, CA: Syntony Publishing.
Lakoff, George and Mark Johnson (1980), *Metaphors We Live By*, Chicago: University of Chicago Press.
Miles, Matthew B. and Michael A. Huberman (1994), *Qualitative Data Analysis*, 2nd Edn, Thousand Oaks, CA: Sage.
Nietsche, Friedrich (1911), 'On truth and falsity in their ultramoral sense', in Oscar Levy (ed.), *The Complete Works of Friedrich Nietsche*, trans. Maximillian Mugge, New York: Macmillan.
Osborn, Michael M. (1967), 'The evolution of the theory of metaphor in rhetoric', *Western Speech*, 31 (Spring), 121–31.
Potter, James, W. (1996), *An Analysis of Thinking and Research About Qualitative Methods*, Mahwah, NJ: Lawrence Erlbaum Associates.
Price, Linda L. and Eric J. Arnould (1998), 'Conducting the choir: representing multimethod consumer research', in Barbara B. Stern (ed.), *Representing Consumers*, London and New York: Routledge, pp. 339–64.
Schon, Donald A. (1979), 'Generative metaphor: a perspective on problem-setting in social policy', in Andrew Ortony (ed.), *Metaphor and Thought*, Cambridge: Cambridge University Press.
Schouten, John W. and James H. McAlexander (1995), 'Subcultures of consumption: an ethnography of the new bikers', *Journal of Consumer Research*, 22 (June), 43–62.
Zaltman, Gerald and Robin H. Coulter (1995), 'Seeing the voice of the customer: metaphor-based advertising research', *Journal of Advertising Research*, July–August, 35–51.

28 Entering entertainment: creating consumer documentaries for corporate clients

Patricia L. Sunderland

The good old days of 'tell 'em what you're going to tell 'em, tell 'em, then tell 'em you told 'em' are clearly over. A more apt dictum for the digital age is 'Don't just tell 'em. Show 'em!' (Sanders, 2002, p. 153)

Let's go to the videotape. (Iconic refrain of Warner Wolf, NY TV Sportscaster)

My concern in this chapter is to bring to light some of the conundrums that occur in the presentation of ethnographic research in moving visual forms or 'movies'. These movies, as a rule now shot on video, then edited and often viewed in digital electronic forms, are frequently referred to with the shorthand of 'video' or 'film', as in 'ethnographic film'. The appellation of movie is rare in the context of research (except that it crops up on our computers via the moniker 'movie file'), yet I have chosen this word as an apt way to begin as I believe that ideas and ideals of entertainment implicit in our cultural notions of movies play a significant role in the production of the conundrums discussed. I will make no pretense of having or providing complete answers to the issues raised here, but wish to discuss them as matters important to consider as we move ahead with more frequent presentation and thus representation of ethnographic analysis in forms beyond (the now increasingly outmoded) prose. I believe that we need to examine ways that cultural and epistemological assumptions reside amidst our (re)presentational choices as well as consider the ways these operate in the reception of ethnographic documentary, or movies.

In this chapter, I draw on experiences that Rita Denny and I have encountered while providing ethnographic cultural analyses for corporate clients. As anthropologists, our practice revolves around culturally inspired ethnographic work conducted to aid our clients in the development of new product, branding and marketing strategies, advertising and the like (see Denny, this volume; Sunderland and Denny, 2003). At times we are hired as expert consultants or trainers (ideally in inspiring locales) but most of our days are spent designing and carrying out ethnographic projects, all of which require some form of (re)presentation to clients.

The videotaping of fieldwork and the creation of composite edited excerpts have been important aspects of our ethnographic work since the late 1990s. Before that time, videotaping of ethnographic interviews and consumer practices was sporadically requested as was the (re)presentation of the results in video format. While from early on we eagerly embraced the values, virtues and creative possibilities of video (in the 1990s, in fact, we rather than the clients were generally the catalysts for the inclusion of an edited videotape), since the early 2000s video has become an assumed requirement not only by us, but also by clients. As Belk and Kozinets (2005a) have noted, there has been a revolution in demand, as well as expectations, for videographic research. Invoking the poignant example of Nissan's insistence to Schouten and McAlexander that they report on commissioned brand community research only in video, not written, format, Belk and Kozinets make the case that these heightened expectations and demands arise out of an appreciation of the power of video-based research as well as a social environment in which not only is video production more feasible, but consumers and clients are also more accustomed to interacting with visual imagery as a result of television, film, computers and the Internet. While we have not yet been asked to produce only a video production, we have had requests from clients to give priority to the video production over the writing (that is, PowerPoint). We have also been asked by a commissioning client to provide video reports that exactly matched the style they had become accustomed to from the work of another research group and we were expected to comply.

In fact, as interest in and benefits of ethnographic video have become more apparent in the corporate world, it has become a selling point for consumer research firms and corporate research departments to hire 'professional videographers'. Many consumer research firms list 'video ethnography' as a research modality they can provide and feature the videographic credentials of their team as a selling point. We have had professional moviemakers contact us, seeking to sell us on the value they could bring to our endeavors.

And certainly, we currently feel the pressure to up the ante on the technical and artistic qualities of our productions even if, *per* Jean Rouch, muse and mentor of many an ethnographic film-maker, one should be less worried about technical aspects and more concerned with content (Colleyn, 2005; Ruby, 2005). In today's climate, especially in corporate circles, not worrying about technical quality does not always seem an option. In our own research we like to put the camera in the hands of the client, thereby increasing their participation in the research process as well as product. This generally means, though, putting the cameras into the hands of 'amateur' videographers which then requires oversight from us in order to maintain the quality of the production. Within our small company, other partners are in fact tired of listening to my reminders to please pay attention to the need for sufficient light and to avoid back lighting, to be sure to capture decent audio from the speaker of interest as well as to pay attention to background noise, and to please not forget the b-roll of telling imagery. And, when I become annoyed in the editing process (which is simultaneously mind-expanding and numbing, not to mention time-intensive) and plead for partners to at least give some attention to the accurate labeling of tapes, what I am really pleading for is the need to keep issues of editing in mind while shooting. Editing is a substantial part of the process when multiple dozens of hours of footage are reduced to minutes' worth of edited excerpts. The editing onus for us has also increased over time as we have shifted from incorporating video into our (re)presentations as mainly highlighting examples to being illustrative of the overall analysis and telling most of the story.

In short, 'video ethnography' now exists as rubric and essential research service that companies currently commission, from us and others. Quite worrisome in these developments is NOT the use of video in ethnographic research but the ways in which, for those commissioning research, videotaping is increasingly becoming not only coterminous, but also synonymous with 'doing ethnography'. The troubling development is when video is rendered synonymous with ethnography via a rendering of observation as synonymous with ethnography. This rendering in turn produces analytically anemic accounts that can pose a danger to the perceived value of ethnography (Wasson, 2000). As has been said before, can we imagine the potential ramifications if quantitative research were rendered synonymous with graphs and tables or, perhaps even worse, with spreadsheets of data?

The concern in this chapter, however, is not to take on the issues which involve profound misinterpretations or misuses of ethnography, but rather to consider the conundrums that notions of entertainment bring to the inclusion and reception of video in ethnographic (re)presentations, even when the epistemological underpinnings of ethnography are comprehended and utilized in all their grandeur.

My point is that we are positioned at a rocky crag in our (re)presentational choices. Video is culturally inflected in a way that foregrounds its value as entertainment, not its value to inform, and thus can be devalued as a medium of information (Belk and Kozinets, 2005a, 2005b). Yet there is also little question that the visual image is a powerful means to transmit and represent ethnographic data (Belk, 1998; Hockings, 2003; Holbrook, 1998; Ruby, 2000; Schroeder, 1998; Taylor, 1994; Peñaloza and Cayla, and others, this volume). And if we are going to achieve phenomenological and sensual understandings, we need to find ways that let us feel cultural issues, ways that allow cultural issues to resonate (Behar, 1999; Joy and Sherry, 2003; Sherry and Schouten, 2002; Stoller, 1997). Gifted and highly evocative writers can create highly sensual and moving imagery in a reader's mind – and this can happen in the writing of academic prose, novels or poetry. But, as Behar (1999) so eloquently points out, anthropologists' productions, the books they write, the 'ethnographies' by which they achieve tenure as well as professional identity, are as a rule not so; nor are they memorable. Instead, as Behar (1999, pp. 482–3) writes, these accounts 'explain rather than show, tell rather than narrate, cite rather than imagine, justify rather than dream, and most tragically, turn vigorous flesh-and-blood people into ponderous slugs of theory'. The poetically told – and shown – is important. As communicators of ethnographic research, a strength and opportunity we now have lies in the access to the production and dissemination of visual imagery. Does not the image of the young customer in Figure 28.1, taken in front of a street cart's medley of offerings while investigating the meaning of beverages in Bangkok, evoke something – something one can feel in the chest – about what a desired beverage can mean on a hot day? Of course, more information is needed. The one photograph does not tell the whole story, nor does it provide the analysis, but it can sufficiently aid the everyday writer in communicating the details, the feelings, the context, the place, the point.

Going beyond still photography, moving imagery allows us the possibilities of narrative flow and storytelling. The value of narrative and stories for uncovering and communicating crucial symbolic meanings has been clearly recognized by consumer research scholars (see chapters in this volume). There is also no question that memorable examples, whether in the form of mnemonics, metaphors or movies, generally help us to remember information. But when it comes to the incorporation of imagery, and especially moving imagery into our (re)presentations, we end up on rocky, difficult terrain. Involved are matters of overcoming modernism's sticky dualisms of objectivity v. subjectivity, method v. theory and data v. speculation, but there is another dualism to overcome. We need also, despite, or perhaps precisely because of, the larger enveloping cultural context of an experience/entertainment economy (Pine, 1999; Wolf, 1999), to overcome the vestigial dualism of entertainment v. information. In anthropological circles there has been considerable discussion of 'blurred genres' and the ways that previously separate (re)presentational forms such as 'factual account' and 'fiction' have been merged into forms such as 'creative non-fiction' (Behar, 1999; Geertz, 1983). As Behar (1999, p. 476) notes, 'the positive result of all this blurring of genres is that we now have a fluid field of hybrid texts

Figure 28.1   Buying beverages on a hot day in Bangkok

that baffle every effort at easy categorization and that respond to the desire, which is the hallmark of our century, for stories based on the testimony of lived experience'. In educational circles we have been entreated to act upon the dictum that, if learning is not fun, students will not learn. We live in a world of edutainment and infotainment. But a lurking dualism of information v. entertainment remains.

The stories that follow invite you to think about the dualism of entertainment and information as it is occurs in the (re)presentation of ethnographic research to corporate clients via video. Again this is not the only issue that could or should be discussed regarding the use of video in corporate consumer research. For instance, the lurking and erroneous promise of video's objectivity or its ability to provide a complete and total (virtual panopticon) of a record are also matters to address (see Belk and Kozinets, 2005a; Sunderland and Denny, 2002). But right now I want us to just think about fun.

In the presentations
We have found that clients – the consumers of our research – expect foremost to be entertained by and with moving images. When we play a moving image snippet during a presentation, the tendency among the assembled audience is not to embrace that video excerpt as the 'real' or 'important' informational resource, but more as the 'fun' stuff. We see evidence of this attitude in gestures and behaviors. As a rule our presentations consist of us talking, i.e., explaining the import of written bullet points and a myriad of accompanying digital photographs, scanned drawings, collages and other images inserted into projected PowerPoint slides. Then, at strategic points, we show edited video clips which are generally five to 15 minutes in duration. A few years ago this meant switching from projected PowerPoint slides to a video player; more recently this has meant simply clicking on the compressed 'movie' file linked to the PowerPoint document. When we do make the switch, people tend to sit back in their chairs and even smile a bit in anticipation. If notes were being taken by pen or into the laptop while we were talking, this tends to stop. To say that we have never seen a client take notes on some aspect of the action occurring in a video involves only a tiny bit of exaggeration.

The difference is due to the pragmatics of the communicative frame (Goffman, 1974; Hymes, 1964; Silverstein, 2004). Even if expository prose and educational lecture are NOT the dominant communication modalities of our time, we do tend culturally to constitute these genres as the 'smarter' stuff, the forms through which serious learning takes place. Moving imagery is not the medium we believe we learn from, even if we do. In fact, moving imagery is itself the contextual key that frames the event as one of 'entertainment'. It is a frame learned from the cultural space of moving imagery in our lives: movies and television programs *are* a dominant form of entertainment in everyday life. Advertising, a prime user of moving imagery, also often foregrounds entertainment. And so, when we switch to the moving imagery of video, assembled audiences may not only smile and sit back in their chairs, but also seize upon those moments as the time when they can stop paying attention to the presentation and instead check – and respond to – messages on their Blackberries. Or it can be seen as the time to make a run out of the conference room for a bathroom break. It is the time when audience members will lean toward each other and have animated short side conversations with those sitting next to them. And, of course, turning off lights in the room, at times a necessity for viewing, only seems to add to the 'now we are at the movies' allure.

As a cultural event, there are undoubtedly many things going on here. Individuals working in corporate worlds frequently live with multiple commitments and extraordinary time pressures. Any kind of a break in an event can be seen as time to check up on things, to answer a message, to get something done. Another contribution to the proliferations of side conversations at that moment could be that we, the presenters/the lecturers, move to the side of the room. In other words, the speaker has given up the floor and thus it is a chance for others to speak. It is a cultural convention that it is rude to have a private, side conversation while someone else is talking to an assembled group (unless, of course, one cannot be seen or heard by the speaker). Audience members were perhaps being thoughtful in waiting for us to finish speaking before talking to each other. But it would also seem that audience members are following learned and practiced behavior from (past) television viewing. From this angle, the move to the videotape (culturally symbolically understood as a 'less crucial' conveyor of information than the main fare of the written word or lecture) is akin to the time out of the current show for the commercial break. Hence the message check, the bathroom break. While I started with the rubric of movies as a useful rhetorical device, it truly is television that we need to be thinking about. As Ruby (1996, p. 201) has written, 'Since viewers spend far more time watching television than they do watching films, it is safe to say that they evaluate all moving pictures in terms of the conventions and expectations they acquire watching television.' And we must take into account that watching television now often means watching while reading a book, magazine, cleaning the house, talking on the phone, browsing on-line and so on, as well as watching considerable numbers of movies for which the ability to start, stop, pause and rewind at will (and thus the ability to do other things while watching) are a given.

With the advent of mobile, individual, digital technologies, the cultural conventions for group face-to-face meetings are in flux; attending to calls, messages or interacting with information stored on a personal device is, in fact, generally becoming more commonplace (Jordan, 2005). We do see evidence of this in the corporate conference rooms before the video goes on as well, but what does not seem to have changed is the relative relationship. The sense remains that there is less need to give as much attention while the video is showing/playing (why do we call it 'playing'?) as when we were lecturing or just talking. More messages are checked. Talk is instituted. Pens and eyes move downward. People leave.

For us, this is a matter of chagrin and unsolved, unresolved dilemmas. Most importantly, we invest our analytic heads and hearts, not to mention time, blood and sweat, in the videos. We see these as productions that illustrate the analytic issues we are trying to make. We rely on the videotape to show cultural and behavioral complexity, in a way we feel we never could with PowerPoint documents filled with bullet points and photographs and accompanied by speech, or even interpretive dance (as one favorite client has quipped should be our next move). By virtue of movies' multimodal presentation of auditory, visual, expository, foreground, background, multi-person and multi-place information, we expect them to inform. Our objective, for us the raison d'être of the video, is the transmittal of truly exciting cultural findings. Our own 'Let's go to the videotape' (like Warner Wolf's) is not supposed to be about spice, it is not just about illustration, it is supposed to be a substantial part of the main course. Yet this common reaction to video segments has provided the space for one of our partners who is slightly less enamored of video (and probably also tired of my admonitions to pay attention to lighting, audio and editing needs) to exact joking revenge. When we recently presented together, and the assembled crowd started checking messages, talking and a few got up to leave just at the moment when we switched to showing video, he leaned over and quipped, 'Yes, Patti, we'll pay more attention to lighting, audio, and labeling the tapes, and maybe one day they'll watch it.'

The conundrum here is that, even if we subscribe culturally to the notion that 'learning must be fun', when the fun times arrive, when the frame of entertainment enters, learning can cease because we cease to pay attention. Moving imagery's association with entertainment and fun means it creates and brackets a time when we feel we do not need to pay attention. As Drotner (1996) observed in relation to her study of Danish teenagers' video productions, while they clearly learned extensively in the process of video-making, they would not speak of it in terms of learning. As she wrote (p. 30), 'the attraction of video to young people . . . lies in its being regarded as non-schooling. It is self-defined, fun, and rarely planned ahead. Watching videos as well as making them are processes lodged outside the realm of regularity. Hence they are deemed insignificant and that is precisely their attraction'.

While 'learning must be fun' is undoubtedly a much too simplistic formulation of what it takes to change or influence our cognitive routes as well as an erasure of the lessons that are all too often learned through pain, there is something to the dictum's implicit sense of involvement. Some of the laughter and side conversations that occur during the moments when video is shown in our presentations are, in fact, important because they are about members of the client team reacting and responding to the viewing of footage for which they had been the videographer. Sometimes colleagues will tease each other, saying things like 'Couldn't keep that camera still could you?' or 'Great filming' in response to some erratic move of the camera. What is good about this is that it gets clients involved in the process, an involvement that can also facilitate investment in the results and help fuel the enthusiasm necessary to see the implications carried through the organization. From developments we see happening around us in applied consumer research (e.g., Sando and Sweeney, 2005) it would seem that one important strategy that researchers are undertaking is to have client teams highly involved in the analysis of the data (we do some of this too), but our main strategy has been to involve them with the video, before and after. We also seek to make our video productions compelling: we do try to find the bits that will illustrate the analysis in the most interesting and engaging, i.e., entertaining, fashion. We feel we must do this if they are ever going to be watched.

And (entertaining) video does have the power to live and involve others in the organization. No question. A number of years ago we had conducted a study on small business owners for a credit card company. Just recently the client for that research requested that we conduct a study that would involve 're-interviews' of those respondents. Most importantly, the desire, the enthusiasm, the impetus was only to re-interview the small business owners who had appeared in the edited tape. As our client contacts told us, these business owners lived within the organization (or more precisely, their edited video images lived, but this was not what was said). They were individuals/customers felt to be known by 'everyone', including the CEO, and 'everyone' wanted to know what happened to them. During the telephone conversation in which we discussed this potential recontacting project with our clients, there was excitement in their voices. The bar owner, the guy who owned the gym, the leather restorer, the antique dealer who had told the story of the furry massage mitts (inspired by a James Bond film) that he had tried to sell in college, the musician, the man in Chicago who owned the toy store – 'We can't wait to hear what happened to them,' they said. 'The real estate manager?,' we asked. 'Oh, don't worry about her, she wasn't that interesting.' Perhaps it goes without stating, but the form of the desired deliverable was not only a written report, but a comparative videotape that would juxtapose footage from the first video we had produced with the newly garnered stories. Notably there was little interest, in fact none, in including material from the original videotapes that had not been included in the original edited version in the new version. These business owners lived as people, their identities were their images from the edited 'movie'.

There is something exceedingly positive in this. There is the glimmer of the gem. It is not only (though importantly) that the video made their consumers seem to come alive. Rather, in this case, it was that *they were watched.* There is no doubt that the lament from marketers about being in competition for the decidedly unpoetic 'share of eyeballs' among consumers in a world of excruciating product, visual and messaging clutter applies within companies as well. Research findings must make their way through the maze. Our analysis, our insights, must rise above the clutter and ideally even be sought out. How perfect would it be if research reports made it to the top of the viral list? Wouldn't it be perfect if they were sent around, inbox to inbox? And sometimes video can make this happen.

There seems to be a truism in the applied consumer research world that video segments should never be longer than a few minutes. This is touted as the length that corporate audiences can endure before boredom (or time crunch) sets in. We have heard this to be the length that even composite edited sequences should be. And we have heard this suggested by established and extremely competent and experienced video editors and producers of work for the corporate world. This information has also been in circulation on the Anthro Design List Serve. It is part of the standard assumption.

But there are ways in which we cannot help but disagree. First, it conflicts with ethnographic epistemologies that would suggest the need of longer, more contextualized ongoing action to understand anything. Second, it seems suspiciously similar to the sound byte lengths that have taken over the news, seemingly both borrowed from and part of advertising. Thirdly, a 'rule' for short clips does not seem to make sense, even in a world of music video inspired and styled quick jump cut editing. Time just does not seem to be the variable, whether in terms of short or long, that can make or break an ethnographic video.

In 1998, we created a composite video focused on fabric refreshers. Febreze was new to the market and our client wanted to understand how and why consumers were using these. What was the 'consumer magic' that was allowing fabric refreshers seemingly to take the world by storm? The tape we produced showed a smoker, who wanted to keep the actualities and volume of her smoking unknown to her husband, demonstrating the permutations she would go through when having a cigarette. She first donned a thick robe that covered her other attire and then tucked her hair into a full coverage plastic shower cap. After slipping a cigarette pack taken from her (not his) bathroom into her pocket, she headed down the hallway, past the kitty litter (for others, the ostensible reason she used Febreze) and went outside to the patio where an ashtray and a bag for wrapping finished cigarette ends were stored in a cabinet. She then showed the routine she went through once finished with her cigarette. For this, she took off her robe and hung it up on the inside of bathroom door and proceeded to spray Febreze (profusely and steadily) on the robe. As she noted, she paid special attention to the cuffs and collar where the smoke would tend to gather and linger. She showed and talked about how, after finishing the spraying of the robe, she would wash her face, brush her teeth and tongue, floss her teeth and so on. She followed up by talking about how, on the occasional times when she would have a cigarette in the bathroom (contradicting what she had told us earlier about never smoking in the house), she would then spray the towels, toilet seat cover and anything else in the bathroom with fabric. If, as sometimes happened, her husband surprised her before she was finished with her routine and was knocking on the door, she would quickly shut her eyes, spray Febreze onto her face and open up the door with a big smile and 'Hi.' Her snippet alone was almost ten minutes, produced out of nearly straight, real time footage.

As we were told later, this tape went around the world. It was passed to far-flung employees of the globally affiliated agencies. People talked to us about it years after its making. We had also included at the end of this tape a snippet of a consumer showing a dead, frozen pet snake pulled from the bottom of the family's freezer. This was included mainly as a joke for the client. We had been together on the interview (she had done the videotaping) and had been freaked and fascinated by the idea that people could keep a now dead snake (wrapped in Ukrainian doll fashion in one used plastic grocery bag in another) in their freezer. The snippet was for her. Clearly she had told others. It was amusement. It was for entertainment. It stuck. About five years later in this case, while working on a job for the same company, a new client mentioned the fabric refresher tape, including the snake snippet. This degree of recall is an advertiser's envy. And we are talking about research footage.

In the representations: integrating analysis, integrating mediums
As noted above, narrative and stories do provide a helpful framework for memory and are a means of conveying phenomenological understandings. Moving images are the American storytellers. Best-selling novels are quickly transformed into films. Classics of literature can be viewed on the television and, even if problematic, successful theatre makes its way to screens. We also believe that the moving images medium can transmit information derived from theoretical insights, yet we often worry about whether the videotaped consumer stories we prepare for clients, the composite edited clips of the ethnographic research, adequately convey to the viewers the theoretical and analytic insights which we hope they will. Here we could invoke the claims of the postmodern outlook that insist on the uncertainty and instability of the interpretive meanings that all agents bring to any kind of text. There is an evident, substantive accuracy to this claim which we cannot help but support. At the same time, it would be disingenuous to leave the matter at that. Not only would it ignore the persuasive arguments of those who have discussed the 'preferred' readings of films constrained by the context and text or discursive space of film even in the case of 'active' viewers (Crawford and Hafsteinsson, 1996), it would be ignoring our own preferences. Those who know us know (or perhaps it is simply discernable from our chapters in this volume) that one of the axes we have been grinding for some time is the value of bringing a cultural analytic outlook into the practice of market research. We want clients to garner this perspective from our ethnographic video productions.

This cultural analysis is always there in our productions, though largely implicitly (e.g., via content and editing decisions and from a few strategically worded section titles) *because* we have decided not to use explanatory voice-over or excessive text among the moving images. We have forgone documentary's traditional voice-over of authority convention in favor of the more *cinéma vérité* tradition that allows the voices of those filmed and the on-going action to be the authorities. The basis of this decision to create edited videos without explanatory text or voice-over is that we want the video to retain its power to portray cultural complexity and texture. In part we are also doing this precisely out of a desire to make the texts (somewhat) open to multiple points of view and interpretations, BUT, and this is purposefully a 'but' in capital letters, in our presentations we bring in cultural analysis and the implications we see via written text and verbally delivered messages. We intersperse these with the showing of the video in order to enhance the appreciation of both. We want the cultural theoretical perspective to be brought to bear.

Yet, again, it is difficult to ensure that it works. Anthropologist Wilton Martínez (1995, 1996) has famously brought to light the ethnocentric readings of anthropological films that occur among anthropology undergraduates in classroom settings. We have our experiences as well. For instance, as wonderful and gratifying as it is that virtually every watcher of our fabric refresher tape remembers that tape and continues to mention it to us years after the fact, countering that elation is the reality that virtually everyone also interprets the actions of the woman described above as those of an obsessive, even slightly mad, individual. We had purposefully tried to counter readings of the tape as about her idiosyncrasies by immediately following her demonstration with the demonstration of another woman, about 20 years her senior and personally quite different, yet conceptually doing the same things. This latter woman was interested in hiding her daytime household smoking not only from her husband, but also from her teenage son. Her routine, started shortly before they were due to arrive home, entailed getting the matches, lighting a candle and spraying Febreze on all fabric furniture as she went on a circular course around the rooms of her home. Febreze spraying was then followed by the spraying of a Glade scented spray. She virtually ran the circular course of her home as she did this, a pace she indicated she would pick up if she heard the garage door sounds that indicated that her husband or son were arriving home earlier than expected. On these occasions she rather hoped that the vanilla, cinnamon and spice scents that she preferred would prompt them to ask what she had been cooking for dinner. This she told us in a slightly out-of-breath voice, given all the spraying and running she had been doing.

Both of these described snippets were ordered under a section in the video that dealt with smoking. There was also a section about new homes (and then one that included the snake). The analytic issues that these video snippets illustrated – issues covered in the written report – included the way that odor was an issue of the moral and social order (Corbin, 1988). Odors considered negative were ones associated with the socially devalued (e.g., cigarettes, deep fried food, inexpensive perfume, disliked houseguests). Also discussed was the way that Febreze fitted into the moral order of the day, as said at the time, one more in line with Oscar Wilde than Dostoevsky. The instances illustrated in the video were not those of idiosyncratic personalities, but of widespread cultural phenomena. Closet smoking, a culturally produced and defined phenomenon, is not idiosyncratic or individual. There are more such phenomena than you think. The woman featured was not anomalous, nor was she nuts. And even if she were, there would be cultural phenomena to discern (Comaroff and Comaroff, 1987).

Questions concerning the (re)presentation of ethnographic data have never been separate from questions of epistemology (Arnould and Thompson, 2004; Belk, 1998; Clifford and Marcus, 1986; Sherry and Schouten, 2002; Geertz, 1988). Anthropologists have long been grappling with the way to negotiate the tacking back and forth between the specific and the general in ethnographic analyses (Maurer, 2005). Ethnography lives, breathes, relies on and finds its strength in the details, in the specifics of individual instances, lives and examples. But the raison d'être has never been understood as only concerning one person, one family, or one small group of people in one place, even when the focus was on one person (Marjorie Shostak's *Nisa*), one family (Oscar Lewis's *The Children of Sanchez*), or the people of one small place (the senior citizens' center of Barbara Myerhoff's *Number our Days*). For anthropologists, ethnography has always been about larger fish to fry, mostly theoretical ones. At issue now is how we write about and represent people without simply turning them into the ponderous slugs of theory, as Behar so aptly put it. It can be done. Myerhoff's (1978) account of Jewish seniors, while perhaps now noticeably outdated from a theoretical perspective, still has the evocative power to bring tears to the eyes, as have some people's deeply resonant poems.

Belk and Kozinets have been active and persuasive agents in trying to move the academic field of consumer research toward a greater embrace and integration of moving imagery (Belk, 1998; Kozinets, 2002; Belk and Kozinets, 2005a, 2005b). As they have pointed out, this embrace and integration entails the epistemological and institutional migration of visual media into the mainstream of the field, an arena in which the field is falling behind relative to popular culture, business and applied consumer research (Belk and Kozinets, 2005b). There is little doubt that, at present, integration is the key word. To choose between one or the other, moving imagery or printed words, is not the answer. Presenting and representing our research and ideas solely in moving imagery would be needlessly counterproductive. This was part of the problem that we saw with the request from the company for a video produced in the style to which they were accustomed. They wanted an on-screen moving list of the objectives and method of the research at the beginning of the video, and at the end of the video, a list of the implications for the company. We could never fathom why a moving list of implications, moving faster than you could write them, made sense on a VHS tape as opposed to one on paper or in a computer document. As a hyperlink on a DVD, yes it would have made sense. But this was prior to the time when it was feasible to give DVDs and expect them to be readable by many.

As Belk pointed out in 1998, new visual and hypermedia technologies would likely give us other possibilities, other means and other conventions for producing, viewing and interpreting visual media (see also Biella, 1993). And new technologies have. It is also noticeable that a high degree of integration of still and moving imagery with written and spoken words is taking place around us. Websites routinely include images as well as words and ever more frequently include video clip options. Television news programs, with their ticker tapes of written information running across the bottom or sides of the screen, sustain (and give priority to) the visual and auditory double-tasker. Our clients expect an integration of written words, spoken words, photographs, collages, drawings and video. At conferences or conference sessions I have attended for practicing consumer researchers, video excerpts are exceedingly common parts of session presentations.

This is not to say that these integrations are necessarily the models we should follow. Yet it still seems that we, as researchers, (re)presenters and consumers of ethnographic research, need to gain a deeper appreciation of the epistemological, cultural and practical intricacies involved in moving imagery. Just as scholars have made us aware of ways written ethnographic accounts are created documents with attention to word choice, inclusion, elisions, rhetoric and so on (in much the same way as any novel, poem or chapter in this volume does), so we need to do for video. We need to be aware of these as created documents and we need to appreciate their semiotic grammars. We also need to be able to incorporate them into our work for the value they hold as vehicles of phenomenological understanding. As viewers and consumers of ethnographic research, we need to appreciate the implicit cultural assumptions and practices that we are bringing to bear.

It is not that I know how this should all be accomplished and there is the jarringly uncomfortable feeling that, as the intertwined technological, cultural and theoretical terrain shifts, how we should – and how we believe we should – (re)present our data will also shift. It is always shifting. A few years ago, Sanders (2002, pp. 141–2), in a kind of rallying call to fellow communications professionals, argued that, given the proliferations of visual messages and mediums, 'communication is increasingly dysfunctional' and that it was a keen moment of opportunity for the communications professional. No doubt. It is probably utopian to think that we will rely on our communications colleagues to help us out – in academic or applied circles – but I do believe this, and what I hope to have accomplished in this chapter is the reminder of the need to look at, recognize and question the cultural and epistemological assumptions that reside within our (re)presentation choices, even when, or especially when, we are entertained.

References

Arnould, Eric and Craig Thompson (2004), 'Consumer culture theory (CCT): twenty years of research', *Journal of Consumer Research*, **31**, 868–82.
Behar, Ruth (1999), 'Ethnography: cherishing our second-fiddle genre', *Journal of Contemporary Ethnography*, **28** (5), 472–84.
Belk, Russell (1998), 'Multimedia approaches to qualitative data and representations', in Barbara B. Stern (ed.), *Representing Consumers*, London: Routledge, pp. 308–38.
Belk, Russell and Robert Kozinets (2005a), 'Videography in marketing and consumer research', *Qualitative Market Research*, **8**, 128–41.
Belk, Russell and Robert Kozinets (2005b), 'Introduction to the resonant representations issue of *Consumption, Markets, and Culture*', *Consumption, Markets and Culture*, **8**, 195–203.
Biella, Peter (1993), 'Beyond ethnographic film: hypermedia and scholarship', in Jack R. Rollwagen (ed.), *Anthropological Film and Video in the 1990s*, Brockport, NY: Institute, pp. 131–76.
Clifford, James and George Marcus (eds) (1986), *Writing Culture*, Berkeley: University of California Press.
Colleyn, Jean-Paul (2005), 'Jean Rouch: an anthropologist ahead of his time', *American Anthropologist*, **107**, 112–15.
Comaroff, Jean and John Comaroff (1987), 'The madman and the migrant: work and labor in the historical consciousness of a South African people', *American Ethnologist*, **14**, 191–209.
Corbin, Alain (1988), *The Foul and the Fragrant*, Cambridge: Harvard University Press.
Crawford, Peter and Sigurjon Hafsteinsson (eds) (1996), *The Constructions of the Viewer*, Højbjerg, Denmark: Intervention Press.
Drotner, Kirsten (1996), 'Less is more: media ethnography and its limits', in Peter Crawford and Sigurjon Hafsteinsson (eds), *The Constructions of the Viewer*, Højbjerg, Denmark: Intervention Press, pp. 28–46.
Geertz, Clifford (1983), 'Blurred genres: the refiguration of social thought', *Local Knowledge: Further Essays in Interpretive Anthropology*, New York: Basic Books.
Geertz, Clifford (1988), *Works and Lives: The Anthropologist as Author*, Stanford, CA: Stanford University Press.
Goffman, Erving (1974), *Frame Analysis*, New York: Harper and Row.
Hockings, Paul (ed.) (2003), *Principles of Visual Anthropology*, 3rd edn, Berlin: Mouton de Gruyter.
Holbrook, Morris (1998), 'Journey to Kroywen: an ethnoscopic auto-auto-auto-driven stereographic photo essay', in Barbara Stern (ed.) *Representing Consumers*, London: Routledge, pp. 231–63.
Hymes, Dell (1964), 'Introduction: toward ethnographies of communication', *American Anthropologist*, **66**, 1–34.
Jordan, Brigitte (2005), 'Managing global teams: Bookkeeping or herding cats?', paper presented at The Society for Applied Anthropology 65th Annual Meeting, 5–10 April, Sante Fe, New Mexico.
Joy, Annamma and John F. Sherry (2003), 'Speaking of art as embodied imagination: a multisensory approach to understanding aesthetic experience', *Journal of Consumer Research*, **30**, 259–82.
Kozinets, Robert (2002), 'Can consumers escape the market? Emancipatory illuminations from Burning Man', *Journal of Consumer Research*, **29**, 20–38.

Martínez, Wilton (1995), 'The challenges of a pioneer: Tim Asch, otherness, and film reception', *Visual Anthropology Review*, **11**, 53–82.
Martínez, Wilton (1996), 'Deconstructing the "viewer": from ethnography of the visual to critique of the occult', in Peter Crawford and Sigurjon Hafsteinsson (eds), *The Constructions of the Viewer*, Højbjerg, Denmark: Intervention Press, pp. 69–100.
Maurer, Bill (2005), 'Introduction to "ethnographic emergences" ', *American Anthropologist*, **107**, 1–4.
Myerhoff, Barbara (1978), *Number Our Days*, New York: Touchstone.
Pine, Joseph (1999), *The Experience Economy*, Boston: Harvard Business School Press.
Ruby, Jay (1996), 'The viewer viewed: the reception of ethnographic films', in Peter Crawford and Sigurjon Hafsteinsson (eds), *The Constructions of the Viewer*, Højbjerg, Denmark: Intervention Press, pp. 193–206.
Ruby, Jay (2000), *Picturing Culture*, Chicago: University of Chicago Press.
Ruby, Jay (2005), 'Jean Rouch: hidden and revealed', *American Anthropologist*, **107**, 111–12.
Sanders, Cameron (2002), 'The case for professional communicators in a digital age', in John Rice and Brian McKernan (eds), *Creating Digital Content*, New York: McGraw-Hill, pp. 141–54.
Sando, Ruth and Donna Sweeney (2005), 'Shedding new light on an old flame', *Quirk's Marketing Research Review*, **19** (5), 30–35.
Schroeder, Jonathan (1998), 'Consuming representation: a visual approach to consumer research', in Barbara Stern (ed.), *Representing Consumers*, London: Routledge, pp. 193–230.
Sherry, John F. and John Schouten (2002), 'A role for poetry in consumer research', *Journal of Consumer Research*, **29**, 218–34.
Silverstein, Michael (2004), ' "Cultural" concepts and the language-culture nexus', *Current Anthropology*, **45**, 621–52.
Stoller, Paul (1997), *Sensuous Scholarship*, Philadelphia: University of Pennsylvania Press.
Sunderland, Patricia and Rita Denny (2002), 'Performers and partners: consumer video documentaries in ethnographic research', *Qualitative Ascending: Harnessing its True Value*, Amsterdam: ESOMAR.
Sunderland, Patricia and Rita Denny (2003), 'Psychology vs. anthropology: where is culture in marketplace ethnography?', in Timothy Malefyt and Brian Moeran (eds), *Advertising Cultures*, Oxford: Berg, pp. 187–202.
Taylor, Lucien (ed.) (1994), *Visualizing Theory*, New York: Routledge.
Wasson, Christina (2000), 'Ethnography in the field of design', *Human Organization*, **59**, 377–88.
Wolf, Michael (1999), *The Entertainment Economy*, New York: Times Books.

PART VII

APPLICATIONS

29 Capturing time

Cele C. Otnes, Julie A. Ruth, Tina M. Lowrey and Suraj Commuri

Imagine if researchers interested in studying consumption- and marketing-related phenomena could do so at only one point in time. Certainly our understanding of concepts such as brand loyalty, consumer socialization, consumers' relationships with brands and the effects of advertising and marketing on brand image would be minimal – if we recognized they existed at all. Simply put, marketing researchers must be able to study phenomena both *over* time (during extended, continuous periods so the lifeworlds of consumers, practitioners and/or marketing organizations can be understood) and *across* time (at different points in time, even those occurring before a study begins). Focusing on the temporal aspects of consumption and marketing enables researchers to make inductively-based inferences about the ways people begin, maintain and end relationships with goods, services, retailers, service providers and other foci of interest – and importantly, how these relationships change over time. Furthermore methods that enable researchers to 'go back in time' and make inferences about the past and the present can help them understand whether and how the psychological, sociological and cultural entities that shape informants' lives have influenced, or continue to influence, interactions with marketplace-related phenomena.

In this chapter we examine the longitudinal and retrospective qualitative techniques that marketing researchers can use when they wish to generate thick descriptions of human behavior. We begin by defining and comparing these research approaches, and describe their potential contributions and limitations. We then examine how studies of marketing-related phenomena have incorporated components of longitudinal qualitative research, and how they have used (or can use) retrospective marketing techniques.

Longitudinal versus retrospective approaches

Definition(s) of longitudinal research
Achieving consensus with regard to what longitudinal qualitative research truly entails is probably elusive, because even in disciplines such as anthropology, sociology and education, where it is a mainstay, the criteria as to what makes a research project longitudinal are often vague. Although all disciplines imply that longitudinal research occurs over a span of time, Saldaña (2003) notes that he could find no agreement as to the minimum span required for a field immersion to be considered longitudinal. Indeed he locates recommended spans of one year, 12 to 18 months and even ' "a substantial calendar time – months or years" ' (Kelly and McGrath, 1998, quoted in Saldaña, 2003, p. 3). Yet he also documents immersions ranging from 50 years to informants' entire life spans. One reason for such a disparate range is that some ethnographers advocate allowing the research design to evolve to meet the demands of the research questions and context being explored. Lincoln and Guba (1985, p. 225) observe:

Timing cannot be predicted for the naturalistic inquiry as it can for the conventional. Events that cannot be described because they have yet to emerge certainly cannot be tied to a particular date. Further, one cannot tell what it is to be 'on track'; the concept of 'milestone events' has no prior meaning . . . the naturalist can be sure [only] that there will be slippage in whatever plans are made; the corollary to Murphy's Law that asserts that 'things always take longer than they do' will never be better exemplified.

Given such conditions, Kottak's (2005, p. 9) definition of longitudinal research as a 'long-term study of a community, region, society, culture, or other unit, usually based on repeated visits', is not as vague as it first seems.

In contrast, a general definition of retrospective research is less problematic, because this method does not require debate over a criterion of prolonged field immersion. Specifically, retrospective research is that which enables the researcher to capture time-infused primary data, by allowing and encouraging participants to tap into one or multiple earlier time periods in their lives post hoc. Because scholars do not want to be limited to the retrospective perspectives available only through secondary data sources such as oral histories, diaries, transaction histories, company data or web-logs, they use a variety of creative retrospective techniques that involve informants (some of which are detailed later in this chapter). Consequently, they can acquire and interpret primary recollections and opinions about past events, to secure perspectives of how these informants believe key events shaped their lives – or, conversely, how these informants believed they or others shaped key events.

Comparison of longitudinal and retrospective methods
Whether one adopts a longitudinal or retrospective approach, both hold the belief that time is ontologically relevant and epistemologically accessible. But thereafter, these two approaches substantively diverge, especially with regard to the conceptualizations of time they embrace and explore. Kant, Husserl and, more recently, Ricoeur elaborate on the distinctions between the two essential notions of time (see Ricoeur, 1985, for a comprehensive discussion). Put simply, cosmological time posits that time is linear and can be measured in terms of minutes and hours. Further, the relative positions of events in cosmological time never change. In contrast, phenomenological time is conceptualized as being composed of the past, present and future. An episode under consideration becomes the present, irrespective of its currency in a cosmological sense. Therefore the status of events as occurring in an individual's past, present or future is not chronologically absolute.

Analysis of data gathered longitudinally often includes assumptions as to the relevance of cosmological time (e.g., minutes, hours, days) through either the specification of a priori relationships between increments of time or the emergent realization that focusing on these increments can provide meaningful insights into the phenomena of interest. For example, prior to entering the field, researchers interested in consumer gift-shopping strategies might assume that givers who spend more minutes or hours shopping for a recipient might be more intimately connected to that recipient, compared to others. Careful recording of increments of time would enable researchers to support or dispute this hypothesis.

Furthermore, since cosmological time progresses linearly, during field immersion scholars who employ longitudinal research typically can specify and gather data on the antecedents of an event before it actually occurs. This fact makes qualitative longitudinal studies ideally suitable for assessing change (e.g., whether consumption increases or decreases over time) and delineating patterns of behavior across similar (or seemingly different) events separated in time. However scholars engaged in longitudinal work must be careful to avoid an overreliance on a priori theorization. As is true with other qualitative techniques, findings based on long-term immersions face a skeptical audience when they purport to establish cause and effect since, in positivistic language, concomitant forces could also contribute to causality. Nevertheless longitudinal qualitative research does offer researchers a panoramic perspective of events unfolding over time, and may enable them to put events into proper perspective that might have been overemphasized during a single or short-term immersion.

Researchers engaged in retrospective investigations use as their starting point present time (which does not necessarily equate to 'current' time in a phenomenological sense). The past is contextually identified with an active emphasis on its relationship to the present. Accordingly, unlike longitudinal studies, retrospective investigations are ideal tools for researching causes of events that have already occurred, because recollections of the past are based on their relevance to the present. Wall and Williams (1970, p. 4) observe that carefully executed qualitative retrospective studies have historically provided such 'detail and precision of information' that 'many, if not most of the hypotheses about the causation of human behavior . . . are based upon . . . retrospective individual studies'. Thus reliable and engaged informants may be able to reflect accurately upon how prior events and people may have shaped and shifted previous events.

However, because the past is identified in the context of the present, retrospective research is often criticized as being subjective, or relying too heavily upon informants' memories as a basis for interpretation. In short, retrospective researchers are often confronted with the criticism that 'human memory is fallible, and events which subsequently prove to be critical in their long-term effects may, at the time of occurrence, appear trivial, and be quickly forgotten' (ibid., p. 8). Also retrospective research is often criticized for what makes it unique: its reliance on idiographic data, or those focusing on discrete facts or events. Thus, in contrast to longitudinal approaches, each participant in a retrospective study may choose to immerse him- or herself in an idiosyncratic, idiographic orientation of the present. Such an approach might hinder researchers from generating nomothetic findings, or those related to the discovery of general patterns or laws, across subjects.

In summary, longitudinal researchers capture time by immersing themselves in a temporal stream that is cosmological, while retrospective qualitative research focuses on capturing and understanding the relative occurrence of events in the past vis-à-vis the present. Furthermore longitudinal researchers are interested more in understanding the emergent relationships between events, rather than establishing how events in the past caused those in the present, as is the case with retrospectively oriented scholars. We now turn to reviewing how these methods have been used in studies of marketing-related phenomena.

Longitudinal research in marketing
Historically most marketing researchers are employed in departments where they are not necessarily encouraged to conduct long-term, longitudinally oriented field immersions. How have they adapted qualitative longitudinal methods to their purposes? To answer this question, we review studies in marketing that feature long-term or multiple ethnographic

immersions, to understand how scholars have maintained or modified the aspects of traditional longitudinal research. The purpose of such scrutiny is not to criticize these studies for their lack of adherence to the standards of longitudinal qualitative research established in other disciplines. Rather we are simply interested in understanding how these longitudinal characteristics are represented in the marketing canon, to acquire a sense of how research that employs longitudinal characteristics is 'done' in marketing.

Table 29.1 summarizes 22 articles or book chapters that explore topics pertaining to marketing (but primarily consumer behavior) and that incorporate one or more elements of traditional longitudinal research in their designs. Although they are not exhaustive of such efforts in marketing, we believe they constitute the majority. We review the following characteristics: total time span of the study, total number of hours in the field, nature of immersion and what type of change (if any) is explored in the study. We also include other key characteristics not considered integral to longitudinal research, but which help contextualize the studies and that we believed would be of interest to readers. These include description of the research site, types of research techniques used, the number of researchers involved and the doctoral degree fields of the author(s).

Time span/total time in the field
The time spans of the immersions recorded in these studies range from one month to 12 years. Eleven of the 22 studies feature immersions of two years or less, with the remainder extending to three years or more. Thus, while field studies that span multiple years have historically not been the norm for marketing researchers, prolonged immersions do exist. Furthermore it is not the case that only the researchers whose doctoral degrees are in anthropology conducted the longer-term field immersions. Another temporal characteristic that is useful to compare is the total time actually spent in the field over the duration of the study, which ranged from 12 hours to over two years. Comparing this range to the total time span of these studies reveals that the field immersions of some scholars may span many years, but in actuality the time they devote to any particular immersion is likely to be relatively brief.

Nature of immersion
Another characteristic of traditional longitudinal qualitative research is that it often requires researchers to relocate to a site that is initially 'foreign' to them (that is, one that is either foreign or domestic, but initially unfamiliar) and therefore requires them to immerse themselves totally in their research context. About half the studies featured such complete immersions, with the rest featuring partial ones, or those where researchers engaged in prolonged or repeat immersions in the sites of interest, but did not actually immerse themselves by living day by day in the research context.

Focus on change
One area of agreement among scholars across social science disciplines is that, regardless of the length of a longitudinal qualitative study, it should satisfy the criterion of focusing on some type of change that occurs within a specified unit of analysis under study (e.g. venues, people, groups; see Saldaña, 2003, pp. 8–9 for a review of how social scientists define change). A little less than half of the studies in Table 29.1 focus on some sort of change, while the others do not. Moreover, as the table reveals, the focus of change is

typically on how consumers change, on changes in a particular marketing-related site, or on a more general topic. Yet, clearly, while not all marketing researchers have incorporated the characteristic of exploring change in their longitudinal studies, we believe that revisiting their voluminous data sets would certainly enable them to offer meaningful, grounded interpretations of the way the observed phenomena changed, if they chose to do so.

In summary, our analysis reveals that marketing scholars who conduct qualitative research that integrates longitudinal components do not feel compelled to enter and remain in the field in the same way as anthropologists such as Mead ([1928] 2001) or Malinowski ([1922] 1984). Rather, they are more likely to design research studies that share characteristics of both cross-sectional and longitudinal research. That is, they collect data and generate text over a period of time (a longitudinal trait), but typically do so with the intent of comparing the experiences of different informants in one or more stages of the life cycle (a hallmark of cross-sectional research; see Baltes, Reese and Nesselroade, 1977). Yet sometimes a study that begins as cross-sectional can evolve into a longitudinal one. For example, after one season of fieldwork, Otnes, Lowrey and Kim (1993) explore which social roles consumers express through Christmas shopping, by conducting interviews and shopping trips with informants in their 20s and 30s. However they became intrigued by the notion that, as these givers and their recipients (who ranged from infants to the elderly) moved through different stages in their life cycles, their gift-giving behavior would undoubtedly adapt to accommodate the changes accompanying this process. As a result, Lowrey, Otnes and Ruth (2004) examine the shopping behavior of five of the original 15 informants during five different Christmas seasons over a 12-year period.

Recommendations for longitudinal marketing research
Earlier we stated that it was not our intention to criticize the studies in Table 29.1 in terms of whether they met certain standards for longitudinal research. Nevertheless we believe it is useful for researchers in marketing to provide clarity on three issues when articulating aspects of their longitudinal designs. First, as Saldaña (2003) recommends, they should specify their stance regarding time. Given that time is a cultural construct, researchers should explicate how and why they understand time, compare their understanding to the ways their informants understand time, and then explain why they believe it is important to record the time devoted to particular activities in the field (if indeed they do so). Second, researchers conducting longitudinal research should address issues pertaining to change in their studies, by (a) focusing on change in some form in their study, (b) articulating the definition of change to which they adhere, (c) providing theoretically sound reasons for focusing on such change, and (d) clearly explicating how changes emerge, and the factors influencing change in the field, by using words and examples that convey the dynamics of the phenomena under study.

Finally Saldaña argues that, in order to truly leverage a long-term study, three sets of questions should be developed, that focus on change. These include *framing* questions (e.g., what is different from one pond or pool of data to the next?), *descriptive* questions (what increases or decreases through time?) and *analytic and interpretive* questions (what changes interrelate through time?). Interested readers should consult Saldaña (2003) for a comprehensive discussion of these types of questions pertinent to longitudinal qualitative research.

Table 29.1 Summary of longitudinal consumer behavior studies

Topic / Author	Total time span	Total time in field	Nature of immersion	Nature of site	Research techniques used	No. of rschers	Focus of change studied (consumers, sites, general topic)	Doctoral fields of authors
Arnould (1989)	9 yrs	Unspecified	Full	Villages in Zinder Province	Interviews (Int.), Observation (Obs.), & Surveys (Surv.)	1 + native speakers	Topic	Anthro
Arnould & Price (1993)	2 yrs	Unspecified	Full	Recreational area	Focus Groups (FG), Obs. & Surv.	2	None	Anthro, Mkting
Belk & Costa (1998)	4 yrs	130 days	Partial	Festivals & retail	Int. & Obs.	2	None	Mkting, Anthro
Belk, Wallendorf & Sherry, Jr. (1989)	2 yrs	90 days	Full	Multiple	Int. & Obs.	3, but 20+ others in Odyssey	None	Mkting, Mkting, Mkting
Communi & Gentry (2005)	2 yrs	Unspecified	Partial	Homes	Int. & Obs.	2	None	Mkting, Mkting
Coupland, 2005	16 mos	48 hrs	Partial	Homes & retail	Obs., Projectives	1	Cons	Mkting
Fournier (1998)	3 mos	75 hrs	Partial	Homes	Int.	1	Cons	Mkting
Fournier & Mick (1999)	8 mos	180 hrs	Partial	Homes & retail	Int. & FG	2	Cons	Mkting
Kozinets (2001)	2 yrs	20 mos	Partial	Conventions & e-sites	Int. & Obs.	1	None	Anthro
Kozinets (2002)	4 yrs	2 yrs	Full	Festivals & e-sites	Int. & FG	1	None	Anthro
Kozinets et al. (2004)	14 mos	14 mos	Partial	Retail & off-site	Int. & FG	5	None	Anthro or Mkting

Study	Duration	Time	Immersion	Setting	Methods	N	Contact	Discipline
Lowrey, Otnes & Ruth (2004)	12 yrs	100 hrs	Partial	Homes & retail	Int., Obs. (shopping w/consumers: SWC)	3	Cons	Comm, Comm, Mkting
Mick & Buhl (1992)	3 mos	12 hrs	Partial	Homes	Int.	2	None	Mkting, Mkting
Mick & Fournier (1998)	1 yr	150 hrs	Partial	Homes & retail	Int., FG & Surv.	2	None	Mkting, Mkting
Otnes, Lowrey & Shrum (1997)	4 yrs	60 hrs	Partial	Homes, retail & off-site	Int., Obs., FG & SWC	3	None	Comm, Comm, Comm
Oswald (1999)	1 yr	3 mos	Partial	Multiple	Int., Obs. & Surv.	1	None	Anthro
Peñaloza (1994)	2 yrs	2 yrs	Full	Multiple	Int. & Obs.	1	Topic	Mkting
Peñaloza (2001)	7 yrs	14 wks	Partial	Events	Int. & Obs.	1	Topic	Mkting
Price & Arnould (1999)	1 mo.	24 days	Partial	Retail	Int. & Surv.	2	None	Mkting, Anthro
Schouten & McAlexander (1995)	3 yrs	Unspecified	Full	Festivals	Int. & Obs.	2	Cons	Mkting, Mkting
Sherry (1990)	5 yrs	2.5 yrs	Full	Retail/event	Int. & Obs.	1	Site	Anthro
Sherry & McGrath (1989)	3 yrs	3 mos	Partial	Retail	Int. & Obs.	2	Site	Anthro, Mkting

Note: Many of the immersions included in the studies above generated numerous journal articles, presentations and book chapters. Due to space limitations, we attempted to include the paper that represented the most 'quintessential' of the authors' longitudinal qualitative endeavors from a particular data set.

Retrospective investigations of time

For several reasons, researchers cannot always implement a longitudinal design to capture primary data, nor is it always appropriate to do so. First, unfolding events often trigger a research interest in the causes of such events. Second, some research opportunities unfold without a forewarning, or so rapidly that current events turn into past ones before a meaningful longitudinal project can be designed and implemented. Third, even with foresight about research-worthy topics, it may not be appropriate or possible to conduct research as events are unfolding, possibly owing to sensitivity of such issues. For example, investigating how children's consumption changes in light of their parents' divorce might be too traumatic for them, and may also be considered unethical. Fourth, research questions sometimes require tapping into reflections upon the way events and phenomena have changed over time. Thus researchers must be able to acquire narratives that recapture time.

Narrative reasoning in retrospective investigations

Narratives are 'how people articulate how the past is related to the present' (Richardson, 1990, p. 125). Such chronology, with an emphasis on sequence, is what distinguishes narratives from others types of data (Cortazzi, 1993). When creating narratives, informants refamiliarize themselves with their past in the context of their present. Such an approach is consistent with the perspective of phenomenological time, and is particularly significant when examining questions of consumer behavior, since the purpose of such research typically is to understand the attributions of the past that consumers ascribe to a focal present state.

Because it subscribes to notions of phenomenological time as understood by past, present and future, narrative reasoning becomes a viable mode of investigation and interpretation in retrospective research. Time-oriented thinking centered on narrative reasoning is a universal mode of cognition that contextually embeds connections between events. Because the participant's voice is central to the quality of the research effort, narratives – and autobiographical narratives in particular – are ideally suited to retrospective investigations. Narratives elicit history and relate and reveal the significance of historical events to the development of a present state of affairs. Organization of experiences into temporally meaningful episodes is at the heart of narratives, as 'narrative meaning is created by noting that something is a "part" of a whole and that something is a "cause" of something else' (Polkinghorne, 1988, p. 6).

Methods facilitating retrospective narratives

Retrospective investigations may be used to investigate three different time frames: (a) a certain time in the past ('How was it to live through the Depression?'); (b) how certain events in the past contribute to an outcome ('How did you come to place such an emphasis on saving?'); and (c) how certain outcomes pertain to an event in the past ('What was the result of losing all your savings?'). Furthermore a single project may integrate one or multiple frames. For example, Ruth (2005) investigates the lived experience of consumers who experienced apartheid in South Africa, as well as changes in their lives since apartheid ended. Table 29.2 summarizes the research approaches available when the researcher wishes to approach the relationship of the past and the present from the perspective of each frame. Each approach – storytelling, retrospective anchoring and profusion, and autobiographies – is summarized below.

Table 29.2 Retrospective approaches to gathering time data

	Storytelling	RAP	Autobiographies
Key purpose	To elicit outcomes in chronological order following a key event or phenomenon	To go back in time and be able to talk about the past	To elicit events in chronological order leading to a key event or phenomenon
Sample research question	How has your life changed since buying a red Mustang convertible?	What car did you aspire to own while in high school?	How did you come to buy a red Mustang convertible?
Key risks	Wishful consequences of a key event may be reported	Heavy reliance on correct and swift identification of an appropriate anchor	Informants may not maintain a first-person perspective throughout the narrative
Suitable format of data	Written or oral	Oral; researcher-assisted data gathering is preferred	Written; informant-driven data gathering
Overarching framework	Chronological and thematic	Thematic	Chronological

Storytelling
Consumer researchers successfully tap into chronological episodes and narrative reasoning by inviting consumers to tell stories of specific consumption-related experiences. The critical incident technique, used to elicit consumer narratives in a number of consumer studies of services (Bitner, Booms and Tetrault, 1990; Iacobucci, Ostrom and Grayson, 1995) and gift giving (Mick and DeMoss, 1990; Ruth, Otnes and Brunel, 1999; Wooten, 2000), has proved to be a successful means of engaging participants in storytelling (see the chapter on storytelling in this book for a complete explication of the method). This technique prompts participants to recall a particular episode that fits certain criteria. Researchers often employ grand-tour prompts (McCracken, 1988) to set the stage for generating these incidents. For example, when investigating the effect of gift receipt on perceptions of giver/recipient relationship quality, Ruth et al. (1999) use a grand-tour prompt that elicits recollections of a past gift-receipt experience involving a 'target' emotion assigned by the researcher (e.g. 'Tell me about a gift receipt when you experienced joy.').

Although a grand-tour prompt can elicit recollection of key episodes fitting the criteria for inclusion in a study, it is not necessarily sufficient for capturing facets of time. Two specific interventions are required: contextual information to situate that event, and insight into how the episode unfolded over time. Regarding this last intervention, time-oriented prompts may facilitate chronological recollection. For example, although a researcher interested in understanding thematic structure may prompt, 'How did that make you feel?', such prompts do not naturally facilitate chronological thinking. In contrast, prompts such as 'What happened next?' will do so. It is important to note that many research methods are not structured by default to facilitate chronological accounts. Thus researchers must be acutely aware that they might have to facilitate the elicitation of chronological structure where needed.

Retrospective anchoring and profusion

Eliciting narratives via the critical incident technique is appropriate when informants can easily recall salient incidents that have taken place in the past. Some research, however, might seek to tap into past behavior that is not necessarily incident-specific. Ruth and Commuri (1998) describe a technique that they call 'retrospective anchoring and profusion' (RAP) that may be useful to researchers under these conditions. Using RAP, the researcher attempts to (re-)situate the participant into a past time period by tapping into a vivid and deeply embedded contextual cue from that period. For example, Ruth and Commuri describe a study of Western influence on spousal decision making in India over an eight-year period. In order to situate husbands and wives in the past, participants were asked where they lived or worked eight years prior to the time the study began. The researchers then used prompts to guide the interviews toward issues of participants' life situations eight years earlier, until the researchers felt confident that participants were sufficiently anchored in that time period. Interviewers then guided participants toward discussing aspects of decision making for product categories in question during that time period. Such retrospective anchoring allowed participants to become resituated in the past so that a profusion of perceptions from that time period were available for recollection. Later in the interview, participants were prompted to describe decision making in the present for similar product categories. Comparing the present to the past allowed for nomothetic research insights grounded in idiographic experiences and recollection.

Retrospective anchoring can also be situated around a specific incident that would be well known to all informants. For example, in the US, many carry vivid memories of what they were doing at the time they heard of President John F. Kennedy's assassination, or of the incidents now known as '9/11'. Ruth (2005) used this type of culturally vivid anchor to study consumption in apartheid and post-apartheid South Africa, by prompting informants to recall and describe their activities at the time that they heard the news that Nelson Mandela was to be released from prison. Because Mandela's plight was well known to South Africans, and his release marked a change in government posture, the Mandela anchor situated all participants in a vivid time that could then elicit a profusion of relevant recollections where events anchored in the past could be contrasted with the present.

Obviously, in both the India and South Africa studies above (or in any studies, for that matter), it was not possible for researchers to go back in time. Furthermore, it may have been difficult to foresee that Western influences would markedly affect spousal decision making among Indians. Moreover, in the case of South Africa during the apartheid era, there was no assurance that the apartheid system of government would ever be dismantled, making a longitudinal investigation one that might never have had a post-apartheid present to contrast to the past. As a result, in both cases, the research teams had to devise a means for participants to go back in time perceptually, by anchoring them to contextually vivid life circumstances or incidents. Once so anchored, consumers were then able to respond (profusely) to prompts about consumption and other aspects of their lives during the time period in question, providing insights into causes and effects of change from past to present.

Autobiographies

An autobiography is a detailed description of a course of events narrated by an informant–protagonist. While such narratives do include other actors or enunciators, it is necessary that all parts maintain the informants' point of view. Further, unlike the narrative
forms discussed above, the informant tells the story *of* a life rather than 'merely reporting
what went on *in* a life' (Harré and Langenhove, 1999, p. 65, emphasis added). In other
words, rather than offer events that are subsequently interpreted by the researcher, the
informant is able to bring closure to the autobiography. As indicated in Table 29.2, autobiographies are well suited for investigating causes of past events: because informants are
expected to reveal the nature *of* events the method naturally grants informants control
over capturing and assessing these events.

When employing autobiography as a retrospective method, the researcher identifies a
key event or phenomenon of interest, and then recruits informants for the study for whom
that phenomenon bears personal meaning. In such a project, the researcher will be interested primarily in unfolding the histories; that is, in how events were interwoven with one
another over the course of time. Thus autobiographies are well suited to investigate how
consumers come to develop certain values or behaviors. Here discrete events are of lesser
consequence than the themes and processes the informant weaves together into a story of
how such values or behaviors emerged.

Because researchers identify the event of interest a priori, they ask the informant to
write the story of how he or she came to be interested in the event or in the outcomes pertaining to it. Three important components of this seemingly simple instruction distinguish autobiographies from other approaches. First, in requesting the story of a key
outcome, the researcher grants the informant complete control, not only with regard to
selecting the antecedents described, but also in the way the author presents the assortment
of such antecedents to the researcher/reader. This procedure stands in sharp contrast to
a depth-interview scenario, where a researcher may prompt and probe the informant to
ensure that all possible causes are unearthed. It also stands in contrast to a social or cultural psychological interpretation that researchers often impose in order to bring closure
to a narration of causes of an event. Thus, in an autobiography, the focus is on the salience
of events to the informant's personal identity, rather than interpretation based on sociology or cultural psychology.

Second, in declaring that the lead actor in the story is the informant, any uncertainty
about the lens through which the story is being recalled is minimized. This is a critical
component in using this method and the issue has been discussed in detail by Peirce (1955)
and adopted for autobiographies by Urban (1989) and Harré and Langenhove (1999; also
see Nunberg, 1993).

Third, it is important that the key outcome or state be clearly specified so that events
and processes leading up to a well-defined, externally valid episode are considered in the
autobiography. In other words, the external validity of the statement of an episode is what
enables researchers to compare multiple antecedents and events in autobiographies, to
arrive at nomothetic inferences.

Conclusion

Our discussion of longitudinal and retrospective qualitative research techniques reveals
that researchers in marketing have many short-term and long-term tools at their disposal

when they wish to incorporate temporal aspects in their studies. Furthermore it does appear that researchers interested in longitudinal qualitative studies have made progress in moving away from what Sherry (1987, p. 371) described as 'blitzkrieg ethnography', or studies that 'provide just enough field exposure to tantalize and to aid hypothesizing, but not enough for comprehensive understanding' (ibid.). Moreover the use of retrospective techniques such as RAP, critical incidents and storytelling is increasing, while autobiography, although seemingly underutilized by marketing researchers, affords great promise for the discipline. As a summary reminder of the benefits of these methods, qualitative longitudinal research seems especially apt when researchers are interested in change, although, clearly, consumer researchers could leverage their data sets more effectively and explore this important issue of how consumers, marketing-related sites or topics in general (e.g. the 'standard package' for consumers) change over time. Furthermore, retrospective techniques offer researchers the opportunity to explore key moments or periods in participants' lives that pertain to their immersion and experience with marketing-related phenomena.

We hope this chapter proves enlightening and encouraging to those scholars interested in capturing and incorporating temporally related phenomena in their research designs.

Acknowledgments

The authors thank Rob Kozinets, L.J. Shrum and Linda Tuncay for their comments on earlier versions of this chapter.

References

Arnould, Eric J. (1989), 'Toward a broadened theory of preference formation and the diffusion of innovations: cases from Zinder Province, Niger Republic', *Journal of Consumer Research*, **16** (September), 239–66.
Arnould, Eric J., and Linda L. Price (1993), 'River magic: extraordinary experience and the extended service encounter', *Journal of Consumer Research*, **20** (June), 24–45.
Baltes, Paul B., Hayne W. Reese and John R. Nesselroade (1977), *Lifespan Developmental Psychology: Introduction to Research Methods*, Monterey, CA: Brooks/Cole Publishing.
Belk, Russell W. and Janeen Arnold Costa (1998), 'The mountain man myth: a contemporary consuming fantasy', *Journal of Consumer Research*, **25** (December), 218–40.
Belk, Russell W., Melanie Wallendorf and John F. Sherry (1989), 'The sacred and the profane in consumer behavior: theodicy on the Odyssey', *Journal of Consumer Research*, **16** (June), 1–38.
Bitner, Mary Jo, Bernard H. Booms and Mary S. Tetreault (1990), 'The service encounter: diagnosing favorable and unfavorable incidents', *Journal of Marketing*, **54**, 71–84.
Commurai, Suraj and James W. Gentry (2005), 'Resource allocation in households with women as chief wage earners', *Journal of Consumer Research*, **32** (September), 185–95.
Cortazzi, Martin (1993), *Narrative Analysis*, Washington, DC: Falmer Press.
Coupland, Jennifer Chang (2005), 'Invisible brands: an ethnography of households and their brands in their kitchen pantries', *Journal of Consumer Research*, **32** (June), 106–18.
Fournier, Susan (1998), 'Consumers and their brands: developing relationship theory in consumer research', *Journal of Consumer Research*, **24** (March), 343–73.
Fournier, Susan and David Glen Mick (1999), 'Rediscovering satisfaction', *Journal of Marketing*, **63** (October), 5–23.
Harré, Rom and Luk van Langenhove (1999), 'Reflexive positioning: autobiography', in Rom Harré and Luk van Langenhove (eds), *Positioning Theory: Moral Contexts of Intentional Action*, Oxford: Blackwell, pp. 60–73.
Iacobucci, Dawn, Amy Ostrom and Kent Grayson (1995), 'Distinguishing service quality and customer satisfaction: the voice of the consumer', *Journal of Consumer Psychology*, **4** (3), 277–303.
Kelly, Janice R. and Joseph E. McGrath (1988), *On Time and Method*, Newbury Park, CA: Sage.
Kottak, Conrad P. (2005), *Cultural Anthropology*, New York: McGraw-Hill.
Kozinets, Robert V. (2001), 'Utopian enterprise: articulating the meanings of *Star Trek's* culture of consumption', *Journal of Consumer Research*, **28** (June), 67–88.
Kozinets, Robert V. (2002), 'Can consumers escape the market? Emancipatory illuminations from Burning Man', *Journal of Consumer Research*, **29** (June), 20–38.

Kozinets, Robert V., John F. Sherry, Diana Storm, Adam Duhachek, Krittinee Nuttavuthisit and Benet Deberry-Spence (2004), 'Ludic agency and retail spectacle', *Journal of Consumer Research*, **31** (December), 658–72.

Lincoln, Yvonna S. and Egon G. Guba (1985), *Naturalistic Enquiry*, Beverly Hills, CA: Sage.

Lowrey, Tina M., Cele C. Otnes and Julie A. Ruth (2004), 'Social influences on dyadic giving over time: a taxonomy from the giver's perspective', *Journal of Consumer Research*, **30** (March), 547–58.

Malinowski, Bronislaw ([1922] 1984), *Argonauts of the Western Pacific*, Long Grove, IL: Waveland Press (reprint edn).

McAlexander, James H., John W. Schouten and Harold F. Hoenig (2002), 'Building brand community', *Journal of Marketing*, **66** (January), 38–54.

McCracken, Grant (1988), *The Long Interview*, Newbury Park, CA: Sage.

Mead, Margaret ([1928] 2001), *Coming of Age in Samoa*, New York: HarperCollins.

Mick, David Glen and Claus Buhl (1992), 'A meaning-based model of advertising experiences', *Journal of Consumer Research*, **19** (December), 317–38.

Mick, David Glen and Michelle DeMoss (1990), 'Self-gifts: phenomenological insight from four contexts', *Journal of Consumer Research*, **17** (December), 322–32.

Mick, David Glen and Susan Fournier (1998), 'Paradoxes of technology: consumer cognizance, emotions, and coping strategies', *Journal of Consumer Research*, **25** (September), 123–43.

Nunberg, Geoffrey (1993), 'Indexicality and deixis', *Linguistics and Philosophy*, **16** (1), 1–43.

Oswald, Laura R. (1999), 'Culture swapping: consumption and the ethnogenesis of middle-class Haitian immigrants', *Journal of Consumer Research*, **25** (March), 303–18.

Otnes, Cele C., Tina M. Lowrey and Young Chan Kim (1993), 'Gift giving for "easy" and "difficult" recipients: a social roles interpretation', *Journal of Consumer Research*, **20** (September), 229–43.

Otnes, Cele, Tina M. Lowrey and L.J. Shrum (1997), 'Toward an understanding of consumer ambivalence', *Journal of Consumer Research*, **24** (June), 80–93.

Peirce, Charles S. (1955), 'Logic as semiotic: the theory of signs', in Justus Bucher (ed.), Philosophical Writings of Peirce, New York: Dover, pp. 98–119.

Peñaloza, Lisa (1994), 'Atravesando fronteras/border crossings: a critical ethnographic exploration of the consumer acculturation of Mexican immigrants', *Journal of Consumer Research*, **21** (June), 32–54.

Peñaloza, Lisa (2001), 'Consuming the American West: animating cultural meaning and memory at a stock show and rodeo', *Journal of Consumer Research*, **28** (December), 369–98.

Polkinghorne, Donald (1988), *Narrative Knowing and the Human Sciences*, Albany: State University of New York Press.

Price, Linda L. and Eric J. Arnould (1999), 'Commercial friendships: service provider–client relationships in context', *Journal of Marketing*, **63** (October), 38–56.

Richardson, Laurel (1990), 'Narrative and sociology', *Journal of Contemporary Ethnography*, **20** (2), 126–35.

Ricoeur, Paul (1985), *Temps et Récit*, vol. 3, Paris: Seuil.

Ruth, Julie A. (2005), 'The "changeover" and the changed: the meaning of product consumption in post-apartheid South Africa', working paper, Rutgers University.

Ruth, Julie A. and Suraj Commuri (1998), 'Shifting roles in family decision making', in Joe Alba and J. Wesley Hutchinson (eds), *Advances in Consumer Research*, Provo, UT: Association for Consumer Research, pp. 400–406.

Ruth, Julie A., Cele C. Otnes and Frédéric F. Brunel (1999), 'Gift receipt and the reformulation of relationships', *Journal of Consumer Research*, **25** (March), 385–402.

Saldaña, Johnny (2003), *Longitudinal Qualitative Research: Analyzing Change Through Time*, New York: Altamira Press.

Schouten, John W. and James H. McAlexander (1995), 'Subcultures of consumption: an ethnography of the New Bikers', *Journal of Consumer Research*, **22** (June), 43–61.

Sherry, John F. Jr (1987), 'Keeping the monkeys away from the typewriters: an anthropologists view of the Consumer Behavior Odyssey', in Melanie Wallendorf and Paul Anderson (eds), *Advance in Consumer Research*, Provo, UT: Association for Consumer Research, pp. 370–73.

Sherry, John F. (1990), 'A sociocultural analysis of a midwestern American flea market', *Journal of Consumer Research*, **17** (June), 13–30.

Sherry, John F. and Mary Ann McGrath (1989), 'Unpacking the holiday presence: a comparative ethnography of two gift stores', in Elizabeth C. Hirschman (ed.), *Interpretive Consumer Research*, Provo, UT: Association for Consumer Research, pp. 148–67.

Urban, Greg (1989), 'The "I" of discourse', in Benjamin Lee and Greg Urban (eds), *Semiotics, Self, and Society*, Berlin: Mouton de Gruyter, pp. 27–51.

Wall, W.D. and H.L. Williams (1970), *Longitudinal Studies and the Social Sciences*, London: Heinemann.

Wooten, David (2000), 'Qualitative steps toward an expanded model of anxiety in gift-giving', *Journal of Consumer Research*, **27** (June), 84–95.

30 Consumption experiences as escape: an application of the Zaltman Metaphor Elicitation Technique
Robin A. Coulter

In the early 1980s, Holbrook and Hirschman (1982) drew attention to the study of experiential consumption and, over the past two decades, numerous scholars have contributed to furthering our understanding of aesthetic, as well as physically challenging and risky, consumption experiences (e.g., Arnould and Price, 1993; Belk, 1988; Belk, Wallendorf and Sherry, 1989; Celsi, Rose and Leigh, 1993; Csikszentmihalyi, 1990; McCracken, 1988; Mick and Buhl, 1992; Shouten, 1991; Thompson, Pollio and Locander, 1994; Wallendorf and Arnould, 1991). Recent work by Arnould and Thompson (2005) proposes a theory of consumer culture that focuses on the experiential and sociocultural dimensions of consumption, and greater interest has been directed to managing customer experiences (Gobé, 2001; Pine and Gilmore, 1999; Lindstrom, 2005; Schmitt, 1999, 2003). Thus understanding more about consumption experiences in the context of consumers' everyday lives is an important undertaking.

The intent herein is to contribute to the literature on consumers' experiences using the Zaltman Metaphor Elicitation Technique (ZMET). ZMET is a hybrid methodology grounded in various domains, including verbal and nonverbal communication, visual sociology, visual anthropology, literary criticism, semiotics, mental imagery, cognitive neuroscience and phototherapy (Zaltman, 1997, 2003; Zaltman and Coulter, 1995). The tenets – thought occurs as a pattern of neural activity, not as words; most human meaning is exchanged nonverbally; much cognition is embodied; emotion and reason are equally important and commingle in decision making; most thought, emotion and learning occur without awareness; mental models guide the selection of, processing of and response to stimuli; cognitions are socially shared, and non-literal language and especially metaphor is central to cognition – suggest that ZMET is an appropriate tool for investigating customer experiences. The method involves semi-structured, in-depth personal interviews centered on visual images that the informant brings to the interview (Denzin, 1989; McCracken, 1988). Because ZMET data are informant-driven rather than researcher-driven, the ZMET interview affords researchers an opportunity to have consumers more freely express and expand on their thoughts and feelings, attitudes and perspectives.

The context of our investigation is consumers' Broadway theatre experiences. Acknowledging that experiences may be different according to frequency and loyalties (Schmitt, 2003), our study involved interviews with 21 US consumers, nine who attend a Broadway show at least once a year (i.e., Frequents), and 12 who attended within the last five years, but not within the last two years (i.e., Infrequents). We begin with a description of the ZMET methodology, as well as of our analytical procedures. Subsequently we report our substantive findings and discuss them in relation to a variety of literature streams.

Using ZMET to understand the Broadway experience

As noted, ZMET uses informants' pictures as the stimuli during in-depth one-on-one interviews to explore and probe informants' thoughts and feelings. The use of pictures is grounded in the facts that most information reaching the brain does so through the visual system, that much communication is nonverbal, and that informant-selected pictures can serve as entry points for exploring customer concepts (Weiser, 1988). Pictures typically represent, not only basic lower-order concepts, but also higher-order constructs that contain extensive information or defining attributes. Owing to the expressive power of pictures, it is not surprising that photographs have been a central part of counseling, sociology, psychology and anthropology (Becker, 1980; Collier and Collier, 1986; Denzin, 1989). Consumer behavior researchers also have employed photographs as stimuli to elicit consumers' subconscious thought processes and/or develop theories relevant to their work (e.g., Belk, Ger and Askegaard, 2003; Belk, Wallendorf and Sherry, 1989; Wallendorf and Arnould, 1991). Validation studies of ZMET applications indicate that four to five depth interviews that are focused on identifying and understanding core themes can provide up to 90 per cent of the information available from a larger set of interviews (Zaltman and Coulter, 1995).

Twenty-one informants from the greater Boston area – nine Frequents and 12 Infrequents – participated in this study of Broadway experience. Both samples included more women, five and eight, respectively; ages ranged from 30 to 50, with an annual income of at least $100 000. Half of the Frequents and Infrequents have attended a Broadway show in New York City; the other half have enjoyed a Broadway show in another city.

One week prior to the interview, participants were sent a letter stating, 'We are interested in your thoughts and feelings about Broadway theatre, and the role that Broadway theatre plays in your life . . . Please bring 6 to 8 pictures that represent these thoughts and feelings about Broadway theatre productions and the role they play in your life.' The images could be pictures from magazines, newspapers, pieces of artwork and/or photographs taken specifically for this assignment or retrieved from photo albums. Each informant was paid $150 to participate in a two-hour, one-on-one audio-taped interview.

Table 30.1 lists six steps in the ZMET interview as related to understanding participants' Broadway experiences. A detailed discussion of ZMET procedures, evaluative criteria and theoretical underpinnings is available in Zaltman and Coulter (1995) and Zaltman (1997).

Metaphor and analyses

A metaphor is the representation of one thing in terms of another (Lakoff and Johnson, 1980) and the importance of metaphor in understanding consumer behavior has received increased attention in recent years (e.g. Belk, Ger and Askegaard, 2003; Burroughs and Mick, 2004; Cotte, Ratneshwar and Mick, 2004; Coulter and Zaltman, 2000; Coulter, Zaltman and Coulter, 2001; Joy and Sherry, 2003). The ZMET interview is grounded in the perspective that metaphor is central to thought (Lakoff and Johnson, 1999; Ortony, 1993) and generates numerous types of metaphors. Of specific interest to this study are image-based metaphors (i.e., visual images participants bring to the interview, sensory images they discuss, and digital images they create). Frequents (F) and Infrequents (I) brought in an average of seven visual images and each created a digital (summary) image. Additionally, the interview transcripts are the source of deep metaphors (i.e., basic, core metaphors that structure consumers' thinking in very fundamental ways and serve to organize a system of concepts); thematic metaphors (or conceptual metaphors that represent consumers' broad

Table 30.1   Steps in the ZMET interview

Storytelling   The informant describes how each image represents his thoughts and feelings about the Broadway experience. Interviewer probe: 'Please tell me how this image relates to your thoughts and feelings about your Broadway experience.'

Missed images   The informant is asked if there were important ideas he wanted to express but for which he could not find relevant images. Interviewer probe: 'Were there any thoughts and feelings for which you were unable to find an image? Please describe the thought or feeling, and tell me about an image that you would use to represent the thought or feeling.'

Metaphor probe/expand the frame   The informant is asked to widen the frame of a selected picture and describe what else might enter the picture to better understand his thoughts and feelings. Interviewer probe: 'If you could widen the frame of this picture in all directions, what else would I see that would help me better understand your thoughts and feelings about Broadway theatre productions and the role they play in your life?'

Sensory metaphors   The informant is asked to express his ideas using various sensory images: color, taste, smell, touch, sound and emotion. Example of interviewer probe: 'What sound could I hear that would represent your thoughts and feelings about Broadway theatre productions and the role they play in your life?'

Vignette   The informant is asked to create a story about the Broadway experience. Interviewer probe: 'I would like you to use your imagination to create a short story. The story should express your thoughts and feelings about Broadway theatre productions and the role they play in your life. Please include at least these characters: (1) you, (2) Broadway theatre productions, and (3) a similar form of entertainment you might enjoy.'

Digital image   The informant, with the skilled assistance of a computer graphics imager, creates a summary collage using his images and supplemental images from a database, as needed.

---

meaning themes and reveal various aspects of deep metaphors); and metaphoric expressions (or surface metaphors, the spoken metaphors consumers explicitly mention). The average transcript word count was 11 770 for Frequents and 10 170 for Infrequents (approximately twice the word length of this chapter).

The analysis of informants' Broadway experiences was iterative. To better understand participants' Broadway experiences, the author first conducted narrative analysis of the stories contained in the transcripts (Riessman, 1993), followed by a metaphoric analysis grounded in qualitative data analytic procedures (Spiggle, 1994; Thompson, Locander and Pollio, 1989).

Findings

Our analyses reveal that informants perceive the Broadway experience as an escape from their daily lives. Although this finding is not a surprise, our analyses reveal very interesting dimensions of escape in terms of deep and thematic metaphors (see Table 30.2). In this section, we use participants' verbatims and images to discuss four aspects of the escape: framing the escape; planning, preparing for and anticipating the escape; the escape; and revisiting the escape.[1]

Framing the escape

The escape is multifaceted: although the focal point is the Broadway production, informants frame the evening more broadly – dinner precedes the theater, and coffee and dessert or

Table 30.2   Summary of deep metaphors and thematic categories

	Deep metaphors	Thematic metaphors
Planning, preparing for and anticipating the escape	System	• Dirty work • Getting 'all dolled up' • Anticipation
The escape	Container	• Sanctuary • Museum
	Resource	• Cognitive stimulation • Sensory stimulation
	Force	• Escape from daily life • Escape to flow experience
	Connection	• Self • Friends and family • Other theatergoers • Performers
Reflecting on the escape	Balance	• Good mental health
	Connection	• Self • Others

drinks follow. 'The dining is important, too. If I couldn't go out to eat before a show, it doesn't mean I wouldn't go to a show, but dining adds to the whole experience. I find it important to be able to enjoy a dinner with my husband or my family beforehand' [F7]. These sentiments were echoed by others: 'You don't just go to a play, you go out for the evening' [F4], and 'When you go to a play . . . you plan from mid-afternoon until the play . . . Where are you going to eat? Where are you going to park? . . . it's the whole evening' [I5].

Planning, preparing for and anticipating the escape
Planning the escape to a Broadway production is best characterized by the deep metaphor, *system* (the set of activities and feelings that precede attendance at a Broadway production) and three thematic metaphors: 'dirty work', 'getting all dolled up', and 'anticipation'. 'Dirty work' has similar meanings for Frequent and Infrequent theatergoers, and includes making arrangements to attend a production: ticket purchase, hotel, travel and childcare arrangements, and related logistics. The complexities, aggravation and related concerns of preparation are captured in the following expression: 'I can dread it, again, because of the money, because of the parking. Is it going to be a rainy night? Are we going to get dinner reservations?' [F6]. Others talk about the effort, as well as the commitment to the particular evening: 'It's something that you definitely need to plan ahead of time . . . you have to actually put effort into it, and a lot more money into it, and you pretty much have to think, "Is this something that I really want to do? Is this something I really have time to do right now?" So, it's also something that like if you buy tickets so far ahead of time, you have to make sure that you're not going to miss out on the opportunity because something else comes up' [I8]; and 'I associate going to a show with having dinner. I associate it with a more planned event . . . It's just more time consuming to get tickets, [and] because you have to go, and you have to plan the event which means you have to put aside a night and you have to say, "Okay, we're definitely doing this on this night" ' [I9]. Another participant, using a picture of a man

Figure 30.1   Preparing for the escape to Broadway

who was climbing a mountain, remarked: 'Preparing for Broadway is a production in itself . . . It's tough, hard work to get there' [F2] (see Figure 30.1).

An important aspect of preparing for the escape is 'getting all dolled up' for the production; extra energies are put toward self-presentation as part of the escape from the ordinary. Women participants, in particular, acknowledged the importance of their dress to attend a show, reporting: 'Everybody knows it's a dress-up event' [F1]; 'You want to dress up . . . to go above and beyond your typical outing kind of stuff. You want to feel classy, a cut above the rest, refined' [I6]; and 'You want to look good for the show. You don't have to get dressed up, but most people do. It's part of the culture' [I1].

Frequents and Infrequents, alike, look forward to their evening out with great 'anticipation', expecting a unique and exciting experience. Numerous participants used the gift metaphor and images of presents and holidays to reflect their anticipation and not knowing quite what to expect of a show: 'I was actually looking at a gift box. I don't know what's in here . . . So you're excited . . . that's what I was thinking, anticipating' [F5]; and 'A show you've never seen before is like a wrapped-up gift, you don't know what you're going to get' [I12]. Another informant, referring to his image of a fisherman (see Figure 30.2), commented: 'He is anticipating a huge fish. That is the anticipation I think of when I think of the fun at the theatre. You don't know what to expect. That makes it exciting' [I7].

Anticipation, one of the fundamental emotions, fuels escape. Our findings suggest that anticipating the escape for Frequents is related to the opportunity to replenish and revitalize themselves:

> The woman in the boat represents the cyclical process where my life started with the introduction of culture, and the exposure to it led to other curiosities. It led to my education, my refinement,

Figure 30.2   Anticipating the fun of Broadway

and my being able to accomplish a great number of things in my life. Those accomplishments afforded me the life experience of being able to afford to do things like taking my family to a show, carrying on this elegant affair, and giving to the grandchildren – just continuing that whole process. [F1] (See Figure 30.3.)

Both Frequents and Infrequents anticipate their escape as a rare treat, as an indulgence, and a reward, particularly given the high Broadway ticket price, coupled with the costs of pre- and post-theater activities. F4 summarizes:

It's really so expensive, so you have to really appreciate the theatre to drop $100 just for the ticket alone. It's a special treat to myself, like I went recently to get Lion King tickets. I wanted the best seats, and they were a hundred whatever dollars but, I said, 'I deserve this.' . . . It's like a reward

Figure 30.3   Reflecting on the cultural experiences of Broadway

to be able to go see it. So that's how I think of it, as a treat to myself that I deserve. If the night costs me $300, it was well worth, it's just I can't do it that often. I go and have a fancy dinner and have a couple of drinks, and I really go all out, because you deserve it so.

Figures 30.4 and 30.5 are also illustrative: 'Broadway is a rich extravagance that I can only have a little bit of at a time. I wouldn't want cake everyday, and I wouldn't want to see a Broadway show every day' [I3]; 'In the middle is a dollar bill with someone's eye kind of tearing it, and that's because the cost of the plays are prohibitive for you to go a lot and for us to take our kids to a lot of them' [I11].

The escape
Four deep metaphors capture the essence of escape via the Broadway production: container, force, resource and connection. Although each is discussed individually, the nature of the escape and these metaphors are inextricably interrelated.

Source: Shutterstock.com.

Figure 30.4 The rich extravagance of Broadway

Source: Olson Zaltman Associates.

Figure 30.5 The prohibitive costs of Broadway

Informants escape from the everyday life *container* to the theater – the *container* or vessel holding the production. Our findings suggest that the theater acts as a sanctuary and a museum. With regard to the former, informants escape from the daily grind to a safe place where they can lose themselves, or protect themselves (and possibly others) from work, the phone, kids, parents, burdens and other travesties. F9's comment is indicative: 'When I think of Broadway, I think of the physical location of Broadway, but more than that I think of the experience of being at a Broadway play . . . It's a place of escape', as represented by the woman walking on a secluded beach (see Figure 30.6).

Source: Shutterstock.com.

Figure 30.6   Broadway is an escape

Figures 30.7 and 30.8 and their expressions are also representative:

> There is a safe sanctuary that I experience at the theater. Everyone's cell phone is off. There are no beepers. There are no interruptions. The guys in the bag are all the distractions that are trying to get to me from the outside world, but inside my sanctuary they are wrapped up in this plastic bag, and they can't get to me. [I5]

> I imagine the rat really running. Kind of looking back at the cat out there, the stress is out there, but hopefully this little guy is safe behind the couch and he may not be thinking about that cat anymore. He may feel safe and just not focus on the craziness that is out there . . . I was thinking the same thing when you are in a theater, and you are not focusing on what is outside the doors. You feel safe . . . I mean safe fun. That is escaping the rat race. [I7]

Additionally, informants envision the theatre as a 'museum', a place to learn, to experience, to become more cultured, to meet people, to expand one's horizons. Pointing to her picture of a museum, one informant enthusiastically reported, 'When you go to a museum you feel cultured. When I go to a play, I feel I am getting some culture, learning something new, something interesting'[I7]. Similarly, F4 commented, 'It's like going to a museum . . . it's just appreciating different things.' Broadway enables our informants to expand their perspectives, as suggested by I11: 'I want to make sure that I experience as much as I can . . . you might enjoy music and all of a sudden, there's a whole new chapter of music you've never considered listening to before . . . I know [attending Broadway productions] has made me a smarter and better person.'

Broadway is a well-orchestrated, captivating *force* that facilitates escape. Several informants employed cooking-related visual metaphors (e.g., cake and recipe) to connote the intricate integration of the many facets of a Broadway production. Referring to these images, informants respectively stated, 'The cake is the bringing together of different ideas or thoughts and presenting them in a new exciting way that people haven't thought of

Source: Olson Zaltman Associates.

Figure 30.7 Broadway is a sanctuary, no one can reach you

Source: Shutterstock.com.

Figure 30.8 At Broadway you escape the rat race

Source: Shutterstock.com.

Figure 30.9   Broadway captivates the audience

before' [I10], and 'the theatre is constructed of a recipe, with different ingredients, char-acters, songs, storylines and experiences going into it . . . when it's put together, it really comes together nicely and it can be really delicious or a total disaster' [F6]. The captivat-ing nature of the production is evident in the following quotes: '[Broadway] captivates the audience and brings them right onto the stage . . . it keeps you involved' [I2]; 'I can only imagine what it takes to be up there and to captivate a live audience' [I6]; '[Broadway] assaults the senses' [I10] and image of the mesmerized owl (see Figure 30.9).

The force of the performance facilitates *escapism from* the 'day-to-day grind' [I8] of work and home, from political and economic aspects of life, from societal problems. From this perspective, escape is very much linked to the theater as a 'sanctuary'. Dominant visual images include pictures of vacation spots and luxury cruise liners, coupled with quotations such as 'When I walk in there and they turn the lights down . . . I forget about work. I forget about home life . . . I forget about money problems . . . it's an escape route' [I1]; 'Going to theatre is like a mini-vacation. I chose a ship as opposed to like a beach scenario because when I'm in a theater, it's almost like I'm escaping. I'm in this little theater and the whole world's outside me, but I don't even notice it' [F6]; and 'You are escaping to someplace beautiful and enjoyable without a care in the world . . . enjoying it and shutting out the outside world . . . where you want no outside distractions' [F1]. I6 used an image of a woman in a yoga pose to illustrate: 'escape, and being able to go to a Broadway play rep-resents escape from mundane day-to-day stuff and typical entertaining activities, like the movies. It's just an escape to something that's not a usual thing for me to do'.

The force of Broadway also facilitates *escapism to* a flow state. Many Frequents described their Broadway experience as flow: their visual images included people floating, soaring, diving and mountain climbing, and their metaphoric expressions referred to 'out of body

Source: Olson Zaltman Associates.

Figure 30.10 Broadway is an out-of-time and out-of-place experience

experiences' and reported on having lost all sense of time. One informant referring to the image of a diver points out, 'The diver represents a sense of surrender. You surrender your sense of disbelief to the artistic experience of being at the theatre . . . an experience of heightened senses' [F8]. Two other powerful images and metaphoric expressions follow:

> The man floating means you get swept up in the emotion of what's going on onstage. You may get swept up in the costumes and the makeup and the sets, or . . . you get really sucked up in just the story itself, just get lost in what's going on, and forget about everyday mundane things, and you're just enjoying the fact that you're at this play. [F4]

> Part of the feeling of a show is experiencing the feel of soaring or flying into the unknown, the anticipation of it, what you're going to see when you're up there, and benefiting from it emotionally, educationally, philosophically . . . you've given yourself permission to forget everything else . . . I won't let myself be interrupted. [F1] (See Figure 30.10.)

The Broadway experience is a *resource* to our informants, offering both sensory and cognitive stimulation, especially well-illustrated by the following image and metaphoric expression: 'You become enmeshed . . . a piece of the energy. Someone else is putting it out there for you but you become a piece of it, and just get very involved mentally and physically' [I10] (see Figure 30.11).

Informants' images representing sensory stimulation include, for example, pictures of fireworks and jumping off cliffs, and their metaphoric expressions reveal the multisensory nature of this escape: 'The Broadway experience involves all your senses. You get to see it. You get to taste it. You're talking to people. You're hearing music. You're listening to the sounds around you. You're in a very extravagant, glamorous setting usually, like in a theater. Most of those venues are very glamorous. It really livens up your senses' [I8]; and 'It's stimulating to the senses' [F8]. I4 titled her digital image, 'A sensory experience',

Figure 30.11   Broadway is unbounded energy

excitedly reporting, 'Broadway plays are very stimulating, the lights, the singing, the dancing, the costumes . . . the firework display represents the sights and sounds of Broadway . . . unfolding before your eyes.'

With regard to the thematic metaphor, 'museum', informants discuss the cognitive and cultural resources related to attending the theater, noting that 'It broadens your horizons . . . Broadway is more cultured. I feel like I am doing something positive, an experience where you're learning or expanding your mind' [I9]. One informant used an image of a light bulb to convey that Broadway represents 'ideas and how plays, particularly ones that have books or history attached to them, affect your opinion or change your mind' [I11]. Several informants also report that attending the theater increases their cognitive creativity, for example, 'You can take this creativity with you from a Broadway show and apply it to every aspect of your life' [I10]; 'When I think if I want to reenergize myself, escape, enjoy myself and forget about whatever else. If I thought about five things I would do, Broadway would be one of them. It stimulates you in different ways, at different levels' [F9].

Connection is a prominent deep metaphor in our data, with several connection-related thematic metaphors: connection to self, connection between theatergoers and friends/family/other theatergoers who are attending the production, and connection between theatergoers and performers (present, as well as past). As we noted, the escape to Broadway provides a quiet and focused time, and informants (particularly Frequents) reported taking this time to reflect on their connection to self, proffering pictures of mirrors: 'Looking in the mirror represents looking into a play, seeing similarities that may happen in your life and others' lives, something that you can relate to' [F3]; 'The mirror is relating it to yourself. It's that, "Oh my gosh, I have experienced that in my life, and so I can relate to it"' [F1]; 'I've seen a play and it's made me think of life, my life and relate to my life, but it gives it a different perspective too' [F6]; and 'It's sort of a mirror on our own experience' [F8].

Escaping to a Broadway production represents a connection to family and friends, an opportunity to have that 'special evening out' with special people. This connection is illustrated primarily with pictures from family albums and discussion about the importance of having quality time, and building a tradition with family members. The salience of having time to appreciate one another was emphasized by numerous participants: '[This is my] family doing something together . . . Broadway was something we did as a family when I was a child and we continue . . . we're sharing something . . . not a routine . . . a ritual' [F1]; 'I would go with my family. Family is important to me and enjoying time with my family is important . . . the core of everything' [F7]; 'What I think of theatre [is] gathering my buddies together and having a good time' [I7]; and 'We're going to go as a family, because although I've been before, it's something that I want to share with you guys' [I6]. All theatergoers, even though they may not be acquainted, co-create a communal experience, collectively experiencing a unique moment in time.

Our theatergoers also sense a strong connection to the Broadway performers, recounting that it is the audience *and* the performers who co-create a forceful experience. Informants enthusiastically reflect, 'They see you. You see them. You are laughing, and they are enjoying themselves. You are part of [the energy] together. You feel you are in the loop' [I7]. The relationship between the deep metaphors, connection and force, is vividly apparent in I2's image (see Figure 30.12) and metaphoric expression:

> It becomes electrifying through the crowd. It is a give and take. It is a relationship between the audience and the performers . . . The adrenaline starts to flow, and I think it makes their performance better because they are going to feed off the crowd.

Interestingly, some Frequents take this connection one step farther, acknowledging their connection to Broadway actors and actresses in general: 'There's a spirit of all the previous actors; you feel a certain energy. All these theaters being next to each other and you're going into one theater, and these people are going into another theater and we're all having this communal experience' [F8].

The meaning of connection to the performers is also informed by informants' stated disconnect with performers. Our theatergoers compliment and admire the unique and extraordinary skills and talents of the performers: 'So, I just become amazed with it. Just in awe. It is something that you don't see [every day] and you appreciate their talent' [I7]. Interestingly other informants reported being somewhat envious of these talents: 'It's different and exciting and [I am] slightly jealous. When they get up there, they have beautiful voices and this ability to embrace a character, and I couldn't do that' [I10]; and 'I have some jealousy . . . I work in corporate America, and I like what I do, but what I do is not all that different. I admire these unique talents who do something very different for a living' [I9].

Revisiting the escape

Two deep metaphors, *balance* and *connection*, capture informants' reflections about their escapes to Broadway. The sanctuary and museum, as well as the force of escapism, provide a countervailing balance to our informants' everyday experiences. I8's digital (summary) image incorporates many images to portray managing mental health through escape:

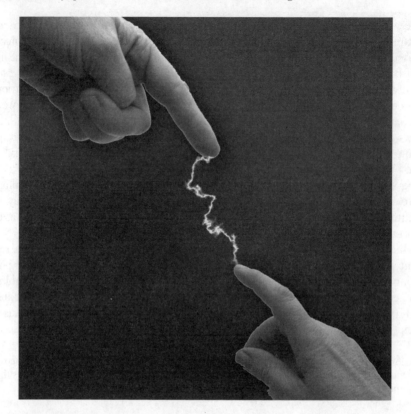

Source: Shutterstock.com.

Figure 30.12   Broadway electrifies the crowd

> You do need a little bit of balance in your life, like you can't work all the time, and again, because it is a special treat to [go to a] Broadway show. You're balancing your hectic life with a sense of taking your life down a couple of notches and giving yourself an opportunity to get away . . . I've done everything I need to do to make this time my time now. You've fulfilled all your obligations to have that time for yourself. (See Figure 30.13.)

Frequents and Infrequents concur about the importance of taking time to escape and to create balance in life. F4 reflects, '[Attending Broadway is] a sort of mentally refreshing – I mean, if you have a stressful job and you have kids, and you say, "I'm going to do this for myself and I'm not going to feel the least bit guilty" . . . so when I do actually do it, I enjoy every second of it and I don't regret it.' I7 echoes the sentiment: 'You work really hard; you have to play hard, too. It is the balance [of] work with play. *(Why is it important to balance those two things?)* Just because the scale will tip and then you will tip . . . I definitely know when I am working too hard and I need to treat myself. I guess that is a way of telling how the balancing goes.' Suspended animation as related to balance is evident in F9's response: 'Just escape into that two-hour performance and really feel it . . . it creates balance in one's life . . . It helps relieve the monotony of doing the same thing always, every day, over and over again without any escape from work or school or whatever it is that we might spend the majority of our life doing.'

Figure 30.13   Broadway brings balance to everyday life

In reliving their escape, informants refer to their memories, as well as their interest in sharing their experiences. The vibrancy of the Broadway experience, the sensory and cognitive stimulation, make for vivid, easily recalled memories. I3 reveals that Broadway 'sticks out . . . [memories] feel more permanent . . . I tend to remember exactly where I was and who I was with. I remember the specific music to it. It gives you a memory to put your finger on'; I8 reports that Broadway 'gives you something to think back on, an enjoyable experience you can relive in your mind, you can share with your friends'. Pictures of people talking, enjoying a party, or a family outing were reflective of informants' interest in sharing their memories. F4 used 'screen beans' to depict a range of emotions and topics that Broadway has to offer noting, 'These little people could also represent the different things you talk about afterwards, which is a big part of it . . . You want to share in it, talk about it, discuss it afterwards.' F2's description is typical: 'After you've gone to see a show, you might have a discussion . . . the idea that [people are] talking and having a mature conversation . . . You can have that conversation about a shared, communal experience.' (See Figure 30.14.)

Figure 30.14   Sharing the escape to Broadway

Discussion

This chapter illustrates the use of the Zaltman Metaphor Elicitation Technique to under-stand consumers' Broadway experiences. Huffman, Ratneshwar and Mick (2000, p. 20) might cast attending a Broadway production as a consumption intention – as a doing goal – one that involves 'allocation and depletion of resources – primarily money, time, and energy – available to the consumer'. Our substantive findings illustrate that the Broadway experience is concurrently an aesthetic (Joy and Sherry, 2003), extraordinary (Arnould and Price, 1993) and flow (Csikzentmihalyi, 1990) experience. Broadway per-formances provide consumers with multisensory, cognitive stimulation, an embodiment such that they are able to escape their everyday lives. Informants willingly expend time and effort to create the escape for which they express intense anticipation. Escape is an indul-gence, a treat, as well as a source of reinvigoration, nutrition for the body and soul. Our informants' descriptions give meaning to Thompson's perspective on postmodernist con-sumer goals (2000, p. 129): 'consumers take flight from the entanglement . . . They seek temporary respite in liminoid spaces offering magic, communion, spiritual enrichment, and the sublime aura of the authentic'. We find inklings of several differences between Frequents and Infrequents in their Broadway experiences that other methods might fruit-fully explore. Importantly escape as consumption is worthy of additional investigation.

The temporality of experiential consumption, from the planning stage to the reflective stage, is evident in our findings. Collectively our findings and those across a variety of con-sumption experiences (Arnould and Price, 1993; Celsi et al., 1993; Joy and Sherry, 2003) affirm that experiential consumption is much more broadly experienced than simply 'the encounter'. The experience (in the form of preparatory activities and anticipation) creeps into consumers' daily lives well before the actual encounter (or performance). Moreover the commanding nature of the Broadway performance provides vivid and dominating memories, long-lasting and easily recalled, that serve to be self-seducing, memories that lurk well after the experience and are also a source of fodder for discussion among family and friends. Future research might examine the broader implications and effects of these experiences, and the balancing of self relative to consumers' everyday lives.

The consumer, co-creator of the Broadway experience, is pre-eminent at all stages, engaging with customer service representatives, baby sitters and reservationists to plan their experiences, with the performers to create their experience, and with their family and friends to plan, create, and remember their experience. They engage in consumption as a means of self-definition (Belk, 1988; Levy, 1981; Schouten, 1991; Thompson, Locander and Pollio, 1989) and escape to create and maintain balance, making time for one's self and important others. Consumers take control, investing the psychic energy to create the optimal experience, offering a gift to self (Mick and DeMoss, 1990).

Being able to access customers' thoughts and feelings, conscious and unconscious, is crucial to elucidating marketing and consumer behavior phenomena. Informants' metaphorical expressions and images of mirrors, floating men, fireworks, vacation spots, decadent cakes and the like offer invaluable insights into the meaning of the Broadway experience, specifically, and escape experiences, more generally. The Zaltman Metaphor Elicitation Technique offers a means to hear the voice of the customer, see through the eyes of the customer, and keep the customer and their experience as a focal point in our research.

Note

1. Thank you to Olson Zaltman Associates and the American League of Theaters and Producers for use of the transcripts in this chapter, and much appreciation to John Bell of Olson Zaltman Associates for the creation of the images: 'Reflecting on the cultural experiences of Broadway', 'The prohibitive costs of Broadway', 'Broadway is a sanctuary, no one can reach you', 'Broadway is an out-of-time and out-of-place experience' and 'Broadway brings balance to everyday life.' The other images in this chapter are representative visual metaphors of the images that participants brought to their interview; source: Shutterstock.com.

References

Arnould, Eric J. and Linda L. Price (1993), 'River magic: extraordinary experience and the extended service encounter', *Journal of Consumer Research*, **20** (June), 24–45.

Arnould, Eric J. and Craig J. Thompson (2005), 'Consumer culture theory', *Journal of Consumer Research*, **31**(March), 868–82.

Belk, Russell W. (1988), 'Possessions and the extended self', *Journal of Consumer Research*, **15** (September), 139–68.

Belk, Russell W., Güliz Ger and Søren Askegaard (2003), 'The fire of desire: a multisited inquiry into consumer passion', *Journal of Consumer Research*, **30** (December), 326–51.

Belk, Russell W., Melanie Wallendorf and John Sherry (1989), 'The sacred and the profane in consumer behavior: theodicy on the Odyssey', *Journal of Consumer Research*, **15** (June), 1–38.

Becker, Howard S. (1980), *Exploring Society Photographically*, Chicago: University of Chicago Press.

Burroughs, James E. and David Glen Mick (2004), 'Exploring antecedents and consequences of consumer creativity in a problem-solving context', *Journal of Consumer Research*, **31** (September), 402–11.

Celsi, Richard L., Randall L. Rose and Thomas W. Leigh (1993), 'An exploration of high-risk leisure consumption through skydiving', *Journal of Consumer Research*, **20** (June), 1–23.

Collier, John and Malcolm Collier (1986), *Visual Anthropology: Photography as a Research Method*, rev. and expanded edn, Albuquerque, NM: University of New Mexico Press.

Cotte, June, S. Ratneshwar and David Glen Mick (2004), 'The times of their lives: phenomenological and metaphorical characteristics of consumers' timestyles', *Journal of Consumer Research*, **31** (September), 333–45.

Coulter, Robin and Gerald Zaltman (2000), 'The power of metaphor', in S. Ratneshwar, David Glen Mick and Cynthia Huffman (eds), *The Why of Consumption: Contemporary Perspectives on Consumers' Motives Goals and Desires*, London: Routledge, pp. 259–81.

Coulter, Robin A., Gerald Zaltman and Keith S. Coulter (2001), 'Interpreting consumer perceptions of advertising: an application of the Zaltman metaphor elicitation technique', *Journal of Advertising*, **30** (Winter), 1–22.

Csikszentmihalyi, Mihaly (1990), *Flow: The Psychology of the Optimal Experience*, NewYork: Harper & Row Publishers.

Denzin, Norman K. (1989), *The Research Act: A Theoretical Introduction to Sociological Methods*, 3rd edn, Englewood Cliffs, NJ: Prentice-Hall.

Gobé, Marc (2001), *Emotional Branding*, New York: Allworth Press.

Holbrook, Morris B. and Elizabeth C. Hirschman (1982), 'The experiential aspects of consumption: consumer fantasies, feelings, and fun', *Journal of Consumer Research*, **9** (September), 132–40.

Huffman, Cynthia, S. Ratneshwar and David Glen Mick (2000), 'Consumer goal stuctures and goal-determination processes: an integrative framework', in S. Ratneshwar, David Glen Mick and Cynthia Huffman (eds), *The Why of Consumption: Contemporary Perspectives on Consumers' Motives Goals and Desires*, London: Routledge, pp. 9–35.

Joy, Annamma and John F. Sherry Jr (2003), 'Speaking of art as embodied imagination: a multisensory approach to understanding aesthetic experience', *Journal of Consumer Research*, **30** (2), 259–82.

Lakoff, George and Mark Johnson (1980), *Metaphors We Live By*, Chicago: University of Chicago Press.

Lakoff, George and Mark Johnson (1999), *Philosophy in the Flesh: The Embodied Mind and Its Challenge to Western Thought*, New York: Basic Books.

Levy, Sidney (1981), 'Interpreting consumer mythology: a structural approach to consumer behavior', *Journal of Marketing*, **45** (Summer), 49–61.

Lindstrom, Martin (2005), *Brand Sense*, New York: Free Press.

McCracken, Grant (1988), *Culture and Consumption*, Bloomington, IL: Indiana University Press.

Mick, David Glen and Claus Buhl (1992), 'A meaning-based model of advertising experiences', *Journal of Consumer Research*, **19** (December), 317–38.

Mick, David Glen and Michelle DeMoss (1990), 'Self-gifts: phenomenological insights from four contexts', *Journal of Consumer Research*, **17** (December), 322–32.

Ortony, Andrew (ed.) (1993), *Metaphor and Thought*, 2nd edn, Cambridge: Cambridge University Press.

Pine, B. Joseph and James L. Gilmore (1999), *The Experience Economy*, Boston: Harvard Business School Press.

Riessman, Catherine K. (1993), *Narrative Analysis*, Newbury Park, CA: Sage Publications.

Schmitt, Bernd H. (1999), *Experiential Marketing*, Hoboken, NJ: John Wiley & Sons, Inc.

Schmitt, Bernd H. (2003), *Customer Experience Management*, Hoboken, NJ: John Wiley & Sons, Inc.

Schouten, John W. (1991), 'Selves in transition: symbolic consumption and personal rites of passage and identity construction', *Journal of Consumer Research*, **17** (March), 412–26.

Spiggle, Susan (1994), 'Analysis and interpretation of qualitative data in consumer research', *Journal of Consumer Research*, **21** (December), 491–503.

Thompson, Craig (2000), 'Postmodern goals made easy', in S. Ratneshwar, David Glen Mick and Cynthia Huffman (eds), *The Why of Consumption: Contemporary Perspectives on Consumers' Motives Goals and Desires*, London: Routledge, pp. 120–39.

Thompson, Craig J., Willian B. Locander and Howard R. Pollio (1989), 'Putting consumer experience back into consumer research', *Journal of Consumer Research*, **16** (September), 1335–46.

Thompson, Craig, Howard R. Pollio and William B. Locander (1994), 'The spoken and the unspoken: a hermeneutic approach to understanding the cultural viewpoints that underlie consumers' expressed meanings', *Journal of Consumer Research*, **21** (December), 432–52.

Wallendorf, Melanie and Eric J. Arnould (1991), ' "We gather together": the consumption rituals of Thanksgiving Day', *Journal of Consumer Research*, **19** (June), 13–31.

Weiser, Judy (1988), ' "See what I mean?" Photography as nonverbal communication in cross-cultural psychology', in Fernando Poyatos (ed.), *Cross-Cultural Perspectives in Nonverbal Communication*, Toronto: Hogrefe Publishers.

Zaltman, Gerald (2003), *How Customers Think*, Boston: Harvard Business School Press.

Zaltman, Gerald (1997), 'Rethinking market research: putting people back in', *Journal of Marketing Research*, **34** (November), 424–37.

Zaltman, Gerald and Robin Higie Coulter (1995), 'Seeing the voice of the customer: metaphor-based advertising research', *Journal of Advertising Research*, **35** (July/August), 35–51.

31 Romancing the gene: making myth from 'hard science'
Elizabeth C. Hirschman and Donald Panther-Yates

Problematizing consumer ethnicity: introduction

What we want to explore in the present chapter is how consumers who are not highly trained in biogenetics weave together the quantitative, technologically produced bits of evidence that result from a personal DNA test with their own pre-existing cultural narratives on race, genealogy and identity (see Appendix). We want also to examine in conjunction with this the social, political and economic tensions that consumers become aware of and must negotiate in their efforts to make sense of their DNA racial ancestry, especially upon discovering ancestry that is not 'white' (Panther-Yates, 2003; Hirschman, 2005; Kennedy, 1997).

In particular we will use consumer commentary about American Indian ancestry to illustrate these issues. American Indian ancestry is particularly interesting for two reasons. First, it is a racial ancestry that was greatly maligned during the early parts of the twentieth century, only to be resurrected as signifying nobility and spirituality during the second portion of that same century (Carvajal-Carmona et al., 2000; Jones, 2002; Smith, 1999). American Indians have now arrived at the status of a revered icon in our national consciousness – the central figures of a nature-based utopian myth that is viewed as sadly wrecked by the onslaught of European colonial hegemony from the 1500s onward (Smith, 1999). This is the type of heroic–tragic narrative which many contemporary American consumers find deeply attractive and to which they would like to attach themselves through genetics (Hall and du Gay, 1996).

Second, once one unexpectedly discovers through the 'hard science' of DNA testing that one is 'carrying' American Indian genetic heritage, one may feel a compulsion to come to terms with this ancestral legacy (Panther-Yates, 2003). To one of the present authors who made just such a discovery, this new knowledge feels somewhat like a benevolent version of the *Aliens* motion picture creature, a life-form that was embedded in unsuspecting human hosts, only to burst out upon completing its gestation period. I, and thousands of other Colonial-era descended Americans, are the sleeper-cells for indigenous genes, once thought to be virtually annihilated, but now, through the wonders of DNA testing, revealed to have been merely hibernating for four or five centuries.[1]

Brodwin (2002, p. 324), an anthropologist working under an NIH grant to study the ethical aspects of the new commercial DNA technologies for consumers, writes that these techniques 'generate knowledge of ancestry: the links between people in the present and their biological forebears. They announce a long-term generational connection . . . Knowledge of these genetic connections alters how we imagine our "significant same", those people who are significantly like me, connected to me . . . Genetic knowledge has the power to change the group with whom we share a deep, horizontal comradeship'.

As Brodwin further declares, such knowledge may either reveal inaccuracies in one's current conception of self-identity or may act to reinforce that identity. In several cases, DNA testing results have created large disruptions in prior perceived racial and ethnic memberships (Panther-Yates, 2003; Hirschman, 2005; Kennedy, 1997). For example, some African-Americans have learned they are partially 'white' or American Indian, or not even 'black' at all. Some white people have learned they have a sizable chunk of African ancestry; some Christians have learned they are carrying the Jewish Cohanim haplotype (Foster and Sharp, 2002). As Brodwin (2002) aptly notes, such discoveries 'set in motion a powerful narrative of loss and redemption' (p. 328). One must sever ties to the comfortable, known racial/ethnic identity with which selfhood was constructed, and cast one's self in a novel narrative.

'Being Indian'
Marketing researchers have generally treated the core issue of ethnic/racial identity as unproblematic (Askegaard, Arnould and Kjeldgaard, 2005; Peñalosa, 1994; Wallendorf and Reilly, 1983; Deshpande, Moyer and Donthu, 1986); that is, in most studies, ethnic affiliation is dichotomous: one either belongs to the ethnic category in question or one does not. While level of commitment to ethnic identity is interrogated in our literature, core belonging/not belonging is not. The advent of DNA testing is likely to challenge this status quo in marketing ethnicity research, as increasing numbers of consumers discover they spring from multiracial, multiethnic ancestries, or even that their entire ethnic identity was in error.

Among American Indians this 'process of problematization' is especially intense, because designation as an Indian and tribal enrollment can bring economic entitlements (Jones, 2002). The discovery via DNA testing that many non-Native-identified persons are actually carrying substantial American Indian ancestry has created a dramatic retrenchment of indigenous ethnic boundaries and stimulated a vigorous debate about who and what is an Indian (Carvajal-Carmona et al., 2000; Tallbear, 2005; Wells, 2003). By examining this debate, we can gain insight into the interpretive strategies consumers use to negotiate their ethnic identity and, more specifically, how DNA data, perceived as especially 'scientific', is used to deconstruct other ethnic criteria.

Within the discussion regarding Native ethnicity, four criteria have been put forward by consumers regarding ethnic identity. These criteria apply, as well, to other ethnicities/races studied within marketing; they are (1) the individual's geographic locale, i.e., is s/he living where members of the group are 'known' to dwell? For American Indians this would imply living on a tribal reservation, i.e., 'the rez'; (2) government-sanctioned documentation and designation; for American Indians this would imply possession of a Bureau of Indian Affairs (BIA) identification card, the listing of one's direct ancestors on the Dawes Rolls, and an acceptable blood quantum level (usually one-eighth or one-quarter American Indian) to qualify for membership in a specific tribe (see cita.Chattanooga.org/bia/cdibFedreg); (3) culture, that is the beliefs, practices, language, spirituality, shared knowledge and history of the specific tribal community (Tallbear, 2005); and the most recent addition, (4) possession of DNA markers which are associated with group members, but not present in members of other groups; i.e., distinctive and distinguishing molecular differences at the genetic level which identify one as an American Indian (Cavalli-Sforza, Menozzi and Piazza, 1994; Collins-Schramm et al., 2002; Foster and Sharp, 2002; Jones, 2002).

We examine the ways in which consumers interpret these four criteria as constituting their ethnic identity. Notably the first three have already been widely used in marketing research, but have not been emically [in the people's terms] examined from the consumers' self-perspective. As we shall show, in the case of newly-discovered Native ancestry (via DNA testing) consumers may seek to deconstruct or dismantle these earlier criteria in order to establish Native identities for themselves. When we consider the new, fourth criterion, DNA testing, we will show that consumers tend to view this form of data as 'hard science', i.e., indisputable evidence of ethnic identity, while the other, earlier, criteria are seen as politically or socially constructed.

Our consumer textual material is drawn from the Rootsweb-DNA-Genealogy website discussion board during the period 2002–4 . This web-board was founded in 2000 and has 750 active subscribers; over 28 000 messages have been posted to the board and are accessible from the archives. It is the largest web-board of its type on the Internet.

Geographic locale

This criterion assumes that American Indians, or members of other ethnic groups, say African Americans or Latinos, 'should' live in a place publicly recognized as appropriate for that group. It is consistently used as an ethnic marker within marketing research. Thus Latinos are expected to dwell in barrios (Peñaloza, 1994), African-Americans in urban ghettoes (Crockett and Wallendorf, 2004) and American Indians on reservations (Tallbear, 2005). To live in this area is taken to imply a higher level of ethnic authenticity for the individual. To live away from this area suggests the possibility or choice of assimilation, lessening the genuineness or depth of the individual's ethnic identity (see Askegaard et al., 2005). By living apart from the ethnic community, one may be suspected of ethnic disloyalty or desertion (see Peñalosa, 1994).

Now let us consider the excerpt below, taken from the Rootsweb DNA discussion board:

> Although I've been a member of the Cherokee Nation [Oklahoma] for a good many years, I have yet to receive any benefits from that membership . . . There is a growing voice by whites that Indians are receiving special privileges and the rez should be dismantled . . . Most of those voices don't understand the U.S.–Native American history . . .
>
> Tribal enrollment also is becoming an increasing problem between non-rez Indians and rez Indians, whether or not you can prove Indian 'blood' . . . So Native Americans are now using whether or not you live on a rez to determine membership in some cases.
>
> Even some of the Cherokee in Oklahoma, who technically don't have a rez, are starting to complain that those living off-rez, outside the Oklahoma Indian Territory [should not] have a say in tribal affairs or participate in tribal elections . . . Although our numbers are added to the need of the tribe for federal funding . . . most Indians living off the rez don't get any benefits of tribal membership. (Charlotte)

What is in play here are interpretive notions of ethnicity *in situ*. Physical location, e.g., on-rez/off-rez, is tangible and concrete, but its ethnic meaning is mutable. While geographic boundaries may be established by some group members (usually those 'inside' the boundary), the validity of these same boundaries may be disputed (usually by those 'outside'). Charlotte argues that, if she is Indian enough to be counted for the tribe's economic benefit, she should not be deemed less-Indian simply because she lives beyond the tribe's physical boundary, i.e., off-rez. Analogously, African-Americans, Latinos and Indo-Pakistanis who dwell in non-typical, 'cross-border' areas within the larger American culture may resent the view of their ethnic comrades that they somehow do not 'count' as group members.

Government issued/sanctioned identification

In the case of American Indians, the external federal and state governments, as well as internal tribal governments, have established a labyrinthine system of certification, documentation and registration intended to identify 'real' or 'genuine' Indians (see Bureau of Indian Affairs, 2005; Tallbear, 2005). Among the institutions involved are the Bureau of Indian Affairs, the Dawes Rolls and the several tribal councils (Bureau of Indian Affairs, 2005). One of the primary qualification devices is the so-called 'blood quantum', a statistic based on the calculated percentage of full blood (i.e., 100 per cent American Indian) ancestry one carries, according to one's 'properly' documented genealogy. Consumers expressed a wide variety of interpretive strategies for this criterion, usually depending upon their own socially positioned vantage point. Consider the comments below:

> I have a documented Cherokee line and I belong to the Cherokee Nation in OK . . . My grandfather was . . . on the Dawes Rolls and when he was born in 1904, he wasn't even considered a US citizen, although he was born in the state of OK . . . The BIA has been using [blood quantum] for the past 200 years and it was specifically designed to breed out Native American blood . . .
> This has created some real problems in the Native American community . . . between full blood and mixed blood . . . You're not quite Indian unless you're full blood, and then there are full bloods that can't be citizens of the Cherokee Nation in OK, because they can't document their family . . . I was in hopes the Native American genetic [DNA] test would lay this theory, i.e. blood quantum, to rest once and for all . . . I don't have a really deep knowledge on genetics, but it seems to me once an Indian always an Indian, and the genes would be there . . . regardless of how far back the full blood Indian was. (Dave)

> For me it is a matter of showing others [that] my ancestors were who our family says they were. The government policy for American Indians has always been – and in many ways still is – genocide. First, it was simply kill us. Then it was 'assimilate' them. And now it is 'ignore the assimilated ones, and pit CDIB (the Indian Board of the Federal Government) carded Indians against those uneligible for CDIB cards, those who were successfully assimilated'. Unfortunate but true. So I look for the day a DNA test can determine American Indian ancestry from the 'Y' [paternal] side of the family tree, since my Dad was three-eighths American Indian. This is a big issue in the Cherokee community, where there are 250 000 registered members, and perhaps that many more who because of tribal requirements are not registered . . . Like cattle, we have to say we are one-half blood, or one-eighth blood, or three-quarter blood; no other nationality has to go under that humiliation. So for American Indian populations, and because of the racist American laws concerning us, it is important for us to show who we are. (Vance)

These commentators represent different identity positions regarding government-sanctioned American Indian ethnicity; some are properly 'carded' and 'enrolled'; some are not. By creating such political distinctions among American Indian descendants, the federal government has effectively prevented this group from organizing itself into a cohesive ethnic unit or identity. Federally recognized tribes act as weak, independent city-states, each carefully guarding its own doorway and jealously blocking entry from outsiders: the mixed bloods and undocumented Native descendants dwelling beyond their boundaries (Jones, 2002).

It is interesting to consider how Native-descended persons interpret this political documentation. For example, Dave views these standards as essentially valid indicators of one's

Indianness. We learn elsewhere in his postings that he can document his Native heritage to the extent necessary to obtain Cherokee tribal membership in North Carolina. Being able to 'meet the standard', he would like to see tribal enrollment determined by this criterion.

However Dave, also a duly registered Cherokee in Oklahoma, perceives more 'evil intent' in the current governmental blood quantum standard. Even though he meets the criterion, he views it as functioning in a negative way, in fact, destroying the Native population. He is reaching out to the believed 'hard science' of DNA testing to provide indisputable claims to Native ancestry for *all* Native descendants: full blood, mixed blood, governmentally documented or undocumented: 'once an Indian, always an Indian'.

In a deeper sense, it is clear that Dave sees Native ancestry as especially powerful, able to outweigh even generations of removal from the 'full-blood Indian'. In Dave's view, once these genes enter one's ancestry, one *is* an Indian.[2]

Vance takes an even more oppositional stance to this criterion. He decries the government's 'divide and conquer' strategy, which he believes has introduced this artificial and destructive boundary into the Native community. Vance would use DNA testing as a fulcrum to group all Native-descended persons together into a cohesive unit. He reasons that, if Indians could 'show who we are', a much larger, more economically and socially powerful entity could be constructed: DNA testing would provide strength, size and unity.

Culture

A third marker of one's ethnicity is culture; cultural practices and artifacts are perhaps the most attended to aspects of ethnicity within the marketing literature (Askegaard et al., 2005; Peñalosa, 1994; Wallendorf and Reilly, 1983). Yet, interestingly, this aspect of one's ancestral identity was the least discussed with respect to American Indian heritage on the Internet board we monitored. When ethnic culture was discussed, it was usually done in general terms or through allusion to romanticized ideas of the Indian lifestyle:

> Culture . . . and kin determine an Indian, not DNA results that indicate someone has 10–15% 'NA'. . . It is one thing to use a DNA test as an indicator of kinship with a specific individual . . .; however to assume that a reading of '15% NA' on a DNA print test indicates that an individual with absolutely no cultural identity *as* an Indian *is* an 'Indian' is ridiculous, and is typically non-Indian as to its understanding of Indians. (Brian)

> One of the things I always found unhelpful in thinking about tribal program development was all of the romanticized environmentalist-talk as it relates to tribes. Particularly, I didn't like the notion that native people were *inherently* environmentalist, rather than having developed environmentally-specific practices – quite often practices based on profound spiritual beliefs – in response to many generations spent engaging with those particular landscapes. I didn't like the idea that it's in our blood or 'genes', rather than our brains and worked out through *practice*. (Kim Tallbear)

Similarly, an article in *Anthropology News* (Sabrina Magliocco, 'Indigenousness and the politics of spirituality', April 2005, **9**, 15) noted that it is the romanticized, sacred aspects of Native peoples' culture that are most likely to be attractive to (and co-opted by) outsiders.

> Spirituality is one of the most important components of any group's identity. Dealing with magical experience and defining the sacred . . . could be said to lie at the core of identity, or a group's ethos. Often, it becomes central to how a group is perceived by others. Many associate

indigenous peoples' *authenticity* with their spirituality, leading to the commodification of indigenous spirituality, reactions against it and various attempts to curtail it . . .

The commodification of spirituality led to outrage on the part of many indigenous peoples that white 'wannabees' were playing at being Indian and appropriating their spiritual traditions. Native Americans were understandably furious that whites were . . . once again profiting at their expense . . .

The Native author (Don Panther-Yates) of the present chapter provides the following reasoning regarding the cultural and spiritual aspects of Indian ethnicity:

From my perspective, you either are or are not an Indian, depending on whether you have an Indian spirit (I intentionally avoid the word 'soul'). As the Lakota Sioux chief Noble Red Man (Matthew King) says, 'Our people don't come in parts.' Indian and white identities, in particular, are opposite right down the line. You cannot be both. Much of it has to do with the great divide between indigenous and colonial mentalities, as set forth by Vine Deloria, Jr (*God Is Red*), Robert Warrior (*Tribal Secrets*), and other American Indian intellectuals (see Linda Tuhiwai Smith, 'Decolonizing indigenous methodologies').

Because of the terrible historical schism that exists between privileged European society and the remnants of Indian tribal civilizations, the twain do not meet in my view. You can become a white person, but you cannot become an Indian. You are born one. You can have the ancestry of Crazy Horse or Chief Tamanend, but be white in your actions and effects. This from an Indian viewpoint is determinative. You can have only a drop of Cherokee blood and be a role model to your people.

These commentaries bring us to a very different facet of ethnic identity interpretation. The excerpt from *Anthropology News* suggests that ethnic culture, because it does not reside in one's genealogy or DNA molecules, is capable of being adopted or hijacked by non-Native persons. Much as suburban white teenagers may mimic or copy hip-hop apparel styles, gestures and language from urban black youth, New Age spiritualists may be seen as co-opting or even stealing Native religious expressions.

We see a different set of interpretive strategies employed by Brian, Kim Tallbear and Don Panther-Yates, who are Native-identifying persons. Brian and Don see Indianness as something intrinsic to the individual (regardless of DNA markers) and embued by participation in Native culture and spiritual traditions. However Tallbear's proposal – that Nativeness is primarily a cognitive and behavioral expression – goes farther and potentially opens the door to entry by non-Native 'joiners' or 'converts'. If Nativeness (or any ethnicity) is *only* mental and behavioral, then it would be possible for, say, 'whites' to become 'blacks', 'Latinos' to become 'Asians' and 'blacks' to become 'whites'. Why won't this work? Because, socially, politically and economically, ethnicity in American society is activated not only by how one *acts and thinks*, but also by how one *looks*; i.e., how one is interpreted physically by others. Let us now consider the fourth criterion of ethnicity: DNA markers.

DNA

The newest, and potentially the most socially and psychologically powerful, criterion for determining ethnic identity is DNA testing, especially autosomal techniques which can calculate the percentage of different racial ancestries in an individual's genotype (Foster and Sharp, 2002; Jones, 2002; Richards et al., 2002; Shriver et al., 1997; Xiao et al., 2002). Because this testing has revealed the presence of American Indian ancestry in persons who previously were not identified (and who did not identify themselves) as Indian, it is viewed by some Indians as potentially a great threat to Native identity, tribal enrollments and economic benefit distribution. Kim Tallbear provides comments which are typical of this thinking:

> It struck me that here was a potentially very disruptive idea that might undermine the whole project of tribal citizenship . . . I was afraid that tribes might consider substituting DNA tests for what I would consider more responsible, and locally productive, enrollment policy – and those would be policies [and regulations] that promote community strength and development . . . I was definitely opposed and still am opposed to the idea that DNA testing is any solution for tribes.
>
> But as I got further into my research, it seemed to me that the greater risk was going to be the way that DNA will by used by *non*-tribally enrolled people, by those who do not have access to that mode (enrollment) of being Native American and who may turn to a DNA test to confirm or establish an NA identity.
>
> In light of the growing popularity of DNA testing . . . the more important question became for me 'how might this growing American cultural practice (genealogy research coupled with DNA testing) *set a new context* for tribal claims to governance and determining their member-ship?' How might identity claims based on DNA, rather than tribal affiliation, eventually come to affect tribal land claims and redress of treaty violations? If, for example, many Americans can 'prove' they have NA DNA, and DNA comes to be taken as proof of NA identity in the public consciousness, where might this leave *tribes* in the long term?

She continues:

> The bigger problem is the equation of [genetic] ancestry *alone* with the social/cultural/political identity category 'NA'. There are no doubt many individuals who possess [genetic] markers, but who are not recognized by anyone – including themselves – as NA *and they should not be recog-nized as such simply because of a marker*. In addition, there are no doubt enrolled Native Americans without the [genetic] markers . . .
>
> We are at a real risk of communicating the idea that genetics and culture are aligned – that living people are animated as Native American through DNA markers . . . What I fear is . . . that as DNA sequencing technologies become more reliable, as the markers that can be investigated become more numerous, and as ancestry DNA testing gains visibility and popularity, that DNA will increasingly be embraced by the courts, media, and state institutions as an authoritative measure of *identity* . . . Decisions that have serious economic and political ramifications.

Tallbear's interpretive reasoning is based upon her self-identity as a 'card-carrying', tribally-affiliated American Indian, whose parents were also tribally affiliated and publicly identified as American Indian. Her reasoning, though understandable given her personal history, would exclude from being considered American Indian the following types of persons:

1. Those whose parents and ancestors were publicly recognized as American Indian, but who did not/do not have the governmentally-approved and/or tribally approved documentation for *tribal* membership. There are tens of thousands such non-enrolled American Indians existing today (Foster and Sharp, 2002; Shriver et al., 1997).
2. Those whose parents were tribally affiliated and documented, but who were adopted as infants by non-American Indian parents and raised without exposure to Native culture.

3. Persons who were viewed [and who saw themselves] as 'white', 'black', or some other non-Native racial category, and who were raised in a non-Native cultural environment, but whom DNA tests reveal to have greater than 12.5% (1/8) American Indian ancestry – percentages likely higher than those of some persons currently dwelling on reservations.

This brings us to the thorny identity issue of persons discovering that they have multiethnic and/or multiracial ancestries. Neither 'fish or fowl', their liminal status may result in non-acceptance by many of the groups from which they spring. It is interesting to consider, for example, whether Asian or Black children adopted by white American families are deemed not-Asian or not-Black because of their lack of culture and location.

Here are some comments by others on Tallbear's (2005) position:

> DNA is . . . *not* the same thing as blood-quantum. It's [actually] a *more accurate indicator* of the quantity of your American Indian genetic inheritance (emphasis added). (John)

In this man's view, the 'officially-sanctioned' blood quantum measure on which most tribes and the federal government rely to establish Indianness is a less valid indicator than the newer, 'hard science' criterion of DNA. Another person comments:

> I see no problem with having NA tribes internally setting their rules for membership. But if membership is a legal thing entitling members to *various benefits and privileges supplied by the larger society*, then something like DNA-defined qualification for membership makes sense to me (emphasis added). (Brian)

In this interpretation, genetic ancestry is a necessary (but not always sufficient) criterion for benefit entitlement, especially when claims for those benefits are derived from past ethnic repression, as described by the writer below:

> I took the [DNA Print] test a couple years ago in order to help determine whether or not my great-grandmother's claim to Indian ancestry could be supported by DNA evidence . . . In my own particular case, there is a 92% probability that my Native American minority ancestry is real. That's pretty good evidence for me. It's not proof, but it is evidence; and I wouldn't have it without this test.
>
> I could care less about enrolling in an American Indian tribe. I am a white man. But, let me tell you, nobody, Indian or non-Indian, is going to take away my birthright, which includes American Indian heritage; and nobody is going to define who I am, except myself, so long as science does not dispute my contention.
>
> Finally, [I agree that] any American Indian tribe has the right to decide who is, and who is not, a member of *that tribe*. But, as long as the government is handing out special rights and government checks (which I agree are owed), it is up to the government to decide who is an Indian for those purposes. I don't want my money going to some blond-haired, blue-eyed, fair-skinned Cherokee, who has less Indian blood quantum than me. (Robert)

And another argues:

> Say that through DNA testing I could demonstrate my grandmother is an Indian by blood and kin. Say that I inherit 22% of her unique genes and a DNAPrint biogeographical test indicates that I have that quantum of Indian genes and hence blood. Do you deny my Indian heritage, because I have no Indian culture? (Malcolm)

These statements bring us to a core issue of consumer ethnicity: which is the *more potent* component of one's identity: culture or genes? In the majority of cases, this is a non-issue; that is, most consumers raised in, say, African-American ethnic culture *are* genetically African, in the majority of their ancestry.[3] Among consumers who identify themselves as 'white', most are 90 per cent or more European in ancestry (Parra, Marcini and Alcey, 1998). Thus most consumers' cultural and ethnic/racial identities are 'in-sync'.

And yet it is at the racial margins that DNA markers are likely to play their most potent role. As we have seen in the foregoing discussions of Native American DNA, one does not have to possess 'a lot' of a discrepant ancestry for it to become disruptive of self-identity. Consumers learning through DNA testing that they have even 'a little' Native or African or European ancestry – when it was unexpected, unknown and unanticipated – can find themselves struggling to make sense of it and to remake their ethnic identities. They may feel that their newly discovered ancestry somehow entitles them to membership of an ethnic culture that previously was deemed to be foreign and off-limits.

As we have also seen, persons who were already members of a given ethnic culture may resent and resist what they view as intrusions by outsiders who just 'happen to have' a few DNA markers in common with them. Novel DNA data tends to loom large to the consumer who has just learned s/he is carrying it, yet loom small (perhaps even paling to insignificance) to those already safely ensconced within ethnic boundaries. Clearly, these interpretive struggles are just beginning. As science, in the form of biogenetic data, becomes more and more widely disseminated and understood, its power to disrupt accepted political and social constructions of ethnicity is likely to become increasingly powerful.

Appendix

A brief history of DNA testing
In 1998, the first commercial DNA testing laboratory, Oxford Ancestors, opened for business, making haplotype testing of paternal (Y-chromosome) and maternal (mitochondrial) DNA available to the general public for the first time (www.oxfordancestors.com 2005; Sykes, 1998). Prior to this, DNA testing had been largely the province of forensic science, e.g., testing crime scene evidence such as blood and semen, and the legal system, e.g., for determining paternity. Oxford Ancestors was founded by biogeneticist Brian Sykes, author of *The Seven Daughters of Eve* (1998), a study which effectively linked all present-day humans to one of seven mitochondrial haplotypes. These seven haplotypes – U (Ursula), K (Katrina), H (Helena), J (Jasmine), etc. – Sykes proposed, could be traced to specific geographic locales across the globe, permitting modern carriers to pinpoint the place from which their ancestral 'mother' originated.

Sykes's description of the prehistoric origins and lifestyles of each of the seven maternal haplotypes provided consumers with a narrative connecting them, via biogenetics, to a near-mythic primordial past. No longer were consumers confined to a three, five, or even 10, generation genealogical chart of their grandparents and great grandparents. They now had access to a personal physical tracer which could transport them back millennia to different regions of the world, all based upon scientifically verifiable scores, taken from molecules they carried in every cell of their bodies (Wells, 2003). By 2000, Sykes had turned his attention to male/paternal descent lines (Sykes and Irven, 2000). Using his own DNA and surname, Sykes identified the specific locale in England where the Sykes haplotype and surname appeared to have originated. A pathway was now opened for identifying one's ancestral father (ibid.).

Autosomal DNA
After establishing technologies for linking consumers to their maternal and paternal ancestries, commercial DNA companies, specifically Ancestry By DNA, developed a technology that permits individuals to learn the percentages of various major racial groups in their genotype (i.e., one's personal genetic composition). This is technically termed 'autosomal DNA' and is marketed to the public as DNA-Print and Euro-Print (www.ancestrybyDNA.com). Because it does obviously re-essentialize race as a social and scientific entity, the test has been widely condemned by anthropologists, as well as some popular culture writers (Foster and Sharp, 2002; Shriver et al., 1997), but embraced enthusiastically by many consumers (for whom the validity of racial essentialism was never in doubt). Especially useful for persons who have an unknown or mixed race background, the autosomal DNA test can provide evidence of one's racial ancestry and support or negate family rumors, origin stories, conflicting accounts or genealogical gaps (Shriver et al., 1997).

Notes

1. By way of contrast, the second author of the present study has been aware of his Native ancestry since childhood.
2. Note that this is a benevolent version of the 'one-drop rule' – the notion that one-drop (a single ancestor) from a particular racial background could irretrievably taint the individual. The 'one-drop' rule was used in the Southern United States to segregate pure 'whites' from those persons having any known African or Native ancestry.
3. Data show that African Americans are, on average, 80 per cent African and 20 per cent European in their genetic ancestry (Oppenheimer, 2003).

References

Askegaard, Soren, Eric J. Arnould and Dannie Kjeldgaard (2005), 'Post assimilationist ethnic consumer research: qualifications and extensions', *Journal of Consumer Research*, **32**, June, 160–70.
Brodwin, Paul (2002), 'Genetics, identity, and the anthropology of essentialism', *Anthropological Quarterly*, **75** (2), 323–30.
Bureau of Indian Affairs (2005), 'Certificate of degree of Indian or Alaska native blood instructions', *Federal Register*, Department of the Interior.
Carvajal-Carmona, Luis G. et al. (2000), 'Strong Amerind/white sex bias and a possible Sephardic contribution among the founders of a population in Northwest Colombia', *American Journal of Human Genetics*, **67**, 1287–95.
Cavalli-Sforza, Luca, Paolo Menozzi and Alberto Piazza (1994), *The History and Geography of Human Genes*, Princeton, NJ: Princeton University Press.
Collins-Schramm, H.E., C.M. Phillips, D.J. Operario et al. (2002), 'Ethnic difference markers for use in mapping admixture linkage disequilibrium', *American Journal of Human Genetics*, **70**, 737–50.
Crockett, David and Melanie Wallendorf (2004), 'The role of normative political ideology in consumer behavior', *Journal of Consumer Research*, **31**, December, 511–28.
Deshpande, Rohit, Wayne D. Moyer and Nareen Donthu (1986), 'The intensity of ethnic affiliation: a study of the sociology of Hispanic consumption', *Journal of Consumer Research*, **13** (September), 214–21.
Foster, M.W. and R.R. Sharp (2002), 'Race, ethnicity and genomics: social classifications as proxies of biological heterogeneity', *Genome Research*, **12**, 844–50.
Hall, Stuart and Paul du Gay (eds) (1996), *Questions of Cultural Identity*, London: Sage, 1996.
Hirschman, Elizabeth C. (2005), *Melungeons: the last lost tribe in America*, Macon, GA: Mercer University Press.
Jones, Peter N. (2002), 'American Indian demographic history and cultural affiliation: a discussion of certain limitations on the use of mtDNA and Y chromosome testing'. Boulder, Coloro.: Bauu Institute, published in *AnthroGlobe Journal* and available online at http://www.bauuinstitute.com/Articles/JonesmtDNA.pdf.

Kennedy, N. Brent (1997), *The Melungeons: The Resurrection of a Proud People*, Macon, GA: Mercer University Press.

Oppenheimer, Stephen (2003), *The Real Eve: Modern Man's Journey Out of Africa*, New York: Carroll & Graf.

Oswald, Laura R. (1999), 'Consumption and ethnogenesis of middle-class Haitian immigrants', *Journal of Consumer Research*, **25** (March), 303–18.

Panther-Yates, Donald N. (2003), 'You will never find the truth', March Feature at Melungeons.com. (available online at http://www.melungeons.com/articles/march2003a.htm).

Parra, E.J., A. Marcini and L. Alcey (1998), 'Estimating African-American admixture proportions by use of population-specific alleles', *American Journal of Human Genetics*, 63, 1839–51.

Peñaloza, Lisa (1994), 'Atravesando Fronteras/Border crossings: a critical ethnographic exploration of the consumer acculturation of Mexican immigrants', *Journal of Consumer Research*, **21** (June), 32–54.

Richards, Martin et al. (2002), 'In search of geographic patterns in European mitochondrial DNA', *American Journal of Human Genetics*, **71**, 1168–74.

Shriver, M.D., M.W. Smith, L. Jin, A. Marcini, J.M. Akey, R. Deha and R.E. Ferrell (1997), 'Ethnic affiliation estimation by use of population-specific D.N.A. markers', *American Journal of Human Genetics*, **60**, 957–64.

Smith, Linda Tuhiwai (1999), 'Decolonizing indigenous methodologies', *Research and Indigenous Peoples*, London: Zed.

Sykes, Brian (1998), *The Seven Daughters of Eve*, Oxford: Oxford University Press.

Sykes, Brian and Charles Irven (2000), 'Surnames and the Y chromosome', *American Journal of Human Genetics*, **66**, 1417–19.

Tallbear, Kim (2005), 'Native American DNA and the search for origins: risks for tribes', presentation to the Stanford University Department of Anthropology, 7 March.

Wallendorf, Melanie and Michael Reilly (1983), 'Ethnic migration, assimilation and consumption', *Journal of Consumer Research*, **10** (December), 293–302.

Wells, Spencer (2003), *The Journey of Man: A Genetic Odyssey*, New York: Random House.

Xiao, Feng-Xia et al. (2002), 'Diversity at eight polymorphic alu insertion loci in Chinese populations shows evidence for European admixture in an ethnic minority population from Northwest China', *Human Biology*, **74** (4) (August), 555–68.

32 Pushing the boundaries of ethnography in the practice of market research
Rita M. Denny

Data are produced, not gathered

This is a chapter on ethnography as it is practiced in the commercial world, how ethnography is conceptualized in practice and the boundaries that limit its utility. I argue that, if ethnography is to live as an analytic and theoretical construct in marketing practice, then its theoretical foundations must be continually made explicit, the opportunity it offers for multi-sitedness and multiple voices must be embraced and, finally, that both the theory and the voices must be pushed through into reporting (and representation more generally). Otherwise, culture as a theoretical construct will remain invisible in commercial practice and ethnography will have little impact on ways of managerial thinking.

Two decades after the (re)introduction of ethnography to the commercial world of marketing not much has changed in its conceptualization in the world of practice, other than the fact that now ethnography is a standard offering of agencies, suppliers and companies. Beyond this currency of familiarity its conceptualization as 'getting below the surface' still reigns. From the *Harvard Business Review* (Leonard and Rayport, 1997) to *U.S. News and World Report* (Koerner, 1998) or *Marketing Week* (2004), whether US-based (Wellner, 2002; Yin, 2001), English (Barrand, 2004) or Canadian (Smallbridge, 2003), the fundamental articulation of ethnography is grounded in metaphors of depth and digging. Truth is somehow fathomable if we just keep on burrowing. Thus ethnography is couched as looking beneath, plumbing psyches, getting to underlying motivations, as it was almost a decade ago (Denny, 1999). Consumer selected images ('ethnography') become metaphors of thought and reveal depth of feeling (Yin, 2001). Because of a (western) folk theory predilection to view actions as more true than words, ethnography 'as a method of observation', 'gets us closer' to consumers and so 'bridges gulfs'. Implicit in these renderings is a myth of objectification (Lakoff and Johnson, 1980), that truth is found in observing v. asking, or behavior v. words, and that the surface is suspect v. the truth lurking below (that digging metaphor once again).

Implicit in these renderings is a belief that bias exists with some methods but not others, (i.e., there is an objective truth), that data are gathered (we just need to know where to go), the subconscious is an objective (v. analytic) reality, that truth is lurking somewhere (but not on the surface), that observations – what we see or hear – are transparent in their marketing implications. Such is the world of practice: muddied, folk-theorized and pragmatic. Whether brand managers, business VPs, R&D engineers, agency planners and account directors or creatives, most are sure and grounded by one thing, the security of what they see and hear. Transparency is the lietmotif; analysis is attenuated. This leads to the Monty Python-like quest for *the* venue (Holy Grail) where truth can be found. Ethnography, because of its apparent 'observational' component, can be embraced by business as a closer accounting of life as it occurs, and thus be seen as a direct line to truth.

'Getting closer', the trope of many an applied ethnographic mission is paradoxically reminiscent of Malinowski-era ethnography, in which the ethnographer, in his/her researcher's role, is the authoritative voice. What one sees, records and transmits is what exists. The force of assumptions is evident in the apparent mistakes of recruiting for ethnographies when othering occurs (e.g., on arrival at a home and neighborhood that does not match a presupposed idea ('this is not my customer'), with attendant consequences for the interview itself (what is heard, observed, even asked). Self-reflexivity, i.e., the constant questioning of one's own assumptions, reactions and distractions, is too often not an integral part of the research process. The fallout, the Malinowski diary equivalent (Malinowski, 1967), is evidenced in the back room of focus groups: laughter, sometimes derision, 'othering' and smothering. In the almost 40 years since the publication of Malinowski's diary, anthropology and ethnographic writing in particular has accepted self-reflexivity: that there is an unmitigated interaction between observer and what is observed, between subject and object, that researcher and research participant are complicit in the research endeavor; and has problematized this implication for fieldwork and writing (see Clifford, 1997; Clifford and Marcus, 1986; Fox, 1991; Marcus, 1998; Van Maanen, 1995). Academic consumer research has problematized representation as well (Sherry, 2000; Stern, 1998; Sherry and Schouten, 2002) and has, more generally, taken on the notion of produced data and its epistemological underpinnings.

The idea of culture remains largely invisible in business articles espousing (or critiquing) ethnography. Rarely is a brand viewed as a symbol for which relevance is the analytic quest (but see Smallbridge, 2003). While anthropology has long ceded ethnography to other disciplines both within and without the academy (Behar, 1999), the lack of any discipline, relying on folk theory, *is* a problem. Without a theoretical wherewithal to make sense of what we hear, we are no further illuminated. Focus groups, the perennial whipping post, are no more superficial (as in false) than an ethnography grounded by a belief that observation (behavior) is truer than talk. It all depends on one's assumptions about human/consumer behavior. Data are produced, not gathered. ('Gathering' is the attendant assumption.)

In commercial work, the issue is not a rigorously applied positivist frame, as much as a vaguely positivist epistemology (observable phenomena, independently viewed) combined with a vaguely humanist agenda (the need to 'really understand', the importance of natural settings) and the vaguely interpretivist axiology (perception is reality). The emphasis here is on 'vaguely'. Despite huge inroads in the last 20 years foregrounding the complex, mutually implicated relationships between culture and consumption (as reviewed by Arnould and Thompson, 2005), ethnographic practice in the corporate world is stymied by the lack of privilege given to analysis in qualitative applied worlds in the US in general, and by the privileged position of folk models of behavior in particular (that are often psychologically based: see Sunderland and Denny, 2003). When 'culture' appears in practice, it often comes with a price. As Mazzarella (2003) has noted, in a globalized advertising world, culture has become an entrenched variable that allows industry (ironically) to become its advocate and make culture into a paying business proposition. In so doing, culture becomes an essentialized construct: that thing that needs decoding for local business strategy applications. The price for the insertion of culture into practice is that the epistemological equation does not change; it simply has another variable.

Native folk theories and the institutionalized practice of 'finding needs' continue apace in this scenario, albeit framed by local 'culture'.

If ethnography, no matter the theoretical discipline that frames it, requires by definition that its purveyors constantly question their own presuppositions and problematize the other, the self, their observations and imaginings, then one would have to conclude there is little ethnography going on in practice. In marketing practice, ethnography is embraced because of its apparent transparency of method, not because it problematizes what one thinks one sees. In our view, observation never lacks a point of view. Even when ethnography is at its most observational, as in usability applications, it is still crucial to remember that actions do not occur in a vacuum, but are framed by cultural notions by both the actors and the interpreters. For example, to keep in mind that notions (and actions) of what a telephone, microwave or computer are, in turn, are predicated on beliefs about offices or kitchens which in turn are informed by beliefs about work, play, place and so on. Theoretical presuppositions are made in the interpretive frame, whether explicitly acknowledged or not.

Pushing boundaries

The first boundary: theory
Full disclosure: we are anthropologists by training and applied market researchers by profession. This means that ethnography, for us, is an inductive process, that our endeavor is a constant questioning of our own presuppositions about the topic under scrutiny, that data are produced in the forms of interaction we have with our research participants and clients. It is a cultural lens and a search for cultural meanings. We would fall in the interpretive or humanistic rather than positivistic camp (Wilk, 2001; Arnould and Thompson, 2005; Hudson and Ozanne, 1988, and countless others). It also means that the kinds of questions we seek to answer are often different from our clients' questions.

In guest lectures to MBAs or marketing professionals we often include a video excerpt from an interview with a New York woman, a respondent in a study whose marketing question was whether gold could be sold on the Internet to the general public. The ultimate client was Anglogold, a large South African mining company looking for new markets. (It was also the late 1990s, in the heyday of Internet commerce possibilities.) In this bit of video, about three minutes long, we see her showing us a jewelry box in which she stores pictures of jewelry torn from catalogues and newspapers. She also discloses that the jewelry box was originally a present to her husband, but that since he did not use it, she did, putting in things that she would like her husband to buy for her. We also hear in the background, interfering with the sound quality of the video at times, a child noisily banging toys. When we show this video, with no introduction other than the project's marketing objective, we ask the audience to answer the question, 'What is gold?' for this woman. The answers we get are along the lines of gold is 'fulfilling a need that her marriage can't provide' or 'her motivation is status'. We also get reactions of laughter and antipathy: they do not like her. 'She's manipulative', 'she's depressed', 'I'd hate to be her husband.' The language is psychological, its terms are needs, motivations and emotional underpinnings. Students and professionals alike are quick to offer a psychographic profile.

I cite this example to demonstrate how pervasive the marketing language of needs and motivation is, to show how observers are implicated agents (even when just watching a video excerpt of an interview) and to show that these answers (and their implicit questions) are not ours. An ethnographic, cultural inquiry focuses on the symbolic meanings of gold (treasure, gifting, investment) versus emotions, on the relevance of these meanings in life as lived (versus motivations) and on opportunities (versus needs) that arise therefrom. We are interested in the meanings that are shared (or contested) among respondents and, while we garner these meanings through ethnographic interviews with individuals, we are not interested in the individual per se. While motivations and needs are ubiquitous marketing terms, the *sine qua non* legitimizing market research projects, they are also analytic constructs tied to psychological models of behavior and, as such, ones that are less relevant to ethnographic inquiry.

The process is one of constantly questioning our own presuppositions, what we think we know. For the Anglogold project, the analytic, cultural questions were What is gold? What is investment? What is the Internet? These are not questions which are asked of our research participants, but the questions we asked ourselves. And we answer them iteratively through what we ask, see, hear, observe, write down, videotape, take photos of and react to, and by what bores, embarrasses or inspires us. The jewelry box-as-treasure-chest, gold-as-jewelry and not currency, the relevance of 'treasure' in harried daily life, were significant 'observations' that were by no means mere observation: they were based on talk, reflections, stories, observed objects and events (a distracting child). From our vantage point, markets are not constituted by segments with specific and profiled 'needs' as they are constituted by symbols of meaning that have resonance or not. Gold, for example, transcends individual life stories of marriage tensions, career angst or the status of being a wife.

The second boundary: methods
If the first boundary we want to cross is pushing explicit cultural theory into ethnographic practice, the second boundary is pushing ethnography's capabilities into just-in-time research. In the last five years, time has become compressed in corporate life. Flatter organizations, portable communications devices, broadband and e-mail have effectively put managers into the perpetual present. While a standard research cycle for product innovation, concept testing, positioning and branding might remain the same, a particular project lies dormant in the pile on the desk until it reaches the surface, at which point it must be put into action. Compression then occurs in every aspect: recruiting, fieldwork, analysis, reporting. The result is aggressive scheduling and intense, compressed time.

In response to time compression, ethnography in practice becomes a multisited endeavor in two ways: multiple methods and multiple vantage points (see Gupta and Ferguson, 1997a, 1997b; Marcus, 1998; Olwig and Hastrup, 1997). In terms of methods we routinely go beyond the ethnographic interview by asking participants to show us, tell us, reflect for us through diaries, essays or poems, whether they be verbal or photographic, still or video. And methods are iterative, both in analytic time and in real time.

In a project focused on out-of-home food consumption among participants aged about 20, we first started with annotated photo diaries and focus groups. Half of the participants were then selected for ethnographic interviews in which our tours of Los Angeles were calibrated by food establishments (including mothers' homes). Realizing in the process that the wee hours were crucial food consumption moments, we then asked our respondents to create video diaries in the following week. We then gathered them all for a debrief – a bit of a party as it turned out. The life events unfolded in the hours bracketed by the focus groups (boy and/or girl friends lost and gained; jobs lost and gained, the palpable singles scene it at times became) were all data produced, between and among ourselves, clients and participants, all speaking to the symbolic construction of food in real time.

Multiple eyes are also invoked routinely. This is a pragmatic decision but also not without theoretical grounding (see Arnould and Wallendorf, 1994). We routinely have clients become part of the ethnographic interview, as videographers, notetakers or observers. Despite their 'apart' status, their presence becomes part of the encounter. It is all data. Thus, for example, the intern who was chastised by us because he floated alone with a camera in spaces beyond the talk of the interview became a source of insight in a study on Mexican American cooking. The respondent, noting our discomfiture and admonishment, came to the intern's defense, likening his behavior to that of children who need encouragement, much as she viewed her own task in cooking (see Sunderland et al., 2004). In this case, wayward behavior became an additional context for crystallizing analytic observations on food. Or we would say that R&D folks look at the world differently, keying into details we might not notice otherwise. In their questioning (and even in what they implicitly prioritize on tape in their role as videographers), we gain an alternative point of view (produced knowledge) that has an impact on what we know, on how we answer the culturally framed questions we started with. Mistakes are data too. In a luxury roadster study in 2003, we neglected to specify that the car be there as a prop and component of the interview. When we arrived, the car was often *not* present: taken by someone else in the household for some errand, some event, some something. This constituted a mistake (in our clients' eyes) that was simultaneously a crucial observation (for us). And so the spaces among researchers, clients who attend and respondents become mutually implicated in the research process (see Sunderland et al., 2004), which in turn allows for additional sources of insight, in the apparent mistakes, disjuncture or tensions that arise.

A cultural analysis is also a bridge into semiotic analysis in which texts (advertising or websites) are subject to the same kinds of scrutiny as our ethnographic data. Unlike ethnography, semiotic analysis has not been easily integrated into or embraced by qualitative marketing research practice in the US. This may be due to its deprioritized status in US academic marketing and consumer research (see Mick et al., 2004) making it an unfamiliar construct for practice, but I suspect it also has to do with its formal analytic requirements. In part, a 'reading' of ads or websites seems utterly transparent – brand audits of such texts are routine in practice – though analysis is confined to marketing terms and categories, such as what are the brand benefits, promise or essence conveyed by the advertising. In part, a more formal analysis invokes what seem to be inscrutable terminologies from the vantage point of its commissioners (brand managers or researchers, agency account directors or planners) and its merits seem hard to articulate. And all too often, if it cannot be communicated internally in easy ways in the US, it does not survive.

In semiotic analyses that we do, we focus on the cultural meanings presupposed by the texts that give meaning to the brand or product. Looked at through the range of the category, one is able to talk about symbolic landscapes, where brands fit and where opportunities might exist. For instance, Apple's print campaign in 2002, in which the Macintosh is presented as art object, introduced a wholly new discourse into computer advertising and the symbolic definitions of the computer itself. As a brand manager, such a shift in discourse cannot be ignored (whether that brand's target audience is similar or different): it requires brands to position themselves accordingly and, if not, they will be repositioned nonetheless.

Following Saussure (paradigmatic analysis), Peirce (symbols, icons or indexes) or Jakobson (communicative relationships presupposed by the texts), we nonetheless convey our findings as a cultural analysis. Indeed this is set up by the research questions themselves. What is presupposed by advertising or media on what it means to be a teen? What is presupposed by New Zealand and Australian car, beer and convenience food advertising about cultural identity? What is business travel, as presupposed in airline advertising? Importantly, while we can observe metaphors, elucidate nuances of cultural symbols, illustrate key icons and so on, our ability to assess relevance of findings for marketing opportunities is not based on and born of the ads (or other texts), but on knowledge produced through years of studying a specific consumer culture.

Can these endeavors – pushing into diaries, essays, consumer-created video documentary, bringing in clients as part of the ethnographic endeavor, semiotic analysis of texts produced by the culture – be construed as ethnography? In themselves, as purely research procedures or 'tools' (see Malefyt and Moeran, 2003), no. Especially in the world of practice, a photo diary or essay, collage, or even a consumer-created video, does not constitute ethnography simply because it occurs outside the focus group room. Bringing in clients to 'get closer' is not itself an ethnographic turn. To paraphrase Geertz (1973), it all depends on the intellectual framing of the task. If the analysis is on the symbols and meanings presupposed by talk, collages, documentaries, essays by research respondents or clients' comments then, yes, these techniques are ethnographic. Each vantage point is a source of illumination. If we put the camera into someone else's hand, we have gained a different voice. If we observe store displays and consumers shopping from these displays we have gained an alternative site for the production of meaning.

In semiotic analysis when ads under scrutiny do not make sense, when decoding can yield formal observations yet result in little corresponding sense (as occurred in both the analysis of messaging to teens and in trans-Tasman reading of advertisements for meanings of cultural identity), it becomes abundantly clear that ads are a kind of performance, verbal art, privileged from day-to-day discourse (Bauman and Briggs, 1990). Advertisements rely on social knowledge outside their frames to create meaning for a brand within societies, much less beyond them. In this sense, delving into the meaning with informants/participants/consumers of what is observed through formal analysis becomes itself an ethnographic exploration. Advertising thus becomes an additional discourse for situating cultural and ethnographic analysis, allowing scrutiny of symbols, meanings, values or metaphors in play in contemporary culture (cf., Denny et al., 2005).

The third boundary: reporting

If the first boundary we want to cross is the integration of explicit theory into practice, and the second is multisited and multivoiced inquiry in a corporate world of compressed time, the third boundary to be breached is reporting. In a recent presentation to Gatorade, of a multivoiced project (including one anthropologist, one PhD in marketing and several industry-experienced clients) that focused on endurance athletes, the senior manager asked at the end of the presentation (with a tone of praise), 'Are all your reports like this? I've never seen a report like it and I've been in this business a long time.' I could wish all our reports were met with such enthusiasm. They are not. Within the world of practice our reports do not, often enough, speak in marketing terms. But they do invoke and evoke a consumer voice (see Sunderland, this volume). They are replete with photographs and they always, but always, start with 'the cultural framework' in which we headline and explicate our point of view as cultural analysts mediated by practical marketing objectives, and take on specific client language and ideas, recasting them in the process. In the case of Gatorade, we recast endurance athletes as a cultural idea, thereby getting beyond an industry descriptor of (and assumptions about) a particular group of people. In the case of food in the lives of people in their twenties, we problematized specific client-articulated 'need states' as cultural constructions whose transparent meanings were limited to the US because the articulation of needs was inherently a cultural formulation, informed by (American) native understandings of human action, mediated by industry language and categories. We spent a lot of reporting time on offering what we viewed as important cultural frameworks for food in the US, namely health, medicine (and drugs), the symbolic recasting of 'fresh', and the fundamental symbolic switch from 'home-made' to professional (or restaurant) cooking.

It would be gratifying to think that what we produce for clients is a form of ethnographic writing and, if so, with voices that are polyphonous and at times dissonant. Unquestionably reporting in practice needs to address clients' marketing objectives, as couched by them. Realism is the unquestionable voice. But consumers' voices, in the form of video, audio diary, photographs or photo diary, essays or poems, loom large in our reporting time ('thick transcription' in Arnould's 1998 terms). Texts such as ours are meant to be evocative. They are meant to bring clients 'closer' without, simultaneously, 'othering' (i.e., exolicizing). They are meant to create a visceral understanding that, because it is couched within an explicit theoretical frame, has the potential to change the way clients comprehend their target and themselves (as professionals and as consumers). While not at all Sherry and Schouten's (2002) poetry or Marcus's (1998) multivoiced and multisited writing, arguably the reports make inroads on issues of representation recently problematized in academic consumer research (Stern, 1998; Belk and Kozinets, 2005). Given the exigency of multiple modalities in the corporate world (visual, video, audio recordings), these reports go further than most representations in 'first tier' (e.g. *Journal of Consumer Research*) or even applied consumer research journals (e.g., *Journal of Marketing*), whose theoretical and representational contributions are still hugely constrained by text, font and indentations (see Brown, 1998).

Conclusion: getting beyond the profanity of practice
In this chapter I have argued that inclusion of multiple points of view as well as muddied, conflicting epistemological groundings are pragmatic realities in practice. I have also suggested that, if theory does not ground the research process and become explicit in the representations of project outcomes, the impact of ethnography in practice is marginalized. In the silence, ethnography in applied circles is reduced to a qualitative tool that is grafted onto prevailing ways of thinking which, in turn, are governed by folk theories, epistemological confusion, psychological constructs of (unmet) needs, and ultimately ethnography becomes a tool that essentializes culture as just another demographic variable. In these concluding paragraphs I would like to ponder the dilemma of practical applications and suggest that the profanity of practice is the fourth boundary that ethnography must get beyond.

If, in the academy, the blend of anthropology and consumer research has fully integrated the notions of complexity between subject and object, has forefronted theory and has preoccupied itself with representational dilemmas, why has practice not done the same? Ethnography in practice is left as the stuff of instrumentality, consulting fees and MBA curricula. Ethnography in practice and ethnography in academic consumer research are parallel but not typically interwoven discourses, as perusal of the trade press versus academic journals will attest. (For exemplars of ethnographic primers, see Desai, 2002; Miriampolski, 1999, 2005; and for a more nuanced contribution of the anthropological perspective see Jordan, 2003.) Trade press articles that truly focus on 'the anthropology' of ethnography in practice (e.g., Kett, 2005; Murphy, 2005) might discuss the morality of anthropologists in commercial enterprises, but not its impact on ways of seeing/understanding. The instrumentality of the commercial world is an accepted status quo. But this attitude or approach risks the proliferation of ethnography as an observational technique whose transparency gives us 'truth' rather than a more complicated understanding of consumers as cultural beings whose behavior is anything other than transparent. Radicalizing representation of both theory and consumer voices is a needed corrective. Anthropologically oriented researchers who work in business cannot afford not to speak of culture as a theoretical construct (with attendant epistemological tenets), yet not speaking seems to happen all too frequently (see also Jordan, 2003).

Ironically, a kind of Malinowski diary equivalent in 2005 is in ethnographic writing (by anthropologists or otherwise) in the trade press and, to some extent, in the academic press about consumer culture. In the distancing of the self from the process, in the lack of reach into theoretical territories in what is produced, and the priority given to ethnography's offering of seemingly new venues for data collection (note the metaphor of gathering), it is apparent that the authoritative frame on which such texts rely is a kind of rhetorical positivism. (The assumption seems to be that this is what 'such' texts need, after all.) The joke, as such, is on us. If, in the attempt to establish authority in a world of prevailing psychological, cognitive or economic models, outmoded tropes of authority have been embraced, one must wonder to what end? The applied side, and here one must include marketing academics as well, then has little effect on the way brand managers or researchers think about their consumers or the process of consumption.

The boundary between pure and applied research, one theoretical and one a practical problem to be solved, is as artificial as the Malinowski-era ethnographer-as-objective-authority in the scientific account, with the sensual and personal self in the diary (cf. Behar, 1999). In the vacuum of (illusory) separateness lies complicity. And the illusion and complicity need to be recognized as such, so that they can be problematized. Practice cannot be done without theoretical implications or theory (no theory *is* a theory), whether this is in the arts (see Castañeda, 2005) or in applied studies of product consumption. While industry is steeped in traditions of its own making (ethnography is but the latest addition) applications of ethnography in commercial practice cannot neglect the needed tension between the practical and the theoretical, and the ensuing reflexivity of our actions in the world at large, as brand manager, industry researcher or academic.

Current efforts in applied ethnographic research to bridge the gap between the academy and industry are to be lauded, but any profound changes are predicated on theory being explicitly a part of practice and managerial concerns and on the ways in which ethnographic work is represented in practice, publicly or privately. We all, collectively in this volume, have a vested interest: we are all practitioners.

References

Arnould, Eric (1998), 'Daring consumer-oriented ethnography', in Barbara Stern (ed.), *Representing Consumers*, London: Routledge, pp. 85–126.
Arnould, Eric and Craig Thompson (2005), 'Consumer culture theory (CCT): twenty years of research', *Journal of Consumer Research*, **31**, 868–82.
Arnould, Eric and Melanie Wallendorf (1994), 'Market-oriented ethnography: interpretation building and marketing strategy formation', *Journal of Marketing*, **31** (4), 484–504.
Barrand, Drew (2004), 'Closer encounters', *Marketing*, 14 July, 48–9.
Bauman, Richard and Charles Briggs (1990), 'Poetics and performance as critical perspectives on language and social life', *Annual Review of Anthropology*, **19**, 59–88.
Behar, Ruth (1999), 'Ethnography: cherishing our second-fiddle genre', *Journal of Contemporary Ethnography*, **28** (5), 472–84.
Belk, Russell and Robert Kozinets (2005), 'Introduction to the resonant representations issue of *Consumption, Markets and Culture*', *Journal of Consumption, Markets and Culture*, **8** (3), 195–203.
Brown, Stephen (1998), 'Unlucky for some: slacker scholarship and the well-wrought turn', in Barbara Stern (ed.), *Representing Consumers*, London: Routledge, pp. 365–83.
Castañeda, Quetzil (2005), 'Between pure and applied research: experimental ethnography in a transcultural tourist art world', *NAPA Bulletin*, **23**, 87–118.
Clifford, James (1997), *Routes: Travel and Translations in the Late 20th Century*, Cambridge: Harvard University Press.
Clifford, James and George Marcus (eds) (1986), *Writing Culture: The Poetics and Politics of Ethnography*, Berkeley: University of California Press.
Denny, Rita (1999), 'Consuming values: the culture of clients, researchers, and consumers', *The Race for Innovation*, Amsterdam: ESOMAR, pp. 375–84.
Denny, Rita, Patricia Sunderland, Jacqueline Smart and Chris Christofi (2005), 'Finding ourselves in images: a cultural reading of trans-Tasman identities', *Journal of Research for Consumers* (www.jrconsumers.com), **8**.
Desai, Philly (2002), *Methods Beyond Interviewing in Qualitative Market Research*, London: Sage.
Fox, Richard (ed.) (1991), *Recapturing Anthropology: Working in the Present*, Santa Fe, NM: School of American Research Press.
Geertz, Clifford (1973), *Interpreting Cultures*, Chicago: University of Chicago Press.
Gupta, Akhil and James Ferguson (eds) (1997a), *Anthropological Locations: Boundaries and Grounds of a Field Science*, Berkeley: University of California Press.
Gupta, Akhil and James Ferguson (eds) (1997b), *Culture, Power, Place: Exploration in Critical Anthropology*, Durham: Duke University Press.
Hudson, Laurel and Julie Ozanne (1988), 'Alternative ways of seeking knowledge in consumer research', *Journal of Consumer Research*, **14**, 508–21.
Jordan, Ann (2003), *Business Anthropology*, Long Grove, IL: Waveland.
Kett, Gillian (2005), 'Lost tribes of Acme accounting', *Financial Times*, 21 May, W1.
Koerner, B. (1998), 'Into the wild unknown of workplace culture: anthropologists revitalize their discipline', *U.S. News and World Report*, 10 August, p. 56.
Lakoff, George and M. Johnson (1980), *Metaphors We Live By*, Chicago: University of Chicago Press.
Leonard, D. and J. Rayport (1997), 'Spark innovation through empathic design', *Harvard Business Review*, November, 102–13.
Malefyt, Timothy and Brian Moeran (eds) (2003), *Advertising Cultures*, Oxford: Berg.
Malinowski, Branislaw (1967), *A Diary in the Strict Sense of the Term*, London: Routledge and Kegan Paul.
Marcus, George (1998), *Ethnography Through Thick and Thin*, Princeton: Princeton University Press.
Marketing Week (2004), 'It's time to get personal', 24 June, p. 43.
Mazzarella, William (2003), 'Critical publicity/public criticism: reflections on fieldwork in the Bombay ad world', in Timothy Malefyt and Brian Moeran (eds), *Advertising Cultures*, Oxford: Berg, pp. 55–74.
Miriampolski, Hy (2005), *Ethnography for Marketers: A Guide to Consumer Immersion*, Thousand Oaks, CA: Sage.
Miriampolski, Hy (1999), 'The power of ethnography', *Journal of the Market Research Society*, **41** (1), 75–86.
Mick, David, James Burroughs, Patrick Hetzel and Mary Yoko Brannen (2004), 'Pursuing the meaning of meaning in the commercial world: an international review of marketing and consumer research founded on semiotics', *Semiotica*, **152** (1/4), 1–74.
Murphy, Richard McGill (2005), 'Getting to know you', *Fortune Small Business*, June, 41–6.

Olwig, Karen Fog and Kirsten Hastrup (1997), *Siting Culture: The Shifting Anthropological Object*, London: Routledge.

Sherry, John F. (2000), 'Place, technology and representation', *Journal of Consumer Research*, **27**, 273–8.

Sherry, John F. and John Schouten (2002), 'A role for poetry in consumer research', *Journal of Consumer Research*, **29**, 218–34.

Smallbridge, Justin (2003), 'The human zoo', *Canadian Business*, **76** (10), 155.

Stern, Barbara (ed.) (1998), *Representing Consumers: Voices, Views and Visions*, London: Routledge.

Sunderland, Patricia and Rita Denny (2003), 'Psychology vs. anthropology: where is culture in marketplace ethnography?', in Timothy Malefyt and Brian Moeran (eds), *Advertising Cultures*, Oxford: Berg, pp. 187–202.

Sunderland, Patricia, Elizabeth Taylor and Rita Denny (2004), 'Negotiating ethnicity in the practice of market research: being Mexican *and* American', *Human Organization*, **63** (3), 373–80.

Van Maanen, John (ed.) (1995), *Representation in Ethnography*, Thousand Oaks, CA: Sage.

Wellner, Alison (2002), 'Watch me now', *American Demographics*, **24** (9), S1.

Wilk, Richard (2001), 'The impossibility and necessity of re-inquiry: finding the middleground in social science', *Journal of Consumer Research*, **28**, 308–12.

Yin, Sandra (2001), 'The power of images', *American Demographics*, **23** (11), 32–3.

33 Autobiography
Stephen Brown

It's a gift!

Call me an old-fashioned romantic, but I always take great care when buying gifts for people. The item has to be 'just right', simply perfect for the person in question. I go to enormous lengths to ensure that the gift and the giftee are compatible at some primal level. Even the most trivial offering gets this treatment, though I wish it didn't, since I've spent many an unhappy hour in gift stores agonizing over the appropriateness of the purchase I'm about to make. I keep telling myself to make do – grab something, anything, Stephen! – but my conscience won't let me leave until I've done the right thing by acquiring the right thing.

My much put-upon wife, as you might expect, is top of my list of recipients. She's a remarkable woman in innumerable respects, not least with regard to home improvement. Unlike your humble scribe, she has a way with hammers, drills, chisels, screwdrivers, spirit levels and all the redoubtable rest. When it comes to putting up shelves, laying wooden floors, making curtain rails and generally painting and decorating, she's in her element. Naturally, I do my bit – bleeding radiators, changing lightbulbs, washing cars, wrestling with recalcitrant lawnmowers – but all things considered I believe such things should be left to the experts, like Linda. Don't you?

Given my wife's natural gifts and given my gift-giving propensities, it is inevitable that the two traits should converge. And, lovestruck sap that I am, I have plied my wife with presents that some may consider mind-bogglingly boorish – cordless drills, set of spanners, multi-purpose workbench, etc. – but that are, in reality, heartfelt tokens of my affection, devotion and deep personal regard.

Anyway, a couple of years ago, I let my amorous side get the better of me and I bought Linda a stepladder for Christmas. Rest assured, compadres, this was no ordinary stepladder. This was the Rolls Royce of stepladders, the Cadillac of stepladders, the Lexus of stepladders. Sturdy, extendible, articulated, anodized aluminium with galvanized steel plates for extra grip, it was perfect for all those tricky tasks and awkward corners. Any construction worker worth his (or her) salt would have been delighted with Coopers' six-star-rated 'Super Step Pro'. I gift wrapped it, what's more, in expensive off-white marbled paper, which made it look, I must confess, a bit like a cartoon bone from *The Flintstones* or, viewed from certain unflattering angles, somewhat akin to a Christmas cracker on steroids.

And so it nestled under the tree, until the extended family foregathered for the traditional gift-opening ritual, one at a time, in front of the others, accompanied by much oohing, aahing and isn't-that-lovely. Surprisingly, however, when the stepladder finally emerged from its marbled sarcophagus, the 'Super Step Pro' was greeted with stunned silence. Even from my wife, who is home improvement incarnate. The silence lasted quite a while, as well. Three weeks in the case of my mortified better half. It was six months or so, before Linda officially 'forgave' me. To this very day she only has to utter the word 'stepladder' to raise a laugh at family gatherings and turn me into an obsequious bearer of jewellery, flowers, chocolate and analogous symbols of my undying ardour. Payback she calls it. Blackmail, says I.

What's in a name?

The foregoing anecdote exemplifies what Sherry, McGrath and Levy (1993) call 'the dark side of the gift', those occasions when individuals misread the signals, or miscalculate the occasion, and give gifts that are inappropriate, offensive, unacceptable. It's the kind of situation we've all been in, some more often than others. Few people, admittedly, are as congenitally, incorrigibly crass as yours truly – I meant well, honest! – but we've all made misjudgments when striking that fine balance between giver, gift and giftee (Belk, 1995; Berking, 1999; Sherry, 1983). As Sherry, McGrath and Levy (1993, p. 225) dryly observe, 'gifts create and exacerbate interpersonal conflict'. Tell me about it.

The problem with the foregoing anecdote, of course, is that it's an anecdote. An auto-biographical anecdote. And autobiographical anecdotes don't count for much in consumer research. Articles on autobiography are conspicuously absent from our journals and conference proceedings. Discussions of autobiography as a research method are even fewer and further between (Brown, 1998a). Aside from occasional analyses of 'autobiographical memory', a distinct subfield of memory research, our autobiographical research cupboard is fairly bare (Escalas, 1998; Stern, 1998). It thus seems that, although the interpretive research tradition has made significant strides in the quarter-century since Belk, Wallendorf and Sherry's (1989) seminal article, autobiography has yet to come out of the closet, as it were.

Autobiography's neglect is no doubt due to many underlying factors, but the principal reason is nomenclatural. Autobiography isn't called autobiography in consumer research. It's called 'introspection' and introspection has proved very controversial (Holbrook, 1995; Levy, 1996; Sherry, 1998). The technique came to prominence in the early 1990s, when Stephen J. Gould drew upon his personal consumption experiences to write an astonishing autobiographical account of perceived vital energy (Gould, 1991). This article was savaged by two prominent consumer researchers, Melanie Wallendorf and Merrie Brucks (1993), who argued that Gould's introspective technique was methodologically suspect, not to say pernicious. The representativeness of the introspector, the reliability of the data, the lack of objective analysis and the availability of alternative research procedures, which could do the same job in a more robust manner, led them to the conclusion that intro-spection, as practised by Gould, was unacceptable in a scientific sense. Such studies, they maintained, 'make for fun reading but may mislead readers if not based on sound, carefully thought out and articulated methods' (Wallendorf and Brucks, 1993, p. 356).

On rereading the exchanges between Gould, his critics, and interested third parties, it is clear that larger issues were at stake (Gould, 1993, 1995; Holbrook, 1995; Wallendorf and Brucks, 1993). The debate wasn't about methodology as such, though it was couched in those terms, it was about the standing of interpretive research within the wider marketing and consumer research community. At that time, interpretive research was widely regarded as suspiciously subjective. Its legitimacy was moot, to put it mildly. Any technique which celebrated subjectivity, especially eroticized subjectivity, was in danger of undermining the disciplinary gains that more sober-sided interpretive researchers, such as Wallendorf and Brucks, had fought long and hard for. Gould's paper had to be crushed, and be seen to be crushed, otherwise the entire interpretive paradigm was endangered.

Regardless of the political circumstances surrounding Wallendorf and Brucks's critique, it had two long-term consequences. On the one hand, it cast a scholarly shadow over the research technique. Introspective analyses rarely feature in the leading journals – even today, when interpretive articles are commonplace in *JCR* – and they're never likely to feature in light of the ineradicable stain on introspection's character (Mick, 2005). On the other hand, it has become something of a *cause célèbre* within consumer research. If anything, the controversy ignited interest in the technique. Countless conference papers have been presented on introspective method. Debate has raged on its merits and demerits, mainly its merits (Levy, 1996; Patterson et al., 1998; Shankar, 2000; Sherry, 1998). Attempts, moreover, have been made to accommodate the concerns of its critics, such as employing it as part of a package, or repertoire, of interpretive research procedures (Gould and Maclaran, 2003). The fact remains, nevertheless, that 'full on' introspections don't get into the leading journals. Introspection was a blood sacrifice that had to be made to propitiate the hard-headed, scientifically minded gods of the marketing academy and no amount of discussion, one suspects, will raise it from the dead.

Arise autobiography
In many ways, however, the most interesting aspect of the introspective technique is that it's a misnomer. The so-called 'introspections' that pepper the consumer research corpus aren't introspections in any psychological or brain science sense. They aren't unmediated outpourings of human consciousness. They are, rather, *artfully rearranged representations* of the outpourings of human consciousness (Brown, 1998b). They are structured, shaped and sifted by the researchers concerned. They may be based on self-conscious introspective reflection, or something similar, but what they really are is autobiographical essays, reflective essays, ruminative essays, introspective essays. They are pieces of creative writing, by and large, not components of a cognitive data set.

To be sure, several researchers have recognized that terminology is a problem. Belk (2000) reserves the term 'life stories' for what others call introspection. Sherry (1998) prefers 'autoethnography', which is akin to the 'confessionalist' mode of fieldwork described by Van Maanen (1988). Mick (2005), moreover, has recently made the case for 'systematic self-observation' (see also Rodriguez and Ryave, 2002). Other researchers use expressions like 'new literary forms', 'creative non-fiction' and so forth (Brown, 1998c; Hackley, 2005). Nevertheless, none of these alternatives has superseded introspection in the nomenclatural scheme of things and I suspect that it's too deeply entrenched to be changed, even though the tainted term guarantees exclusion from top-tier consumer research journals. The expression, in truth, is becoming increasingly amorphous, as it is being indiscriminately applied to a host of ever more eclectic approaches (see Gould and Maclaran, 2003), so much so that it is surely time to untangle the extant introspective array. A typology wouldn't go amiss, for starters.

Irrespective of the terminological tangle, autobiographical writing is more common in consumer research than many suppose. It simply trades under the guise of introspection. Indeed, when the on-going debates are set aside, it is clear that some of the autobiographical writing in consumer research is uncommonly insightful. It achieves everything that all good autobiographical writing is supposed to achieve. It gives us a real sense of lived experience, of what it feels like to be a consumer. It connects on an emotional level and, in so doing, provides something that is allegedly absent from more conventional research methods, interpretive methods included.

A fine example of the power of autobiographical writing is provided by Holbrook's (1992) ruminations on flying, an everyday consumer experience that is stressful for some and loathsome for others:

> On an airline, the conventional rules of civility and sociability are suspended and replaced by planespeak and aerologic. From the moment they enter the airport, people are treated like aliens, enemies and animals – or sometimes all three simultaneously. At the check-in counter, I encounter the first in a series of lines. It will be followed in all-too-rapid succession by the line getting onto the plane, the line of aircraft at the takeoff runway, the line getting off the plane, the line at the baggage claim area, and the ultimate exasperation of the line at the taxi stand – a veritable line of lines or a sort of metaline that knows no end. Air travel involves a level of enforced patience that makes Type-A personalities sorry they came.
>
> The result of my first queuing experience is a personal transfiguration from the qualitative status of human to the quantitative rank of numerical digit: Flight 483, Gate 6, Seat 39A. As I proceed toward the gate, I pass through a transitional state as suspected alien intruder. My briefcase, hand luggage, shoulder bag, and overcoat must pass through an X-ray machine. My body must pass through metal detectors miraculously sensitive to the most minute amounts of pocket change or the smallest number of house keys, but apparently not able to detect arsenal-sized collections of handguns and grenades. Amazingly, as I am detained, or relieved of the contents of my pockets, and perhaps even frisked or strip-searched, I experience something approaching gratitude. Perhaps one instinctively interprets these security precautions as a sign of safety: 'If they treat *me* like this, then surely they would catch a vicious terrorist before he or she got onto the plane.' Naturally, we know that often they do not. (Holbrook, 1992, pp. 96–7)

Many readers, I reckon, will recognize themselves, or at least part of themselves, in Holbrook's anti-aeronautical outburst. The same, I suspect, is true of Aherne's (2003) calamitous service encounter in the lobby of a tacky theme hotel in the wilds of Wisconsin. We've all embarrassed ourselves in retail situations and, on reading Aherne's autobiographical account of his hapless behaviour in the Great Wolf Lodge, a brief frisson of recognition passes through us:

> Next morning, still groggy from my night on the logs, I staggered around the lobby in search of a cup of coffee, while the kids were getting ready for Great Wolf's '70 000 sq ft of indoor and outdoor waterparks!' A swimming pool with plastic appendages, basically. Fortunately, a traditional Bear Trapper's Coffee Stand stood sentinel in the corner, complete with the comestibles that kept the mountain men going when the going got tough – donuts, bagels, muffins, cinne-buns, and an ice bucket brimming with sodas and fruit juices. With vittles like that, it's no wonder the West was won. Clearly, it rolled over and couldn't get up again. Now I know what put the middle into Middle America.
>
> However, when in Rome. 'A Howling Wolf double decaff and a Grizzly Cinnebun to go, my stout fellow,' I requested politely. The attendant looked at me as if I had two heads and, to be honest, the way I felt I could well have had. Maybe I'm supposed to make my request in Moose. Maybe I've committed a terrible social gaffe by not ordering extra cheese on top. Maybe calling her a stout fellow wasn't a smart move. Maybe it's a self-service operation.
>
> 'It's self-service sir,' she said curtly. D'oh. I grabbed a plastic cup, opened the spigot and, while waiting for the fabulous fountain to fill my eco-friendly Styrofoam receptacle, I reached over for one of the frosted cinnebuns perched on top of the elaborate display. Not a good move in my groggy condition. I caught the edge of the platter and a cascade of cinnebuns, donuts, and muffins plunged into the half-melted ice bucket below. The attendant looked at me, aghast.

Luckily, I have a quip for every occasion. 'Dunkin donuts?' I ventured. Silence. 'At least the bagels didn't take a bath.' Not a flicker. 'How much does all that come to?' Works every time. (Aherne, 2003, p. 164)

These examples could be multiplied many times over, since the vast majority of introspective analyses in consumer research are autobiographical essays of one kind or another. A noteworthy exception, interestingly enough, is Gould's (1991) classic *JCR* article, the one that catalysed the controversy that had been building since Holbrook's (1986, 1987, 1988) 'ACR Trilogy'. According to Stern (1998, p. 72), Gould's paper 'forgoes the opportunity to reveal the contents of his mind in his own words . . . which casts doubt on the value of using the form'. This statement says much about the introspective method's stage of development and of the pressing need to itemize and classify extant contributions. Reframing at least some of these studies as 'autobiography' may help in this regard.

Waxing autobiographical
Making the nomenclatural leap from 'introspection' to 'autobiography' is no easy solution, unfortunately. Autobiography itself is riven with controversy. As a glance at the academic literature on autobiography attests, the field is no less fragmented than that of introspective consumer research (e.g. Conway, 1998; Edel, 1984; Folkenflik, 1993). Smith and Watson (2001), for instance, identify 52 different types of autobiography, ranging from Confessions and Captivity Narratives to Scriptotherapy and Testamonio. Distinctions, what's more, are ordinarily made between life writing, life narrative, autobiography and, naturally, autobiography's near yet very different neighbour, biography (Rhiel and Suchoff, 1996). The history of autobiographical writing has also been studied in detail, as have the literary devices used to compose them (plot, suspense, conflict, humour, chronology and suchlike), as indeed have the profound implications of postmodern notions of the fragmented self, expired authors, conditions of possibility et cetera (Ashley, Gilmore and Peters, 1994; Stanley, 1992). Is autobiography even possible these days?

Still, at least autobiographers have explored these issues, which is more than can be said for most introspective consumer researchers. Another issue that exercises autobiographers, and is directly relevant to the consumer research situation, is the relationship between truth and fiction in autobiographical writing. How reliable are autobiographies? Can we trust what they tell us? In our purportedly post-Freudian world, is an autobiographer really capable of writing cogently about him or herself? The answer to these questions, which echo those raised about introspection by Wallendorf and Brucks (1993), is that most autobiographies are a mixture of truth and fiction, a combination of what Virginia Woolf (1960) aptly terms 'granite' and 'rainbows', hard facts and literary flourishes, respectively (quoted in Smith, 1994, p. 292).

To be sure, searching for granite at the end of rainbows is an exercise in pot-of-gold futility. The treasure trove that autobiography provides is not the truth, the whole truth and nothing but the truth, so help us Saint Patrick. It's experiential. It's true to life, not true to an enforceable legal standard or established scientific protocol. The resonance of the above excerpts from Holbrook and Aherne has nothing to do with veridicality, or representativeness, though they undoubtedly describe occurrences that are common in consumer society. They work, rather, through exaggeration. The experiential frisson comes, not from the accuracy of the accounts – this is exactly what happened – but from the heightened, larger-than-life, just-like-reality-only-more so aspect of the writing. They give a sense of what consumption activities are 'really like' but in order to do so they must depart from the truth, the incontestable scientific truth that consumer researchers are ordinarily expected to aim for and, ideally, attain. In other words, they are truth-like, not truth-full. Truthfulness has its place, especially in the upper turrets of the ivory tower, but it isn't the be all and end all of autobiographical writing.

Consumer researchers with autobiographical inclinations are thus faced with a dilemma. Making their accounts more truthful, and therefore academically acceptable (see Mick, 2005), can only come at the cost of their truth-likeness and, if they don't convey some kind of emotional or experiential truth, then the potential contribution of autobiographical approaches is compromised. Why bother with autobiographical reportage when similar 'findings' can be extracted from less controversial interpretive research methods? Taming the technique is no solution either, as a glance at many interpretive articles in *JCR* attests. The exuberance of early interpretive publications has latterly been smothered in layers of impenetrable theory and emergent models of the processes under investigation. It seems to me that the voice of the consumer – authentic, unmediated, impactful – is rarely heard nowadays.

Tall tales, short stories
The alternative option facing would-be autobiographers is to follow the rainbow rather than chip away at the granite. That is to recognize, after Young and Caveney (1992, p. viii), that 'fiction is now the closest we're likely to come to truth and as such it should be loved and cherished'. Searching for truth in fiction may seem like a singularly quixotic exercise. Yet, if we accept the verdict of autobiographical scholarship that autobiographies are fictional to some degree, as indeed are biographies and other forms of life writing, then scouring works of fiction for nuggets of truth doesn't seem too far-fetched. Given that most novelists draw on their personal experiences to some degree and are specifically encouraged to do so in creative writing classes, it is fair to infer that 'truth' will out. Given, moreover, that consumer society is a particularly popular topic among contemporary novelists, the pickings are potentially rich (Brown, 2005). Instead of writing our own amateurish autobiographical accounts of the consumer experience, why not let the professionals do it for us?

Consider, for example, David Flusfeder's (2003) novel, *The Gift*. It describes the descent into near madness of Phillip, a penurious translator of instruction books for Korean household appliances. Happily married to Alice, a rebranding consultant, with beautiful twin daughters, he gets caught up in an increasingly destructive gift-giving contest with two close acquaintances, Barry and Sean. Big in the movie production business, Barry and Sean have unlimited gift-giving resources and, obliged not only to reciprocate but to surpass their tokens of friendship, Phillip can't compete with their boundless generosity. He buys them a rare Italian poster of one of their movies, only to find that they have hundreds of spare copies in the office. They respond with an all-expenses-paid skiing holiday in France. Phillip fights back with two pedigree chinchilla rabbits (which the twins fall in love with and beg pop not to give away). The producers retaliate with a pair of ponies for the girls. Phillip promptly arranges for their portraits to be secretly painted, only to be trumped by a beautiful Chinese bibelot:

> Their gift was gorgeous. Unanswerable. A carving in jade, maybe as recent as Qing. The date didn't matter. What mattered was beauty. This was more than beautiful. A miniature sculpture of three mountains, three peaks, the highest one in the middle with a figure that was part bird and part river curling around it. The carving was so beautiful that it made my heart lift and then sink. It made me feel sorry for everything inept I or anyone else had ever done in this or any life. The gift was cruelly perfect.
>
> That is so gorgeous, Alice said.
> It's for you. We want you to have it.
> Oh we couldn't possibly. It must be very valuable.
> No it's for you. You're our friends. Our best friends. Phil?
> This gift shames me.
> Don't be silly.
> We want it to give you pleasure.
> How can it?
> I detected in their concerned expressions benevolence triumphant. And my own utter servility confirmed and condemned.
> Did you say you had something for us?
> No. Sorry. You misunderstood.
> The game was over. I had lost. I had been defeated utterly. Routed. I tried to think clearly. How could I beat this? I couldn't. I was the inferior man. (Flusfeder, 2003, pp. 143–4)

So destructive is this descent into gifticide, that on discovering Barry's love of early Pink Floyd, Phillip foolishly decides to kidnap Syd Barrett, former lead singer of the supergroup. He drives to Cambridge, where he hunts down the eccentric recluse, tricks him into compliance and takes Syd to Barry's movie set, where the producer is appalled by his friend's unforgivable action. Having squandered his family's savings and having all but destroyed his marriage, Phillip finally finds out that Barry and Sean employ sourcers, professional shopping scouts who scour the world for perfect gifts for their wide circle of showbiz contacts. He had been fighting a battle against people who didn't know they were fighting a battle. And, just as Syd Barrett quit the madness of the music business, which was even crazier than that notoriously 'crazy diamond', Phillip successfully steps back from the madness of apocalyptic gift-giving.

Flusfeder thereby dramatizes the dark side of the gift. Cogent though scholarly studies of the gift's dark side undoubtedly are, they cannot compete with the complete lunacy captured by Flusfeder. Even the most carefully conducted interpretive research, diligently hewn from the granite of real-world consumer behaviour, suffers when set beside the rhetorical rainbow woven by Flusfeder. By drawing on his autobiographical experiences and exaggerating them for effect, Flusfeder gives us a very real sense of what the dark side of the gift entails.

To be sure, the insights available from novels and analogous works of art have long been recognized by consumer researchers. It is 20 years since Belk (1986) loudly announced that we can 'learn more from a reasonably good novel than from a "solid" piece of social science research'. Morris Holbrook, Beth Hirschman, Bob Grafton Small and many more have culled the canon on behalf of the consumer research community (see Brown, 2005). Everything from content analyses to managerially oriented self-help studies have been produced, though such is the scale and scope of literary endeavour that these investigations represent but a drop in the academic ocean. Nevertheless, the extracted experiential insights are steadily seeping into consumer research consciousness. Calls have even been made for the novelization of research findings, or turning them into poetry at least (Sherry and Schouten, 2002), but if the pitiful literary endeavours of autoethnographers are anything to go by (e.g. Bochner and Ellis, 2002), perhaps we should leave creative writing to the professionals. Unlike Flusfeder, we don't have the gift.

Novels, then, are an important source of autobiographical insight, but they have limitations too, not least lack of control. Consumer researchers can't dictate the agendas of creative writers, nor would we wish to. The best we can hope for is that our particular area of academic interest has been addressed by a creative writer at some point – like Flusfeder – and that his or her reflections are worth extracting, either scientifically (as a repository of researchable ideas) or cosmetically (as a source of juicy quotes for our articles). Novelists have their own agendas, aspirations and aesthetic imperatives and they may or may not coincide with those of autobiographically minded consumer researchers.

So, what can we do? Where should we go from here? Is Mick's solution, more rigorous, truthful, systematic approaches to introspection, the best way forward? Should we cease writing autobiointrospective observations, or whatever we choose to call them, and start classifying them instead? Why not simply wipe the scholarly slate clean and rebrand ourselves as autobiographical consumer researchers? How about letting the current free-for-all continue and relying on the Darwinian review process to winnow our field? Maybe it's time to write an autobiographical novel about doing introspective research in a hostile academic environment. Hey, who cares about the accusations of solipsism, self-indulgence, samples-of-one and so forth. Keep writing, amigos, and the devil take the hindmost!

Greetings from autobiographia

It remains to be seen which, if any, of these possibilities will come to pass. If it were my decision, I'd opt for a model that combined the best of autobiographical writing (creative, iconoclastic, insightful) while avoiding what many conventional consumer researchers consider its biggest weakness (self-selected sample of one). To this end, I've been building a collection of autobiographical essays. That is, autobiographical writings by many consumers on a wide range of research topics: brands, adverts, product categories, retail environments, purchasing behaviour etc. These consumer anthologies are then analysed and salient themes extracted. The approach thus retains the liveliness of the writing and the depth of insight that self-observation bestows, while ensuring that the solipsistic propensities of any individual essayist are kept in check.

One such anthology concerns greeting cards. My 'cards collection' is made up of 118 autobiographical essays. These range from 1000 to 6000 words in length and average approximately 2500, which is quite impressive compared to equivalent storytelling techniques. The essays show, as might be expected, a very strong gender divide. Buying cards is women's work, by and large, though there are enough exceptions to suggest that we're dealing with 'feminine' and 'masculine' purchasing behaviours rather than 'male' and 'female' traits. The essays also show just how stressful the card acquisition process is. Although greeting cards don't involve large financial outlays (in absolute terms) the emotional outlays are prodigious. Greetings cards form part of the gift-giving circuit and thus take on a degree of importance that far transcends their monetary value. For many consumers, greetings cards are symbols of the sender, the recipient and the precise state of their relationship. Enormous care is taken to ensure that the right card is selected and, although time is often at a premium in today's fast-moving world of juggling lifestyles, enormous amounts of precious time are committed to this cardboard quest.

Commitment is one thing, admittedly, choosing is something else again. The wealth of cards on offer nowadays and the sheer number of factors that have to be taken into account – the image on the front, the verse on the inside, the overall tone of the message, the size, shape and texture of the card, the appropriateness of the envelope, the price in relation to the recipient's standing within the sender's circle of friends, et cetera – make the selection decision extremely stressful, as near to impossible as makes no difference.

No less anxiety-inducing is the actual purchasing experience, which frequently takes place in crowded retail stores during peak card-sending occasions such as Christmas or Valentine's Day. This problem is compounded by stores' refusal to price their products (in Britain, most cards are given cryptic price codes), which often comes as a shock at the checkout, though many consumers are too embarrassed to back out of the transaction at that late stage, especially if a line is building up behind:

> It was my brother's birthday last month and I remember when going in to purchase a card for him, I really didn't want to spend long in there. I wanted to go in, find a reasonably cheap and funny card . . . I ended up spending half an hour in the card shop fumbling through the different sections looking for one I think he would like, thinking to myself: 'This is pointless, he probably won't even read the joke!' So I grabbed one that looked quite cheap and slightly funny, and brought it to the till. To my astonishment the card I selected was well over a fiver, and it was already too late to leave it back, because the shop assistant had already scanned it through. With the queue behind me becoming more hostile, I was searching through my pockets for coins, then realized I had forgotten the envelope and had to go back to get it. So I dumped my money on the counter, marched to the other end of the shop and back, to get the envelope and then with great relief I took my change and left the shop, getting dirty looks from everyone in the queue. (David McG)

Resentment, therefore, is rife. There is a strong sense that Hallmark's marketers are inventing occasions and card categories simply to instil a sense of obligation and generally bilk their customers through guilt trip inculcation. On top of that, there's an overwhelming sense of frustration and futility, not to say self-loathing. Many consumers feel that they take card shopping far too seriously, that the recipient won't appreciate all the effort that's gone into it, and that their carefully selected card will be displayed for a day or two at most, only to be binned before the week is out. Yet, because the giver's sense of self, as well as the card, is slipped into the envelope, it is impossible to escape the interpersonal pressures that accompany this often loathsome process:

> 'Give what you expect to receive.' Whoever said this is nuts! I actually believed this until I realized that I never receive anything remotely near what I give. I spend hours pouring over cards, pay a reasonable price for them and maybe even throw in an additional token gift. What do I get in return? Yep you guessed it, a 50p card from Poundstretchers! The nerve of some people! Perhaps it's time to enjoy the giving a bit more like I used to before the prices went up, before we were bombarded with different days throughout the year, when there was only a Mother's Day. Now there is a Father's Day, even a Grandparent's Day, where is it all going to end? I think as I stand here looking at this vast array of cards 'It's not going to stop.' The marketers have to keep coming up with these new ploys to drag people into their shops, trying to entice us into buying senseless cards that mean very little to so many people. (Angela H.)

Indeed, even those who claim to set little store by greeting cards – men, in the main – can't avoid the burdens they impose. Certain occasions, usually those involving the opposite sex (e.g. Mother's Day, Valentine's Day, partner's birthday, etc.), are minefields that have to be negotiated very carefully. Any failing on the dutiful husband/boyfriend/son front will be remembered forever and mentioned many times thereafter. The mortification of a mis-judged card, or gift, is etched on many a male psyche, as in the case of an inattentive husband who thought he'd bought his wife her first Mother's Day card, on behalf of their new-born son. Only it wasn't a Mother's Day card:

> Mother's Day is a particularly traumatic time for me as it is the anniversary of a mistake most foul. On the wife's first Mothering Sunday I forgot to buy a card . . . Once I had realized my folly, I rushed round to the local newsagent, I chose a card which looked nice, and this was where the main mistake was made. I brought it home pleased with my swift response, wrote it with my foun-tain pen and triumphantly handed it to my wife. Slowly she opened it and read the card. Then she blew a gasket. I had purchased a 'You're Like a Mother to Me' card. I never even knew such a card even existed. It took me months to claw back the damage and everyone still keeps me going about it. Always select carefully. (David L.)

At least his heart was in the right place. Not so one tightwad, who foolishly recycled an unsigned Valentine's card from an ex-girlfriend, only to find that his new girlfriend noticed his handwriting had changed:

> Valentine cards are the only cards I have ever kept for sentimental value, every other type of card gets binned within a week or two. One year I got a Valentine Card from a girlfriend, who I was in love with at the time, so I kept the card. We finished about six months later but I never got round to throwing the card out. About another year or two later, Valentine's Day was approach-ing and I happened to notice the Valentine's card from my old girlfriend, lying at the bottom of my cupboard. I picked it up and gave it a read, noticing that there were no names on it, just a couple of love poems. To cut a very long story short, I gave it to my new girlfriend for Valentine's Day, but she caught me out as I had already given her a birthday card a couple of months before-hand. Unbeknown to me she kept the card and noticed the writing was different. She said to me the card was lovely and asked did I write it myself. I said yes. She then confronted me about the other card, catching me off-guard, so I had to own up. (Ryan D.)

Needless to say, there are many more excruciating excerpts where the foregoing come from. And that, of course, is part of the problem with this research technique. As auto-biographical essays are carefully crafted – much more so than, say, the stories consumers tell during depth interviews or focus groups – there is an overwhelming temptation to let the essays speak for themselves. Extensive quotation, however, is all but debarred from latter-day academic articles, largely because of the space constraints imposed upon inter-pretive researchers by pagination-preoccupied journal editors. Short of stitching together entire books based on autobiographical excerpts (e.g. Brown, 1998b), much of the best material – the stuff that makes autobiography really sing – is lost in the academic article assembly process. The voice of the consumer is all-but extirpated, which is ironic given that interpretivism was first embraced because it brought us closer to the living, breath-ing consumers who were being silenced by positivistic research methods.

Another problem with autobiographical essays is getting people to write them. Penning 5000 words on greeting cards or book buying or whatever is extremely time-consuming. The technique asks a lot of its informants and, consequently, it is confined to situations where mutually beneficial exchange relationships can be established (autobiographical essays in return for course credit, principally). Although story writing tasks have been attempted in traditional focus groups and form part of ever-popular projective techniques, the resultant essays tend to be short and specific (compared, that is, to the lengthy reflexive essays that autowritings typically produce). The autobiographical approach, therefore, tends to be limited to student samples and, while this has never stopped experimental consumer researchers, the inherent unrepresentativeness of most data sets has to be acknowledged.

A third difficulty with the procedure is the essay form itself. In our society of the spectacle, where visual images are becoming ever more important, essay writing is something of a lost art. This has led some to advocate an increasingly visual approach to autobiographical consumer research – Morris Holbrook's photoessays, the use of disposable cameras, asking consumers to assemble collages, and what have you (Gould and Maclaran, 2003). However the art of writing hasn't disappeared completely. Email, blogging, text messaging, chatroom conversations and suchlike suggest that penning plangent prose will be with us for some time yet. The essay writing tasks that form part of SAT and college admission procedures are another sign that there's more potential in autobiographical writing than is commonly supposed (e.g. Graff, 2003).

The crucial question, however, is whether the ends justify the means. Do autobiographical essays tell us anything we don't already know or that can be learned from more traditional interpretive procedures? Until comparative tests are undertaken, it is impossible to answer this question with any degree of confidence. Having attempted both, my feeling is that autobiographical essays *don't* tell us anything new but they tell it in a way that is wonderfully rich and entertaining and alive. They bring us back to the point made by Belk (1986) 20 years ago, when he argued that novels provide the kind of emotional insights that traditional research approaches can't. Autobiographical essays do the same, only, unlike novels, which rely on the idiosyncrasies of the novelist, they deal with topics that the researcher controls, to some extent at least. They're more focused, in a consumer research sense, though, as they are penned by non-professional writers, they lose in literary élan what they gain in specificity.

There is, nevertheless, one enormous benefit that flows from autobiographical essay writing. The act of writing about their personal consumer behaviours is emancipatory for the writers themselves. Being required to reflect on what they do, often without thinking, raises consumer consciousness. In the process of gathering autobiographical essays, I often ask my informants to introspect on their introspections, as it were, and again and again the answers come back: 'The experience was an eye-opener'; 'I didn't realize I did that'; 'I surprised myself'; 'I reckoned I was wise to marketers' wiles but now I appreciate that I'm susceptible too.' Clearly, some of these responses may have been diplomatically phrased – telling the researcher what he wants to hear – but as they are often prefaced with remarks like, 'I thought this was going to be a pointless exercise,' 'It felt like I was back at school writing "what I did on my holidays" ', or 'My professor is completely crazy', they're obviously not unduly concerned about the collator's sensibilities. If, as Cialdini (2001) observes, the act of writing something down makes it more believable, more meaningful, more truthful for the person doing the writing, then penning autobiographical essays about consumer behaviour may do more to raise consumer consciousness than all the huffing and puffing by prominent anti-capitalist campaigners like Naomi Klein (2000) or Kalle Lasn (2000). It may also help us understand the intensity of feelings felt by brand communities, since they are inclined to write at length about their relationship, on webpages, in chatrooms, etc. (e.g. Muniz and O'Guinn, 2001). It thus seems that there's more to autobiography than meets the eye. We've hardly begun to tap the wellsprings of autobiography. Autobiography is the event horizon of consumer research. Honest to Holbrook.

By the way, did I ever tell you about my trip to Universal Studios, where one of my darling daughters had a panic attack during 'Earthquake', another stood way too close to the Jurassic Park water splash and the other was sick in the car on the way home? Another time, perhaps . . .

References

Aherne, Aedh (2003), 'Travels in retroreality', in S. Brown and J.F. Sherry (eds), *Time, Space, and the Market: Retroscapes Rising*, Armonk, NY: M.E. Sharpe, pp. 158–70.
Ashley, Kathleen, Leigh Gilmore and Gerald Peters (1994), *Autobiography and Postmodernism*, Amherst, MA: University of Massachusetts Press.
Belk, Russell W. (1986), 'Art versus science as ways of generating knowledge about materialism', in D. Brinberg and R.J. Lutz (eds), *Perspectives on Methodology in Consumer Research*, New York: Springer-Verlag, pp. 3–36.
—— (1995), 'Studies in the new consumer behaviour', in D. Miller (ed.), *Acknowledging Consumption*, London: Routledge, pp. 58–95.
—— (2000), 'A cultural biography of my Groucho glasses', in S. Brown and A. Patterson (eds), *Imagining Marketing: Art, Aesthetics and the Avant-Garde*, London: Routledge, pp. 249–59.
——, Melanie Wallendorf and John F. Sherry (1989), 'The sacred and the profane in consumer behavior: theodicy on the Odyssey', *Journal of Consumer Research*, **16** (June), 1–38.
Berking, Helmuth (1999), *Sociology of Giving*, trans. P. Camiller, London: Sage.
Bochner, Arthur P. and Carolyn Ellis (2002), *Ethnographically Speaking: Autoethnography, Literature and Aesthetics*, Walnut Creek, CA: AltaMira Press.
Brown, Stephen (1998a), 'The wind in the wallows: literary theory, autobiographical criticism and subjective personal introspection', in J.W. Alba and J.W. Hutchinson (eds), *Advances in Consumer Research*, Vol. XXV, Provo, UT: Association for Consumer Research, pp. 25–30.
—— (1998b), *Songs of the Humpback Shopper (And Other Bazaar Ballads)*, www.sfxbrown.com.
—— (1998c), *Postmodern Marketing Two: Telling Tales*, London: International Thomson.
—— (2005), 'I can read you like a book! Novel thoughts on consumer behaviour', *Qualitative Market Research*, **8** (2), 219–37.
Cialdini, Robert B. (2001), *Influence: Science and Practice*, Boston, MA: Allyn and Bacon.
Conway, Jill Ker (1998), *When Memory Speaks: Exploring the Art of Autobiography*, New York: Vintage Books.
Edel, Leon (1984), *Writing Lives: Principia Biographica*, New York: Norton.
Escalas, Jennifer Edson (1998), 'Advertising narratives: what are they and how do they work?', in B.B. Stern (ed.), *Representing Consumers: Voices, Views and Visions*, London: Routledge, pp. 267–89.
Flusfeder, David (2003), *The Gift*, London: Fourth Estate.
Folkenflik, Robert (1993), *The Culture of Autobiography: Constructions of Self-Representation*, Stanford, CA: Stanford University Press.
Gould, Stephen J. (1991), 'The self-manipulation of my pervasive, perceived vital energy through product use: an introspective-praxis perspective', *Journal of Consumer Research*, **18** (September), 194–207.
—— (1993), 'The circle of projection and introjection: an investigation of a proposed paradigm involving the mind as "Consuming Organ" ', in R.W. Belk and J.A. Costa (eds), *Research in Consumer Behavior*, Volume 6, Greenwich, CT: JAI Press, pp. 185–230.
—— (1995), 'Researcher introspection as a method in consumer research: applications, issues, and implications', *Journal of Consumer Research*, **21** (March), 719–22.
—— and Pauline Maclaran (2003), 'Tales we tell about ourselves and others: heteroglossic perspectives on introspective self-report applications in consumer research', in D. Turley and S. Brown (eds), *European Advances in Consumer Research*, Vol. 6, Valdosta, GA: Association for Consumer Research, pp. 72–5.
Graff, Gerald (2003), *Clueless in Academe: How Schooling Obscures the Life of the Mind*, New Haven, CT: Yale University Press.
Hackley, Chris (2005), 'A Celtic crossing: a personal, biographical exploration of the subjective meaning of the Celtic brand and its role in social identity formation', *Journal of Strategic Marketing*, in press.
Holbrook, Morris B. (1986), 'I'm hip: an autobiographical account of some musical consumption experiences', in R.J. Lutz (ed.), *Advances in Consumer Research*, Vol. 13, Provo, UT: Association for Consumer Research, pp. 614–18.

Holbrook, Morris B. (1987), 'An audiovisual inventory of some fanatic consumer behavior: the 25-cent tour of a jazz collector's home', in M. Wallendorf and P.F. Anderson (eds), *Advances in Consumer Research*, Vol. 14, Provo, UT: Association for Consumer Research, pp. 144–9.

—— (1988), 'Steps toward a psychoanalytical interpretation of consumption: a meta-meta-meta-analysis of some issues raised by the consumer behavior odyssey', in M.J. Houston (ed.), *Advances in Consumer Research*, Vol. 15, Provo, UT: Association for Consumer Research, pp. 537–42.

—— (1992), 'Morris fears flying', in E.C. Hirschman and M.B. Holbrook, *Postmodern Consumer Research: The Study of Consumption as Text*, Newbury Park, CA: Sage, pp. 96–100.

—— (1995), *Consumer Research: Introspective Essays in the Study of Consumption*, Thousand Oaks, CA: Sage.

Klein, Naomi (2000), *No Logo: Taking Aim at the Brand Bullies*, London: HarperCollins.

Lasn, Kalle (2000), *Culture Jam: How to Reverse America's Suicidal Consumer Binge – And Why We Must*, New York: Quill.

Levy, Sidney J. (1996), 'Stalking the amphisbaena', *Journal of Consumer Research*, **23** (3), 163–76.

Mick, David Glen (2005), 'I like to watch', Presidential Column, *ACR Newsletter*, Spring (www.acrwebsite.org).

Muniz, Albert and Thomas C. O'Guinn (2001), 'Brand community', *Journal of Consumer Research*, **27** (March), 412–32.

Patterson, Anthony et al. (1998), 'Casting a critical 'I' over Caffrey's Irish Ale', *Journal of Marketing Management*, **14** (7), 733–48.

Rhiel, Mary and David Suchoff (1996), *The Seductions of Biography*, New York: Routledge.

Rodriguez, Noelie and Alan Ryave (2002), *Systematic Self-Observation*, Thousand Oaks, CA: Sage.

Shankar, Avi (2000), 'Lost in music: subjective personal introspection and popular music consumption', *Qualitative Marketing Research: An International Journal*, **3** (1), 27–37.

Sherry, John, F. (1983), 'Gift giving in anthropological perspective', *Journal of Consumer Research*, **10** (September), 157–68.

—— (1998), 'The soul of the company store: Niketown Chicago and the emplaced brandscape', in J.F. Sherry (ed.), *Servicescapes: The Concept of Place in Contemporary Markets*, Chicago: NTC Books, pp. 109–46.

—— and John W. Schouten (2002), 'A role for poetry in consumer research', *Journal of Consumer Research*, **29** (2), 218–34.

——, Mary Ann McGrath and Sidney J. Levy (1993), 'The dark side of the gift', *Journal of Business Research*, **28**, 225–44.

Smith, Louis M. (1994), 'Biographical method', in N.K. Denzin and Y.N. Lincoln (eds), *Handbook of Qualitative Research*, Thousand Oaks, CA: Sage, pp. 286–305.

Smith, Sidonie and Julia Watson (2001), *Reading Autobiography: A Guide for Interpreting Life Narratives*, Minneapolis, MN: University of Minnesota Press.

Stanley, Liz (1992), *The Auto/Biographical I*, Manchester: Manchester University Press.

Stern, Barbara B. (1998), 'Narratological analysis of consumer voices in postmodern research accounts', in B.B. Stern (ed.), *Representing Consumers: Voices, Views and Visions*, London: Routledge, pp. 55–82.

Van Maanen, John (1988), *Tales of the Field: On Writing Ethnography*, Chicago, IL: University of Chicago Press.

Wallendorf, Melanie and Merrie Brucks (1993), 'Introspection in consumer research: implementation and implications', *Journal of Consumer Research*, **20** (December), 339–59.

Woolf, Virginia ([1927] 1960), *Granite and Rainbow*, London: Hogarth.

Young, Elizabeth and Graham Caveney (1992), *Shopping in Space: Essays on American 'Blank Generation' Fiction*, London: Serpent's Tail.

34 The consumption of stories
Sidney J. Levy

Modern marketing thought broadly interprets consumption to include all objects, ideas and experiences. This chapter explores how stories, like anything else, are consumed, that is, taken up, internalized and transformed. It reports a qualitative inquiry into the stories that college undergraduates remember from their childhood and what those and subsequent tales mean to them. The study has two general aims: one, it seeks insight into the main ways consumers internalize and interpret stories as meaningful to them; two, I was especially curious about how, given their historic and pervasive importance, religious tales are ardently believed and lead to a desire to proselytize on their behalf.

It is useful to start by recognizing that the word 'story' has many implications. It is evident that anything we tell one another is a story of some kind. A common dictionary lists eight definitions that range from facts to fiction, truth to lies, rumors to news, amusement to drama, and use such synonyms as history, account, statement, anecdote, narrative, article, etc.; and we could add a long list of other terms: tale, myth, gossip, chronicle, report, gospel, scriptures, saga, etc. These terms indicate the multitude of ways people express themselves by telling stories, and justify the exchange of stories as a marketing activity.

Varieties and levels of analysis
There are also many ways of explaining how people consume stories. Within our field are scholars who examine the effects of commercials as persuasive stories, or the appeal of particular forms of entertainment as kinds of products. A classic study by W. Lloyd Warner and William E. Henry (1948) of the radio daytime serial showed its role in the lives of its listeners. Glick and Levy (1962; reissued 2005) interpret the appeal of shows and commercials to different market segments. More recent work gave us analyses such as Hirschman on *Dallas* and *Dynasty* (1988); or such as Holbrook and Grayson on the symbolic consumer behavior in *Out of Africa* (1986) and in their consideration of 'The role of the humanities in consumer research: *Close Encounters* and *Coastal Disturbances*' (1989). Some researchers focus on literary techniques and the character of the language used, such as in the work of Stern (1993), McQuarrie and Mick (1999), Sherry and Camargo (1987) and O'Guinn and Shrum (1997). Escalas and Bettman (2000) explore the role of narratives, with special attention to their effects on consumers' identities. Levy (1963) analyzes executives' stories to interpret their personalities as offerings in the labor market.

Other interpreters of stories may not think of readers as consumers, but analyze the effects of reading and explain the use of it to suit their own purpose. As a psychotherapist, Bruno Betelheim (1977) relates how fairy tales benefit children. Empirically oriented researchers analyze how readers or listeners speak for themselves. Using secondary data of several kinds – memoirs, library records, periodicals, etc. – Jonathan Rose (2001) interprets the provocative effects of reading on the British working classes. The *Journal of Marketing* and the ACR Newsletter provide examples in which Sidney Levy (1998), Everett Rogers

(2001), Elizabeth Hirschman (2001), Morris Holbrook (2001) and Russ Belk (2001) tell how they 'bought into', as we say, stories they found important in their lives.

A qualitative exploration

The study reported here made use of a university subject pool. To gain understanding of how consumers incorporated stories and believe in them, a first wave of interviews with undergraduates was taken in February 2001. The project gained greater salience when people claiming zealous belief in the story told by Mohammad attacked the World Trade Center and the Pentagon on 11 September 2001. Consequently, to observe what affect those events might have on respondents, a second wave of interviews was conducted at the end of September, using the same interview approach. The subjects are primarily men and women college juniors in their twenties who range in income and vary in ethnic and religious background. The characteristics of the sample and the interview approach are detailed in the Appendix.

The study focuses on three realms of attention to stories. The first part looks to the past, to the recollection and influence of stories from childhood, stories that had been read or told to them or that they had read themselves. The second focus is on the subjects' perceptions of particular stories taken from well-known tales of historical, religious and literary character, asking how favorably the stories are regarded, how true they are, and how important they are. A third aspect is about the weight respondents placed on their belief in the stories. This issue was explored by asking how likely the respondents were to try to convince other people of the truth and value of a favored story. Finally, to highlight this issue, respondents were told an incomplete story that posed a conflict of religious beliefs and were asked to finish it. These various approaches illuminated the ways consumers absorb the stories that they experience, remember and act upon. Subjects show basic patterns in the kinds of stories recalled and reactions to them. The following report is a content analysis that summarizes, categorizes and interprets these patterns.

Why people exchange stories

We asked how consumers explain their need for stories, 'why we read stories, watch them on TV and in the movies, in the news, and tell them to each other'. Respondents offered the following explanations to indicate the importance of story telling.

1.   The need to communicate: people tell stores because doing so is essential.
2.   Stories create social memory: as thinking creatures with a history, receivers of stories absorb them to build character, to sustain family identity and cultural tradition; and to conceptualize their relationship to the cosmos.
3.   Stories transmit information: although the word *story* often signifies fictional ideas, respondents accept the notion that even a bare-bones statement of facts is a form of story telling. News is provided, facts are learned, the mind is expanded.
4.   Stories test reality: appreciating stories, whether happy or sad, is a way of recognizing life. Beyond bringing facts, they help to organize reality and give it purpose. They teach ways to cope, enabling rehearsal of how to deal with potential situations.
5.   Stories stimulate fantasy: beyond giving the news, stories help people to think about experiences that are novel and unlike their own. They foster imagination and creativity, and escape from everyday life.

6. Stories stimulate emotions: there is a sense of amusement and entertainment associ-
    ated with stories. The involving character of stories justifies them because they can
    stir different feelings, exciting the teller and the receiver. Even stories of disaster or
    horror, that may not seem enjoyable per se, may fascinate readers or viewers.

The earliest story
Almost everyone responds to the invitation to tell 'the earliest story you remember'; only
a few people say they cannot do that. Although most of the stories are taken as instruc-
tive, designed to teach a lesson, they may be grouped into these main categories: family
myths, edification stories, and foundation stories.

Family myths
Family myths are stories that have traditional, legendary and epitomizing qualities. Levi-
Strauss (1969) similarly distinguishes myths of origin from village myths. There are three
kinds of family myths. One sort includes stories that are less basic than foundation stories
but close to them, being part of the *folklore* in the society. They are linked to the local
culture, express its tone and are told to awe the child or express some cautionary purpose.
These stories often arouse fear: sometimes the 'boogie man' is used as a concretion of the
harm that threatens the child who misbehaves.

A second type of family myth embraces family *history*, having to do with its ancestral
background. These stories are genealogical, telling about the family's national or ethnic
origins. They express who we are, where we came from, and remind us of the lineage that
will be passed on to future generations.

Levy (1981) explored the third kind of family myth in 'Interpreting consumer mythology'. They are called *little myths* to distinguish them from the grander myths of origin,
migration and folklore described by Claude Levi-Strauss (1969). Little myths inform
about the family and its specific members, drawn from the fund of past experiences. They
serve to humanize and individualize the parents and grandparents, to amuse, arouse nostalgia, pride and other sentiments, foster family solidarity, transmit values, etc. They
usually make people laugh, although they often seem trivial and outsiders are likely to feel
one had to belong or 'to have been there' to appreciate the humor. The laughter may also
be a way of reconciling oneself to long remembered mistreatment, to mitigate teasing,
humiliation or bullying.

Edification stories
Most stories have the potential to play a role in enlightening, instructing, improving and
informing the audience. But edification stories are those that are specifically identified as
aiming to build moral direction or strength of character. Respondents relate how family
members sought to instill virtuous behavior.

Several well-known edification stories are identified. Frequently mentioned are 'The
Little Engine That Could', and 'The Boy Who Cried Wolf'. Then there are mentions of
'Charlotte's Web', 'Cinderella', 'Little Red Riding Hood', 'Humpty-Dumpty', 'The Cat
in the Hat', 'Green Eggs and Ham', 'Where the Wild Things Are', 'James and the Giant
Peach', 'Three Little Pigs', 'Bambi', 'Goldilocks and the Three Bears', 'The Rescuers',
'The Ugly Duckling', 'Beauty and the Beast', 'The Tortoise and the Hare', 'Aladdin and
his Magic Lamp', 'Mrs Twiggly's Tree', 'Goodnight Moon', 'Wacky Wednesday',

'Hansel and Gretel', 'Pokey the Little Puppy', 'The Little Mermaid' and 'The Proud Little Puppy'.

These stories commonly use animals to exemplify the traits typically associated with them and they symbolize the young, primitive, inchoate aspect of children. Subjects point out the moral of the story and see it as part of their character formation or as a general guide to living. They cite such themes as confidence, honesty, teamwork, tolerance, creativity, courage, daring, caution, sharing, sympathy, hope and returning good for evil.

Some individuals give a less conventional twist to the point of a story. For example, to most readers, 'The Little Engine That Could' represents the values of determination, self-confidence, perseverance and achievement. But it can also be a spur to competing with other people: 'I remember that I always liked the ending, especially after none of the other engines were able to perform the task and the little engine came through and outshined everyone. It no longer consciously affects me but I know my personality type pushes me to outperform others around me or show them that I am capable of anything, especially when it's not considered possible.' Few people criticized the stories they were told or read, whether for character building or as family myth, but readers sometimes react intensely to their influence, as illustrated in this woman's passionate expression:

> My mother used to tell me about a young lady in our family. She gave birth to a child at 16 and then died at 17. She was beautiful, nice and tender. Yet, the whole value of her life turned to be a birth-machine. I hate people who think of woman as nothing but a pretty thing that must belong to someone else.

Foundation stories
Foundation stories are religious in nature, with people distinguishing them for their profundity, their supernatural, sacred, ultimate or essential significance. (Science offers foundation stories, also, but they were not asked about in this study.)

Truth and the strength of belief
After discussing their early recollections, the respondents were presented with a list of popular stories (see Appendix) and asked to consider them for their truth and their importance. The list included histories (e.g., *Gettysburg*, *Holocaust*), fiction (e.g., *Cinderella*, *Catcher in the Rye*), and foundation stories (*Moses*, *Jesus*, *Mohammed*, *Buddha*). With this aided recall, the subjects were asked to select an important story and to discuss why it was important, and similarly to select a story they believed to be true. For each instance, they were also asked how they felt about other people disbelieving or hating that story and how hard they would try to convince them of it.

Fiction and symbolic truth
Among the fictional tales, *Romeo and Juliet* and *Cinderella* are chosen mainly by women, who enjoy their theme of love and related issues of hope, rebellion and reward. *Robin Hood* is selected by men especially for its theme of helping people and stealing from the rich, and is appreciated as a social message. Recommending a story, a film, a book, a television show, is common, but only a few ardent fans of a fiction tale feel strongly enough to promote it actively to other people. 'I am fairly offended when people dislike *Hamlet*, although I have met few that did. I try as hard as I can to convince them otherwise, sometimes spouting lines myself.'

Although fiction is understood not to be literally true, enduring fictions such as *The Great Gatsby*, *Hamlet*, *Romeo and Juliet* and *Catcher in the Rye* are said to be true in that they depict the period or capture the truth of human situations, thereby reinforcing the readers' appreciation and edification.

History and hard truth
When the stories cited are historical episodes such as *The Holocaust*, *The Battle of Gettysburg* or *The Storming of the Bastille*, reactions are different. These stories are believed to be literally true, factual, tales of real events; of their truth it seems sufficient to state that they are history, maybe self-evidently so. When pressed to explain this belief, subjects cite records, people who knew people who were there, common knowledge and the authority of school. Something called history seems so inherently true that there is nothing to dispute.

Common among the sample is an attitude of *laissez-faire* toward disbelief in any stories, and old battles do not arouse fervor; but disbelief in history seems particularly irrational or recalcitrant and can call for some efforts to inform or persuade. The prominence given to *The Story of the Holocaust* in various forms, news stories, film, museums, etc., and its horrific character, gives it salience to the subjects.

Foundation stories and basic truth
The foundation stories listed are of religious figures, Moses, Jesus, Mohammed, Rama and Buddha. The members of the sample who characterize themselves as devout or faithful believers choose these stories as important and true, as do some of the 'casual' believers. Being listed as a 'story', *The Story of Jesus* is accepted as such and almost half of the sample (all Christians) chooses to discuss it. The strength of the belief in foundation stories derives from a combination of factors, among which early instruction is said to be primary. (None in the sample claimed to have converted after childhood, although some fell away.)

Family tradition   Subjects attribute religious training to the family environment and early exposure that govern so much social learning and the incorporation of any behavior. Respondents sound like any consumers explaining their devotion to Heinz catsup or Tide detergent when they refer to early maternal and familial influence: 'I learned it from my mother', 'People important in my life told me the story of Jesus.' Subjects may state this acceptance and identification as a basic fact of life that is so ingrained that it is ineffable; it requires no other explanation and becomes inarguable. They have faith in it because it is true – or it is true because they have faith in it: 'I'm Catholic. My whole religion is based on the story of Jesus' life', 'I'm Catholic and believe that Jesus is our Savior and I just simply believe, it's not a question.'

Reinforcement   Not only are religious stories introduced early under family auspices, but also they are given frequent repetition and reinforcement. As one grows up, the environment of religious schools, church attendance, literature and numerous social institutions, as well as everyday language, serve to make belief in religious stories seem correct and natural: 'My grandfather was a very devoted Buddhist. He used to tell me Buddha's stories over and over again.' 'This story is important to me because ever since

I was young I have been brought up in the faith. Religion and church have always been important to me.'

The message   The inherent validity of the message and its own power are cited as beyond indoctrination and reinforcement and as intrinsically worthy of adherence. Gordon Allport's concept of functional autonomy (1940, p. 545) describes how motives gain separation from their historical roots. The adult comes to justify belief or disbelief by maturing cognitive processes of comprehension or insight. Of course, this developmental process may lead to a skeptical perception: 'I do sort of believe the story of Moses because I was told it back when I would believe almost anything. In my rational mind I think "probably not too accurate", but in my heart it seems true.' 'The stories I was told most often are religious related. But I turned out to be not religious. I believe religion is a product of history and society, which have nothing to do with God.'

The believers reason otherwise, saying the story must be true because it has endured so long and has been so influential. Consumers of foundation stories explain their conviction that the truth of their story is history, apparent or demonstrable, that there is evidence of its truth, or they fall back on its widespread acceptance: 'Because it is one of the oldest and most influential books ever, it has been important to humans since the time it actually happened.' 'I have thoroughly studied the Story of Jesus . . . I can back up the validity of this story with secular works written at this time.'

The urge to persuade
Subjects are almost unanimous in denying that they would try hard to persuade non-believers of a foundation story's truth. One might expect otherwise, given that foundation stories are regarded as divinely inspired and are expected to affect the way of life of the community. In addition, believers are often exhorted to engage in proselytizing, as shown in the world's history of mission, coercion and conflict. But members of this sample, including all the strong Christians and the sprinkling of Jews, Muslims and Buddhists, consistently express tolerance and assert the principle of respect for other people's right to hold different opinions and alternative beliefs: 'It's their right to choose in this situation.' 'I respect other people's religions and I would not try to dissuade them from their own beliefs.'

Nevertheless about a third of the sample do claim stronger identification with their foundation story than with any other, and feel the urge to tell it. They emphasize its importance, its validity and its influence. In the face of opposing views they are passionate enough that they express sorrow, regret and want to be evangelical, to do something positive to spread their word. Such actions include telling and explaining the story, encouraging a rereading, praying and being a role model.

Projective reactions to a narrative threat
To explore the issue of conflict between beliefs in different foundation stories, the interview offered a projective device in the form of an incomplete narrative, as follows.

> Here is a story: 'A man, Divol, believes in a God who explains how the world came to be and how people should behave in that world or suffer greatly. He meets a man, Testard, who believes in a similar God, but One who has provided different rules for how to behave. Testard says Divol should change his beliefs and join Testard's group or he will endanger the lives of Divol's family.' Finish the story, telling what Divol will do and why he will do that.

When the issue of foundation stories is thus described as urgent and threatens harm to those who believe in a different story, respondents see the resolution of the conflict in these primary ways.

1. *Conversion*: A small subgroup of people extend their reasonableness – or fear – to project the thought that Divol might consider converting to Testard's views or at least pretend to do so.
2. *Reasonable discussion*: about a fourth of the sample is optimistic about talking things over. They say Divol will reason with Testard about freedom of belief, cause him to change his views, inform him of Divol's own sturdy belief, ameliorate the situation and arrive at a live-and-let-live compromise.
3. *Adamancy*: about half of the members of the sample insist that Divol will flatly refuse to change his beliefs. As the most devout and faithful subjects, they determinedly ignore the threat of harm to his family, minimize or deny it, have him leave the area, or leave his fate in his own God's powerful – even fearful – hands. They believe their virtue will protect them or they will suffer if they must.
4. *Combat*: about 20 per cent of the sample thinks that Divol's and Testard's adherence to the rules put forth by their God will lead them to forceful assertion or aggression. The more faithful observers in this group limit Divol to defensive response with retaliatory threats to Testard's family or having Testard go to jail for murder. 'Divol does nothing and continues practicing and preaching his beliefs. In turn Testard kills his family and goes to jail.'

Those who claim to be agnostic, atheistic or casual believers, describe the greatest violence on the part of Divol or Testard. These subjects offer their stories to observe that such strong beliefs are futile, evil and have enduring consequences: 'Divol gathers the worshippers of his God and battles Testard and his people. Strong beliefs in God have caused many wars.' 'Divol will get more mindless people to follow him. They will all be brainwashed until they do everything that Divol's "Book" tells them to do. Divol and Testard will engage in a holy war that will be carried on from generation to generation. He will do this because that is the only common ground that all religions share . . . I'm right, you're wrong, change to my way or die.'

After 11 September 2001, the respondents still give pronounced expression to traditional American values regarding freedom of religion in their discussions of foundation stories. A few subjects saw in Divol and Testard the potential for active conflict that is manifest in September 11. 'Divol should research the subject and find out the truth. Testard should be killed. Endangering one's family over religion is ridiculous. Like those damn Muslims who killed 4,000 people in New York. Blah, it sickens me.' 'Divol will then argue with the other man, eventually leading to great disagreement between the two. At one point, two different organizations of each belief will rise to power and constantly question the other's belief, causing hatred, fear and discrimination. Much like what religion has done to the world of today.'

Discussion

It is evident that stories are powerful products that affect consumers as they internalize them and fashion them into their personalities, philosophies and sources of action. The

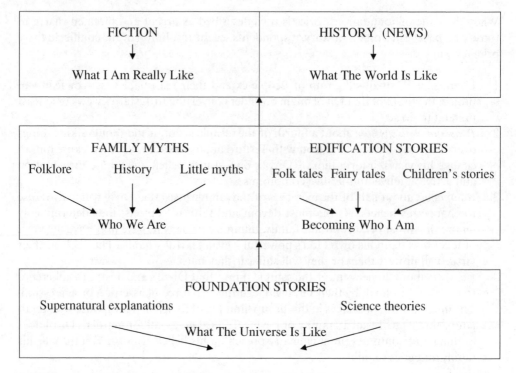

Figure 34.1   Developmental scheme

findings of this inquiry into the consumption of stories point to a developmental scheme, illustrated in Figure 34.1. Families teach their children ways of thinking and feeling about their identities. Through the vehicles of ethnic folklore, history and family episodes, family myths tell about the genealogy and the tradition of which the child is a part. The emphasis is on ancestors, forebears, relatives, the family's nationality, what the grandparents, the aunts, uncles, cousins, parents and siblings did. The child incorporates the content of knowing '*who we are*'.

The children's edification stories come along with this input. They often use animals as anthropomorphic vehicles to carry their morals and specific injunctions to persevere, tell the truth, be brave, obey your parents, be kind and loving, be smart, oppose evil, overcome adversity, or even to be rebellious and break the rules (e.g., like Pippi Longstocking). These stories are seen to become part of one's personal character; they are remembered as lessons that helped one in becoming '*who I am*'.

Attending to fiction serves the process of personality development, of learning more about people and how to cope with situations in life. Warner and Henry (1948) said of listeners' reactions to the daytime radio soap opera, 'the effect of the Big Sister program is to direct their hopes into confident and optimistic channels . . . there is an underlying assumption that this is a moral universe where evil is punished and virtue is rewarded' (p. 58). The range is great: there are myths, legends, fables, folk and fairy tales, parables, old wives' tales, novels, plays, poems and sitcoms. Beyond the examples used in the study are all the other varied and repeated experiences such as *West Side Story*, Harlequin romances, Ellery Queen's mystery stories, John Grisham, *La Traviata*, Tom Clancy, the

Marquis de Sade, Larry Flynt, etc., *ad infinitum*. They affirm or challenge their audiences' views about moral dilemmas, sex, true love, violence, social justice, obsessions, pursuing adventure and diverse aspirations. These tales are fantasies, decorated and metaphorical, which means they are symbolic vehicles for representing truths. They carry lessons that enable people to identify with or reject the persons, the animals, the events and the import of the stories, and thereby better to know the truth of themselves. All this is basically a process of testing reality, identities, and values, and affirming 'what I am really like'.

Some stories are regarded as true by definition, because they are called true stories and ordinarily accepted as that: facts, histories, chronicles, annals, documentaries, biographies, non-fiction and the provisional assertions of truth called science. History and the news (and other non-fiction) bring facts, supposedly true stories about the past and the present, feeding the consumers' cultural awareness. Respondents said *The Holocaust* was true, horrific and important to remember so as not to be repeated. Like the *Battle of Gettysburg*, the *Storming of the Bastille* and the destruction of the World Trade Center, these things have 'really' happened and show us 'what the world is like'.

Foundation stories are basic and have strong effects. They are learned early and grow, change or fade along the way. The truth of the cosmos is hard to understand, seeming miraculous, ineffable and composed of grand assertions (in the beginning was the Word, $e = mc^2$, the big bang, black holes, *The Origin of Species*) that are accepted as either scientific truths or non-provable articles of faith. They provide the most comprehensive and most profound explanations of life and death. They give supernatural accounts of life's origins and numinous grounds for human purpose and behavior, or scientific descriptions and theories that consumers absorb as opposed, parallel or compartmentalized understandings of 'what the universe is like'.

When consumers are strong believers, they want to evangelize, that is, to be angels broadcasting the good news. But about the truth of stories there are also dispute, deniers, controversy, critics, heretics and journal reviewers. Often there are social struggles about access to consuming these opportunities, including censorship attempts when school libraries are asked not to circulate *Huckleberry Finn* or *Catcher in the Rye* and disagreement about the support of schools where preferred foundation stories are taught: e.g., evolution versus creationism or intelligent design. Elaboration of the Divol/Testard scenario showed the seeds of such conflicts in the apperceptions of adamant or violent responses.

Nevertheless the study did not elicit much negativism toward any stories, because it asked about truth and belief but did not explore falsehood and disbelief. Such demand characteristics of the interview probably joined with the compliance of the subjects to give exaggerated emphasis to the positive aspects of stories and the subjects' claimed tolerance for stories they do not believe. To provide a fuller picture, further study is needed that samples segments of the population who are more aggressive and vehement, and willing to admit it.

The importance of foundation stories and their significance to consumers are highlighted by the events of 11 September 2001, and since. Although started before that time, the study gained more contemporary salience. A consequence is much discussion in the media about the character of religious belief, especially in Islam, highlighting the tension between belief in a religious truth and tolerance for alternative beliefs. Commentators, politicians and clergy debate the nature of the conflicts that have grown out of the stories told in the

Hebrew Bible, the Christian Bible and the Quran, and the divergent ways mainstream and militant believers interpret these stories and act upon them. Writing in *The New York Times Magazine*, Andrew Sullivan (2001) observes, 'If you believe that there is an eternal afterlife and that endless indescribable torture awaits those who disobey God's law, then it requires no huge stretch of imagination to make sure that you not only conform to each *diktat* but that you also encourage, and, if necessary, coerce others to do the same . . . It seems almost as if there is something inherent in religious monotheism that lends itself to . . . terrorist temptation' (p. 46). In the *Arizona Daily Star*, Thomas L. Friedman (2001) expresses sur-prise that such conditions are not worse in the United States. 'Whenever I encounter the reality of religious tolerance in America, it strikes me almost as a miracle. I know religious intolerance is also alive and well in this country, but it is not the norm' (p. B5). Similarly, despite the historic conflicts in the US between Protestants and Catholics, anti-Semitism and the violent assertions of their values by some extremist groups, Pete Eckerstrom (2001) points out that, 'Unlike many nations of the world, we do not define ourselves with refer-ence to a specific ethnic heritage or religious doctrine. Instead, our national identity arises from a set of shared core values: a belief in individual human rights' (p. B5).

The study reported here supports Eckerstrom's thought. Half the sample shows skept-icism about the truth of non-secular foundation stories. In addition, the subjects are vir-tually unanimous in expressing a transcendent respect for diversity of individual belief systems and the alternative narratives these represent. They would agree with Robert A. Sirico (2001), writing in the *Wall Street Journal* on 'Faith and Freedom', who says that 'In many parts of the world, religion inspires despotism, unending bloodshed, and war; but here, many faiths, each vigorous in its truth-claims, live at peace with each other and form the foundation of society' (A18). As a priest, he also regrets that 'Most popular Christian literature, for example, is superficial as compared with the great popular writings of saints and theologians of the past. The line between religious writing and the pop psychology is increasingly difficult to detect.' However that may be another reason why the subjects in the study express as much tolerance as they do, and agree with him, 'that American faiths are reconciled to freedom, and indeed serve as a bulwark of that freedom'. Still, along with these peaceful protestations, half the sample claim to be faithful or devout in the intensity of their belief in their foundation stories and they really would like to have others share in their belief. They also tend to express adamancy about their true tales and resolve to defend the values propounded by these stories, as they project in their stories about Divol and Testard. Such adherence and determination is what generally underlies the potential for struggle (*jihad*) and litigation (e.g., about the Ten Commandments and 'under God' in the pledge of allegiance) that is ever present when groups intensely prefer different stories about the nature of the universe and how one should live in it.

Appendix

Procedure
The study is a typical qualitative inquiry. Respondents were given the following introduc-tion to the project. 'We are conducting a study of people's ideas about stories and we'd like your opinions. This is not a test. There are no right or wrong answers. We want to know what you think. Please answer frankly and fully, on the back or added pages if necessary. Take the questions in order and do not look ahead. Your responses will be

completely confidential and not be individually identified with you in any way.' Respondents were asked about the earliest stories they recall reading or having told to them. They were asked what influence these stories had on them, and how strongly they felt about them. The list below was used to stimulate recall and discussion. They selected stories they thought were true and important and were asked to explain why they thought so, and how hard they would try to persuade others of their truth.

At the outset the subjects were told in a straightforward manner that the purpose of the study was to learn what people's experience with stories had been and how they felt about them. The subjects filled out a questionnaire that asked these questions and provided space to write their responses. Most of them were cooperative and responsive. They wrote relatively long replies, with lively individual detail. Afterwards, they were debriefed, told there was no ulterior purpose to the questions, and asked what they thought of the experience. They generally replied that the study seemed interesting, especially for a marketing study, and they had enjoyed doing it.

Table 34A.1   List of stories

The Cat in the Hat
Cinderella
Romeo and Juliet
Moses and the Exodus
Luke Skywalker
Harry Potter
The Life of Prophet Mohammed
Catcher in the Rye
The Ramayana
Hamlet
Don Quixote
The Story of Jesus
The Storming of the Bastille
Moby Dick
The Holocaust
Mary Poppins
Robin Hood
The Life of the Buddha
The Battle of Gettysburg
The Great Gatsby
(Other) _____

Note: The following is a summary description of the samples, with an N of 123: sex: female 58, male 60, non-response 5; age: 19–28 years 106, 29+ years 12, NR 5; education: sophomore 9, junior 85, senior 23, masters and doctoral level 2, NR 4; income: under \$45K 41, 45K–75K 17, 75K+ 53, NR 12; ethnicity: Asian 18, African 3, European 44, Latin 11, East Indian 3, Pacific 2, mixed American 39, NR 4; religion: Catholic 45, Protestant 20, a few each of Jewish, Muslim, Buddhist and mixed backgrounds 33, none 15, NR 10; range in belief: devout 9, faithful 41, casual 44, lapsed 4, agnostic 5, atheist 6, other 9, NR 10.

References

Allport, Gordon W. (1940), 'Motivation in personality', *Psychological Review*, **47**, 533–54.
Belk, Russ (2001), 'ACR Fellows' bookshelf', *ACR News* (Winter), 38–40.

Betelheim, Bruno (1977), *The Uses of Enchantment*, New York: Vintage.
Eckerstrom, Pete (2001), 'U.S. should live its values', *Arizona Daily Star*, 18 December.
Escalas, Jennifer Edson and James R. Bettman (2000), 'Using narratives to discern self-identity related consumer goals and motivations', in Ratti Ratneshwar, David Mick and Cynthia Huffman (eds), *The Why of Consumption: Perspectives on Consumer Motives, Goals, and Desires*, New York: Routledge, pp. 237–58.
Friedman, Thomas L. (2001), 'West needs a spiritual missile shield', *Arizona Daily Star*, 18 December.
Glick, Ira O. and Sidney J. Levy (1962), *Living with Television*, Chicago, IL: Aldine.
Hirschman, Elizabeth C. (1988), 'The ideology of consumption: a Structural–syntactical analysis of *Dallas* and *Dynasty*', *Journal of Consumer Research*, **15**, 344–59.
—— (2001), 'ACR Fellows' bookshelf', *ACR News* (Winter), 36.
Holbrook, Morris B. (1989), 'The role of the humanities in consumer research: *Close Encounters* and *Coastal Disturbances*', in E.C. Hirschman (ed.), *Interpretive Consumer Research*, Provo, UT: Association for Consumer Research.
—— (2001), 'ACR Fellows' bookshelf', *ACR News* (Winter), 36–9.
—— and M.W. Grayson (1986), 'The semiology of cinematic consumption: symbolic consumer behavior in *Out of Africa*', *Journal of Consumer Research*, **13**, 374–81.
James, William (1911), *The Meaning of Truth*, New York: Longman.
Levi-Strauss, Claude (1969), *The Raw and the Cooked*, New York: Harper.
Levy, Sidney J. (1963), 'Thematic assessment of executives', *California Management Review*, **V** (4), 3–8.
—— (1981), 'Interpreting consumer mythology: a structural approach to consumer behavior', *Journal of Marketing* (Summer), 49–61.
—— (1985), 'Dreams, fairy tales, animals, and cars', *Psychology and Marketing* (Summer), 67–81.
—— (1998), 'The enjoyment of reading books', *Journal of Marketing* (October), **62** (4), 99–101.
—— and Gerald Zaltman (1975), *Marketing, Society, and Conflict*, Englewood Cliffs, NJ: Prentice-Hall.
McQuarrie, Edward F. and David Glen Mick (1999), 'Visual rhetoric in advertising: text-interpretive, experimental, and reader-response analyses', *Journal of Consumer Research*, **26** (1), 37–54.
O'Guinn, Thomas C. and L.J. Shrum (1997), 'The role of television in the construction of consumer reality', *Journal of Consumer Research*, **23** (4), 278–94.
Rogers, Everett (2001), 'ACR Fellows' bookshelf', *ACR News* (Winter), 34.
Rose, Jonathan (2001), *The Intellectual Life of the British Working Classes*, New Haven: Yale University.
Sherry, John F. and Eduardo Camargo (1987), ' "May your life be marvelous": English language labeling and the semiotics of Japanese promotion', *Journal of Consumer Research*, **14** (3), 174–88.
Sirico, Robert A. (2001), 'Faith and freedom', *Wall Street Journal*, 24 December.
Stern, Barbara B. (1993), 'Feminist literary criticism and the deconstruction of ads: a post-modern view of advertising and consumer responses', *Journal of Consumer Research*, **19** (March), 556–66.
Sullivan, Andrew (2001), 'Who says it's not about religion?', *The New York Times Magazine*, 7 October.
Wall Street Journal (2001), 'Nigerian Christians and Muslims clash; army is called out', 9 September.
Warner, W. Lloyd and William E. Henry (1948), 'The radio day time serial: a symbolic analysis', *Genetic Psychology Monographs*, **37**, 3–71.

35 Discerning marketers' meanings: depth interviews with sales executives
June Cotte and Geoffrey Kistruck

How do sales executives think about, visualize and talk about customers? What if the metaphor that a sales executive uses to describe customers influences ultimate sales success? These are the questions we address in this chapter. Appearing in the *Applications* part of this book, our obvious goal is to offer an example of qualitative research in action. In our case, while focusing on some positive and negative aspects of the use of qualitative methods with marketing and sales executives, we also explore intriguing questions concerning sales success.

We focus on depth, or long, interviews (McCracken, 1988). We do not set out to discuss how to conduct these interviews, as many other sources, in both this book and others, already do this very well. What we focus on are the unique challenges and opportunities associated with using depth interviews with marketing executives. While we use depth interviews as a way of understanding the executives, we also acknowledge 'the possibility that interview statements reveal less about the interiors of the interviewees or the exteriors of organizational practices and more about something else' (Alvesson, 2003, p. 17). In highlighting some of the issues with depth interviews with executives in particular, we examine this 'something else'. That is, we use our data to illustrate the value of the technique as well as the potentially troublesome underlying assumptions inherent in its use with executives.

First, we briefly overview how earlier researchers have used depth interviews with executives. Next, using data from a recent study, we will explore the metaphors that marketers use to describe their customers and in the process we will answer some specific questions about using this method with executives. What are the *unique* benefits of this method with this group? What are the *unique* limitations and pitfalls of using this method with executives? What we hope to do here is offer a frank and honest discussion of issues that rarely, if ever, make it to the pages of journals, the methodological concerns that are often edited out or simply not considered in the final resulting write-up of the study (see also Macdonald and Hellgren, 2004).

Our organization of the chapter is as follows: we first outline who tends to conduct depth interviews with executives in academic research, and how they do so. Summarizing this review, we draw on the work of Alvesson (2003) as an organizing framework to outline some broad concerns with this approach. This framework is a useful, if somewhat limited, overview of the relevant methodological issues. We then draw on a recent study, completed by the first author, for an application of depth interviews with executives. This study is used as an illustrative example of the benefits to this qualitative technique (understood and contrasting meanings, openness) as well as some of the often unstated shortcomings (secrecy, face, representativeness) of its application with executives.

Depth interviews with executives

A review of the marketing, management and sociology literature reveals that the use of depth interviews with executives as a data collection method is both widespread and varied. It is important for the purpose of our overview to identify alternative terms that are used in research to refer to depth interviews. When we talk about the challenges and benefits of depth interviews in this chapter, we include several types of interviews that do vary in specific methods and underlying philosophies: in-depth interviews (Konrad and Linnehan, 1995), phenomenological interviews (Thompson, 1997) and long interviews (McCracken, 1988). When we discuss executives we have a similarly loose definition; we include, as interchangeable, terms used by researchers such as manager, CEO and team leader. The commonality across the studies we review is that we are discussing a key figure within the organization that was studied.

While virtually all studies using depth interviews have a common goal of deep under-standing of the phenomenon of interest by the researcher, the manner in which the depth interviews are employed differs from study to study. Some researchers use depth interviews with executives as a stepping stone to other quantitative methods within the study (Bunn, 1993), or to build theoretical models to be quantitatively tested at a later date (Sashittal and Jassawalla, 2001), while some make no attempt to quantify the data (Fine, 1996). Some researchers code the collected data to produce statistical results (Gibson and Zellmer-Bruhn, 2001) or to create common categories or typologies (Ranft and Lord, 2002), while others include an abundance of textual data for rich, insightful description, as we do in our study.

A depth interview with an executive of an organization can be a particularly useful tool for discovering the 'cause and effect maps of managers' (Kohli and Jaworski, 1990). Depth interview research is usually directed towards answering the question why something occurred, and towards theory building rather than theory testing (Guba and Lincoln, 1994). Sometimes it is useful to study individual-level phenomena with interviews with executives, but depth interviews with executives are also valued for their ability to gain key insights into more organizational-level phenomena (see Marschan-Piekkari et al., 2004). We take an individual-level approach in our research to offer some reasoning on why some sales executives may be more successful than others.

If depth interviews are used as part of a multiple method study designed from a more positivist stance, they are usually used prior to the construction of a questionnaire (Mentzer, Flint and Hult, 2001; Morgan and Piercy, 1998; Sarkar, Echambadi and Harrison, 2001). The typical usage in these situations involves a depth interview with a small representative sample of the population being investigated in order to garner infor-mation to be used for developing a large-scale survey (Noble and Mokwa, 1999; Slater and Narver, 2000). However, other researchers incorporate depth interviews into their study design in unusual ways. One researcher conducted depth interviews first, but then followed up with a survey more as a means of confirmation of their initial findings than as a means to an end (Gioia and Thomas, 1996). In one study researchers conducted depth interviews as a first step, but then followed up with a series of experiments (Morrin et al., 2002). Another team chose to conduct a survey of respondents first, and then followed up with depth interviews of the executives to gain a better understanding of the survey results (Ibeh and Young, 2001). These examples help to illustrate the increased variety in which depth interviews with executives are being used, rather than simply as a precursor to collecting large-scale quantitative data.

In interpretive approaches, depth interviews are also often used within a multi-method context. For example, depth interviews are generally used as part of a larger ethnography (Barker, 1993), case study (Yan and Gray, 1994) or a grounded theory approach (Bansal and Roth, 2000), although certainly many researchers use depth interviews as a sole method of data collection (Dougherty and Hardy, 1996; Henry, 2005; Madhavan and Grover, 1998; Thompson, Pollio and Locander, 1994). So while the dominant usage of depth interviews with executives in both interpretive and other approaches appears to be in conjunction with other methods, a multi-method approach is certainly not necessary to gain useful insights into the phenomenon.

Having provided a brief review of where and how depth interviews are mainly used, it is useful now to outline recent work that questions the quality of data we get from interviews. After all, every research method has its trade-offs and shortcomings, and acknowledging these is crucial to understanding just where the boundaries of the knowledge we gain from using the method may be. Alvesson (2003) identifies three dominant philosophical approaches to depth interviews, which he calls neopositivism romanticism and localism. Most interview work in marketing and consumer behavior is conducted from one of the first two approaches. Simplifying, the first approach imitates quantitative approaches, with emphases on rigorous coding and analysis and large quantities of data, member checks and peer debriefing, in an attempt to find the truth in a situation. The metaphor for the depth interview under this approach would be *interview as an instrument*. The approach Alvesson labels as romantic is more focused on understanding the world as the informant in an interview sees it, and emphasizes an understanding of social reality gained through a true communal sharing of information with rapport and understanding built between interviewer and informant. The research metaphor most apt here is the *interview as a human encounter*. This is, arguably, now the dominant metaphor for depth interviews in consumer research, and it is primarily the one we use in our approach.

Illustrative study: depth interviews with sales executives

We now present data from a study that used depth interviews to explore the meaning of a customer to sales and marketing executives. Although we present some initial findings concerning the relationship between sales success and the customer metaphor used by the executive, in this chapter we primarily use these data as a backdrop to offer a frank and open discussion of the problems, as well as the benefits, of depth interviews with executives.

In this exploration of the way sales executives think and talk about their customers, the research motivation was searching for any possible links between the metaphors used for talking about customers and ultimate sales success. A professional researcher, trained and debriefed by the first author, completed depth interviews with 12 senior sales and marketing executives with a range of eight to 40 years of experience, and an average experience level in sales of about 15 years. The companies and industries whence these informants came varied considerably, from global firms operating in many countries and offering high-technology products, to small Canadian companies operating in the hospitality industry. Seven men and five women were interviewed. Interviews averaged about one and a half hours, and were mainly conducted on-site at the executives' firms, although several were done at home offices. The data from the interviews were almost 350 pages of single-spaced transcription, including the verbatim interviews as well as field notes about the executives themselves and their physical surroundings and atmosphere.

The interviews started with very broad questions concerning the experience of the informant, past history in sales and his or her current situation (type of industry, customer segments, etc.). When informants were discussing customers especially, probing was very extensive, asking for elaboration and more discussion about customers. Non-directive probes were used to encourage a frank discussion of customer strengths and weaknesses (e.g., 'That's interesting, what's it like to work with a customer like that?'). If necessary, the interviewer asked a sentence completion task in the form of the question, 'Can you finish this sentence for me: my customers are like ———?' This question led to a productive discussion concerning the customer, and how the informant thought about customers. The interview concluded with a discussion of sales performance, including how the sales executive was evaluated, and how well they were currently doing concerning their sales targets and quotas.

The metaphors that emerged from these depth interviews were insightful, and appear connected to the ultimate performance of the sales executive. In essence, what a customer *means* to a marketer helps determine his or her stance towards dealing with customers in a sales setting, and seems related to their success in converting potential customers into sales. While exploring this connection, the metaphors we uncovered in our research are presented as examples of the richness of data possible from well-executed depth interviews with executives; they illuminate our discussion about the strengths and weaknesses of this qualitative approach.

Some benefits of depth interviews with executives

Understood organizational meaning
Often the assumption of the researcher, stated or otherwise, is that the executive they are interviewing is a proxy voice for the organization. As we will discuss below, this can lead to problems. However, making this assumption, at least initially, means that we can interrogate the understood organizational meaning behind key marketing concepts. For example, it is only through actually speaking with executives at a firm that we can determine what market orientation means to that firm. This is the phenomenological understanding that is the great hallmark of well-executed depth interviews. If we seek to understand any particular marketing phenomenon from the perspective of the organization, then depth interviews with well-placed executives can be insightful and often the only route to this sort of understanding.

In addition, we can often find the data indicating a conflict between the understood organizational norms and meanings of a certain behavior, and the meanings understood by a unique informant executive. For example, in our study, many sales executives raised the issue of excellent sales training as integral to their being able to serve their customers. On the surface, this would appear to be a 'motherhood' sort of comment, not worthy of further analysis and interpretation. It is in fact the stated organizational goal of most sales training programs (the organizational meaning). However, this method of interviewing allows for considerable probing, and what became clear in many of these interviews is that training is valued not only because it helps salespeople to serve customers very well, but because it allows salespeople to do this better than anyone else in the organization. Daniel, the veteran technology sales executive, talks about training as an edge for himself:

> after my first month of training, I never missed quota for three years . . . I was the top rep two years in a row . . . I ask myself what can I take away, that on my own time, practice, learn and teach myself so that I can get *better than anybody else on my team*.

Sales training then becomes understood as a benefit which, if used properly, can allow you to outperform your peers in your own organization. Indeed, for at least a quarter of the sales executives we talked with, customer service or a better focus on the customer was initially mentioned when discussing sales training, but, when probed, the discussion of training benefits evolved into a less benign, more self-centered story. This is in contrast to the commonly understand goal of sales training as a way to better meet customer needs, and is an effective illustration of the way depth interviews allow for an interrogation of commonly understood organizational meaning. Interpreting the data in this way makes use of one of Alvesson's (2003) metaphors for interview research, namely, that the interview is an opportunity for informants to reproduce 'cultural scripts' about the subject, in this case, sales training. It is very important for an interpreter of interview data, therefore, to understand the accepted/acceptable cultural scripts underlying the subject in order to question whether one is being told what the interviewee expects a researcher would want to hear.

Contrasts with customer meaning
Many customers would arguably assume that the sales executive they deal with on an ongoing basis treats them, and visualizes them, as individuals. This would be bolstered by the popular business press accounts of one-to-one marketing and mass customization of which sophisticated business buyers would be aware. Somewhat overlapping with the cultural scripts issue above, executives may try and guess what the interview is about, and frame their answers to 'establish and perpetuate basic assumptions', as Alvesson (2003) puts it; that is, to give the expected answer concerning the individual importance of each and every customer.

However, depth interviews offer the potential to tap into a deeper meaning of a customer. Some executives expressly do not see their customers as individuals, but use a metaphor of a *collective* to describe their convictions about customers. Several salespeople talked about their customers almost as an organic whole, a collective that needed to be handled as a whole entity, although made up of individual pieces. Gillian, a salesperson in the entertainment industry, saw her customers as a garden, while David, a technology sales executive, saw his customers as a collection.

> . . . they are like a garden. Sometimes we have weeds that have medicinal values and uh, sometimes they are just pretty flowers and sometimes they are noxious . . . but they all have value in one place. Absolutely in nature. (Gillian)

> You don't think of them as individual people, you think of them more, an analogy would be a hobby, I am just going to use that word hobby . . . And you have to look at your customer as a project. What are you doing with this project, what are you doing with this hobby? . . . It does become like a hobby, it's like a stamp collection, a coin collection . . . how do you make it grow, how do you organize it, how do you work with it, how do you catalogue it, how do you work with an existing account that you have, or one that you would like to have, if you are going to be a coin or stamp, or whatever collector or matchbox series trucks . . . it is all about people but it's broader and it becomes a project. (David)

Both Gillian and David treat their customers as a collective project. What this allows them to do, in contrast to others who think of their customers quite differently, is manage the loss of a customer, or difficulties with a specific customer, in an arguably healthier way. What we mean is that these reps saw the whole collection of customers as what they were managing, and tended not to focus on single customers too much. Good customers compensated for 'noxious' ones, valuable stamps compensated for relatively worthless ones. Interestingly these two sales executives were two of the most successful (in terms of quota achieved and other financial measures of sales success) in the group of informants we spoke to. But, for the researcher, these types of insights will only emerge if one can get beyond the interviewee's attempts to tell you what he or she thinks you are studying.

Openness

If an interviewer can gain rapport and break down some of the barriers to communication that exist between researcher and informant, this form of data gathering can result in insights simply not possible (we argue) with any other method. For example, several sales executives admitted, somewhat sheepishly, that they treated one-time customers differently from longer term relationship customers. David is a 25 year veteran of the computer industry. About an hour into the interview, he began to discuss the differences between minor and major accounts. Although initially reluctant to outline his meaning clearly, over about five minutes his meaning becomes clear.

> *Interviewer*: Could you describe how you treat these major accounts versus a minor account, for example?
> *David*: Um, I think, just to be specific . . . um, the difference is . . . on a major account you go back and see the same person day after day, week after week, year after year, and the question of ethics is large because you can't, um, and I don't want to use the word lie, you can't slide on issues on a major account that perhaps you could in an account where you see the person once and you sell a machine and move on. [. . .] If you are talking to someone at (a major account) you pretty well have to be honest and ethical . . . you have to be really careful to be honest and ethical, because if you are not, it's easy to get caught (at a major account).

Often implicitly, but sometimes explicitly, sales executives think of their customers as simply proxies for their own financial well-being, a *customer as wealth* metaphor. We argue that this sort of open and candid insight into a marketer's understanding of a customer would simply be unattainable with more common data collection formats, like a mail survey. Daniel's quote here is illustrative. He is an 18 year sales veteran with various technology firms: 'My customers are gold. Because they offer me extreme value and wealth, but I have to take care of it.' John, our most senior informant in his mid-sixties, with forty years' experience in a large variety of sales roles and industries, was perhaps most explicit with his use of this metaphor:

> I think that the customer is the most important person in my life. Without him, either big or small, I am not going to survive. I can't live without him, quite literally. [. . .] They are the most important part of my life. Without them I don't have a living.

Michael, our least experienced informant, with three years' experience, also reflects this metaphor in his interview, with possibly the most candid assessment of a customer one might like to encounter: 'My favorite customer is the one you make the most money off of.' The sales executives using this customer as wealth metaphor, including Michael and John, were in fact some of the least successful (in terms of meeting or exceeding their set sales targets). Indeed the customer as collection metaphor seems more apt to help a salesperson cope psychologically with periodic downturns in sales than the use of a customer as wealth metaphor, which focuses the executive on the short-run financial implications of each interaction with an individual customer.

Thus far, we have used our elicitation of the customer metaphors to highlight the unique insights that we believe would simply be unattainable with the more common methods of researching marketing executives. These benefits argue strongly for the inclusion of depth interviews when the goal is a deeper understanding of a phenomenon, both with an individual executive and within the organizational setting. However we would be remiss to offer depth interviews as a panacea for research with executives without examining some very serious issues that can arise when interviewing this group that may not be as problematic when interviewing consumers.

Some limitations of depth interviews with executives

Secrecy
In direct contrast to the openness that is more possible with this method than with many others, the in-person nature of a typical depth interview can put some informants on guard against revealing too much. For example, some executives saw themselves as psychologists; we deemed this a *customer as patient* metaphor. From our analysis perspective, this very interesting metaphor opened the possibility of customers who hide information from a salesperson, who may misrepresent their true situation and who require a lot of in-depth analysis to understand and to help, in the sales executive's role of analyst. Mark, our highest-ranking informant (part of the top executive team at a national wholesaler), used the metaphor this way:

> where you almost become a psychologist. And you have to read between the lines and you have to dig a little deeper as to finding out a little more . . . the test is not necessarily what happens when things run smoothly, but how things are resolved when things run poorly . . . the customer feels a certain amount of confidence and security . . . knowing that the confidentiality of the information (shared) will not be broached.

However informants using this metaphor for thinking about customers were reluctant to reveal much detail about their customers (the supposed topic of our interview) because of issues of confidentiality. Echoing a doctor–patient situation, this is perhaps not surprising, but it circumvented our ability to discuss pertinent details of the customer relationship, and even in some cases led to an early conclusion of the interview.

Even more troubling for this metaphor, Alvesson (2003) theorizes that this sort of identity creation (e.g., a sales executive likening themselves to a psychologist) happens as the interview happens; thus the social situation and the probing questions could lead to the use of a customer metaphor *only because of the interview*. It behooves a researcher to be cognizant of the potential for this to happen during the interview itself and at least admit the possibility in the interpretation/analysis phase. In reviewing the progress of the interviews wherein we initially identified the customer as patient metaphor, we are concerned that this sort of contextual identity creation is an issue for us. As we proceed, we will need to make educated judgments as to whether secrecy concerns, combined with the social context of the interview setting, created a one-time-use customer metaphor that really does not accurately assess the sales executives' day-to-day views.

A further concern with secrecy and executives can arise during the interview. In our study, the data from one very informative interview were very difficult for us to use because of confidentiality and secrecy concerns, an issue that can arise most particularly with executives, and arguably more with depth interviews than with other forms of data collection. In our case, once we were granted access to this executive, and she agreed to the interview, rapport was established and the interview proceeded quite well. However it became apparent, both to the interviewer and to the informant, that the conversation was increasingly 'on dangerous ground', in the words of the informant, because her industry is very small, very insular and very well known. In this case, ensuring confidentiality meant that most of the data could not be used publicly, as they would likely identify both the informant and her company and customer base.

Of course, a related problem regarding secrecy is not being granted access for interviews at all, circumventing the confidentiality issue before it can arise. This is usually a less difficult problem to deal with, assuming one can replace reticent informants with others. The problem of not being able to use data after the effort (time, money and travel) has been made is a more serious one for qualitative researchers. Compounding the difficulty, this problem cannot always be discerned in advance and can lead to wasted effort and frustration on the part of the researcher, and concern and worry on the part of the informant.

Face

In-person depth interviews, of anyone, can lead to issues of self-presentation, or what Alvesson (2003) calls 'impression management'. That is, in face-to-face interviews, informants want to put their best face forward. However, in a consumer setting, it may not be as obvious to an informant what the appropriate response, or best face, may actually be. That may also be the case in a cleverly developed survey, where there are several viable alternative answers for a respondent to choose from. However, in a face-to-face business setting with real executives, we argue that there is an assumed best script for what a marketing or sales executive should be. That can lead to potential issues for the interpreter, for he or she must decide whether the executive being interviewed is actually saying what they feel or know, or whether indeed they are parroting what they believe is the appropriate response for someone in their position. For an example, we look to Mark, a 15 year veteran of sales and sales management positions. In talking about himself as a salesperson, as well as the salespeople he now leads, he reiterates a very well known story, the party line, so to speak, on salespeople:

> being a salesperson . . . you hate to lose. You never hire a salesperson who is complacent about losing. That is one of the things that is part of our makeup or persona, that we have a drive and a need to win . . . usually salespeople are type-A personalities . . . you always want to be better.

However, closely analyzing the rest of Mark's narrative, one can find many more instances where he indeed belies this logic, showing a calm, logical approach when deals are not going to work out. He himself appears quite capable of handling defeat with equanimity, and does not in fact see sales as a win or lose scenario, as his earlier discussion implies. About an hour after he claims that all salespeople need to win, he talks about his sales approach to customers: 'we ultimately want . . . the exchange of value for value for mutual gain . . . if we perceive that there is going to be a win/lose circumstance, then we tend to shy away from that'.

There are many times when Mark discusses the need for mutual cooperation, and the seeking of mutual benefits with customers. So we have a face dilemma: is Mark really so desperate to win, as he claims all sales executives are, or is he simply reproducing for the interviewer the official management story about what a salesperson should be like? Much more of his interview revolves around a mutually cooperative stance with customers.

As another example of face, or impression management, issues with sales executives we present an example of self-contradiction that occurred, in a very similar way, in several interviews in the study. There appears to be, for these informants, a tension between being themselves and being what the customer wants. Numerous people called this having to be 'a chameleon' in front of various diverse customers. Early in his interview, when David is talking about how different his customers are, he contrasts that with his rather more consistent self:

> *David*: I am just that, they buy me, they get me. I am, for better or worse, that's what they get.
> *Interviewer*: So you don't tailor your response from one person to another?
> *David*: No, I don't. Were you thinking that I should? (laughing)

However, it is apparent later that indeed David does considerably alter his behavior from one customer to another, an inconsistency in his interview text that perhaps he is not aware of, or that does not appear to bother him. In fact, this tailored approach is one of the difficulties that he identifies about his job:

> *David*: The number one thing a sales rep has got to be is really a chameleon to make it. You have got to sort of change your psyche to match the buyer . . . they are not going to change to match me, *I have to change to match them* . . . that's the hard part . . . sometimes you can't do it very well, or sometimes it is a strain.

Thus one of the key drawbacks to interviews like these with executives is the potential clash between the acceptable norms for a person in their position, as reproduced in countless popular press business books and put forth by the informant, and their potentially different sense of self, which hopefully also will be elicited by a skilled interviewer. During the analysis phase, this face, or presentation, issue must be seriously considered.

Representativeness
Often executives are interviewed as a way of capturing the organization's views, as a sort of proxy. There are inherent risks here, however, when one or even several executives are assumed to stand for the organization. The researcher can never really be sure that these informants are indicative of the organization. Our recommendation here is rather straightforward, yet may be difficult to adhere to: do not make the assumption. Stand grounded in the reality of your informants, and their organizational context, while remembering that with a depth interview study (in contrast to prolonged engagement in an organizational ethnography) what you gain is an understanding of your informants' understanding of the firm, and nothing more.

For example, in our study two informants came from the same large consumer packaged goods firm. Their approaches to customers, and the metaphors they use to describe them, are very different and illustrate that, whatever the overall emphasis of the organization, individual executives will reflect their own orientation, not just that of the firm.

Laura, a former marketing executive, moved to a sales role in her packaged goods firm a decade ago to get closer to the customers. She, as well as several other informants from other organizations, sees the firm's customers as partners. For Laura, the partner metaphor is contrasted with a hard sell approach, and customers seen as partners take a much longer time to develop:

> I think they sense devotion in you. It's rapport building . . . it takes a long time to get established like that . . . it takes years. [. . .] There's old school, which is a hard sell. Then there is the new school that's a softer sell . . . you can't push people . . . it's a longer approach, but it's more of a winning approach . . . Together we can come up with something that's great for everyone. I think that hard sell, I don't think relationship building is part of it. It can't be, I don't see how that can develop a partnership . . . how it can get to trust . . . I think you have to have that passion that has to come out of a relationship that is a good, strong back and forth partnership. [. . .] My customers are more good solid business partners.

However Larry is at the same firm, with roughly the same experience and background as Laura, although with not quite as much experience in marketing before moving to sales. In contrast to the partner metaphor, Larry uses the customer as wealth metaphor outlined earlier in his attempt to maximize his own financial well-being, certainly at the expense of a partnership approach:

> Look, it's sometimes hard to really maintain a long-term thing. I do the best I can for customers knowing they will switch on me for a better deal, and knowing that I want to get the best deal for myself from them. There's not a lot of loyalty out there, and I can't count on them for anything more than what's happening today.

Larry's views on customers, contrasted with Laura's, highlight the very real danger of relying too heavily on an informant as a representative of an overall organizational outlook. (As an important aside, Laura is a more successful salesperson, which we theorize is related to her use of the partner metaphor.) While we are not suggesting that there is some privileged vantage point from which one could actually discern the organization as a whole, we are cautioning against representing the firm on the basis of one or two informant interviews. While they are steeped in the context of their organization, it would take a more prolonged engagement, with more informants, to really get to the heart of organizational meaning.

Summary

As this volume so ably illustrates, qualitative research in marketing is vigorous, varied and valuable. Focusing on one tool (depth interviews) with a unique set of constituents (marketing and sales executives) we have offered some guidance concerning the cautions necessary for successful usage. It should be apparent that we strongly believe in the benefits of depth interviews. In other research, we have used quantitative techniques with executives, and they certainly have their place and usefulness. However, when one is searching for a deeper understanding, seeking to go beyond what can be achieved with other methods, depth interviews offer a valuable, and still underused, window into our understanding of marketers. Here, our use of depth interviews allows us to theorize about the role that customer metaphors play in sales success, an intriguing result that we believe could only have emerged from this sort of approach.

References

Alvesson, Mats (2003), 'Beyond neopositivists, romantics, and localists: a reflexive approach to interviews in organizational research', *Academy of Management Review*, **28** (1), 13–33.

Bansal, Pratima and Kendall Roth (2000), 'Why companies go green: a model of ecological responsiveness', *Academy of Management Journal*, **43** (4), 717–36.

Barker, James R. (1993), 'Tightening the iron cage: concertive control in self-managing teams', *Administrative Science Quarterly*, **38** (3), 408–38.

Bunn, Michele D. (1993), 'Taxonomy of buying decision approaches', *Journal of Marketing*, **57** (1), 38–57.

Dougherty, Deborah and Cynthia Hardy (1996), 'Sustained product innovation in large, mature organizations: overcoming innovation-to-organization problems', *Academy of Management Journal*, **39** (5), 1120–53.

Fine, Gary Alan (1996), 'Justifying work: occupational rhetorics as resources in restaurant kitchens', *Administrative Science Quarterly*, **41** (1), 90–116.

Gibson, Cristina B. and Mary E. Zellmer-Bruhn (2001), 'Metaphors and meaning: an intercultural analysis of the concept of teamwork', *Administrative Science Quarterly*, **46** (2), 274–303.

Gioia, Dennis A. and James B. Thomas (1996), 'Identity, image, and issue interpretation: sensemaking during strategic change in academia', *Administrative Science Quarterly*, **41** (3), 370–404.

Guba, Egon G. and Yvonna S. Lincoln (1994), 'Competing paradigms in qualitative research', in N.K. Denzin and Y.S. Lincoln (eds), *Handbook of Qualitative Research*, 1st edn, Thousand Oaks, CA: Sage Publications, pp. 105–17.

Henry, Paul C. (2005), 'Social class, market situation, and consumers' metaphors of (dis)empowerment', *Journal of Consumer Research*, **31** (4), 766–78.

Ibeh, Kevin I.N. and Stephen Young (2001), 'Exporting as an entrepreneurial act: an empirical study of Nigerian firms', *European Journal of Marketing*, **35** (5/6), 566–88.

Kohli, Ajay K. and Bernard J. Jaworski (1990), 'Market orientation: the construct, research propositions, and managerial implications', *Journal of Marketing*, **54** (2), 1–18.

Konrad, Alison M. and Frank Linnehan (1995), 'Formalized HRM structures: coordinating equal employment opportunity or concealing organizational practices?', *Academy of Management Journal*, **38** (3), 787–821.

Macdonald, Stuart and Bo Hellgren (2004), 'The interview in international business research: problems we would rather not talk about', in Rebecca Marschan-Piekkari and Catherine Welch (eds), *Handbook of Qualitative Research Methods for International Business*, Cheltenham, UK and Northampton, MA, USA: Edward Elgar, pp. 264–81.

Madhavan, Ravindranath and Rajiv Grover (1998), 'From embedded knowledge to embodied knowledge: new product development as knowledge management', *Journal of Marketing*, **62** (4), 1–12.

Marschan-Piekkari, Rebecca, Catherine Welch, Heli Penttinen and Marja Tahvanainen (2004), 'Interviewing in the multinational corporation: challenges of the organisational context', in Rebecca Marschan-Piekkari and Catherine Welch (eds), *Handbook of Qualitative Research Methods for International Business*, Cheltenham, UK and Northampton, MA, USA: Edward Elgar, pp. 244–63.

McCracken, Grant (1988), *The Long Interview*, Beverly Hills, CA: Sage Publications.

Mentzer, John T., Daniel J. Flint and G. Tomas M. Hult (2001), 'Logistics service quality as a segment-customized process', *Journal of Marketing*, **65** (4), 82–104.

Morgan, Neil A. and Nigel F. Piercy (1998), 'Interactions between marketing and quality at the SBU level: influences and outcomes', *Academy of Marketing Science*, **26** (3), 190–208.

Morrin, Maureen, Jacob Jacoby, Gita Johar, Xin He, Alfred Kuss and David Mazursky (2002), 'Taking stock of stockbrokers: exploring momentum versus contrarian investor strategies and profiles', *Journal of Consumer Research*, **29** (2), 188–98.

Noble, Charles H. and Michael P. Mokwa (1999), 'Implementing marketing strategies: developing and testing a managerial theory', *Journal of Marketing*, **63** (4), 57–74.

Ranft, Annette L. and Michael D. Lord (2002), 'Acquiring new technologies and capabilities: a grounded model of acquisition and implementation', *Organization Science*, **13** (4), 420–41.

Sarkar, M.B., Raj Echambadi and Jeffrey S. Harrison (2001), 'Alliance entrepreneurship and firm market performance', *Strategic Management Journal*, **22** (6/7), 701–11.

Sashittal, Hemant C. and Avan R. Jassawalla (2001), 'Marketing implementation in smaller organizations: definition, framework, and propositional inventory', *Academy of Marketing Science*, **29** (1), 50–69.

Slater, Stanley F. and John C. Narver (2000), 'Intelligence generation and superior customer value', *Academy of Marketing Science*, **28** (1), 120–28.

Thompson, Craig J. (1997), 'Interpreting consumers: a hermeneutical framework for deriving marketing insights from the texts of consumers' consumption stories', *Journal of Marketing Research*, **34** (4), 438–55.

Thompson, Craig J., Howard Pollio and William Locander (1994), 'The spoken and the unspoken: a hermeneutic approach to understanding the cultural viewpoints that underlie consumers' expressed meanings', *Journal of Consumer Research*, **21** (3), 432–52.

Yan, Aimin and Barbara Gray (1994), 'Bargaining power, management control, and performance in Uni', *Academy of Management Journal*, **37** (6), 1478–518.

36 Photo essays and the mining of minutiae in consumer research: 'bout the time I got to Phoenix
Morris B. Holbrook

Introduction

This chapter recommends and justifies an approach to qualitative consumer research that, though used relatively infrequently, has much to recommend it. Specifically, I propose the usefulness of the photo essay (PE), the collective photo essay (CPE), and/or the collective stereographic photo essay (CSPE) as a way of eliciting material drawn from subjective personal introspection (SPI) in a manner suitably expressed by means of a reflexive self-revelatory narrative.

The style of my chapter is itself reflexive in that it presents an essay about essays. Hence it illustrates its subject matter in a way that I hope readers will find meaningful. It begins with a brief description and defense of SPI and of PE-CPE-or-CSPE. It then presents an example drawn from an interpretation of some of my own recent photographs, especially those of animals at the Phoenix Zoo.

Owing to lack of space, this chapter does not include detailed bibliographic references to the literature on photography or to its use by social scientists in general and by consumer researchers in particular. Readers interested in pursuing my own work should consult the list of publications posted online at www1.gsb.columbia.edu/mygsb/faculty/research/pubfiles/1100/Holbrook_VITA2004.pdf, where it will be helpful to search for such keywords as 'photo(graphy)', 'stereo(graphy)', 'photo essay', 'autoethnograph(y)', and 'subjective personal introspection'. These publications contain extensive references to the relevant literature. Meanwhile excellent and highly esteemed treatises on photography appear in the work of Susan Sontag (*On Photography*) and John Berger (*Ways of Seeing*; *About Looking*; *Another Way of Telling*). Jac. G. Ferwerda provides an especially helpful discussion of stereography (*The World of 3-D*). The role of abstraction surfaces with special clarity in the books by Freeman Patterson (*Photography and the Art of Seeing*; *Photography For the Joy of It*). Garry Winogrand visits the zoo in *The Animals*. Frans Lanting presents amazing close-ups of wild creatures in *Eye to Eye*. Hans Silvester does something similar in his fetching photos of alley cats (*Cats in the Sun*; *Asleep in the Sun*). Specific applications to the social sciences have appeared in the burgeoning literature on the uses of photography in psychology (*Photographing* THE SELF by Robert C. Ziller); sociology (*Doing Things Together* by Howard S. Becker; *Images of Information* by Jon Wagner; *Sociology and Visual Representation* by Elizabeth Chaplin); and anthropology (*Visual Anthropology* by John Collier and Malcolm Collier; *Analyzing Visual Data* by Michael S. Ball and Gregory W.H. Smith). The latter two disciplines produce their own journals devoted to the subjects of *Visual Studies* (formerly *Visual Sociology*) and *Visual Anthropology*. Aspiring marketing and consumer researchers should be warned that publishing in these journals from the basic disciplines is harder than getting a rich man into heaven (*Matthew*, 19:23–6). Targeting our marketing-related outlets is far more likely to meet with success, thanks to the pioneering efforts of Sid Levy, Deb Heisley, Dennis

Rook, Jerry Zaltman, Melanie Wallendorf, Russ Belk, John Sherry, Tom O'Guinn, Ron Hill and many others (with apologies to those whose names I have omitted).

Subjective personal introspection (SPI)
The various types of photo essays advocated here all depend on the use of what I call 'subjective personal introspection' or SPI. This approach draws on one's own impressionistic experiences (subjective) to compose a self-revealing essay (personal) based on essentially private insights (introspective). SPI stems from a tradition of writing essays in the humanities that traces its line of descent all the way back to Michel de Montaigne in the sixteenth century. Even prior to the time of Shakespeare, this father of the essay pursued a focus centered above all else on himself and on his penchant for colorfully describing his own unique and sometimes even bizarre consumption experiences. As a defense of this practice, he voiced the justification that he wished to plumb the depths of the human condition; that he himself was human; and therefore that, in writing about himself, he inevitably explored the topic of interest.

This quintessential statement of priorities in the humanities led to a literary form – the essay – that has become something of a lost art in consumer research but that offers one potentially revealing window onto the nature of consumption experiences. Occasional practitioners of SPI in consumer research (listed alphabetically) have included, among others, Dan Ariely, Stephen Brown, Steve Gould, Beth Hirschman, Robert Kozinets, Dennis Rook, Clint Sanders, John Schouten, John Sherry and George Zinkhan. All forms of the photo essay described in this chapter draw on SPI in one way or another, either by eliciting SPI-based mini-essays from informants or by delving more deeply into the researcher's own SPI-inspired self-reflections.

The photo essay (PE)

The collective stereographic photo essay (CSPE)
My earliest applications of the collective stereographic photo essay (CSPE) were inspired by grapevine accounts of some work by Jerry Zaltman and were encouraged by the collaboration of my colleague from Japan, Professor Takeo Kuwahara, who did much to implement the visual-imaging technology involved. Specifically, Takeo and I proceeded by lending large samples of informants stereographic cameras (two disposable 35 mm. cameras fastened together in a way that permitted them to take side-by-side left/right pictures); by asking them to shoot stereo photos that represented some topic of interest (the meaning of happiness, the experience of living in New York, the nature of complexity); by requesting that they write brief vignettes explaining their intentions in taking these stereographs (short mini-essays probing the relevant SPIs of each informant); and by interpreting the resulting photos and vignettes via a collective stereographic photo essay (a report presented in the CSPE format and illustrated by three-dimensional photographs).

We believed at the time and still do believe that stereography offers a worthwhile approach to enhancing the vividness, clarity, realism and depth of pictorial representations in ways that deepen our understanding of the relevant visual components of experience. However we also began to recognize that the cumbersome nature of stereography – that is, the greatly complicated shooting, mounting, displaying and viewing of the 3-D images – partially vitiated the usefulness of this method.

The collective photographic essay (CPE)

These practical difficulties associated with stereography encouraged me to turn increasingly to a simpler approach using ordinary photos – still by means of lending disposable cameras to large samples of informants and asking them to take pictures explained by SPI vignettes – to create a collective photographic essay (CPE) on one or another consumption-related topic (the experience of animal companionship, the meaning of beauty). Though the beauty project was a solo effort, I was greatly aided on the pets project (which also included some stereographs) by a worthy cast of co-authors (Debra Stephens, Ellen Day, Sally Holbrook and Gregor Strazar). Again, the challenge in the CPE approach lay in interpreting the SPI vignettes to discover themes illustrated, often quite vividly, by the relevant photographs.

The photo essay (PE)

But in my heart I have a not-so-secret side that cares about what I myself think or feel and that believes the rest of the world should care about this as well – just as I care about the thoughts of others because, after all, we are all humans and share together in highly similar consumption experiences of one sort or another. This penchant for self-reflection has encouraged me to dabble in an approach that I call the photo essay (PE) focused on the SPI-inspired interpretation of my own photographs and of photographs accessible to me through efforts by members of my immediate family or other privileged sources. Thus far, in this spirit, I have twice focused on a collection of photos taken by my grandfather Arthur T. Holbrook during the 1940s and bequeathed to me in a rather voluminous collection of black-and-white negatives plus several boxes of Kodachrome slides. The color slides, which have magically retained their pictorial vividness for roughly 60 years, still await detailed interpretation in a prospective project that I am quite eager to pursue. Meanwhile, in one application of the SPI-based PE, I have reflected on meanings in the B&W photos of ATH's experiences on the Brule River in Northern Wisconsin. In another, I have used ATH's photographic œuvre to illustrate eight major types of interactive relativistic consumption experiences distinguished by my Typology of Customer Value (efficiency, excellence, status, esteem, play, aesthetics, ethics and spirituality).

Future directions for the SPI-based PE

In future work with photo essays in general and with SPI-based PEs in particular, I hope to explore further aspects of this approach using the aforementioned color slides provided by ATH and to delve into similar themes emerging from the interpretation of a comparable set of stereographic photos taken by my father, Arthur A. Holbrook, in glorious Kodachrome during the 1950s, 1960s and 1970s. Moreover, I would encourage other consumer researchers to undertake similar explorations based on their own photographic family heirlooms. Many or even most of us have treasure troves of photos piled up in an attic or basement where a parent or grandparent deposited them 50 or 100 years ago and where nobody has bothered to look for the past few decades or longer. These pictures promise to reveal interpretive insights that we, as a field of inquiry, have barely begun to investigate but owe it to ourselves and to posterity to explore in depth.

Meanwhile the present chapter adds another aspect to the approach just described by providing an illustration of an SPI-based PE elicited by my own photographs from a recent excursion with my new digital camera. Before turning to that example, however, I should perhaps say a few words about the rationale supporting the validity or worth of the SPI-based CSPE, CPE and PE or (for short) SPI/PE methods advocated here. In this connection, I have four major justifications to offer.

Four justifications for SPI/PE

My four justifications appear roughly in declining order of their respectability vis-à-vis the philosophy of science.

(1)   The postpositivistic defense

First, we encounter a species of what I shall call the 'postpositivistic defense'. Here we recognize that recent thinkers on the philosophy of science (Kuhn, Feyerabend, Rorty, McCloskey and others) have questioned the existence of Universal Objective Truth (capitalized and singular) and have come to regard scientific truths (small letters and plural) as a collection of multiple intersubjective agreements among members of alternative scientific communities. In such a view, the foremost criterion of validity concerns one's ability to persuade other participants in a scientific community that one's statements are true, thereby engendering intersubjective if not objective consensus. As we all know, the art of persuasion in general and the art of winning agreement among the members of a scientific community in particular flies under the banner of what we call rhetoric.

Participants in a given scientific community therefore deploy various rhetorical devices for the sake of enhancing the persuasiveness of their arguments on behalf of the various truths that they wish to espouse. Depending on the constituency of the relevant reference group, these rhetorical devices might take the form of structural equations, ANOVA tests, multidimensional scaling, hedonic pricing models, computer simulations, or . . . anecdotes, personal narratives, stories, poems, songs, or . . . whatever. Whichever mode of persuasion is adopted – mathematics, multivariate statistics, metaphysics, metaphors, poetry or music – it's all just one or another form of rhetoric. The same goes for the photo essay or PE based on subjective personal introspection or PSI.

If my self-reflective pictorial narrative persuades members of my scientific community that my claims to truth are valid, these claims enjoy exactly the same kind of scientific status attained by truth claims based on structural equation models, seven-way factorially designed experiments or rigorous ethnographic procedures. OK, I admit, the latter will more easily persuade a scientific community composed of (say) Alice Tybout, Bobby Calder, Melanie Wallendorf and Merrie Brucks. But the former will more successfully convince a scientific community consisting of my wife Sally, our neighbor Fred, my dentist Edgar and our cat Rocky. And if you don't think that Rocky the Cat is a scientist, you have not witnessed the sophisticated methods by which he unobtrusively observes the behavior of chipmunks.

So rest easy, O, ye neopositivistic colleagues, because your own intersubjectivity is no better than the intersubjectivity of the postpositivistic folks who believe in SPI, PE and related self-reflective approaches.

(2)   The I-am-a-camera defense

Second, we encounter what I call the 'I-am-a-camera defense'. This justification was originally conceived as a rationale for SPI, but it strikes me as especially felicitous when applied to the case of SPI-based PE (relying on one or another kind of photographic image). Specifically, consider the fact that we typically attribute a high degree of objective accuracy to a visual representation produced by a camera. Thus, in a close horse race, we trust the decisive evidence from the stop-action image that records a 'photo finish'. We believe the implications from an instant video replay of a contested call at second base in a televised baseball game. We accept the verdict of the Mac Cam at the US Open. We acknowledge the verity in those familiar aphorisms to the effect that a photo allows us to see ourselves as others see us and that the camera doesn't lie.

Of course, we all know that, in a sense, the camera *does* lie or, in other words, that it can be manipulated to misrepresent the truth, as when we purposely crop out relevant parts of an image, frame the picture in a misleading way, doctor a photo with the use of airbrushes or PhotoShop, deploy soft-focus lenses to mask wrinkles or blemishes in the portrait of a senior citizen, and so forth.

But the point is that, in general, society trusts a photographic image because its members have themselves constructed the camera as a reliable instrument for observing and recording visual reality. Knowledgeable members of society (though certainly not yours truly) understand the relevant optics of the camera lenses, the physics of the light-registering exposure mechanism, the chemistry of the film-development process and other pertinent technical details. Because of this understanding, those who design cameras and consequently we who use them trust the resulting photographs that document objective features of the world around us (which horse finished first, whether Derek Jeter reached second base before the tag, where the tennis ball landed on Serena's serve, whether you were wearing a striped shirt at lunch last Wednesday). Put simply, society trusts the camera because society itself has constructed the camera as an instrument of observation.

Analogously, I believe, society has constructed me (also, Dear Reader, you) as an instrument of observation capable of recording the truths constructed by society as valid representations of the world around us. Yes, all truth is socially constructed. And, yes, society constructs us as observers suitable for recording such truths via various aspects of our enculturation into the relevant social norms and mores – as taught by our parents, siblings, friends, teachers, clergy, colleagues, communications media and so forth.

In short, society has reason to trust our claims to truth because society has itself constructed us as instruments of observation for recording various aspects of its own socially constructed reality. So my reply to the earnest ethnographers who do not trust introspective methods would take the form of suggesting that, hey, society built me and I am just reporting the insights that society has pre-programmed into my powers of observation. Not trusting my introspections would be comparable to pointing your camera at the Grand Canyon and then insisting that the resulting photo is really a picture of Niagara Falls.

(3)   The autoethnography defense
Third, even the most rigorous ethnographers agree on the merits of participant observation as a route to emic understanding of cultural or subcultural meanings. From this perspective, according to the 'autoethnography defense', it makes sense to regard SPI as a form of self-directed cultural anthropology; that is, as participant observation of oneself or, perhaps more accurately, as observant participation in one's own life. And who, might I ask, is more qualified than I myself or you yourself to undertake such an investigation? Hence, rather than following the widely approved ethnographic methods of observation

via participation in the lives of others, we pursue an essentially autoethnographic approach to observant participation in our own existence.

(4)   The 'who cares?' defense
Fourth, just in case you don't happen to buy any of the first three rationales for the scientific status of SPI-based PE, I offer what I call the 'who cares? defense'.

Specifically, when we come right down to it, what's so great about science anyway? True, science has given us certain life-saving health-protecting happiness-inducing medications; highly useful electronic computers; very worthwhile communications media; promising stem-cell research; and, most spectacularly, E-ZPass. But science has also given us the hydrogen bomb, cosmetic surgery, SUVs, the Atkins diet and cell phones. Clearly, as evinced by Botox, Vioxx, Krispy Kreme, Microsoft, the Ford Motor Company and the Pentagon, for starters, science is not the repository of all truth and goodness.

By contrast, the humanities have given us *Hamlet*, *Hard Times* and *Ulysses*; 'Mona Lisa' and 'Guernica'; *The Well-Tempered Klavier* and *Eine Kleine Nachtmusik*; Satch, Bird, Diz and Miles. Indeed, as vociferously argued by such poets as John Sherry, John Schouten and George Zinkhan, we might well turn for insights and inspiration to the humanities. I myself have found as many truths (small 't' and plural) about consumer behavior in the television series by David Kelly, the plays by Tina Howe, the movies by Robert Altman, the novels by Nicholson Baker and the songs by David Frishberg as in the factorially designed lab experiments or maximum-likelihood structural equation models of the folks who believe that the latter approaches represent the royal road to Truth (capital 'T' and singular). In the last analysis, I opt for truths (with a minuscule 't' and an 's' on the end) which I find scattered around in all sorts of places that the scientistic neopositivists fear to tread.

Illustration: 'bout the time I got to Phoenix
Everything I have said thus far will, I trust, have indicated my faith in an approach to consumer research that draws on the collective stereographic photo essay (CSPE) or just the collective photo essay (CPE) or even only the photo essay (PE) as a way of developing insights into consumption experiences by exploring the subjective personal introspections (SPI) of either informants or researchers themselves. In what follows, I shall illustrate this SPI/PE approach by means of its specific application to a set of photos that emerged from a recent trip on which I accompanied my wife Sally and son Chris to Phoenix, AZ during the Spring of 2005.

Lens is more
Briefly, we traveled to Phoenix with plans to visit such scenic locations as Sedona (home of majestic mountains and amazing rock formations) and the Phoenix Zoo (home of exotic animals and swarming tourists). I had decided to use this excursion to break in a new camera, namely, a Nikon D-70 digital SLR equipped with a semi-telephotographic 75–240 mm. zoom lens. Now most people would not take a telephoto lens on a tour planned for the purpose of shooting mountains and other scenic wonders. For this mission, a wider-angle lens – say, 28-to-50 mm. – would typically be considered ideal and would produce the sorts of images normally found on picture postcards and other expressions of popular scenery-centered sensibilities.

Figure 36.1   Cactus and rock formation in postcard pose

Pretty as a picture postcard

A typical photograph taken from such a postcard-like vantage point might resemble that shown in Figure 36.1, which presents a cactus and rock formation characteristic of the Phoenix environs. OK, I admit that I probably could have found a more impressive mountainscape. Indeed, during our detour to Sedona, I did attempt to shoot a whole memory chip full of such postcard wannabes, aimed at capturing the splendor of the beautiful red rock formations found in that area. Unfortunately for my scenery-focused aspirations, this entire set of Sedona souvenirs was obliterated owing to my incompetence in learning to work my new digital equipment. Specifically, sitting in the back seat while Chris drove our rented Taurus back from a sidetrip to Paolo Soleri's Arcosanti on the outskirts of Phoenix, I amused myself by pressing various buttons on the new Nikon D-70, just to see what functions they performed. It turns out that there is a button that performs the function of erasing the entire memory card and reformatting it for the purpose of taking a new set of photos. This button performs that function in less time than it takes to say, 'Damn it, I just destroyed three days' worth of Sedona photographs.' Which is exactly what happened to me, I'm sorry to say. (In retrospect, this seems rather ironic given that my whole reason for going digital was to forestall the damage done to film when it passes through the x-ray machines at airports. Well, it turns out that there's damage to film, and then there's damage to digits – far more devastating than anything a measly machine at the airport might cook up, indeed comparable to opening the back of a 35-mm. SLR camera in bright sunlight before the film has rewound.)

In the details

Destructive as it was for my ambitions to capture pretty images of scenic beauty, this autodidactic button-pushing card-formatting episode had the advantage of refocusing my attention on my true purpose as a photographer, with the result that my pictures of our Phoenix trip gravitated back toward my normal imaginative instincts, namely, the visual inspection of details as minute as I am able to manage. Specifically I enjoy taking pictures at the most microscopic possible level (subject to the limits of the equipment at hand). I would rather shoot the eye of a bird than the bird's head; the face of a person than the person's body; the body of a lion than the whole pride of lions; the pride of lions than the sweeping savanna. In other words, my preferred point of view is up-close-and-personal. The voyeuristic invasion of private space is my favorite vantage point.

This inclination runs against the postcard-dedicated ethos and also against the macroscopic orientation that typically guides much of our thinking in consumer research or other branches of the social sciences. In general, we aspire to comprehending a phenomenon in the context of its relationships with broader aspects of its situation. We wish to understand the individual consumer within the domain of the household or the household as one component of the larger marketplace. We hope to grasp the connections between a firm and its environment: how its actions affect (say) its physical habitat, how they fit or clash with government regulations, how they shape the surrounding cultural climate. We try to view the local industry within the scope of the national scene, the national economy within its global setting. In short, for virtually every problem, we move toward contemplating key issues with an eye to assessing their impact on the larger system within which they are embedded. This is the essence of the ecological focus that commends itself to our attention, both from the perspective of intellectual curiosity and from the viewpoint of social responsibility in the service of sheer survival.

But, contrary to that admirably macroscopic orientation, I wish to say a word or two on behalf of the opposite inclination – namely, a push toward the more microscopic view of things in which God or, if you prefer, the Devil is in the details. In this connection, the photos that came home with me from our trip to Phoenix have taught me something about myself and about ways of looking at the world – including the world of consumer behavior – that I did not fully grasp until I loaded these pictures onto the computer, selected them as my rotating screensavers, and spent a couple of months occasionally glancing in their direction while wondering what I was thinking of when I shot them and pondering how they affect me now.

Would you like to see my travel photos?
Even the most polite account of my Phoenix photos would note that they give absolutely no sense of the Arizona experience. From the viewpoint of tourism, they provide an absurdly sketchy travelogue. Instead of mountains and cactuses and bright blue skies, we see a series of pictures that, quite frankly, could have been taken anywhere at all as long as the venue happened to have a handy supply of flora, fauna and other curiosities to photograph. In numerous cases, I have pursued the close-up as a means of abstracting from the surrounding context. Rather than photographing the cactus on a hillside, I have aimed at its thistles. Rather than focusing on the lounging lion, I have dwelled on her whiskers and paws. Rather than shooting the zebra, I have captured his stripes.

Of course, there are limits to how close you can get to a lounging lion and therefore limits to how much you can focus on her whiskers with a 75-to-240 mm. zoom lens. But within those limits, in virtually every case, I find that I have pursued the up-close-and-personal perspective. Occasionally this orientation has been further assisted by the judicious use of PhotoShop for purposes of cropping pictures down to an even more microscopic level of detail. In such cases, the Adobe-adjusted images represent what I wanted to capture, sometimes beyond the physical capabilities of the lens at my disposal.

Disembodied details

One symptom of my preoccupation with the in-your-face vantage point appears in various bizarre juxtapositions, as in close-ups that include only a bird's head and feet, giving it a somewhat disturbingly disembodied appearance. In this vein, Figure 36.2 shows such a photo of a pink–orange flamingo, whose body – by implication – is somewhere else. Notice how this visual effect focuses our attention on the bird's constant preoccupation with seed pecking. Something similar happens in a comparable photo, not shown here, that features an ostrich whose legs and neck appear as three separate entities – like three columns of a Roman amphitheater – reminding us of the somewhat dysfunctional design of this creature's flightless physique. For both these birds, at different scales on the size continuum, it's all about eating. Foraging forever for ground-level goodies is the name of the consumption-oriented game. Lest we forget.

Stripes and thorns

Another illustration moves even farther in the direction of abstraction at the expense of capturing the whole beast. Thus Figure 36.3 depicts the side of a zebra in a shot showing the wonderfully intricate pattern of markings – the beautiful combination of regularity and irregularity – that distinguishes this creature from all others of its kind. (OK, so it's sort of like snowflakes. I mean, how do we really *know* that no two are exactly alike? Have we actually inspected all N of them and considered all N(N-1)/2 comparisons? I think not.)

Figure 36.2   Flamingo's head and feet

Figure 36.3   Zebra close and personal

Figure 36.4   Cactus close-up

Similarly close scrutiny is rewarded by rather beautiful patterns of design that characterize cactuses and other plants. For example, Figure 36.4 shows the intricate geometrical design embodied by the thorns of a cactus, a nearly perfect specimen of vegetative patterning in which clean regimentation into columns confronts and fuses with obliqueness and disarray. Most cactuses and many other plants can be fruitfully regarded as a juxtaposition of these tendencies; that is, ordered regularity commingled with constant irregularity. Hence their beauty. And hence their reflexive ability to comment on the essence of creativity as a synthesis of thesis and antithesis, an integration of structure and departure, a combination of theme and variation, a balancing of symmetry and asymmetry or a reconciliation of order and chaos. Somehow, despite its picturesque visual impression, I don't get the same insights when looking at the cactus in front of a rock formation, as seen earlier in Figure 36.1.

No free lunch
Every serious consumer researcher should go to the zoo, take a photo of a lion or tiger, enlarge it, and hang it on the wall. Preferably, as in Figure 36.5, try to catch a pose in which the lion glowers at you and licks her chops. Very importantly, you should make sure to take this photo yourself so that you can retain a deep visceral sense of the fact that it is *you* whom the lion is looking at, thereby achieving a profound SPI-based PE-enhanced

Figure 36.5   Lion with relaxed paws

recognition that there is at least one animal in the kingdom whom you have met and who would dearly love to eat you for lunch. Where lions, tigers and even house cats are concerned, this is a truism that we too easily forget. Witness the horrifying attack on Roy Horn of Siegfried-&-Roy by a tiger whom he had raised from infancy and whom he thought he could trust unequivocally.

This sense of being regarded as potential food is a perspective that deserves cultivation by all those with an interest in the ways of consumption. It helps alert us to how a deer might feel when regarded as venison, a calf as veal, a shrimp as scampi or a lobster as thermidor. Actress Mary Tyler Moore has voiced her empathy for lobsters. But most of us remain fairly relaxed about all this and cheerfully consume our next gluttonous feast with little concern for the fact that the fish or cow does not necessarily relish being regarded as prospective bouillabaisse or Beef Wellington. In this spirit, note the casual limpness of the lion's paws, masking claws that could cut you to shreds with one well-placed swipe, but conveying a sense of total relaxation comparable to what most of us human creatures display at the dinner table.

Framing the bend

As long as I'm engaging in shameless anthropomorphism, albeit in the service of what I hope is greater self-understanding, let us consider the close-up of a kneeling pink-orange flamingo in Figure 36.6. At first blush, this picture presents a deeply disquieting appearance – at least to a naïve spectator such as myself – because it gives the indelible impression that the bird's knees are bending backwards. Even if we consciously 'know' that birds and indeed many animals have backward-bending knees, this perfectly normal creature somehow looks 'broken' or even 'mutilated.' The first few hundred times I looked at it, I felt strongly disturbed by this troubling impression. Then I rediscovered the power of framing.

Figure 36.6   Flamingo kneeling

Formerly I have always thought of wings as analogous to arms. Flapping my arms would be comparable, if I had feathers, to beating my wings. This leaves the bird's legs as analogous to my own legs. After all, didn't Plato say that humans are two-legged creatures without feathers? From this habit of mind, it follows that the flamingo's knees appear to bend backwards. Ouch!

But equally plausibly (at least, to one more concerned with suggestive metaphors than with accurate ornithology), it makes sense to think of the bird's wings as legs and to conceive of his talons as hands. From this perspective, our flamingo is resting on his arms with his elbows bent in the usual direction. No sooner did I realize the possibility of this reframing than the photo began to look perfectly normal to me.

Bending the frame

My new understanding of bird knees as comparable to human elbows is illustrated in Figure 36.7, in which I attempt to replicate the posture adopted by the flamingo in my earlier photo. Even the most skeptical reader will doubtless concede that I look remarkably like a kneeling bird, especially if taking due account of my protruding proboscis, which so strongly resembles a beak. O, sure, the flamingo doesn't wear eyeglasses or a wristwatch. But if you look closely at Figure 36.6, you will observe a metal band above the flamingo's left elbow. So, like Morris, the flamingo wears a sort of arm bracelet.

Moreover, via this interpretive exercise, I have gained a valuable SPI-influenced insight. Specifically, I now perceive that my legs – not my arms – are analogous to wings, especially because they are the means by which I propel myself forward so that the otherwise

Figure 36.7   Morris kneeling

Figure 36.8   Fennec fox sleeping

dirty, ugly, repulsive NYC sidewalks metaphorically become the wind beneath my wings. If you get sufficiently blown away by this breezy simile, it literally changes your outlook on the abstract human condition, not to mention the concrete public pavement.

Sleep
Sleep is surely a blessed event, especially for those of us who suffer chronic deprivation from anywhere near enough of it. For this reason, we tend to regard a sleeping beast – say, our cat stretched out on the hearth – as enjoying a kind of voluptuous bliss that inspires in us no small degree of envy. For me, the up-close image shown in Figure 36.8 (a furry Fennec fox from Africa, blissfully asleep in the sun) stirs such powerful feelings. Studying his air of utterly restful repose – the way, flooded with sunlight, he uses his paws as a pillow – my sense of wistful longing to achieve a similar state of tranquility makes me aware that, in some seldom-realized way, I must be very . . . very . . . very . . . tired.

Conclusions

The aesthetics of minutiae
Thus far, we have said nothing much about the artistic merits of the various photos under consideration. Obviously, one's aesthetic appreciation for (say) my Flamingo Kneeling (Figure 36.6) or my Lion With Relaxed Paws (Figure 36.5) depends on questions of taste about which reasonable people may differ. There is, as the old saying conventionally goes, no arguing about taste because, hey, beauty is in the eye of the beholder. But despite these clichés,

people have been doing exactly that – arguing about taste – for centuries. So I might at least express my own self-reflective thoughts about which types of photographs I happen to prefer.

In this connection, let us assume that we are comparing two pictures of roughly equal quality in terms of lighting, resolution and composition (clarity, balance, unity-in-variety, etc.). Given close comparability on these important dimensions, my own preferences tend to gravitate in the direction of abstraction; that is, purely visual elements taken from their surrounding context in ways that focus on the formal arrangements of patterns, contours or other components rather than on their literal meaning or worldly significance. In general, this process of abstraction benefits from a more micro-level focus; that is, from an up-close-and-personal point of view, the more detailed the better.

Thus the face of the lion (Figure 36.5) moves in the right direction, but is still too representational to be entirely satisfying. The flamingo's head and feet (Figure 36.2) take a welcome step toward greater abstraction in the sense that the legs and face form a three-component display that loses the representational aspects of the creature's body. The cactus thorns (Figure 36.4) begin to suggest a welcome degree of abstraction in which our attention is drawn to the shape of their pattern. Better yet, the stripes of the zebra (Figure 36.3) encourage a disinterested focus on the visual configuration of black-and-white lines appreciated purely for its own sake, to such an extent that, unless somebody reminds us, we might not even notice or care that the visual composition comes from a zebra.

It is this state of appreciation for its own sake that philosophers of art identify as a true aesthetic experience. The ability of an artwork or, in this case, a photographic image to lead us toward this sort of self-justifying attention to an experience valued as an end in itself strikes me as the crux of its greater or lesser aesthetic excellence.

The mining of minutiae

All this combines to suggest what I regard as the main takeaway from the present chapter for those interested in the study of consumer behavior, namely, whether in photo essays based on subjective personal introspection or elsewhere, the value of observing the phenomena of interest at different levels of scale in general (from the most macroscopic to the most microscopic) and of drilling down to the most small-scaled level of detail in particular (the mining of minutiae). Put in a rather obvious way, in consumer research, it pays to look not just at the level of aggregate consumption (thank you, J.M. Keynes); not just at the level of segment-specific behavior (thank you, Wendell R. Smith); not just at the individual consumer's decision-oriented choice processes (thank you, John Howard and Jim Bettman) or at a person's unique consumption experiences (thank you, Lawrence Abbott and Wroe Alderson). Rather, it pays to keep pushing down to more and more minute levels of analysis, plumbing the depths and probing the details of everyday consumer reality: which hand we use to hold the toothbrush; how many squares of toilet paper we devote to each wipe; what utensil we use to beat eggs; which combinations of ties and shirts are viewed as stylish or unfashionable; how many bites we invest in eating one 3.7-ounce Snickers bar; how many bytes we need to save one 26-page Word document.

It took me five years to ask my psychoanalyst why she wore her wedding ring on her right hand. I would have learned a lot more about her a lot faster if I had examined this detail a lot sooner. (She was a member of the Greek Orthodox Church, where apparently this is the custom.) When she got pregnant, my verbal ramblings on the couch immediately turned to issues related to conception, birth and growth, even though I delayed for at least four or five months before recognizing consciously that she was with child. I still wonder what telling details, observed only at the unconscious level, gave her away initially. Wouldn't it be nice to understand this hidden, secret, unaware level of scrutiny? This clandestine language? Those tell-tale signs that propel this submerged mode of communication?

Voyeurism and sensitivity

Of course, such questions lead us in the direction of observations that become increasing personal – and, therefore, sensitive – as we energetically and even voyeuristically probe deeper and deeper levels of privacy. It is one thing to ask someone what brand of toilet tissues she uses and another to ask her how many squares she tears off at a time or which hand wields the wipes. Clearly, from the viewpoint of Kimberly-Clark executives, who would dearly love to get every citizen to use just one more square of tissue per wipe, the question has or ought to have a profound resonance of undeniable relevance to the profit motive. Yet we humans remain sensitive in the extreme to such detailed scrutiny of our private selves.

I find this fear of personal revelation quite conspicuously when I take portraits of friends. As always, my instinct is to go for the close-up, even at the expense of capturing every wrinkle, blemish and tell-tale sign of age or maturity. I am always surprised at how resistant people can be to this approach. One of our most beautiful friends expressed horror at what was revealed by an intimate portrait of her loveliness. Admittedly such photographs do not show off people in their most glamorous light. Investing some diligent time with PhotoShop – for example, the 'blur more' command – I could make them look more conventionally handsome or pretty according to the norms promulgated by the fashion magazines. I could photograph them through a Vaseline-coated lens. Or I could hire Bachrach to produce a typical exercise in airbrushed iconography. But the point is that the more in-your-face photos show our beloved family and friends with revealing intimacy, warts and all, in a way that invites all sorts of interesting questions about where each little laugh line or worry wrinkle came from. I find such pictures both attractive and suggestive of important consumption-related questions.

Exhibitionism and beyond

Ultimately, as I have argued elsewhere at length, voyeurism and exhibitionism are reciprocal or indeed symbiotic phenomena. The impact of an exhibitionist's conspicuous consumption *depends* on the responses of one or more voyeurs – and vice versa. So I end with an example of a more cooperative informant encountered at the Phoenix Zoo, namely, a charmingly gregarious scarlet-faced mandrill who entertained a picture window full of delighted school children and shocked their astonished parents by mounting a magnificent demonstration of mandrillian masturbation when, without the slightest shred of inhibition or modesty, he cheerfully performed a dazzling display of self-fellatio for the admiring crowd. While appalled mothers fled with their baby carriages and I happily snapped photos with bemused dedication, this prestidigital primate executed a highly-practiced onanistic routine that one could not help but regard with a feeling of fascination bordering on jealousy. Let's just say that he found an autoerotic use for the prehensile powers of his opposing thumbs that added a new dimension to the concept of toolmaking.

Obviously such a demonstration raises important questions about the role of consumption experiences in evolution. Does this monkey's behavior confer some sort of

Figure 36.9   Mandrill smiling

survival advantage (a selfish gene)? Or does it represent a cultural habit that works against propagation of the gene pool (a selfish meme)? By interfering with procreation, does it help to explain why humans have evolved in the direction of standing upright rather than bending over? The issues raised by this exhibitionistic display seem almost limitless, the point being that they would not have arisen had we not pursued our photographic goals down to the most microscopic level of reciprocally voyeuristic observation. Yes, meaning emerges from the mining of minutiae. Yes, I have the pictures to prove it. And, no, I'm not going to show them to you. But I will show you the ecstatic expression on the mandrill's face. As revealed by Figure 36.9, his smiling visage pretty much says it all.

Two concluding thoughts
In sum, all this suggests two conclusions with which I shall leave the patient reader. First, as a general proposition, I recommend use of the photographic essay (CSPE, CPE or PE) as a window onto the sorts of subjective personal introspections (SPI) that often raise questions about consumer behavior not elicited by other sorts of empirical approaches. Put simply, photos stimulate introspections in ways that shed light on consumption-related phenomena. Aspects of consumption experiences are illuminated precisely because photography shines a light on them.

Second, as a specific example, I believe that my photographs of Phoenix illustrate one aspect of consumer research that deserves our attention, namely, the sense in which we have much to gain by reversing our usual obsession with macroscopic themes (environmental impacts, social effects, managerial implications) in favor of a preoccupation with small-scale details that interest us because of the manner in which such minutiae illuminate various facets of everyday experience (stripes, thorns and paws). To my eyes, the fine-grained patterning of a cactus plant represents something more profound than the scene typically featured on a picture postcard. If we insist on pursuing the subjective personal introspective photo essay as an approach to research – which, I believe, we should – then it apparently pays to focus at least part of our attention on the tiniest cracks and crevices in the world around us.

Acknowledgment

The author gratefully acknowledges the support of the Columbia Business School's Faculty Research Fund.

PART VIII

SPECIAL ISSUES

37 The emergence of multi-sited ethnography in anthropology and marketing

Karin M. Ekström[1]

Although multi-sited ethnography is an exercise in mapping terrain, its goal is not holistic representation, an ethnographic portrayal of the world system as a totality. Rather, it claims that any ethnography of a cultural formation in the world system is also an ethnography of the system, and therefore cannot be understood only in terms of the conventional single-site mise-en-scène of ethnographic research, assuming indeed it is the cultural formation, produced in several different locales, rather than the conditions of a particular set of subjects that is the object of study. (Marcus, 1998, p. 83)

1 Introduction

Ethnography has traditionally involved spending a long time in a remote location far away from home, seeking a deeper cultural understanding of a certain phenomenon. Recently, or more specifically since about the mid-1980s, there has been a paradigm shift in anthropology. It has stimulated a discussion about representation of the field as well as the researcher and has led to new ways of seeking knowledge (e.g., Gupta and Ferguson, 1997). New ways of conducting ethnography have been introduced, and today multi-sited ethnography challenges the long-established approach for conducting ethnographic fieldwork. Rather than focusing on one location, fieldwork can now be conducted in a number of sites. Although fieldwork has historically been an imperative ingredient for the definition of anthropology and ethnography, the change to multiple sites has not occurred without opposition. Some researchers express their concern regarding the direction that the discipline of anthropology is leading for, being afraid of losing the 'thick description' to a more superficial interpretation of cultural meaning. Others point to benefits such as the possibility of producing and disseminating knowledge throughout the world in new ways. In a changing world, conventional ethnography is not sufficient for studying 'circulation of cultural meanings, objects and identities in diffuse time-space' (Marcus, 1998, p. 2). Others express their concern regarding the direction that the discipline of anthropology is heading, being afraid of losing the 'thick description' to a more superficial interpretation of cultural meaning. The paradigm shift has led to a debate about the nature of fieldwork. The purpose of this chapter is to illuminate the emergence of multi-sited ethnography in anthropology and to provide suggestions for the way this can be used in marketing. Before doing so, there will be a brief introduction to ethnography.

2 Single-site ethnography

2.1 Ethnography

'Ethnography is that form of inquiry and writing that produces descriptions and accounts about the ways of life of the writer and those written about' (Denzin, 1997, p. xi). Since the turn of the twentieth century, fieldwork has been a vital component of ethnography.

The picture of the traditional ethnographer, investigating cultural meaning in a remote rural village, both looking and dressing differently than the natives studied, is often what comes to mind when thinking of ethnographic fieldwork. Around the turn of the twentieth century, studies of ethnography developed simultaneously with Western interest in non-Western societies (e.g., Atkinson and Hammersley, 1994). The anthropologists in the United States focused on the American Indians and the British anthropologists studied colonies (Garbarino, 1983). Research was often funded from government departments or vested economic interests (Garbarino, 1983). Prominent researchers involved in developing early ethnographic fieldwork were Malinowski, Boas and Radcliffe-Brown. It should be recognized, however, that ethnography has a history (e.g., Atkinson and Hammersley, 1994; Gupta and Ferguson, 1997). For example, Carl von Linné, during his fieldtrips to Lapland in 1732 and to Dalarna, Sweden in 1734, wrote not only about botany, but also about ways of life (Hallbert, 2003). What characterizes the ethnographic method during the twentieth century is the need to study social surroundings and not merely rely on historicism (Atkinson and Hammersley, 1994). Geertz's (1973) emphasis on thick description in interpretation of cultural meaning characterizes how he thinks fieldwork should be conducted in anthropology.

The definition of ethnography is not unambiguous. For some people, it implies a method and for others a philosophical paradigm (Atkinson and Hammersley, 1994). In an attempt to define ethnography, Atkinson and Hammersley try to identify different features characterizing ethnography. The first characterizing feature is exploring the nature of a particular social phenomenon rather than testing hypotheses. A second is working mainly with unstructured data rather than with pre-coded data. Third is the feature of investigating a small number of cases in detail, and a fourth feature is an analysis involving explicit interpretation, mainly in the form of verbal descriptions and explanations rather than quantification and statistical analysis. It should also be added that participant observation has been an important part of ethnography.

Different views on ethnography have evolved over time (e.g., Denzin, 1997). The traditional period from the early 1900s to World War II focused on ' "objective" colonializing accounts of field experiences reflective of the positivistic science paradigm' (ibid., p. 16). Although early ethnographers argued that their approach had a greater capacity to represent the nature of social reality accurately, this argument is seldom advanced today as a result of the prevalence of constructivism, philosophical hermeneutics or poststructuralism (Atkinson and Hammersley, 1994).

2.2   Fieldwork

Fieldwork has always been considered necessary for anthropologists (e.g., Hannerz, 2001; Clifford, 1997). It is a fundamental disciplining function (Clifford, 1997). To leave home is central. Hannerz writes: 'The anthropologist who never conducts fieldwork is perceived as just as odd as a theoretical swimmer' (Hannerz, 2001, p. 8). The conventional picture of fieldwork and more specifically local fieldwork is Malinowski's (1922) work in the Trobriand Islands. Traditionally, going into the field doing fieldwork implied a spatial distinction between home and a place of discovery (Clifford, 1997). These types of conventional fieldwork usually lasted for at least a year. Hannerz (2001) discusses several reasons for this. First of all, if the life form studied was closely linked to nature, it might be of interest to see how the seasonal changes affected the topic of study. Second, it took time to build knowledge about the topic studied and to establish a good relationship with the people studied. Third, the possibility of traveling during the beginning of the twentieth century was limited.

In anthropological fieldwork, the emphasis has been on staying in one site rather than passing through a field site. As Clifford (1997, p. 199) puts it: 'The fieldworker was a homebody abroad, not a cosmopolitan visitor.' Ethnography is about getting close to the experiences of people studied. Emerson, Fretz and Shaw (1995, p. 2) write: 'The ethnographer seeks a deeper immersion in others' worlds in order to grasp what they experience as meaningful and important.' However the nuances in fieldwork need to be pointed out. It is easy to think of the fieldworker in a more stereotypical way as the person who stayed a long time in the field, speaking local languages and participating in local life. Clifford (1997, p. 201) emphasizes that this was not always the case: 'The range of actual social relations, communicative techniques and spatial practices deployed between the poles of fieldwork and travel is a continuum, not a sharp border.' Over the years, there have been different views on how much the ethnographer should participate in local culture. For example, should the ethnographer stand out, dress in white as Malinowski did and thereby communicate not going native? Or should the ethnographer emphasize total immersion by taking on the roles of the culture studied?

Fieldwork has historically been conducted with a variety of methods, such as observation, participation, interviewing and archival analysis. Different ways of recording fieldnotes have been noticed. Sanjek (1990) discusses ethnographers having used headnotes, scratch notes, fieldnotes proper, fieldnote records, texts, journals and diaries, letters, reports and papers. The traditional anthropologist's fieldwork has been distinguished from the work of the missionary, the colonial officer and the travel writer (journalist or literary exoticist) (Clifford, 1997). Clifford (ibid., p. 196) writes: 'It is often easier to say clearly what one is not than what one is.' Anthropologists have for the last two decades discussed what fieldwork is for them today. It is still a crucial bone in the anthropologist's body of research, but a part which is in the process of change. Clifford states (p. 194): 'Fieldwork has become a problem because of its positivist and colonialist historical associations (the field as "laboratory", the field as place of "discovery" for privileged sojourners).' Over time, the fieldwork of disciplinary distinction for anthropology might change. The paradigm shift in anthropology that became evident around the mid-1980s has led to questions about traditional fieldwork, including to what extent reality is or can be represented in fieldwork, and whose voices are made explicit in the fieldwork – the researcher, the informants, males, females – as discussed below. Also there has been criticism that ethnography changes societies by subtly introducing new technology or ideas.

Ethnography involves both emic and etic experience. Emic is the subjective experience of the informants, while etic is the researcher's interpreted cultural meaning or theoretical accounts of this experience (e.g., Denzin, 1989; Arnould and Wallendorf, 1994; Arnould, 1998). Murray (2005) emphasizes the importance of balance between emic and etic in ethnography: if too much emic, the researcher is just focusing on the description of the informants, and if too much etic, the researcher is just summarizing a theory, the consequence being that there is no theoretical advance made. Also Goulding (2005) claims that ethnographic analysis needs to move beyond thick description, such as informant's stories and case studies, and that the analytical phase of theorizing should be separated from the descriptive discourse.

Finally, even though the origin of ethnography is anthropological, ethnography is today conducted in many disciplines. The practice of ethnography in marketing is widespread (e.g., Kozinets, 2001; Schouten and McAlexander, 1995; Thompson and Arsel, 2004). It is, however, likely that the notion of doing fieldwork differs between disciplines. Crossovers between disciplines exist, for example, between anthropology and cultural studies.

2.3   The paradigm shift

New ways of conducting fieldwork have been introduced as a consequence of the paradigm shift that has taken place in anthropology, beginning in the mid-1980s. Whereas fieldwork historically implied a clear distinction between home and place of discovery, today the border is unstable and is constantly renegotiated (Clifford, 1997). Spatial practices involving moving to and from, passing through and dwelling (rapport, initiation, familiarity) is changing (ibid.). A newer suggestion is to think of the field as habitus instead of place, involving embodied dispositions and practices. Clifford (1997, p. 195) writes: 'Anthropology has always been more than fieldwork, but fieldwork has been something an anthropologist should have done . . . Perhaps fieldwork will become merely a research tool rather than an essential disposition or professional marker.'

Society has changed and much has happened since the early anthropological studies. Traditional anthropological fieldwork is best suited for conditions in which the people studied communicate orally and do not move around, making it easier to keep track of them (Hannerz, 2001). The possibility of traveling and communicating in many different ways opens up new ways of conducting fieldwork. The meaning of 'local' can also be questioned, particularly in today's society in which media and popular culture from around the world reaches us even if we are in remote places. Giddens (1991, p. 188) writes: 'Although everyone lives a local life, phenomenal worlds for the most part are truly global.' He emphasizes that 'localities are thoroughly penetrated by distanciated influences'. Also Grewal and Kaplan (1994, p. 11) write: 'the parameters of the local and global are often indefinable or indistinct – they are permeable constructs. How one separates the local from the global is difficult to decide when each thoroughly infiltrates the other'.

The traditional emphasis on 'hanging out' deeply in the field in one site can today be developed by including several sites. It is no longer necessary for an anthropologist to travel to a very remote place, but the fieldsite can be a neighborhood, an office, or a laboratory, store, brand community, coffee shop or franchise such as McDonalds. Gupta and Ferguson (1997) advocate that the anthropology of today focus on shifting locations rather than on bounded fields. However the emphasis on conducting a significant piece of fieldwork persists. Clifford (1997, p. 209) writes 'Ethnography is no longer a normative practice of outsiders visiting or studying insiders but, in Narayan's words, of attending to "shifting identities in relationship with the people and issues an anthropologist seeks to represent"'. Transcultural studies require cosmopolitan fieldworkers often fluent in more than one language and familiar with different cultures (Marcus, 1998).

Ethnography of today looks different than in earlier days. Today we can witness use of a variety of methods including long-term and shorter-term stints in the field, interviews, participant observation, netnography, videography, photography, narratives and story telling. The Arnould and Price (1993) study on river-rafting provides an example of use of multiple ethnographic accounts.

The paradigm shift involves a discussion about the researcher's role in producing and creating knowledge. Rabinow (1977) argues that the participant observer is influenced by the collection of cultural data. He made it scientifically legitimate to include the researcher's own experience in a study. Clifford (1997) writes that a certain degree of auto-biography is now accepted, but wonders about how much. He thinks encounters in the field are still important and writes: 'Travel, redefined and broadened, will remain consti-tutive of fieldwork at least in the near term. This will be necessary for institutional and material reasons. Anthropology must preserve not only its disciplinary identity, but also its credibility with scientific institutions and funding sources' (ibid., p. 217). Also Marcus views reflexivity as a dimension of method.

As mentioned previously, the paradigm shift has also led to questions about traditional fieldwork, for example, to what extent reality is or can be represented in fieldwork, and whose voices are made explicit in the fieldwork. The debate that went on during the mid-1980s (e.g. Clifford and Marcus, 1986) made both research and writing more reflexive and questioned gender, class and race (Denzin, 1997). Reflexivity encompasses not only concern about how data are collected and analyzed and how theories used in the analysis are written, but also a concern about how the ethnography is written up. Denzin (2001, p. 324) writes: 'writing is not an innocent practice. Men and women write culture differently'. 'Reflexivity thus implies that the orientations of researchers will be shaped by their socio-historical locations, including the values and interests that these locations confer upon them' (Hammersley and Atkinson, 1995, p. 16). Also thick descriptions emphasized in realistic ethnographies have been criticized for an inability to recognize power relationships and factors behind such relationships (e.g. Arnould, 1998).

Van Maanen (1988) discusses different ways to present research, such as the realist, confessional and impressionist tales. The interplay of literary and rhetorical, historical and ideological influences on the production and reception of ethnographies in anthro-pology is discussed by Clifford and Marcus (1986). Also Geertz (1973) mentions that anthropological writings are fiction, shaped by literary conventions and devices. However, Atkinson and Hammersley (1994) indicate that the conventions deployed in constructing anthropological and sociological styles need to be identified.

Although ethnographic texts historically have been monologic, there is a shift toward a text allowing for a multiplicity of voices (Atkinson and Hammersley, 1994). An example is Dwyer's (1982) study on Moroccan dialogues. This change is in line with postmodern ethnography. Tyler (1986, p. 126) writes, as cited in Atkinson and Hammersley (1994, p. 256): 'The postmodern author seeks to dissolve that disjuncture between the observer and the observed. The trope of "participant observation", which captures the ambivalence of distance and familiarity, is replaced by one of "dialogue", showing "the cooperative and collaborative nature of the ethnographic situation" '. He is critical of the contention that ethnography represents the social world and prefers evoking (Atkinson and Hammersley, 1994). Also Strathern (1991) discuss evocation and ethnographic complexity. The postmodern movement has led to experimentation with textual styles and formats, a focus on textuality which may privilege the rhetorical over the 'scientific' (Atkinson and Hammersley, 1994). In the future, it is important to focus on strategies of reading and writing ethnography in order to evaluate the quality of arguments and the use of evidence (Hammersley, 1991, 1993). Fischer (1999) empha-sizes that ethnographic practice in the future needs to juxtapose, complement or supplement other genres of writing such as those used by historians, literary theorists and photographers.

Finally the paradigm shift did not occur without concern in anthropology. There have been attempts to recapture anthropology in writing culture (e.g., Clifford and Marcus, 1986). Clifford (1997) expresses a concern that multilocale field studies are a symptom of postmodern fragmentation. He wonders if it can be collectively fashioned into something more substantial and emphasizes critical dialogue and respectful polemic.

3   Multi-sited ethnography

3.1   Multilocale ethnography
The concept of multilocale ethnography was introduced into anthropology by Marcus (1986, 1989) near the end of the 1980s, but later on he chose to use the term 'multi-sited' (Marcus, 1995, 1998), a term that has become commonly used internationally.

Hannerz (2001) was also an early proponent of multilocale ethnography. He emphasizes not only that this type of ethnography is about involving several field sites, but that the fields are linked together in a coordinated structure. He calls it a network of localities or 'several fields in one'. This is also exemplified in this chapter's introductory quotation. It is of interest to try to identify which types of chains and patterns of social relations exist in the network (e.g., Hannerz, 1996, 2001). Furthermore the field is not only multilocale, but translocale, the latter focusing on identifying the relationships between the localities (Hannerz, 2001). The social anthropologists at Stockholm University started early to work along this line and Hannerz (2001) indicates that they probably have a wider selection of studies than most anthropological institutions in the world. An example is Garsten's (1994) doctoral dissertation 'Apple World', in which she studied the organizational culture of the computer company Apple in its office in a suburb of Stockholm, in the international head-quarters in Silicon Valley and in the European headquarters in Paris.

3.2   Multi-sited ethnography
Marcus (1995) describes the emergence of multi-sited ethnography in anthropological research and explains that it is used in particular in new spheres of interdisciplinary work, for example various strands of cultural studies. He states (1995, p. 97): 'such interdisciplinary arenas do not share a clearly bounded object of study, distinct disciplinary perspectives that participate in them tend to be challenged.' He also emphasizes that conventional ethnography is not sufficient for studying circulation of cultural meanings, objects and identities in diffuse time–space (Marcus, 1998). Marcus writes (p. 90): 'Multi-sited research is designed around chains, paths, threads, conjunctions, or juxtapositions of locations in which the ethnographer establishes some form of literal, physical presence, with an explicit, posited logic of association or connection among sites that in fact defines the argument of the ethnography.'

Different areas in which multi-sited research has emerged include media studies and the social and cultural study of science and technology (Marcus, 1998). Some examples are Latour (1993, 1998) and Haraway (1991), both of whom have published multi-sited research. In consumer research, a recent example of multi-sited research is Canniford (2005), who reassesses the experience of global cultures with reference to the global surfing scene. By talking to and interviewing surfers in different surfing locations in Indonesia, by reviewing surfing films and other media, and by the use of historical data, he demonstrates how local sovereignty is pooled on a global stage. Other examples of multi-sited consumer research are Schouten and McAlexander (1995), who studied bikers, Belk and Costa (1998), who did multiple location case studies over several years, focusing on the mountain man myth, and Belk, Ger and Askegaard (2003), who studied desire in the United States, Turkey and Denmark.

There are different techniques for conducting multi-sited ethnography, such as 'follow the people', things, metaphor, plot, story, allegory, life, biography or conflict (Marcus, 1998). An example of using 'follow the people' technique is in migration studies, and in studies involving shadowing people who move around in multinational contexts (e.g., Czarniawska, 1998). An example of 'follow the thing' is Curasi, Price and Arnould (2004), who studied how objects pass across generations. Appadurai (1986) writes about how the status of commodities shifts in different contexts. An example of 'follow the metaphor' is presented in Martin's (1994) study on the body's immune system. Her work also illustrates renegotiation of identities in different sites: being an AIDS volunteer at one site, a medical student in another and a corporate trainee at a third. An example of following the formation of the plot and thereby the story can be found in the work of Czarniawska (2004a). An example of 'follow the life or biography' is illustrated in an on-going study on the meanings of food among elderly at different ages and life situations (Brembeck et al., 2005). 'Follow the conflict' can involve, for example, legal issues or media issues. Hardtmann (2001) studied resistance activists in India and England who are against the caste system.

One of the benefits of multi-site ethnography is the different perspectives provided compared to a single-site study. Marcus (1998, p. 99) writes: 'This condition of shifting personal positions in relation to one's subjects and other active discourses in a field that overlap with one's own, generates a definite sense of doing more than just ethnography, and it is this quality that provides a sense of being an activist for and against positioning in even the most self-perceived apolitical fieldworker.'

Multi-sited research is challenging both the way to conduct fieldwork and the way to write ethnography (Marcus, 1998). Multi-sited strategies require creative process. Marcus calls this research imaginary, influencing how research ideas are formulated and how fieldwork is conceived.

3.3 Translocale ethnography

The translocale ethnography focuses on identifying the relationships among the localities (Hannerz, 1996, 2001). However the term 'translocale' is seldom used. In Hannerz's (2001) anthology on translocale fieldwork, he says that it might be possible to say that the fieldwork is multilocale, but the analysis is translocale. In international anthropology, it is more common to use the term 'multi-sited', which also includes translocale. However it might still be of interest to try to identify to what extent the character of a specific field study is multi-sited or translocale.

Appadurai (1996, p. 192) uses the term 'translocalities' to characterize places at which people circulate through rather than at which they anchor themselves. He writes: 'The challenge to producing a neighborhood in these settings derives from the inherent instability of social relationships, the powerful tendency for local subjectivity itself to be commoditized, and the tendencies for nation-states, which sometimes obtain significant revenues from such sites, to erase internal, local dynamics through externally imposed modes of regulation, credentialization, and image production.' A good example of

504 *Handbook of qualitative research methods in marketing*

a translocale study is Garsten's (2001) study on Olsten Staffing Services in which the project employed consultants who worked for different companies and continuously changed offices. In translocale field studies, the process of transfer and the motion is particularly interesting (Hannerz, 2001). The participants' inputs and relations can be just as short-term as the anthropologists' in translocalities such as conferences, courses and festivals (Hannerz, 2001). Czarniawska (2004b) introduces the concept of mobile ethnologies for studying the life and work of people who move in contemporary organizations.

3.4 Implications for conducting multi-sited research
There are several important aspects to consider when conducting multi-sited, multilocale or translocal fieldwork. First there is a need *to define and rethink the field*. Gupta and Ferguson (1997) write: ' "The field" is a clearing whose deceptive transparency obscures the complex processes that go into constructing it.' Second, there is a need to *determine what localities to include*. Sometimes the choice of which localities to include might be quite obvious, at least, at the beginning of the study. At other times, the choice of localities might develop during the study.

Again, to define and rethink the sites requires creativity (e.g., Marcus, 1998). *Interdisciplinary* research can be expected to contribute to this, in that new perspectives, theories and methods are made visible. Johansson (2004) discusses how creativity and innovations can be found in intersections across disciplines. Also multi-sited research can challenge disciplinary perspectives (Marcus, 1998).

The extent to which the localities are *comparable* varies. Not all sites are uniform and they require different practices and opportunities (Marcus, 1998). Comparisons not previously thought about come to mind. They develop throughout movement and discovery among sites rather than being predetermined (ibid.). The effects of simultaneity can be exemplified by looking at the action happening in different locales as a consequence of an event such as a scandal (ibid.).

Hannerz's (2001) term, 'translocale', emphasizes the importance of identifying the *relationships between the localities*. It is important for the researcher to think about relationships, associations and connections before, but also during, the fieldwork.

A crucial component in multi-sited research is translation from one cultural idiom or language to another. This concerns all interpretive research, but is in particular significant in multi-sited research. Marcus (1998, p. 84) writes: 'This function is enhanced since it is no longer practiced in the primary, dualistic "them–us" frame of conventional ethnography but requires considerably more nuancing and shading as the practice of translation connects the several sites that the research explores along unexpected and even dissonant fractures of social location.' Translation has also been applied by Latour (e.g., 1986) and Czarniawska (2001). The process of translation may help us to understand change better in that it considers watching, for example, ideas, objects and humans travel. It is not about reception, rejection, resistance or acceptance; rather it is about on-going interpretations and relationships (Czarniawska, 2001). The process of translation is applied by Peñaloza (1994) when describing Mexican immigrants' consumer acculturation process, in other words, their use of cultural signs and heuristics from the previous system in the new system.

Literal language learning is as important in multi-sited ethnography as in single-sited ethnography, and it may explain why multi-sited fieldwork has been developed in monolingual, primarily Anglo-American contexts (Marcus, 1998).

Participant observation has always been a significant part of anthropology. Gusterson (1997) has emphasized that it is important to consider the character of polymorphous engagements in contemporary fieldwork rather than participant-observation fetishism. Hannerz (2001) mentions that several of the studies in his anthology on translocale field studies include more interviews and fewer observations than is common in traditional anthropology. He gives several explanations. First, there might be less time to spend in observation for the multilocale fieldworker. Second, texts and media are a large part of many contemporary field studies. Hannerz (2001) emphasizes that, even if studies of today have less participant observation, they may have many other types of materials, which was not possible long ago. This does, however, demand new skills in composition and synthesis. Also media play an important role in keeping the translocale fields together, by making them translocale instead of merely multilocale.

Reflexivity is an important aspect in multi-sited research (e.g., Marcus, 1998): 'The identity of anyone or any group is produced simultaneously in many different locales of activity by many different agents for many different purposes' (ibid., p. 62). The identity of the ethnographer requires negotiation across sites. Because ethnography is about being in the field as well as writing up the fieldwork, it is important to consider reflexivity for both parts.

Multi-sited research can also allow new ways of conducting research, such as new methods and media, but also bringing in a multiplicity of voices. Arnould and Price (1993), Joy and Sherry (2003) and Peñaloza (2001) have previously used multivocal techniques in consumer research. Voices can imply not only the researcher and the informants, but also the things studied. Material culture studies (e.g., Miller, 1987) will allow for things to make their voices heard. The separation between humans and nonhumans has been criticized by Latour (1993, 1998), who means that people and things, nature and culture should be studied in relationships.

Also a researcher's previous experience can affect how research is conducted, something which concerns all types of ethnographic research. However, access to the field may be easier if one has previous experience. For example, Huss (2001) probably benefited from his background as a music producer when he conducted field studies of reggae music.

Although ethnography in general requires immersion in the field, in multi-sited research it is necessary to be able to immerse in different contexts and relations, both in and across sites. Furthermore the above discussion of balance considering emic and etic is important to consider here. Multi-sited research will allow the researcher to develop a better understanding of cultural phenomena.

4 Conclusions and challenges ahead
Multi-sited, multilocal and translocal ethnography have brought new ideas into the field of ethnography and the discipline of anthropology. It is developing the way to conduct fieldwork and to write ethnography. Multi-sited ethnographic research is useful for studying global markets as well as for focusing on local markets. It can be seen as a way to understand micro–macro relationships. Rather than viewing consumers and marketers as binary opposites, multi-sited research allows for them to be seen as interdependent and for researchers to develop an understanding of cultural formation. Multi-sited research can contribute to making consumers, producers, marketers, consumer advocates and different authorities aware of their different experiences and relationships. There is a need

to develop multi-sited ethnographic research in marketing in order to understand the circulation of meanings, objects and identities in today's society. There is also a need to develop multi-sited locale research, since seemingly local and bounded phenomena are created and performed in a multi-sited field.

A major challenge involved in using multi-sited ethnography is the time and embedded cultural knowledge it requires. Apart from doing multi-sited research individually, it is possible to construct teams performing multi-sited research that supplements each other's knowledge and provides access to different sites. If this is a chosen alternative, it is important to recognize different degrees of cooperation among researchers within as well as across disciplines. This opens opportunities for multidisciplinary research (working together in parallel), interdisciplinary research (working closer together with a higher integration) and transdisciplinary research (also borrowing theories and methods from each other). Regardless of the choice made, multi-sited research is a promising way to explore new fields and phenomena in marketing.

Note
1. The author wishes to thank the Bank of Sweden Tercentenary Foundation for support of this research project.

References

Appadurai, Arjun (1986), 'Introduction: commodities and the politics of value', in Arjun Appadurai (ed.), *The Social Life of Things, Commodities in Cultural Perspective*, Cambridge: Cambridge University Press.
Appadurai, Arjun (1996), *Modernity at Large*, Minneapolis: University of Minnesota Press.
Arnould, Eric J. (1998), 'Daring consumer-oriented ethnography', in Barbara B. Stern (ed.), *Representing Consumers*, London and New York: Routledge, pp. 85–126.
Arnould, Eric J. and Linda L. Price (1993), 'River magic: extraordinary experience and the extended service encounter', *Journal of Consumer Research*, **20** (1), 24–45.
Arnould, Eric J. and Melanie Wallendorf (1994), 'Market-oriented ethnography: interpretation building and marketing strategy formulation', *Journal of Marketing Research*, **31** (4) (November), 484–504.
Atkinson, Paul and Martyn Hammersley (1994), 'Ethnography and participant observation', in Norman K. Denzin and Yvonna S. Lincoln (eds), *Handbook of Qualitative Research*, Thousand Oaks, CA: Sage.
Belk, Russell W. and Janeen Arnold Costa (1998), 'The mountain man myth: a contemporary consuming fantasy', *Journal of Consumer Research*, **25** (December), 218–40.
Belk, Russell W., Güliz Ger and Sören Askegaard (2003), 'The fire of desire: a multisited inquiry into consumer passion', *Journal of Consumer Research*, **30** (December), 326–51.
Brembeck, Helene, MarieAnne Karlsson, Eva Ossianson, Helena Shanahan, Lena Jonsson and Kerstin Bergström (2005), 'Vin, växthus och vänskap' (Wine, Greenhouses and Friendship), Center for Consumer Science, School of Business, Economics and Law, Report 2005:04.
Canniford, Robin (2005), 'Moving shadows: suggestions for ethnography in globalised cultures', *Qualitative Market Research: An International Journal*, **8** (2), 204–18.
Clifford, James (1997), 'Spatial practices: fieldwork, travel and the disciplining of anthropology', in Akhil Gupta and James Ferguson (eds), *Anthropological Locations, Boundaries and Grounds of a Field Science*, Berkeley, Los Angeles and London: University of California Press, pp. 185–222.
Clifford, James and George E. Marcus (eds) (1986), *Writing Culture, The Poetics and Politics of Ethnography*, Berkeley, Los Angeles and London: University of California Press.
Curasi, Carolyn Folkman, Linda L. Price and Eric J. Arnould (2004), 'How individuals' cherished possessions become families' inalienable wealth', *Journal of Consumer Research*, **31** (December), 609–22.
Czarniawska, Barbara (1998), 'A narrative approach to organization studies', *Qualitative Research Methods*, vol. 43, Thousand Oaks, London and New Delhi: Sage Publications.
Czarniawska, Barbara (2001), 'Anthropology and organizational learning', in Meinolf Direkes, Ariane Berthain Antal, John Child and Ikuijra Naraka (eds), *Handbook of Organizational Learning and Knowledge*, Oxford: Oxford University Press.
Czarniawska, Barbara (2004a), 'The uses of narrative in social science research', in Melissa Hardy and Alan Bryman (eds), *Handbook of Data Analysis*, London: Sage Publications Ltd.

Czarniawska, Barbara (2004b), 'On time, space, and action nets', *Organization*, **11** (6), 773–91.

Denzin, Norman K. (1989), 'Interpretive interactionism', *Applied Social Research Method Series*, vol. 16, Newbury Park, CA: Sage Publications.

Denzin, Norman K. (1997), *Interpretive Ethnography, Ethnographic Practices for the 21st Century*, Thousand Oaks, London and New Delhi: Sage.

Denzin, Norman K. (2001), 'Reflections and reviews – the seventh moment: qualitative inquiry and the practices of a more radical consumer research', *Journal of Consumer Research*, **28** (September), 324–30.

Dwyer, Kevin (1982), *Morroccan Dialogues: Anthropology in Question*, Baltimore: Johns Hopkins University Press.

Emerson, Robert M., Rachel I. Fretz and Linda L. Shaw (1995), *Writing Ethnographic Fieldnotes*, Chicago: University of Chicago Press.

Fischer, Michael M.J. (1999), 'Emergent forms of life: anthropologies of late or postmodernities', *Annual Review of Anthropology*, **28**, 455–78.

Garbarino, Merwyn S. (1983), *Sociocultural Theory in Anthropology*, Prospect Heights, IL: Waveland Press Inc.

Garsten, Christina (1994), *Apple World*, Stockholm Studies in Social Anthropology 33, Stockholm: Almqvist and Wiksell International.

Garsten, Christina (2001), 'Bland "äpplen" och "änglar" i translokala organisationer' (Among 'apples' and 'angles' in translocale organizations), in Ulf Hannerz (ed.), *Flera fält i ett, socialantropologer om translokala fältstudier* (Several Fields in One, social anthropologists about translocale field studies), Stockholm: Carlssons.

Geertz, Clifford (1973), *The Interpretation of Cultures, Selected Essays*, New York: Basic Books Inc.

Giddens, Anthony (1991), *Modernity and Self-Identity; Self and Society in the Late Modern Age*, Cambridge: Polity Press.

Goulding, Christina (2005), 'Grounded theory, ethnography and phenomenology, a comparative analysis of three qualitative strategies for marketing research', *European Journal of Marketing*, **39** (3/4), 294–308.

Grewal, Inderpal and Caren Kaplan (eds) (1994), *Scattered Hegemonies: Postmodernity and Transnational Feminist Practices*, Minneapolis: University of Minnesota Press.

Gupta, Akhil and James Ferguson (1997), 'Discipline and practice: "the field" as site, method and location in anthropology', in Akhil Gupta and James Ferguson (eds), *Anthropological Locations, Boundaries and Grounds of a Field Science*, Berkeley: University of California Press.

Gusterson, Hugh (1997), 'Studying up revisited', *Political and Legal Anthropology Review*, **20** (1), 114–19.

Hallbert, Britt-Marie (2003), *Linné och hans resor* (Linné and his travels), Stockholm: LL-förlag.

Hammersley, Martyn (1991), *Reading Ethnographic Research: A Critical Guide*, London: Longman.

Hammersley, Martyn (1993), 'The rhetorical turn in ethnography', *Social Science Information*, **32** (1), 23–37.

Hammersley, Martyn and Paul Atkinson (1995), *Ethnography, Principles in Practice*, 2nd edn, London and New York: Routledge.

Hannerz, Ulf (1996), *Transnational Connections*, London: Routledge.

Hannerz, Ulf (2001), *Flera fält i ett, socialantropologer om translokala fältstudier* (Several Fields in One, social anthropologists about translocale field studies), Stockholm: Carlssons.

Haraway, Donna (1991), *Simians, Cyborgs, and Women: The Reinvention of Nature*, New York: Routledge.

Hardtmann, Eva-Maria (2001), 'Motståndsrörelse mot kastväsendet: glimtar från Indien och England', (Resistance movement against the caste system: glimpses from India and England), in Ulf Hannerz (ed.), *Flera fält i ett, socialantropologer om translokala fältstudier* (Several Fields in One, social anthropologists about translocale field studies), Stockholm: Carlssons.

Huss, Hasse (2001), 'I reggaens kvarter: på jakt efter ett fält' (In the quarter of reggae: hunting for a field), in Ulf Hannerz (ed.), *Flera fält i ett, socialantropologer om translokala fältstudier* (Several Fields in One, social anthropologists about translocale field studies), Stockholm: Carlssons.

Johansson, Frans (2004), *The Medici effect: Breakthrough Insights at the Intersection of Ideas, Concepts, and Cultures*, Cambridge, MA: Harvard Business School Press.

Joy, Annamma and John F. Sherry (2003), 'Speaking of art as embodied imagination: a multisensory approach to understanding aesthetic experience', *Journal of Consumer Research*, **30** (2), 259–83.

Kozinets, Robert V. (2001), 'Utopian enterprise: articulating the meanings of Star Trek's culture of consumption', *Journal of Consumer Research*, **28** (June), 67–88.

Latour, Bruno (1986), 'The powers of association', in J. Law (ed.), *Power, Action and Belief*, London: Routledge and Kegan Paul, pp. 264–80.

Latour, Bruno (1993), *We Have Never Been Modern*, Hemel Hempstead, Hertfordshire: Harvester Wheatsheaf and the President and Fellows of Harvard College.

Latour, Bruno (1998), *Artefaktens återkomst; Ett möte mellan organisationsteori och tingens sociologi* (The return of the artifact; a meeting between organisational theory and the sociology of things), Stockholm: Nerenius och Santérus förlag.

Malinowski, Bronislaw (1922), *Argonauts of the Western Pacific*, London: Routledge and Kegan Paul.

Marcus, George E. (1986), 'Contemporary problems of ethnography in the modern world system', in James Clifford and George E. Marcus (eds), *Writing Culture, The Poetics and Politics of Ethnography*, Berkeley, Los Angeles and London: University of California Press.

Marcus, George E. (1989), 'Imagining the whole: ethnography's contemporary efforts to situate itself', *Critical Anthropology*, **9**, 7–30.

Marcus, George E. (1995), 'Ethnography in/of the world system: the emergence of multi-sited ethnography', *Annual Review of Anthropology*, **24**, 95–117.

Marcus, George E. (1998), *Ethnography through Thick and Thin*, Princeton, NJ: Princeton University Press.

Martin, Emily (1994), *Flexible Bodies: Tracing Immunity in American Culture from the Days of Polio to the Age of AIDS*, Boston: Beacon.

Miller, Daniel (1987), *Material Culture and Mass Consumption*, Oxford: Basil Blackwell.

Murray, Jeff B. (2005), 'Understanding existential-phenomenology as method, in consumer research', unpublished lecture notes presented at the Center for Consumer Science, School of Business, Economics and Law at Gothenburg University, Sweden.

Peñaloza, Lisa (1994), 'Atravesando Fronteras/border crossings: a critical ethnographic exploration of the consumer acculturation of Mexican immigrants', *Journal of Consumer Research*, **21** (June), 32–54.

Peñaloza, Lisa (2001), 'Consuming the West: animating cultural meaning and memory at a stock show and rodeo', *Journal of Consumer Research*, **28** (3), 369–98.

Rabinow, Paul (1977), *Reflections on Fieldwork in Morocco*, Berkeley and Los Angeles: University of California Press.

Sanjek, Roger (1990), 'A vocabulary for fieldnotes', in Roger Sanjek (ed.), *Fieldnotes, the Makings of Anthropology*, Ithaca and London: Cornell University Press.

Schouten, John and John H. McAlexander (1995), 'Ethnography of the new bikers', *Journal of Consumer Research*, **22** (1), 43–61.

Strathern, Marilyn (1991), *Partial Connections*, Lanham: Rowan and Littlefield.

Thompson, Craig J. and Zeynep Arsel (2004), 'The Starbucks brandscape and consumers' (anticorporate) experiences of glocalization', *Journal of Consumer Research*, **31**, 631–42.

Tyler, Stephen A. (1986), 'Post-modern ethnography: from document of the occult to occult document', in J. Clifford and G.E. Marcus (eds), *Writing Culture: The Poetics and Politics of Ethnography*, Berkeley: University of California Press, pp. 122–40.

Van Maanen, John (1988), *Tales of the Field, On Writing Ethnography*, Chicago and London: University of Chicago Press.

38 Doing research on sensitive topics: studying covered Turkish women
Güliz Ger and Özlem Sandikci

Scholars studying sensitive topics encounter various challenges at different stages of the research. Although any topic can be perceived as sensitive, areas where the potential of physical and/or emotional threat to the researcher and the researched is substantial are generally regarded as highly sensitive. These include, for example, studies on terminal illnesses, death and dying (e.g., Alty and Rodham, 1998; Cannon, 1989; Johnson and Plant, 1996), deviant and criminal behavior (Bergen, 1993; Braithwaite, 1985; Herzberger, 1993) and political and interest groups (Brewer, 1990; Hoffman, 1980; Punch, 1989). Despite the fact that many of the topics that are addressed by the marketing scholars, such as the homeless (Hill and Stamey, 1990; Hill, 1991), aids (Raghubir and Menon, 1998), breast cancer (Pavia and Mason, 2004) and subcultures (Schouten and McAlexander, 1995; Kates, 2004) are all potentially sensitive, there is little guidance on how to conduct research on sensitive topics (Hill, 1995).

The purpose of this chapter is to discuss potential dilemmas that marketing researchers might encounter while studying sensitive topics and to present possible solutions. However we should stress that our discussion draws from our personal experiences and does not claim to encompass all possible complexities experienced during different phases of research. Specifically, we talk about the problems we faced while we were studying the consumption practices of covered women in Turkey. We believe that the study of covered women provides a good case to trace how methodological, ethical and political problems are interrelated and emerge unexpectedly at various stages of inquiry. Given the intricate and unpredictable nature of the research process, we prefer to present a self-reflective, critical and contextualized narrative of our fieldwork rather than a totalizing check-list of what to do and what not to do. In line with the spirit of critical and feminist ethnographies, our account seeks to emphasize the conditional nature of scientific investigation, the validity of personal experiences as a method of inquiry, the power dynamics influencing the research process and the importance of the subjectivities of both the researcher and the researched (Clifford and Markus, 1986; Marcus and Fischer, 1986; Nielsen, 1990; Roberts, 1981).

Studying covered Turkish women
We have been studying the Islamist[1] consumptionscape in Turkey since 2000. Our project involved researching various domains of daily life, such as fashion, leisure, home decoration and entertainment in which differences between secularist and Islamist consumption styles are particularly visible. By exploring diverse practices and meanings, we sought to portray the plurality, hybridity and tensions which characterize the Islamist consumptionscape and advance our understanding of how individuals negotiate modernity and tradition through their consumption practices (for a detailed discussion, see Sandikci and

Ger, 2001, 2002, 2005). Our study has been an ethnographic inquiry with multiple sources of data and multiple methods of investigation. Over a period of five years, we conducted in-depth interviews with covered and uncovered women, interviewed owners and personnel of Islamist-style clothing stores, attended several Islamist fashion shows, carried out fieldwork at an Islamist summer resort, undertook observations at various sites such as shopping centers, mosques and women's associations, took pictures whenever we were allowed to, and compiled an archive that consisted of news articles, advertisements and company catalogues.

Although the population we are studying consists of men and women from different socioeconomic backgrounds, we are interested mainly in the middle/upper-middle, educated urban women who define and defend their decision to cover as a personal choice. There are a number of reasons for such a focus. First of all, one of the most prominent signs of the Islamist identity and consumption culture is the female headscarf. Beginning in the mid-1980s, a new style of head covering, *türban* as it is referred to in Turkish, emerged in the cities. The *türban* is adopted by urban, educated and relatively well-off young women, who wanted to set themselves apart from rural women who are covered out of tradition. Observing the increasing demand for headscarves and accompanying religiously appropriate garments, several companies catering to the urban women emerged. Soon, religiously appropriate dressing became a lucrative business field with several companies operating in the sector. The 1980s also witnessed the emergence of an Islamist bourgeoisie who developed a taste for conspicuous consumption. Hotels and summer resorts, hypermarkets and gated communities catering to the conservative clientele developed in different parts of Turkey. In almost all sectors of the economy Islamist companies competing head-on with their secular counterparts flourished.

Researching the Islamist consumption culture has been very rewarding and challenging. It has been rewarding because it exemplified a consumptionscape in which aesthetics and politics, modernity and tradition are continuously confronted and negotiated. What we found compelled us to question our own assumptions and re-evaluate existing theories. The study offered a rich case through which to rethink our understanding of the linkages between modernity, postmodernity, globalization and consumption in non-Western societies. The challenges, on the other hand, have been equally compelling. For us, two secular Turkish women, to research covered women in Turkey was an adventure. We faced numerous challenges at different stages of the research: some expected, some not. Researching the Islamists is a sensitive topic, not because of the private and sacred nature of religious practices but, on the contrary, because of their very public and political nature. Turkey has a secular legal system and covering is banned in public spaces and institutions including universities, hospitals and courts. While many rural and elderly women are covered in what is regarded as the 'traditional' style, the urban *türban* is perceived as the symbol of political Islam. For many, the *türban* represents a threat to the secular Republic and should be confined to the private realm. Images of covered students demonstrating in front of the universities, where they are not allowed access, frequently appear in both secular and Islamist media, aggravating the issue even further. Whenever there is an attempt to lift the ban, there is instant political turmoil in the country. Given the intense polarization of views between the secularists[2] and the Islamists, and the symbolism of *türban* and other forms of Islamist consumption practices, the topic is highly political and controversial. Furthermore, for those who study Islamists, there is a significant threat of being categorized as a sympathizer with political Islam by colleagues, the media and the general public. In the following pages, we discuss some of the method-ological problems that we and other researchers have encountered while conducting research on sensitive topics, and also point to some solutions.

Researching a sensitive topic
Renzetti and Lee (1993) define a sensitive topic as 'one that potentially poses for those involved a substantial threat, the emergence of which renders problematic for the researcher and/or the researched the collection, holding and/or dissemination of research data' (p. 5). They argue that the sensitive character of a particular piece of research lies less in the topic itself but rather in the relationship between the topic and the social context in which the research is conducted. From this perspective, any topic can become sensitive, depending on the social milieu. Nonetheless the authors suggest that certain areas of research have a higher probability of being perceived as threatening and contro-versial than others. These areas include research that delves deeply into the private and stressful experiences of people; explores deviant and illegal activities; exposes political alignments and the vested interests of powerful persons; and deals with sacred and reli-gious matters (Lee, 1993; Renzetti and Lee, 1993).

Sensitivity can introduce different issues at different stages of the research process. The problems can be methodological, ethical, political or legal, and can arise during the design and implementation phases or during the dissemination of the findings (Brewer, 1990; Seigel and Bauman, 1986; Sieber and Stanley, 1988). Adequate conceptualization of a particular topic, or finding informants who are willing to talk, can be difficult. Studying sensitive topics can be threatening to both the researched and the researcher; even the per-sonal security of the researcher may be jeopardized. Trust often becomes difficult to main-tain, especially when the research is perceived as threatening, and the relationship between the informant and the researcher can easily turn into one of concealment and deception. The fieldworker can even be perceived to be a spy (Warren, 1988). Nonetheless research on sensitive topics 'addresses some of the society's most pressing social issues and policy questions' (Sieber and Stanley, 1988, p. 55), potentially throws light on taboos and the darker corners of society, and challenges taken-for-granted ways of seeing the world.

Duelli Klein (1983) points out that 'the "what" to investigate must come prior to the decision of "how" to go about doing one's research' (p. 38). However, in many respects sensitivity can constrain what is studied. For example, powerful gatekeepers includ-ing funding agencies, universities and research institutions, and sometimes politicians, can impose restrictions on researchers (Broadhead and Rist, 1976; Moore, 1973). Furthermore asking questions about a particular social issue can have major social impli-cations even if the research is never performed (Sieber and Stanley, 1988). How an inquiry is framed shapes the nature and direction of attention and, in some cases, may mislead-ingly affect conceptions of significant social issues. The framing of the research questions may also carry the risk of classifying the researcher as an accomplice or an apologist, in the minds of informants, colleagues or the public. Consider, for instance, the case of covered women. While there is a vast amount of literature on veiled women and women in Islam, this field of inquiry tends to focus on why women choose to cover themselves, and whether covering is emancipative or restrictive. While there are exceptions, many studies do favor one or the other, and become classified as sympathetic or antipathetic towards covering and, by extension, Islam. In our own research, we shifted the question from why to how, and sought to understand how women who choose to cover of their own free will adorn themselves. Our interest was in the aesthetic and material aspects of the headscarf and other garments, and of consumption in general, yet, our colleagues, friends and the media kept questioning us about our position on the politics of Islam and whether we were Islamists or secularists; our informants had a similar mentality too. Despite our emphasis on the aesthetics and material culture, informants frequently drifted into discussing the politics of the headscarf ban and other issues during the interviews, and we were often required to clarify our position on the politics of the headscarf. However clarifying our position as an 'objective researcher' has been particularly challenging as we had our own identity politics, and 'objectivity', as it always has been, was rather illusionary and flimsy.

Researcher's position
A major challenge was posed by our subjective positions. When we began the study, we engaged in lengthy discussions about our position as researchers, our biases and preconceived notions. While we were striving to be 'neutral' researchers and respect the way of life of our informants, we could not help but feel distaste towards the women we were to talk to, observe and understand. They were 'them' and surely different from 'us'? No matter how much we tried to empathize and see them as 'normal,' deep down, we could not. It was an enigma for us why modern urban educated women would choose to cover out of their own volition.

We employed a variety of interpretive methods to capture the diverse aspects of the lives and the milieu of the covered women. We observed women in public spaces such as the streets and shopping malls, at fashion shows, political party headquarters and in women's clubs, in the urban environments of Ankara and Istanbul, as well as at seaside vacation resorts. We spent an extended weekend at a popular summer resort for families of covered women. We swam in the all-female pool and eavesdropped on the conversations around us. We joined in their conversations about computers, sports and dieting. Yet we felt most comfortable when we were on the balcony of our room, watching them promenade below, at a distance. After we left the hotel and were waiting for our bus, we looked at each other and realized that we both desperately wanted the same thing: a drink. No alcoholic beverages were served at the resort and, while in our daily lives neither of us drink on a daily basis, and we sometimes go without a drink for a week or longer, those few days without a drink were different. We truly enjoyed that glass of cheap wine and we enjoyed being away from that environment that had not felt comfortable, even though the word we heard most often from the covered women when they talked about the resort was that it was a very comfortable place.

Similar feelings of discomfort existed during the fashion shows we attended and the interviews we conducted with retail shop owners and designers. We felt that they were being distant but perhaps we were being distant too. Interviews with women at their homes were more 'comfortable', maybe because they were uncovered at home. These interviews lasted between two and four hours and were accompanied by tea and cookies.

Furthermore, while not many, a few of our informants attempted to engage us in discussions about religion per se, the virtues of Islam and being a believer, and accused us of not practicing our religion. While we wanted to be unattached researchers, they wanted to be missionaries. While we wanted to be participant observers at significant female gatherings such as book readings, theological discussion meetings and social meetings at clubs, we faced the awkward situation of being drawn into the position of being potential recruits. Hence we could not do the immersion or the prolonged engagement in the field that are typically the preferred ways of being in the (ethnographer's) field. Nor could we be participant observers in meetings and gatherings that had a religious significance for these women.

What did we learn? One can still obtain rich data despite not being able to be a fully-fledged participant observer and not being able to attain prolonged engagement with the same group of people. But this can only be achieved by spending a longer period of time in the field, talking to larger numbers of people, and observing a broader range of places and social contexts. Our study took more than four years to complete and entailed talking to over 60 informants in different contexts until we felt confident about what we learned. We also found that interviewing some of the informants as a team, especially in the earlier stages of the fieldwork, was very fruitful: while one of us focused on the interview, the other focused on the observations of the home as well as the nonverbal communication of the informant, that is, paralinguistics, chronemics and kinesics. Team interviewing not only improved our observations but also made us feel more comfortable in the informant's territory. Finally we each read and interpreted each transcription independently and then iterated our interpretations. Hence we could check and question each other's lenses.

Finding informants who will talk and gaining their trust
We anticipated that access and negotiating the research relationship would be difficult. The way we look, that is, uncovered, placed us in a box in the minds of the covered women, just as they were in a box in our minds when we began the study. Given the political context and that we are professors at an institution, the university, where headscarves are banned, it was a major challenge to gain their trust. We knew that we would have to be ready to answer all sorts of questions and repel all sorts of suspicions. We could have been taken (and sometimes were) for journalists, or as spies working for secularist feminist organizations, or as political party members, or more commonly, just as the 'Other'. so we had to give a detailed account of who we were and why we were interested in their clothing and consumption practices. We assured them of confidentiality and anonymity, and offered them copies of their interview transcripts and the paper when it is written, which they could edit if they wished. This worked sometimes but not always.

However, before dealing with the problems of gaining access, we needed to deal with the basics: deciding who should be included in our study. There are well-developed methods and strategies for selecting respondents who are representative of the population under study or who are relevant for theoretical purposes. Sampling, however, becomes more difficult when the topic under investigation is sensitive. As Lee (1993) argues, when an issue is perceived as sensitive people tend to conceal their identities and activities; thus obtaining sample elements becomes both more difficult and costly. Furthermore, since the selection of informants and research sites is informed by theoretical purposes and expectations, sampling always requires a sound theoretical framework to begin with. In the case of researching sensitive topics, theoretical reflection and available knowledge can be limited (Lee, 1993), and complex patterns of social organization 'may not be obvious to the researcher *before* the research has begun' (p. 61, emphasis in original).

At the beginning, because their *türban* was more noticeable and prominent than anything else, covered women appeared to us to be a homogeneous group of people. The only available distinction mentioned in the literature was that between peasant women wearing *başörtüsü* (headscarf) out of habit and urban women wearing *türban* out of political motivation. This, of course, amounted to millions of women who looked alike but turned out to be, as any group, much more heterogeneous. There were further complexities to be resolved. In addition to the women who wore *türban* there were also a small number of covered women who wore the black chador, a loose garment that covers the body from head to toe. Should we include them in our research as well, or were they too marginal and distant from our middle-class focus? Black chador wearers are typically associated with *tarikats* (religious sects) which are regarded as highly radical and secretive. Gaining access would be extremely difficult, and potentially, dangerous. On the other hand *türban* wearers are associated more with the Islamist political party members and the middle class. We decided to focus on them, and get access to urban middle-class covered women. Below is the path to research (Sanjek, 1990) which we took.

We started out with a key informant who was the wife of an academic colleague. Our colleague was active in the Islamist party and, soon after, become a member of parliament and quit his job at the university. His spouse is a computer scientist with an MS degree. She comes from a family of uncovered women and she herself used to wear shorts when she was a young adult. We visited her at her home where she was wearing tight jeans and a t-shirt and had her long hair down, uncovered. She was already familiar with some of the research of one of the co-authors. After we explained to her what we were interested in she was very forthright and we had a pleasant conversation about clothes, fashion and consumption in general. She talked at length about different styles and patterns prevalent among different social groups and alerted us to the differences among university students, middle-class professional women, the wealthy and the newly rich. She was willing to introduce us to her female covered colleagues at work, so we succeeded in finding our first six informants, who in turn led us to other informants in their social milieu.

However things got more difficult after that. For example, how were we to find informants from among the wealthy and the newly rich? How were we to find students who would talk to us? In instances when those being studied are members of vulnerable, stigmatized or deviant groups or are difficult of access, snowball sampling proves to be useful, and 'it often represents the only way of gathering a sample' (Lee, 1993, p. 66). In snowball sampling the key informant initiates the links of the referral chain. While bias is almost inevitable in snowball samples, the issue of trust is better handled. As 'the intermediaries who form the links of the referral chain are known to potential respondents and trusted by them' they are 'able to vouch for the researcher's *bona fides*' (ibid., p. 67). Biernacki and Waldorf (1981) suggest that researchers pace and monitor chains of referral in order to maximize sample variability and the theoretical utility of snowball sampling. As they point out, while at the beginning the aim is simply to make sufficient contacts to get the project started, in the later stages, a variety of starting points needs to be utilized in order to ensure extensive coverage of the population. Eventually, certain referral chains may be developed in preference to others because they help in illuminating and developing theoretical formulations.

In the next phase of informant search, we sought to interview university students. Lacking a key informant who would refer us to others, we tried to contact covered students at our university on our own. When we explained our research, we were politely refused or stood up. Disillusioned and disappointed, we asked our doctoral students to interview any covered women (university graduate or student, urban and covered by choice) they knew personally or could access via their friends, in order to throw a wider net for snowballing. We were able to get some informants but not many. Even when we were able to do an interview with a covered student, she would be anxious and very reserved. By that time, we had realized that it was important for us to interview students because it is during the university years that these women get involved in religious organizations, their convictions become stronger and they eventually decide to cover. So theirs would be a perspective different from the women who have been already settled into covering. However we had also discovered that both our doctoral students and we ourselves had an extremely difficult time finding university students who would talk to us in an open, sincere manner and without fear or anxiety.

Depth interviewing and participant observation, which rely on sustained or intensive interactions with those studied, appear to be ideal methods for building trusting relationships between the researcher and the researched. Yet, as Renzetti and Lee (1993) point out, 'the establishment of trustful relations is never easy', and '[i]n many situations, researchers face hostility and sometimes danger' (p. 101). In the case of sensitive topics, it is common for informants to treat the researcher with skepticism and provide only superficial answers. Several researchers have also noticed that exploration of sensitive information could lead some informants to lie (Bleek, 1987; Nachman, 1984). To minimize this problem, it is suggested that one engages in prolonged interactions with informants, observes them in their daily life, raises related issues after a while, and uses different sources to check the accuracy of the information (Shahidian, 2001). In our case, the difficulty we encountered was not informants who lied but informants who would not talk to us. Ultimately it was luck that got us out of this loop.

Through our contacts in other universities, we managed to locate a recent sociology graduate who was covered and looking for a job. We had a meeting and discussed at length and very openly with her what we were doing and why we needed her help. As she related the topic to the readings she had done, she became excited and was willing to help us until she found a job. She did about 20 interviews for us, all with university students. We worked closely with her, training her and sensitizing her to the theoretical concepts we were interested in, especially before and after her first interview, after the third interview and when she had completed all the interviews. She herself became a second key informant.

If it were not for these two key informants who trusted us, one of whom introduced us to her friends who in turn became our informants, and the second who actually conducted 20 interviews herself, we could not have completed the fieldwork. We were also able to reach several wealthy informants and feminists, again thanks to the spouse of the first informant acting as an intermediary. These two informants made us aware of the popular stores, seaside resorts and other spaces that covered women frequent as well as the fashionable brands of headscarves.

We also interviewed sales clerks and owners of stores that sell headscarves and clothing appropriate for covered women, interviewed designers and formed an archive of virtual, visual and textual material from the media and advertising. We learned about the popular books and magazines covered women read and the television channels they watch, the more intellectual/scholarly journals their role models read and write in. We read those books, magazines and journals, and watched those programs ourselves. While these were not among the challenges of our research, the familiarity we were able to gain through these means about their social, political, cultural and ideological milieu and interests helped us deal with the challenging moments of the fieldwork. When we could refer to a popular Islamist novel or a television show during the interview, a smile often appeared on the informant's face, and we became less the 'Other'.

Hence finding even two souls who trust the researcher and who are willing to help because they find the topic intriguing makes the fieldwork possible, even in topics that are difficult to research, even when most people are unwilling to talk. What is invaluable is also the media: newspapers, books, advertising, television and magazines, as well as the websites and Internet discussion groups that sensitize the researcher to the mindset of the informants and the discourses that surround them.

Struggling with ethical issues

Ethical issues such as harm, consent, privacy, anonymity and confidentiality (Berg, 2004; Fetterman, 1998; Lofland and Lofland, 1995; Silverman, 2005; Weiss, 1994) multiply and pose major dilemmas in investigating sensitive topics. Ethics provide the basis for conduct in any research (Punch, 1986) and 'research that harms or offends, or that appears to be conducted incompetently, invalidly, or without due regard for consequences, is likely to result in someone . . . questioning the prerogative of the scientist to conduct such research' (Sieber, 1993, p. 15). Perceptions of sensitivity and harm are highly subjective and it is likely that different groups perceive risks and benefits differently. Risks include the invasion of privacy, breach of confidentiality and embarrassment, whereas benefits can be in the form of information and services provided to the informants (Sieber, 1993). It is the responsibility of the researcher to make sure that participants fully understand what it means to participate in terms of risks and benefits; and that they are aware of their right not to participate or to withdraw from the research at any time. As Sieber points out, 'being ethical in the conduct of sensitive research also means being *culturally sensitive* in the way one designs the research and interacts with research participants, community members, gatekeepers, and relevant others' (p. 19, emphasis in original). This requires the researcher to be attentive to the life-styles of individuals being studied and respect their beliefs, habits, values and fears. Such considerations may make or break the research.

Even a basic requirement of doing any ethnography, the deep respect for people's way of life (Fetterman, 1998) can become very difficult in researching topics such as drug addiction or criminality, or even in consumption among Islamist women. As we discussed above, we constantly had to reflect upon our distaste and consciously attempt to empathize with our informants.

The simplest research tool, taking photographs, may become impossible for confidentiality and privacy purposes. We were confronted by ethical issues especially when we tried to acquire visual data. This was one research project where taking pictures or videotaping was next to impossible in most situations, except in the public spaces. Most of our informants did not want to be photographed, yet they allowed us to take pictures of their homes and their clothes on hangers. Whenever it was possible, we took pictures of women walking on the streets, sitting in cafes or strolling through shops. Even though we used these pictures only for investigative purposes and never made them public, we always felt somewhat intrusive and covert while shooting. As Lipson (1994) points out, asking for consent may alter the course of events at times when certain events unfold in their natural setting and, in such situations, it is better to continue collecting data while making observations rather than interrupting the flow of actions. Deciding on how to proceed and use information gathered in this manner depends ultimately on the researcher's own code of ethics. However, it appears that 'the best way to proceed is to obtain post hoc consent to use the information as data' (Corbin and Morse, 2003, p. 349).

The extended weekend at the five-star summer resort, Caprice Hotel, posed many ethical dilemmas. This is a summer resort designed for Islamist families, with separate swimming pools for men and women, separate discos and separate beaches. Tennis hours alternate to accommodate male and female tennis players. Caprice Hotel frequently appears in the Islamist and secularist media, drawing both praise and criticism from the former and criticism from the latter. All of our informants had heard of this resort, had clear favorable or unfavorable opinions about it, and some had actually been there.

We put headscarves in our luggage although we were keen not to wear them, as we did not want to engage in any deception. But we did not pack as we would normally do when going on our summer holidays: we carefully chose the loosest clothes and long-sleeved shirts. We did not know whether or not we would be allowed into the hotel without headscarves. We were also wondering if and when we should tell the hotel management that we were there for research; if we did not we could not interview the managers and hotel personnel; but, if we did, what if they wanted us out? We decided not to say anything upfront. With our hair exposed, we walked in timidly and approached the reception desk slowly, watching the reaction of the people in the lobby. We registered with no questions asked and felt better from that moment on.

We saw that there were a few other uncovered women whom we eventually realized to be relatives or friends of the family they were vacationing with. Although we were not the only uncovered women at the resort we definitely were in the minority. We checked in and spent a day at the resort without telling anyone that we were there for research. However other hotel guests and waiters kept asking us why we were there, some speculating that we were likely to be journalists or researchers. We answered that we were researchers, academics, spending the weekend there. On the second day we made appointments with the public relations manager and another manager and interviewed them at their offices. We also interviewed sales clerks of the clothing shop located in the hotel.

At the pool, where no one is covered, we were able to be less visible. Since most people were there with their sisters, cousins or mothers, they were sitting in groups and chatting – a great opportunity for eavesdropping. However we could not take any pictures at the pool: no cameras were allowed. In the gardens, restaurants and cafés, we saw great photo opportunities but could not take any pictures even though cameras were allowed: it would have been too disruptive, too rude, and inappropriate. However, there was a professional photographer, as in all resorts, who was shooting constantly. He displayed his photos on bulletin boards located next to the restaurant area and the display looked like a goldmine. We selected about 30 photos and ordered copies. That night, still unsure whether we would be allowed to purchase them, we approached the counter. The photographer was not present. We handed in the receipt to his assistant. The pictures were ready; we paid, got the envelope and headed off for dinner. Fifteen minutes or so later, while we were still at the restaurant, the photographer approached us. He was intrigued by the fact that we were not included in any of the photos which we had bought. He asked if we were journalists writing a piece about the resort. We disclosed our identities and assured him that the pictures would only be used for investigative purposes and would not to be published. Despite our assurance he stated that he could not sell the photos to us for ethical reasons and insisted on having them back. We handed over the pictures; he gave us a refund and he walked back to his studio. Puzzled, embarrassed and somewhat frightened that we would be asked to leave the hotel as well, we sat quietly at our table for a while. Somehow, we had lost our appetite. Nothing else happened. All the visual data we have from the resort is video footage from the balcony of our room – everything was taken at a distance.

Conclusion

Our aim in this chapter was to reflect on some of the particular problems which we have encountered when we, two secular (or uncovered) Turkish female academics, set out to study covered Turkish women. Even the choice of the word to describe ourselves in the preceding sentence, 'secular' or 'covered', became a point of discussion as 'secular' implies a more political stance than 'uncovered', yet it is associated with 'secularism', a dogmatic position which we do not identify with. What we discuss in this chapter is neither prescriptive nor prescribed but rather highly autobiographical. However our observations reiterate that doing research on sensitive topics involves many complexities, some of which are difficult to predict and often require a creative approach to resolve. In the initial phase of our research we wondered whether or not it would be at all possible to find informants who would talk to us Being Turkish and female did not help us much in terms of access as the 'us' versus 'them' distinction lingered in the minds of our informants as well as us. Trust, however difficult, was eventually established and with the help of our two key informants we managed to gather data.

When we conducted interviews ourselves we often felt that we were perceived as interested newcomers, spies or potential converts. We realized, in line with Johnson (1975), that access is not an initial phase of entry but a continuing process of negotiation and renegotiation. Whenever our informants attempted to indoctrinate us, we highlighted our positions as researchers, not as potential recruits, and tried to cultivate distance in the interaction. Yet the pressure was strong, and after such interviews we engaged in lengthy conversations with each other in order to try and handle the culture shock and reflect upon the impressions that each of us had gathered. When our informants were hesitant, thinking that we were spies of the media or a secularist political party, we reiterated our role as researchers and talked about this research and other research we do. Once again, doing research with a colleague helped in the constant process of negotiating the field.

In sum, the challenges we faced included finding informants willing to talk, collecting visual data, gaining trust, respecting the informants, dealing with the way the informants perceived us and our own subjective position, and not being able to do prolonged engagement and participant observation in some situations. These issues, which are at the junction of methodological, political and ethical concerns, intermingled and appeared at various stages of the research. The way we attempted to deal with the challenges and the dilemmas was by reflexivity, teamwork and constant negotiation and renegotiation.

Ethical issues are ubiquitous in sensitive research. While it is impossible to foresee all ethical problems, it is important that researchers consider possible concerns and plan their course of action. Otherwise breach of trust, embarrassment and eventually withdrawal of the informant is almost inevitable. As Ayella (1993) states, 'Field research highlights the researcher. Some researchers, like informants, are simply better able to establish rapport and to feel at ease in a new, let alone strange, setting' (p.. 112). We were not one of them, not in this fieldwork. Unlike the case in any other research we have done and any other new and strange field setting we have been in, in this case, we felt uncomfortable in all the settings where we conducted our research, less in some and more so in others. We encountered several ethical problems. At times, we felt most embarrassed, yet we learned a lot. We learned not only the dynamics of the Islamist consumptionscape in Turkey, not only the intricacies of doing research on sensitive topics, but also about ourselves as researchers, our own prejudices and biases.

Notes

1. We use the term 'Islamist' to refer to those who are politically religious, to distinguish it from secular Muslims who are believers without an affiliation to political Islam.
2. Secularists refer to both practicing and non-practicing Muslims and non-believers, some of whom are dogmatic in their view of secularism.

References

Alty, A. and K. Rodham (1998), 'The ouch! factor: problems in conducting sensitive research', *Qualitative Health Research*, **8**, 275–82.
Ayella, Marybeth (1993), ' "They must be crazy": some of the difficulties in researching "cults" ', in Claire M. Renzetti and Raymond M. Lee (eds), *Researching Sensitive Topics*, Newbury Park, CA: Sage, pp. 108–24.
Berg, Bruce L. (2004), *Qualitative Research Methods for the Social Sciences*, Boston, MA: Pearson.
Bergen, R.K. (1993), 'Interviewing survivors of marital rape: doing feminist research on sensitive topics', in Claire M. Renzetti and Raymond M. Lee (eds), *Researching Sensitive Topics*, Newbury Park, CA: Sage, pp. 197–211.
Biernacki, P. and D, Waldorf (1981), 'Snowball sampling: problems and techniques of chain referral sampling', *Sociological Methods and Research*, **10**, 141–63.
Bleek, W. (1987), 'Lying informants: fieldwork experiences from Ghana', *Population and Development Review*, **13**, 314–22.
Braithwaite, J. (1985), 'Corporate crime research: why two interviewers are needed', *Sociology*, **19**, 136–8.
Brewer, John D. (1990), 'Sensitivity as a problem in field research: a study of routine policing in Northern Ireland', *American Behavioral Scientist*, **33**, 578–93.
Broadhead, R.S. and R.C. Rist (1976), 'Gatekeepers and the social control of research', *Social Problems*, **23**, 325–36.
Cannon, S. (1989), 'Social research in stressful settings: difficulties for the sociologist studying the treatment of breast cancer', *Sociology of Health and Illness*, **11** (1), 66–77.
Clifford, J. and G.E. Marcus (1986), *Writing Culture: The Poetics and Politics of Ethnography*, Berkeley: University of California Press.
Corbin, Juliet and Janice M. Morse (2003), 'The unstructured interactive interview: issues of reciprocity and risks when dealing with sensitive topics', *Qualitative Inquiry*, **9** (3), 335–54.
Duelli Klein, R. (1983), 'How to do what we want to do: thoughts about feminist methodology', in G. Bowles and R. Duelli Klein (eds), *Theories of Women's Studies*, London: Routledge & Kegan Paul.
Fetterman, David M. (1998), *Ethnography*, Thousand Oaks, CA: Sage.
Herzberger, S.D. (1993), 'The cyclical pattern of child abuse: a study of research methodology', in Claire M. Renzetti and Raymond M. Lee (eds), *Researching Sensitive Topics*, Newbury Park, CA: Sage, pp. 33–51.
Hill, R.P. (1991), 'Homeless women, special possessions, and the meaning of "home": an ethnographic case study', *Journal of Consumer Research*, **18** (December), 298–310.
Hill, R.P. (1995), 'Researching sensitive topics in marketing: the special case of vulnerable populations', *Journal of Public Policy and Marketing*, **14** (1), 143–8.
Hill, R.P. and M. Stamey (1990), 'The homeless in America: an examination of possessions and consumption behaviors', *Journal of Consumer Research*, **17** (December), 303–21.
Hoffman, J.E. (1980), 'Problems of access in the study of social elites and boards of directors,' in William B. Shaffir, Robert A. Stebbins and Alan Turowetz (eds), *Fieldwork Experience: Qualitative Approaches to Social Research*, New York: St Martin's Press.
Johnson, B.M. and H. Plant (1996), 'Collecting data from people with cancer and their families', in L. De Raeve (ed.), *Nursing Research: An Ethical and Legal Appraisal*, London: Bailliere Tindall, pp. 85–100.

Johnson, J.M. (1975), *Doing Field Research*, New York: Free Press.
Kates, S.M. (2004), 'The dynamics of brand legitimacy: an interpretive study in the gay men's community', *Journal of Consumer Research*, **31** (September), 455–64.
Lee, Raymond M. (1993), *Doing Research on Sensitive Topics*, London: Sage.
Lipson, J.G. (1994), 'Ethical issues in ethnography', in Janice M. Morse (ed.), *Critical Issues in Qualitative Research Methods*, Thousand Oaks, CA: Sage, pp. 333–55.
Lofland, John and Lyn H. Lofland (1995), *Analyzing Social Settings*, Belmont, CA: Wadsworth Publishing.
Marcus, G.E. and M.M.J. Fischer (1986), *Anthropology as Cultural Critique: An Experimental Moment in Human Sciences*, Chicago: University of Chicago Press.
Moore, J. (1973), 'Social constraints on sociological knowledge: academics and research concerning minorities', *Social Problems*, **21**, 65–77.
Nachman, S.R. (1984), 'Lies my informants told me', *Journal of Anthropological Research*, **40**, 536–55.
Nielsen, J.M. (ed.) (1990), *Feminist Research Methods: Exemplary Readings in Social Sciences*, Boulder: Westview Press.
Pavia, T.M. and M.J. Mason (2004), 'The reflexive relationship between consumer behavior and adaptive coping', *Journal of Consumer Research*, **31** (September), 441–54.
Punch, M. (1986), 'The politics and ethics of fieldwork', *Qualitative Research Methods*, vol. 3, Beverly Hills, CA: Sage.
Punch, M. (1989), 'Researching police deviance: a personal encounter with the limitations and liabilities of fieldwork', *British Journal of Sociology*, **40**, 177–204.
Raghubir, P. and G. Menon (1998), 'AIDS and me, never the twain shall meet: the effects of information accessibility on judgments of risk and advertising effectiveness', *Journal of Consumer Research*, **25** (June), 52–63.
Renzetti, Claire M. and Raymond M. Lee (eds) (1993), *Researching Sensitive Topics*, Newbury Park, CA: Sage.
Roberts, H. (ed.) (1981), *Doing Feminist Research*, London: Routledge & Kegan Paul.
Sandikci, Özlem and Güliz Ger (2001), 'Fundamental fashions: the cultural politics of the turban and the Levi's', in Mary C. Gilly and Joan Meyers-Levy (eds), *Advances in Consumer Research*, vol. 28, Salt Lake City, UT: Association for Consumer Research, pp. 146–50.
Sandikci, Özlem and Güliz Ger (2002), 'In-between modernities and postmodernities: investigating Turkish consumptionscape', in Susan Broniarczyk and Kent Nakamoto (eds), *Advances in Consumer Research*, vol. 29, Salt Lake City, UT: Association for Consumer Research, pp. 465–70.
Sandikci, Özlem and Güliz Ger (2005), 'Aesthetics, ethics, and politics of the Turkish headscarf', in Suzanne Kuechler and Daniel Miller (eds), *Clothing as Material Culture*, London: Berg, pp. 61–82.
Sanjek, Roger (1990), 'On ethnographic validity', in Roger Sanjek (ed.), *Fieldnotes: The Makings of Anthropology*, Ithaca, NY: Cornell University Press, pp. 385–418.
Schouten, J.W. and J.H. McAlexander (1995), 'Subcultures of consumption: an ethnography of the new bikers', *Journal of Consumer Research*, **22** (June), 43–61.
Seigel, K. and L.J. Bauman (1986), 'Methodological issues in AIDS-related research', in D.A. Feldman and T.M. Johnson (eds), *The Social Dimension of AIDS*, New York: Praeger.
Shahidian, Hammed (2001), ' "To be recorded in history": researching Iranian underground political activists in exile', *Qualitative Sociology*, **24** (1), 55–81.
Sieber, J.E. (1993), 'The ethics and politics of sensitive research', in C.M. Renzetti and R.M. Lee (eds), *Researching Sensitive Topics*, Newbury Park, CA: Sage, pp. 14–26.
Sieber, J.E. and B. Stanley (1988), 'Ethical and professional dimensions of socially sensitive research', *American Psychologist*, **43**, 49–55.
Silverman, David (2005), *Doing Qualitative Research*, London: Sage.
Warren, Carol A.B. (1988), *Gender Issues in Field Research*, Newbury Park, CA: Sage.
Weiss, Robert S. (1994), *Learning from Strangers*, New York: The Free Press.

39 Grasping the global: multi-sited ethnographic market studies
Dannie Kjeldgaard, Fabian Faurholt Csaba and Güliz Ger

Introduction

In recent years, the field of marketing and consumption research has seen a rise in studies applying ethnographic methods (Arnould and Wallendorf, 1994; Arnould and Thompson, 2005). A number of these studies have utilized a multi-sited research approach (Marcus, 1995). This chapter discusses the emergence and principles of multi-sited ethnography: how it differs from cross-cultural and single-sited ethnographic research, and how it applies to marketing and consumer research. A central argument is that multi-sited ethnographic market studies are particularly pertinent in investigations which specifically attempt to grasp global or globalizing market conditions and relations. Describing and analyzing the complexities of market phenomena of an inter-linked and interdependent social world, a multi-sited ethnographic approach studies globalization 'from within' rather than as an external influencing factor on local market realities. Where traditional ethnographic work in anthropology suggests the deep immersion in and thick description of a single locality, multi-sited ethnography argues that to immerse oneself deeply in a transnational phenomenon one must abandon the privilege of the locality, embrace mobility and 'go with the flow' (Burawoy, 2000; Hannerz, 2003).

Globalization challenges the units of analysis of traditional cross-cultural research as well as the objects and premises of traditional ethnography. Multi-sited ethnographic inquiry can bring out the multifaceted character of globalization through the analysis of different experiences of its impact on communities, but also by studying the specific networks, flows and connections that constitute the social–cultural and economical infra-structure of globalization. Rather than merely describing the imprints of globalization, multi-sited ethnography moves with it, tracing its networks, flows and interconnections and the modes of interaction, institutions and stratification that characterize it. Multi-sited research hence represents an attempt to adjust ethnography and make it viable and relevant under the conditions of globalization. Multi-sited Ethnographic Market Studies (MEMS hereafter) is a set of guiding principles that can be followed more or less rigorously when studying global phenomena of the market.

We begin our discussion of MEMS by situating it in relation to the cross-cultural research tradition in marketing and consumer research, the challenges posed by an emergent transnational market reality and how this has led to suggestions in anthropology to move from single-sited to multi-sited research. In the second part of the chapter we introduce research strategies (drawn from Marcus, 1995) and relate these to existing research in marketing and consumer research. Finally we discuss some of the practical and analytical challenges posed by MEMS.

Marketing and consumer research: from cross-cultural to ethnographic perspectives
The continuous expansion of international trade over several decades has given rise to a large body of academic and commercial research in international consumer behavior and marketing. In the effort to map international consumer and market variations and finding out how consumers in different countries react to marketing efforts, cross-cultural research has assumed great importance (van Herk, Poortinga and Verhallen, 2005; Malhotra, Agarwal and Peterson, 1996). But, as globalization has intensified and researchers have come to realize better its complex ties to culture and consumption, serious doubts have been raised about dominant theoretical models in the field. As Douglas and Craig noted in 1997, 'traditional approaches to studying cross-cultural behavior which are typically grounded in a comparative or cross-sectional approach have become increasingly inadequate to capture the complexity of cultural influences' (p. 381). Criticism has pointed to the lack of explanatory power and rigor, which, of course, are interrelated. We might distinguish between two veins of criticism: one that addresses the technical, methodological problems arising when collecting comparable data in different cultures, and a more fundamental critique, addressing the very theoretical premises behind cross-cultural consumer and marketing research.

The methodological problems in cross-cultural studies can be framed in terms of the distinction between etic and emic. An etic approach is based on criteria from outside a particular culture, often scientific procedure and norms. In contrast, 'emic' explains the behavior of members of a culture according to their own, indigenous concepts and definitions. Cross-cultural researchers are faced with the emic/etic dilemma: they might adapt research instruments to each national culture (emic approach) at the expense of the cross-cultural comparability and external validity, or stick to tests applicable to several countries at the expense of reliability and internal validity (Douglas and Craig, 1997; Usunier, 2000). Since comparison and generalization across cultures is a central aim of most studies, cross-cultural research has leaned towards the etic approach, but sought to alleviate problems of the comparability of data by identifying ways of establishing cross-cultural equivalence. Usunier (2000) lists six main categories of cross-cultural equivalence, designating areas in which non-equivalence may arise in comparative research. These are conceptual, functional, translation, measurement, sample and data collection equivalence. Construct equivalence refers to the similarity of the interpretation of objects or behavior, and the comparability of the categories in which objects are placed. Functional equivalence has to do with similarity of the functions or purposes of use of objects across cultures. Translation equivalence is concern with lexical, idiomatic, syntactical and experiential similarity across languages and dialects. Measurement equivalence concerns translation, calibrating the equivalence of the units of measurement, and metric equivalence or the equivalence of the scale or the scoring procedure. Sample and data collection equivalence address the practical challenges of collecting survey data under different circumstances where the availability and accessibility of informants may vary greatly. Of these, construct equivalence or specification error is arguably the most important issue (Cavusgil and Das, 1997; van Herk, Poortinga and Verhallen, 2005). Although the equivalence categories demonstrate the numerous potential sources of error in and the complex nature of cross-cultural research, the effort to address equivalence issues reflects a belief that careful research procedures can help minimize non-equivalence and produce valid and reliable findings. While scholars have emphasized the critical role of taking steps to minimize non-equivalence or to measure the extent of non-equivalence and have warned researchers that, unless equivalence exists, the findings and conclusions of a study are worthless (e.g., Cavusgil and Das, 1997; van Herk, Poortinga and Verhallen, 2005; Steenkamp and Baumgartner, 1998), studies abound in journals which either ignore this issue or pay lip service to it. Even the rare studies which follow a rigorous approach and accept equivalence only if serious attempts to find non-equivalence have failed, are at a loss in explaining why non-equivalence occurs when it does. So, while acknowledging that many studies do not exhibit the necessary methodological rigor, this vein of criticism does not fundamentally question the central premises of cross-cultural research.

In a more far-reaching critique, Holt reflects on evidence that cross-cultural consumer research has little success in describing and explaining cultural differences in consumption patterns across countries, and attributes this to three underlying flaws in the predominant values/personality conception of culture. First, he argues that its nomothetic approach – which seeks to measure, describe and compare cultures according to a limited set of purportedly universal traits, values or needs – is too reductive to uncover differences and meaning in consumption. Secondly, the focus on preferred end-states ignores what is arguably the very essence of consumption: how consumers reach these end-states. Similar points have been made by other interpretivist scholars, in advancing anthropological and ethnographic approaches in consumer and marketing research. Venkatesh (1995) reproaches cross-cultural consumer research for imposing its positivistic research tools and measures developed in Western countries uncritically on other cultural settings and thus being ethnocentric. Sherry (1995, p. 15) implies that anthropological methods offer a better way of fulfilling marketing's ideal of 'getting closer to the consumer' (or other marketplace stakeholders) and to deal with challenges of cultural propriety and appropriate development in international marketing. Holt's final point of criticism regards the level-of-analysis and conceptions of self and culture as holistic entities. The values/personality approach takes both self and culture to be rather coherent, stable and well-defined constructs, but much of contemporary thought on social identity rejects this view, and suggests that 'self' is a contingent, situational and contradictory structure. This, of course, raises serious questions about the validity of survey research based on the responses of capricious individuals. And the classical assumption of cultures as unified wholes has become more and more dubious in complex, differentiated societies, especially, as we shall argue, with the continuous advancement of globalization. The acknowledgment that today multiple and diffuse cultural systems operate across a given population poses fundamental challenges to both anthropological thought and cross-cultural consumer and marketing research (Holt, 1994, p. 81). Douglas and Craig (1997) recognize that the evolving globalization of cultures demands new research designs for cross-cultural consumer inquiry, and suggest studies of cultural units at various levels and 'multiple site studies' as paths forward. In taking stock of two decades of what they label 'consumer culture theory' (CCT), Arnould and Thompson (2005) argue that a new concept of culture now reigns in the field, which 'explores the heterogeneous distribution of meanings and the multiplicity of overlapping cultural groupings that exist within the broader socio-historic frame of globalization and market capitalism' (p. 869).

Global market realities
Globalization and the processes and changes associated with the term are said to change the nature of social life and hence the reality of markets and consumption. The central

issue in marketing has been whether international marketing strategies should follow the principle of global standardization or local adaptation (e.g. Levitt, 1983; Usunier, 2000). The issue echoes a wider debate in social theory about the homogenization or heterogenization of social life (for a review and critique of the debate, see Askegaard and Kjeldgaard, 2002). Approaches resisting the either–or position have also emerged. One example is Robertson's (1992) notion of 'glocalization', which argues that the local is always also global and the global is always local in its manifestations. While many accounts view the local and the global as separate entities, others imply that the dichotomy of the local and the global is broken down. Waters, for example, defines globalization as 'a social process in which the constraints of geography on social and cultural arrangements recede and in which people become increasingly aware that they are receding and in which people act accordingly' (2001, p. 5). This definition implies, first of all, that the decreasing constraints of geography mean that the social processes entailed essentially reconfigure notions of time and space. Secondly, it implies reflexivity on behalf of both institutional and individual actors.

One way of describing the processes of globalization is Appadurai's (1990) seminal account of the global cultural economy. Appadurai argues that economy, polity and culture increasingly operate disjunctively and detached from localities and nation states. They operate through cultural flows in five 'scapes': ethnoscapes (the flow of people), technoscapes (the flows of technology: both conventional and also social technology, such as management principles and theories), finanscapes (flows of money), mediascapes (the flow of images and, more importantly, representations of a greater variety of imagined lives) and ideoscapes (the flow of ideas). Within marketing Ger and Belk (1996) have since added the term 'consumptionscapes' in order to highlight the specific flow of cultures of consumption. Often the global in marketing and consumer research is (more or less explicitly) understood as something external to the local. Ger and Belk (1996) argue that global consumer culture is used together with local culture to navigate and positioning the individual in the local identity hierarchies. Askegaard, Arnould and Kjeldgaard (2005) analyse the acculturation processes of Greenlanders in Denmark by identifying three ideologies that are formative of identity negotiation, one of which is global consumer culture. Thompson and Arsel (2004) analyze the glocalization of consumer culture by Starbucks in a given locality. While these studies take globalization seriously, both as consequence for and object of the study of market phenomena, with the theories just outlined above, however, we argue that the social reality is by and large deterritorialized and hence has become transnational. This means that the global culture is an all-encompassing system of which what we call the local is a part (Hardt and Negri, 2000). Then any study of a locality is a study of the lived meaning of the system.

Globalization represents 'a multifaceted or differentiated social phenomenon', which 'cannot be conceived as a singular condition but instead refers to patterns of global interconnectedness within all the key domains of social activity' (Held et al., 1999, p. 27). Any meaningful account of contemporary globalization and its unique attributes or dominant features requires that a set of key spatiotemporal and organizational dimensions are analyzed. This involves studying the organization of networks of relations and connections, flows and levels of activities, interchanges and the impact of these phenomena on communities (ibid., p. 17). Since the processes of globalization lead towards an increased transnational social reality, marketing and consumption phenomena can no longer be understood sufficiently through reliance on single-sited analysis. The globalized condition calls for 'innovative forms of multi-locale ethnography necessary to do justice to transnational political, economic and cultural forces that traverse and constitute local and regional worlds' (Clifford, 1997, p. 27).

Transformations of ethnography: the emergence of multi-sited research

The concept of multi-sited ethnography was advanced by Marcus (1986, 1995, 1999) as a designation for an emergent stream in anthropological research, which, in the face of the challenges posed by globalization, breaks with conventional ethnographic methodology (for a discussion of wider methodological debates in anthropology, see Ekström in this volume). Marcus distinguishes multi-sited ethnography from the conventional, 'single-sited research' approach to fieldwork which relies on the intensive investigation of one particular place or a local situation. The multi-sited approach, he argues, has emerged in response to empirical changes in the world and therefore to transformed locations of cultural production (1995, p. 97). In a world in which few places are untouched by global forces and flows, ethnographic research focusing on single sites and local experiences, culture and roots is constrained and constraining (Gupta and Ferguson, 1997). While conventional single-sited research is capable of registering the impact of globalization in the local context of its research settings, it must rely on theoretical work (on world systems, globalization) to frame the experiences of local subjects and cultural impact of encounters with the global. With such a 'one-sited' perspective, intercultural connections are conceived mainly in terms of the way local cultures accommodate and resist the encroachments of modernity, Western (neo-) colonialism, or global capitalism. Multi-sited research, on the other hand, through the study of multiple locales, extends the scope of ethnography to include not only the life world of situated subjects, but also associations and connections among sites that make up the system. While acknowledging macrotheoretical accounts of globalization, multi-sited research engages in its own empirical investigations of the relationships, discourses, infrastructures and agents that connect, constitute and construct the global (and local).

Multi-sited fieldwork does not represent an entirely new conception, yet it marks a break with the norms and assumptions instituted by classical anthropology. Hannerz (2003) discusses these fieldwork norms in terms of the prescriptions of Evans-Pritchard. This classical model demands prolonged and close contact with the people in the site, communication through the natives' language, and the study of their entire culture and social life. It represents the idea of a thorough, formative, exclusive engagement with a single field. Hannerz suggests that, while this ideal has been important for the identity of the discipline, it does not represent the full range of research practices anthropologists have engaged in. Ethnographic practice outside anthropology has conformed even less to this ideal. Hannerz offers examples of multi-sited research even in pioneering anthropology studies, such as Malinowski's trailing of the Kula ring among the Trobriander Islanders. He also argues that the transnational, translocal and global themes addressed through multi-sited ethnography have appeared in anthropological studies of diffusion, acculturation, culture contact, social change and modernization throughout much of the twentieth century. The common premise of these studies, as for multi-sited ethnography, is the recognition that the 'world is not a mosaic of bounded identities, existing in isolation from each other' (Hannerz, 1998, p. 237). Transnational research rejects the classical quest for pure traditions and discrete cultural differences, which Clifford deems 'exoticist' and 'orientalist' (1997, p. 5).

Single-sited ethnography should not be identified too closely with the classical quest, however. Hannerz discusses a genre of transnational anthropology 'communities open to the world', which addresses the local impact of outside forces. Using rather conventional research approaches, such studies have looked at the way local cultures have resisted, accommodated or made creative use of powerful foreign cultural influences. While analysis of resistance tends to reflect the desire to preserve cultural integrity and resist external influences, the genre also acknowledges the capacity of globalization to produce new cultural forms and diversity in the local context, through creolization and hybridity. The genre does seem to maintain certain taken-for-granted notions of the local rooted in an emic perspective. Other genres of transnational anthropology are translocalities (places such as airports, world cities, world's fairs which are hubs or nodes in transnational social and cultural processes), border studies, migration, diasporas, transnational corporations and occupations, cyberspace and commodities (Hannerz, 1998). Mobility, flows and relations between places are central to each of these genres and call for multi-sited approaches.

Table 39.1 provides an overview of the main contrasts between single-sited ethnography and the multi-sited approach. We might, however, ask whether there really is a significant difference in the methodology of fieldwork in the two approaches. Moeran, commenting on Marcus's distinction, suggests that even what he calls 'frame-based' fieldwork, conducted in easily identified physical locations, involves following people and things around. Although he implies that *network-based* fieldwork, which involves following a flow of social interaction along networks of people and things, is much less solidly anchored in a locality, he does not believe that the character of the fieldwork or the fieldworker changes fundamentally (Moeran, 2005).

While the theories on culture have generated a new line of consumption and market research based on single-sited research (see Arnould and Thompson, 2005, for a selective summary), theories of globalization have not generated a similar line of multi-sited research, at least not to the same extent. This is curious as there have been repeated calls to 'demystify and 'ground' globalization in the theoretical literature on globalization (Freidberg, 2001, p. 354). Perhaps the challenges posed by multi-sited research are greater than those of single-sited research. However, if we want to understand globalization, as well as international marketing informed by theories of globalization, multi-sited ethnographical research provides a rewarding route.

MEMS: methodological principles and challenges
Although few aspects of social life are unaffected by the processes of globalization, MEMS will not be applicable to all types of research questions. However, more and more research questions will emanate from the phenomena of the market that are increasingly transnational.

Research strategies
Following Marcus (1995), we introduce five strategies for constructing multi-site ethnographic studies. These are avenues to be pursued in order both to accomplish a generation of knowledge of transnational phenomena and to establish a transnational terrain for

Table 39.1 Comparison of single-sited and multi-sited ethnography

	Single-sited	Multi-sited
Approach to fieldwork	Intensively-focused upon single site of ethnographic observation and participation	Objects of study are mobile and multiply situated Fieldwork conducted at multiple sites. Not all sites are treated by a uniform set of fieldwork practices. Varying intensities and qualities of fieldwork
Central themes of the research	Illuminating the entire culture and social life of a people or the perspective of the subaltern. Resistance and accommodation. Groups' encounter of and responses to displacement of their culture	The circulation of cultural meanings, practices, objects and identities in diffuse time–space
Research perspective	Committed localism, holistic Dualistic them–us frame	Self-consciously embedded in a world system. Exercise in mapping terrain, goal not holistic representation
Comparative perspective	Comparative studies are generated for homogeneously conceived conceptual units, on the basis of separate projects of fieldwork	Comparative dimension is integral to study. It involves juxtaposition of phenomena previously seen as 'worlds apart'
Reliance on theory of globalization (world system)	Relies on theory of world system for contextualizing portraiture in terms of which experiences of local subjects are described and analyzed	Acknowledges narratives of world system but does not rely on them. Constructs the lifeworld of situated subjects, but also ethnographically constructs aspects of the system itself through the connections among sites

studying global consumer culture. We relate these strategies to studies in marketing and consumer research which are exemplars of multi-sited research, although not necessarily explicitly framed as such.

Follow the people   The flow of people is a particular aspect of the global cultural system that lends itself to a multi-site approach. In line with Appadurai's (1990) notion of the ethnoscapes, certain groups of consumers and marketers are particularly mobile and construct their identities transnationally. Studies that can be said to have used the 'follow the people' strategy are studies of transmigrants (Ücok and Kjeldgaard, 2006), marketers' transnational activities and their structuring of global markets (Applbaum, 2000) and the study of surfer culture (Canniford, 2005). These studies acknowledge that market phenomena are constructed and lived transnationally. Hence one must follow the people as they move to, from and through multiple sites or their multiple local manifestations.

Follow the thing   Material manifestations of contemporary consumer culture are results of the output of transnational commodity chains. In order to get beyond the surface brand identities of mass consumer goods, Klein (1999) traced, for example, Nike shoes back through the chain of commodification and hence uncovered previously unknown brand meanings. Similarly Marcus points to Sidney Mintz's study of sugar. Csaba and Ger (2000) have followed the Turkish carpet and the meanings attached to this commodity from its culture of production to culture of distribution and consumption. Tracing these commodity chains generates knowledge of the workings and linkages of transnational marketing networks and consumer culture and thereby a way of entering the transnational flows of global culture.

Follow the metaphor[1]   Similar to following things, this mode obtains when the things followed are signs, symbols or metaphors, that is, the transnational aspects of discourse. Here we can point to studies of consumer desire (Belk, Ger and Askegaard, 2003) and consumer cosmopolitanism (Thompson and Tambyah, 1999) which trace elements of discourse which shape consumer identities and lifeworlds. Furthermore the construction and production of transnational brand identities have been studied: for example, how a common cultural identity of Asianness is constructed by brand managers and advertising executives (Eckhardt and Cayla, 2005). Another possibility is to study certain market metaphors or terminology in multiple sites: for example, how certain segments are represented globally and appropriated locally (e.g. Kjeldgaard and Askegaard's 2006 study of the glocalization of the transnational ideology of youth culture in Denmark and Greenland and in urban and rural contexts in each of these cultural contexts. This facilitated an analysis of how an ideological market phenomenon may be appropriated and creolized according to local culture but this occurred according to certain structural constraints).

Follow the life or biography   The biographical method involves tracing the emergence of a given phenomenon through multiple sites. This could be the historical emergence of certain phenomena of the market in one cultural context and its cultural history and its diffusion and morphology throughout global cultural economy (for example the emergence and spread of youthful consumption: Liechty, 1995). Another example is the tracing of commodities as suggested by Kopytoff (1986) or brand histories such as Holt's (2004) tracing of the biography of certain iconic brands and their relation to popular culture.

Follow the conflict   While Marcus primarily makes reference to the anthropology of law in connection with following conflicts, global consumer culture is generative and partly constituted by conflicts. Culture jamming and the rise of alternative global brands which define themselves as a negation of dominant brands – so-called 'Doppelgänger' brands (Thompson, Rindfleisch and Arsel, 2006) – illustrate that the tensions created by the logic of marketing are negotiated through resistance based on the very same logic. Furthermore the resistance to the form of contemporary global market and its semi-state institutions (such as the alternative to the World Economic Forum, the World Social Forum, or the way protestors follow the G8 summits around the world) represents examples of social relations constituted by conflict that are stretched across traditional sociogeographic boundaries.

The strategically situated single-site study   Although the tracing and following across multiple sites lie at the heart of multi-sited ethnography, there can be instances when the mapping of the broader system is best studied in particular contexts. One example of strategically situated (single-site) ethnography is the study of how glocalization shapes a particular brand competition domain and hence generates new local variation as the outcome (Thompson and Arsel, 2004). Another is the study of the social technique of branding in market cultures where branding is an emergent phenomenon (Askegaard, 2005). Such studies provide knowledge of the logic of transnational markets and hence provide knowledge of the system as it becomes manifest in local cultural contexts.

Challenges
Multi-sited fields pose various challenges in research design, depth, reflexivity and interpretation.

Research design   One issue is the unforeseen connections discovered in the field which lead to unexpected trips at unexpected times. For example, a carpet fair held once a year at a particular town, the link of an Ankara retailer to a middleman from Kayseri who buys from weavers in mountain villages two hours' driving distance from Kayseri, and a Philadelphia-based owner–manager visiting the Eastern Anatolian villages three times a year require great flexibility on the part of the researcher (see Csaba and Ger, 2000). Furthermore unforeseen sites lead to unforeseen topics and conceptual foci such as the weavers' dilemmas and gender relations entailed in global carpet production and consumption. Thus research designs will be highly emergent.

Another major issue is achieving depth. In order to achieve a relatively satisfactory understanding of the given phenomenon, research can be undertaken individually or in teams. When done individually, what could be termed 'ethnographic nomadism', one has the advantage of constantly improving understanding based on previous understandings. The disadvantage of this is the risk of not achieving sufficient detail, not following the phenomenon extensively enough. This strategy was applied in Ücok's study of Turkish transmigrants (Ücok and Kjeldgaard, 2006) by following informants in multiple sites (their homes, at work, at social occasions) as well as doing this in the multiple cultural contexts which informants moved to and from (Denmark and Turkey). This nomadism facilitated a fuller understanding of an identity forged as 'in-between' being constituted by the very movement between localities.

Another option is to conduct the research in a team in which one or more researchers study each site in depth and then compare and combine the findings. For example, three researchers from three different countries working on consumer desires (Belk, Ger and Askegaard, 2003) generated a multi-site study by each one doing essentially a single-site study but in a coordinated way. The coordination involved methodological as well as theoretical concerns. While following the phenomenon, 'desire', each of the three countries posed different challenges. For example, in Turkey, the researchers needed to sample from among lower-class informants with a rural background as the notion of modern subjectivity is important for the phenomenon of desire, and this group would provide a comparison and counterpoint to the middle-class informants. However this was not called for in Denmark or the USA. On the other hand, Denmark posed a greater problem than Turkey or the USA in terms of access to informants, owing to the institutional structures and expectations. This study benefited from having an insider doing the fieldwork in each of the three sites combined with researchers cross-checking each other's assumptions, perspectives and interpretations in various ways. In this way, it is possible to study each site in more detail, but there is the danger of this becoming a comparative study based on a standardized methodology, not capturing the flows and connections among the sites.

A third option is to follow the phenomenon in teams, for example a group of researchers with multiple cultural and/or disciplinary backgrounds, as Csaba and Ger (2000) did in their study of networks of production and consumption relationships of carpets. The advantage is that each site can be studied in more detail, that there is the possibility of constructing and reconstructing the interpretation as the team moves from site to site and having a multiplicity of perspectives on the phenomenon. Hence working on a topic as a multi-culture team not only enables multi-sited research but also brings additional benefits: as the researchers have different cultural lenses, the ultimate interpretation of the data goes through more as well as more interesting iterations and these iterations are subjected to each other's criticisms.

The last option is one in which the individual researcher does the following but teams up with locally based collaborators in each site. This strategy was followed in a study of heritage and theme parks in diverse localities (Hendry, 2003).

There might be more options and obviously combinations of the four outlined above. A study that exemplifies the reliance on both teamwork and ethnographic nomadism is Ger and Belk's (1999) work on materialism in four sites. With each researcher investigating two sites, this research followed a conflict-ridden phenomenon and the conflict itself: how is it that people consume excessively while they think that placing a lot of emphasis on consumption is bad? Unlike the study on consumer desire, this one involved each co-author working in a site where s/he was an insider and another one in which s/he was an outsider. Again, the study benefited from divergent cultural perspectives of the researchers. The very fact that there were multiple sites and that the researchers were themselves from different cultures enabled uncovering the underlying culturally specific ethics that justify, moralize and legitimize consumption.

Trustworthiness and glocal reflexivity   In terms of trustworthiness, MEMS pose the question of how to achieve in-depth knowledge of geographically and culturally dispersed phenomena. How is one to balance the requirement of thick description of the local versus the need to map the relations and connections? While this to some extent is determined by the goals of the research, it points to the need to negotiate 'the distribution of attention' (Hannerz, 1998). On one hand, ethnography is incomplete if it does not take into account the experiences of local actors. On the other hand, if there is no account of relations and connections among sites and life world experiences in these sites, the results will be parochial.

One important aspect of multi-sited ethnographic studies is the constant reflexivity required by the researcher as she moves, traces and follows the connections and relations of the phenomenon across sites. How are variations of the phenomenon constructed in the global–local dialectic (Thompson and Arsel, 2004)? Which local cultural or political economical contexts enter into the dialectical process? Moving across sites and thinking through the different experiences in the various sites not only requires but also facilitates a depth in reflexivity. For example, noteworthy differences in the nature of the relationships among the carpet weavers and the dealers in different villages helped Csaba and Ger (2000) identify and interpret the link between carpet quality and power relations in carpet production networks. Reflexivity therefore is a matter of distinguishing similarities from differences so that the study of the phenomenon in one site adds to the totality of understanding of the overall phenomenon. Therefore each local instantiation must be studied intratextually and then read intertextually across sites – much like what is suggested when studying a phenomenon by interviewing individuals (Thompson et al., 1989); however, in this case this must be done specifically with a glocal perspective.

In summary, MEMS pose challenges such as time, access to multiple fields, logistics of numerous trips, lack of prolonged engagement in any particular locale and the accompanying interpretive challenges. These challenges can be overcome by flexibility, negotiating the diverse fields, teamwork, intratextual and intertextual reading of the multiple sites, as well as intraresearcher and interteam glocal reflexivity.

Conclusion

The key aspects of globalization, namely, global interconnectivity, the transnational nature of social reality and the local-as-part-of-the-global compel us to use multi-sited methods. Multi-sited ethnography is more than a necessary adjustment to ethnography; it can contribute greatly to our very understanding of the complex phenomenon of globalization and the application of this approach in marketing and consumer research offers rich insights into the processes and contours of economic and cultural globalization. A multi-sited approach can contribute to refining our picture of globalization. When studying phenomena of the market which is constituted transnationally it makes less sense to carry out the single-sited ethnography or cross-cultural comparative studies. Rather, to offer adequate accounts of such phenomena one approach is to utilize MEMS. How particular projects are to be designed depends on the nature of the research question and which, or which combination of, phenomena are to be investigated. The important thing is that by constructing a research setup one also constructs the particular terrain or part of the terrain one wants to research. It is therefore more a matter of applying a 'multi-sited imaginary' as a perspective on market phenomena that does not have localities as privileged units of analysis. Rather the unit of analysis is the relations that emerge from the manifestations of the global in the local.

MEMS allow us to get into the global flows, to study the consumptionscapes and marketscapes of the global cultural economy from within rather than as an external cultural representation entering specific localities. While following the phenomenon through the flows poses various methodological challenges, these challenges are not insurmountable. Thus MEMS provide the capacity to make theoretical arguments through revealing and demarcating connections and relational categories rather than essentialized differences.

Note
1. Here we have collapsed 'follow the metaphor' with Marcus's 'follow the plot/story/allegory', since this is defined as a subset of the 'follow the metaphor' mode.

References

Appadurai, Arjun (1990), 'Disjuncture and difference in the global economy', in M. Featherstone (ed.), *Global Culture: Nationalism, Globalization and Modernity*, London: Sage, pp. 295–310.

Applbaum, Kalman (2000), 'Crossing borders: globalization as myth and charter in American transnational consumer marketing', *American Ethnologist*, **27** (2) (May), 257–82.

Arnould, Eric J. and Craig J. Thompson (2005), 'Consumer culture theory (CCT): twenty years of research', *Journal of Consumer Research*, **31** (March), 868–82.

Arnould, Eric J. and Melanie Wallendorf (1994), 'Market-oriented ethnography: interpretation building and marketing strategy formulation', *Journal of Marketing Research*, **XXXI** (November), 484–504.

Askegaard, Søren (2005), 'Brands as a global ideoscape', in J. Schroeder and M. Salzer-Moerling (eds), *Brand Culture*, London: Routledge.

Askegaard, Søren and Dannie Kjeldgaard (2002), 'The water fish swim in: relations between marketing and culture in the age of globalization', in S. Askegaard, N. Jøgensen and T. Kaudson (eds), *Perspectives on Marketing Relations*, Copenhagen: Thomson, pp. 13–35.

Askegaard, Søren, Eric J. Arnould and Dannie Kjeldgaard (2005), 'Post-assimilationist ethnic consumer research: qualifications and extensions', *Journal of Consumer Research*, **32** (1) (June), 160–71.

Belk, Russel W., Güliz Ger and Søren Askegaard (2003), 'The fire of desire: a multisited inquiry into consumer passion', *Journal of Consumer Research*, **30** (December), 326–51.

Burawoy, Michael (2000), *Global Ethnography. Forces, Connections, and Imaginations in a Postmodern World*, Berkeley: University of California Press.

Canniford, Robin (2005), 'Moving shadows: suggestions for ethnography in globalized cultures', *Qualitative Market Research: An International Journal*, **8** (2), 204–18.

Cavusgil, S. Tamer and A. Das (1997), 'Methodological issues in empirical cross-cultural research: a survey of the management literature and a framework', *Management International Review*, **37** (1), 71–96.

Clifford, James (1997), *Routes. Travel and Translation in the Late Twentieth Century*, Cambridge: Harvard University Press.

Csaba, Fabian Faurholt and Güliz Ger (2000), 'Global village carpets: marketing, tradition and the oriental carpet renaissance', in Clifford J. Schulz and Bruno Grbac (eds), *Marketing Contributions to Democratization and Socioeconomic Development*, Phoenix: Arizona State University.

Douglas, Susan P. and C. Samuel Craig (1997), 'The changing dynamics of consumer behaviour: implications for cross-cultural research', *International Journal of Research in Marketing*, **14**, 379–95.

Eckhardt, Giana M. and Julien Cayla (2005), 'Asian brands without borders: recentering models of international marketing', working paper, Australian Graduate School of Management.

Freidberg, Susanne (2001), 'On the trail of the global green bean: methodological considerations in multi-site ethnography', *Global Networks*, **1** (4), 353–68.

Ger, Güliz and Russell Belk (1996), 'I'd like to buy the world a Coke: consumptionscapes of the "less affluent world"', *Journal of Consumer Policy*, **19** (3), 271–304.

Ger, Güliz and Russell Belk (1999), 'Accounting for materialism in four cultures', *Journal of Material Culture*, **42**, 183–204.

Gupta, Akhil and James Ferguson (1997), *Anthropological Locations. Boundaries and Grounds of a Field Science*, Los Angeles: University of California Press.

Hannerz, Ulf (1998), 'Transnational research', in H. Russell Bernard (ed.), *Handbook of Methods in Cultural Anthropology*, London: Sage, pp. 235–58.

Hannerz, Ulf (2003), 'Being there . . . and there . . . and there! Reflections on multi-site ethnography', *Ethnography*, **4** (2), 201–16.

Hardt, Michael and Antonio Negri (2000), *Empire*, Cambridge, MA: Harvard University Press.

Held, David, Anthony McGrew, David Goldblatt and Jonathan Perrathon (1999), *Global Transformations*, Cambridge: Polity.

Hendry, Joy (2003), 'An ethnographer in the global arena: globography perhaps?', *Global Networks*, **3** (4), 497–512.

Holt, Douglas B. (1994), 'Consumers' cultural differences as local systems of tastes: a critique of the personality/values approach and an alternative framework', *Asia Pacific Advances in Consumer Research*, **1**, 178–84.

Holt, Douglas B. (2004), *How Brands Become Icons. The Principles of Cultural Branding*, Boston, MA: Harvard Business School Publishing.

Kjeldgaard, Dannie and Søren Askegaard (2006), 'The glocalization of youth culture: the global youth segment as structures of common difference', *Journal of Consumer Research*, **22** (September), 231–47.

Klein, Naomi (1999), *No Logo. Taking Aim at the Brand Bullies*, London: Flamingo.

Kopytoff, Igor (1986), 'The cultural biography of things: commoditization as process', in A. Appadurai (ed.), *The Social Life of Things: Commodities in Cultural Perspective*, Cambridge: Cambridge University Press, pp. 64–91.

Levitt, Theodore (1983), 'The globalization of markets', *Harvard Business Review*, May/June.

Liechty, Mark (1995), 'Media, markets and modernization. Youth identities and the lived experience of modernity in Kathmandu, Nepal', in Vera Amit-Talai and Helena Wulff (eds), *Youth Cultures. A Cross-cultural Perspective*, London: Routledge, pp. 166–201.

Malhotra, Naresh K., James Agarwal and Mark Peterson (1996), 'Methodological issues in cross-cultural marketing research: a state-of-the-art review', *International Marketing Review*, **13** (5), 7–43.

Marcus, George E. (1986), 'Contemporary problems in ethnography and in the modern world system', in James Clifford and George E. Marcus (eds), *Writing Culture*, Berkeley: University of California Press, pp. 165–93.

Marcus, George E. (1995), 'Ethnography in/of the world system: the emergence of multi-sited ethnography', *Annual Review of Anthropology*, **24**, 95–117.

Marcus, George E. (1999), 'What is at stake – and is not – in the idea and practice of multi-sited ethnography', *Canberra Anthropology*, **22** (2), 6–14.

Moeran, Brian (2005), *The Business of Ethnography. Strategic Exchanges, People and Organization*, Oxford: Berg.

Robertson, Roland (1992), *Globalization: Social Theory and Global Culture*, London: Sage.

Sherry, John F. (ed.) (1995), *Contemporary Marketing and Consumer Behavior: an Anthropological Sourcebook*, London: Sage.

Steenkamp, Jan Benedict and H. Baumgartner (1998), 'Assessing measurement invariance in cross-national consumer research', *Journal of Consumer Research*, **25** (June), 78–90.

Thompson, Craig J. and Zeynep Arsel (2004), 'The Starbucks brandscape and consumers' (anti-corporate) experiences of glocalization', *Journal of Consumer Research*, **31** (December), 631–42.

Thompson, Craig J. and Siok K. Tambyah (1999), 'Trying to be cosmopolitan', *Journal of Consumer Research*, **26** (December), 214–40.

Thompson, Craig J., William B. Locander and Howard R. Pollio (1989), 'Putting consumer experience back into consumer research: the philosophy and method of existential phenomenology', *Journal of Consumer Research*, **16** (September), 133–46.

Thompson, Craig J., Aric Rindfleisch and Zeynep Arsel (2006), 'Emotional branding and the strategic value of the doppelgänger brand image', *Journal of Marketing*, **70** (January).

Üçok, Mine and Dannie Kjeldgaard (2006), 'Consumption in transnational social spaces: a study of Turkish transmigrants', in Karin Ekström and Helene Brembeck (eds), *European Advances in Consumer Research*, vol. 7, Duluth, MN: Association for Consumer Research, pp. 431–6.

Usunier, Jean-Claude (2000), *Marketing Across Cultures*, 3rd edn, London: Pearson Education.

Van Herk, Hester, Ype H. Poortinga and Theo M.M. Verhallen (2005), 'Equivalence of survey data: relevance for international marketing', *European Journal of Marketing*, **39** (3/4), 351–64.

Venkatesh, Alladi (1995), 'Ethnoconsumerism: a new paradigm', in Janeen A. Costa and Gary J. Bamossy (eds), *Marketing in a Multicultural World. Ethnicity, Nationalism, and Cultural Identity*, London: Sage, pp. 26–67.

Waters, Malcolm (2001), *Globalization*, London: Routledge.

40 In pursuit of the 'inside view': training the research gaze on advertising and market practitioners
Daniel Thomas Cook

In recent years, a number of academic researchers have turned their attention toward inspecting the beliefs and practices of advertising and marketing professionals, particularly as these are enacted in organizational contexts. Led mainly by historians, anthropologists and communication scholars, the turn to the 'inside view', as I call it, represents an alternative to research that seeks to determine the 'effects' of advertising and marketing on consumer behavior (Barry and Howard, 1990; Naples, 1979; Pechmann and Stewart, 1989; Vakratsas and Ambler, 1999) and to research that studies the content and structure of advertisements themselves (Williamson, 1978; Goffman, 1979; Goldman, 1993; O'Barr, 1994). That said, one should not get the impression that the works examined in this chapter necessarily hang together seamlessly as a body of thought or that the scholars discussed would group themselves together in the manner I have chosen. Rather I suggest that the research described herein is best conceptualized as comprising an emergent arena of inquiry organized around the effort to render accessible the various ways of knowing and doing of market and advertising practitioners.

The works examined below fall roughly into two kinds of studies, historical and ethnographic. Most take the advertising industry as their research site. Some focus on how those in the industry, currently and historically, create and re-create their subject, 'the consumer', and concomitant notions of 'need' and 'desire'; others on how they manage their relations with clients through the strategic deployment of 'research'; and still others on how the internal relations within agencies figure in production and use of 'knowledge'. All authors share an ambition to enter into the mindset and practices of those involved in the creation of commercially informed and commercially motivated knowledge, meaning and expression. Trade journals, company papers and letters, interviews and personal observation are exploited in different ways by scholars, all in an attempt to make their entrée into a world that is not otherwise readily accessible.

The efforts in this regard strive to gain an inside or emic view, not of 'the natives' or 'the people', but of the worlds of professionals whose jobs involve the fabrication of images, texts and semantic associations intended to result in the creation of social meanings which will serve as vehicles for the realization of economic exchange value and, ultimately, profit. Not entirely novel, the impetus to study advertising and business industries from within has an affinity with several extant lines of thinking. The 'production of culture' perspective (Crane, 1992; Hirsch, 1981; Peterson, 1978; diMaggio, 1977; see also du Gay and Pryke, 2002), associated mainly with American sociology, has tended to examine the organizational dimensions of the so-called 'culture industries', art markets and popular music, in particular. Works in this area seek to demonstrate how those cultural products which ultimately come into social use have been selected and shaped by the structures and imperatives of their respective industries and thus are not pure reflections of unmitigated social process. Those grouped in the closely aligned 'production of consumption' approach are seen similarly to focus on the productive apparatus of goods, often to the exclusion of the meanings and use of consumers (Miller, 1995; Warde, 1992); see Martens et al., 2004, pp. 157–62, for a review specifically applied to children's consumption. In the field of communication, there is a rich history of garnering the inside view on media industries (see Gitlin, 1983; Dornfeld, 1998).

In what follows, I offer a description and assessment of studies which I have grouped into something of a bounded arena of inquiry. I do so with an eye toward evaluating their import as methodologies and methodological positions. Not intended as an exhaustive survey of work in this area, the works discussed herein represent the range of thought and effort that has been put into pursuing the inside view over the last two decades. Among the questions guiding this inquiry are the following. What forms of seeing and knowing do historical and ethnographic approaches offer when the tools of observation are trained on industry creators and practitioners of consumption and advertising, rather than on the everyday, lived settings of consumers? How does the status of 'truth' and truth claims change when producers explain or otherwise annunciate their reasons for production? What can be said about the status, shape and veracity of 'knowledge' (academic or otherwise) when researchers enter the worlds of practitioners and attempt to assess their contexts and meanings?

Histories
In both substance and approach, Roland Marchand's *Advertising the American Dream: Making the Way for Modernity, 1920–1940* stands as the *locus classicus* of the inside view. Published in 1985, this volume examined some 180 000 advertisements along a number of dimensions including design, visual clichés in art and photography, color as a symbolic device as well as written and visual content. He gave dimension and analytic utility to concepts like ensembling, stylistic/progressive obsolescence and the consumption ethic as he identified devices such as parables and social tableaux that were deployed by an emerging industry bent on defining the good life in its own image.

To my mind, and for purposes of the present discussion, Marchand's most significant contribution resides in the angle of vision and epistemological standpoint he brought to bear on the interpretation of advertisements, the industry and American consumer culture. He tells his own story as one of discovery. As an historian wishing to apply the tools of his field to the then overlooked realms of advertising and consumption, Marchand made the assumption that advertisements served as a social mirror that 'completely and vividly' reflected the times (p. xvi). Unhampered at first by the relatively undifferentiated depictions of social life found in the first set of advertisements he had collected, Marchand expanded his scope to include newspapers and additional magazines and extended the historical chronology. His efforts were to no avail as significant scenes from everyday life, such as religious services, the lives of factory workers or even sports fans enjoying a game, remained unrepresented in advertising depictions.

Marchand forced himself to question his naïve assumption of an unproblematic social mirror, a process that led him to confront the contexts, identities, circumstances and motivations of those involved in the production of advertisements. Consequently he sought research materials which could give him insight on the industry, but found that the papers kept by many agencies were inaccessible, unorganized or 'deficient in materials that bear on the development of advertising and public relations strategies' (p. 420). Other supplemental sources like autobiographies of or correspondences between key industry members were sparse or favored an 'anecdotal' treatment of industry or agency history. Ultimately he turned to trade journals – *Advertising Age, Advertising and Selling, Printer's Ink*, among others – the articles of which were written by and for advertising managers and agency leaders. Because these organs were produced for other professionals, they were both 'self-serving and uncritical' and allowed access to 'frank' discussions and debates within the trade (ibid.).

Examining these materials, Marchand found himself faced with a double distortion of sorts: the ads themselves 'distorted' social reality and, as well, the discussions of them by those who were on the production side were also 'biased' or misrepresentative in various ways. His ingenuity as a social thinker and researcher is evident from the way in which he responded to what seems like a conundrum:

> it is a bias that, paradoxically, offers us the prospect of using advertisements . . . more confidently as a key to understanding certain realities of American culture . . . . Constantly and unabashedly, [ad creators] championed the new against the old, the modern against the old-fashioned. This bias, inherent in their economic function, ensured that advertisements would emphasize dispro-portionately those styles, classes, behaviors, and social circumstances that were changing. (p. xxi)

Rather than harping on about this 'bias' or trying to circumvent it to any significant degree (although see Marchand, 1985, p. xx) he treated industry discourses somewhat as an anthropologist would an informant's statements. He sought in their discourses (in their quasi-public declarations and discussions found on the pages of these publications) evidence of their subject positions, their structural perspective and ultimately of their socio-historical location.

No postmodernist, Marchand had faith that reality existed somewhere underneath the images of advertisements and rhetoric of advertising practitioners. It simply was not a transparent reality but one that had to be excavated, dusted off and examined with a schooled eye: 'This bias toward modernity, although it further amplified advertising's distortions of typical social circumstances, ironically served to enhance the fidelity of ads as mirrors of a wider cultural ethos' (p. xxi). In a sense, he tried to look over advertisers' shoulders – from a distance of 50 or 60 years – and learn how they learned, to appreciate their stance toward consumers and toward the social world. Because of their apostolic posture vis-à-vis modernity, he reasoned, those in the industry were particularly alert to signs of consumer acceptance and resistance, to vacuums of advice in a changing social world and to the tensions between portraying 'life as it is' and 'life as one might wish'. They and their creations could thus be marvelously informative about social life in particular because Marchand saw them as exhibiting an 'innocent self-assurance about their culture mission' (p. xxii) and thus, at some level, he thought that their practices (discourses and advertisements) were without guile. A truth could be read off bias and distortion.

A few examples will have to suffice. In his chapter on the consumption ethic (Chapter 5), Marchand understands that the use of color and ensembling are integral to the efforts to move away from values of utility to those of personal pleasure and fashion, and thus increasing turnover of styles leading to increased sales. He 'reads' the ads most often from the advertisers', rather than the consumers', point of view, describing to the reader the thoughts and strategies behind, say, the absence of a car in an automobile ad (p. 122) or providing the context to understand why, for instance, a woman would be dressed to match her bathroom (p. 125). When examining sketches of women for higher class goods from the late 1920s and early 1930s in Chapter 6, Marchand notes that the torso and legs were greatly out of proportion to the standard human form (pp. 179–185). Dubbed 'grotesque moderne', he interprets these 'distortions' as indicative of a shift toward emphasizing the style over function, modern art over literalism and toward reinscribing 'woman' as decoration or accessory to material objects – all of which says 'modern'.

Always attuned to the differences between 'real life' and that depicted in advertisements, Marchand successfully crafts a lens which 'corrects', to his mind, the distortions and frag-mentations that advertisements pose by consulting the views and perspectives of creators. In a sense, advertisements for Marchand were akin to Freud's dreams (1900), Turner's symbols (1967) and Geertz's cultures (1973), to the extent that he saw in them extant truths that needed to be deciphered. His post-positivist stance notwithstanding, Marchand's work offers a model of sorts to approach the 'bias' of trade materials as indications of 'per-spective' rather than merely as simple distortions.

Susan Porter Benson's *Counter Cultures* (1986) pursues a different kind of inside view than Marchand. Focusing on the intersection of labor and gender relations in the heyday of the department store (1890–1940), Benson sought to explore the 'cultures of the three major presences on the selling floor – saleswomen, managers, and customers – and the ways in which their patterns of interaction shaped large-scaling retailing for a half-century' (p. 2). It was on the retail floor and at the service counter that struggles between these cultures were played out on a daily basis, posing a common methodological problem of historical research, namely, how to gain entrée into everyday life encounters and inter-actions which may be decades or centuries in the past.

Benson turned to trade journals, in particular *The Dry Goods Economist*, as well as to house organs of department stores and archival material from individual department stores and from merchants' associations like the National Dry Good Retail Association. Trade journals offered insights on the problems and concerns facing managers and owners in the process of running a store or department. In these somewhat technical discussions about stock turnover and flow of customers through a store, Benson (pp. 31–74) found an institution, a cultural form, in the making.

More than a simple forum for the exchange of information, the trade press encouraged the development of managerial virtues as part of the development and self-assessment of an emergent industry (p. 32). The public self-assessments, Benson argued, provided an entry way into the managerial mindset which was, at the time, suffused, with detail about the micro-organization of a relatively new commercial site: the retail floor. In particular manager and owners displayed a consistent concern about the 'behavior and outlook' (p. 314) of the saleswomen and female clientele who patronized the stores.

In their discussions about the 'problem' of customers or the 'shopgirl', Benson found a portal into everyday life on the retail floor. Thus, with virtually no first-hand testimo-nials, we learn the extent to which the female middle-class customer pushed stores' return policies to the limit and how she could send a male manager scurrying about to right a wrong order or to discipline an impolite clerk (p. 95). The ability of a patron to demand style, service and 'appropriate' treatment, for Benson, highlights the extent to which the consumption setting served as an arena where middle-class women could exercise power out of proportion to what they could wield in the home.

Something of the clerks' everyday world could also be gathered when discussed as a managerial 'problem', as managers 'complained with gusto and candor about the failings of their employees' on the pages of trade journals (p. 230). Benson uncovered a 'clerking sisterhood' of resistance among saleswomen by combining material from trade journals, a few social science reports and some testimonials of shopgirls in consumer women's magazines. Of note are clerks' own stories taken from *Echo*, a Filenes's employee newspaper, where everything from poetry to expressions of pride in their skill to stories of outright refusals to comply with management strictures give a textured sense of the everyday battles and 'culture' of saleswomen. Here we learn that, at Filenes's, clerks had elaborate forms of communication, from code words to the tapping of pencils, to signal each other about, for instance, an approaching customer or manager (p. 245).

Through it all, Benson gives little indication of concern about questions of the partiality or trustworthiness of materials beyond stating that 'careful' use of them will reveal more than one point of view (p. 314). Her success in conveying a sense of the everyday 'work culture' of department stores resides in her inventive and intelligent combination of sources allowing her to offer multiple views of multiple 'insides.'

Not all historians of advertising and consumer culture who use trade materials are on the prowl for the inside view, or are keen to problemitize it. William Leach's history of modern American consumer culture swims in materials from the trade press, numerous business and advertising archives and, notably, the papers of the John Wanamaker collection. But, in *Land of Desire: Merchants, Power and the Rise of a New American Culture* (1993), he states that the book is not about behavior or social consensus but about the creation of a new culture through the efforts of a small set of business elites (p. xiv). Impressive in its scope and detail and laudable for its comprehensive reach, Leach's work nevertheless presents something of a grand narrative about the spread and eventual triumph of the new undemocratic, but obviously appealing, consumer culture. In a sense, the story that *Land of Desire* tells is told from the business and cultural elites' perspectives and rarely steps out of that viewpoint to find other voices to counterbalance or at least contextualize the dominant account.

My own work, influenced and inspired by those discussed above, examines the interplay between the children's clothing industry and the rise of the 'child consumer' from 1917 to 1962. In *The Commodification of Childhood* (2004), I examine in some detail a key (and for a time the only) trade journal devoted to the children's wear industry, now known as *Earnshaw's Review*. Paging through the publication, I began to discern several orders of 'data'. These ran from articles discussing the seemingly 'technical' considerations concerning staffing, the flux of sales, the best location for an infants' and children's department to more ideological and cultural descriptions of the social role of mothers, their 'desires' and foibles, the appropriateness of certain styles for children (mainly girls) and children's influence on the choice of their own clothing.

I became keen to the epistemological status of 'the child' and 'the mother' in these discussions as there was no hint of market research to inform the writers' statements. In particular, children, even infants, were discussed as if they had pre-existent tastes and desires for specific kinds of clothes and retail settings. It occurred to me that 'child' and, to a different extent, 'mother' were functioning as symbolic currencies – morally inflected to be sure – that were exchanged among buyers, managers and merchants who wrote for and read the publication.

Not in any way 'false' or 'less real' than a living biographical child, these constructs came to be seen as fabrications of figurative persons, what I called 'commercial personae', which assisted in making the commercialization of childhood and motherhood a morally palatable undertaking. Commercial personae consist of 'assemblages of characteristics – known or conjectured, "real" or imagined – constructed by and traded among interested parties in the service of their industry' (p. 19). I present materials and cases in support of my argument that children have gained increasing degrees of social personhood largely, but not exclusively, through market processes and trade constructions by being legitimized as agentive economic actors, i.e., in various commercial personae as 'consumer', over the better part of the last century.

Trade publications can reach beyond their immediate constituency and have a larger, civic impact. In her history of the clashes between the advertising industry and what is commonly referred to as the 1930s consumer movement, Inger L. Stole shows how the advertising trade press served as a microphone or prosthesis for business interests over and against those of the public. *In Advertising on Trial: Consumer Activism and Corporate Public Relations in the 1930s* (2006), she documents the industry's efforts to debunk and marginalize a movement that demanded a high degree of corporate accountability and laws to protect consumers in the marketplace. Industry groups, threatened by the popularity of independent watchdog groups, set out on their own campaigns to 'sell advertising' itself as a form of 'education' while delegitimizing the consumer movement as being unrepresentative of consumers as a whole.

To the chagrin of the advertising industry, consumer advocates found their message particularly welcome in schools and institutions of higher learning, a trend which prompted one trade journal to move beyond its traditional function. Stole recounts the role played by *Advertising Age* as a defender of the industry's interests as it took action by reporting on research 'designed to measure anti-advertisement sentiments and classroom treatment of advertising on several major university campuses' (pp. 126–7). The publication also initiated an annual writing contest to encourage high school and college students to write essays on 'How Advertising Benefits the Consumer' (p. 133) and encouraged instructors to make the activity a part of the curriculum.

Stole's approach to the trade press takes it as a political vehicle, rather than being simply internally oriented. In this way, her work expands the boundaries of 'advertising' to include its own promotional organs and thereby provides insight into how the industry built its own image by fighting against the consumers it proposed to serve.

Not emphasized to any extent above is how each author took pains to compare, verify or otherwise triangulate the views and technical facts proffered by the trade with other forms of evidence, including government reports and stories in consumer magazines and newspapers. Whether imperfect reflections of reality to be deciphered, sources of multiple perspectives, microphones of commercial interest or a forum for the exchange of symbolic currencies, trade materials were examined by each author so as to discern the particular viewpoints made possible by their consultation.

Ethnographies

Since the latter part of the 1990s, there has been a growing interest in the inner workings of the advertising industry. Public images of the advertising profession, images which unfortunately many academics often accept uncritically, have presented it in one of two general ways: either as a highly scientized and therefore manipulating undertaking where researchers have their finger on the pulse of consumer desire, or as a thoroughly creative endeavor arising from the inspiration and perhaps genius of creatives. Indeed any conversation with entering undergraduate advertising majors will confirm that both of these views still hold sway. Perhaps owing to the explosion of electronic and globalized media, to the aggressive corporate sponsorship of events and to the never-ending efforts to make brands a ubiquitous part of public culture (Klein, 1999), some scholars have sought to penetrate the façade of readily visible advertisements in an effort to grapple with the pervasive societal power of the advertising industry.

Sean Nixon points out that researchers have tended to subsume advertising under a larger rubric of 'consumption', thereby turning out 'a rather flat and untroubled picture of the economic and cultural rise of advertising practitioners', as if the industry had an unproblematic, 'functional necessity' about it (1997, 2000, p. 56). Moreover, studies of advertising's 'effects' on consumers as well as many analyses of advertisements – some quite detailed and sophisticated (Williamson, 1978; Goffman, 1979) – focus intently on the finished product but do not and can not speak to the processes involved in their fabrication. Recognizing that much of the work done by advertising professionals has been opaque to scholars as well as to the public, it is not surprising that the turn to the inside view in recent years has taken an ethnographic tendency.

Through interviews, participation and observation, a number of scholars have trained their research gaze on the persons, contexts and social relations informing the creation of advertisements and ad campaigns, rather than only on the ads themselves.[1] Ethnographic inquiry understands advertising as a form of socially informed and embedded production where commercial meanings are manufactured, organized and ultimately deployed in tight packets of images, words and sounds to a potentially global audience. The thrust of this research is to study 'producer behavior' with the intent of demystifying an industry increasingly on the defensive from intensifying public scrutiny.

When researchers approach advertising practitioners as informants and conceptualize their profession as a field site, questions of the social use and status of knowledge come to the fore in a number of ways. For one, advertisers, as Lury and Warde (1997) show, must convince potential clients that they 'know' consumers and the market, and that this knowledge is expert (not folk) knowledge that is derived from calculable and replicable operations (pp. 89–90). The point and function of advertising, they claim, is to reduce producer anxiety (see also Mazzarella, 2003a, 2003b). Advertising firms rely on market research firms who, in a similar manner, sell not only their particular service or product, i.e., their data sheets, but also a sense of their competence and of the robustness of their findings to advertising firms who, in turn, use these claims to alleviate client concerns.

Anne Cronin's (2004a) interviews with British advertising practitioners and market researchers points to the multiple audiences and multiple motivations for undertaking advertising campaigns. A 'good' campaign to her respondents was not necessarily measured in increased sales but in peer recognition of the innovativeness of the effort. Practitioners engaged in a process of 'post rationalization' whereby research is deployed after the fact to assure clients as to the prudence of their choice of the agency (pp. 347–8). Indeed, Cronin found that account planners and consumer researchers took a decidedly anti-intellectual stance on 'book' knowledge, preferring at times even 'badly run' focus groups (p. 348). She concludes that brand managers deploy research to manage their clients and that the validity of research in this context comes to be defined in terms of its utility (pp. 350–52).

In a similar vein, a number of scholars who have entered advertising agencies as researchers have pointed out the power dynamic between client and agency, the competitive environment in which agency exists vis-à-vis other agencies and how these frame the structure, status and use of 'knowledge' (Nava, 1997; Nixon, 2002; Malefyt, 2003; Mazzarella, 2003a, 2003b; see also chapters in Malefyt and Moeran, 2003). Certainly the researcher's ability to query and observe practitioners in this way enables a view of advertising as practice, rather than as product, and thus facilitates analysis of the extent and nature of mediation that occurs within firms and among those engaged in advertising work (see Cronin, 2004b). The presence of the researcher who can follow campaigns and decisions as they change in response to changing situations and priorities, or who can interview about these processes, brings into relief the multiple actors and positions involved in the making of an advertisement, such as clients, creatives, account planners and research firms (Malefyt and Moeran, 2003). Consequently, as Kover (1995) points out in his study of implicit theories of advertising copyrighters, interpretive inquiry details how knowledge is a co-creation which cannot be simply located within individuals or in mere creative genius.

Problems of knowledge always accompany any kind of study and any sort of method regardless of topic or technique. In the study of advertising and markets, knowledge arises as a particular kind of problem to the extent that many practitioners in these professions draw upon their own understandings and beliefs about the people and markets they sell – something which Marchand addressed in his own way. The difference here resides in the fact that, in ethnographic research, the researcher also must deal with the way her or his cultural position and presence inform the social shape and character of the materials gathered, a point barely touched upon in the studies discussed above. A number of recently published ethnographic studies on advertising, marketing and marketplaces offer different takes on problems of knowledge, or knowledges, in the context of commercial enterprise.

Arlene Davila (2001), in *Latinos, Inc.*, examines the historical and contemporary marketing of Latinidad, focusing particularly on the way commercial representations 'may shape people's cultural identities as well as affect notions of belonging and cultural citizenship in public life' (p. 2). Interviewing and conversing with advertising practitioners, observing marketing presentations to clients and examining market reports and other materials allows Davila to trace the dynamics through which the construction of a generic 'Hispanic' consumer continues to persist despite the diversity of Latin ethnicities of US consumers and practitioners themselves. Market research, she notes, which should give a fuller picture than a cultural stereotype, tends to be presented in 'digests', 'fact sheets' and 'snapshots', invariably ignoring class differences in favor of privileging cultural uniqueness to clients interested in marketability. Notably marketers and advertisers deploy 'commercial personae' of Latino consumers who are often presented as communally and family oriented, brand loyal, respectful of elders and preferring Spanish over English, among other characteristics (pp. 68–74).

The tensions and interactions reinforcing the tendency toward generic depictions are multiple and cross-cutting. Latino marketers and advertisers often scrutinize the authenticity of newcomers to their agencies in terms of country of origin, skin tone and the kind of Spanish they speak (pp. 23–55). Consequently many creatives, account mangers and researchers need to demonstrate or perform their Latin-ness to each other, sometimes in stereotypical ways. Davila's entrée into the Latino marketing and advertising worlds was facilitated by her own self-presentation as a Spanish-speaking, light-skinned and fashionably dressed Latina who thus posed 'no threat' to her informants' 'normative ideal of Latinidad' (pp. 18–19). She finds that the overwhelming preference for light-skinned models in advertisements is shared by creatives, account managers and clients alike who believe in and therefore enable a 'pan-Hispanic look' (pp. 56–87), despite preferences to the contrary expressed in focus groups (pp. 201–15).

Davila argues that it is the profit-making impetus, rather than simple politics or simple racism (although clearly evident), that drives the effort to present a distinct, manageable, non-threatening 'Latin look'. She concludes that ethnic marketing remains politicized as 'the last bastion of representation for minority populations' all the while concealing and contaminating multifaceted ethnic subjects (p. 240).

The distinctive contours and trajectory involved in the making and remaking of the 'gay market', detailed by Katherine Sender (2004) in *Business, Not Politics*, point to some tensions shared by Latino/as: namely, there exists an ever-present push and pull between the strong tendency of marketing practice to narrow representations of a 'group' into a publicly palatable, commercially viable persona and the diverse and changing expressions of those living members of the 'group'. Some of the key, defining issues for self-identified gay, lesbian, bisexual and transgender (GLBT) people center on visibility, i.e., the extent to which GLBT people can, should and want to be publicly identified, in what contexts and the extent to which this identity is or should be connected to sex and sexuality.

Through the interviews, combined with analyses of advertisements, attendance at marketing presentations and examination of trade press articles, Sender finds that the routines of production encode ideologies that reproduce dominant images (p. 96). Because GLBT identity is not necessarily as publicly apparent as, say, racial or ethnic identities, there is a need to produce, and thus reproduce, a recognizable 'gayness', an effort which quickly slides into stereotypes of overly style-conscious and sexually obsessed gay *men* in particular. In addition, the typification required for marketing and advertising to reinscribe the GLBT consumer (and again gay men in particular) as affluent, conspicuous consumers, essentially erases the non-flamboyant and poor (pp. 95–9). Ultimately, she concludes, the construction of the gay consumer – by GLBT *and* general marketers and media – functions as a form of ideological containment through a policed and often self-policed form of market-appropriate visibility.

Sender reports that her struggle with the problem of knowledge centered on issues of proprietary information where she sometimes had to settle for general discussions and overviews instead of the detail an ethnographer seeks (pp. 243–52). Perhaps most encompassing was the manner of posture of marketing and advertising practitioners who are bent on 'pitching' themselves, their products and organizations. Sender became acutely aware that she, as a specific audience in interpersonal interviews and as part of a larger audience at presentations, was often targeted with persuasive, marketing 'pitches' by those invested in the 'credibility of the gay market' who wished to put their organization, work and own professional image in the best light (pp. 248–51). Recognizing that 'the pitch' framed the discursive context of all communications with professionals led her to treat all documents from industry as forms of marketing appeal, not just those explicitly marked as such.

Anthropologist William Mazzarella spent time in the 1990s at a Bombay advertising agency, participating in strategy sessions, creative meetings and agency–client consultations (2003a, p. 296, n. 34). He encountered similar practical, epistemological and ideological problems faced by practitioners as those described by Sender, Davila and others. Like Sender, he found that practitioners were uncomfortable being the object of inquiry, often making him an audience for pitches regarding their ingenuity, competence and prowess (2003b).

In *Shoveling Smoke*, Mazzarella (2003a) examines the successful and provocative Kama Sutra condom campaign of the early 1990s, notable both for its explicit sexual imagery and for its appropriation of the spiritual sex manual *Kamasutra*. Participant recollections of the campaign, including those of the photographer, reveal the multiple tensions they faced and which the ads addressed. Appeals to the new middle-class, 'aspirational' consumer using 'modern', sexy images and lifestyle implications were counterbalanced by concerns about public 'good taste', a balance partly achieved in the aesthetic of the black-and-white photography used. Any threats to national and ethnic identity that might be invoked by appeals to a 'modern', perhaps Western, consumer were eased by the references to and the quoting of *Kamasutra*, which worked to keep the product image and referent decidedly 'Indian' (pp. 117–46).

Mazzarella argues that a key purpose of a coherent brand image (besides managing the relationship between client and customer) relates to the agency's 'capacity to manage its relationship with the client' (p. 170). For instance, in relating his observations of agency presentations to the client about the launch of a cellular phone brand, Mazzarella describes the shape of the performance presented by the agency team as an effort to 'heighten the client's flow of adrenaline and sense of expectation' (p. 168). In the meeting, seemingly inspirational and spontaneous solutions were offered in the heat of the moment. The account executive and agency manager played good-cop, bad-cop with the client to give a sense of dynamic, just-in-time mediations to problems (pp. 172–5). These moves served to create drama in the meeting. Practitioners in this way apply their persuasive skills to their own clients (as well as to the researcher), a practice which can extend beyond the meeting room to the launch of the product in a spectacular techno-display staged to dazzle the client and hopefully give reassurance that he chose the right agency (pp. 180–83).

Mazzarella makes the case that examining advertising and marketing practice by attending to the very detailed and situated contexts is the only way to grasp their larger implications and extensions. Ethnographic inquiry problemitizes the meaning of any advertisement: how it can and should be 'read' and, as well, whether an ad *can* be read with any sense of confidence without attending to the behavior and contexts of those involved in the process of its production. Echoing Marchand, albeit with a quite different temperament and focus, he concludes that, 'Because commodity images do not show everything, we should not think that they are obscure' (p. 287).

Conclusion
Taken together, the works examined here invite us to consider 'advertising' and 'marketing' as phenomena that cannot be located solely on the magazine page, television screen, corporate logo or brand mascot. Indeed none of the insights offered above could be gleaned from scrutinizing advertisements or consumers, however intensely, in isolation.

Through often quite inventive uses of trade materials, interviews and personal observation, scholars in pursuit of the inside view offer a glimpse into practices, process and considerations not readily accessible from one's everyday, public position as a magazine reader or television enthusiast. Historians deal mainly with extant and somewhat static and scarce resources, having to infer behavior, attitudes and practices from them (oral histories aside). Ethnographers, on the other hand, often find themselves awash in encounters, conversations and observations of those whose lives and worlds they study. Both face questions of knowledge and perspective – of their multiplicities and selectivity – and thus the problem of representation.

In training the research gaze upon those who have been and are involved in the making of the images, spaces and social relations of commerce, these scholars offer an understanding of practitioners as astute cultural observers who, like interpretive researchers themselves, read the culture for pattern and meaning. As sociologist Don Slater (2002) observes, practitioners do not see and, importantly, do not experience the 'market' separate from 'culture', but understand that both calculable strategies and larger meaning systems inform each other in the everyday, pragmatic activities (p. 63). The many insights achieved by those discussed above are made possible precisely because practitioners were 'humanized' and seen, not as 'cultural dupes' within their fields, but as meaning-making agents who are members of the larger culture who occupy distinct and strategic positions in powerful professions.

To take this interpretive stance toward practitioners, however, is not to excuse or exonerate their activities as benign simply because they are not outright vilified. As Mazzarella (2003b, p. 68) points out, the important parallel between anthropologists and practitioners is not that they both study 'culture' so much as they engage in 'public cultural practices'. Indeed Stole's descriptions of the advertising industry's successful efforts to stifle a consumer movement, Benson's feminist analysis of power relations on the department store 'shop floor' and Davila's and Sender's discussions of the complex interplay between identity and commercial practice, among others, all speak to the public and political consequences of professions whose main purpose is to create and circulate particular versions of the good life for their own benefit.

It should come as no surprise that the turn to the inside view in the last 20 years comes at time when advertising, branding, electronic communications and capitalism are ascendant over the globe. There is an increasingly felt need to understand, penetrate and criticize the brokers of a dominant public order of images and commercial meaning. To strive continually to understand them and to attempt to see the world through their eyes to the extent possible assists in demystifying, and hopefully de-deifying, advertisers and marketers. However minute compared to the scale of the reach of these industries, these efforts by scholars nevertheless are sincere and innovative attempts continually to hold back the curtain and pull down the veil of images, practices and proscriptions that often present themselves as inevitable and natural. The turn to the inside view rejects claims to naturalness and inevitability in favor of making visible the relentless presence of the 'hand of the market' in everyday life.

Note
1.   Not focused on advertising or marketing but not to be neglected is Lisa Peñaloza and Mary Gilly's (1999) interesting study, 'market acculturation', on a multi-ethnic street market in southern California.

References

Barry, Thomas and Daniel Howard (1990), 'A review and critique of the hierarchy of effects in advertising', *International Journal of Advertising*, **9** (April–June), 121–35.

Benson, Susan Porter (1986), *Counter Cultures*, Bloomington: Indiana University Press.

Cook, Daniel Thomas (2004), *The Commodification of Childhood*, Durham: Duke University Press.

Crane, Diana (1992), *The Production of Culture*, London: Sage.

Cronin, Anne (2004a), 'Regimes of mediation: advertising practitioners as cultural intermediaries?', *Consumption, Markets and Culture*, **7** (4) (December), 349–70.

Cronin, Anne (2004b), 'Currencies of commercial exchange: advertising agencies and the promotional imperative', *Journal of Consumer Culture*, **4** (3) (November), 339–60.

Davila, Arlene (2001), *Latinos, Inc.*, Berkeley: University of California Press.

DiMaggio, Paul (1977), 'Market structure, the creative process, and popular culture: toward an organizational reinterpretation of mass-culture theory', *Journal of Popular Culture*, **3**, 436–52.

Dornfeld, Barry (1998), *Producing Public Television, Producing Public Culture*, Princeton: Princeton University Press.

du Gay, Paul and Michael Pryke (eds) (2002), *Cultural Economy*, London: Sage.

Freud, Sigmund (1950), *The Interpretation of Dreams*, trans. A.A. Brill, New York: Modern Library.

Geertz, Clifford (1973), *The Interpretation of Cultures*, New York: Basic Books.

Gitlin, Todd (1983), *Inside Prime Time*, New York: Pantheon.

Goffman, Erving (1979), *Gender Advertisements*, New York: Harper.

Goldman, Robert (1993), *Reading Ads Socially*, New York: Routledge.

Hirsch, Paul M. (1981), 'Processing fads and fashions: an organization-set analysis of cultural industry systems', in Chentra Mukerji and Michael Schudson (eds), *Rethinking Popular Culture*, pp. 313–34.

Klein, Naomi (1999), *No Logo*, New York: Picador/St Martin's Press.

Kover, Arthur J. (1995), 'Copyrighters' implicit theories of communication: an exploration, *Journal of Consumer Research*, **21** (March), 596–611.

Leach, William (1993), *Land of Desire*, New York: Pantheon.

Lury, Celia and Alan Warde (1997), 'Investments in the imaginary consumer: conjectures regarding power, knowledge and advertising, in Mica Nava, Andrew Blake, Iain MacRury and Barry Richards (eds), *Buy This Book*, London: Routledge, pp. 87–102.

Malefyt, Timothy Dewaal(2003), 'Models, metaphors and client relations: the negotiated meanings of advertising', in Timothy Dewaal Malefyt and Brian Moeran (eds), *Advertising Cultures*, Oxford: Berg, pp. 139–64.

Malefyt, Timothy Dewaal and Brian Moeran (eds) (2003), *Advertising Cultures*, Oxford: Berg.

Marchand, Roland (1985), *Advertising the American Dream: Making the Way for Modernity*, Berkeley: University of California Press.

Martens, Lydia, Dale Southerton and Sue Scott (2004), 'Bringing children (and parents) into the sociology of consumption', *Journal of Consumer Culture*, **4** (2) 155–82.

Mazzarella, William (2003a), *Shoveling Smoke: Advertising and Globalization in Contemporary India*, Durham: Duke University Press.

Mazzarella, William (2003b), 'Critical publicity/public criticism: reflections on fieldwork in the Bombay ad world', in Timothy Dewaal Malefyt and Brian Moeran (eds), *Advertising Cultures*, Oxford: Berg, pp. 55–74.

Miller, Daniel (1995), 'Consumption as the vanguard of history: a polemic by way of an introduction', in Daniel Miller (ed.), *Acknowledging Consumption*, London: Routledge, pp. 1–57.

Naples, Michael J. (1979), *Effective Frequency: The Relationship Between Frequency and Advertising Effectiveness*, New York: Association of National Advertisers.

Nava, Mica (1997), 'Framing advertising: cultural analysis and the incrimination of visual texts', in Mica Nava, Andrew Blake, Iain MacRury and Barry Richards (eds), *Buy This Book*, London: Routledge, pp. 34–50.

Nixon, Sean (1997), 'Advertising executives as modern men: masculinity and the UK advertising industry in the 1980s', in Mica Nava, Andrew Blake, Iain MacRury and Barry Richards (eds), *Buy This Book*, London: Routledge, pp. 103–19.

Nixon, Sean (2000), 'In pursuit of the professional ideal: advertising and the construction of commercial expertise in Britain 1953–64', in Peter Jackson, Michelle Lowe, Daniel Miller and Frank Mort (eds), *Commercial Cultures: Economies, Practices, Spaces*. Oxford: Berg, pp. 55–75.

Nixon, Sean (2002), 'Re-imagining the ad agency: the cultural connotations of economic forms', in Paul du Gay and Michael Pryke (eds), *Cultural Economy*, London: Sage, pp. 132–47.

O'Barr, William M. (1994), *Culture and the Ad*, Boulder, CO: Westview Press.

Pechmann, Cornelia and David, W. Stewart (1989), 'Advertising repetition: a critical review of wearin and wearout', *in* James H. Leigh and Claude R. Martin (eds), *Current Issues and Research in Advertising*, Ann Arbor, MI: University of Michigan, pp. 285–9.

Peñaloza, Lisa and Mary C. Gilly (1999), 'Marketer acculturation: the changer and the changed', *Journal of Marketing*, **63** (3) (July), 84–104.

Peterson, Richard (1978), 'The production of cultural change: the case of contemporary country music', *Social Forces*, **45**, 292–314.

Schor, Juliet (2004), *Born to Buy*, New York: Scribner.

Sender, Katherine (2004), *Business, Not Politics: The Making of the Gay Market*, New York: Columbia University Press.

Slater, Don (2002), 'Capturing markets from the economists', in Paul du Gay and Michael Pryke (eds), *Cultural Economy*, London: Sage, 59–77.

Stole, Inger L. (2006), *Advertising on Trial: Consumer Activism and Corporate Public Relations in the 1930s*, Urbana: University of Illinois Press.

Turner, Victor (1967), *The Forest of Symbols*, Chicago: University of Chicago Press.

Vakratsas, Demetrios and Tim Ambler (1999), 'How advertising works: what do we really know?', *Journal of Marketing*, **63** (1) (Jan.), 26–43.

Warde, Alan (1992), 'Notes on the relation between production and consumption', in R. Burrows and C. Marsh (eds), *Consumption and Class: Divisions and Change*, London: Macmillan, pp. 15–31.

Williamson, Judith (1978), *Decoding Advertisements*, London: Boyars.

41 Researching ethnicity and consumption
Lisa Peñaloza

Introduction

> To analyze how white Americans thought about the west, it helps to think anthropologically. One lesson of anthropology is cultural persistence . . . beliefs and values will persist even when the supporting economic and political structures have vanished . . . Among those persistent values, few have more power than the idea of innocence. The dominant motive for moving west was improvement and opportunity, not injury to others. Few white Americans went west intending to ruin the natives and despoil the continent. Even when they were trespassers, westering Americans were hardly, in their own eyes, criminals; rather they were pioneers. The ends abundantly justified the means; personal interest in the acquisition of property coincided with national interest in the acquisition of territory, and those interests overlapped in turn with the mission to extend the domain of Christian civilization. Innocence of intention placed the course of events in a bright and positive light; only over time would the shadows compete for our attention. (Patty Limerick, *Legacy of Conquest*)

Ethnicity is a pressing topic in the world today, as most nations grapple with issues related to ethnic difference in increasingly multicultural societies. Many of these issues have a long history stemming from patterns of settlement, competing territorial claims, wars, colonization and slavery among different ethnic, racial and/or religious groups within national borders, e.g., Arabs and Jews in Israel; or Latinos/as, Blacks and Whites in the US. Other issues relate to immigration, legal and illegal, and guest worker programs, as differences between nations in level of development are reflected in business activity in labor and consumption markets. Examples of the former are Mexicans and Cubans in the US, Indians and Pakistanis in the UK, Algerians in France and the Chinese in Indonesia and the Philippines; while examples of the latter are Turks in Germany and Denmark.

This chapter discusses methodological challenges at the nexus of ethnicity and consumption. In approaching these challenges I overview contributions from various disciplines to the study of ethnicity, and highlight examples regarding Latinos/as in the US, my area of study over the last 15 years. The largest minority group in the US, Latinos/as accounted for 14.2 per cent of the national population growth in 2004 (US Census, 2004). Latinos/as exhibit sociodemographic differences and differences in consumption patterns and processes from white mainstream consumers in the country that are of interest to consumer researchers. Further, situating such study within markets is important as well, as marketers' work in addressing ethnic subgroups plays upon existing distinctions, at times aggravating and/or ameliorating them.

Like ethnic studies, studies of consumption have benefited from work spanning the spectrum of academic disciplines: psychology, sociology, history, marketing, economics, political science and the humanities. I point to a combination of factors (sociodemographic, religious, national policy and international business dynamics) igniting smoldering tensions between groups in increasingly multicultural societies, and discuss methodological challenges related to subjectivity, agency, social relations and market relations for minority ethnic groups.

Then, rejecting popular notions and research conventions that reserve ethnicity for minorities and that have colluded in the innocence of Whites intimated in the opening quotation, I discuss issues in investigating mainstream ethnic groups, in this case, white ethnicity and culture in the US and abroad in relation to market culture. As more and more societies in the world are multicultural and as markets gain ground as cultural institutions, it is increasingly important that studies of ethnicity and consumption take a good look at patterns of social relations between mainstream and marginal groups, and how such social relations are played out in markets. In closing I point to further directions in research, extending from two major views of ethnic consumers: market niche versus marginal group, in incorporating research reflexivity and exploring relations between democracy and capitalism.

From ethnic consumption to consuming ethnicity

> As Roman imperialism laid the foundations of modern civilization, and led the wild barbarians of these islands [Britain] along the path of progress, so in Africa today we are repaying the debt and bringing to the dark places of the earth, the abode of barbarism and cruelty, the torch of culture and progress, while ministering to the material needs of our own civilization . . . We hold these countries because it is the genius of our race to colonise, to trade, and to govern. (Lugard, 1922)

A sordid past
To understand ethnic consumption it is helpful to contrast what ethnicity represents today with its earlier connotations. Today ethnicity is fundamentally tied to social subgroups of people and expresses their range of physical characteristics, contested subjectivities and social positions. It encompasses the ways of being and knowing of the group, and reverberates in the way one relates to oneself as a group member and interacts with others in society. Relations between social groups are fundamental to ethnicity as well, particularly how members of other groups treat the group in question and its members, both informally in personal interactions and formally on the job, in the marketplace, in education and in local and national government programs, to name but a few institutional sites.

As with many other basic social concepts such as nation, city, community, family, class and gender, ethnic scholars emphasize that ethnicity takes on particular meanings with respect to particular social subgroups, and at particular historical times and geographic places, and that it is increasingly affected by market forces and representations in an increasingly global economy. Today we are steadily moving towards a place where ethnicity is something both mainstream and marginal groups have (Delgado and Stefancic, 1997), but it was not always seen in this way, and remnants of the way of thinking of the ethnic as minority and as different remain in ethnic studies of consumption.

Early mention of ethnicity is strongly entrenched in the social order and world view of colonialism (Foucault, 1970), as illustrated in the quotation opening this section. 'Ethnics' were those who, from different countries, particularly those less developed, and characterizing their early treatment was exploration and categorization, culminating in the caging, labeling and display of 'specimens' in museums and World Expos (Harris, 1993). Significant for our purposes here is the mix of fascination for the other coupled with the zealous, ethnically unbridled use of the scientific method in accumulating knowledge of the other and using it in the pursuit of social and economic interests.

Manifestations of this social order can be traced through the slave trade of Blacks in Europe and in the US and the genocide of indigenous peoples throughout the Americas. Slavery, perhaps the ultimate commodification of the other in trade, vaulted European nations to richessse through the fifteenth and sixteenth centuries. Slave labor was as fundamental to the agricultural economy of the US Southeast as well, just as racial distinctions were to its civil society. Over time, accounting measures of slaves' physical characteristics and sale prices morphed into strict social codes and laws segregating business, residence and marriage that were not overturned until the Civil Rights legislation of 1965 (Elkins, 1968).

For Latinos/as, the benefits of Spanish colonization quickly turned to losses as the US took territory in the Southwest in the mid-1800s (Acuña, 1988). Echoing past diatribes against savage Indians, Whites formulated a doctrine of Manifest Destiny (Limerick, 1987). Its advantageous positioning for the US in relation to Latin America reverberates to the present in the Central American Free Trade Agreement debated on the House floor as I write this (February 2006).

There are stark lessons for consumer researchers in studying relationships between ethnic groups. Much has changed for minority ethnic groups in the US, from the enslavement of Blacks, genocide of Native Americans and colonization of Latinos that fueled US nation-building and consolidation, through the Emancipation Proclamation of 1862 and the Civil Rights Legislation of 1965, to the present institutionalization of ethnic groups in the marketplace.

Social relations are a convoluted legacy of the best and worst that we can treat each other. Historically and at present scholars have made advances in understanding social difference by examining discourses of superior civilization against opportunistic treatments of others at home and abroad. This barometer of what a society values and devalues is vital to consumer research. The next section overviews writings across a number of disciplines, tracing various developments on ethnic subjectivity, agency and social relations and extending them to topics related to contemporary consumption and markets.

Multidisciplinary developments
In discussing the contributions of various disciplines to the study of ethnicity, I begin with individual-level conceptualizations and constructs and continue to social ones. I proceed from outsider to insider views, and from disciplines in the social sciences to marketing and to political science.

Important among the psychological contributions to our understandings of ethnicity is work on identity and values. Amado Padilla (1980) and Henry Triandis (1998) invigorated conceptualizations of cultural identity and values by incorporating the experiences and perspectives of Latinos/as. They built upon earlier work distinguishing between ascribed and prescribed ethnic social characteristics, to feature how ethnic members deal with their ethnicity. Knowledge of the culture and experiences with it are important considerations in ethnic identity and affiliation (i.e., desires to claim or disavow themselves from an ethnic group), as is the treatment of the group in society.

Their work adds flesh and blood to the psychological canon of values profiles. Hofstede's (2002) profiles of national cultures bridges macro and micro elements in emphasizing contrasts in values and priorities: collectivist/individual orientation, fate/ agency, present/future time and hierarchical/egalitarian social relations. The scale is commonly used in consumer research to profile ethnic groups and measure cultural influences on consumption patterns. Its challenges lie in considering different levels of development across rural/urban regions within nations, untangling international class differences and investigating how people understand and feel about social difference.

In contrast to the individual level of analysis in psychological studies, sociological studies build on the coherence of the group. Some of this work profiles Latinos/as sociodemographically, as with Borjas and Tienda's (1985) survey work drawing attention to persistent income gaps. At the time of this writing the median family income for Hispanics was $34 968, as compared to $55 885 for Whites and $34 293 for Blacks. Rates of poverty follow a somewhat similar pattern; 39.8 per cent of Hispanic workers earned wages below that level for a family of four, compared to 30.4 per cent of Blacks and 20.4 per cent of Whites (Mishal et al., 2005). The wealth gap is more striking. By 2001, the median net worth of Hispanic families totaled $10 563, compared to $17 537 for Blacks and $111 532 for Whites (Robles, 2004).

Another area of important work has been on the Latino family. Baca-Zinn (1995) stressed the importance of correcting false universals based on white, middle-class family forms. Difference all too often has been treated as culture, she argues, criticizing influential work by the Chicago School of Sociology through the 1970s that was itself a product of its time, emphasizing social problems of displacement related to urbanization and modernization from the implicit ideal of the organizational man and his dedicated housewife and children inhabiting the suburbs.

Instead Baca-Zinn exhorts researchers to include various family forms in a more general framework that incorporates social conventions based on gender and race, and attends to adaptation to specific historical, social and market conditions. Rethinking the family as an adaptive social structure reclaims some of the benefits from pejorative accounts of resource sharing, cooperation and sacrifice for Latino/a families, without romanticizing or idealizing them (Zambrana, 1995). Attention to internal variations remains important in these studies, owing to wide diversity in national origin, socioeconomic status and language use/acquisition. As examples, although there are general trends in Latino/a families as having younger, larger families with more children and extended family members; families spanning national borders as a result of diasporic movements of people; and resources topping 12 billion annually in remittances (Robles, 2004), families differ in cultural and language challenges for recent generations as compared to longer-term US residents, and even within households, given differences between parents and children and among children (Massey et al., 1995).

Another feature of sociological work is serious attention to social relations, particularly relations of power between mainstream and marginal social groups. Our understandings of consumers can benefit from a stronger sociological orientation in attending to group interactions and how they change over time as the result of birthrates, immigration, the state of domestic economy and changing representations of the groups. A growing force affecting social relations is the market (Slater and Tonkiss, 2001) and media representations (Rodriguez, 1998). Dávila's (2001) study of Cuban-owned ad agencies institutionalizing Latino/a identity is an excellent case in point.

Since the civil rights movements Latinos/as have experienced some social incorporation, as evident in increasing friendships and marriages between Latinos/as and nonLatinas/os. Workplace interactions are increasingly common with the presence of more minorities in the labor force, although such growth continues disproportionately for the working classes in various construction and service sectors and in agriculture (Robles, 2004). Even so, Latinos/as continue to experience discrimination and segregation in social interactions and in the marketplace (Peñaloza, 1994a, 1994b, 2005), pointing to important consumer research issues in keeping social relations at the fore.

Culture is the central focus of anthropology. Because this includes a fairly comprehensive embrace of the way members of a group see the world, their social realities, values, and priorities, anthropological approaches have generated key insights regarding ethnicity and consumption. Among these are the ways members reproduce cultural forms in consumption discourses and rituals (Appadurai, 1986), how the knower is always implicated in the known (Rosaldo, 1989) and how the market is itself a culture (du Gay and Pryke, 2002).

Anthropologists grapple with the challenges of comparing and valuing societies at different levels of development. Rosaldo (1989) observed a peculiar ratio, such that those who tend to be studied the most as having the most culture tend to be the most different and have the fewest resources, while those studied the least tend to be closest to researchers, and have the most resources and the least culture. He challenged myths of detachment and constructions of the innocent scholar documenting the culturally different as smokescreens for complicity with colonialism and imperialist national development, and urged the field to adopt more relational ways of knowing and writing the other.

Reflexivity, then, is not just the position of the researcher vis-à-vis the researched, but it also increasingly concerns his/her relations to them as a function of his/her ethnicity, socioeconomic background, and experience in the developed/developing worlds. These dimensions of researcher subjectivity and agency are important tools in generating more consciousness regarding how we see and study social relations of power. Further these skills render knowledge production more transparent in ethnographic texts by addressing explicitly who writes cultural knowledge, about whom, for whom, who is implicated in it and who benefits.

Globalization studies highlight rapid alterations in relations of culture and place. No longer anchored but far from free-floating, cultures deterritorialize and reterritorialize, altering both groups and places. Flows of technology, people and cultural products do not move solely West to East, but also move from the 'Third World' to the 'First World' and even circumvent the West entirely, in moving East to East and from Third to Third World nations (Inda and Rosaldo, 2002). Some of the pressing concerns: tensions between cultures and nations, and cultures and markets; lopsided distributions of wealth in societies; breakdowns of traditional institutions with modernization; religious conflicts; poverty; infrastructural development; and international relations and policy.

Work in marketing is marked by a historical split between that employing a marketing gaze and that oriented more towards consumers, following in the traditions of the social sciences. Examples of the former blur distinctions between academics and practitioners, using the plural pronoun 'we' in measuring associations between key sociodemographic variables and consumption behavior in the form of purchases, or related psychological processes, such as attitudes or intentions, towards the goals of identifying distinct consumption patterns and processes for firms to better target members of ethnic groups (Tharp, 2001). The interested view of marketers in looking at consumers is far from the unbiased ideals of science, but, like other applied disciplines, skirts these research issues and other ethical questions in the interest of developing 'best practices'.

In contrast, qualitative consumer researchers tend to follow the second path, examining in detail ethnic consumers' subjectivity and agency. There is a flourishing group of qualitative consumer researchers across the globe; for example: Askegaard et al.'s (2005) study of Icelanders in Denmark; Ger and Sandicki's (2005) study of Muslim women in Turkey, Bonsu and Belk's (2003) study of funeral practices in Ghana, Venkatesh's (1995) work in Southern India, and my own with Mexican immigrants (1994a) and Mexican Americans (2005) in the US. This work combines meticulous study of ethnic cultures with attention to intranational social relations and global market forces.

The ethnic studies literature is a veritable well of insights on ethnic subjectivity and agency, as is kindred work in critical race studies, Asian studies, gay and lesbian studies and studies of working-class culture. A central problematic in the ethnic studies literature examines the ways in which ethnic groups are represented and ordered in particular societies. The social context is both the object of study in documenting social conditions and the frame for better understanding subjectivity and agency.

Ethnic studies departments were launched in US universities as part of the Civil Rights Movements in the 1970s and 80s. Activist-scholars pushed their universities into providing space to study various marginalized groups, documenting their experiences from their perspectives towards the dual goals of understanding and developing their communities. By the mid-1990s, these departments had come under attack by groups such as the euphemistically named Academics for Freedom; their very action orientation and challenge to white dominance labeled them as divisive and interested.

Ethnic studies work is characterized by a blend of academic, literary and popular culture approaches across the humanities and social sciences (Aldama and Quiñones, 2004). *Testimonios* (personal testimony) are a vital tool for scholars in validating Latinos'/as' experiences and critiquing disciplinary canons, for example, anthropologist Jose Limon (1992), writer Gloria Anzaldúa (1987), and historian Emma Pérez (1999). Cutting-edge work entails partnering with organizations for community development, and forging international links to ethnic diaspora, labor organizations and anti-globalization activists (San Juan, 2002; Velez-Ibañez et al., 2002).

Historical work has been foundational in building knowledge of ethnic groups useful in mobilizing future generations of community members and academics, and in taking on historical canons of national identity and market development. Examples include Acuña's (1988) studies of violence to Mexicans and the taking of their land throughout the US Southwest, and Montejano's (1987) work recognizing Mexicans and Mexican Americans in US. Western history and countering popular mythologies of democracy with crass business interests, such as the defense of the slave economy in the Texas battle for independence. Viewed from historical approaches, diaspora movements of people, products and capital in the US are anything but unique in comparison with other national, colonial powers. Such work is invaluable in making theoretical contributions regarding complex relations of nationalism, colonialism and ethnicity with gender (Ruiz, 1987, 1998) and class (Garza-Falcon, 1998).

Economic activity is a lifeline for ethnic communities. Even so, work on ethnic economies highlights the convoluted processes of economic development in minority communities in societies characterized by discrimination and segregation (Light and

Gold, 2000). Such development features a mix of industry specialization and community sustenance, as 'ethnic vendors' tailor their offerings via the use of language and cultural symbols in the product and service mix.

Challenges here include investigating how ethnic economies are organized and regulated for community and cultural development and survival. For example Borjas (1999) contrasted Cubans in Florida with Mexicans in California and Texas. Class composition is the biggest difference between the groups impacting their economic development, with labor isses crucial for Mexicans and Mexican Americans, the majority of whom are located in the working classes; while Cubans and Cuban Americans, whose early migration was primarily middle-class and who were already well integrated into US firms operating in Cuba, dominate the economic and political scene in Florida.

Political Science work is useful in bringing forth the political dimensions of ethnicity. It directs attention to national circumstances, with ethnic relations intimately tied to nation building. Examples include Hero's (1992) work on Latinos'/as' voting patterns across the US and Rosales' (2000) work on political representation and participation in San Antonio, Texas. The mixed race category added to the 2000 US Census is a good example of the nation incorporating changing categories to reflect dynamic social relations.

To recap, interdisciplinary work has proved invaluable to ethnic studies and consumption in challenging disciplinary canons and knowledge practices, building theory, and etching new methods and topics by revaluing what has been historically devalued. In the next section I hope to show that we can learn a lot by scrutinizing our perspectives, our topics and our questions, ultimately examining what consumer behavior and marketing can and cannot do for ethnic communities.

Where to go from here

> And of course, the ideal form of ideology of this global capitalism is multiculturalism, the attitude which, from a kind of empty global position, treats each local culture the way the colonizer treats colonized people – as 'natives' whose mores are to be carefully studied and 'respected'. (Slavoj Zizek, 'Multiculturalism')

Where we go from here in studying ethnicity and consumption, that is, the questions we ask and the answers we formulate, are partially a matter of the approach we take. There are problems with the view of targeting ethnic groups as a market and that of studying ethnic consumers as marginalized, as Zizek touches upon in the quotation above. Academics operating from the viewpoint of marketers seldom dig far enough to appreciate how ethnic consumers are impacted by the issues affecting their communities, while academics studying ethnic minority consumers often ignore the work minorities do for themselves and the role of mainstream institutions in reproducing white privilege. Both are precarious positions.

Studies of ethnic consumers have benefited and will continue to benefit from attending to the subjectivity and agency of ethnic members and communities with respect to the phenomena of interest, as Venkatesh (1994) urged years ago. By 'subjectivity' I refer to the way one locates oneself and the group(s) to which one is a member within the social order, how they feel about the group, their position in it, its issues and the position of the group in relation to others. 'Agency' refers to the way people act with respect to the group in its relation to other groups, and what they do in the interest of sustaining their culture and developing their communities.

It remains important to study ethnic group members psychologically, not just as individuals dealing with their culture, but also in families and as communities, and with attention to their relations with other groups. Especially important is how members of ethnic groups see consumption. It is crucial that we expand work on ethnic identity to include ethnic group members' sense of themselves as consumers. We have detoured theoretically in separating ethnic identity as an individual phenomenon apart from consumer subjectivity and agency as a member of an ethnic group.

Sociologically it is important to go beyond the package of ethnic traits, perspectives and values in their influence on consumption behavior to situate consumption within the social domain, viewing ethnicity as a key dimension of the social matrix within which consumption is intelligible. From this view social relations of power are inherent to ethnic consumption, and consumption becomes the terrain in and through which social relations are expressed and negotiated in multicultural societies.

Cultural cross-overs are an emerging area of importance, as Firat (1995) anticipated. Consuming ethnicity, that is, consuming the artifacts and sentiments of a culture, does validate that ethnic group socially. But there are distortion effects, as the market tends to select those artifacts and traits that are more marketable over those less so. This is especially an issue when the larger group consuming a culture is composed of nonmembers, as in tourism (Peñaloza, 2005).

The market is a key institution administering, regulating and reproducing social difference. Our work needs to go much further in developing conceptualizations and constructs of market literacy that capture consumers' understandings of consumption as it affects their communities and social relations. A promising avenue is incorporating insights from critical theory in taking consumers and market processes into account and considering social relations of power with an action orientation in consumers' interests.

We can learn from ethnic studies by refusing to treat ethnicity as solely a person of color issue. Studying ethnic minorities remains important in validating and understanding their experiences, and we can do much better in investigating the issues of ethnic minority communities and how they are furthered and/or compromised via social and market dynamics. But this is only part of the phenomenon.

To better understand ethnicity, we must look at the mainstream cultures of nations, paying attention to their consumption behavior. We must investigate the subjectivity and agency of 'whiteness', examining its discourses and rituals in detail and in relation to market culture with all the disciplinary tools at our disposal. As consumer researchers we can no longer tolerate our complicity with 'whiteness'. Leaving it unexamined reinforces its invisibility as the barometer of normality, permits white people to be innocent, standing apart from ethnic/racial dynamics that benefit them, and cripples our knowlege of ethnicity and consumption.

Instead, we must interrogate white values of individual autonomy, achievement and meritocracy, contrasting them with the structural advantages and privileges of being white. As Lipsitz observed and as doctoral student Michelle Barnhart and I are documenting in a current study, many Whites deny that they have a culture. Like many consumer researchers, Whites tend to think of ethnicity as something people of color have. If asked for their cultural roots, many will claim European descent, but they stop short of claiming the historical and institutional legacy of being the ones against whom all others are measured, the ones from whom all others are different and, still too often, inferior. Such denial of identity may well be part of the legacy of imperialism, as one way of dealing with the contradictions of democratic values and colonial and imperialist actions. Such denial may also arise because white groups, for example White Aryan Nation, tend to be represented as extremists. Interestingly those who identify strongly with a minority ethnic group tend to be represented as radicals as well. Both sets of representations are likely part of the larger phenomenon of ethnicity.

An emerging category in the US is mixed race, making its debut in the 2000 US Census. While there is good reason to be wary of its impacts on ethnic groups in diluting them or further mystifying whiteness, such cross-categories can put a valuable check on the identity politics and nationalisms of individual groups, minority and mainstream.

Social relations remain a pressing topic as well. The one-to-one matching of identity to consumption is hopelessly outdated in multicultural societies, as identity with one group is inherently defined in terms of its difference from other groups. We need further work in the US and other nations that better understands how relations between and within ethnic groups are reproduced and altered in consumer behavior and markets. Examples include class differences within white and minority subcultures (Storper, 2000) and those between rural and urban locations.

Chua (2003) has pointed to the nexus of social hierarchies and market hierarchies in national development. Historical work on Latinos/as in the US shows how the market has reinforced social distinctions as well as lowered them at times. There are pressing challenges for Latinos/as in reproducing their cultural values/system within a market system that incorporates culture selectively. Yet we are far from alone in this. Ethnic social domains are not discrete, distinct entities, but rather operate with blurred edges in and through markets within and across other nations in the world, as Velez-Ibañez et al. (2002) note in their study of transnational Latino communities, in their shared discourses and practices and those with the other groups with which they are in contact.

Ultimately ethnic consumption work interrogates the relationship between capitalism and democracy. At least in the US, with the Civil Rights movements, ethnic groups have gained rights accorded white citizens. Latinos/as' beliefs in equal opportunity and progress can be among their strongest points in working towards individual and community survival. These are not solely the purview of white culture, but rather have energized and mobilized Blacks and Latinos/as in holding this nation to its promises – for all. Strong family values and practices, such as pooled assets, tastes in food, music, film, clothes and lifestyles need not be viewed as cultural obstacles to individual development, but rather as vital to the health of families and communities.

To avoid nostalgic, romantic characterizations of ethnic cultures, we must avoid either/or dichotomies, but rather retain mixed elements of interdependence and sacrifice with independence and autonomy. Furthermore such work should avoid separating consumption from community issues including unemployment and underemployment, teen pregnancy, drugs, nutrition and poverty and attend to larger social patterns of subordination, subjugation and segregation, as well as legitimization and valuing.

We can draw a valuable lesson from historians in refusing to forget that attaining Civil Rights entailed long-term struggles, violent at times, and that gaining such rights was not and never will be a one time ordeal, but continues at present and will likely continue well into the future. While some alarmists caution that the current 'post-affirmative action' era signifies a return to the assimilationism of the 1950s, we have come too far in recognizing ethnic groups socially, in the expectations and values of all residents, citizens as well as those many who come here to live, and institutionally in enthusiastic and comprehensive work developing markets.

Even so, we must revisit conventional economic wisdom and populist common sense that capitalism equals democracy. While democratic developments in political processes have been important in engendering individual agency, and democratic institutions are invaluable in tempering capitalism (Becker and Becker, 1997), this is but one side of the coin and badly needs updating with respect to multicultural consumer (Baudrillard, 1988) and market societies (Slater and Tonkiss, 2001).

More research is called for, investigating re/productions of the social and market systems. Such work will make headway in juxtaposing beliefs in equal opportunity and the American dream of working for a better life, owning a house and making progress for oneself and one's family, with experiences of ethnic groups as consumers and in relation to markets. Markets grant social legitimacy to ethnic groups in targeting them as market niches (Dávila, 2001; Peñaloza and Gilly, 1999; Peñaloza, 1994a) and this will only accelerate as markets grow in relation to nations in terms of assets. At the same time, national governments maintain important roles in legitimating ethnic subjects and groups, enacting social and market relations in budgets, policies and procedures (Lipsitz, 1998; San Juan, 2002).

Turning to the other side of the coin, it is equally important to ask what capitalism does to democracy. In the US, the unique blend of democracy and capitalism has brought about unheralded rights for minority groups, as well as bloated lobbyist organizations and Tamany Hall-scale political action committees that dwarf individual representation. Globally further work is of the utmost importance, examining the spread of capitalism to better understand its market cultures and how they favor the US. and Europe by means of the World Bank and IMF institutions and global trade policy (Wade, 2003).

Regarding addressing relations between white culture and market culture, a pressing issue is reflexivity (see Joy et al., this volume) and it, too, is at once a global and a local issue. We must begin to look at ourselves as researchers who are also ethnic, and we must examine our positions relative to consumers and our roles in reproducing social and market systems as we study them. We must look at the impact of debt practices and institutions on cultural values and consumption expectations and experiences in the US. We must examine overlaps and contradictions between white culture and market culture, looking into what the market does for the white community, and examining what roles Whites play in the market and in our research conventions.

To begin, the most immediate thing we can do is qualify our studies of white, first-world consumer behavior as the minority this group represents in the world. Learning from anthropology, it is high time we recognized how our quest for universals masks our own provincialism and renders us complicit with a value hierarchy that places the US at the invisible center of global consumer behavior and consumer culture, and either ignores or devalues the vast differences between ourselves and others.

A promising avenue for further work is investigating forms of otherness as institutionalized in markets and trade treaties. Other nations in the world grappling with cultural difference look to us (researchers) with roughly equal parts of admiration and consternation: admiration for our principles and actions in institutionalizing equal opportunity and a fair shake in life, consternation where we have fallen short, and what these principles mean in nations where mainstream groups remain entrenched in privilege.

In closing, we can do a much better job documenting and imagining consumption alternatives valuing ethnic groups in developing communities, societies and markets. We must work harder to hold capitalist markets to the democratic principles of participation, equal representation and equal opportunity, even as we work to better understand these as particular social and historical US developments.

Richard Rodriguez penned a recent book entitled *Brown: The Last Discovery of America*. While based on sound demographic forecasting, this title exploits white fears of becoming a minority and being treated as different, as less. There are other alternatives. Tempering US excesses of individual achievement and private gain is not necessarily bad. Simply put, humankind has advanced by sharing, caring and giving as well. Mainstream and minority ethnic subcultures are likely to benefit from contact and cross-fertilization with each other, individually, socially and institutionally in markets and governance to get to the point where we see each other in ourselves and work to better integrate each other into our particular versions of national identity and consciousness.

References

Acuña, Rodolfo (1988), *Occupied America: The Conquest and Colonization of the U.S. Southwest*, New York: Harper Collins.

Aldama, Arturo J. and Naomi H. Quiñones (2004), *Decolonial Voices: Chicana and Chicano Cultural Studies in the 21st Century*, Bloomington, IN: Indiana University Press.

Anzaldúa, Gloria (1987), *Borderlands/La Frontera: The New Mestiza*, San Francisco, CA: Spinsters/Aunt Lute Press.

Appadurai, Arjun (ed.) (1986), *The Social Life of Things: Commodities in Cultural Perspective*, Cambridge: Cambridge University Press.

Askegaard, Soren, Eric J. Arnould and Dannie Kjeldgaard (2005), 'Postassimilationist ethnic consumer research', *Journal of Consumer Research*, **32** (1), June, 160–70.

Baca-Zinn, Maxine (1995), 'Social science theorizing for Latino families in the age of diversity', in Ruth E. Zambrana (ed.), *Understanding Latino Families: Scholarship, Policy, and Practice*, Thousand Oaks, CA: Sage, pp. 177–89.

Baudrillard, Jean (1988), 'Consumer society', in Mark Poster (ed.), *Jean Baudrillard, Selected Writings*, Stanford, CA: Stanford University Press, pp. 29–57.

Becker, Gary S. and Guity Nashat Becker (1997), *The Economics of Life*, New York: McGraw-Hill.

Benhabib, Seyla (1996), 'The democratic moment and the problem of difference', in Seyla Benhabib (ed.), *Democracy and Difference: Contesting the Boundaries of the Political*, Princeton, NJ: Princeton University Press, pp. 3–18.

Bonsu, Samuel and Russell Belk (2003), 'Do not go cheaply into that good night: death-ritual consumption in Asante, Ghana', *Journal of Consumer Research*, **30** (June), 41–55.

Borjas, George (1999), *Heaven's Door: Immigration Policy and the American Economy*, Princeton, NJ: Princeton University Press.

—— and Marta Tienda (eds) (1985), *Hispanics in the U.S. Economy*, Orlando, FL: Academic Press.

Brah, Avtar and Annie Coombes (eds) (2000), *Hybridity and its Discontents*, London: Routledge.

Chua, Amy (2003), *World on Fire: How Exporting Free Market Democracy Breeds Ethnic Hatred and Global Instability*, New York: Doubleday.

Churchill, Ward (1994), *Indians Are Us? Culture and Genocide in Native North America*, Monroe, MA: Common Courage Press.

Costa, Janeen and Gary Bamossy (eds) (1995), *Marketing in a Multicultural World*, Thousand Oaks, CA: Sage.

Cromer, Evelyn Baring (1916), *Political and Literary Essays*, 2nd edn, London: Macmillan.

Dávila, Arlene (2001), *Latinos Inc.: The Marketing and Making of a People*, Berkeley, CA: University of California Press.

Delgado, Richard and Jean Stefancic (1997), *Critical White Studies: Looking Behind the Mirror*, Philadelphia, PA: Temple University Press.

Despandé, Rohit, Wayne Hoyer and Naveen Donthu (1986), 'The intensity of ethnic affiliation: a study in the sociology of Hispanic consumption', *Journal of Consumer Research*, **13** (September), 214–20.

du Gay, Paul and Michael Pryke (2002), *Cultural Economy*, London: Sage.
Elkins, Stanley M. (1968), *Slavery: A Problem in American Institutional and Intellectual Life*, 2nd edn, Chicago: University of Chicago Press.
Firat, Fuat (1995), 'Consumer culture or culture consumed?', in Janeen Costa and Gary Bamossy (eds), *Marketing in a Multicultural World*, Thousand Oaks, CA: Sage.
Foucault, Michel (1970), *The Order of Things: An Archaeology of the Human Sciences*, New York: Random House.
Gabriel, John (1994), *Racism, Culture, Markets*, London: Routledge.
Garza-Falcon, Leticia (1998), *Gente Decente: A Borderlands Response to the Rhetoric of Dominance*, Austin, TX: University of Texas Press.
Ger, Güliz and Özlem Sandicki (2005), 'Representing the Islamist consumer: transformation of the market', presented to the Association for Consumer Research, San Antonio, Texas, 28 September–2 October.
Harris, Neil (1993), *Grand Illusions: Chicago World's Fair of 1893*, Chicago: Chicago Historical Society.
Hero, Rodney (1992), *Latinos and the U.S. Political System*, Philadelphia, PA: Temple University Press.
Hofstede, Geert (2002), *Exploring Culture: Exercises, Stories, and Synthetic Cultures*, Yarmouth, ME: Intercultural Press.
Inda, Jonathan Xavier and Renato Rosaldo (2002), *The Anthropology of Globalization*, Oxford: Blackwell.
Jacobs, Jane (1984), *The Economy of Cities*, New York: Vintage Books.
Lamont, Michele and Marcel Fournier (1992), *Cultivating Differences: Symbolic Boundaries and the Making of Inequality*, Chicago: University of Chicago Press.
Light, Ivan and Steven J. Gold (2000), *Ethnic Economies*, San Diego: Academic Press.
Limerick, Patricia (1987), *The Legacy of Conquest: The Unbroken Past of the American West*, New York: W.W. Norton.
Limon, José (1992), *Mexican Ballads, Chicano Poems: History and Influence in Mexican American Social Poetry*, Berkeley, CA: University of California Press.
Lipsitz, George (1998), *The Possessive Investment in Whiteness: How White People Profit from Identity Politics*, Philadelphia, PA: Temple University Press.
Lugard, Frederick John D. (1922), *The Dual Mandate in British Tropical Africa*, Edinburgh: Blackwood.
Luna, David and Laura Peracchio (2001), 'Moderators of language effects in advertising to bilinguals: a psycholinguistic approach', *Journal of Consumer Research*, **28** (September), 284–95.
Massey, Douglass, Ruth E. Zambrana and Sally Alonzo Bell (1995), 'Contemporary issues in Latino families: future directions for research, policy, and practice', in Ruth E. Zambrana (ed.), *Understanding Latino Families: Scholarship, Policy, and Practice*, Thousand Oaks, CA: Sage, pp. 190–204.
Mishal, Lawrence, Jared Bernstein and Sylvia Allegretto (2005), *The State of Working America 2004/2005*, Washington, DC: Economics Policy Institute.
Montejano, David (1987), *Anglos and Mexicans in the Making of Texas, 1836–1986*, Austin, TX: University of Texas Press.
Moraga, Cherríe and Gloria Anzaldúa (1981), *This Bridge Called my Back: Writings by Radical Women of Color*, New York: Kitchen Table Press.
Padilla, Amado (1980), *Acculturation: Theory, Models, and Some New Findings*, Boulder, CO: Westview Press.
Peñaloza, Lisa (1994a), 'Atravesando fronteras/Border crossings: a critical ethnographic exploration of the consumer acculturation of Mexican immigrants', *Journal of Consumer Research*, **21** (June), 32–54.
—— (1994b), '¡Ya Viene Atzlan! Images of Latinos in U.S. advertising', *Media Studies Journal*, **8** (3), 133–42.
—— (1995), 'Immigrant consumers: marketing and public policy implications', *Journal of Public Policy and Marketing*, **14** (1), 83–94.
—— (2005), *Generaciones/Generations: Cultural Identity, Memory, and the Market*, documentary film, 48 min. Minidv.
—— and Mary Gilly (1999), 'Marketers' acculturation: the changer and the changed', *Journal of Marketing*, **63** (3), 84–104.
Pérez, Emma (1999), *The Decolonial Imaginary: Writing Chicanas Into History*, Bloomington, IN: Indiana University Press.
Robles, Barbara (2004), 'Latinos in the U.S.: diverse policies for a diverse population', monograph, University of Texas Center for Mexican American Studies, Austin, TX.
Rodriguez, Clara (ed.) (1998), *Latin Looks: Images of Latinas and Latinos in the U.S. Media*, Boulder, CO: Westview Press.
Rodriguez, Richard (2002), *Brown: The Last Discovery of America*, New York: Viking.
Rosaldo, Renato (1989), *Culture and Truth: the Remaking of Social Analysis*, Boston: Beacon Press.
Rosales, Rodolfo (2000), *The Illusion of Inclusion: The Untold Political Story of San Antonio*, Austin, TX: University of Texas Press.
Ruiz, Vickie (1987), *Cannery Women, Cannery Lives: Mexican Women, Unionization, and the California Food Processing Industry, 1930–1950*, Albuquerque, NM: University of New Mexico Press.

Ruiz, Vickie (1998), *From Out of the Shadows: Mexican American Women in Twentieth Century America*, Oxford: Oxford University Press.

Sandoval, Chela (2000), *Methodology of the Oppressed*, Minneapolis, MN: University of Minnesota Press.

San Juan, E. (2002), *Racism and Cultural Studies: Critiques of Multiculturalist Ideology and the Politics of Difference*, Durham, NC: Duke University Press.

Slater, Don and Fran Tonkiss (2001), *Market Society: Markets and Modern Social Theory*, Malden, MA: Blackwell Publishers Inc.

Sotomayor, Marta (ed.) (1991), *Empowering Hispanic Families: A Critical Issue for the 90s*, Milwaukee, WI: Family Service America.

Storper, Michael (2000), 'Lived effects of the contemporary economy: globalization, inequality, and consumer society', *Public Culture*, **12** (2), 375–409.

Tharp, Marye C. (2001), *Marketing and Consumer Identity in Multicultural America*, Thousand Oaks, CA: Sage.

Triandis, Harry (1998), *Individualism and Collectivism*, Boulder, CO: Westview Press.

US Census Bureau (2004), American Community Surveys, Washington, DC. US Printing Office.

Velez-Ibañez, Carlos, Anna Sampaio and Manolo Gonzalez-Estay (2002), *Transnational Latino Communities*, New York: Rowman and Littlefield.

Venkatesh, Alladi (1994), 'Gender identity in the Indian context: a socio-cultural construction of the female consumer', in Janeen Costa (ed.), *Gender Issues and Consumer Behavior*, Thousand Oaks, CA: Sage, pp. 42–62.

Wade, Robert Hunter (2003), 'The invisible hand of the American empire', *Ethics and International Affairs*, **17** (2), 77–88.

Zambrana, Ruth E. (1995), *Understanding Latino Families: Scholarship, Policy, and Practice*, Thousand Oaks, CA: Sage.

Zizek, Slavoj (1999), 'Multiculturalism', *The Ticklish Subject: The Absent Centre of Political Ontology*, London: Verso, pp. 215–21.

42 The etiquette of qualitative research
Julie A. Ruth and Cele C. Otnes

Good manners are part of working smart. (Baldrige, 1985, p. 4)

Most advice on how to enhance interactions between researchers and informants homes in on two issues: gaining access and helping researchers employ techniques as skillfully as possible (e.g., explaining when, where and how to use 'grand tour' questions; McCracken, 1988). So it is fair to say that the quality of researcher/informant interactions is typically considered from the researcher's perspective and not from that of the informant. But no matter how willingly participants engage in interviews, observations, shopping trips and other activities, the research process always involves researchers imposing on, and requiring sacrifices from, informants for a (short or long) time. So how can researchers create research experiences that will be remembered by informants, not as burdens, but as interpersonal encounters that were reasonable in scope, beneficial in some way, and possibly even enjoyable?

We believe one clear way is for researchers to understand the roles etiquette can play at different stages of interacting with informants, and to realize that etiquette practices should not be regarded as optional, but rather as integral, to the research process. Furthermore, by approaching etiquette as more than a tool, and as a way for researchers to demonstrate their humanity and to reinforce the humanistic ideology that underlies qualitative research, researchers and informants alike can reap practical and relational benefits from their interchanges.

Our motivations for writing this chapter stem from situations where we wished we had been better equipped with an understanding of the etiquette of fieldwork. Furthermore we felt such a chapter was important because the anthologies and books pertaining to qualitative research are largely silent on this topic. Thus, in this chapter, we (1) explore the general benefits of incorporating practices of etiquette in qualitative research; (2) describe in both practical and theoretical terms particular practices of etiquette that can enhance the research experience over its various stages; and (3) provide a checklist that will make remembering and implementing practices of etiquette easier for the researcher.

General benefits of etiquette in qualitative research

Etiquette is defined as 'the forms, manners, and ceremonies established by convention as acceptable or required in social relations, in a profession, or in official life [and] the rules for such forms, manners, and ceremonies' (*Webster's*, 1988, p. 467). Most writers who address issues of etiquette stress that understanding expectations and executions of manners in various social situations enables both parties to communicate more effectively and paves the way for deeper relationships, two goals that are fundamental to qualitative research. Compared to 'more formal and socially distant methods', qualitative research is heavily dependent upon successful social interactions, and ones that typically occur in participants' everyday lives, in order to achieve the goal of understanding phenomena in contexts in which they occur (Punch, 1994, p. 93). If we reframe qualitative research not merely as a series of interactions, but as opportunities for interpersonal communication and relationship building with informants, it becomes immediately obvious that etiquette will be integral to any qualitative research effort.

Many of our colleagues whom we consulted on why etiquette is important to qualitative research argue, first and foremost, that practices of etiquette are simply expected, that we would expect to be treated in the same manner if we were the informants and others were the researchers, and that to ignore etiquette may delay completion of a research project, or put it in jeopardy altogether. Respecting our informants and their stories must be at the forefront of our research efforts, and etiquette is one primary mechanism for demonstrating we have done so.

In addition, while researchers typically present themselves as professionals with individual research agendas, at a macro level they also personify other entities, namely, universities, sponsoring organizations or corporations for whom they work or consult, and perhaps even 'researchers' at large. On a micro level, researcher behavior may also reflect upon gatekeepers or intermediaries that may have made introductions to informants. Thus a second reason for incorporating etiquette practices is that, when we conduct research, we are representing interests of others besides ourselves, and that these 'others' typically may be in positions to benefit when we act respectfully and deferentially, and to be tarnished when we do not.

The third reason we offer for educating oneself and adhering to etiquette practices, even (and especially) if these practices are foreign because of cultural distance between the lifeworlds of researcher and participant, is that etiquette can make fieldwork proceed more efficiently. Given the arduousness of gaining access, retaining informants and managing and analyzing the text, we believe efficiency concerns alone would be sufficient motivation for this chapter. As one etiquette expert observes, 'when people . . . adhere to the rules of social behavior . . . there is an absence of confusion and wasted time . . . a minimum of stumbling about, feeling awkward, groping for words, or wondering what to do next' (Baldrige, 1985, pp. 6–7).

In summary, in the words of one research colleague, qualitative research 'is no different than the rest of the world, in requiring a decent, honest, and reliable mode of conduct to keep it well-oiled' (personal communication, 2005). We now explore etiquette practices researchers should consider at three stages of interacting with informants: before, during and after the focal interaction(s). In addressing etiquette issues arising in each phase, we draw upon two bodies of research that can enlighten us on how and why etiquette is important in interacting with informants: namely, interpersonal relationship theory and gift exchange. Moreover we concur with colleagues who interpret the time, effort and access that informants grant as real gifts, ones that enable us to 'secure an in-depth understanding of the phenomenon in question' (Denzin and Lincoln, 1994, p. 2). We have tried to make our comments general enough to apply to a wide variety of interactions occurring in qualitative research; that is, with consumers, retailers, CEOs, the media, or whomever the researcher believes to represent the richest source of information for the topic at hand. We also offer examples that highlight situations where practicing etiquette (or failing to) shaped social encounters and relationship building with informants. Table 42.1 summarizes etiquette practices across the three stages.

Table 42.1 Etiquette checklist

The 'Before' Phase: Making and Managing Contact with Informants

---

Locating informants and making contact
- Decide whether it is best to approach prospective informants directly or through a third party
- Determine whether research context is open/closed
- Determine whether research context is formal/informal
- Determine best channel for initial contact (e.g., email, in-person)
- Determine appropriate tone and content of initial communication

Specifying the nature of the interaction
- Describe (orally or in writing) the proposed interaction, including what you expect of participant and what participant can expect
- What will the participant be asked to do?
- What are the costs and who will pay for them?
- What is the time commitment?
- What is the remuneration?
- Where, when, and under what circumstances should researcher and participant interact?
- Send summary and consent form to participant in advance, if applicable
- Provide a reminder of the time/place of interaction, if applicable
- Provide your contact information/acquire informant's contact information to enable communication

Introductions and self-presentation
- Conduct cultural sleuthing necessary for making a good first impression
- Consider proper introductions and role you wish to portray
- Consider most appropriate way to present credentials
- Attend to self-presentation, including dress

Meeting face-to-face for the first time
- Be on time, or early
- Adhere to agreements regarding meeting time, place and identifying characteristics
- Be focused on arrival of informant
- Demonstrate deference with seating, refraining from annoying habits, etc.
- Be prepared with knowledge of local manners and social graces

---

The 'During' Phase: Respect and Deference during the Focal Interaction

---

Effective listening
- Prepare in advance by bolstering relevant background knowledge
- Allow informant to talk
- Follow lead of informant
- Keep opinions to yourself

Minimizing researcher-oriented distractions
- Turn off cell phones, pagers, etc.
- Have all research-related materials ready
- Monitor venue for distractions and minimize them

Keeping promises
- Note any requests that emerge during interaction, such as providing a summary of findings
- Be attentive to time and your promise regarding time commitment
- Offer and provide assistance to informant, as appropriate

Table 42.1 (continued)

Parting rituals
- Make a sincere verbal expression of gratitude
- Process paperwork
- Provide remuneration or gift, as promised
- Consider any optional or additional gifts to express gratitude
- Ensure informant receives care in moving to his/her next appointment
- Lay groundwork for subsequent contact, if applicable

The 'After' Phase: Enhancing the Chances for Prolonged Relationships

---

Continue to treat informant with respect and deference
- Provide additional thank-you notes for informant, as appropriate
- Express gratitude to third parties, as appropriate
- Respect informants and their experiences in presentations and publications
- Make good on any promises for follow-up (e.g., summary of findings)

The 'before' phase: making and managing contact with informants

Before text can be collected, etiquette comes into play as researchers plan their approach to relating to informants. The overarching etiquette concerns in making and maintaining contact are to demonstrate respect for the informant's time and effort, and to build relational trust and rapport (Fontana and Frey, 1994; Kleinman and Copp, 1993). Accomplishing both of these tasks will generally facilitate greater openness and intimacy in interpersonal communications (see Duck, West and Acitelli, 1997). It is important to note that Human Subjects Review (HSR) and Institutional Review Board (IRB) policies have been developed to protect informants' rights, including avoiding harm and deception, obtaining informed consent and maintaining informant privacy and confidentiality of text. Qualitative researchers are well aware that informants are 'partners in the research process. To dupe them in any way would be to undermine the very processes one wants to examine' (Punch, 1994, p. 89). At a minimum, then, researchers should attend to HSR/IRB considerations so that informants' rights are respected.

Researchers should understand, however, that conforming to HSR/IRB rules does not mean they have taken care of any or all salient issues pertaining to etiquette. Most HSR/IRB rules are designed primarily as prevention-focused strategies (e.g., to avoid harm or possible litigation). However practices of etiquette can be regarded more as promotion-based strategies, those that will help us 'make the fine distinctions that arise at the interactional level' (Punch, 1994, p. 89) during initial contact and text collection, and to build relationships proactively rather than merely minimizing negative outcomes.

All research-related encounters–not merely attempts to obtain informed consent, for example – should communicate respect and gratitude for informants' time, information and energy. Kirk and Miller (1986) recommend that the earliest stages of research require preparing for 'an opening for data collection . . . [including] strategic presentation of the ethnographer's persona . . . the location of key and other informants, and the coordination of a research situation . . . Success in this endeavor is no mean feat of cultural choreography' (Kirk and Miller, 1986, p. 66). To assist in choreographing the etiquette of making and managing contact, we divide the discussion into four topics: locating informants, specifying the nature of informant/researcher interaction, introductions and self-presentation, and meeting face-to-face for the first time.

Locating informants and making contact
While advice abounds on gaining access to informants, our perspective on this issue is motivated more by the need to show respect and deference rather than on quickly and efficiently acquiring participants. Consequently, even if it may be within acceptable bounds to ask people directly to participate, social norms might support a more deferential strategy of securing an introduction or permission from an influential third party (see Milardo and Helms-Erikson, 2000, regarding third-party effects).

Also to be considered are the appropriate channels (e.g., email, phone, in-person), tone (i.e., formal versus informal) and content of such communication. Consistent with our own experience, 'Field research conducted without attention to the native perception and local cultural context . . . is a contradiction in terms' (Kirk and Miller, 1986, p. 66). Thus decisions on channel, tone and content of contact communication are often conditional upon the cultural context of target informants. One salient issue in this regard is whether the research context is 'closed' or 'open' (i.e., if access requires more negotiation for entry versus little to no negotiation; Jorgensen, 1989). For example, most researchers seeking to conduct depth interviews with CEOs will likely seek out a third-party introduction. Furthermore the mode of communication with target CEOs might be formal, such as a letter on letterhead from the researcher, contact from a firm hired to recruit informants or a query from an intermediary who invites participation and includes an abstract of the purpose of the study. Also norms in certain cultures require introductions to be made even in more casual social situations. One of our informants told us that, even at gatherings such as hobby clubs in England, where the motivation for attendance is almost purely social and all attendees are united by a common interest, 'the British have to be introduced; they won't just speak to one another'. Even for target informants who are likely to expect less formality, a third-party introduction recognizes rights of informants, tends to equalize status differences, lends credibility and can often pay off in informants introducing the researcher to other helpful parties.

Specifying the nature of the interaction
One way to indicate respect and deference is to alleviate any potential anxiety by clearly and completely explaining expectations for participation. One of the most efficient ways to accomplish this task is to prepare a short handout or verbal explanation that summarizes expectations of the study (e.g., how long the encounter will last; whether the researcher would like to record the encounter; remuneration offers). Furthermore providing informants with the consent form in advance can also demonstrate that an institution such as a university has informants' best interests at heart. This gesture also provides an opening for informants to ask questions in advance, saving valuable time in the field. Explaining the study in advance also involves informants as relational partners earlier rather than later in the process, and can foster a perception that researchers hold informants in high regard.

Another aspect of setting expectations is specifying the *quid pro quo* in the research relationship. A good rule of thumb is that researchers should never expect informants to spend any money on the encounter. Therefore, if travel to a specific place is required, researchers should immediately make it clear that those costs will be covered. Likewise, the researcher's willingness to reimburse any costs for food, beverages or other expenses (e.g., shopping with an informant) should be specified up front. Researchers also should anticipate that, if informants are asked to give up time during their workday, chances of success are increased by offering to buy the participant food (e.g., lunch) or drink (e.g., coffee) during a reasonable break from work.

Similarly the researcher should address the issue of where the participant would like to meet (sometimes at the expense of researcher preferences). Etiquette regarding meeting locations and whether the meeting is public or private must be balanced with practical matters such as a possible desire to record the interaction. Although public meetings may be preferred for some reasons, informants may be more comfortable in private settings, particularly if sensitive topics are to be discussed. While it goes without saying that the chosen venue should be clean and free of clutter, what is not always so obvious is that, even if the research setting is clean, safe and well-lit, venues containing political or religious messages that could prove offensive, or could make informants uncomfortable because of the clientele, music, art or other environmental aspects, should be avoided.

It is worth noting that the researcher may have to indulge the informants' whimsies in this regard in order not to immediately shut down the possibility of a relationship. Recently one of our participants declared he had a 'surprise' quiet location for an interview, which turned out to be concrete steps under the hot sun inside the largest cemetery in London! In another research setting, a third party provided introductions and the venue for interacting with informants, a setting that was populated by a pet bird named 'Poopie' that flew to and from the heads of the third party, informants and researcher. Although the researcher certainly did not anticipate Poopie's presence, everyone else was well acquainted and comfortable with the bird, and so the interviews continued apace (photo available from the authors).

Finally, the researcher should remind informants of meeting arrangements, preferably the day before or morning of a meeting. Providing a reminder not only will ensure greater informant commitment but is a courteous way to demonstrate respect for the informant's time and effort. Of course, to the extent possible, if informants are late for a meeting, researchers should be as accommodating as possible. It is important to make sure that researchers and informants have contact information for each other in case anything goes awry while both are in transit to meetings (e.g., cell phone numbers, email addresses).

Introductions and self-presentation

At initial encounters with participants, it is important to attend to introductions and to be sensitive to any potential status differences that might foster discomfort between researcher and informant. Researchers should consider what role(s) they wish to express (e.g., esteemed academic, researcher, listener, or 'friend') and how communication might be affected by these roles (see Marshall and Rossman, 1989). The researcher may opt to present a persona that attempts (at least seemingly) to place all parties on a par with one another socially (Fontana and Frey, 1994), because such similarity has been observed to foster relational development (Duck et al., 1997). For example, when conducting interviews with US consumers, we have found it helpful to de-emphasize our university roles and educational background so participants feel comfortable in sharing intimate experiences of their lives. In such cases, researchers may choose to wait until the interview is over to provide a business card with contact information so that differences in role statuses are de-emphasized. The opposite may be true if an informant occupies a higher status than the researcher; for example, with CEO informants, presenting credentials upon introduction will likely enhance researcher credibility and demonstrate that the researcher knows what is proper in business settings.

Furthermore researchers should also attend to dress and other aspects of self-presentation. Although in one's own culture it may be fine to wear, for example, shorts, sandals or perfume, such choices might offend informants or affect perceptions of the researcher's manners or credibility. In many cases, a researcher may merely wish to deflect attention and 'blend in' with the culture of the informant in order to put informants at ease and set a common foundation for the informant/researcher relationship (see Duck et al., 1997).

Coming face-to-face with informants
At the first (and subsequent) face-to-face encounters, it is typically appropriate to stand up and shake hands when meeting informants. Although researchers may automatically assume it is acceptable to engage in direct eye contact and use an informant's first name, it is best to assess whether cultural norms sanction such behavior. In addition, simple principles of respect and deference discussed by Baldrige (1985), that will save time and face, and that the researcher should consider incorporating into his or her greeting rituals, include (1) being on time (which the researcher should probably interpret as 'being 15 minutes early') to allow for traffic jams, last-minute delays at the office, etc.; (2) adhering to any description given to the informant that will help him or her easily identify the researcher (e.g., 'I'll be wearing a red sweater and grey pants and I'll be at the front door of the restaurant'); (3) while waiting for participants, refraining from behavior that could distract researchers from proper greeting rituals, or that could be offensive (e.g., talking on a cell phone, smoking, eating a meal before the participant arrives); and (4) practicing good manners that demonstrate deference (e.g., allowing participants to step onto an elevator first, asking them where they might like to sit in restaurants or on transportation).

In summary, we have deliberately stressed that cultures can differ on details associated with etiquette of making and maintaining contact. In many cases, researchers will have a great deal of knowledge of the culture to be studied (e.g., Christmas gift givers in North America) and so will have good understanding of etiquette practices. In other contexts, researchers may have less knowledge of the target culture. In such cases, it is wise to seek advice from someone embedded in the informant culture. In addition, it is wise to brush up on any language or cultural rules or norms that could make researchers seem rude if not followed (e.g., understanding when to use 'Madame' versus 'Mademoiselle' in French; honorifics like 'Auntie'). Moreover, it is important to remember that, in some cultures, there are strict rules about proper interactions between men and women. In India, for example, if a man wishes to interview a woman, others must be in the room, or the interview must occur outdoors.

The 'during' phase: respect and deference during the focal interaction
The true test of whether the way has been paved for successful interaction will not occur until researcher and informant get down to the business at hand: engaging in the focal

research interaction(s). Once in that context, it is paramount to remember two main goals of etiquette: demonstrating respect and deference for the participant. We divide our discussion of etiquette practices associated with this stage into four topics: effective listening, minimizing researcher-oriented distraction, keeping promises and parting rituals.

Effective listening

Quite simply, effective listening is probably the most important indicator of respect and deference a researcher can offer a participant. Almost every colleague whom we consulted about the topic of etiquette and qualitative research mentioned that *truly* listening to the informant is the most important practice of etiquette to follow during the encounter. Effective listening has been discussed in the qualitative canon more as a means of garnering high-quality text (e.g., McCracken, 1988). However its benefits from the perspective of demonstrating respect and deference have not been highlighted.

So what is effective listening? Our colleagues offer the following components: (1) being grounded sufficiently in the topic so as to understand what the informant is truly saying (e.g., if the research topic involves the experience of certain medical procedures, the researcher must acquire knowledge of such procedures in advance rather than requiring the informant to explain these); (2) allowing the informant to say everything he or she desires on a topic or question, even if this is not particularly central to the research at the outset; (3) allowing the informants to talk, period – and not coming away with researcher-dominated text; (4) if the researcher is engaging in autodriving, focusing on the specific item the informant wants to show the researcher, rather than being distracted by other artifacts that might seem more interesting; (5) following up on issues that are clearly important to the informant, whether or not these issues are included on the research protocol; and (6) keeping one's opinions to oneself (see Fontana and Frey, 1994). For example, the proper response to an informant's question of 'What do you think?' is often a neutral comment such as 'I really haven't thought about it enough.' Especially in the early stages of a researcher's career, or in a situation where a graduate student might be conducting fieldwork for a supervising professor, the burden is on the senior researcher to ensure that all members of the research team understand, and can employ, principles of effective listening.

Minimizing researcher-oriented distractions and interruptions

Because most research encounters take place in social or quasi-social settings, the likelihood of 'real life' seeping into an encounter can be quite high. However both the researcher and the participant theoretically have control over how much other aspects of their lives emerge. Researchers are well advised to exercise as much control as possible to keep their own real life from invading the research encounter. On the other hand, there may be little researchers can do from an etiquette perspective if participants do not exercise similar control. For example, during a mutually agreed upon interaction, a bed-and-breakfast proprietor was consistently interrupted: the telephone rang constantly, other guests made requests and conversation, and the proprietor was always halfway listening to the television in the background. However the researcher had to remind herself that this experience was also a privileged foray into the lifeworld of this informant, and might prove to be infinitely more revealing than an uninterrupted interview at a more distant venue. Nevertheless it was a reminder that the goal of minimizing distractions is not necessarily one that is shared by participants.

For researchers, however, this issue has become even more critical because a plethora of technologies such as cellular telephones, Blackberries, pagers and so on could potentially wreak havoc on the encounter. Researchers' failure to manage these devices, by turning them off or putting them in vibrate or silent mode, may be regarded by informants as nothing short of rude. Of course, if a researcher is expecting a critically important call (e.g., a family medical emergency), he or she can explain to the participant in advance that a situation is pending that may require attention. Alternatively it may be more respectful to reschedule the meeting.

In that same vein, any researcher action that could serve to delay or prolong the encounter, and could therefore be construed as being inconsiderate of the informant's time, should be avoided. For example, if an informant suggests a coffee shop on campus as a place to meet, the researcher should consider whether s/he will be subject to multiple interruptions by students and colleagues, which could be perceived as 'wasted time' by the informant. Other distractions or interruptions controlled by the researcher could include cigarette breaks; having to search (frantically) for research materials such as tapes, interview guides or consent forms; or having an illness such as a cold that is distracting or possibly contagious.

Again it is worth remembering that, because researchers impose themselves on the lives of participants, especially in the early stages of the research relationship, there should be no expectation of the same level of self-monitoring on the part of participants. In fact, in some cultures, what may be considered a distraction to the researcher may be a very normal part of everyday life. When we have conducted research outside of North America (e.g., Great Britain, South Africa), we have observed that the desire of American researchers to delve into the interview guide with gusto almost immediately after introductions is often interpreted as behavior that is too abrupt, and perhaps even borderline rude. Although it is probably always appropriate to have some 'small talk' at the beginning of an encounter, in some cultures informants want to engage in 'medium' or 'large' talk, an experience that could eat up a seemingly large chunk of time. Once again, it is useful to reframe these experiences, not as irritants, but as glimpses into the lifeworld of the informant that may, in the long run, enrich research quality. Therefore researchers should consider inquiring about a person's well being, their background, their family, and the like. Furthermore, it is important to take cues from informants as to when they are ready to proceed to the task at hand, rather than rushing to conclude seemingly irrelevant conversation. The important point to remember is that, if researchers keep their end of the bargain, that is, if they minimize distractions that would make them appear inconsiderate while patiently accepting distractions emanating from informants, the informants are likely to align their behavior to that of researchers.

Keeping promises
While setting the stage and minimizing distractions are about demonstrating deference, keeping promises is about building and maintaining relational trust. It is a given that researchers must adhere to HSR/IRB policies and procedures reflected in consent forms. However any promises made to participants that are not included in these protocols must also be kept. For example, informants frequently inquire about the research and ask to learn about the findings. Make a note of such requests and be sure to follow up. Rather

than regarding such requests as a nuisance, remember that it is often useful to have participants serve as external auditors of the interpretation, and such promise keeping goes a long way toward cementing longer-term relationships.

The one promise that researchers are frequently tempted to break involves how much of the participant's time the study requires. The best strategy involves estimating (realistically) and stating the expected time commitment in a range (e.g., 'about 45 to 60 minutes'). In the event that the interaction approaches the end of this range, the researcher can offer the participant several choices: continue if possible, terminate at the scheduled time or schedule a follow-up meeting. In the same vein, researchers should make sure their own schedules are clear after the established end time so that, if participants are willing to extend the interaction, it is not the researcher who keeps that opportunity from being realized.

If one is conducting an in-depth immersion (e.g., staying at or near the participant's home), an implicit promise is that researchers are expected to help the participant with chores or tasks that might emerge in their everyday lives (Marshall and Rossman, 1989). For example, one of us acted as secretary and hostess to a participant while she ran errands, answering the telephone and letting in visitors to her B&B. Furthermore, when such needs arise, it is worth noting that the researcher may have to sacrifice his or her own activities (e.g., visiting another site to make field notes) so as to engage in whatever helping behavior is requested, in order to accommodate the informant's wishes.

Parting rituals
As the encounter itself draws to a close, the researcher should incorporate etiquette practices into parting rituals in order to communicate gratitude to the participant, and pave the way to maintain contact if desired. First and foremost among required etiquette practices is the researchers' acknowledgment of sincere appreciation for the informant's contribution to the research endeavor. Researchers should offer a verbal expression of gratitude as the focal interaction is concluding.

Moreover the researcher should also complete any necessary paperwork (e.g., copies of consent forms, payment and signatures required for payment) so the participant will not have to be inconvenienced at a later date. It is also important to provide the remuneration or gift that was promised. As much as possible, researchers' offerings should attend to the wants and needs of the recipient, and researchers should be aware that some items may be seen as 'too much', 'too little' or inappropriate and may tend toward damaging rather than acknowledging or fostering a relationship (Ruth et al., 1999; Jorgensen, 1989). For example, we are aware of a situation where informants were given an item of small monetary but high sentimental value. Some informants expressed uneasiness in accepting the gift because it was perceived as difficult to acquire and, thus, 'too much' for an hour-long interview. In determining appropriate gifts, researchers can ask someone embedded in the informant culture for insight into how best to express appreciation. Money may generally be frowned upon, but it may be best for certain groups of informants. Researchers also have the option of doing something beyond what was promised. We have sometimes observed that adult informants thoroughly appreciate and enjoy the gesture of gifts offered to their children, such as a t-shirt or small toy. This may be especially true in informant cultures that place greater emphasis on family relations.

Just as was suggested for introductions, leave taking should also involve smiling, standing and extending a hand to shake (if cultural norms permit) after the encounter is clearly over, even if the researcher plans to remain at the research venue afterwards. If the informant has traveled to the venue, the researcher should make appropriate offers to walk them to their car or other transport, pay for travel-related expense (e.g., parking, taxi) or reasonably escort them to their next appointment. If instead the engagement has been conducted in the informant's sphere of operation, the researcher should give due respect to norms of exiting in that cultural milieu (e.g., saying goodbye according to cultural norms to any elders or family members present).

Finally researchers may wish to set groundwork for future communication originating from either party (e.g., 'Please call me with questions' or 'Might I call you with any questions?'). If the participant is going to be considered as a source of additional informants, it is probably best not to pin him or her down for names at the time, but to ask them to consider such a request, and ask for an appropriate time to contact them. Also do not contact anyone mentioned by an informant as a potential participant until the informant has given permission for this to occur, or has offered to serve as an intermediary. These simple but effective aspects of parting rituals ensure that the informant leaves feeling his or her input was valued, and that the interaction has transcended what might have been motivated by an information-for-remuneration exchange.

The 'after' phase: enhancing the chances for prolonged relationships
In this phase, investigators should attend to the etiquette of thanking participants, extending gratitude to third parties, and maintaining respectful representation in subsequent stages of the extended research process.

Thanking participants
As noted earlier, verbal expressions of appreciation and making good on promised remuneration may be the most appropriate ways of acknowledging informants' contributions. In many cultures, it may be appropriate to follow up with a written expression of gratitude. A thank-you note or letter will be perceived as a sign that the researcher truly values the informant as a person, and not just as a 'participant'. Such thank-you notes can refer to an interesting incident shared between researcher and informant, or thank them for a particular lead or suggestion of a research venue. Written acknowledgments also serve a second purpose of laying relational groundwork, should additional contact be desired. Furthermore, if informants provide ongoing assistance to researchers, multiple expressions of gratitude over time may be required. In addition to thanking informants for their contributions, it is also important to provide an opportunity for informants to comment or ask questions about the research, and to respond with appropriate honesty and openness. In addition to treating informants' interest with genuine respect, continued communication often produces additional text or insight into the topic at hand.

Extending gratitude to third parties involved
It is generally appropriate to express gratitude (i.e., verbal thanks, gift) to individuals or organizations that have been helpful in the research process (e.g., drivers, secretaries). Such gratitude can take the form of written thank-you notes and may not require remuneration

or gifts, depending upon the level of assistance provided. Such gestures serve to acknowledge the influence of third parties in making and maintaining relationships with informants (see Lowrey et al., 2004, regarding third-party influence in social networks).

Representation
A final but important arena where researchers must practice etiquette is in treating informants with respect in discussions and representations of their experiences at presentations and in publications (see Atkinson and Hammersley, 1994). Such representation goes beyond merely preserving confidentiality of text. Rather, as scholars continue to explore more postmodern methods of textual presentation (e.g., short stories, plays and forms that could easily intrude into informants' lifeworlds, such as videography), it is important to place respect and deference at the forefront of researchers' goals of representation. Furthermore, when writing interpretations of text, researchers should place their desire to portray informants respectfully ahead of goals pertaining to highlighting their own cleverness through the use of metaphors, tropes, nicknames for informants and the like in their publications. One test for whether representation has overstepped the bounds of propriety is whether a researcher would feel comfortable sharing the textual representation with informants.

Conclusion
Attending to etiquette in qualitative research underscores the importance of Fontana and Frey's observation that researchers should ensure that 'the "other" is no longer a distant, aseptic, quantified, sterilized, measured, categorized and catalogued faceless respondent, but has become a living human being' (1994, p. 373). Although this chapter addresses what we believe to be an overlooked issue in conducting research, we certainly do not wish to convey the impression that incorporating etiquette into the research design is insurmountable or burdensome. To that end, Table 42.1 serves as an etiquette checklist for the novice or experienced researcher. We hope this chapter is useful for understanding how and why etiquette is not only good research practice, but also in line with the humanistic perspective that undergirds qualitative research.

References
Atkinson, Paul and Martyn Hammersley (1994), 'Ethnography and participant observation', in Norman K. Denzin and Yvonna S. Lincoln (eds), *Handbook of Qualitative Research*, Thousand Oaks: Sage, pp. 248–61.
Baldrige, Letitia (1985), *Letitia Baldrige's Complete Guide to Executive Manners*, New York: Macmillan.
Denzin, Norman K. and Yvonna S. Lincoln (1994), 'Introduction: entering the field of qualitative research', in Norman K. Denzin and Yvonna S. Lincoln (eds), *Handbook of Qualitative Research*, Thousand Oaks: Sage, pp. 1–17.
Duck, Steve, Lee West and Linda K. Acitelli (1997), 'Sewing the field: the tapestry of relationships in life and research', in Steve Duck (ed.), *Handbook of Personal Relationships: Theory, Research, and Interventions*, Chichester, NY: John Wiley & Sons, pp. 1–23.
Fontana, Andrea and James H. Frey (1994), 'Interviewing: the art of science', in Norman K. Denzin and Yvonna S. Lincoln (eds), *Handbook of Qualitative Research*, Thousand Oaks: Sage, pp. 1–17.
Jorgensen, Danny L. (1989), *Participant Observation*, Newbury Park, CA: Sage.
Kirk, Jerome and Marc L. Miller (1986), *Reliability and Validity in Qualitative Research*, Newbury Park, CA: Sage.
Kleinman, Sherryl and Martha A. Copp (1993), *Emotions and Fieldwork*, Newbury Park, CA: Sage.
Lowrey, Tina M., Cele C. Otnes and Julie A. Ruth (2004), 'Social influences on dyadic giving over time: a taxonomy from the giver's perspective', *Journal of Consumer Research*, **30** (4), 547–58.
Marshall, Catherine and Gretchen B. Rossman (1989), *Designing Qualitative Research*, Newbury Park, CA: Sage.
McCracken, Grant (1988), *The Long Interview*, Newbury Park, CA: Sage.

Milardo, Robert M. and Heather Helms-Erikson (2000), 'Network overlap and third-party influence in close relationships', in Clyde Hendrick and Susan S. Hendrick (eds), *Close Relationships*, Thousand Oaks, CA: Sage, pp. 33–46.
Personal communication with various research colleagues, September 2005.
Punch, Maurice (1994), 'Politics and ethics in qualitative research', in Norman K. Denzin and Yvonna S. Lincoln (eds), *Handbook of Qualitative Research*, Thousand Oaks: Sage, pp. 83–97.
Ruth, Julie A., Cele C. Otnes and Frédéric F. Brunel (1999), 'Gift receipt and the reformulation of interpersonal relationships', *Journal of Consumer Research*, **25** (March), 385–402.
Webster's New World Dictionary, 3rd College edn (1988), New York: Simon & Schuster.

Index

Abelson, Raziel 70
Ableson, Herbert 256
Abrams, Mark 255
Acknowledging Consumption (D. Miller) 220
ACR (Association for Consumer Research),
   see Association for Consumer Research
   (ACR)
actor network theory 356
Adair, John 338
adamancy, and religious stories 459
Adkins, Natalie Ross 112, 113
advertising
   Benetton advertisements 315
   Burberry advertisement 317
   campaigns 540
   'centerfold' format of advertisements 308
   CK One advertisements 303–10, 306, 307,
      312, 313, 315–19
   and consumption 540
   Dolce & Gabbana advertisement (2004)
      314
   and focus groups 255
   as form 62–3
   inner workings of industry 539–43
   and market research 64
   public images of advertising profession
      539–40
   qualitative research in 59–69
   reader responses 60–62
      cultural influences 61
   rhetoric 34, 312
   semiotics 34, 40–41, 435
   studying advertising practice 63–5
   and text 59, 60, 62, 73
   theory/criticism 65–7
   and visuals 73
Advertising Age 539
advertising agencies 6–7
Advertising the American Dream
   (R. Marchand) 535
*Advertising on Trial: Consumer Activism and
   Corporate Public Relations in the 1930s*
   (I.L. Stole) 539
Affluent Society, The (J. Galbraith) 4
African Charter on Human and People's
   Rights (1986) 47
Agar, Michael 347, 348
Aherne, Aedh 443–4
Ahuvia, Aaron C. 11, 61

Albrecht, Terence L. 260
Alexander, C.S. 234
Alford, Robert R. 106
Allen, Douglas E. 112, 179–80
Allport, Gordon W. 5, 458
'Alternative Approaches in the Study of
   Complex Situations' (R. Weiss) 7–8
alterpieces 308
Altman, Robert 367, 481
Alvesson, Mats 53, 465, 467, 469, 471, 472
AMA (American Marketing Association) 84
Ambler, Tim 63, 64
American Indian ancestry 419, 420
   culture 423–4
   geographic locale 421–2
   identification, government issued/sanctioned
      422–3
   Indian identity 420–21
   Native-descended persons 422–3
   'process of problematization' 420
   see also DNA testing; United States
American Marketing Association 84
American Psychological Association 323
analytic questions/strategies 27–9, 391
Ancestry By DNA 428
Anderson, Paul 48–9
Andreasen, Alan R. 324
anecdotes 441
Anglogold (South African mining company)
   432, 433
Anthro Design List Serve 378
anthropology
   and culture 551
   and documentary creation 380–81
   fieldwork 246, 499
   paradigm shift 500–502
   participant observation 505
   and photography 279
   and reflexivity 347
      radical 348–52
   transnational 526
Anthropology News 423, 424
antitheory 227
Appadurai, Arjun 503, 524, 527
Apple Computer 102, 336
   OSX operating system (Tiger) 140
   print campaign (2002) 434
applied research 437
Archer, R.L. 238